The New Book of American Rankings

The New Book of American Rankings

FYI Information Services

Facts On File Publications
New York, New York ● Bicester, England

The New Book of American Rankings

Library of Congress Cataloging in Publication Data

Main entry under title:

The New book of American rankings.

   Rev. ed. of: The book of American rankings/by Clark S.
Judge. c1979.
   Bibliography: p.
   Includes index.
   1. United States—Statistics.   I. Judge, Clark S.,
1948-   . Book of American rankings.   II. For Your
Information Services, Inc. III. Facts on File, Inc.
HA214.N49   1984   317.3   84-4115
ISBN 0-87196-254-3

Printed in the United States of America

10 9 8 7 6 5 4 3 2 1

Composition by Text Processing
Printed By Maple Press

TABLE OF CONTENTS

Preface

The New Book of American Rankings is not a complete digest of all available information on these United States. While the coverage is broad in scope it is, necessarily, selective. For some items of interest there are no up-to-date data on a state by state basis. The production of this new edition has been hampered by long delays in the disclosure of detailed results of the 1980 census. On the positive side, the reader will encounter many items that are not usually found in standard reference works. For example, there are tables on the popularity of certain magazines and television programs. These tabulations are included because they offer clues to otherwise intangible variations in tastes, preferences and modes of thought.

Data are presented in a form—generally involving the use of percentages and per capita rates—that allows meaningful comparisons among the states. When states differ by a wide margin on basic variables like population and area, comparisons based on simple counts can be very deceptive. If, for example, we rank states by the *number* of voters in a national election, we will produce a listing that closely corresponds to the ranking of states by population. This only makes the trivial point that states with large populations also have many residents of voting age. But if the states are ranked by *percentage* of voting age residents who actually vote, we obtain a ranking independent of population size that gives a far more accurate indication of the level of interest in politics in each state.

This is a book for both browsers and serious students. The browser will find all the material that is necessary to start or to settle thousands of arguments. The student will find an introduction to the general issue of regional differentiation and variation in America that is easy to understand and easy to use. The discussion attached to each table speaks to issues raised by the data. The statistical indicators are defined and specific cautions against misinterpretation are introduced. An effort has been made to raise questions, not to have the last word on interpretation of evidence. The reader is brought to the point at which an analysis of the statistics can begin. Insight, intelligence and a willingness to consult more specialized sources of information will be needed to carry on from here.

Skepticism and caution are the watchwords for any serious efforts to grapple with statistical data. The numbers in a statistical series are only "true" in relation to the specific questions that they are designed to answer. It is perfectly reasonable to argue and disagree about which questions are the best ones to ask about a given topic and which statistical indicators are the best measures for a given question. Some of the rankings presented below may seem surprising. Your home state may turn up in an unexpected ranking position. Before concluding that your assumptions have been mistaken all along be sure to double-check the definition of the indicator to see if it is really measuring what you think it is measuring.

The assemblage of information in this book is the work of many hands. First of all there are the men and women responsible for the research that led to the results reported here. One of our great unsung national resources is the network of quiet, diligent people and organizations who produce this kind of information. Then there are the many men and women in libraries and offices around the country who spent so much time seeking the information requested by a voice over a telephone. We wish to acknowledge the patient help received from the following information specialists: Beverly Wright and Maria Morales-Harper of the Bureau of the Census, Mr. Stuart Werner of the International Trade Administration of the U.S. Department of Commerce, and Patricia Bommicino and Lillian Kohlreiser of the Bureau of Labor Statistics. For her good humor, support and guidance, we offer special thanks to our editor, Eleanora Schoenebaum.

Pat Bear
Naomi Bernstein

September 1984

INTRODUCTION

The New Book of American Rankings celebrates the enormous variety of the United States of America. The book is both a handy collection of reference materials and a statistical scorecard that presents in tabular form comparisons of the 50 states in over 300 different geographic, demographic and cultural categories. The organization of the statistical tables is based on the idea that to understand our nation as a whole it is important to be aware of the great diversity of conditions in different parts of the country. The information presented here can be used to test assumptions and to form new impressions of American institutions and the American people. Each one of us has only a limited range of personal experience, but we can extend this range and learn to understand some of its limitations by comparing conditions in familiar places with conditions in more remote parts of this great nation of ours.

Many generalizations about the United States are based on simple national averages. For example, we are said to be a wealthy nation or a well-educated nation. The very specific data presented in this book allow us to examine the extent to which such general statements apply equally to all parts of the country. It often turns out that national average figures conceal great variations from place to place, and that what is true "for the nation as a whole" is not true for very many places in particular. The abundance of the material presented here will reveal the precariousness of many generalizations about America and challenge the reader to make use of the material to expand his or her own vision of the country. Some assumptions and stereotypes will survive this test, but others will surely fail.

Some of the tables below present data for cities or metropolitan areas,* but in most cases the tables contain information on a particular topic for each one of the 50 states. The ranking order of states in a table depends on the topic or item in question. If the topic is area, for example, Alaska ranks as number one and Rhode Island as number 50.

Tables covering similar topics are arranged in sections dealing with an overall theme, such as education, health, agriculture or religion. Each section begins with a general introduction and there is a short discussion prefacing each table. Along with data for particular states (or cities or SMSAs), tables include national totals or averages and state median values (that is, the average of values for states that rank in the middle for the category being measured—i.e., at positions 25 and 26). At the end of the book there is a separate section containing thumbnail sketches of each of the states. These sketches are based on the combination of a selection of rankings shown in certain tables from the main sequence of tables.

*Metropolitan areas are those classified by the Census Bureau as Standard Metropolitan Statistical Areas (SMSAs), consisting of large central cities plus their suburbs. A definition of these units is found in the section on population, where SMSAs are ranked by population.

GEOGRAPHY

Geographically, the United States is a giant among nations, ranking fourth in total area after the Soviet Union, Canada and China. The nation spans the continent of North America from east to west and reaches out into the heart of the Pacific, thus incorporating immense geographical variety. The dense settlement of the states of the eastern shore stands in sharp contrast to the sparsity of areas of human habitation separated by vast distances in Alaska and many western states. Americans live in the deserts of Death Valley, around the lakes of Minnesota, on the plains of Kansas and in the forests of the Pacific Northwest.

The great variety of American lifestyles is based in part on the variety of geographical conditions found in America. In any given state, geographical and other environmental conditions help to determine the range of available occupations and leisure pursuits. The resources of the earth, the air and the water set limits upon what *can* be done in a given state, and thus provide the framework for the political process of discussion and decision as to what *should* be done. Natural conditions also have a profound effect on everyday experiences and attitudes. Recognition of the effects of geographical factors on lifestyles has become an increasingly important factor both for families and for economic enterprises faced with relocation decisions.

The tables in this section describe the states as physical entities. Together with statistics on climate, agriculture, energy, and pollution presented in subsequent chapters, they provide a concise overview of the major interactions between inhabitants and environment that set the stage for studying other patterns of variation among the states.

1. Area

The familiar jumble of sizes and shapes on a map of the United States reminds even the casual observer that no two states are alike. Louisiana and Mississippi are the states most nearly equal in area, but a difference of some 63 square miles still remains between them. Comparing extremes, it seems that mighty Alaska could be broken up into as many as 487 districts as large as little Rhode Island (or, if you prefer, into two states of Texas plus one Illinois). The 20 largest states are west of the Mississippi. The 20 smallest states (except Hawaii) lie to the east of or, in the case of Louisiana, astride the river.

The 48 contiguous states cover just over three million square miles. National territory increased by nearly 20% when Alaska and Hawaii entered the Union in 1959. The 49th and 50th states are presently the only ones without neighboring states on their borders, but this situation is not historically unique. California, which entered the Union in 1850, was isolated until the entry of Oregon in 1859. Nevada was added as a neighbor to both states in 1864, but this western group remained isolated until the admission of Idaho and Wyoming in 1890 added the final links in a chain of states joining the West Coast to the East.

In the East, state boundary lines are generally irregular; in the West, most state lines are straight. There is a story behind every state line. In the East and South, the political map was fashioned by colonial charters, border disputes and the Indian wars of the 17th and 18th centuries. Arrangements with foreign powers have shaped the borders of many states, including Alaska (purchased from Russia in 1867), Florida (ceded by Spain in 1819), Montana and North Dakota (acquired by treaty with Great Britain in 1818), and the states of the Southwest (acquired from Mexico in the mid-19th century). National issues have also shaped state lines. The politics of slavery helped to fix the Kansas-Nebraska border. Efforts to contain Mormon influence led to the formation of Utah. Texas, which after breaking away from Mexico, had claimed the status of an independent nation from 1836 to 1845, received its final form in the give and take of domestic politics.

Table: Area of States
Date: 1980
Source: Census Bureau
Description: Total area of each state in square miles.

AREA OF STATES

Rank	State	Square miles
1	Alaska	591,004
2	Texas	266,807
3	California	158,706
4	Montana	147,046
5	New Mexico	121,593
6	Arizona	114,000
7	Nevada	110,561
8	Colorado	104,091
9	Wyoming	97,809
10	Oregon	97,073
11	Utah	84,899
12	Minnesota	84,402
13	Idaho	83,564
14	Kansas	82,277
15	Nebraska	77,355
16	South Dakota	77,116
17	North Dakota	70,702
18	Oklahoma	69,956
19	Missouri	69,697
20	Washington	68,139
21	Georgia	58,910
22	Florida	58,664
23	Michigan	58,527
24	Illinois	56,345
25	Iowa	56,275
26	Wisconsin	56,153
27	Arkansas	53,187
28	North Carolina	52,669
29	Alabama	51,705
30	New York	49,108
31	Louisiana	47,752
32	Mississippi	47,689
33	Pennsylvania	45,308
34	Tennessee	42,144
35	Ohio	41,330
36	Virginia	40,767
37	Kentucky	40,409
38	Indiana	36,185
39	Maine	33,265
40	South Carolina	31,113
41	West Virginia	24,231
42	Maryland	10,460
43	Vermont	9,614
44	New Hampshire	9,279
45	Massachusetts	8,284
46	New Jersey	7,787
47	Hawaii	6,471
48	Connecticut	5,018
49	Delaware	2,044
50	Rhode Island	1,212

2. Area in Water

Surface water resources are an important element in the economic geography of the states. Centers of commerce are found on the coasts and around the Great Lakes, but also along such inland waterways as the Mississippi and Ohio rivers and on the routes of the great 19th-century canals, of which the Erie Canal in New York is the foremost example. Natural and artificial lakes are the sites of many resort areas and also furnish water for metropolitan centers. The scarcity of water looms as an important constraint on the further development of the American Southwest. Plans to carry the waters of northern California to the booming but thirsty cities of the southern part of the state by means of a grand canal have touched off political disputes involving sectional interests as well as the issue of environmental integrity versus economic development.

Inland water is found in several forms. The areas in this table include streams, canals, lakes and ponds, with 40 or more acres of open water, and coastal waters protected by headlands. All of this area is included in the measurement of total state area given above. Swamps, bogs and marshland are officially classified as land area and not included here.

When the states are ranked by percentage of total area occupied by open water, the top of the list is dominated by states along the eastern coast and in the district of the glacial lakes along the northern border from Minnesota— "the land of 10,000 lakes"—eastward. Utah, with its Great Salt Lake, is the only western state in the top 20. The inland waters of the six states at the head of the list include extensive estuaries and other coastal waters. When the particularly large portion of water area is deducted from the small total area of Rhode Island, barely 1,000 square miles of land remains. The complex interplay of weather and geology that determines the amount of surface water in a given state is suggested by the geographical variety at the bottom of the list. Here, mountainous West Virginia and Hawaii, with its volcanic terrain, join desert states and states of the Central Plains. State boundaries also play their part; for example, if California were to be divided appropriately, the two resulting states would appear in positions near the top and the bottom of the list.

Table: Area in Water
Date: 1980
Source: Census Bureau
Description: Percentage of each state in inland water area.

AREA IN WATER

Rank	State	Percent of total area	Square miles
1	Rhode Island	13.0	158
2	Florida	7.7	4,511
3	North Carolina	7.3	3,826
4	Maine	7.0	2,270
5	Louisiana	6.8	3,230
6	Maryland	6.0	623
7	Minnesota	5.8	4,854

Rank	State	Percent of total area	Square miles
8	Massachusetts	5.6	460
9	Delaware	5.5	112
10	New Jersey	4.1	319
11	New York	3.5	1,731
11	Vermont	3.5	341
13	Alaska	3.4	20,171
14	Utah	3.3	2,826
15	New Hampshire	3.1	286
15	Wisconsin	3.1	1,727
17	Connecticut	2.9	147
17	South Carolina	2.9	909
19	Michigan	2.7	1,573
20	Virginia	2.6	1,063
21	Washington	2.4	1,627
22	Tennessee	2.3	989
23	Arkansas	2.1	1,109
24	North Dakota	2.0	1,403
25	Oklahoma	1.9	1,301
26	Alabama	1.8	938
26	Texas	1.8	4,790
28	Kentucky	1.8	740
29	California	1.5	2,407
29	South Dakota	1.5	1,164
31	Georgia	1.4	854
31	Idaho	1.4	1,153
33	Illinois	1.2	700
34	Missouri	1.1	752
34	Montana	1.1	1,657
36	Mississippi	1.0	457
37	Nebraska	.9	711
37	Oregon	.9	889
39	Pennsylvania	.9	420
40	Ohio	.8	325
40	Wyoming	.8	820
42	Hawaii	.7	46
42	Indiana	.7	253
44	Kansas	.6	499
44	Nevada	.6	667
44	Iowa	.6	310
47	Colorado	.5	496
47	West Virginia	.5	112
49	Arizona	.4	492
50	New Mexico	.2	258

3. Coastline

The general outline of the seacoast of the United States measures 12,383 miles. About 62% of this mileage is on the Pacific Coast from Alaska to California, 17% on the Atlantic Coast from Maine to Florida, 13% on the Gulf Coast from Florida to Texas, and the remainder on the Arctic Coast of Alaska.

Twenty-two states have coastline frontage, with Alaska accounting for about 54% of the total. Two additional states also touch the oceans according to a more detailed measure of "tidal shoreline": Connecticut (the part extending beyond Long Island) and Pennsylvania (at the head of Delaware Bay). The shoreline measure, based on a survey done at the beginning of World War II, traces the contours of inlets, offshore islands and other irregularities that are ignored in the determination of "general coastline." Total shoreline—amounting to 88,633 miles for the nation as a whole—is some seven times greater than general coastline. For Maryland, which encompasses Chesapeake Bay, the ratio of shoreline to coastline stands at more than 100 to 1.

The 26 states without ocean frontage are not all completely landlocked. Oceangoing vessels have access to six of them (Ohio, Michigan, Indiana, Illinois, Wisconsin and Minnesota) via the St. Lawrence River and the Great Lakes.

Table: Coastline of the United States
Date: 1975
Source: National Oceanic and Atmospheric Administration
Description: Statute miles of general coastline for 22 states.

COASTLINE OF THE UNITED STATES

Rank	State	Statute miles
1	Alaska	6,640
2	Florida	1,350
3	California	840
4	Hawaii	750
5	Louisiana	397
6	Texas	367
7	North Carolina	301
8	Oregon	296
9	Maine	228
10	Massachusetts	192
11	South Carolina	187
12	Washington	157
13	New Jersey	130
14	New York	127
15	Virginia	112
16	Georgia	100
17	Alabama	53
18	Mississippi	44
19	Rhode Island	40
20	Maryland	31
21	Delaware	28
22	New Hampshire	13

4. Area in Forest Land

Forests cover 1.15 million square miles of the American landscape, about one-third of the land. The bulk of forestland is located in the South and the West (from the

Rockies to the Pacific Coast and Alaska). Absence of woodlands is characteristic of the Midwest, the Southwest and the High Plains: the 12 states with under 20% forestland are all located in these areas. Arizona and New Mexico are not part of this group; woodland in the mountainous northern portions of these two states contrasts sharply with desert conditions to the south.

Southern states, with extensive mountain and coastal forests, figure prominantly among the group of 21 states with over half of their land in forests. New England is the most heavily forested region in the country on a percentage basis, although the total amount of forest here is but a small part of the national total. (Note that the combined area of the six New England states—66,672 square miles—is smaller than that of the state of Washington, ranked 20th in Table 1.) In 1845, when Henry Thoreau retired to a hut near Concord, Mass. to gather the experiences he later described in *Walden; or, Life in the Woods*, there was in fact very little woodland left in New England. More than 80% of the region was open farmland in 1850, but in succeeding decades crops produced in the Midwest and shipped back east by means of the new railroad systems gradually undermined the agricultural economy of the Northeast. Farmland reverted to woodland, and today over 75% of New England is forest once again. Most of this forest is privately held in relatively small parcels, which hinders efficient use of its resources. The energy shortages of the 1970s however, gave an impetus toward further commercial development, as wood-burning stoves once again become a fixture in many Yankee households.

Ecological, recreational and commercial interests intersect and often conflict in their concerns with forest resources. About two-thirds of the American forest, whether under public or private ownership, is considered to be commercial timberland, a source of lumber, paper products, fuel and other goods. The noncommercial forest is almost entirely in the Far West—88% in the Rockies or further westward, 42% in Alaska alone.

Table: Area in Forestland
Date: 1977
Source: Department of Agriculture, Forest Service
Description: Percentage of area in forestland, with total number of acres of forestland in thousands.

AREA IN FORESTLAND

Rank	State	Area forested (thousands of acres)	Percent forested
1	Alaska	119,145	33
2	California	40,152	48

Rank	State	Area forested (thousands of acres)	Percent forested
3	Oregon	29,810	49
4	Georgia	25,256	69
5	Texas	23,279	14
6	Washington	23,181	55
7	Montana	22,559	24
8	Colorado	22,271	34
9	Idaho	21,726	41
10	Alabama	21,361	66
11	North Carolina	20,043	65
12	Michigan	19,270	63
13	Arizona	18,494	25
14	Arkansas	18,282	55
15	New Mexico	18,060	23
16	Maine	17,718	90
17	New York	17,218	57
18	Florida	17,040	50
19	Pennsylvania	16,826	59
20	Mississippi	16,716	56
21	Minnesota	16,709	33
22	Virginia	16,417	65
23	Utah	15,557	30
24	Wisconsin	14,908	43
25	Louisiana	14,558	51
26	Tennessee	13,161	50
27	Missouri	12,876	29
28	South Carolina	12,249	64
29	Kentucky	12,161	48
30	West Virginia	11,669	76
31	Wyoming	10,028	16
32	Oklahoma	8,513	19
33	Nevada	7,683	11
34	Ohio	6,147	24
35	New Hampshire	5,013	87
36	Vermont	4,512	76
37	Indiana	3,943	17
38	Illinois	3,810	11
39	Massachusetts	2,952	59
40	Maryland	2,653	42
41	Hawaii	1,986	40
42	New Jersey	1,928	40
43	Connecticut	1,861	60
44	South Dakota	1,702	4
45	Iowa	1,561	4
46	Kansas	1,344	3
47	Nebraska	1,029	2
48	North Dakota	422	1
49	Rhode Island	404	61
50	Delaware	392	32

5. State Parks and Recreation Areas

Areas set aside for public use, managed by state governments, were first created at the turn of the 19th century. Progressives, responding to the closing of the frontier and to the environmental inefficiencies and damages resulting from prevailing patterns of private land use, pressed for greater public control over land.

Conservationists successfully promoted federal legislation that permanently removed public lands from the marketplace by creating the National Park Service. National parks on a grand scale were established in the unsettled western states; the idea was also successful in a number of the densely settled states in the East.

State parks and recreation areas take in about 15,000 square miles of territory across the nation, and the National Park Service administers over seven times as much area. Alaskan state parks account for just over one-third of the total state park area and for more than one-half of all national park territory.

Table: State Park and Recreation Areas
Date: 1980
Source: General Services Administration
Description: Percentage of area designated as state park and recreation areas with total number of acres in thousands so designated.

STATE PARK AND RECREATION AREAS

Rank	State	Percent of total area	Total area (thousands of acres)
1	Connecticut	6.30	198
2	New Jersey	5.39	260
3	Massachusetts	4.72	238
4	Vermont	2.64	157
5	Rhode Island	1.77	12
6	Maryland	1.31	83
7	New Hampshire	1.21	70
8	California	1.00	1,005
9	West Virginia	.97	194
10	Pennsylvania	.95	275
11	Illinois	.91	327
12	Alaska	.90	3,314
13	Florida	.82	286
13	New York	.82	253
15	Ohio	.72	188
16	Delaware	.71	9
17	Michigan	.67	244
18	Hawaii	.60	25
19	Tennessee	.49	131
20	Minnesota	.37	189
21	South Carolina	.35	68
22	Maine	.34	67
22	North Carolina	.34	117
24	Nebraska	.27	131
25	Colorado	.24	160
26	Indiana	.23	54
27	Missouri	.22	96
27	Oklahoma	.22	95
29	Nevada	.21	151
29	Virginia	.21	53
31	Wisconsin	.20	69
31	Wyoming	.20	123
31	Washington	.20	86
34	South Dakota	.18	90
35	Idaho	.16	83
35	Kentucky	.16	41
37	Iowa	.15	52
37	Oregon	.15	92
39	Alabama	.14	48
39	Georgia	.14	52
41	Arkansas	.13	42
41	Utah	.13	69
43	Louisiana	.10	30
44	New Mexico	.09	71
45	Mississippi	.07	21
45	Texas	.07	134
47	Kansas	.05	29
47	Montana	.05	43
49	North Dakota	.04	16
50	Arizona	.03	29

6. Federal Government Land

The federal government holds title to about 34% of all land in the United States. Private interests hold about 58%, and the rest is divided among state and local governments and native Americans. In 1979, Alaska was almost exclusively a federal preserve; nonfederal Alaska was no larger than the state of Maryland (ranked 42nd in Table 1). This situation has changed somewhat, as distributions of land to state government and native corporations have occurred. By 1986 federal ownership is expected to drop to about 60%, which means that nonfederal Alaska will be almost as large as Texas.

Leaving Alaska and Hawaii aside, federal land accounts for 21.6% of all land in the 48 contiguous states. Federal holdings are concentrated in the West. The 13 westernmost states are at the head of this list and the drop-off in federal ownership east of Montana, Wyoming, Colorado and New Mexico is very sharp.

The present pattern of federal holdings was established early in the 20th century under President Theodore Roosevelt. Surveys of the western lands by John Wesley Powell, published in 1879, had shown that traditional farming patterns were unsuited to conditions in much of the area. Under Roosevelt, land sales to private individuals, as provided under the Homestead Act of 1862, were suspended. The new federal policy, guided by presidential aide and prominent conservationist Gifford Pinchot, called for retaining title to public lands and introducing coordinated resource management. Private use of federal land was regulated under leasing arrangements. The scope of federal resource management tasks has since expanded, and other policy aims have been developed, such as the preservation of forests, wildlife and endangered species and the provision of sites for national defense.

Under the Reagan administration, Secretary of the Interior James Watt was an advocate of renewed sales of federal land. It was argued that private concerns now have the technical expertise to manage land more efficiently than the federal government and that sales would therefore provide both short-term revenue to the Treasury and long-run increases in national output. Only a tiny fraction of federal land has actually been sold so far, but the new course marked a dramatic shift in the ideas that have guided land policy for the past 75 years.

Table: Land Owned by the Federal Government
Date: 1979
Source: General Services Administration
Description: Percentage of state area owned by the federal government.
United States average: 33.9%

LAND OWNED BY THE FEDERAL GOVERNMENT

Rank	State	Percent of state area
1	Alaska	98.3
2	Nevada	86.1
3	Idaho	63.7
4	Utah	63.6
5	Oregon	52.4
6	Wyoming	48.6
7	California	46.6
8	Arizona	44.0
9	Colorado	35.5
10	New Mexico	33.2
11	Montana	29.7
12	Washington	29.2
13	Hawaii	16.1
14	New Hampshire	12.5
15	Florida	11.6
16	Arkansas	9.9
17	Michigan	9.5
18	Virginia	9.4
19	South Dakota	7.1
19	West Virginia	7.1
21	Tennessee	6.9
22	Minnesota	6.6
23	North Carolina	6.5
24	Georgia	6.1
25	South Carolina	6.0
26	Mississippi	5.7
27	Kentucky	5.6
28	North Dakota	5.3
28	Wisconsin	5.3
30	Missouri	4.9
30	Vermont	4.9
32	Louisiana	3.8
33	Oklahoma	3.6
34	Alabama	3.4
35	Delaware	3.2

Rank	State	Percent of state area
35	Maryland	3.2
37	New Jersey	3.1
38	Pennsylvania	2.5
39	Indiana	2.1
40	Texas	2.0
41	Illinois	1.6
41	Massachusetts	1.6
43	Nebraska	1.4
44	Kansas	1.3
44	Ohio	1.5
46	Rhode Island	1.1
47	New York	.8
48	Maine	.7
49	Iowa	.6
50	Connecticut	.3

7. Indian Lands

The native peoples who once dominated this continent now control only about 2% of the land—some 83,000 square miles—and this land stands under the legal jurisdiction of the United States Bureau of Indian Affairs. Established under hundreds of specific treaties, Indian lands are scattered across 27 states: the 24 listed below plus Louisiana, Maine and New York, with less than 1,000 acres apiece. The affairs of Native Alaskans, organized in corporations which are receiving distributions of federal lands, are managed separately under the Native Claims Settlement Act of 1971.

The principal Indian reservations are in the West, a geographical legacy of numerous campaigns of forced resettlement. The most radical of these campaigns (mandated by Congress under terms of the Indian Removal Act of 1830) transferred all Indians east of the Mississippi River to lands in the West. The extent of these lands was in turn reduced following a series of military operations that culminated at the battle of Wounded Knee, in 1890.

The largest reservation belongs to the Navajo. It occupies over 20,000 square miles in parts of Arizona, New Mexico and Utah. Indian lands make up 27% of the territory of Arizona, 10% of New Mexico and South Dakota, 5% of Montana (where Custer was defeated at the battle of the Little Bighorn in 1876), and much smaller fractions elsewhere.

About 80% of the Indian lands are owned collectively by tribal authorities. Almost all of the Indian lands in Arizona and 90% of those in New Mexico are owned in common. Federal efforts to turn Indians into farmers, under the Dawes Act of 1887, were finally abandoned in 1934, but not before 20% of present Indian lands had been carved out and assigned to individual proprietors. Individual ownership is predominant in Oklahoma. Montana (with 60% individual ownership) and South Dakota (where the two forms are about evenly split) stand between the extremes.

Table: Lands under Jurisdiction of Bureau of Indian Affairs
Date: 1980
Source: Bureau of Indian Affairs
Description: Lands under jurisdiction of Bureau of Indian Affairs, in thousands of acres, for 24 states.

INDIAN LANDS

Rank	State	Acres (in thousands)
1	Arizona	20,036
2	New Mexico	7,864
3	Montana	5,249
4	South Dakota	5,093
5	Washington	2,520
6	Utah	2,286
7	Wyoming	1,888
8	Oklahoma	1,230
9	Nevada	1,154
10	North Dakota	853
11	Idaho	827
12	Colorado	783
13	Minnesota	764
14	Oregon	762
15	California	573
16	Alabama	428
17	Wisconsin	410
18	Florida	79
19	Nebraska	65
20	North Carolina	57
21	Kansas	29
22	Michigan	21
23	Mississippi	18
24	Iowa	4

8. Mean Elevation

Mean elevation figures smooth out sharp local variations within the states. Consider the case of California. Ranked 11th overall (mean elevation 2,900 feet above sea level), California includes both the highest point in the 48 contiguous states (Mt. Whitney, 14,494 feet) and the lowest point in the entire nation (282 feet below sea level in Death Valley). The highest point in all 50 states is in Alaska (Mt. McKinley, 20,320 feet), but the state also includes large coastal areas at sea level and thus ranks only 15th in mean elevation. Louisiana is the only state except California with territory below sea level (the city of New Orleans, –5 feet). It is also a relatively flat state, with no elevation above 535 feet, and thus it is found at the bottom of this list along with the two lowest and flattest states in the nation: Florida (sea level to 345 feet) and Delaware (sea level to 442 feet).

The top states on the list all include parts of the Rockies. The first five are over one mile high on the average. Volcanic Hawaii stands high on the list, but the only eastern states found in the top half are West Virginia and Pennsylvania, with their Appalachian mountain ranges. States along the Atlantic and Gulf coasts occupy the 11 lowest positions on the list, with mean elevations not above 500 feet.

Table: Mean Elevation
Date: 1980
Source: Geological Survey
Description: Mean elevation, in feet, of each state.

MEAN ELEVATION

Rank	State	Mean elevation (in feet)
1	Colorado	6,800
2	Wyoming	6,700
3	Utah	6,100
4	New Mexico	5,700
5	Nevada	5,500
6	Idaho	5,000
7	Arizona	4,100
8	Montana	3,400
9	Oregon	3,300
10	Hawaii	3,030
11	California	2,900
12	Nebraska	2,600
13	South Dakota	2,200
14	Kansas	2,000
15	Alaska	1,900
15	North Dakota	1,900
17	Texas	1,700
17	Washington	1,700
19	West Virginia	1,500
20	Oklahoma	1,300
21	Minnesota	1,200
22	Iowa	1,100
22	Pennsylvania	1,100
24	Wisconsin	1,050
25	New Hampshire	1,000
25	New York	1,000
25	Vermont	1,000
28	Virginia	950
29	Michigan	900
29	Tennessee	900
31	Ohio	850
32	Missouri	800
33	Kentucky	750
34	Indiana	700

Rank	State	Mean elevation (in feet)
34	North Carolina	700
36	Arkansas	650
37	Georgia	600
37	Illinois	600
37	Maine	600
40	Alabama	500
40	Connecticut	500
40	Massachusetts	500

Rank	State	Mean elevation (in feet)
43	Maryland	350
43	South Carolina	350
45	Mississippi	300
46	New Jersey	250
47	Rhode Island	200
48	Florida	100
48	Louisiana	100
50	Delaware	60

CLIMATE

Although the 48 contiguous states all lie in the Temperate Zone, the variety of climates found here would guarantee that some of the most severe as well as some of the most pleasant weather conditions in the world lie within the American experience—even if Arctic Alaska and Subtropical Hawaii were not members of the Union. Contrasts between warm and chilly, wet and dry climates have become a part of our national folklore. We know where hurricanes rage and tornados whirl, where snow piles up winter after winter, and where to find our place in the sun.

Except for tables on record high and low temperatures for the states, weather information here is given for those cities among the 50 most populous urban centers in 1980 for which data are available. The big cities have the best historical data series, and the local variations in many states are so great that average values would not be very informative in any case. (Compare, for example, rainfall in El Paso and Houston in Texas.)

Climatic conditions are represented as long-term averages that discount variations in the weather from year to year. The major influences on local climate are latitude and geography (altitude, position with respect to the oceans or other large bodies of water, the location of mountains, etc.). Weather obviously influences the agricultural economy of an area, but has important effects on other aspects of the economy (e.g., on energy costs for heating and cooling) and on styles of life. The attractiveness of warm weather lifestyles helps to explain recent interregional migration. Lifestyle changes in regions where seasonal variations are strongly pronounced—where summer vacations mark a high point of the year for example—differentiate the sensibilities of people who live in these regions from those of people who live where seasonal change is almost imperceptible.

9. Average Annual Temperature

Houston and Honolulu, with 30-year average temperatures of 76.1°, are the warmest of the 50 largest cities in the nation. Miami (75.5°), Tampa (72.3°), Phoenix (70.3°)

and San Antonio (69.1°) follow closely. Although average temperature in these cities is similar, the extremes are quite different. Honolulu experiences no seasons as mainlanders know them. The temperature in the coldest months drops only to the middle 60s, while in the hottest it rises to the middle 80s. In Phoenix, on the other hand, the temperature can fall to the 20s in the winter and go over 100° in the summer. Florida, too, experiences winter. Temperatures often drop near freezing, forcing citrus growers to burn smudge pots to warm their orchards and protect their crops.

Cities around the Great Plains and Great Lakes regions are the coldest in the nation, often getting the bitter winter storms that come down from Canada. Minneapolis-St. Paul has the lowest average temperature—44.9°. It is preceded closely by Milwaukee with 46.5° and Buffalo with 47.3°.

Alaskan cities do not appear on the chart because none are among the 50 largest in the nation. Juneau, the state's capital, is colder than any city on the list with an average temperature of 40.3. Surprisingly, though, it does not have the coldest winters in the nation. A number of cities in the lower 48 states have average minimum temperatures below Juneau's 33.5°. Bismarck, N.Dak. is at the bottom of the list of cities surveyed by the National Oceanic and Atmospheric Administration. Its average annual minimum temperature is 29.3°.

Table: Average Annual Temperature
Date: 1941–75
Source: National Oceanic and Atmospheric Administration
Description: Average annual temperature for the 50 largest cities.

AVERAGE ANNUAL TEMPERATURE

Rank	City	Temperature (Fahrenheit)
1	Honolulu	76.1°
1	Houston	76.1°
3	Miami	75.5°
4	Tampa	72.3°
5	Phoenix	70.3°

Rank	City	Temperature (Fahrenheit)
6	San Antonio	69.1°
7	New Orleans	69.0°
8	Jacksonville	67.9°
9	Fort Worth	65.7°
9	Dallas	65.7°
11	El Paso	63.8°
12	Los Angeles	63.6°
13	Birmingham	63.2°
14	Long Beach, Calif.	62.8°
15	San Diego	62.0°
16	Memphis	61.9°
17	Atlanta	61.5°
18	Tulsa	60.5°
19	Oklahoma City	60.1°
20	Norfolk	59.8°
21	Nashville-Davidson	59.6°
22	Washington, D.C.	57.3°
23	Oakland	57.1°
24	Louisville	56.9°
25	St. Louis	56.2°
25	San Francisco	56.2°
27	Kansas City, Mo.	55.6°
28	Baltimore	55.0°
29	Philadelphia	54.6°
30	New York	54.5°
31	Cincinnati	53.9°
32	Newark	53.8°
33	Seattle	53.3°
34	Pittsburgh	52.7°
35	Indianapolis	52.6°
36	Portland, Oreg.	52.5°
37	Columbus, Ohio	52.3°
38	Omaha	51.1°
39	Boston	50.3°
40	Denver	50.2°
41	Chicago	49.9°
41	Cleveland	49.9°
43	Toledo	49.7°
44	Detroit	49.2°
45	Rochester,N.Y.	47.8°
46	Buffalo	47.3°
47	Milwaukee	46.5°
48	Minneapolis	44.9°
48	St. Paul	44.9°
48	San Jose	44.9°

10. Sunshine

Most big cities have kept records for many years of the amount of sunshine that reaches the surface of the earth. These figures are expressed as a percentage of the maximum amount of sunshine (which varies by latitude as well as season) that would reach the surface between dawn and dusk in the absence of clouds, fog, smoke and other blockages in the atmosphere. Data are available through 1980 for 43 of the top 50 cities. The figure for New York represents a 100-year average of observations in Central Park, the time series for 38 of the cities is longer than 20 years.

Four of the southwestern cities are at the top of the list, with over 75% reception of light sent by the sun. The minimum value for all big cities is just under 50%. The low group includes cities in two regions: the Great Lakes and the Pacific Northwest. Sunshine prevails throughout the Southwest, although there are great variations among Texas cities according to their location—in the desert or near the Gulf. Boston and New York are the sunniest of the northeastern cities. The values for 22 of the 43 cities lie in a narrow range between 55% and 62%.

Table: Sunshine
Date: Through 1980
Source: National Oceanic and Atmospheric Administration
Description: Average percentage of possible sunshine in 43 large cities.

SUNSHINE

Rank	City	Percent of possible sunshine
1	Phoenix	86
1	Tucson	86
3	El Paso	83
4	Albuquerque	77
5	Los Angeles	73
6	Denver	70
6	Miami	70
8	Honolulu	68
8	San Diego	68
10	Kansas City, Mo.	67
10	Oklahoma City	67
10	San Francisco	67
13	Charlotte	66
14	Memphis	65
15	Jacksonville	62
15	Omaha	62
15	Tulsa	62
18	Atlanta	61
18	Austin, Tex.	61
18	San Antonio	61
21	Boston	60
22	New Orleans	59
22	New York	59
22	St. Louis	59
25	Birmingham	58
25	Indianapolis	58
25	Minneapolis	58
25	Washington, D.C.	58
29	Baltimore	57
29	Louisville	57
29	Houston	57
29	Nashville	57
29	Philadelphia	57
34	Cincinnati	56
34	Milwaukee	56

Rank	City	Percent of possible sunshine
36	Toledo	55
37	Detroit	54
38	Buffalo	52
38	Columbus, Ohio	52
40	Cleveland	51
41	Portland, Oreg.	49
42	Pittsburgh	48
42	Seattle	48
	Chicago	no data
	Dallas	no data
	Fort Worth	no data
	Long Beach, Calif.	no data
	Newark	no data
	Oakland	no data
	San Jose	no data

11. Average Annual Inches of Rainfall

Miami is the wettest among the top 50 cities, receiving 59.2 inches of rainfall on the average. Ironically, the other cities that lead the list in rainfall—New Orleans, Birmingham, Jacksonville and Tampa—are also in what is known as the Sunbelt—the South and Southwest.

Phoenix, located near a desert, is not surprisingly, the nation's driest large city, with an average of only 7.41 inches of rain per year. The second driest city is El Paso with 8.47 inches. Honolulu, despite its reputation as a lush, subtropical paradise, received only 24.05 inches, less than New York (42.92), Chicago (33.47), or Detroit (31.49).

Table: Average Annual Inches of Rainfall
Date: 1941–70
Source: National Oceanic and Atomspheric Administration
Description: Average annual inches of rain for the 50 largest cities.

AVERAGE ANNUAL INCHES OF RAINFALL

Rank	City	Average annual inches
1	Miami	59.21
2	New Orleans	58.93
3	Birmingham	53.46
4	Jacksonville	51.75
4	Seattle	51.75
6	Tampa	48.99
7	Memphis	48.74
8	Atlanta	48.66
9	Houston	47.07
10	Nashville-Davidson	46.61
11	Norfolk	45.22
12	Louisville	42.94

Rank	City	Average annual inches
13	New York	42.94
14	Newark	41.82
15	Baltimore	41.62
16	Boston	41.55
17	Philadelphia	41.18
18	Cincinnati	40.40
19	Washington, D.C.	40.00
20	Indianapolis	39.98
21	Tulsa	38.04
22	Portland, Oreg.	37.98
23	Columbus, Ohio	36.98
24	St. Louis	36.70
25	Kansas City, Mo.	36.66
26	Pittsburgh	36.21
27	Buffalo	35.19
28	Cleveland	34.15
29	Chicago	33.47
30	Rochester, N.Y.	32.61
31	Dallas	32.11
32	Oklahoma City	31.71
33	Fort Worth	31.53
33	Toledo	31.53
35	Detroit	31.49
36	Milwaukee	30.18
37	Omaha	28.48
38	San Antonio	27.56
39	Minneapolis	26.62
39	St. Paul	26.62
41	Honolulu	24.05
42	San Francisco	18.88
43	Oakland	17.97
44	Los Angeles	14.78
45	Denver	14.60
46	Long Beach, Calif.	9.77
47	San Diego	9.71
48	El Paso	8.47
49	Phoenix	7.41
50	San Jose	—

12. Average Annual Inches of Snowfall

Snowfall data, like those for sunshine, are long-term averages through 1980, covering at least 20 years for all of the 49 cities with available information. Buffalo is the unchallenged snow capital among the big cities, averaging over seven and a half feet per annum since 1944. Ten cities get over three feet of snow in an average year, including Denver and Boston along with a number of Buffalo's neighbors near the Great Lakes. The 13 cities with average snowfall between one and three feet are found on the eastern seaboard and in the Midwest. The South, the Southwest and the Pacific coast see relatively little snow, but—except for Miami and Houston—at least a trace of snow has been observed at some point in the past. Cities in these three regions are generally unprepared for snow and icy roads, so that moderate dustings that would be laughed at in Buffalo can create emergencies.

Table: Average Annual Inches of Snowfall
Date: Through 1980
Source: National Oceanic and Atmospheric Administration
Description: Average annual inches of snow (including ice pellets) in 49 large cities.

SNOWFALL

Rank	City	Average annual inches
1	Buffalo	92.8
2	Denver	59.6
3	Cleveland	52.0
4	Milwaukee	47.0
5	Minneapolis	46.4
6	Pittsburgh	45.3
7	Boston	42.0
8	Chicago	40.2
9	Detroit	39.7
10	Toledo	38.2
11	Omaha	31.6
12	New York	29.0
13	Columbus, Ohio	28.7
14	Newark	28.4
15	Indianapolis	22.4
16	Baltimore	21.9
17	Philadelphia	21.8
18	Kansas City, Mo.	20.1
19	St. Louis	19.8
20	Cincinnati	18.9
21	Louisville	18.3
22	Washington D.C.	17.0
23	Seattle	13.4
24	Nashville	11.6
25	Albuqerque	10.8
26	El Paso	9.6
27	Tulsa	9.3
28	Oklahoma City	9.0
29	Portland, Oreg.	7.3
30	Charlotte	5.8
31	Memphis	5.7
32	Dallas	3.5
32	Fort Worth	3.5
34	Atlanta	1.7
35	Tucson	1.4
36	Birmingham	1.1
37	Austin, Tex.	1.0
38	Houston	.4
38	San Antonio	.4
40	New Orleans	.2
41	Jacksonville	trace
41	Long Beach, Calif.	trace
41	Los Angeles	trace
41	Oakland	trace
41	Phoenix	trace
41	San Diego	trace
41	San Francisco	trace
48	Honolulu	0
48	Miami	0

13. Record High Temperatures

On July 10, 1913, at Greenland Ranch in Death Valley, a temperature of 134° was recorded. No higher temperature has even been recorded in the United States. The world record is held by Azziaia, Libya: 136°. All 50 states have been at or above the 100° mark at some moment in the past.

Table: Record High Temperatures
Date: 1981
Source: National Oceanic and Atmospheric Administration
Description: Highest temperatures ever recorded.

RECORD HIGH TEMPERATURES

Rank	State	Temperature (Fahrenheit)	Date
1	California	134	1913
2	Arizona	127	1905
3	Nevada	122	1954
4	Kansas	121	1936
4	North Dakota	121	1936
6	Arkansas	120	1936
6	Oklahoma	120	1943
6	South Dakota	120	1936
6	Texas	120	1936
10	Oregon	119	1898
11	Colorado	118	1888
11	Idaho	118	1934
11	Iowa	118	1934
11	Missouri	118	1954
11	Nebraska	118	1936
11	Washington	118	1961
17	Illinois	117	1954
17	Montana	117	1937
19	Indiana	116	1936
19	New Mexico	116	1934
19	Utah	116	1892
22	Mississippi	115	1930
23	Kentucky	114	1930
23	Louisiana	114	1936
23	Minnesota	114	1936
23	Wisconsin	114	1936
23	Wyoming	114	1900
28	Georgia	113	1978
28	Ohio	113	1934
28	Tennessee	113	1930
31	Alabama	112	1925
31	Michigan	112	1936
31	West Virginia	112	1936
34	Pennsylvania	111	1936
34	South Carolina	111	1954
36	Delaware	110	1930
36	New Jersey	110	1936
36	Virginia	110	1954
39	Florida	109	1931
39	Maryland	109	1936
39	North Carolina	109	1954
42	New York	108	1926
43	Massachusetts	107	1975

Rank	State	Temperature (Fahrenheit)	Date
43	New Hampshire	106	1911
45	Connecticut	105	1926
45	Maine	105	1911
45	Vermont	105	1911
48	Rhode Island	104	1975
49	Alaska	100	1915
49	Hawaii	100	1931

14. Record Low Temperatures

The national record low of –80° was recorded at Prospect Creek, Alaska on January 23, 1971. The world record is much lower: –127° at Vostok, a Soviet weather station in the Antarctic. Forty-nine of the 50 states have had subzero weather at some moment in the recorded past, but as far as is known the only ice ever found in Hawaii has been in refrigerators.

Table: Record Low Temperatures
Date: 1981
Source: National Oceanic and Atmospheric Administration
Description: Lowest temperatures ever recorded.

RECORD LOW TEMPERATURES

Rank	State	Temperature (Fahrenheit)	Date
1	Alaska	-80	1971
2	Montana	-70	1954
3	Wyoming	-63	1933
4	Colorado	-60	1951
4	Idaho	-60	1943
4	North Dakota	-60	1936
7	Minnesota	-59	1903
8	South Dakota	-58	1936
9	Oregon	-54	1933
9	Wisconsin	-54	1922
11	New York	-52	1934
12	Michigan	-51	1934
13	Nevada	-50	1937
13	New Mexico	-50	1951
13	Utah	-50	1933
13	Vermont	-50	1913
17	Maine	-48	1925
17	Washington	-48	1968
19	Iowa	-47	1912
19	Nebraska	-47	1899
19	New Hampshire	-47	1934
22	California	-45	1937
23	Pennsylvania	-42	1904
24	Arizona	-40	1971
24	Kansas	-40	1905
24	Maryland	-40	1912
24	Missouri	-40	1905
28	Ohio	-39	1899
29	West Virginia	-37	1917
30	Illinois	-35	1930
30	Indiana	-35	1951
32	Kentucky	-34	1963
32	Massachusetts	-34	1957
32	New Jersey	-34	1904
35	Connecticut	-32	1943
35	Tennessee	-32	1917
37	Arkansas	-29	1905
37	North Carolina	-29	1966
37	Virginia	-29	1899
40	Alabama	-27	1966
40	Oklahoma	-27	1930
42	Rhode Island	-23	1942
42	Texas	-23	1933
44	South Carolina	-20	1977
45	Mississippi	-19	1966
46	Delaware	-17	1893
46	Georgia	-17	1940
48	Louisiana	-16	1899
49	Florida	-2	1899
50	Hawaii	14	1961

POPULATION

Knowledge of the growth and distribution of population is the indispensable foundation for understanding other elements of American society. The tables on the size, growth and density of population presented in this section are used over and over again in evaluating the indicators that appear in other sections.

When the first U.S. census was taken in 1790, this was a nation of small farmers. Only 5% of the total population lived in towns that specialized in coastal and international trading of agricultural products. Philadelphia, the largest city, counted 68,000 residents. In 1980 there were 169 cities with populations of 100,000 or more. Today there are 21 *states* with populations in excess of 3.9 million, the total national population in 1790. A small outpost of European civilization has been transformed into a major population center and economic power. The population first exceeded 100 million in 1915, reaching a total of 216 million in the bicentennial year of 1976. China, India and the Soviet Union are the only nations on earth with populations larger than that of the United States.

15. Population of the States

The 1980 census found 226.5 million people in the United States, an average of about 4.5 million per state. The actual distribution of persons among states is very uneven. The top three states—California, New York and Texas—account for about 25% of the population. Additional 25%-segments are found in the six states ranked four through nine, the 11 states ranked 10 through 20, and the remaining 30 states ranked 21 through 50. The total population of the 20 states at the bottom of the list is smaller than the population of California. Californians account for about one American in 10 and they outnumber New Yorkers by over six million. Alaskans, on the other hand, are rare creatures. Fewer than one American in five hundred lives in Alaska, and there are about fifty-nine Californians and forty-four New Yorkers per Alaskan.

Different rates of population change caused several changes in the ranking of states between 1970 and 1980. Near the top of the list, Texas moved ahead of Pennsylvania, Florida moved ahead of Michigan and New Jersey, and North Carolina captured the 10th position by overtaking Massachusetts and Indiana. Each one of these cases illustrates the dominant pattern of population change in the 1970s, when growth in the West and South ran far ahead of development in the Northeast and Midwest. Near the bottom of the list, Nevada vaulted ahead of Montana, South Dakota, North Dakota and Delaware to claim position 43.

Table: Population of the States
Date: 1980
Source: Census Bureau
Description: Population (including members of the armed forces) and state population as a percentage of the total U.S. population.
United States total: 226.5 million
State average: 4.5 million
State median: 3.1 million

POPULATION OF THE STATES

Rank	State	Population (in thousands)	Percent of total population
1	California	23,669	10.45
2	New York	17,557	7.75
3	Texas	14,228	6.28
4	Pennsylvania	11,867	5.24
5	Illinois	11,418	5.04
6	Ohio	10,797	4.77
7	Florida	9,740	4.30
8	Michigan	9,258	4.09
9	New Jersey	7,364	3.25
10	North Carolina	5,874	2.59
11	Massachusetts	5,737	2.53
12	Indiana	5,490	2.42
13	Georgia	5,464	2.41
14	Virginia	5,346	2.36
15	Missouri	4,915	2.17
16	Wisconsin	4,705	2.08

Rank	State	Population (in thousands)	Percent of total population
17	Tennessee	4,591	2.03
18	Maryland	4,216	1.86
19	Louisiana	4,204	1.86
20	Washington	4,130	1.82
21	Minnesota	4,077	1.80
22	Alabama	3,890	1.72
23	Kentucky	3,661	1.62
24	South Carolina	3,119	1.38
25	Connecticut	3,108	1.37
26	Oklahoma	3,025	1.34
27	Iowa	2,913	1.29
28	Colorado	2,889	1.28
29	Arizona	2,718	1.20
30	Oregon	2,633	1.16
31	Mississippi	2,521	1.11
32	Kansas	2,363	1.04
33	Arkansas	2,286	1.01
34	West Virginia	1,950	.86
35	Nebraska	1,570	.70
36	Utah	1,461	.65
37	New Mexico	1,300	.57
38	Maine	1,125	.50
39	Hawaii	965	.43
40	Rhode Island	947	.42
41	Idaho	944	.42
42	New Hampshire	921	.41
43	Nevada	799	.35
44	Montana	787	.35
45	South Dakota	690	.31
46	North Dakota	653	.29
47	Delaware	595	.26
48	Vermont	511	.23
49	Wyoming	471	.21
50	Alaska	400	.18

16. Population Change 1970–1980

The population of the nation increased by 23.3 million, or 11.4%, during the 1970s. New York and Rhode Island were the only states with negative population growth. The fact that 30 of the 50 states had rates of increase above the national average indicates that there was a moderate tendency toward a more even distribution of population among the states during the decade, since the smaller states were growing more rapidly on the average.

Arizona and especially Nevada were well ahead of the rest of the country in relative growth, with increases of more than 50% in just 10 years. The largest increases in numbers were recorded in California (3.71 million), Texas (3.03 million) and Florida (2.95 million). The absolute increase of 310,000 persons in Nevada was small by comparison.

Some of the population change in a given state occurs because the number of births is greater than the number of deaths among residents; but net migration—the balance between people moving to and from a state—is usually more important in accounting for change. The key pattern of migration during the 1970s was a flow between regions, from the Northeast and Midwest toward the West and South. This interregional stream of persons, the larger pattern that lies behind different growth rates in the states, can be more clearly displayed if states are collected into the nine standard census division groups. The standard divisions are made up as follows:

(1) *New England* (6 states): Connecticut, Maine, Massachusetts, New Hampshire, Rhode Island, Vermont.
(2) *Middle Atlantic* (3): New Jersey, New York, Pennsylvania.
(3) *East North Central* (5): Illinois, Indiana, Michigan, Ohio, Wisconsin.
(4) *West North Central* (7): Iowa, Kansas, Minnesota, Missouri, Nebraska, North Dakota, South Dakota.
(5) *South Atlantic* (8 plus the District of Columbia): Delaware, Florida, Georgia, Maryland, North Carolina, South Carolina, Virginia, West Virginia.
(6) *East South Central* (4): Alabama, Kentucky, Mississippi, Tennessee.
(7) *West South Central* (4): Arkansas, Louisiana, Oklahoma, Texas.
(8) *Mountain* (8): Arizona, Colorado, Idaho, Montana, Nevada, New Mexico, Utah, Wyoming.
(9) *Pacific* (5): Alaska, California, Hawaii, Oregon, Washington.

The pattern in the census divisions is clear and striking. Throughout the northeast and north central areas state populations changed very little. New Hampshire, Vermont and Maine were the only states among 21 included in these "frostbelt" divisions with rates of increase above the national average. They are also the least urbanized and least economically developed states in the Northeast, so their growth actually corresponds to the large-scale trends of dispersion of economic activity and movement of population to areas with rich natural amenities that have contributed to the boom in the five Sunbelt divisions. Among the 29 states assigned to the five divisions of the West and South, there were 27 with rates of population increase above the national average. Once again, the exception proves the pattern: Delaware and Maryland are located at the extreme northeastern tip of the South Atlantic division and in general they have more in common with the Middle Atlantic states than with the others in their division.

The surprising feature of the ranking by divisions is that

the Pacific division, which led all others in relative growth during each decade between 1920 and 1970, fell to fourth place. The astounding growth of the Mountain division, which still has the smallest population among the nine, was based on both the continuation of long-term high growth rates in some states (Arizona, Colorado, Nevada) and a revival of growth in some states that had been relatively stagnant in previous decades (Idaho, Montana, Wyoming). In these three reviving states, the key development was increased exploitation of energy resources that resulted from changes in oil prices. All of the Mountain states have benefited from changing national attitudes and preferences in recent years. The growing interest in winter sports stimulated development of ski resort areas, while the growing public concern with ecology increased the attractiveness of mountain environments for vacationing and living.

Table: Population Change (A)
Date: 1970–1980.
Source: Census Bureau
Description: Percent of population change 1970–1980.
National rate: 11.4%
State median: 13.7%

POPULATION CHANGE

Rank	State	Percent of change
1	Nevada	63.5
2	Arizona	53.1
3	Florida	43.4
4	Wyoming	41.6
5	Utah	37.9
6	Alaska	32.4
6	Idaho	32.4
8	Colorado	30.7
9	New Mexico	27.8
10	Texas	27.1
11	Oregon	25.9
12	Hawaii	25.3
13	New Hampshire	24.8
14	Washington	21.0
15	South Carolina	20.4
16	Georgia	19.1
17	Arkansas	18.8
18	California	18.5
19	Oklahoma	18.2
20	Tennessee	16.9
21	North Carolina	15.5
22	Louisiana	15.3
23	Vermont	15.0
24	Virginia	14.9
25	Kentucky	13.7
25	Mississippi	13.7
27	Montana	13.3
28	Maine	13.2

Rank	State	Percent of change
29	Alabama	12.9
30	West Virginia	11.8
31	Delaware	8.6
32	Maryland	7.5
33	Minnesota	7.1
34	Wisconsin	6.5
35	Indiana	5.7
35	Nebraska	5.7
37	North Dakota	5.6
38	Kansas	5.1
38	Missouri	5.1
40	Michigan	4.2
41	South Dakota	3.6
42	Iowa	3.1
43	Illinois	2.8
44	New Jersey	2.7
45	Connecticut	2.5
46	Ohio	1.3
47	Massachusetts	.8
48	Pennsylvania	.6
49	Rhode Island	-.3
50	New York	-3.8

Table: Population Change (B)
Date: 1980
Source: Census Bureau
Description: Population and percent of change from 1970 to 1980, by Census Divisions.

POPULATION CHANGE BY CENSUS DIVISIONS

Rank	Census division	Percent of change	1980 Population (in thousands)
1	Mountain	37.1	11,368
2	West South Central	22.9	23,743
3	South Atlantic	20.4	36,943
4	Pacific	19.8	31,797
5	East South Central	14.5	14,663
6	West North Central	5.2	17,184
7	New England	4.2	12,348
8	East North Central	3.5	41,670
9	Middle Atlantic	-1.1	36,788

17. Large Metropolitan Areas

The first 50 of the 318 Standard Metropolitan Statistical Areas (SMSAs) identified in the 1980 census are listed below. Just to be on the list requires a population of about 800,000, twice the population of Alaska. Even among this group of very large centers of population, size differences are enormous. Ten SMSAs as large as Memphis could be carved out of the New York SMSA.

The true giants—New York, Los Angeles and Chicago—would stand even further above the others if neighboring SMSAs were included to give a comprehensive picture of the urban regions in their vicinities. Two other SMSAs in the top 20 are neighbors of New York—Nassau-Suffolk, or Long Island (11th) and Newark (17th). Two neighbors of Los Angeles also appear on the list—Anaheim (18th) and Riverside (25th).

Rates of population change in the top SMSAs during the 1970s varied between 63.5% (Fort Lauderdale) and −8.6% (New York). Eleven of the top 50 lost population. SMSA central cities have been losing population for several decades, but widespread declines for entire SMSAs, central cities plus suburbs, is a new phenomenon. America's metropolitan areas are no longer developing in a uniform fashion. The big Sunbelt SMSAs continue to grow rapidly, while low or negative growth rates are now the norm in the Northeast and Midwest. In the first group, only Los Angeles and San Francisco have slowed notably in their growth, while the (relatively) high fliers among the second group are Washington, D.C., Baltimore, Minneapolis, Indianapolis and Columbus.

Table: Large Metropolitan Areas
Date: 1980
Source: *American Demographics*
Description: Population of the 50 largest Standard Metropolitan Statistical Areas on April 1, 1980 and percent of population change 1970–1980.

LARGE METROPOLITAN AREAS

Rank	SMSA	Population (in thousands)	Percent of change
1	New York	9,120	−8.6
2	Los Angeles-Long Beach	7,478	6.2
3	Chicago	7,102	1.8
4	Philadelphia	4,717	−2.2
5	Detroit	4,353	−1.9
6	San Francisco-Oakland	3,253	4.6
7	Washington, D.C.	3,060	5.2
8	Dallas-Fort Worth	2,975	25.1
9	Houston	2,905	45.3
10	Boston	2,763	−4.7
11	Nassau-Suffolk (Long Island)	2,606	2.0
12	St. Louis	2,355	−2.3
13	Pittsburgh	2,264	−5.7
14	Baltimore	2,174	5.0
15	Minneapolis-St. Paul	2,114	7.6
16	Atlanta	2,030	27.2
17	Newark	1,965	−4.5
18	Anaheim-Santa Ana-Garden Grove, Calif.	1,932	35.9
19	Cleveland	1,899	−8.0
20	San Diego	1,862	37.1
21	Miami	1,626	28.3
22	Denver-Boulder	1,620	30.7

Rank	SMSA	Population (in thousands)	Percent of change
23	Seattle-Everett	1,607	12.8
24	Tampa-St. Petersburg	1,569	44.2
25	Riverside-San Bernardino-Ontario, Calif.	1,557	36.7
26	Phoenix	1,508	55.3
27	Cincinnati	1,401	1.0
28	Milwaukee	1,397	−0.5
29	Kansas City	1,327	4.2
30	San Jose	1,295	21.6
31	Buffalo	1,243	−7.9
32	Portland, Oreg., Wash.	1,242	23.3
33	New Orleans	1,187	13.4
34	Indianapolis	1,167	5.0
35	Columbus, Ohio	1,093	7.4
36	San Antonio	1,072	20.7
37	Fort Lauderdale-Hollywood	1,014	63.5
37	Sacramento	1.014	26.2
39	Rochester, N.Y.	972	1.1
40	Salt Lake City-Ogden	936	32.7
41	Providence-Warwick-Pawtucket, R.I., Mass.	919	1.1
42	Memphis	913	9.4
43	Louisville	906	4.5
44	Nashville-Davidson	851	21.6
45	Birmingham	847	10.4
46	Oklahoma City	834	19.3
47	Dayton	830	−2.6
48	Greensboro-Winston-Salem-High Point	827	14.3
49	Norfolk-Virginia Beach-Portsmouth	807	10.1
50	Albany-Schenectady-Troy	795	2.2

18. Metropolitan Population

The population density of a state depends on just two numbers—total population and total area. If these numbers are held constant, the measured density is the same whether homes are uniformly scattered across a state or concentrated in just a few places. When most Americans were farmers, homes were widely scattered and local population densities were similar throughout any given state. An increasingly uneven distribution of population and a more concentrated pattern of settlement began to be established over 150 years ago, as industrialization and commercial development led to the rapid growth of towns and cities. Concentration increased continually, but Americans were never fully reconciled to life in urban agglomerations. In recent times people have taken advantage of automobiles and highway systems, and the opportunities presented by the shift from production of goods to production of services and information to establish a more scattered or "counterurbanized" pattern of residential settlement that marks a departure from the long historical trend toward concentration.

The degree of population concentration in a given state is an indicator suggestive of the typical lifestyles and everyday experiences of its population. We have a rough, intuitive sense of what it means to live among more or less concentrated groups of our fellow beings, and a corresponding sense that the degree of concentration must vary to a wide extent in different parts of the country. It is difficult, however, to define and measure concentration in a way that accords with everyone's intuition and satisfies everyone's curiosity. The Bureau of the Census has wrestled with this problem for many years. Two different measures of concentration or "urbanization" are produced by the bureau. The degree of *large-scale* concentration may be expressed as the percentage of state population found within one of the SMSAs. This is presented in the first table given below. In the next table, the focus shifts to pick up concentration on a relatively *small scale*, expressed as the percentage of state population found in "urban" areas (whether or not they are also part of "metropolitan" or SMSA areas).

Between 1970 and 1980, the proportion of population found in the 318 SMSAs actually *declined* from 75.6% to 74.8%. Total SMSA population did increase (by 10.2%), but not as rapidly as nonmetropolitan population (15.1%). The apparent relative scattering or dispersion of population during the 1970s marked the first measured countermove in a trend toward concentration that had remained unbroken, even during the frontier-settlement period of our history, since about 1815. This is one of the major findings of the 1980 census and there has been much debate as to its meaning. Some argue that small towns and areas rich in natural amenities have been leading the way in nonmetropolitan growth. Others claim that sprawling fringes of SMSAs now simply escape across their statistical frontiers, giving a false impression of growth unrelated to the major centers. In either case, a scattering of one type or another is implied, and further dispersion seems to be in line for the 1980s.

Comparing states, it is clear that the size of metropolitan segments varies across a wide range. In 16 states, including the nine most populous states that account for over half of the national population, the degree of metropolitan concentration is 80% or above. Many of these states lie within the Boston-Washington corridor, but California stands at the top of the list and the only major regions not represented in this group are the Great Plains and the South. At the bottom of the list, Vermont joins four states from the Mountain-High Plains area in the group with less than 25% metropolitan population. The national trend toward a slight decline in the

metropolitan segment was also observed in 27 individual states. Among the 23 states that bucked the trend of the 1970s by becoming relatively *more* metropolitan, the most significant gains were made in North Dakota, New Mexico, Idaho and Mississippi. In the States of Massachusetts, New Jersey, New York, Ohio and Pennsylvania there was both a loss of metropolitan population in relation to nonmetropolitan areas and a decline in the total number of metropolitan residents.

Table: Metropolitan Population
Date: 1980
Source: Census Bureau
Description: Percent of state population living in standard metropolitan statistical areas.
National rate: 74.8%
State median: 64.8%

METROPOLITAN POPULATION

Rank	State	Percent of population living in SMSAs
1	California	94.9
2	Rhode Island	92.2
3	New Jersey	91.4
4	New York	90.1
5	Maryland	88.8
6	Connecticut	88.3
7	Florida	87.9
8	Massachusetts	85.3
9	Michigan	82.7
10	Nevada	82.0
11	Pennsylvania	81.9
12	Illinois	81.0
13	Colorado	80.9
14	Washington	80.4
15	Ohio	80.3
16	Texas	80.0
17	Hawaii	79.1
18	Utah	79.0
19	Arizona	75.0
20	Indiana	69.8
21	Virginia	69.6
22	Delaware	67.0
23	Wisconsin	66.8
24	Missouri	65.3
25	Oregon	64.9
26	Minnesota	64.6
27	Louisiana	63.4
28	Tennessee	62.8
29	Alabama	62.0
30	Georgia	60.0
31	South Carolina	59.7
32	Oklahoma	58.5
33	North Carolina	52.7
34	New Hampshire	50.7
35	Kansas	46.8
36	Kentucky	44.5

Rank	State	Percent of population living in SMSAs
37	Nebraska	44.2
38	Alaska	43.2
39	New Mexico	42.4
40	Iowa	40.1
41	Arkansas	39.1
42	West Virginia	37.1
43	North Dakota	35.9
44	Maine	33.0
45	Mississippi	27.1
46	Montana	24.0
47	Vermont	22.3
48	Idaho	18.3
49	South Dakota	15.9
50	Wyoming	15.3

19. Large Cities

Cities are political units with legally established boundaries, unlike SMSAs or "urban areas." This table presents the 1980 populations of the 50 largest units of municipal government in the United States.

New York is far and away the largest city, more than twice as big as second-city Chicago. If New York City were a state, it would have the 10th largest state population in the country. (Chicago or Los Angeles would rank 27th, just ahead of Iowa.) New York maintained its lead over all other cities even though its population declined by more than 800,000 during the 1970s—by more, that is, than the entire 1980 population of Nevada.

A list of the top 50 cities in 1970 is included below for comparison. There have been several changes in the top 10. Houston moved ahead of Detroit and drew close to Philadelphia. Dallas moved from the eighth to the seventh position, and San Diego and San Antonio entered the top 10 for the first time. Baltimore fell from the seventh to the ninth position, while Washington and Cleveland not only dropped from the top 10, but fell to positions below Phoenix, Honolulu (which incorporated a great amount of new area), Indianapolis, San Francisco and Memphis. New additions to the top 50 are Austin, Albuquerque, Tucson and Charlotte. St. Paul, Rochester, Tampa and Norfolk are no longer on the list. The rise of the Sunbelt cities is clearly evident.

Table: Population of the 50 Largest Cities (A)
Date: 1980
Source: Census Bureau
Description: Population of the 50 largest cities in 1980.

POPULATION OF THE 50 LARGEST CITIES IN 1980

Rank	City	Population (in thousands)
1	New York	7,071
2	Chicago	3,005
3	Los Angeles	2,967
4	Philadelphia	1,688
5	Houston	1,594
6	Detroit	1,203
7	Dallas	904
8	San Diego	876
9	Baltimore	787
10	San Antonio	785
11	Phoenix	765
12	Honolulu	763
13	Indianapolis	701
14	San Francisco	679
15	Memphis	646
16	Washington, D.C.	638
17	San Jose	637
18	Milwaukee	636
19	Cleveland	574
20	Columbus, Ohio	565
21	Boston	563
22	New Orleans	557
23	Jacksonville	541
24	Seattle	494
25	Denver	491
26	Nashville-Davidson	456
27	St. Louis	453
28	Kansas City, Mo.	448
29	El Paso	425
29	Atlanta	425
31	Pittsburgh	424
32	Oklahoma City	403
33	Cincinnati	385
33	Fort Worth	385
35	Minneapolis	371
36	Portland, Oreg.	366
37	Long Beach, Calif.	361
37	Tulsa	361
39	Buffalo	358
40	Toledo	355
41	Miami	347
42	Austin, Tex.	345
43	Oakland	339
44	Albuquerque	332
45	Tucson	331
46	Newark	329
47	Charlotte	314
48	Omaha	312
49	Louisville	298
50	Birmingham	284

Table: Population of the 50 Largest Cities (B)
Date: 1970
Source: Census Bureau
Description: Population of the 50 largest cities in 1970.

POPULATION OF THE 50 LARGEST CITIES IN 1970

Rank	City	Population (in thousands)
1	New York	7,894
2	Chicago	3,366
3	Los Angeles	2,816
4	Philadelphia	1,948
5	Detroit	1,511
6	Houston	1,232
7	Baltimore	905
8	Dallas	844
9	Washington, D.C.	756
10	Cleveland	750
11	Indianapolis	744
12	Milwaukee	717
13	San Francisco	715
14	San Diego	696
15	San Antonio	654
16	Boston	641
17	Memphis	623
18	St. Louis	622
19	New Orleans	593
20	Phoenix	581
21	Columbus, Ohio	539
22	Seattle	530
23	Jacksonville	528
24	Pittsburgh	520
25	Denver	514
26	Kansas City, Mo.	507
27	Atlanta	496
28	Buffalo	462
29	Cincinnati	452
30	Nashville-Davidson	448
31	San Jose	445
32	Minneapolis	434
33	Fort Worth	393
34	Toledo	383
35	Newark	382
35	Portland, Oreg.	382
37	Oklahoma City	366
38	Louisville	361
38	Oakland	361
40	Long Beach, Calif.	358
41	Omaha	347
42	Miami	334
43	Tulsa	331
44	Honolulu	324
45	El Paso	322
46	St. Paul	309
47	Norfolk	307
48	Birmingham	300
49	Rochester, N.Y.	296
50	Tampa	277

20. Urban Population

The Census Bureau defines an "urban" settlement as a place with at least 2,500 residents, although smaller places may also be so defined when they belong to urbanized areas with a certain population density. This differs from the definition of an SMSA in two major respects. First, small towns outside large population centers are included. Second, urban areas need not be whole political units like cities and counties. The low density sections of SMSA counties are not urban under this definition. (Check the *Statistical Abstract of the United States* for technical details.)

At the national level, the percent of urban and the percent of metropolitan populations in 1980 were about the same—73.77% and 74.8%. The relationship between the two measures is also strong at the state level. The proportion of national population classified as urban increased by a fraction of a percentage point (73.5% to 73.7%) during the 1970s, but comparison of the figures is not entirely warranted since the particular urban areas compared are not the same in both 1970 and 1980 (whereas the 318 SMSAs used for this analysis are the same ones for both 1970 and 1980).

In states with low metropolitan segments, somewhat higher figures are often found for urban segments because of the inclusion of smaller towns. Wyoming is only 15.3% metropolitan, but 62.8% urban. The same pattern is found in states like Idaho (18.3% and 54.0%), Maine (33.0% and 47.5%) and Mississippi (27.1% and 47.3%). In states with high metropolitan segments, on the other hand, smaller urban segments are often observed because of the exclusion of rural portions of the SMSA counties. Connecticut, 88.3% metropolitan, is just 78.8% urban. The same pattern appears for Pennsylvania (81.8% and 69.3%) and Michigan (82.7% and 70.7%). Hawaii is an exception to the rule that states with high metropolitan proportions have relatively lower urban segments. Hawaii is highly metropolitan (79.1%), but even more urban (86.5%), since very little rural territory is included in the island SMSA. California is at the top of both the urban and the metropolitan lists. West Virginia and Vermont, not Wyoming, prove to be the most rural states.

Table: Urban Population
Date: 1980
Source: Census Bureau
Description: Percent of population living in urban areas.
National rate: 73.7%
State median: 67.0%

URBAN POPULATION

Rank	State	Percent of urban population
1	California	91.3
2	New Jersey	89.0

Rank	State	Percent of urban population
3	Rhode Island	87.0
4	Hawaii	86.5
5	Nevada	85.3
6	New York	84.6
7	Utah	84.4
8	Florida	84.3
9	Arizona	83.8
9	Massachusetts	83.8
11	Illinois	83.0
12	Colorado	80.6
13	Maryland	80.3
14	Texas	79.6
15	Connecticut	78.8
16	Washington	73.6
17	Ohio	73.3
18	New Mexico	72.2
19	Delaware	70.7
19	Michigan	70.7
21	Pennsylvania	69.3
22	Louisiana	68.6
23	Missouri	68.1
24	Oregon	67.9
25	Oklahoma	67.3
26	Minnesota	66.8
27	Kansas	66.7
28	Virginia	66.0
29	Alaska	64.5
30	Indiana	64.2
30	Wisconsin	64.2
32	Wyoming	62.8
33	Nebraska	62.7
34	Georgia	62.3
35	Tennessee	60.4
36	Alabama	60.0
37	Iowa	58.6
38	South Carolina	54.1
39	Idaho	54.0
40	Montana	52.9
41	New Hampshire	52.2
42	Arkansas	51.6
43	Kentucky	50.8
44	North Dakota	48.8
45	North Carolina	48.0
46	Maine	47.5
47	Mississippi	47.3
48	South Dakota	46.4
49	West Virginia	36.2
50	Vermont	33.8

21. Population Density

The eight states with the highest average population density, that is, population per square mile of land area, form a geographical block along the East Coast from Boston to Washington, D.C. The small, urbanized states crowd close to the top of the list. Geographically, New York and Pennsylvania are the biggest states in this group,

although their large "upstate" (rural) sections, spread between high density areas in the eastern and western parts, hold down overall statewide density. Four of the five states holding positions 9 through 13 are clustered around the Great Lakes. Variations in density among the states are so great that it helps to think in multiples. To approximate the density of Alaska in Wyoming (rank 49), six of every seven residents of Wyoming would have to leave. To approximate current Wyoming density in Maine (rank 36), or current Maine density in Ohio (rank 9), a similar operation which left only one in seven residents in place in the more densely inhabited state would be required. Going the whole route and approximating Alaska density in Ohio would involve displacing almost everybody in Ohio. (About 375 would have to go for each person who remained.) The 10 low-density states in positions 40 through 49 are found, like the high-density groups of states, in a distinct geographical block. This block extends from Mexico to Canada along both sides of the Rockies.

Overall state population density smooths out extreme local variations to provide a useful yardstick for comparisons on a broader scale among the states. This will be obvious to anyone who has trekked through the empty Pine Barrens in New Jersey, where average density approaches 1,000 per square mile, or who has lived as a town dweller in Alaska, where average density figures suggest that one square mile is available for each resident. Measures of average density should not be confused with measures of population concentration (presented above under the headings of Metropolitan Population and Urban Population). A comparison of average densities nevertheless presents a clear picture of some important facts. Average density of settlement various enormously as one moves across the country, and the "wide open spaces" are still to be found in the West (if you do not venture too close to the coast).

Table: Population Density
Date: 1980
Source: Census Bureau
Description: Population per square mile of land area.
United States average: 64.0 (76.2 without Alaska)
State median: 78.7

POPULATION DENSITY

Rank	State	Persons per square mile
1	New Jersey	986.1
2	Rhode Island	897.6
3	Massachusetts	733.3

POPULATION DENSITY

Rank	State	Persons per square mile	Rank	State	Persons per square mile
4	Connecticut	637.9	28	Washington	62.1
5	Maryland	428.6	29	Vermont	55.1
6	New York	370.6	30	Texas	54.3
7	Delaware	308.0	31	Mississippi	53.4
8	Pennsylvania	264.4	32	Iowa	52.1
9	Ohio	263.3	33	Minnesota	51.3
10	Illinois	205.2	34	Oklahoma	44.1
11	Florida	179.9	35	Arkansas	43.9
12	Michigan	162.8	36	Maine	36.3
13	Indiana	152.8	37	Kansas	28.9
14	California	151.4	38	Colorado	27.9
15	Hawaii	150.2	39	Oregon	27.4
16	Virginia	134.6	40	Arizona	23.9
17	North Carolina	120.3	41	Nebraska	20.5
18	Tennessee	111.6	42	Utah	17.8
19	South Carolina	103.3	43	Idaho	11.5
20	New Hampshire	102.4	44	New Mexico	10.7
21	Louisiana	94.4	45	North Dakota	9.4
22	Georgia	94.1	46	South Dakota	9.1
23	Kentucky	92.3	47	Nevada	7.3
24	Wisconsin	86.4	48	Montana	5.4
25	West Virginia	80.8	49	Wyoming	4.9
26	Alabama	76.6	50	Alaska	.7
27	Missouri	71.3			

HOUSING

This section surveys the number of housing units in each state, trends in new construction, and certain characteristics of the housing stock, including current prices.

The trend toward smaller households played an important part in the housing markets of the 1970s. Population increased by 11.4% during the decade, but the number of dwellings rose by 28.1% in response to the demand generated by young people for residences separate from their parents, by older people for residences separate from their children, and by formerly married people for residences separate from their ex-spouses. The fragmentation of families means good business for the builders. A further impetus for construction came from regional shifts of population and industry toward the West and South, where new housing had to be developed to receive the influx.

Booming business in construction came to an abrupt halt, however, in the late 1970s. Recession combined with mortgage interest rates in the neighborhood of 17% slammed the door on housing. The savings and loan institutions, severely tested by competition from money market funds and general financial conditions, can now no longer provide affordable mortgages at fixed interest rates. New financing schemes that involve more risk for borrowers are increasingly prevalent. American households face the prospect of spending at least 30% to 35% of their incomes for housing in the future. The old 25% rule of thumb is now just a memory. Higher housing costs result not just from high interest rates (which could become permanent if federal deficits remain high), but also from trends toward higher costs of land and buildings. Traditional construction methods simply cannot be made more productive to the same degree as other industrial and service activities, so the relative cost of construction necessarily increases. One solution to the productivity squeeze is to build houses in factories. The data on mobile homes given below indicate that there is indeed a shift in this direction.

The present combination of trends in household makeup, finance and production of housing have led many analysts to assert that a fundamental reorientation in American housing is now under way. The baby-boom generation is reaching the age for buying a home at a time when prospects for homeownership are relatively bleak. Many younger Americans will have to settle for a home that falls far short of their dreams and expectations, and this promises to make the politics of housing during the 1980s increasingly volatile.

22. Number of Year-Round Housing Units and Percentage of Change from 1970 to 1980

In 1980 there were over 86 million separate dwellings suitable for year-round occupancy in the United States. There were about two million other dwellings that were used only on a seasonal basis. Between 1970 and 1980 about 19 million units were added to the year-round housing stock. This represented a 28% increase during the decade, well above the 20% rate of increase during the 1960s. Two-thirds of the housing stock consisted of single-family homes, freestanding or attached (including row houses). One home in six was found in a structure containing five or more dwelling units, and one home in twenty was a mobile home.

The greatest increases in the housing stock during the 1970s occurred in the West and the South. New Hampshire was the only state outside these regions with an unusually high rate of increase.

Table: Year-Round Housing Units
Date: 1980
Source: Census Bureau
Description: Total number of year-round housing units and percentage of change from 1970 to 1980.
United States total: 86.7 million
United States increase 1970–1980: 28.1%

YEAR-ROUND HOUSING UNITS

Rank	State	Percent of change	Total number of units (in thousands)
1	Nevada	96.6	337
2	Arizona	84.3	1,066
3	Alaska	74.1	154
4	Florida	71.4	4,270
5	Wyoming	59.2	182
6	Colorado	57.3	1,169
7	Utah	54.1	481
8	Hawaii	53.9	332
9	New Mexico	53.1	493
10	Idaho	51.0	360
11	Oregon	45.6	1,071
12	Texas	43.9	5,480
13	New Hampshire	40.4	349
14	South Carolina	39.3	1,121
15	North Carolina	37.3	2,223
16	Georgia	37.2	2,013
17	Washington	37.0	1,650
18	Virginia	34.6	1,999
19	Louisiana	34.0	1,535
20	Tennessee	33.9	1,737
21	California	32.2	9,220
22	Arkansas	32.1	889
23	Delaware	31.5	230
24	Oklahoma	31.0	1,229
25	Montana	30.8	315
25	Vermont	30.8	196
27	Alabama	30.1	1,450
28	Mississippi	29.7	904
29	Kentucky	27.7	1,355
30	North Dakota	26.0	253
31	Maine	25.9	427
32	Maryland	25.5	1,549
33	Minnesota	25.4	1,529
34	West Virginia	24.2	736
35	Wisconsin	23.8	1,753
36	South Dakota	21.6	269
37	Michigan	21.2	3,448
38	Nebraska	21.0	619
39	Kansas	20.7	950
40	Indiana	20.5	2,063
41	Ohio	18.3	4,077
42	Connecticut	18.1	1,144
43	Rhode Island	18.0	363
44	Missouri	17.8	1,961
45	Iowa	17.4	1,121
46	New Jersey	16.6	2,688
47	Illinois	16.5	4,303
48	Massachusetts	16.4	2,140
49	Pennsylvania	16.2	4,509
50	New York	8.8	6,699

23. Construction of New Housing Units

Authorizations for the construction of about one million new housing units were issued during 1982. Over 99% of this work was for the private sector; contracts for only 6,204 new units of public housing were awarded. The amount of construction in 1982 was only slightly greater than that of 1981, with levels for both years well below the average of close to two million units per year during the 1970s. Permits for single-family structures came to 54% of the total in 1982. Since in 1980, single-family structures made up 66% of the total housing stock, this signals a shift away from the single-family home, caused by the rising costs of land and construction. About 82% of new construction was located in SMSAs—30% in central cities and 52% in the suburbs.

Texas was the locus of slightly over 20% of all new residential construction in the United States in 1982. Two of every five homes being built were found in just three states: Texas, Florida and California.

Table: New Housing Units Authorized
Date: 1982
Source: Census Bureau
Description: Preliminary estimates of the number of new housing units authorized by building permits and public contracts.
United States total: 998,892

NEW HOUSING UNITS AUTHORIZED

Rank	State	Units authorized
1	Texas	203,230
2	Florida	103,735
3	California	85,423
4	Georgia	40,771
5	Arizona	36,839
6	North Carolina	31,614
7	Colorado	31,466
8	Virginia	29,711
9	Oklahoma	28,178
10	New York	24,290
11	New Jersey	23,647
12	Pennsylvania	20,912
13	Maryland	20,361
14	Louisiana	20,030
15	Minnesota	17,699
16	Washington	17,285
17	South Carolina	17,237
18	Massachusetts	16,822
19	Ohio	16,735
20	Illinois	16,365
21	Tennessee	15,088
22	Michigan	13,848
23	Indiana	12,534
24	Missouri	11,100
25	Wisconsin	10,820
26	Connecticut	10,376
27	Alabama	9,557
28	Nevada	9,011

Rank	State	Units authorized
29	Kansas	8,977
30	Alaska	7,994
31	New Mexico	7,927
32	Kentucky	7,397
33	Oregon	7,334
34	Utah	6,950
35	Arkansas	6,333
36	Mississippi	6,064
37	Hawaii	5,790
38	Iowa	5,284
39	New Hampshire	4,167
40	Nebraska	4,072
41	Vermont	3,675
42	Wyoming	3,386
43	Delaware	3,050
44	Maine	2,843
45	Rhode Island	2,486
46	North Dakota	2,417
47	Idaho	2,385
48	West Virginia	1,979
49	Montana	1,906
50	South Dakota	1,360

24. New Housing Units Completed in Selected SMSAs

Generally speaking, rates of new construction are highest in the West and the South, but there are sharp variations from one locality to another. In southern California, for example, the rates reported below vary from 3.7 units per thousand population in Los Angeles to 6.2 in neighboring Anaheim and 11.4 in the Riverside SMSA further to the east. Washington, D.C. is the only eastern SMSA on this list with a rate above 4.0 news units per thousand population. And moving into a brand-new home is a truly rare event in the New York City area.

Table: New Housing Units Completed in Selected SMSAs
Date: 1981
Source: Census Bureau
Description: Housing units completed per 1,000 population in 20 large SMSAs.

NEW HOUSING UNITS COMPLETED

Rank	SMSA	Completions per 1,000 population	Units completed
1	Las Vegas	19.3	8,900
2	Phoenix	14.3	21,500
3	Riverside-San Bernardino-Ontario, Calif.	11.4	17,700
4	Denver-Boulder	10.4	16,800
5	Miami	10.2	16,600
6	Sacramento	9.3	9,400
7	Seattle-Everett	8.6	13,900
8	San Diego	6.8	12,600
9	Washington, D.C.	6.5	19,800
10	Portland, Oregon-Washington	6.3	7,800
11	Anaheim-Santa Ana-Garden Grove, Calif.	6.2	11,900
11	Salt Lake City-Ogden	6.2	5,800
13	New Orleans	6.0	7,100
14	San Jose	5.1	6,600
15	Baltimore	3.8	8,300
16	Los Angeles-Long Beach	3.7	28,000
17	Cincinnati	3.6	5,000
18	Chicago	2.2	15,900
19	Detroit	1.8	7,800
20	New York	1.3	11,700

25. Value of All Construction

The data in this table represent the total value of all construction work done in the United States during 1981. About 43% of the total value was in residential construction, 36% in construction of nonresidential buildings, and 21% in construction of facilities other than buildings. California, Texas and Florida clearly emerge as the states in which the development of the manufactured environment is proceeding most rapidly.

Table: Value of Construction
Date: 1981
Source: Dodge Construction Potentials
Description: Value of construction in billions of dollars.

VALUE OF CONSTRUCTION

Rank	State	Value (in billions of dollars)
1	California	17.19
2	Texas	16.10
3	Florida	12.29
4	New York	6.46
5	Illinois	4.80
5	Ohio	4.80
7	Pennsylvania	4.77
8	Colorado	4.38
9	Georgia	3.80
10	Louisiana	3.77
11	Washington	3.64
12	New Jersey	3.47
13	Virginia	3.45
14	Kentucky	3.42
15	North Carolina	3.35

Rank	State	Value (in billions of dollars)
16	Michigan	3.30
17	Massachusetts	3.16
18	Arizona	3.10
19	Oklahoma	2.84
20	Minnesota	2.66
21	Tennessee	2.56
22	Maryland	2.55
22	Missouri	2.55
24	Indiana	2.37
25	Wisconsin	2.12
26	South Carolina	2.10
27	Oregon	2.05
28	Montana	2.00
29	Connecticut	1.82
30	Idaho	1.80
31	Alabama	1.70
32	New Mexico	1.35
33	Mississippi	1.34
34	Kansas	1.28
35	Iowa	1.25
36	Arkansas	1.22
37	Nevada	1.20
38	Utah	1.10
39	Alaska	1.08
40	Nebraska	.77
41	West Virginia	.68
42	Wyoming	.57
43	New Hampshire	.54
44	North Dakota	.51
45	Delaware	.49
46	Maine	.42
47	Rhode Island	.38
48	South Dakota	.35
49	Vermont	.24
50	Hawaii	.09

26. Older Year-round Housing Units

One of every four year-round dwellings in the United States was built prior to the World War II, and 37.4% of all such dwellings have been in place since 1950. The proportion of older housing in a given state depends on the pattern of population growth during the past few decades. Although many older dwelling units in the East and the Midwest have been replaced by new ones, large segments of the populations of states in these areas are still living in the same housing that served an earlier generation. The highest proportions of postwar housing are found in areas with high postwar population growth, especially Florida, Alaska, Hawaii and the Southwest. In Nevada, Alaska and Arizona about nine of every 10 of today's homes did not exist before 1950. Across the South newer housing accounts for 70% to 75% of the total, with lower percentages along the mountainous northern edge of the region in Kentucky and especially West Virginia.

Table: Year-round Housing Prior to 1950
Date: 1980
Source: Census Bureau
Description: Percentage of year-round housing units built prior to 1950.
United States average: 37.4%

YEAR-ROUND HOUSING PRIOR TO 1950

Rank	State	Percent built
1	New York	57.2
2	Massachusetts	56.9
3	Maine	56.2
4	Pennsylvania	54.8
5	Rhode Island	54.1
6	Vermont	53.5
7	Iowa	52.4
8	Nebraska	48.3
9	West Virginia	48.1
10	New Hampshire	47.7
11	South Dakota	47.5
12	New Jersey	46.9
13	Wisconsin	46.5
14	Illinois	46.1
15	Kansas	45.3
16	Connecticut	44.4
17	Ohio	44.3
18	Indiana	43.3
19	Michigan	42.4
20	North Dakota	41.6
21	Missouri	41.0
21	Minnesota	41.0
23	Montana	37.4
24	Maryland	35.9
25	Oregon	35.1
26	Idaho	34.7
26	Oklahoma	34.7
28	Washington	34.5
29	Kentucky	34.0
30	Wyoming	33.0
31	Delaware	31.9
32	Utah	29.7
33	Louisiana	29.1
34	Alabama	28.8
35	Arkansas	28.5
36	North Carolina	28.4
36	Virginia	28.4
38	California	28.0
39	Tennessee	27.8
40	Mississippi	27.6
41	Georgia	27.5
42	South Carolina	26.3
43	Colorado	25.1
44	Texas	25.0
45	New Mexico	23.6
46	Hawaii	17.9
47	Florida	14.3
48	Arizona	12.3
49	Alaska	11.3
50	Nevada	11.1

27. Percentage of Housing Units Occupied by Owners

Prior to the World War II, the percentage of housing units occupied by their owners varied between 40% and 50%. Federal loan programs and general prosperity during the postwar period raised the figure to 55% in 1950, 62% in 1960, and 63% in 1970. The percentage of owner-occupied units peaked at 65.4% in 1979. Owner occupancy seems destined to remain stable or to decline gradually in the future. New forms of cooperative and condominium ownership, combined with intricate financing schemes and tax incentives, account for the maintenance of high ownership rates despite the acute affordability crisis in homeownership.

Throughout much of the country rates of owner occupancy are fairly similar. For the top 40 states on the list the figures fall within a range of five percentage points on either side of the 68.4% national median value. (West Virginia is just a shade beyond this range on the high side.) Half of the remaining states with low rates of ownership are in the East. The group also includes Illinois and California, with their huge urban rental markets, and the states of Nevada, Alaska and Hawaii, where areas of settlement tend to be highly concentrated. New York is the only state where rental occupancies are in the majority.

Table: Owner-occupied Housing Units
Date: 1980
Source: Census Bureau
Description: Percentage of all housing units occupied by owners.
United States average: 64.4%
United States median: 68.4%

OWNER-OCCUPIED HOUSING UNITS

Rank	State	Percent owner-occupied
1	West Virginia	73.6
2	Michigan	72.6
3	Idaho	72.0
4	Iowa	71.8
5	Indiana	71.7
5	Minnesota	71.7
7	Mississippi	71.0
8	Maine	70.9
9	Oklahoma	70.7
9	Utah	70.7
11	Arkansas	70.5
12	Alabama	70.2
12	Kansas	70.2
12	South Carolina	70.2
15	Kentucky	70.0
16	Pennsylvania	69.9

Rank	State	Percent owner-occupied
17	Missouri	69.6
18	South Dakota	69.3
19	Wyoming	69.2
20	Delaware	69.1
21	North Dakota	68.7
21	Vermont	68.7
23	Montana	68.6
23	Tennessee	68.6
25	Nebraska	68.4
25	North Carolina	68.4
25	Ohio	68.4
28	Florida	68.2
28	Wisconsin	68.2
30	New Mexico	68.0
31	New Hampshire	67.6
32	Arizona	66.4
33	Virginia	65.6
33	Washington	65.6
35	Louisiana	65.5
36	Georgia	65.0
36	Oregon	65.0
38	Colorado	64.5
39	Texas	64.3
40	Connecticut	63.9
41	Illinois	62.6
42	Maryland	62.0
42	New Jersey	62.0
44	Nevada	59.6
45	Rhode Island	58.8
46	Alaska	58.3
47	Massachusetts	57.5
48	California	55.9
49	Hawaii	51.7
50	New York	48.6

28. Median Value of Owner-Occupied Homes

The value of owner-occupied homes is generally high in the West and low in the South. In Hawaii, where the rate of ownership is relatively low, those who do own homes have, typically, poured three to four times more money into their properties than homeowners in the South. The affluent suburbs of New York City and Washington, D.C. account for the fact that Connecticut, New Jersey, Maryland and Virginia show values much higher than those for their regional neighbors.

Table: Median Value of Owner-Occupied Homes
Date: 1980
Source: Census Bureau
Description: Median value of owner-occupied homes.
United States average: $47,200
United States median: $45,000

MEDIAN-VALUE OF OWNER-OCCUPIED HOMES

Rank	State	Median value
1	Hawaii	$118,100
2	California	84,500
3	Alaska	76,300
4	Nevada	68,700
5	Connecticut	65,600
6	Colorado	64,100
7	New Jersey	60,200
8	Washington	59,800
9	Wyoming	58,900
10	Maryland	58,300
11	Utah	57,300
12	Oregon	56,900
13	Arizona	54,700
14	Minnesota	53,100
15	Illinois	52,800
16	Wisconsin	48,600
17	Massachusetts	48,400
18	New Hampshire	48,000
18	Virginia	48,000
20	Rhode Island	46,800
21	Montana	46,500
22	Idaho	45,600
22	New York	45,600
24	New Mexico	45,300
25	Florida	45,100
26	Ohio	44,900
27	Delaware	44,400
28	North Dakota	43,900
29	Louisiana	43,000
30	Vermont	42,200
31	Iowa	40,600
32	Pennsylvania	39,100
32	Texas	39,100
34	Michigan	39,000
35	West Virginia	38,500
36	Nebraska	38,000
37	Maine	37,900
38	Kansas	37,800
39	Indiana	37,200
40	Georgia	36,900
41	Missouri	36,700
42	South Dakota	36,600
43	North Carolina	36,000
44	Oklahoma	35,600
44	Tennessee	35,600
46	South Carolina	35,100
47	Kentucky	34,200
48	Alabama	33,900
49	Mississippi	31,400
50	Arkansas	31,100

29. Median Purchase Prices for Housing in Selected SMSAs

There was wide variation among SMSAs in the typical price paid for a home during 1981. The highest prices were those in California, Honolulu, Dallas and Washington, D.C. Typical monthly mortgage payments are keyed to purchase prices, but they also reflect prevailing mortgage rates in local areas. Average payments were over $500 per month in all but eight of the 50 SMSAs covered here. The median income of buyers in 1981 was $39,196, up sharply from $28,110 in 1979. High interest rates reduced the pool of potential buyers considerably, selectively excluding those with lower incomes.

Table: Housing Costs
Date: 1981
Source: The United States League of Savings Associations
Description: Median purchase prices and monthly payments for housing in 50 SMSAs.
United States median: $72,000

HOUSING COSTS

Rank	SMSA	Median purchase price	Median monthly payment
1	Anaheim, Calif.	$130,998	$1,053
2	San Francisco-Oakland	121,833	1,053
3	Dallas-Fort Worth	114,025	953
4	Los Angeles-Long Beach	111,001	1,053
5	Honolulu	108,122	926
6	Washington, D.C.	99,000	824
7	San Diego	93,775	946
8	Phoenix	89,500	795
9	Denver	87,452	717
10	Houston	86,500	803
11	Oklahoma City	83,500	744
12	Newark	83,003	699
13	New York City	82,505	642
14	Hartford	81,500	758
15	Atlanta	80,447	718
16	New Orleams	80,050	657
17	Fort Myers, Fla.	76,015	639
18	Portland, Oreg.	75,950	699
19	Memphis	75,000	641
20	Minneapolis-St. Paul	74,500	629
21	Tampa-St. Petersburg	73,003	653
22	Las Vegas	71,525	657
23	Milwaukee	71,499	540
24	Boston	70,992	659
25	Bradenton, Fla.	70,025	693
26	Albuquerque	70,002	610
27	Chicago	65,900	530
28	Seattle	65,505	631
29	Miami	64,999	641
30	Baltimore	64,903	573
31	Jackson, Miss.	63,500	585
32	Jacksonville	63,100	567
33	Sioux Falls, S. Dak.	63,050	541
34	Nassau-Suffolk (Long Island)	62,505	542
35	Omaha	62,025	573
36	Louisville	61,988	577

Rank	SMSA	Median purchase price	Median monthly payment
37	St. Louis	$60,000	$546
38	Detroit	58,998	505
39	Cleveland	58,004	461
40	Des Moines	57,985	550
41	Indianapolis	56,905	488
42	Salt Lake City	56,331	539
43	Philadelphia	55,901	462
44	Pittsburgh	55,008	469
45	Birmingham	54,998	505
46	Burlington, Vt.	54,600	506
47	Kansas City	54,102	472
48	Fort Smith, Ark.	50,025	452
49	Portland, Maine	49,025	452
50	Greensboro-Winston-Salem-High Point	44,042	440

30. Mobile Homes

The number of year-round mobile homes has risen sharply in recent years. Factory-built homes, transported intact to residential sites, are simply much less expensive than structures built in the traditional way. The contemporary mobile home, which evolved from the trailer, is located, typically, at a given site on a more or less permanent basis. More elaborate factory-built dwellings called 'modular homes' are now coming on the market. These are built room by room, then shipped to a site and assembled into a house resting on a permanent foundation. Given the realities of construction costs, it is clear that in the future the American housing stock will include a relatively larger portion of mobile homes and other factory-built units. Local zoning regulations are currently the main obstacle to this development.

A mobile home is defined as a movable dwelling at least 8 feet wide and 40 feet long that has built-in transportation gear and does not require a permanent foundation. Travel trailers, motor homes and modular housing do not count as mobile homes in the statistics.

At present, the highest percentages of year-round mobile homes are found in the housing stocks of states in the western part of the country and in the upper South. Many warm-weather states have above average proportions of mobile homes, but so do energy-producing states with more severe climates, states that have experienced sudden population booms in recent years: Wyoming (nearly one mobile home in every five), Montana, Alaska and Idaho. Mobile homes are relatively rare in Hawaii and in the states along the northeastern seaboard.

Table: Mobile Homes
Date: 1980
Source: Census Bureau
Description: Mobile homes as a percentage of all year-round housing units.
United States average: 5.0%

MOBILE HOMES

Rank	State	Percent of mobile homes
1	Wyoming	18.8
2	Montana	13.6
3	New Mexico	12.6
4	Arizona	12.1
4	Nevada	12.1
6	Alaska	10.5
6	West Virginia	10.5
8	Idaho	10.2
9	South Carolina	9.9
10	North Carolina	9.7
11	Kentucky	9.2
12	Arkansas	9.0
13	North Dakota	8.9
14	Florida	8.7
15	South Dakota	8.5
16	Oregon	8.4
17	Delaware	8.3
18	Alabama	8.2
19	Mississippi	8.1
20	Georgia	7.7
21	Maine	7.4
22	Louisiana	7.3
22	Vermont	7.3
24	Tennessee	6.5
25	Kansas	6.2
25	Washington	6.2
27	New Hampshire	5.7
27	Oklahoma	5.7
29	Colorado	5.6
30	Virginia	5.2
31	Missouri	5.1
31	Nebraska	5.1
33	Indiana	4.8
34	Utah	4.6
35	Texas	4.4
36	Michigan	4.2
37	Ohio	4.1
38	Minnesota	4.0
39	California	3.6
39	Wisconsin	3.6
41	Iowa	3.4
42	Pennsylvania	3.2
43	Illinois	3.1
44	New York	2.0
45	Maryland	1.6
46	Massachusetts	.8
47	Connecticut	.7
47	Rhode Island	.7
49	New Jersey	.5
50	Hawaii	.2

31. New Mobile Homes

Nearly one-quarter million new mobile homes were set up for residential use during 1981, better than one new mobile home for every five traditional, site-constructed homes on which work was begun in the same year. The average sales price of new mobile homes in 1981 was $19,900. New installations in Texas and Florida accounted for 26% of the national total.

Table: New Mobile Homes
Date: 1981
Source: Department of Commerce
Description: New mobile homes placed for residential use.
United States total: 229,200

NEW MOBILE HOMES

Rank	State	Number
1	Texas	33,600
2	Florida	25,700
3	Louisiana	12,900
4	North Carolina	12,800
5	California	11,400
6	Oklahoma	10,800
7	Georgia	9,200
8	South Carolina	7,900
9	Washington	6,500
10	Arizona	6,000
11	Ohio	5,500
12	Pennsylvania	5,400
13	Alabama	4,900
13	Kentucky	4,900
15	Virginia	4,700
16	Michigan	4,100
16	Mississippi	4,100
18	Illinois	3,900
18	Tennessee	3,900
20	Oregon	3,700
20	New Mexico	3,700
22	Colorado	3,600
22	Indiana	3,600
22	New York	3,600
25	Kansas	3,100
25	West Virginia	3,100
27	Wyoming	2,900
28	Missouri	2,800
29	Arkansas	2,600
30	Wisconsin	2,500
31	Nevada	2,000
32	Minnesota	1,700
33	Maryland	1,300
34	Idaho	1,200
34	Montana	1,200
34	Utah	1,200
37	Delaware	1,000
37	North Dakota	1,000
39	Iowa	800
39	Nebraska	800

Rank	State	Number
39	New Hampshire	800
42	Maine	700
43	New Jersey	500
44	Vermont	400
45	Massachusetts	300
45	South Dakota	300
47	Alaska	200
47	Connecticut	200
49	Rhode Island	100
50	Hawaii	0

32. Incomplete Plumbing

The components of a complete plumbing system are defined by the Bureau of the Census as hot and cold running water, a flush toilet, and a bathtub or shower. About 98% of all American housing units contain all of these facilities. In Alaska, Maine and much of the South, however, above average proportions of households are making do without one or more of these basic plumbing conveniences. Elsewhere in the country there is not much variation from state to state.

Table: Lack of Plumbing
Date: 1980
Source: Census Bureau
Description: Percentage of occupied housing units lacking complete plumbing facilities.
United States average: 2.2%
United States median: 1.9%

LACK OF PLUMBING

Rank	State	Percent
1	Alaska	10.4
2	Kentucky	6.5
3	Mississippi	5.9
4	West Virginia	5.7
5	Maine	4.9
6	Alabama	4.2
6	Arkansas	4.2
6	Virginia	4.2
9	North Carolina	4.1
9	South Carolina	4.1
11	Tennessee	3.7
12	New Mexico	3.6
13	Georgia	3.2
14	South Dakota	2.7
14	Vermont	2.7
16	New Hampshire	2.5
16	New York	2.5
16	North Dakota	2.5
19	Louisiana	2.4
20	Montana	2.3

Rank	State	Percent
21	Hawaii	2.2
22	Arizona	2.1
22	Minnesota	2.1
22	Missouri	2.1
25	Maryland	1.9
25	Texas	1.9
25	Wisconsin	1.9
28	Pennsylvania	1.8
29	Delaware	1.7
29	Illinois	1.7
29	Iowa	1.7
29	Ohio	1.7
29	Rhode Island	1.7
34	Indiana	1.6
34	New Jersey	1.6
34	Wyoming	1.6
37	Massachusetts	1.5
38	Idaho	1.4
38	Oklahoma	1.4
38	Oregon	1.4
41	Colorado	1.3
41	Connecticut	1.3
41	Michigan	1.3
44	California	1.2
44	Kansas	1.2
44	Nebraska	1.2
44	Nevada	1.2
44	Washington	1.2
49	Florida	1.1
50	Utah	.9

33. Vacancy Rates

Vacancies, especially in the rental sector, are a normal feature of all housing markets; they create the indispensable slack that enables people to move from one place to another. If we take the national vacancy rate of 7.1% as a norm, lower rates indicate tight markets and higher rates indicate loose markets where the process of construction has momentarily outrun the processes of population increase and household formation. In general, the highest vacancy rates are found in the western part of the country (plus Delaware), while low rates appear in the East and parts of the Midwest (but also California, Washington and Utah). The fact that higher rates tend to appear in states with high recent population growth is a sign of increasing mobility rates and heavy activity among builders who have good reason to expect future sales and rentals.

Table: Housing Vacancies
Date: 1980
Source: Census Bureau
Description: Vacant housing units as a percentage of total housing units.
United States average: 7.1%

HOUSING VACANCIES

Rank	State	Percent vacant
1	Alaska	13.9
2	Florida	12.0
3	Hawaii	11.4
4	New Mexico	10.2
5	Arizona	9.9
5	Texas	9.9
7	Nevada	9.8
8	Delaware	9.7
8	South Dakota	9.7
10	North Dakota	9.6
11	Idaho	9.5
11	Montana	9.5
13	Colorado	9.0
14	Oklahoma	8.9
14	Wyoming	8.9
16	Mississippi	8.4
17	Kansas	8.2
18	Arkansas	8.1
19	Louisiana	8.0
20	North Carolina	7.9
20	South Carolina	7.9
20	Vermont	7.9
23	Nebraska	7.6
24	Alabama	7.4
24	Oregon	7.4
26	Michigan	7.1
27	Georgia	7.0
28	Tennessee	6.8
29	Kentucky	6.7
29	New Hampshire	6.7
29	Virginia	6.7
29	West Virginia	6.7
33	Utah	6.6
34	Indiana	6.5
34	Rhode Island	6.5
34	Washington	6.5
37	California	6.4
37	Maine	6.4
37	Missouri	6.4
40	Pennsylvania	6.3
41	Illinois	6.0
41	Iowa	6.0
43	Ohio	5.9
44	Maryland	5.6
45	Wisconsin	5.4
46	Minnesota	5.2
46	New York	5.2
48	New Jersey	5.0
49	Massachusetts	4.9
50	Connecticut	4.3

FOREIGN RESIDENTS (IMMIGRATION)

Only about 1.5 million Americans can claim descent from the peoples who inhabited our national territory in prehistoric times. For everyone else, the family tree includes an immigrant from some other part of the world. Between 1829 and 1980 some 50 million immigrants entered the country. The vast majority of these people came from Europe. Census Bureau studies show that about 29% of all Americans consider themselves to be at least partly of German ancestry. This is the largest ancestral group in the country, but people with hereditary links to Ireland (25%) and England (22%) are also numerous. (Many people trace their ancestry to several different nations, so the sum of percentages for each one comes to well over 100%.)

European predominance in immigration occurred spontaneously at first, but later it was artificially maintained under restrictive quotas introduced during the 1920s. When the quota system was revised in the mid-1960s, the present predominance of people from Asia and Latin America was quickly established. The economic growth of the Southwest has drawn millions of job seekers from Mexico, and political catastrophies in Southeast Asia and the Caribbean have propelled many refugees to our shores. During the decade of the 1970s, over 1.5 million Asians were admitted to the United States.

Immigrants are defined as persons who have established permanent residence in the United States but have not yet established citizenship. The total number thus depends both on the rate of new immigration from abroad and the rate at which such people obtain citizenship, at which point they are no longer included. The figures presented in this section cover residents of the United States who registered with the Immigration and Naturalization Service in 1979 as citizens of foreign countries. The total for the nation stood then at just under 5 million. The ten leading nations of origin were Mexico (990,000), Cuba (281,000), Canada (266,000), the United Kingdom, i.e. England, Wales, Scotland, and Northern Ireland (265,000), the Philippines (209,000), Italy (178,000), Germany (155,000), Korea (153,000), China and Taiwan (136,000), and Portugal (128,000).

Important groups *not* included in the total immigration figure are foreign tourists (about 10 million per year), foreign nationals who are in the United States only to conduct business and, especially, nonregistered or illegal foreign residents. There are no accurate figures on the number of unregistered aliens presently in the country, and there is not even general agreement on whether their number has increased much over the past decade. It is certain, however, that American concern about illegal immigrants—inspired both by the unfamiliarity of the new ethnic mix among immigrants and the fear that they will absorb jobs during this extended period of high unemployment—is greater now than it has been since the wave of nativism that gave birth to the quota system in the 1920s. The highest plausible estimates of the total number of unregistered aliens suggest a number less than the 5 million registered aliens. Everyone agrees that over half of unregistered aliens are from Mexico. Arrests of illegal foreign residents amounted to about one million in 1981.

Although the quota for legal immigration was set at less than 300,000 in 1968, exceptions to certain special quotas together with illegal immigration led to an estimated 800,000 new arrivals in 1980. In 1982, a Presidential Task Force working to set guidelines for a new immigration policy estimated that about 500,000 unregistered aliens are added to the population each year, a figure at the high end of the range of expert estimates. New immigration policy is expected to include a higher quota for Mexico, some form of amnesty for persons who have been in the country illegally for several years, and possibly a formal "guest worker" system for Mexicans. The effect of illegal immigration on government finances has been beneficial for the taxpayer, according to most experts, since unregistered aliens rarely claim social services benefits even though they usually pay income taxes and always pay sales taxes.

Tables in this section provide an overview of registered foreign residents. A summary for the 50 states appears in the first table, followed by tables for key national groups showing the 10 states in which they reside in greatest numbers.

34. Registered Alien Residents

The five million residents of the United States registered as of 1979 as citizens of other countries are concentrated in only a few states. New York City has traditionally been the major port of entry for immigrants, and about 22% of all foreign residents can still be found in states close to the port—New York, New Jersey and Connecticut. New immigration from Mexico and the Pacific has lifted California to the top of the list, but the attraction of the California lifestyle for skilled and affluent people from affluent countries also contributes to the total; California has the most resident citizens of Britain, Canada, Germany and Japan. Mexican residents represent a smaller fraction of all foreign residents in California (39%) than in Texas (68%). The other states among the top 10 in this table include Florida, where Cubans account for about half of all foreign residents, and a number of industrial states with large metropolitan centers: Illinois, Massachusetts, Michigan and Pennsylvania. All together, the first 10 states account for 80% of all foreign residents.

The ratio of foreign residents to state population is presented as a supplementary table, where the states are ranked accordingly. Hawaii and California stand out above the other states on a percentage basis. Throughout the South and the nonindustrial Midwest, foreign residents make up less than 1% of state population. The 10 states with the greatest number of foreign residents are also found near the top in percentage terms (Michigan and Pennsylvania excepted), joined by Rhode Island and a group of western states where the influence of Pacific migrations is felt—often as outflow from California—and where migrant farm labor plays a big part in the state economy.

Table: Registered Alien Residents
Date: 1979
Source: Immigration and Naturalization Service
Description: Number of registered alien residents and percentage of U.S. total.

United States total: 4,931,779
United States average: 98,635

REGISTERED ALIEN RESIDENTS

Rank	State	Alien population (in thousands)	Percent of U.S. total
1	California	1,317	26.0
2	New York	763	15.1
3	Texas	425	8.4
4	Florida	376	7.4
5	Illinois	290	5.7
6	New Jersey	269	5.3
7	Massachusetts	167	3.3
8	Michigan	136	2.7
9	Pennsylvania	110	2.2
10	Connecticut	95	1.9
11	Ohio	86	1.7
12	Washington	77	1.5
13	Hawaii	70	1.4
14	Arizona	67	1.3
15	Maryland	57	1.1
16	Virginia	55	1.1
17	Colorado	35	.7
17	Louisiana	35	.7
19	Oregon	34	.7
20	Rhode Island	33	.7
21	Indiana	32	.6
21	Wisconsin	32	.6
23	Minnesota	28	.6
24	Georgia	25	.5
24	Missouri	25	.5
26	North Carolina	23	.5
27	New Mexico	22	.4
28	Nevada	20	.4
29	Oklahoma	19	.3
30	Kansas	17	.3
31	Utah	16	.3
32	Iowa	15	.3
32	Tennessee	15	.3
34	Maine	14	.3
35	South Carolina	13	.3
36	Kentucky	11	.2
36	New Hampshire	11	.2
38	Alabama	10	.2
39	Nebraska	8	.2
40	Arkansas	7	.1
40	Idaho	7	.1
40	Mississippi	7	.1
40	Vermont	7	.1
44	Alaska	6	.1
44	Delaware	6	.1
44	West Virginia	6	.1
47	Montana	4	.1
48	North Dakota	3	.1
48	Wyoming	3	.1
50	South Dakota	2	.1

Table: Ratio of Registered Alien Residents to State Population
Date: 1979

Source: Immigration and Naturalization Service
Description: Percentage of state population that are registered aliens.

RATIO OF REGISTERED ALIEN RESIDENTS

Rank	State	Percent of state population
1	Hawaii	7.4
2	California	5.7
3	New York	4.3
4	Florida	4.0
5	New Jersey	3.7
6	Rhode Island	3.5
7	Connecticut	3.1
7	Texas	3.1
9	Massachusetts	2.9
10	Nevada	2.6
11	Arizona	2.5
11	Illinois	2.5
13	Washington	2.0
14	New Mexico	1.7
15	Alaska	1.5
15	Michigan	1.5
17	Vermont	1.4
18	Maryland	1.3
18	Oregon	1.3
20	Colorado	1.2
20	Maine	1.2
20	New Hampshire	1.2
23	Utah	1.1
24	Delaware	1.0
24	Virginia	1.0
26	Louisiana	.9
26	Pennsylvania	.9
28	Idaho	.8
28	Ohio	.8
30	Kansas	.7
30	Minnesota	.7
30	Wisconsin	.7
30	Wyoming	.7
34	Indiana	.6
34	Oklahoma	.6
36	Georgia	.5
36	Iowa	.5
36	Missouri	.5
36	Montana	.5
36	Nebraska	.5
36	North Dakota	.5
42	North Carolina	.4
42	South Carolina	.4
44	Alabama	.3
44	Arkansas	.3
44	Kentucky	.3
44	Mississippi	.3
44	South Dakota	.3
44	Tennessee	.3
44	West Virginia	.3

35. British

The British are represented about as often as the Canadians among foreign residents and, save perhaps for their accents, are similarly invisible. They are just as concentrated as the Canadians—71% of them in 10 states—but the tendency to settle along the northern border is absent. Colonies of Britons in California and Florida suggest the importance of sunny and warm retirement homes for citizens of a damp nation. Other concentrations are found in states with large metropolitan centers in the eastern half of the country.

Table: Registered Aliens Born in the United Kingdom
Date: 1980
Source: Immigration and Naturalization Service
Description: Number of registered aliens born in the United Kingdom, and percentage of the U.S. total, for the 10 states with the largest population of registered U.K. aliens.
United States total: 265,171
State average: 5,303

REGISTERED ALIENS BORN IN THE UNITED KINGDOM

Rank	State	Number	Percent of total number of U.K. aliens
1	California	57,583	21.7
2	New York	43,149	16.3
3	Florida	15,734	5.9
4	New Jersey	13,737	5.2
5	Michigan	11,333	4.3
6	Massachusetts	10,681	4.0
7	Illinois	10,099	3.8
8	Pennsylvania	9,601	3.6
9	Connecticut	7,996	3.0
10	Ohio	7,662	2.9

36. Canadians

Canadians, the third largest group of foreign residents, are not readily identifiable as members of an ethnic or linguistic minority and so ordinarily escape notice. The U.S.-Canadian border has been open for many years, resulting in the formation of business ties and a friendliness that lead to much of the immigration that occurs. Most of the states on this list are on or near the Canadian border, suggesting that immigration has occurred as a natural outgrowth of everyday relationships. Canadian residents are scattered, however, across many states, with a proportion of just over 70% of them in 10 states. The presence of California and Florida at the top of the list shows that lifestyle considerations—especially for relatively affluent Canadians who have retired—have also inspired immigration.

Table: Registered Aliens Born in Canada
Date: 1979
Source: Immigration and Naturalization Service
Description: Number of registered aliens born in Canada and percentage of the U.S. total for the 10 states with the largest population of registered Canadian aliens.
United States total: 265,956
State average: 5,319

REGISTERED ALIENS BORN IN CANADA

Rank	State	Number	Percent of total number of Canadian aliens
1	California	56,932	21.4
2	Florida	24,662	9.3
3	New York	22,601	8.5
4	Michigan	22,232	8.4
5	Massachusetts	15,290	5.7
6	Washington	15,011	5.6
7	Connecticut	8,708	3.3
8	Texas	7,503	2.8
9	Maine	7,304	2.7
10	Illinois	6,834	2.6

37. Chinese (including Taiwanese)

People of Chinese ancestry, most of them American citizens, numbered over 800,000 in 1980, up from 435,000 in 1970. This is the largest group of Asian origin in the American population. Residents of the United States in 1979 who were still citizens of China or Taiwan were, however, fewer in number than their Filipino or Korean counterparts. With 86% of the Chinese and Taiwanese population living in 10 states, they were less concentrated geographically than the Filipinos but more so than the Koreans. Los Angeles, San Francisco and New York City are the main centers of settlement. Other states on the list either have major urban centers or touch the Pacific.

Table: Registered Aliens Born in China and Taiwan
Date: 1979
Source: Immigration and Naturalization Service
Description: Number of registered aliens born in China and Taiwan and percentage of the U.S. total for the 10 states with the largest population registered Chinese and Taiwanese aliens.
United States total: 136,258
State average: 2,725

REGISTERED ALIENS BORN IN CHINA AND TAIWAN

Rank	State	Number	Percent of total number of Chinese aliens
1	California	56,936	41.8
2	New York	33,922	25.0
3	Illinois	5,008	3.7
4	Massachusetts	4,863	3.6
5	Texas	3,625	2.7
6	New Jersey	3,252	2.4
7	Washington	3,104	2.3
8	Hawaii	3,041	2.2
9	Pennsylvania	1,930	1.4
10	Maryland	1,893	1.4

38. Cubans

Cubans form the second largest group of foreign residents, although they represent a group less than one-third as large as the Mexicans. Like the Mexicans, they are highly concentrated geographically. Over 97% of Cubans are found in the nine states listed below. Most are in Florida, but there are significant subgroups in the New York City vicinity and in the metropolitan centers of California and Illinois. As a group, the Cubans are far wealthier and more securly established than the Mexicans. Many wealthy and middle-class Cubans arrived in Florida following the revolution in 1960. They have come to form the center of the Spanish-speaking sector, which is increasingly predominant in the commercial and political life of Miami. Cuban immigrants of all classes are, typically, far more familiar with the skills and styles of urban life when they arrive in the United States than the villagers who make up most of the group entering from Mexico.

Table: Registered Aliens Born in Cuba
Date: 1979
Source: Immigration and Naturalization Service
Description: Number of registered aliens born in Cuba and percentage of the U.S. total for the nine states with the largest population of registered Cuban aliens.
United States total: 280,812
State average: 5,616

REGISTERED ALIENS BORN IN CUBA

Rank	State	Number	Percent of total number of Cuban aliens
1	Florida	176,627	62.9
2	New Jersey	32,710	11.6

Rank	State	Number	Percent of total number of Cuban aliens
3	California	24,096	8.6
4	New York	22,796	8.1
5	Illinois	6,508	2.3
6	Texas	3,068	1.1
7	Louisiana	2,371	.8
8	Connecticut	2,073	.7
9	Massachusetts	1,497	.5

39. Dominicans

Citizens of the Dominican Republic, a small nation that shares an island in the Caribbean with Haiti, form the 12th largest group of foreign residents in the United States. Only a small fraction of this group is found anywhere outside the New York metropolitan area. Dominicans began to migrate north during the 1950s, in the final years of the Trujillo dictatorship. Immigration has accelerated in recent years due to the pressures of unrelieved poverty and political violence. Public officials in some areas of the United States, especially in New York City, contend that the total number of Dominican aliens is considerably larger than the group registered with the Immigration Service.

Table: Registered Aliens Born in the Dominican Republic
Date: 1979
Source: Immigration and Naturalization Service
Description: Number of registered aliens born in the Dominican Republic and percentage of the U.S. total for the 10 states with the largest population of registered Dominican aliens.
United States total: 92,707
State average: 1,854

REGISTERED ALIENS BORN IN THE DOMINICAN REPUBLIC

Rank	State	Number	Percent of total number of Dominican aliens
1	New York	73,925	79.7
2	New Jersey	8,905	9.6
3	Florida	2,995	3.2
4	Massachusetts	2,270	2.1
5	Rhode Island	936	1.0
6	California	679	.73
7	Illinois	554	.60
8	Connecticut	372	.40
9	Pennsylvania	296	.32
10	Texas	287	.31

40. Filipinos

The largest group of Asian immigrants who have not yet become citizens comes from the Philippines. With 87% of the entire group residing in the 10 states on this list, concentration remains high. California and Hawaii are the main locations of settlement groups, but Filipino communities have also been established in Chicago and the New York City area. Except for the state of Washington, a West Coast port of entry, the pattern presented by the remaining states is not easy to interpret. In 1980, there were some 775,000 Filipinos in the United States, including naturalized citizens and their descendents, an increase of 126% since 1970.

Table: Registered Aliens Born in the Philippines
Date: 1979
Source: Immigration and Naturalization Service
Description: Number of registered aliens born in the Philippines and percentage of the U.S. total, for the 10 states with the largest population of registered Filipino aliens.
United States total: 208,877
State average: 4,178

REGISTERED ALIENS BORN IN THE PHILIPPINES

Rank	State	Number	Percent of total number of Filipino aliens
1	California	93,706	44.9
2	Hawaii	32,165	15.4
3	Illinois	16,516	7.9
4	New York	10,769	5.2
5	New Jersey	8,024	3.8
6	Washington	5,869	2.8
7	Virginia	4,320	2.0
8	Texas	4,186	2.0
9	Michigan	3,847	1.8
10	Florida	3,195	1.5

41. Italians

The great migration of Italians to the United States began about 100 years ago and lasted until World War I. New York City was the dominant port of entry, and the major areas of settlement were established in the cities of the Northeast. This pattern is still reflected in the statistics today, since a large part of current Italian immigration involves bringing members of the immediate or extended family into established Italian-American homes (as is the case for current migration from other European countries with kin groups already established in the United States).

The New York City area remains the focal point, and the level of population concentration, 92% in ten states, is unusually high for a European country. Among the European nationalities, only the Portuguese, with colonies in Massachusetts and Rhode Island, show a higher degree of concentration.

Table: Registered Aliens Born in Italy
Date: 1979
Source: Immigration and Naturalization Service
Description: Number of registered aliens born in Italy and percentage of the U.S. total, for the 10 states with the largest population of registered Italian aliens.
United States total: 177,853
State average: 3,557

REGISTERED ALIENS BORN IN ITALY

Rank	State	Number	Percent of total number of Italian aliens
1	New York	65,527	36.8
2	New Jersey	21,917	12.3
3	Connecticut	13,464	7.6
4	Illinois	12,761	7.2
5	Massachusetts	12,589	7.2
6	Pennsylvania	12,158	6.8
7	California	11,134	6.3
8	Michigan	6,848	3.9
9	Ohio	5,667	3.2
10	Florida	2,502	1.41

42. Jamaicans

Jamaican residents of the United States are only slightly less concentrated than the Dominicans, with 93% in just ten states. The vast majority of Jamaicans live in the greater New York area, with a key secondary center in Florida. Economic and political troubles in Jamaica continue to speed the flow of citizens to the United States, where Jamaicans arrive with the advantage that English is their native language. (Jamaica, once part of the British Empire, became independent of Great Britain in 1962 when it joined the Commonwealth of Nations.)

Table: Registered Aliens Born in Jamaica
Date: 1979
Source: Immigration and Naturalization Service
Description: Number of registered aliens born in Jamaica and percentage of the U.S. total for the 10 states with the largest population of registered Jamaican aliens.
United States total: 82,329
State average: 1,647

REGISTERED ALIENS BORN IN JAMAICA

Rank	State	Number	Percent of total number of Jamaican aliens
1	New York	41,947	51.0
2	Florida	12,746	15.5
3	New Jersey	5,185	6.3
4	Connecticut	4,917	6.0
5	Massachusetts	2,464	3.0
6	Pennsylvania	2,457	3.0
7	Illinois	2,083	2.5
8	California	1,948	2.4
9	Maryland	1,942	2.4
10	Missouri	990	1.2

43. Koreans

The Koreans form the second largest group of new Asian immigrants and the eighth largest of the 10 leading immigrant groups. They are much less concentrated geographically than other Asian groups, with just 75% of the total in 10 states. Like the Chinese but in contrast to the Filipinos, Koreans have made their way across the Pacific directly to the mainland; relatively few Koreans have chosen to settle in Hawaii. A focus on the very largest metropolitan centers is indicated by the size of the colonies in California, New York and Illinois, as well as the groups in Maryland and Virginia, which border the nation's capital, and in Pennsylvania. The total number of Koreans in the United States, including American citizens of Korean ancestry, increased by a phenomenal 413% to over 350,000 during the 1970s.

Table: Registered Aliens Born in Korea
Date: 1979
Source: Immigration and Naturalization Service
Description: Number of registered aliens born in Korea and percentage of the U.S. total, for 10 states with the largest population of registered Korean aliens.
United States total: 153,009
State average: 3,060

REGISTERED ALIENS BORN IN KOREA

Rank	State	Number	Percent of total number of Korean aliens
1	California	47,120	31.0
2	New York	14,706	10.0
3	Illinois	11,776	7.7
4	Maryland	7,410	4.8
5	Virginia	5,936	3.9

Rank	State	Number	Percent of total number of Korean aliens
6	Texas	5,919	3.9
7	Pennsylvania	5,781	3.8
8	Hawaii	5,702	3.7
9	Washington	5,295	3.5
10	New Jersey	5,117	3.3

44. Mexicans

Mexicans are by far the largest single group of foreign residents in the United States. They also form one of the most highly concentrated groups in terms of their geographical location. Outside of California, Texas and the other two border states, Chicago, Illinois is the only other significant place of residence. Over 96% of all Mexicans in the United States are located in the 10 states listed here. Mexican immigrants were at one time employed primarily as migrant farm laborers in the Southwest, but the proliferation of low-wage industrial jobs and urban service jobs that have accompanied the Sunbelt boom now offer them many other forms of work. Rural areas in central Mexico, relatively overpopulated and still lacking in economic opportunity despite more than a decade of rural development programs, are the primary source of the stream of immigrants.

The demand for Mexican labor in the Southwest has for many years been running ahead of the number of immigrants permitted by the quota system, leading to high levels of illegal immigration. Business interests have been the only clear beneficiaries of this situation, since unregistered residents have little bargaining power in the face of possible disclosure and deportation and therefore often must make do with substandard employment and housing conditions. On the whole, however, many immigrants apparently still prefer this situation to conditions in Mexico. Efforts to reorganize the institutions that govern the flow of Mexicans to this country have been initiated by both the Carter and Reagan administrations and, as noted above, immigration reform legislation is forthcoming.

Table: Registered Aliens Born in Mexico
Date: 1979
Source: Immigration and Naturalization Service
Description: Number of registered aliens born in Mexico and percentage of the U.S. total for the 10 states with the largest population of registered Mexican aliens.
United States total: 990,243
State average: 19,805

REGISTERED ALIENS BORN IN MEXICO

Rank	State	Number	Percent of total number of Mexican aliens
1	California	513,086	51.8
2	Texas	291,193	29.4
3	Illinois	71,519	7.2
4	Arizona	41,642	4.2
5	New Mexico	12,584	1.3
6	Florida	5,653	.57
7	Michigan	5,642	.57
8	Colorado	5,384	.54
9	Washington	5,156	.52
10	Indiana	5,096	.52

ETHNIC AND RACIAL DIVERSITY

Jean de Crevecoeur, a French nobleman who became a gentleman farmer and a naturalized citizen of the United States, was the first (in 1782) to describe the country as a "melting pot." People from all parts of the globe continued to arrive in America during the intervening 200 years. They have indeed blended together to form a single society, but the traces of their origins have not all melted away. Inspired by the growing awareness among black Americans of their special cultural heritage, native-born descendents of immigrants from many nations of the world have taken a greater interest in matters of their own cultural origins and traditions. The ties that bind Americans to their kin in other parts of the world have stimulated concern in connection with such issues as the uprising in Poland and the status of Northern Ireland. Racial and ethnic diversity, always a central feature in American life, will continue to be a vital factor in shaping the American future.

Heterogeneity is the rule in the United States, but some parts of the country are more heterogeneous than others. The tables in this section portray the degree of diversity found in the 50 states. Language diversity is considered in the first three tables, where states are ranked according to the percentage of persons in the adult population who speak English mainly (89% nationwide), or Spanish (5%), or some other language (6%). The other tables examine diversity by ethnicity and race, showing how members of selected population groups are distributed around the country. Some general information on racial designations is included in the discussion of the table on the black population.

45. English Language

This table and the two that follow are based on responses to the 1980 census, indicating the language that people ordinarily speak at home. Responses from persons 18 years of age or above have been used to derive percentages for each state. Since many Americans speak two or more languages, the fact that they do not speak English at home does not mean that they cannot use it outside the home. About 11% of American adults normally speak a language other than English at home, but only about 2% report that they cannot use English very well or at all.

Throughout the South and the farming country of the lower Midwest the sounds of languages other than English are rarely heard. The Gulf states of Florida and Louisiana and the state of Illinois, which includes Chicago, are the only states in their areas where the fraction of English-speakers is below the national average. The 18 states under the national average also include Alaska, Hawaii, several East Coast states that have been traditional ports of entry for immigrants, three states on the Canadian border and four states on the Mexican border. Rural life and an inland location protected from immigrant streams by buffer states on the coasts and borders are characteristic of those states where English is overwhelmingly predominant.

Table: English-Speaking Population
Date: 1980
Source: Census Bureau
Description: Percentage of persons 18 years and older who speak only English at home.
United States average: 88.7%

ENGLISH-SPEAKING POPULATION

Rank	State	Percent
1	Arkansas	98.2
1	Kentucky	98.2
1	Tennessee	98.2
4	Alabama	98.1
5	Mississippi	97.9
6	West Virginia	97.5
7	North Carolina	97.4
7	South Carolina	97.4
9	Georgia	97.3
10	Iowa	96.7
10	Missouri	96.7
12	Oklahoma	96.0
13	Virginia	95.4
14	Indiana	95.1
15	Kansas	94.9
16	Nebraska	94.7
17	Ohio	94.4
18	Idaho	94.2
19	Oregon	94.1
20	Delaware	94.0
21	Montana	93.9

Rank	State	Percent
22	Wisconsin	93.7
23	Minnesota	93.6
24	Maryland	93.4
25	Washington	92.9
25	Wyoming	92.9
27	Michigan	92.4
27	Pennsylvania	92.4
27	Vermont	92.4
30	Utah	92.1
31	South Dakota	92.0
32	Nevada	89.7
33	Colorado	88.6
34	Louisiana	88.5
35	New Hampshire	88.1
36	Illinois	87.7
37	Alabama	87.5
38	Maine	86.7
39	Florida	86.5
40	North Dakota	86.0
41	Massachusetts	85.9
42	Connecticut	84.8
43	New Jersey	83.6
44	Rhode Island	81.8
45	Arizona	80.9
46	New York	79.9
47	Texas	79.1
48	Colorado	77.6
49	Hawaii	71.1
50	New Mexico	61.6

46. Spanish Language

The Spanish language has been spoken by Americans in the Southwest for hundreds of years. Spanish explorers established outposts at Santa Fe and Taos, New Mexico several years before the Pilgrims landed at Plymouth Rock in 1620. Although commerce and contact with Mexico was sharply reduced after the United States acquired the territory of the border states in the 1840s, the Spanish-speaking population remained large (still half of the population of New Mexico just 40 years ago). English-speaking migrants from the East swept into the border area in increasing numbers after World War II, and the continuing acceleration of this influx through the 1970s has tended to reduce the proportion of Spanish-speakers in border state populations. The influence of this new migration on language was not as great as it might have been, however, because the Spanish-speaking group was largely excluded or isolated from social contact with the newcomers. Recently, the trend toward declining use of Spanish has been balanced (and actually reversed in states such as California and Texas) by renewed migration from Mexico.

Spanish is the primary language of large segments of the population in the four border states. Ten other states have Spanish-speaking segments amounting to at least 3% of the general population. These include several western states and the states in which the metropolitan areas of New York City, Chicago and Miami are located. Populations tracing their origins to Puerto Rico, Mexico or Cuba form the main Spanish-speaking groups in these cities.

Table: Spanish-Speaking Population
Date: 1980
Source: Census Bureau
Description: Percentage of persons 18 years and older who speak Spanish at home.
United States average: 3.2%

SPANISH-SPEAKING POPULATION

Rank	State	Percent
1	New Mexico	30.6
2	Texas	18.7
3	California	13.4
4	Arizona	12.3
5	Florida	8.4
6	New York	8.0
7	Colorado	7.0
8	New Jersey	5.3
9	Nevada	4.8
10	Illinois	4.4
11	Utah	3.1
11	Wyoming	3.1
13	Connecticut	3.0
13	Idaho	3.0
15	Kansas	1.9
16	Alaska	1.8
16	Washington	1.8
18	Massachusetts	1.7
19	Hawaii	1.5
19	Louisiana	1.5
21	Maryland	1.4
22	Indiana	1.3
22	Michigan	1.3
22	Oklahoma	1.3
25	Delaware	1.2
25	Nebraska	1.2
25	Virginia	1.2
28	Pennsylvania	1.1
28	Rhode Island	1.1
30	Georgia	1.0
30	Wisconsin	1.0
32	Montana	.9
32	Ohio	.9
32	South Carolina	.9
35	Missouri	.8
35	North Carolina	.8
37	Iowa	.7
37	Minnesota	.7
37	Mississippi	.7

Rank	State	Percent
40	Alabama	.6
40	Arkansas	.6
40	New Hampshire	.6
40	North Dakota	.6
40	South Dakota	.6
40	Tennessee	.6
46	Kentucky	.5
46	Vermont	.5
46	West Virginia	.5
49	Maine	.2
50	Oregon	.1

47. Other Languages

The group of Americans who speak neither English nor Spanish at home is larger than the group of Spanish-speakers and more widely distributed around the country. There are 37 states where people who use some other language make up more than 3% of the population. In Hawaii, the languages of Asia and the Pacific islands are well represented. In Louisiana and the five New England states where more than 10% of the population uses language other than English, French (or Canadian French) is the most important tongue, with Italian close behind in Massachusetts, and Italian and Portuguese well represented in Rhode Island. German is the forerunner in North Dakota (where the Lutheran church is also strong) and native American tongues lead the way in Alaska. Italian is the foremost language other than English in New York and New Jersey, but great linguistic diversity is the real hallmark of the greater New York City area.

Table: Population Speaking Other Languages
Date: 1980
Source: Census Bureau
Description: Percentage of persons 18 years and older who speak a language other than English or Spanish at home.
United States average: 6.3%

POPULATION SPEAKING OTHER LANGUAGES

Rank	State	Percent
1	Hawaii	27.3
2	Rhode Island	16.9
3	North Dakota	13.4
4	Maine	13.1
5	Alaska	12.5
5	Massachusetts	12.5
7	Connecticut	12.1
8	New York	12.0
9	New Hampshire	11.3
10	New Jersey	11.1

Rank	State	Percent
11	Louisiana	10.0
12	California	9.0
13	Illinois	7.9
14	New Mexico	7.8
15	South Dakota	7.4
16	Vermont	7.1
17	Arizona	6.8
18	Pennsylvania	6.5
19	Michigan	6.3
20	Minnesota	5.7
21	Nevada	5.3
21	Wisconsin	5.3
23	Maryland	5.2
23	Montana	5.2
23	Washington	5.2
26	Florida	5.1
27	Utah	4.8
28	Delaware	4.7
29	Ohio	4.6
30	Colorado	4.3
31	Nebraska	4.2
32	Oregon	4.1
33	Indiana	3.5
34	Virginia	3.4
34	Wyoming	3.4
36	Texas	3.3
37	Kansas	3.2
38	Iowa	2.7
39	Oklahoma	2.6
40	Missouri	2.5
41	Idaho	2.4
42	West Virginia	2.0
43	Alabama	1.9
44	Georgia	1.8
44	North Carolina	1.8
46	South Carolina	1.7
47	Mississippi	1.4
48	Kentucky	1.3
49	Tennessee	1.2
49	Arkansas	1.2

48. Black Population

The data in this table and its supplement and in the three following tables are drawn from the provisional results of the 1980 census. Asked to indicate the racial group with which they identified themselves, 83.2% of the U.S. population selected "white" and 11.7% selected "black." The other 5.1% of the population chose a designation from one of the native American groups (American Indian, Eskimo, Aleut), or the Asian/Pacific Islander groups (Chinese, Filipino, Japanese, Indian, Korean, Vietnamese, Hawaiian, Samoan, Guamanian), or some other group not specified above. White Americans thus form the largest racial group in the country—the majority—and black Americans constitute the largest racial minority. In 1980, 55% of self-identified Hispanics also identified themselves as white, 3% as black and 42% chose neither designation.

The black population of the United States was at one time concentrated almost exclusively in the slave-holding states of the South. Emancipation established the precondition for changes in this pattern, but the migration of blacks from the rural South to the northern cities was not significant before World War I. This stream of migration gathered force following the second world war, when blacks seeking employment opportunities in the urban economy also played an important part in migration to southern California. The largest groups of black Americans are presently found in the metropolitan areas (mainly the central cities) of the most populous states, but the highest percentages of blacks in state populations are still found in the South: Mississippi (35.2%), South Carolina (30.4%), Louisiana (29.4%), Georgia (26.8%), and Alabama (25.6%). States outside the South without major urban centers have few black residents.

In 44 of 318 SMSAs, black population exceeds 100,000. These SMSAs are ranked in a supplementary table according to total black population. A majority of the 50 largest SMSAs is represented here, along with a number of smaller SMSAs in the South.

Table: Black Population
Date: 1980
Source: Census Bureau
Description: Black population and percentage of the total state population.
United States total: 26,488,218
Percent of U.S. population: 11.7%

BLACK POPULATION

Rank	State	Black population (in thousands)	Percent of total state population
1	New York	2,402	13.7
2	California	1,819	7.7
3	Texas	1,710	12.0
4	Illinois	1,675	14.7
5	Georgia	1,465	26.8
6	Florida	1,342	13.8
7	North Carolina	1,316	22.4
8	Louisiana	1,237	29.4
9	Michigan	1,199	12.9
10	Ohio	1,077	10.0
11	Pennsylvania	1,048	8.8
12	Virginia	1,008	18.9
13	Alabama	996	25.6
14	Maryland	958	22.7
15	South Carolina	948	30.4
16	New Jersey	925	12.6
17	Mississippi	887	35.2

Rank	State	Black population (in thousands)	Percent of total state population
18	Tennessee	726	15.8
19	Missouri	514	10.5
20	Indiana	415	7.6
21	Arkansas	373	16.3
22	Kentucky	259	7.1
23	Massachusetts	221	3.9
24	Connecticut	217	7.0
25	Oklahoma	205	6.8
26	Wisconsin	183	3.9
27	Kansas	126	5.3
28	Washington	106	2.6
29	Colorado	102	3.5
30	Delaware	96	16.1
31	Arizona	75	2.8
32	West Virginia	65	3.3
33	Minnesota	53	1.3
34	Nevada	51	6.4
35	Nebraska	48	3.1
36	Iowa	42	1.4
37	Oregon	37	1.4
38	Rhode Island	28	2.9
39	New Mexico	24	1.8
40	Hawaii	17	1.8
41	Alaska	14	3.4
42	Utah	9	.6
43	New Mexico	4	.4
44	Idaho	3	.3
44	Maine	3	.3
44	North Dakota	3	.4
44	Wyoming	3	.7
48	Montana	2	.2
48	South Dakota	2	.3
50	Vermont	1	.2

Table: Black Population of Selected SMSAs
Date: 1980
Source: Census Bureau
Description: SMSAs with black population over 100,000, ranked by size of black population.

BLACK POPULATION OF SELECTED SMSAs

Rank	SMSA	Black population
1	New York	2,363,807
2	Chicago	1,710,173
3	Los Angeles-Long Beach	1,288,468
4	Philadelphia	1,079,183
5	Detroit	833,070
6	Washington, D.C.	749,995
7	Baltimore	597,855
8	Houston	561,704
9	Newark	543,971
10	San Francisco-Oakland	491,212
11	St. Louis	462,571
12	Dallas-Fort Worth	433,094
13	Atlanta	420,388
14	New Orleans	411,084
15	Cleveland	410,157
16	Memphis	324,310

Rank	SMSA	Black population
17	Miami	249,161
18	Boston-Lowell-Broxton-Lawrence-Haverhill	246,302
19	Norfolk-Virginia Beach-Portsmouth	209,631
20	Kansas City	203,036
21	Birmingham	196,382
22	Pittsburgh	180,131
23	Milwaukee	177,880
24	Indianapolis	171,785
25	Cincinnati	169,299
26	Nassau-Suffolk (Long Island)	163,707
27	Gary-Hammond-East Chicago	149,525
28	Tampa-St. Petersburg	149,455
29	Buffalo	148,742
30	Greensboro-Winston-Salem-High Point	141,989
31	Richmond	141,802
32	Jacksonville	137,367
33	Mobile	135,636
34	Columbus, Ohio	127,140
35	Charlotte-Gastonia	120,534
36	Nashville-Davidson	118,847
37	Louisville	115,918
38	Shreveport, La.	114,359
39	Raleigh-Durham	112,926
40	Dayton	110,549
41	Baton Rouge	107,969
42	Jackson, Miss.	106,849
43	San Diego	104,452
44	Fort Lauderdale-Hollywood	101,857

Table: Asian and Pacific Islander Population
Date: 1980
Source: Census Bureau
Description: Asian and Pacific islander population and percentage of total state population in 28 states with more than 15,000 members of this group.
United States total: 3,500,636
Percent of U.S. population: 1.5%

ASIAN AND PACIFIC ISLANDER POPULATION

Rank	State	Population	Percent of state population
1	California	1,253,987	5.3
2	Hawaii	583,660	60.5
3	New York	310,531	1.8
4	Illinois	159,551	1.4
5	Texas	120,306	.8
6	New Jersey	103,842	1.4
7	Washington	102,503	2.5
8	Virginia	66,209	1.2
9	Pennsylvania	64,381	.5
10	Maryland	64,276	1.5
11	Florida	56,756	.6
12	Michigan	56,731	.6
13	Massachusetts	49,501	.9
14	Ohio	47,813	.4
15	Oregon	34,767	1.3
16	Colorado	29,897	1.0
17	Minnesota	26,533	.7
18	Georgia	24,461	.4
19	Louisiana	23,771	.6
20	Missouri	23,108	.5
21	Arizona	22,098	.8
22	North Carolina	21,168	.4
23	Indiana	20,488	.4
24	Connecticut	18,970	.6
25	Wisconsin	18,165	.4
26	Oklahoma	17,274	.6
27	Kansas	15,078	.6
28	Utah	15,076	1.0

49. Asian/Pacific Islander Population

Nine of the racial choices offered on the 1980 census forms came under this general heading. In order of population size, the places of origin designated by these nine groups were: China, the Phillipines, Japan, India, Korea, Vietnam, Hawaii, Samoa and Guam. The 806,000 Chinese form the largest of these groups, the 32,000 Guamanians the smallest. All together, 3.5 million persons, 1.5% of the total population of the United States, identified themselves with these designations.

The Asian/Pacific population is highly concentrated, with over 60% of all such persons living in the three states of New York, California and Hawaii. In Hawaii, people of Asian/Pacific extraction are in the majority. Elsewhere, members of this group make up more than 2% of the population only in the two coastal states of California and Washington.

50. American Indian Population

American Indians today constitute less than 1% of the population of the United States; they total about 1.3 million people. American Indian population exceeds 5% of state population only in New Mexico (8.0%), South Dakota (6.5%), Oklahoma (5.6%), Arizona (5.6%), and Alaska (5.5%). The groups of Eskimo and Aleuts, classified separately, consist of fewer than 60,000 people in the nation as a whole. They are mainly located in Alaska, where they make up 10.5% of the population. The bulk of the American Indian population is found in the West and the upper Midwest, with outlying groups in North Carolina, New York and Florida.

Table: American Indian Population
Date: 1980
Source: Census Bureau
Description: American Indian population for 21 states with American Indian population of 15,000 or more.
United States total: 1,361,869
Percent of U.S. population: 0.6%

AMERICAN INDIAN POPULATION

Rank	State	Population	Percent of total American Indian population
1	California	198,095	14.5
2	Oklahoma	169,297	12.4
3	Arizona	152,610	11.2
4	New Mexico	104,634	7.7
5	North Carolina	64,519	4.7
6	Washington	58,159	4.3
7	South Dakota	45,081	3.3
8	Michigan	39,702	2.9
9	Texas	39,374	2.9
10	New York	38,117	2.8
11	Montana	37,153	2.7
12	Minnesota	34,841	2.6
13	Wisconsin	29,318	2.2
14	Oregon	26,587	2.0
15	Alaska	21,849	1.6
16	North Dakota	20,119	1.5
17	Utah	19,158	1.4
18	Florida	18,981	1.4
19	Colorado	17,726	1.3
20	Illinois	15,833	1.2
21	Kansas	15,254	1.1

51. Spanish/Hispanic Population

The Spanish/Hispanic segment of the American population is classified as a group according to ethnicity and national origin. Forty percent of the individuals who identified their origins as Spanish/Hispanic in the 1980 census did not choose any of the standard racial classifications offered on the census form. These persons make up over 85% of the group appearing in the residual racial category "Other" in census reports.

The state by state distribution of Spanish/Hispanic individuals parallels the distribution of people speaking Spanish at home that was reported above. The majority of Hispanics live in the Southwest. Florida and the metropolitan areas of New York City and Chicago are the other major centers of residence. In every state, the population of those of Spanish/Hispanic *origin* is greater than the population using the Spanish *language* at home. Where the difference between these two measures is small (e.g., in Florida and Texas), it is clear that many recent arrivals are included in the Hispanic population. In states where populations of Spanish/Hispanic origin have been established for a long time (e.g., throughout the Southwest and in Hawaii), the percentage of members who regularly speak Spanish is much smaller.

Table: Hispanic Population
Date: 1980
Source: Census Bureau
Description: Hispanic population, and percentage of total state population.
United States total: 14,609,000
Percent of U.S. population: 6.4%

HISPANIC POPULATION

Rank	State	Hispanic population (in thousands)	Percent of total state population
1	California	4,544	19.2
2	Texas	2,986	21.0
3	New York	1,659	9.5
4	Florida	858	8.8
5	Illinois	636	5.6
6	New Jersey	492	6.7
7	New Mexico	476	36.6
8	Arizona	441	16.2
9	Colorado	339	11.7
10	Michigan	162	1.8
11	Pennsylvania	154	1.3
12	Massachusetts	141	2.5
13	Connecticut	124	4.0
14	Ohio	120	1.1
15	Washington	110	2.7
16	Louisiana	99	2.4
17	Indiana	87	1.6
18	Virginia	80	1.5
19	Hawaii	71	7.4
20	Oregon	66	2.5
21	Maryland	65	1.5
22	Kansas	63	2.7
22	Wisconsin	63	1.3
24	Georgia	61	1.1
25	Utah	60	4.1
26	North Carolina	57	1.0
26	Oklahoma	57	1.9
28	Nevada	54	6.8
29	Missouri	52	1.1
30	Idaho	37	3.9
31	Tennessee	34	.7
32	Alabama	33	.8
32	South Carolina	33	1.1
34	Minnesota	32	.8
35	Nebraska	28	1.8
36	Kentucky	27	.7
37	Iowa	26	.9
38	Mississippi	25	1.0
39	Wyoming	24	5.1
40	Rhode Island	20	2.1
41	Arkansas	18	.8
42	West Virginia	13	.7
43	Delaware	10	1.7
43	Montana	10	1.3
45	Alaska	9	2.3
46	New Hampshire	6	.7
47	Maine	5	.4
48	North Dakota	4	.6
48	South Dakota	4	.6
50	Vermont	3	.6

FAMILY

The tables in this section consider the American family from a variety of perspectives. The first table compares the average size of the groups in which people live in different states, tracing the advance of more independent, that is, small-group lifestyles. A pair of tables then indicates the degree to which the population includes family members who have their roots in the states where they presently reside. A table on the age structure of state populations serves as an introduction to a series of tables on birth, marriage and divorce, the "vital statistics" that are most closely connected with the family. The average age of a population is often the key to explaining the rates at which "vital" events occur. It has been some time since the typical American family included children, parents, and grandparents living under the same roof. Recent patterns of divorce and increases in births to unmarried women suggest that families including children and a pair of married parents are now becoming less typical. With higher proportions of persons of all ages living alone, and an increase in single-parent families leading the way, the form of the typical grouping in which people live is changing rapidly. Included in the statistics on births are tables on abortion, providing some indication of the extent of a procedure that is now the subject of intense discussion.

52. Marriage

Nevada, where there is a well-organized marriage trade, displays a marriage rate that is entirely out of line with rates in the rest of the country. Chapels by the roadside can provide witnesses and all the other fixings for a wedding on a moment's notice. A ceremony can be performed in about the time it takes to pump a tankful of gas. Out of state couples account for almost all marriages in Nevada.

Elsewhere, there is a ratio of about 2 to 1 between the highest and lowest state marriage rates. Higher rates are found in the West and the South, with lower rates in the East and the Midwest. The age structure of the population is the key to the marriage rate, even more important than regional variations in the propensity to get married. With the baby-boom generation arriving at marriageable ages in recent years, the marriage rate for the nation has edged upward, despite the fact that people are choosing to remain single longer. The average age at first marriage increased between 1970 and 1979 (from 22.5 to 23.4 for men; from 20.6 to 21.6 for women). During the same period, however, the average age of remarriage declined sharply (from 39.6 to 35.3 for men; from 35.5 to 31.9 for women). For 33 states, using data that separate first marriages from remarriages for brides, it appears that about 32% of the 2.3 million marriages in 1979 were remarriages for the bride. In 1960 only about 23% of all marriages fell into this category.

Table: Marriage Rates
Date: 1979
Source: National Center for Health Statistics
Description: Marriage rate per 1,000 population.
United States average: 10.6 per 1,000
State median: 10.7 per 1,000

MARRIAGE RATES

Rank	State	Rate per 1,000 population
1	Nevada	147.4
2	South Carolina	18.2
3	Oklahoma	15.4
4	Idaho	14.8
5	Wyoming	14.4
6	Tennessee	13.5
7	Georgia	13.4
8	New Mexico	13.1
9	South Dakota	13.0
10	Alabama	12.9
10	Texas	12.9
12	Hawaii	12.8
13	Alaska	12.3
14	Utah	12.2
15	Arizona	12.1

Rank	State	Rate per 1,000 population
16	Washington	12.0
17	Arkansas	11.9
18	Colorado	11.8
19	Florida	11.7
20	Virginia	11.3
21	Mississippi	11.2
22	Maryland	11.1
23	Indiana	11.0
24	Maine	10.9
24	Montana	10.9
24	Rhode Island	10.9
27	Kansas	10.5
27	Vermont	10.5
29	Montana	10.4
30	Louisiana	10.3
31	New Hampshire	10.2
32	Illinois	9.7
32	Michigan	9.7
34	Iowa	9.6
34	Kentucky	9.6
36	West Virginia	9.4
37	Ohio	9.3
38	North Dakota	9.2
39	Minnesota	9.1
40	Nebraska	8.9
41	California	8.8
42	Oregon	8.7
43	Wisconsin	8.4
44	Connecticut	8.2
45	New York	8.1
46	North Carolina	8.0
46	Pennsylvania	8.0
48	Massachusetts	7.8
49	Delaware	7.5
49	New Jersey	7.5

53. Divorce and Annulment

Divorce rates per 1,000 population doubled between 1965 and 1976. The 1979 total of about 1.2 million divorces and the 1979 divorce rate of 5.4 divorces per 1,000 population are both all-time highs for the United States. The median duration of marriages ending in divorce was 6.8 years in 1979. This figure has remained about the same throughout the great upswing in divorce of the past 20 years. The median age of men and women at the time of first divorce has also stayed about the same (31.0 for men and 28.7 for women in 1979). The average number of children involved in divorces has declined, however, from 1.32 per divorce in 1965 to 1.00 per divorce in 1979; this reflects the rise in the number of marriages with few or no children.

State regulations on grounds and procedures for divorce vary. Leaving aside Nevada, where a quickie divorce industry complements the fast-marriage trade, the ratio between the highest and lowest state divorce rates is about 3 to 1, with generally higher levels in the West.

Table: Divorce and Annulment Rates
Date: 1979
Source: National Center for Health Statistics
Description: Divorce and Annulment rate per 1,000 population.
United States average: 5.4 per 1,000
State median: 5.5 per 1,000

DIVORCE AND ANNULMENT RATES

Rank	State	Rate per 1,000 population
1	Nevada	16.8
2	Arkansas	9.3
3	Alaska	8.6
4	Arizona	8.2
5	New Mexico	8.0
6	Florida	7.9
6	Oklahoma	7.9
8	Wyoming	7.8
9	Indiana	7.7
10	Idaho	7.1
11	Alabama	7.0
11	Oregon	7.0
13	Texas	6.9
13	Washington	6.9
15	Tennessee	6.8
16	Georgia	6.5
16	Montana	6.5
18	California	6.1
19	Colorado	6.0
20	New Hampshire	5.9
21	Missouri	5.7
22	Maine	5.6
22	Mississippi	5.6
22	Utah	5.6
25	Hawaii	5.5
25	Ohio	5.5
27	Kansas	5.4
28	Delaware	5.3
28	West Virginia	5.3
30	North Carolina	4.9
31	Michigan	4.8
32	South Carolina	4.7
33	Illinois	4.6
33	Vermont	4.6
35	Connecticut	4.5
35	Kentucky	4.5
35	Virginia	4.5
38	Maryland	4.1
39	Nebraska	4.0
40	Iowa	3.9
40	Rhode Island	3.9
40	South Dakota	3.9
43	Louisiana	3.8
44	Minnesota	3.7
44	New York	3.7
46	Wisconsin	3.6

Rank	State	Rate per 1,000 population
47	Pennsylvania	3.4
48	New Jersey	3.2
48	North Dakota	3.2
50	Massachusetts	3.0

54. Divorce/Marriage Ratio

The ratio of divorces to marriages can be viewed as a rough index of how well things are going for couples in a given state. It simply compares the number of married couples breaking up to the number of couples entering marriage. Note, however, that roughly one of every three members of the group of persons getting married was formerly a partner in a marriage that broke up. The data for Nevada should be ignored in this regard, since they merely trace the relative fortunes of two specific types of business.

Marriage formation is still running ahead of marriage breakup in every state of the union, although the two categories are edging toward equality in Arkansas and breakups are generally running at a high rate in the western part of the country and in a few eastern states. Marriages are still well ahead of breakups in most states found in a large region extending from the East Coast through the Midwest as far as the Dakotas. The average age of state population plays a role here. People in these states tend to be older and therefore married before 1977. Projections indicate that about one of every three marriages formed in 1952 will eventually end in divorce. For marriages formed 25 years later, in 1977, it seems that one of every two marriages will end up this way.

Table: Divorce/Marriage Ratio
Date: 1980
Source: National Center for Health Statistics
Description: Number of divorces for every 1,000 marriages for 48 states.
48 State average: 490
48 State median: 490

DIVORCE/MARRIAGE RATIO

Rank	State	Divorces per 1,000 marriages
1	Arkansas	864
2	Oregon	775
3	Alaska	677
4	Arizona	659
5	Florida	646
6	New Mexico	640

Rank	State	Divorces per 1,000 marriages
7	California	615
8	Washington	610
9	North Carolina	608
10	Montana	593
11	Ohio	585
12	Wyoming	582
13	West Virginia	568
14	New Hampshire	562
15	Alabama	548
16	Kansas	537
17	Colorado	533
18	Delaware	523
19	Oklahoma	521
20	Texas	519
21	Tennessee	512
22	Idaho	508
23	Rhode Island	503
24	Missouri	500
25	Kentucky	495
26	Vermont	486
27	Georgia	485
28	Mississippi	480
29	New Jersey	470
30	Utah	466
31	Nebraska	457
32	Illinois	456
32	Michigan	456
34	Connecticut	444
35	Wisconsin	436
36	Maine	435
37	Iowa	427
38	Minnesota	400
39	Virginia	392
40	New York	384
41	Hawaii	376
42	Pennsylvania	365
43	Maryland	354
44	North Dakota	349
45	Massachusetts	336
46	South Dakota	316
47	South Carolina	256
48	Nevada	118

55. Household Size and Percentage of Change 1970–1980

The Bureau of the Census defines households as groups of people who share a common dwelling. Most households consist simply of families, but persons living alone count as separate households, and persons living as lodgers, foster children or employees are counted as household members even though they are not related to the people they live with. Persons who live in "group quarters" such as jails, hospitals, nursing homes, dormitories, barracks and rooming houses are not included in the household statistics.

The average size of households declined in all 50 states during the 1970s. In 1975 a historic milestone was reached when average size slipped below three persons per household. The 1980 average of 2.75 persons is the lowest ever recorded in this country. Declining rates of birth are the major factor in this trend, but several other factors cannot be overlooked, including the affluence that enables Americans to afford separate living quarters, increasing preference for lifestyles that involve separating different generations of a family, and rising rates of divorce and marital separation.

Utah and Hawaii are the only states in which more than three people are still found in a typical household. Since most large households are based on relationships in which parents care for young children, it is not surprising that high average household size tends to be associated with high birthrates and low median ages.

Table: Household Size
Date: 1980
Source: Census Bureau
Description: Average household size and the percentage of decrease in size from 1970 to 1980.
United States average size: 2.75
United States median size: 2.76
United States average decrease 1970 – 1980: −11.6%

AVERAGE HOUSEHOLD SIZE

Rank	State	Average household size 1980	Percent decrease 1970–1980
1	Utah	3.20	− 7.5
2	Hawaii	3.15	−12.3
3	Mississippi	2.97	−12.4
4	Alaska	2.93	−16.8
4	South Carolina	2.93	−13.6
6	Louisiana	2.91	−13.6
7	New Mexico	2.90	−15.5
8	Idaho	2.85	−10.1
9	Alabama	2.84	−12.6
9	Georgia	2.84	−12.6
9	Michigan	2.84	−13.1
9	New Jersey	2.84	−10.4
13	Kentucky	2.82	−11.0
13	Maryland	2.82	−13.2
13	Texas	2.82	−11.0
16	Arizona	2.79	−12.8
16	Delaware	2.79	−13.6
16	West Virginia	2.79	−10.6
19	North Carolina	2.78	−14.2
19	Virginia	2.78	−13.1
19	Wyoming	2.78	−10.0
22	Indiana	2.77	−11.8
22	Tennessee	2.77	−12.1

Rank	State	Average Household Size 1980	Percent Decrease 1970–1980
22	Wisconsin	2.77	−14.0
25	Connecticut	2.76	−12.7
25	Illinois	2.76	−10.7
25	Ohio	2.76	−12.7
28	Maine	2.75	−13.0
28	New Hampshire	2.75	−12.4
28	North Dakota	2.75	−15.4
28	Vermont	2.75	−14.3
32	Arkansas	2.74	−10.2
32	Minnesota	2.74	−14.4
32	Pennsylvania	2.74	−11.6
32	South Dakota	2.74	−13.8
36	Massachusetts	2.72	−12.8
37	Montana	2.70	−12.9
37	New York	2.70	−10.3
37	Rhode Island	2.70	−12.1
40	California	2.68	− 9.2
40	Iowa	2.68	−12.1
42	Missouri	2.67	−10.4
43	Nebraska	2.66	−11.9
44	Colorado	2.65	−14.0
45	Kansas	2.62	−11.8
45	Oklahoma	2.62	− 9.7
47	Washington	2.61	−12.4
48	Oregon	2.60	−11.6
49	Nevada	2.59	−13.4
50	Florida	2.55	−12.1

56. Interstate Mobility

One way to gauge the importance of mobility in a given state is to look at the proportion of the population that was born in a different state. This neglects, of course, the everyday mobility within a given state. Overall, about one in every four Americans lives outside the state of his or her birth, but there are sharp differences among the states in this respect. Nevada is the outstanding example of a magnet state, drawing three-quarters of its population from elsewhere in the country. Patterns in the ranking of the other states are more regular than they appear to be at first glance. The general rule is that the proportion of population born out-of-state increases from east to west. The eastern states in the top half of the table, however, all represent specific exceptions to this rule. Florida is a retirement center; New Hampshire and Vermont have added migrants from lower New England to their small populations over the years; and the influx of people from around the country who have come to seek their fortunes in New York City and Washington D.C. and live in their suburbs, explains the positions of Connecticut, New Jersey, Maryland, Virginia and probably Delaware.

Table: Interstate Mobility
Date: 1980
Source: Census Bureau
Description: Percentage of State Population born in one state and now residing in another.
United States median: 27.3%
United States average: 33.7%

57. Stability

Stability, the proportion of state population born within the state, is for the most part the opposite side of the coin of mobility. The inverse relationship is not perfect, however, since persons born outside the United States are not included in the figures reported in either this table or the previous table. This foreign-born group can be very large in certain states (especially California, Hawaii and New York), so the sum of the figures in these two tables may fall far short of 100%.

High stability quotients are found in states along the Appalachian range and in several states in the South and the Midwest. These are areas that have experienced little in-migration in recent decades. The low levels of stability are found in the West and in those eastern states discussed in the introduction to the previous table.

Table: Stability
Date: 1980
Source: Census Bureau
Description: Percentage of population born and still residing in the same state.
United States average: 63.8%
States median: 68.8%

INTERSTATE MOBILITY

Rank	State	Percent
1	Nevada	76.0
2	Alaska	63.6
3	Arizona	60.5
4	Wyoming	59.1
5	Florida	56.4
6	Colorado	52.6
7	Oregon	51.4
8	Idaho	47.8
9	New Hampshire	45.4
9	Washington	45.4
11	New Mexico	44.0
12	Delaware	43.6
13	Maryland	41.2
14	Montana	40.2
15	California	38.9
16	Virginia	35.7
17	Kansas	35.1
18	Oklahoma	34.6
19	Vermont	34.0
20	Connecticut	32.2
21	New Jersey	31.6
22	Utah	30.0
23	Arkansas	29.7
24	Missouri	28.1
25	South Dakota	27.6
26	Nebraska	27.0
27	Georgia	26.7
28	Indiana	26.4
28	Tennessee	26.4
30	Hawaii	25.8
31	South Carolina	25.4
32	North Dakota	24.7
32	Ohio	24.7
34	Texas	24.6
35	Michigan	23.9
36	Rhode Island	23.5
37	Illinois	22.8
38	Maine	22.3
38	Minnesota	22.3
38	North Carolina	22.3
41	Iowa	21.2
42	Mississippi	20.3
43	West Virginia	20.1
44	Wisconsin	19.7
45	Alabama	19.5
46	Kentucky	19.3
46	Louisiana	19.3
48	Massachusetts	18.9
49	Pennsylvania	14.8
50	New York	14.3

STABILITY

Rank	State	Percent
1	Pennsylvania	81.0
2	Kentucky	79.4
3	Alabama	79.0
4	West Virginia	78.6
5	Mississippi	78.5
6	Louisiana	78.1
7	Wisconsin	77.2
8	Iowa	76.8
9	North Carolina	75.8
10	Minnesota	74.7
11	Maine	72.9
12	South Carolina	72.7
13	North Dakota	72.6
14	Tennessee	72.3
15	Ohio	72.1
16	Massachusetts	71.6
17	Indiana	71.3
17	Michigan	71.3
19	Georgia	70.8
20	Nebraska	70.5
20	South Dakota	70.5
22	Missouri	69.8
23	Arkansas	69.0
23	New York	69.0
25	Illinois	68.9
26	Texas	68.6
27	Rhode Island	67.0
28	Utah	65.8

Rank	State	Percent
29	Oklahoma	63.0
30	Kansas	62.3
31	Vermont	61.3
32	Virginia	60.0
33	Hawaii	57.8
34	Connecticut	57.2
35	Montana	56.8
36	New Jersey	56.1
37	Maryland	53.3
38	Delaware	52.0
39	New Mexico	51.2
40	New Hampshire	49.7
41	Idaho	49.4
42	Washington	47.8
43	California	45.3
44	Oregon	43.7
45	Colorado	42.7
46	Wyoming	38.3
47	Arizona	32.5
48	Alaska	31.6
49	Florida	31.1
50	Nevada	21.3

58. Median Age

In 1820 the median age of the American population was 16.7 years. This figure crept higher with declining birthrates and increasing length of life. The figures for 1860, 1900 and 1940 were 19.4 years, 22.0 years and 29.0 years, respectively. The median age of the population has fluctuated within a narrow range of about 1.5 years on either side of the 1940 figure ever since. Recent trends in the birthrate indicate, however, that the median age will soon break out of this range and begin climbing again. The "average American" is aging and the Social Security system will not be the only institution affected by this change.

Data on median age are included here because they provide some insight into the situation of families in different states. Except for Florida, where a very large contingent of retired persons boosts the median value, the seven states where median age is more than one year higher than the national median are found in the Northeast. Almost all of the 15 states with a median age more than one year lower than the national median are located in the South and the West. High birthrates characterize most of these states.

Table: Median Age
Date: 1980
Source: Census Bureau
Description: Median age.
United States median: 30.0

State median: 29.6

MEDIAN AGE

Rank	State	Median age
1	Florida	34.7
2	New Jersey	32.2
3	Pennsylvania	32.1
4	Connecticut	32.0
5	New York	31.9
6	Rhode Island	31.8
7	Massachusetts	31.2
8	Missouri	30.9
9	Arkansas	30.6
10	Maine	30.4
10	West Virginia	30.4
12	Maryland	30.3
12	Nevada	30.3
14	Oregon	30.2
15	Kansas	30.1
15	New Hampshire	30.1
15	Oklahoma	30.1
15	Tennessee	30.1
19	Iowa	30.0
20	California	29.9
20	Illinois	29.9
20	Ohio	29.9
23	Virginia	29.8
23	Washington	29.8
25	Delaware	29.7
25	Nebraska	29.7
27	North Carolina	29.6
28	Vermont	29.4
28	Wisconsin	29.4
30	Alabama	29.3
31	Arizona	29.2
31	Indiana	29.2
31	Minnesota	29.2
34	Kentucky	29.1
35	Montana	29.0
36	South Dakota	28.9
37	Michigan	28.8
38	Georgia	28.7
39	Colorado	28.6
40	Hawaii	28.4
41	North Dakota	28.3
42	South Carolina	28.2
42	Texas	28.2
44	Mississippi	27.7
45	Idaho	27.6
46	Louisiana	27.4
46	New Mexico	27.4
48	Wyoming	27.1
49	Alaska	26.1
50	Utah	24.2

59. Birthrate

The birthrate of the United States as a whole in 1910

was the same as the extraordinary birthrate of the state of Utah in 1979. A downward trend set in following World War I. By 1935, in the midst of the Depression, the rate had dropped to 18.7 live births per 1,000 population. The baby boom brought a revival, to a rate of 25.0 in 1955, but the general trend ever since has been toward fewer births. A slight upturn from a low of 14.8 in 1975 and 1976 has recently occurred, but this is mainly because there happens to be a relatively large segment of women in the population at the present time (the baby-boom girls) who have reached childbearing age.

States in the West and the South have the highest birthrates. The lowest rates are observed in states along the East Coast.

Table: Birthrate
Date: 1979
Source: National Center for Health Statistics
Description: Total number of births and birthrate per 1,000 population.
United States average: 15.9 per 1,000
State median: 16.4 per 1,000

BIRTHRATE

Rank	State	Birthrate per 1,000 population	Total birth-rate (in thousands)
1	Utah	30.1	41
2	Alaska	22.4	9
3	Idaho	22.1	20
4	Wyoming	21.7	10
5	New Mexico	20.6	26
6	Louisiana	19.7	79
7	Hawaii	19.2	18
8	Arizona	19.1	47
9	Texas	19.0	255
10	Mississippi	18.9	46
10	South Dakota	18.9	13
12	Montana	17.9	14
12	North Dakota	17.9	12
14	Nevada	17.6	12
15	South Carolina	17.3	51
16	Georgia	17.2	88
17	Colorado	17.0	47
17	Oklahoma	17.0	49
19	Arkansas	16.7	36
19	California	16.7	379
19	Kentucky	16.7	59
19	Nebraska	16.7	26
23	Alabama	16.6	63
24	Kansas	16.5	39
24	Oregon	16.5	42
26	Illinois	16.4	184
26	Washington	16.4	64
28	Indiana	16.2	87
29	Iowa	16.1	47

Rank	State	Birthrate per 1,000 population	Total birth-rate (in thousands)
29	Minnesota	16.1	65
31	West Virginia	15.9	30
32	Michigan	15.7	145
32	Missouri	15.7	76
34	Ohio	15.6	167
34	Tennessee	15.6	68
36	Wisconsin	15.5	73
37	Delaware	15.3	9
38	Vermont	15.2	8
39	North Carolina	15.0	84
40	Maine	14.9	16
41	Virginia	14.8	77
42	New Hampshire	14.5	13
43	Maryland	14.0	58
44	Florida	13.7	121
45	Pennsylvania	13.5	158
46	New York	13.4	236
47	New Jersey	13.2	97
48	Rhode Island	12.8	12
49	Connecticut	12.4	39
50	Massachusetts	12.2	71

60. Average Number of Births per 1,000 Women

The data in this table indicate the number of children already born per thousand women in the age-group 15 to 44. The figures range from about 1.6 births per thousand women in the states of Utah and Idaho (where Mormon influence is strong) to a low of about 1.1 births per thousand women in lower New England (where, surprisingly, Catholics are well represented). California and Colorado have rates that contrast sharply with those of other states in the West.

These data do not cover children not yet born to the women surveyed, but calculations of the total fertility rate for 1979 (which projects the number of babies that would be born if women continue to have babies at the 1979 age-specific rates for the rest of their childbearing years) indicate that current levels of fertility are not high enough to maintain the present level of population. This has been true since 1972. About 2.11 lifetime births per woman are needed to hold population at a constant level over the long run. Continuation of the age-specific birth pattern of 1979 would result in a total of only about 1.86 lifetime births per woman. It is true that there has been an upsurge recently in births among women in their early 30s, but many of the babies that these women did not have when they were in their 20s will never be made up for in this way.

Table: Average Number of Births
Date: 1980
Source: Census Bureau
Description: Average number of births to each 1,000 women aged 15 to 44.
United States average: 1,301
State median: 1,336

AVERAGE NUMBER OF BIRTHS

Rank	State	Average births per 1,000 women
1	Utah	1,638
2	Idaho	1,561
3	Arkansas	1,514
3	Mississippi	1,514
5	Louisiana	1,483
6	New Mexico	1,464
6	Wyoming	1,464
8	Alabama	1,417
9	Montana	1,416
10	Texas	1,405
11	Kentucky	1,400
12	South Dakota	1,395
13	Oklahoma	1,392
14	Georgia	1,389
15	Indiana	1,388
15	West Virginia	1,388
17	Iowa	1,369
18	South Carolina	1,364
19	Kansas	1,360
20	Tennessee	1,358
21	Maine	1,356
22	Alaska	1,346
23	Michigan	1,342
24	Arizona	1,338
24	North Dakota	1,338
26	Missouri	1,334
27	Ohio	1,330
28	Illinois	1,327
29	Oregon	1,310
30	Nebraska	1,309
31	Wisconsin	1,297
32	Nevada	1,291
33	North Carolina	1,288
34	Minnesota	1,284
34	Washington	1,284
36	Delaware	1,264
37	Florida	1,261
38	New Hampshire	1,241
39	Virginia	1,236
40	Vermont	1,234
41	Pennsylvania	1,230
42	California	1,229
43	Maryland	1,221
44	New Jersey	1,213
45	Colorado	1,195
46	New York	1,193
47	Hawaii	1,186
48	Connecticut	1,183
49	Rhode Island	1,140
50	Massachusetts	1,110

61. Births to Unmarried Women: Total Births to White Women and Births to Black Women

There has been a sharp upward trend in births to unmarried women over the past 29 years. The historical pattern of births to unwed mothers as a percentage of all births may be summarized as follows: 1950, 4.0%; 1960, 5.3%; 1970, 10.7%; 1975, 14.2%; 1979, 17.1%. To some extent, the higher share of births to unmarried women appears because married women are planning their families with increasing care and therefore reducing their share, but several other factors have combined to cause increases in the rate of births to unwed mothers. These include increased difficulties in making marriages work, increased social acceptance of unwed mothers and their children and even, in some cases, a preference on the part of mothers for remaining unmarried.

The separate tables for births to unmarried white and black women indicate striking differences. Over half of all black births in 1979 were to unmarried women, who are about five times as likely as unmarried white women to have a child. About 1.5 of every 100 unmarried white women in the age group 15 to 44 gave birth in 1979. The comparable figure for black women was about 8.5 per 100. Viewed in another way, however, it appears that births to unwed women are now increasing more rapidly among white women. Between 1974 and 1979 the number of births to unmarried white women increased by 56.1%, while the increase among black women was 32.2%.

The state by state patterns are complex. The ratio between the highest and the lowest value is about 5 to 1 in the overall table, 2.5 to 1.0 in the table for whites, and 10 to 1.0 in the table for blacks. The seven states at the bottom of the table for blacks have very small black populations. There is no strong overall relationship between the rankings in the two race-specific tables. Data for the following 11 states were unavailable: California, Connecticut, Georgia, Maryland, Michigan, Montana, Nevada, New Mexico, New York, Ohio and Texas.

Table: Births to Unmarried Women
Date: 1979
Source: National Center for Health Statistics
Description: Births to unmarried women as a percentage of all births for 39 states.
39-state average: 17.1%
39-state median: 14.0%

BIRTHS TO UNMARRIED WOMEN

Rank	State	Percent of all births
1	Mississippi	27.2
2	Delaware	22.9
3	Louisana	22.8
4	Florida	22.4
5	Illinois	21.9
6	Alabama	21.8
7	New Jersey	20.2
8	Arkansas	19.6
9	Tennessee	19.0
10	North Carolina	18.5
11	Virginia	18.4
12	Pennsylvania	17.2
13	Arizona	17.1
14	Missouri	16.9
15	Hawaii	16.3
16	Massachusetts	14.8
17	Indiana	14.6
18	Rhode Island	14.3
19	Kentucky	14.0
19	Oklahoma	14.0
21	Alaska	13.9
22	Oregon	13.4
23	South Carolina	12.9
24	Wisconsin	12.8
25	Maine	12.7
26	Washington	12.6
27	Colorado	12.3
28	West Virginia	11.9
29	Kansas	11.8
29	South Dakota	11.8
31	Vermont	11.5
32	Nebraska	10.8
33	Minnesota	10.5
34	New Hampshire	10.1
35	Iowa	9.4
36	North Dakota	8.3
37	Wyoming	7.8
38	Idaho	7.0
39	Utah	5.5

Table: Births to Unmarried White Women
Date: 1979
Source: National Center for Health Statistics
Description: Births to unmarried white women as a percentage of all white births for 39 states.
39-state average: 9.4%
39-state median: 8.8%

BIRTHS TO UNMARRIED WHITE WOMEN

Rank	State	Percent of all white births
1	Arizona	12.9
2	Maine	12.6
3	Oregon	12.5
4	Hawaii	12.4
5	Massachusetts	11.9
6	Rhode Island	11.5
7	Vermont	11.4
8	Washington	11.1
9	Colorado	11.0
10	West Virginia	10.4
11	Delaware	10.3
11	New Hampshire	10.3
13	New Jersey	10.2
14	Illinois	9.9
14	Pennsylvania	9.9
14	South Dakota	9.9
17	Florida	9.6
18	Kentucky	9.5
19	Indiana	9.4
20	Wisconsin	9.2
21	Minnesota	8.8
22	Missouri	8.7
23	Nebraska	8.5
24	Oklahoma	8.4
25	Iowa	8.2
26	Kansas	8.1
27	Tennessee	8.0
28	Alaska	7.8
29	Arkansas	7.7
30	Virginia	7.6
31	Wyoming	6.9
32	Idaho	6.7
33	Louisiana	6.6
34	North Dakota	6.0
35	South Carolina	5.9
36	North Carolina	5.7
37	Alabama	5.4
38	Mississippi	5.1
39	Utah	5.0

Table: Births to Unmarried Black Women
Date: 1979
Source: National Center for Health Statistics
Description: Births to unmarried black women as a percentage of all black births for 39 states.
39-state average: 54.6%
39-state median: 51.3%

BIRTHS TO UNMARRIED BLACK WOMEN

Rank	State	Percent of all black births
1	Pennsylvania	66.3
2	Illinois	65.4
3	Delaware	63.1
4	Wisconsin	63.0
5	Missouri	62.5
6	New Jersey	59.6
7	Nebraska	59.4
8	Florida	58.4
9	Kentucky	57.6

Rank	State	Percent of all black births
10	Indiana	57.1
11	Tennessee	56.5
12	Rhode Island	55.3
13	Arkansas	54.3
14	Iowa	52.8
15	Minnesota	52.7
16	Massachusetts	52.1
17	Kansas	51.6
17	Oklahoma	51.6
19	Virginia	51.4
20	Alabama	51.3
21	Mississippi	50.8
22	West Virginia	50.2
23	Arizona	48.9
24	Louisiana	48.6
25	Oregon	47.9
26	North Carolina	47.4
27	South Carolina	45.7
28	Washington	40.1
29	Utah	39.1
30	Colorado	38.8
30	Vermont	38.8
32	Wyoming	36.1
33	Idaho	20.0
34	Alaska	19.2
35	North Dakota	14.8
36	New Hampshire	14.2
37	Maine	11.7
38	Hawaii	10.8
39	South Dakota	6.0

62. Abortions

In 1973 the Supreme Court ruled that women have a constitutional right to an abortion, at least during the first six months of any pregnancy. This established a national legal standard where previously there had been varying state laws that ranged from prohibiting all or most abortions to allowing abortions on demand in most cases. During the past several years a passionate debate has been waged between "pro-life" and "pro-choice" advocates. The "pro-life" forces have focused their efforts on obtaining a constitutional amendment that would guarantee legal protection to the fetus from the moment of conception. "Pro-choice" arguments support the legal status quo, holding that the moral decision of whether or not to have an abortion is essentially a private choice in which the government should not interfere. There have been no changes in the law as yet, but the issue has not yet been resolved.

There were over 1.2 million legal abortions in 1979—a ratio of 358 abortions to 1,000 live births. These figures mean that approximately 26% to 30% of all pregnancies are terminated by abortion. Variations among the states are very great. Roughly speaking, high rates of abortion are found in states close either to the East Coast or to the West Coast (including Nevada), with lower rates in the center of the country. The geographical pattern is actually rather complex and the data should be interpreted cautiously, since many women leave the state in which they live in order to have an abortion. Data for 1978 indicate that over 40% of abortions among women who reside in West Virginia, Kentucky, Mississippi and South Dakota were performed out of state. Figures for states with well-developed medical facilities may be somewhat overstated for the same reason.

Table: Abortions
Date: 1979
Source: Department of Health and Human Services
Description: Ratio of Abortions to 1,000 live births.
United States average: 358
State median: 278

ABORTIONS

Rank	State	Ratio
1	New York	666
2	Massachusetts	602
3	Nevada	539
3	Washington	539
5	California	515
6	Maryland	510
7	Florida	465
8	Rhode Island	440
9	Virginia	426
10	Georgia	409
11	Pennsylvania	407
12	Delaware	399
13	Vermont	395
14	Connecticut	385
15	Illinois	376
16	Hawaii	351
17	North Carolina	349
18	Colorado	345
19	Oregon	337
20	Kansas	332
21	Tennessee	324
22	Michigan	313
23	Alaska*	292
24	Texas	290
25	Minnesota	288
26	New Jersey	269
27	Ohio	255
28	Alabama	252
28	Maine	252
30	Montana	250
31	Wisconsin*	244
32	New Hampshire	243
33	Oklahoma	227

Rank	State	Ratio
34	Missouri	220
34	South Carolina	220
36	New Mexico	203
37	Kentucky	188
38	Nebraska	177
39	Arkansas	173
40	Arizona	171
41	Louisiana	170
42	Indiana	168
42	North Dakota*	168
44	Idaho	124
45	Iowa	111
45	South Dakota	111
47	West Virginia	98
48	Mississippi	96
49	Utah	87
50	Wyoming	84

*Latest Available 1978

63. Abortions Among Married Women

Approximately three-fourths of all abortions occur among unmarried women. Data for the states show that this is true of at least two-thirds of all abortions in every case.

Among women in their childbearing years, married women vastly outnumber unmarried women. The fact that married women have fewer abortions results both from the fact that on the average, they practice contraception more carefully than unmarried women, and that they are more likely than unmarried women to carry through with unwanted pregnancies. Married women in America are far less likely to have abortions than married women in certain other countries. In the USSR, for example, where contraceptives are hard to obtain and unpopular, the average women has about six abortions during her lifetime. In 1970 there were an estimated 180 abortions per 1,000 Soviet women aged 15 to 44. The figure for the United States, in 1979, was 30 abortions per 1,000 women.

Table: Abortions among Married Women
Date: 1978
Source: Center for Disease Control
Description: Percentage of married women having abortions for 31 states.
31-state Average: 25.9%
31-state Median: 25.0%

ABORTIONS AMONG MARRIED WOMEN

Rank	State	Percent
1	North Carolina	31.2
2	Alaska	30.9
3	Hawaii	30.8
4	Louisiana	28.2
5	New York	27.9
6	Tennessee	27.2
7	South Carolina	27.0
8	Illinois	26.7
9	Arkansas	26.5
10	Rhode Island	26.4
11	Mississippi	26.1
12	Oregon	26.0
13	Georgia	25.8
13	Maryland	25.8
15	Nevada	25.7
16	Missouri	25.0
17	Colorado	24.9
18	Kansas	24.7
19	Indiana	23.8
19	Washington	23.8
21	New Mexico	23.6
22	Ohio	23.1
23	Arizona	23.0
24	Virginia	22.6
25	South Dakota	22.1
26	Vermont	21.7
27	Utah	20.1
28	New Hampshire	20.0
29	Nebraska	19.6
30	Montana	19.3
31	Minnesota	17.2

64. Abortions Among Very Young Women

About 30% of all reported abortions in 1978 occurred among teenage women. Pregnancies among young women (under 20) and older women (40 and up) are more likely to terminate with an abortion than pregnancies among women aged 20 to 39. The birth of a child to a girl under 15 years of age can pose many problems both for the child and the mother. Data for 37 states in 1978 show that there were 1,149 abortions to every 1,000 births among girls under 15, with at least a small number of abortions among members of this group in every one of the 37 reporting states.

Table: Abortions among the Very Young
Date: 1978
Source: Center for Disease Control
Description: Total number of abortions among the very young (from 10 to 14 years of age) for 37 states.
37-state total: 7,755

ABORTIONS AMONG THE VERY YOUNG

Rank	State	Number
1	New York	1267
2	Illinois	703
3	Pennsylvania	642
4	Georgia	600
5	North Carolina	465
6	Maryland	425
7	Virginia	404
8	Washington	284
9	Tennessee	251
10	New Jersey	249
11	Ohio	248
12	Missouri	215
13	Massachusetts	193
14	Louisiana	164
15	South Carolina	155
16	Colorado	131
17	Indiana	117
18	Kansas	111
19	Oregon	106
20	Connecticut	96
21	Minnesota	94
22	Arkansas	66
23	Mississippi	63
24	Arizona	58
25	Nebraska	50
26	Nevada	49
27	New Mexico	36
28	Hawaii	32
29	Rhode Island	24
30	Montana	23
31	New Hampshire	22
32	Idaho	17
33	Vermont	14
34	Utah	12
35	Wyoming	8
36	Alaska	6
37	South Dakota	5

RELIGION

Religious influences in American life can be traced back to the initial European settlement of the land. Radical or unorthodox groups of believers, unhappy in their homelands, played a vital part in the early transatlantic migration. Although religious leaders and their congregations have always helped to focus attention on the moral aspects of momentous public issues—such as slavery, civil rights and the justification of wars—the religious sphere in the United States has been clearly separated in principle from affairs of state ever since the beginning of the Republic. Religious freedom and tolerance of a variety of beliefs is a cornerstone of the American tradition and one of the principal reasons why the country has succeeded in providing opportunities for peoples of diverse cultural backgrounds.

The variety of religious communities in the United States today is simply astonishing. The 1980 survey of Judeo-Christian denominations* (from which most data in this section are drawn) identified 228 different church bodies, the coordinating agencies for groups of local churches. The responses received from 111 denominations included 17 from bodies representing over one million adherents and 25 from bodies representing between 100,000 and one million adherents. Roman Catholics accounted for about 42% of the total, Southern Baptists for 14.5% and United Methodists for 10.3%. The remaining 31% of religious adherents were divided among 108 other denominations, none of which claimed more than 2.6% of the total. Organizational decentralization and the great variety of beliefs are demonstated by this breakdown, but this is only part of the story.

Thousands of local churches are not affiliated with any umbrella organization; these congregations and movements are not represented in the summary statistics. Many religious organizations that prospered during the 1970s *Bernard Quinn, et al., *Churches and Church Membership in the United States 1980: An Enumeration by Region, State and County Based on Data Reported by 111 Church Bodies* (Atlanta: Glenmary Research Center, 1982)

stand partly or entirely outside the sphere of Judeo-Christian beliefs. Examples include the Unification Church of Rev. Sun Myung Moon, the Scientologists, the International Society for Krishna Consciousness or Hare Krishna movement, and the tragic, doomed congregation that followed Rev. Jim Jones to Guyana. Television evangelists rose to new prominence during the 1970s. Their "video congregations" are difficult to enumerate, and it is uncertain whether they are actually enlarging the Christian community or simply draining the strength of ordinary churches. In any case, they helped to mobilize the dollars and the political participation that allowed a conservative "moral majority" to become a factor in national elections and to channel attention to their views on such issues as women's rights, abortion, school prayer, creationism and "secular humanism." Spiritual development pursued outside of religious communities on an individualized basis, often associated with therapeutic or exercise techniques such as transcendental meditation or Yoga, were also important in the 1970s.

All in all, the revival of interest in religion during the last decade represents an even more extreme extension of the characteristic pattern of American religious diversity. The traditional churches of the nation have continued to exist and to do their work during this period of social upheaval, serving as focal points for community life and carrying on the programs of charity that provide spiritual and material support for individuals. Much of the new activity, however, has occurred outside such established churches. While national religious surveys were documenting rising religious interests in the mid-1970s, they were also indicating a moderate decline in regular church attendance; about 40% of the population attends services regularly. The momentum of the revival seemed to slow in the early 1980s. The concerns of the nation shifted from spiritual to material matters as a prolonged recession battered the country, and the moral focus of the churches shifted from other social issues to the question of nuclear war.

The data on church affiliation in this section are taken from a 1980 survey sponsored by an interdenominational committee. Data on "adherents" (full members, plus an allowance for the number of children of members, if this number was not reported) have been provided by the central offices of 111 denominations. One hundred and twelve million Americans, or 49.7% of the 1980 population of the United States, are reported to be adherents of churches organized in these denominations. Following a table on total adherents of all denominations in each state, several denominational groups are presented separately, showing their relative strength in various states.

Information on the Jewish population of the states is drawn from a separate source. It represents persons of Jewish ethnicity, not religious adherents.

65. Church Adherents

The 109 Christian and two Jewish denominations participating in the 1980 survey of religious bodies represented 231,708 individual churches and synagogues. Almost one-half of the American population is affiliated with one of these churches. The data should be interpreted cautiously. Many denominations were not included in the survey, including 11 with over 100,000 adherents each: and other congregations have no denominational affiliation. The figures for all states are probably low by a few percentage points, and perhaps a bit lower for states in the West and South where unaffiliated or unconventional congregations are more prevalent. It would be a mistake, of course, to confuse the level of association with church bodies in a given state with the level of religious commitment. Commitment is difficult to measure and there are no reliable data for the states.

Levels of adherence to church bodies vary to a surprising extent across the country, ranging from about 30% to 75.5% of state population. The lowest levels are observed in the far West, where state populations include few residents who have remained in a given community since childhood and many who have migrated during their lifetimes. Other states with levels of adherence below the national average are scattered around the country with no clear regional pattern. The states of the South (except Georgia, Virginia and Florida) are found in the range between 51% and 57%. Nearly half of all church adherents in the South are Baptists.

The 13 states at the top of the list are all outside the South. They fall into three general groups. First there are one-church states, where the great majority of adherents belong to a single denomination: Utah (Latter Day Saints, or Mormons) and Rhode Island, Massachusetts and Connecticut (all Roman Catholic). Then there are

two-church states where Catholic and Lutheran adherents together constitute a large majority. These are located in the upper Midwest where persons of German and Scandinavian extraction make up a large part of the population: North Dakota, South Dakota, Minnesota and Wisconsin. Finally, there are states with a more mixed denominational profile, often a weaker version of the one- or two-church pattern. Nebraska and Iowa add a large segment of Methodists to the Catholic-Lutheran pattern of the upper Midwest. In Pennsylvania a Catholic majority is combined with Methodists, Lutherans and Presbyterians in great numbers. The Catholic majority in New Mexico is joined by a strong Baptist minority. Oklahoma, really an extension of the South in religious terms, combines a Baptist majority with a strong Methodist minority.

Table: Church Adherents
Date: 1980
Source: *Churches and Church Membership in the United States 1980*
Description: Percentage of church adherents in the population.
United States average: 49.7%

CHURCH ADHERENTS

Rank	State	Percent of total state population
1	Rhode Island	75.5
2	Utah	75.2
3	North Dakota	73.9
4	South Dakota	67.0
5	Minnesota	65.1
6	Massachusetts	64.7
7	Wisconsin	64.6
8	Nebraska	63.2
9	Connecticut	61.6
10	Iowa	61.2
11	Pennsylvania	60.9
12	New Mexico	59.1
13	Oklahoma	58.0
14	Alabama	57.5
15	Louisiana	57.4
16	Arkansas	56.2
17	Illinois	55.2
18	Mississippi	55.0
19	Texas	54.7
20	Tennessee	54.3
21	Kentucky	54.2
21	New Jersey	54.2
23	North Carolina	54.0
24	Missouri	53.6
25	Kansas	53.5
26	South Carolina	51.5
27	Idaho	50.1

Rank	State	Percent of total state population
28	New York	49.7
29	Ohio	49.5
30	Vermont	47.8
31	Georgia	47.0
32	Indiana	44.8
33	New Hampshire	44.3
34	Wyoming	44.1
35	Montana	43.3
36	Michigan	42.7
37	Virginia	41.8
38	Maine	41.0
39	Delaware	40.2
39	Maryland	40.2
41	West Virginia	39.7
42	Arizona	39.5
43	Florida	38.5
44	Colorado	36.6
45	Oregon	36.1
46	California	34.5
47	Hawaii	33.2
48	Washington	31.0
49	Alaska	30.8
50	Nevada	29.3

66. Roman Catholics

Roman Catholics make up 21% of the population of the United States and 42% of all church adherents. The close historical association between Catholicism and the immigration of specific national groups is still reflected in the state by state pattern. In New England and the Middle Atlantic states the descendents of earlier Catholic groups from the Caribbean are heavily represented in the metropolitan areas. The Catholic population of Maryland (just 17.5% of the population today) traces its origins to the establishment of a refuge for Catholics created by Lord Baltimore in 1632.

Catholics of German descent account for the high rankings of states in the upper Midwest; and the descendents of Polish and Irish immigrants in the Chicago area explain the position of Illinois. The heritage of French Catholicism is directly expressed in the figures for Louisiana and indirectly, through residents of French-Canadian origin, in northern New England. The influence of Spanish Catholicism is evident in the data for New Mexico. New immigration from Mexico is gradually increasing the Catholic segments of the border states. California Catholics account for only 20% of the state population, but in a largely unchurched state (adherents representing just 34.5% of the state population) they are a majority of the church-affiliated population. In Texas, there are still more Baptists than Catholics (18.9% to 16.4% of general population), but this relationship may soon be reversed.

Table: Roman Catholics
Date: 1980
Source: *Churches and Church Membership in the United States 1980*
Description: Percentage of Roman Catholics in the population.
United States average: 21.0%

ROMAN CATHOLICS

Rank	State	Percent of total state population
1	Rhode Island	63.7
2	Massachusetts	53.0
3	Connecticut	44.7
4	New Jersey	40.2
5	New York	35.6
6	New Mexico	33.5
7	Wisconsin	32.8
8	Pennsylvania	32.7
9	Illinois	31.5
10	Louisiana	31.0
10	New Hampshire	31.0
12	Vermont	30.6
13	North Dakota	26.7
14	Minnesota	25.6
15	Maine	24.5
16	Ohio	22.5
17	Michigan	22.1
18	Hawaii	21.8
19	Nebraska	21.2
20	California	20.1
20	South Dakota	20.1
22	Iowa	18.5
23	Arizona	17.8
23	Montana	17.8
25	Maryland	17.5
26	Delaware	17.3
27	Texas	16.4
28	Missouri	16.3
29	Kansas	14.3
30	Colorado	14.0
31	Florida	13.9
32	Nevada	13.8
33	Indiana	13.2
33	Wyoming	13.2
35	Oregon	12.2
36	Kentucky	10.0
37	Alaska	9.9
38	Washington	9.2
39	Idaho	7.5
40	West Virginia	5.4
41	Virginia	5.3
42	Utah	4.1
43	Mississippi	3.8

Rank	State	Percent of total state population
44	Oklahoma	3.6
45	Alabama	2.7
46	Georgia	2.6
47	Arkansas	2.5
47	Tennessee	2.5
49	South Carolina	1.9
50	North Carolina	1.6

67. Methodists

Denominational subdivisions are less important among Methodists than among other Protestant groups. Figures given here represent adherents of one dominant denomination—the United Methodist Church. Organized in 38,465 churches, United Methodists comprise 5.1% of the population and 10.3% of all church adherents nationwide. Strong Methodist representation is found in a broad band of states stretching from Delaware, Maryland and Virginia to Nebraska, Kansas and Oklahoma, and in states to the south of this band. This pattern probably traces migration routes favored by descendents of early Methodist settlers in the Chesapeake Bay area. Few Methodists are found in New England or in the West; Methodist families either stopped migrating west of Oklahoma and Texas, or they ceased to be Methodists as they pushed further on.

Table: Methodists
Date: 1980
Source: *Churches and Church Membership in the United States 1980*
Description: Percentage of United Methodists in the population.
United States average: 5.1%

METHODISTS

Rank	State	Percent of total state population
1	West Virginia	11.3
2	Kansas	11.1
3	Iowa	10.9
4	Oklahoma	10.4
5	Delaware	10.2
6	North Carolina	10.1
7	Nebraska	10.0
8	Mississippi	9.9
9	South Carolina	9.5
10	Arkansas	9.4
10	Virginia	9.4

Rank	State	Percent of total state population
12	Tennessee	9.0
13	Alabama	8.9
13	Georgia	8.9
15	Maryland	7.6
16	Indiana	7.0
17	Ohio	6.9
18	South Dakota	6.7
19	Pennsylvania	6.6
19	Texas	6.6
21	Kentucky	6.4
22	Missouri	5.5
23	Vermont	5.2
24	Florida	4.4
24	Illinois	4.4
26	New Mexico	4.1
26	North Dakota	4.1
28	Louisiana	4.0
29	Minnesota	3.6
30	Wisconsin	3.5
31	Colorado	3.4
31	Maine	3.4
33	Wyoming	3.2
34	Michigan	3.1
34	Montana	3.1
36	New York	2.9
37	New Jersey	2.5
38	Idaho	2.4
38	Washington	2.4
40	New Hampshire	2.2
41	Connecticut	2.0
42	Arizona	1.9
42	Oregon	1.9
44	Massachusetts	1.3
45	California	1.2
46	Alaska	1.1
47	Nevada	.9
47	Rhode Island	.9
49	Hawaii	.7
50	Utah	.4

68. Baptists

The figures presented here are based on data for two specific denominations—the Southern Baptist Convention (35.552 churches, 16.3 million adherents) and the American Baptist Churches in the U.S.A. (5,792 churches, 1.9 million adherents). There are a number of other Baptist organizations that could not be included here because of incomplete data. Among them are two large denominations of black Baptist churches—the National Baptist Convention U.S.A. and the National Baptist Convention of America—that reported a combined membership of over eight million when last surveyed in the late 1950s. Their membership is probably distributed in such a way that the relative rankings given here would not change much if they were included, although the figures for most states might be over 50% higher.

Baptists are the largest non-Catholic religious grouping in the country. As defined here, Baptist adherents amount to 8% of the total U.S. population and 16.2% of all church adherents. They are highly concentrated in the South, with important geographical extensions westward into Missouri, Oklahoma, Texas, New Mexico and to some extent Kansas. The Baptist segment of state populations drops off sharply outside this region.

Table: Baptists
Date: 1980
Source: *Churches and Church Membership in the United States 1980*
Description: Percentage of Baptists in the population.
United States average: 8.0%

BAPTISTS

Rank	State	Percent of total state population
1	Alabama	30.4
2	Mississippi	30.2
3	Oklahoma	26.5
4	Tennessee	26.3
5	South Carolina	25.7
6	Georgia	25.4
7	Kentucky	24.3
8	North Carolina	23.0
9	Arkansas	22.9
10	Texas	18.9
11	Louisiana	15.5
12	Missouri	14.5
13	Virginia	13.6
14	New Mexico	10.1
15	Florida	9.7
16	West Virginia	9.5
17	Kansas	6.2
18	Alaska	4.6
19	Arizona	4.5
20	Indiana	4.4
21	Maryland	3.8
21	Wyoming	3.8
23	Maine	3.5
24	Colorado	3.3
25	Illinois	3.2
26	Rhode Island	2.7
27	Ohio	2.6
28	California	2.5
28	Nevada	2.5
30	Vermont	2.2
31	Idaho	2.1
31	New Hampshire	2.1

Rank	State	Percent of total state population
33	South Dakota	2.0
33	Washington	2.0
35	Nebraska	1.8
36	Montana	1.7
36	Oregon	1.7
38	Iowa	1.6
39	Connecticut	1.5
39	Hawaii	1.5
41	Michigan	1.4
42	Delaware	1.3
42	Massachusetts	1.3
42	New York	1.3
45	Pennsylvania	1.2
46	New Jersey	1.1
47	North Dakota	.9
47	Utah	.9
49	Wisconsin	.6
50	Minnesota	.5

69. Presbyterians

The Presbyterian adherents enumerated here belong to The United Presbyterian Church in the U.S.A. (8,633 churches, three million adherents) and The Presbyterian Church in the United States (4,068 churches, one million adherents). The latter denomination is found only in the South and the bordering states of Kansas and Missouri, while the former is scattered around the country. These two denominations account for 1.8% of the total U.S. population and 3.5% of all church adherents.

The geographical distribution of Presbyterians is similar to that of Methodists, with strength focused along a broad band stretching from Pennsylvania through Ohio into the Midwest. The migration of Presbyterians had its origin among Scotch-Irish settlers in the region of Philadelphia, to the north of the Chesapeake Bay base of the Methodists. The Presbyterian migration stream turned northward after crossing the Mississippi, while Methodists tended to turn south. The southern denomination of Presbyterians is focused in the Carolinas, Virginia and West Virginia. Presbyterians, like Methodists, are infrequently found in New England and the Southwest.

Table: Presbyterians
Date: 1980
Source: *Churches and Church Membership in the United States 1980*
Description: Percentage of Presbyterians in the population.
United States average: 1.8%

PRESBYTERIANS

Rank	State	Percent of total state population
1	Pennsylvania	4.0
2	Nebraska	3.7
3	Iowa	3.6
4	North Carolina	3.5
5	Kansas	3.3
6	South Carolina	3.0
7	Delaware	2.8
8	South Dakota	2.7
8	Virginia	2.7
10	New Jersey	2.4
10	Ohio	2.4
10	West Virginia	2.4
13	North Dakota	2.2
13	Wyoming	2.2
15	Colorado	2.0
15	Indiana	2.0
17	Minnesota	1.9
17	Missouri	1.9
19	Tennessee	1.8
20	Georgia	1.7
20	Illinois	1.7
20	Michigan	1.7
20	Montana	1.7
20	Washington	1.7
25	Florida	1.6
25	Oklahoma	1.6
25	Oregon	1.6
28	Alaska	1.4
28	Kentucky	1.4
28	New York	1.4
28	Texas	1.4
32	Arkansas	1.3
32	Idaho	1.3
32	Maryland	1.3
32	New Mexico	1.3
36	Arizona	1.2
36	Wisconsin	1.2
38	Alabama	1.1
38	California	1.1
38	Mississippi	1.1
41	Louisiana	.8
42	Nevada	.6
43	Utah	.5
44	Connecticut	.3
44	Rhode Island	.3
46	New Hampshire	.2
46	Vermont	.2
48	Hawaii	.1
48	Maine	.1
48	Massachusetts	.1

70. Lutherans

The strong denominational divisions among Lutherans reflect both theological differences and ethnic groupings (e.g., German, Swedish or Norwegian). Data for several denominations are combined in this table, but just three of them account for almost all adherents—The American Lutheran Church (4,845 churches, 2.3 million adherents), The Lutheran Church in America (5,762 churches, 2.9 million adherents), and The Lutheran Church – Missouri Synod (5,686 churches, 2.6 million adherents).

Lutherans are heavily represented in states of the upper Midwest, where people of German and Scandinavian stock form a large segment of the population. The Lutheran population drops off sharply outside this region, although Pennsylvania and to a lesser extent Washington and Maryland, are outlying areas of strength.

Table: Lutherans
Date: 1980
Source: *Churches and Church Membership in the United States 1980*
Description: Percentage of Lutherans in the population.
United States average: 3.6%

LUTHERANS

Rank	State	Percent of total state population
1	North Dakota	31.9
2	Minnesota	26.0
3	South Dakota	23.4
4	Wisconsin	20.0
5	Nebraska	15.9
6	Iowa	14.2
7	Montana	9.0
8	Pennsylvania	6.7
9	Illinois	5.5
10	Michigan	5.1
11	Kansas	4.4
12	Washington	4.3
13	Ohio	4.0
14	Wyoming	3.9
15	Colorado	3.6
15	Maryland	3.6
17	Indiana	3.5
18	Missouri	3.3
19	Oregon	3.0
20	Idaho	2.8
21	Alaska	2.4
21	Arizona	2.4
23	South Carolina	1.9
24	Texas	1.8
25	Connecticut	1.7
25	Delaware	1.7
25	New Jersey	1.7
25	New York	1.7
29	North Carolina	1.5
30	California	1.4

Rank	State	Percent of total state population
30	Florida	1.4
30	Virginia	1.4
33	Nevada	1.2
34	New Mexico	1.1
35	Oklahoma	.9
36	West Virginia	.8
37	Arkansas	.7
37	Louisiana	.7
37	Rhode Island	.7
40	Georgia	.6
40	Utah	.6
42	Massachusetts	.5
42	Tennessee	.5
44	Alabama	.4
44	Hawaii	.4
44	Kentucky	.4
44	New Hampshire	.4
48	Mississippi	.3
48	Vermont	.3
50	Maine	.1

71. Mormons

The Golden Tablets of the Book of Mormon were revealed to Joseph Smith at Palmyra, N.Y. in 1830. Combining these revelations with elements of Judeo-Christian doctrine derived from the Bible, Smith gathered his followers into a community that relocated several times during the 1830s as a result of conflicts with outsiders and state authorities. The great Mormon city of Nauvoo, Ill. dissolved after Smith was murdered by a mob in the aftermath of civil disorders in 1847. A crisis of succession followed his death, dividing the community into two parts, but the majority moved on to the valley of the Great Salt Lake under the leadership of Brigham Young. The isolated Utah community petitioned for statehood in 1849; not until the church renounced its doctrine sanctioning polygamy, however, was it admitted to the Union in 1896.

There are 6,771 separate churches organized under The Church of Jesus Christ of the Latter Day Saints. Their adherents comprise 1.2% of the American population and 2.4% of all church adherents. Everyone knows that the church is centered in Utah, but it is surprising that only 37% of its adherents are residents of Utah. Mormons account for about half of all church adherents in Idaho and there are sizable numbers of adherents in several other western states. They are the most geographically concentrated major religious group, although there are some members in every one of the 50 states.

Table: Mormons
Date: 1980
Source: *Churches and Church Membership in the United States 1980*
Description: Percentage of Mormons in the population.
United States average: 1.2%

MORMONS

Rank	State	Percent of total state population
1	Utah	67.4
2	Idaho	25.5
3	Wyoming	8.6
4	Nevada	6.9
5	Arizona	5.1
6	Montana	3.3
7	Hawaii	2.9
8	Oregon	2.8
9	Washington	2.5
10	Alaska	2.2
10	New Mexico	2.2
12	Colorado	1.8
13	California	1.7
14	Oklahoma	.5
14	Texas	.5
14	Virginia	.5
17	Florida	.4
17	Georgia	.4
17	Kansas	.4
17	Maine	.4
17	Missouri	.4
17	Nebraska	.4
17	North Carolina	.4
17	South Carolina	.4
17	South Dakota	.4
17	West Virginia	.4
27	Alabama	.3
27	Arkansas	.3
27	Indiana	.3
27	Iowa	.3
27	Kentucky	.3
27	Louisiana	.3
27	Maryland	.3
27	Mississippi	.3
27	New Hampshire	.3
27	Vermont	.3
37	Connecticut	.2
37	Delaware	.2
37	Illinois	.2
37	Michigan	.2
37	Minnesota	.2
37	North Dakota	.2
37	Ohio	.2
37	Pennsylvania	.2
37	Tennessee	.2
37	Wisconsin	.2
47	Massachusetts	.1

Rank	State	Percent of total state population
47	New Jersey	.1
47	New York	.1
47	Rhode Island	.1

72. Seventh-Day Adventists

Fundamentalist, Pentecostal Protestant groups are hard to include in state by state rankings because they are not generally organized under wider denominational headings. The Seventh-Day Adventists, a denomination with 3,676 churches and over 650,000 adherents, are included here to suggest the typical geographical distribution of such groups. The denomination traces its origins to the mid-19th century and to a man named William Miller who originally predicted a definite and imminent end of the world and a Second Coming. Seventh-Day Adventists today still look forward to the return of Jesus and the arrival of the millennium, but at an unspecified time in the near future. They are active evangelists with a worldwide following and strong U.S. representation in the West and parts of the South.

Table: Seventh-Day Adventists
Date: 1980
Source: *Churches and Church Membership in the United States 1980*
Description: Percentage of Seventh-Day Adventists in the population.
United States average: 0.3%

SEVENTH-DAY ADVENTISTS

Rank	State	Percent of total state population
1	Oregon	1.2
2	Washington	.8
3	Idaho	.7
4	California	.6
4	North Dakota	.6
6	Colorado	.5
6	Hawaii	.5
6	Montana	.5
6	Nebraska	.5
6	Tennessee	.5
6	Wyoming	.5
12	Alaska	.4
12	Maryland	.4
12	Michigan	.4
12	South Dakota	.4

Rank	State	Percent of total state population
16	Alabama	.3
16	Arizona	.3
16	Florida	.3
16	Georgia	.3
16	Kansas	.3
16	New Mexico	.3
16	North Carolina	.3
16	Oklahoma	.3
24	Arkansas	.2
24	Delaware	.2
24	Illinois	.2
24	Indiana	.2
24	Iowa	.2
24	Louisiana	.2
24	Maine	.2
24	Minnesota	.2
24	Mississippi	.2
24	Missouri	.2
24	Nevada	.2
24	New York	.2
24	New Jersey	.2
24	Ohio	.2
24	South Carolina	.2
24	Texas	.2
24	Virginia	.2
24	West Virginia	.2
24	Wisconsin	.2
42	Vermont	.1
42	Utah	.1
42	Rhode Island	.1
42	Pennsylvania	.1
42	New Hampshire	.1
42	Massachusetts	.1
42	Kentucky	.1
42	Connecticut	.1

73. Jewish Population

Churches and Church Membership in the United States 1980 identified about 800,000 persons (0.3% of the population) as adherents of either Conservative or Reformed Jewish congregations. Estimates of the total Jewish population in 1981 are much larger—about 5.9 million individuals, or 2.6% of the total population. The Jewish population is highly concentrated, with 37% of the total in New York state alone and 88% in the 10 states with over 100,000 members of the group. New York City has always been the principal port of entry for Jews from Central and Eastern Europe. Many of these people and their descendants have remained in the tri-state area around the port. Other concentrations are found in states with major metropolitan areas, since very few Jewish immigrants ever settled in rural areas or small towns.

Table: Jewish Population
Date: 1981
Source: *American Jewish Yearbook*
Description: Jewish population by state: estimated total and percentage of the population.
United States total: 5,881,115
United States average: 2.6%

Rank	State	Jewish population	Percent of total state population
45	North Dakota	1,080	.2
46	Alaska	960	.2
47	Montana	645	.1
48	South Dakota	600	.1
49	Idaho	510	.1
50	Wyoming	310	.1

JEWISH POPULATION

Rank	State	Jewish population	Percent of total state population
1	New York	2,139,090	12.2
2	California	754,480	3.2
3	Florida	466,980	4.8
4	New Jersey	436,865	5.9
5	Pennsylvania	413,630	3.5
6	Illinois	266,190	2.3
7	Massachusetts	240,805	4.2
8	Maryland	185,915	4.4
9	Ohio	143,960	1.3
10	Connecticut	101,700	3.3
11	Michigan	90,200	1.0
12	Texas	72,570	.5
13	Missouri	71,770	1.5
14	Virginia	59,340	1.1
15	Arizona	45,285	1.7
16	Georgia	35,980	.7
17	Minnesota	35,220	.9
18	Colorado	31,765	1.1
19	Wisconsin	30,280	.6
20	Indiana	23,460	.4
21	Rhode Island	22,000	2.3
22	Washington	21,885	.5
23	Tennessee	16,715	.4
24	Louisiana	16,200	.4
25	Nevada	14,700	1.8
26	North Carolina	14,450	.2
27	Kentucky	11,585	.3
28	Oregon	10,835	.4
29	Kansas	10,760	.5
30	Delaware	9,500	1.6
31	Alabama	9,010	.2
32	South Carolina	8,660	.3
33	Iowa	8,130	.3
34	Nebraska	7,905	.5
35	West Virginia	7,340	.4
36	New Mexico	7,155	.6
37	Maine	6,800	.6
38	Oklahoma	6,565	.2
39	Hawaii	5,625	.6
40	New Hampshire	4,480	.5
41	Arkansas	3,375	.1
42	Mississippi	3,080	.1
43	Vermont	2,470	.5
44	Utah	2,300	.2

74. Fifteen Counties with Highest Percentage of Church Attendance

The National Council of Churches collects attendance figures by place of congregation; thus, people who live in one county but worship in another are included in the county in which they attend services. As a result, every one of the top 15 counties here listed has more worshipers than residents. Five of these 15 counties are scattered throughout Texas.

Table: Fifteen counties with the Highest Percentage of Reported Church Membership
Date: 1980
Source: *Churches and Church Membership in the United States 1980*
Description: Fifteen counties with the highest percentage of reported church membership, as recorded by the National Council of Churches.

FIFTEEN COUNTIES WITH THE HIGHEST PERCENTAGE OF REPORTED CHURCH MEMBERSHIP

Rank	County	Percent of county population
1	Wichita, Kansas	169.8
2	Starr, Texas	143.6
3	Willacy, Texas	141.0
4	Guadelupe, New Mexico	138.7
5	Jeff Davis, Texas	136.4
6	Harding, New Mexico	136.1
7	Throckmorton, Texas	125.4
8	Hancock, Tennessee	124.5
9	Rolette, North Dakota	122.1
10	Morgan, Utah	121.0
11	Mora, New Mexico	118.9
12	Dallam, Texas	114.7
13	Franklin, Georgia	113.1
14	Kalawaco, Hawaii	112.5
15	Taos, New Mexico	111.0

THE ELDERLY

All of us will be (or hope to be) counted among the elderly one day. Improvements in diet and medical care during the past century have given most of us, in fact, a very good chance of reaching the age of 65. The fraction of the American population at or above this age has increased from 4% in 1900 to over 11% at present, with the prospect of rising above 20% within the next 40 years. Lower birth rates and longer lives are combining to make us an older population, and this process will continue (barring disaster) in the decades to come.

As the elderly population increases, the problem of providing income support and medical care becomes ever more acute. The first round of what promises to be an ongoing process of reforming the Social Security system was fought out in 1982 and 1983. In much the same way that the rising level of "technological unemployment" requires new thinking on how to achieve a fair distribution of income to persons who cannot find jobs, we will need innovative solutions to the problems of providing adequate financial support to increasing numbers of senior citizens.

Tables in this section cover state by state distribution of older Americans, recent patterns of increase among this group, life expectancy, employment, poverty and Social Security benefit levels. The final table documents the influence of an important interest group for the elderly.

75. The Elderly as a Percentage of Population

Except for the extreme cases of Florida and Alaska, the fraction of people aged 65 and over varies between 13.7% and 7.5% of state population. States with high fractions of older persons are found in the center of the country, in Florida and in the Northeast. In general, these states have seen the out-migration of younger people in recent years and relatively little new economic development. Several states with lower fractions of the elderly are found in the

Mountain States of the western interior. The others are Alaska, Hawaii and a group of states on the East Coast south of Washington, D.C. In general, these states either have relatively high birth rates or they have experienced heavy economic development and population influx in recent years.

Overall, about 45% of Americans aged 65 and over live in just seven states: California, New York, Florida, Illinois, Ohio, Pennsylvania and Texas. The proportion of persons 65 and over in the general population is expected to top 13% in the year 2000 and to rise to about 21% in the year 2020 (higher than in any given state, including Florida, at present).

Table: Where Americans 65 and Over Live
Date: 1980
Source: Census Bureau
Description: Population of those 65 years of age and over and percentage of the total state population.
United States total: 25.5 million
United States average: 11.3% of population

WHERE AMERICANS 65 AND OVER LIVE

Rank	State	Percent of total state population	Population (in thousands)
1	Florida	17.3	1,685
2	Arkansas	13.7	312
3	Rhode Island	13.4	127
4	Iowa	13.3	387
5	Missouri	13.2	647
5	South Dakota	13.2	91
7	Nebraska	13.1	206
8	Kansas	13.0	306
9	Pennsylvania	12.9	1,531
10	Massachusetts	12.7	727
11	Maine	12.5	141
12	Oklahoma	12.4	376
13	New York	12.3	2,161
13	North Dakota	12.3	80

Rank	State	Percent of total state population	Population (in thousands)
15	West Virginia	12.2	238
16	Wisconsin	12.0	564
17	Minnesota	11.8	480
18	Connecticut	11.7	365
18	New Jersey	11.7	860
20	Mississippi	11.5	289
20	Oregon	11.5	303
22	Vermont	11.4	58
23	Alabama	11.3	440
23	Arizona	11.3	307
23	Tennessee	11.3	518
26	Kentucky	11.2	410
26	New Hampshire	11.2	103
28	Illinois	11.0	1,261
29	Ohio	10.8	1,169
30	Indiana	10.7	585
30	Montana	10.7	85
32	Washington	10.4	431
33	North Carolina	10.3	602
34	California	10.2	2,415
35	Delaware	10.0	59
36	Idaho	9.9	94
36	Michigan	9.9	912
38	Louisiana	9.6	404
38	Texas	9.6	1,371
40	Georgia	9.5	517
41	Maryland	9.4	396
41	Virginia	9.4	505
43	South Carolina	9.2	287
44	New Mexico	8.9	116
45	Colorado	8.6	247
46	Nevada	8.2	66
47	Hawaii	7.9	76
47	Wyoming	7.9	38
49	Utah	7.5	109
50	Alaska	2.9	12

76. Recent Increase in the Elderly Population

The percentage of older Americans 65 years of age and over is now rising more rapidly than the general population level. From 1970 to 1980, general population rose 11.4%, but the numbers of the elderly went up 27.9%. Rates of increase varied sharply across the states. Deviations of up to about 10 percentage points from the national average increase may be explained by different basic age structures in the states, but larger deviations definitely mean that significant numbers of older persons were moving to or from the states in question during the 1970s.

The top 13 states on the list are clearly those to which older people have been moving, often shortly after they retire from work. On a proportional basis, Nevada and Arizona are the most favored locations for elderly migrants, followed by Hawaii, Alaska (a surprise), Florida and New Mexico. The bottom 10 states are the ones from which elderly individuals are most likely to move. Eight midwestern states are joined by New York and Massachusetts in this group.

Table: Population Increase among the Elderly
Date: 1980
Source: Census Bureau
Description: Percentage of increase from 1970 to 1980 of population 65 years of age and over.
United States average: 27.9%
State median: 28.8%

POPULATION INCREASE AMONG THE ELDERLY

Rank	State	Percent of increase
1	Nevada	112.9
2	Arizona	90.7
3	Hawaii	72.7
4	Alaska	71.4
5	Florida	71.1
6	New Mexico	65.7
7	South Carolina	51.1
8	North Carolina	46.1
9	Georgia	41.6
9	Utah	41.6
11	Idaho	40.3
12	Texas	38.8
13	Virginia	38.7
14	Alabama	35.8
15	Tennessee	35.6
16	California	34.8
17	Washington	34.7
18	Delaware	34.1
18	Oregon	34.1
20	Maryland	32.9
21	Louisiana	32.5
22	Colorado	32.1
22	New Hampshire	32.1
24	Arkansas	31.6
25	Mississippi	30.8
26	Connecticut	26.7
26	Wyoming	26.7
28	Oklahoma	25.8
29	Montana	25.0
30	New Jersey	23.9
31	Maine	23.7
32	Vermont	23.4
33	West Virginia	22.7
34	Rhode Island	22.1
35	Kentucky	22.0
36	Michigan	21.8
37	North Dakota	21.2
38	Pennsylvania	20.8

Rank	State	Percent of increase
39	Wisconsin	19.7
40	Indiana	18.9
41	Minnesota	17.9
42	Ohio	17.7
43	Missouri	16.1
44	Illinois	15.8
45	Kansas	15.5
46	Massachusetts	14.8
47	South Dakota	13.8
48	Nebraska	12.6
49	Iowa	10.9
50	New York	10.8

77. Life Expectancy for White Males at Age 65

People are living longer than ever these days, and people who survive to age 65 can generally look forward to many more years of life. The life expectancy data in this table and the following table were computed by the Metropolitan Life Insurance Company for the year 1975. The average further life expectancy for a white male who turned 65 in 1975 was 13.7 years. This means that *half* of all such men are expected to survive to age 78.7 (which would be reached in the year 1988 or 1989). Well over half of the 65-year-old white men as of 1975 are probably still alive today. (The technical explanation of life-expectancy data is complex, but what has been said will not put you on the wrong track. Since life-expectancy figures change only a tiny bit from one year to the next, these figures are also about right for all men who have turned 65 since 1975. If there has been a change, it would most likely involve *adding* a fraction of a year for people who are turning 65 at present.)

The Alaskan data in this table are based on very few cases and, although Alaskans may indeed be the heartiest people among us, the number given here should be viewed skeptically. For the rest of the nation, further life expectancy varies between 16.2 years in Florida (that is, to age 81.2 in 1990 or 1991) and 12.9 years in Ohio (to age 77.9 in 1987 or 1988). The states of Florida, Arizona and Hawaii are clearly a cut above the rest when it comes to surviving beyond age 65. From Oklahoma to Ohio the values decline smoothly and the overall difference is just 1.5 years (though 1.5 years is nothing to scoff at when speaking of human lives). Perhaps the climates in the three top states below Alaska really are healthier. A more likely explanation of the figures for these states, however, is that the people who move there are either healthier than

the average to begin with or wealthier than the average elderly American, and so able to afford better medical care.

Table: Further Life Expectancy for White Males Aged 65
Date: 1975
Source: Metropolitan Life Insurance Company
Description: Expectation of life at age 65 for the white male population.
United States average: 13.7 years
State median: 13.5 years

FURTHER LIFE EXPECTANCY FOR WHITE MALES AGED 65

Rank	State	Years
1	Alaska	18.0
2	Florida	16.2
3	Arizona	15.7
4	Hawaii	15.4
5	Oklahoma	14.4
6	Minnesota	14.2
7	Colorado	14.1
7	Connecticut	14.1
7	Oregon	14.1
7	South Dakota	14.1
11	New Jersey	14.0
11	North Dakota	14.0
13	Nebraska	13.9
13	Utah	13.9
15	California	13.8
15	Kansas	13.8
15	New York	13.8
15	Wisconsin	13.8
19	Massachusetts	13.7
19	Montana	13.7
19	Rhode Island	13.7
19	Texas	13.7
23	Delaware	13.6
23	Iowa	13.6
25	Arkansas	13.5
25	Maryland	13.5
25	Nevada	13.5
25	Tennessee	13.5
25	Washington	13.5
25	Wyoming	13.5
31	New Mexico	13.4
31	Missouri	13.4
31	Virginia	13.4
34	Vermont	13.3
35	Idaho	13.2
35	Illinois	13.2
35	Michigan	13.2
35	Pennsylvania	13.2
39	Alabama	13.1
39	Georgia	13.1
39	Indiana	13.1
39	Maine	13.1
39	Mississippi	13.1
39	New Hampshire	13.1

Rank	State	Years
45	Louisiana	13.0
45	North Carolina	13.0
47	Kentucky	12.9
47	Ohio	12.9
47	South Carolina	12.9
47	West Virginia	12.9

78. Life Expectancy for White Females at Age 65

Average life expectancy for white females who turned 65 in 1975 was 4.4 years longer than that for men who turned 65 in the same year. This means that *half* of all such women are expected to survive to age 83.1 (in 1993 or 1994).

Leaving aside the Alaskan data, and observing that the three states of Florida, Arizona and Hawaii are again grouped at the top, we see that there is a difference of 1.9 years separating the extreme cases among the remaining 46 states (North Dakota and Vermont). Comparison of this table to the preceding table for men shows that the rankings are roughly parallel, with a few interesting shifts up or down. To trace these shifts, subtract the figures for men from the figures for women and compare the results to the average national differential of 4.4 years.

Table: Further Life Expectancy for White Females Aged 65
Date: 1975
Source: Metropolitan Life Insurance Company.
Description: Expectation of life at age 65 for the white female population.
United States average: 18.1 years
State median: 18.0 years

FURTHER LIFE EXPECTANCY FOR WHITE FEMALES AGE 65

Rank	State	Years
1	Alaska	21.4
2	Florida	20.7
3	Arizona	20.2
4	Hawaii	19.1
5	North Dakota	19.0
6	Colorado	18.9
7	Idaho	18.8
7	Minnesota	18.8
7	Nebraska	18.8
10	Missouri	18.6
10	Utah	18.6
12	Oregon	18.5
12	North Carolina	18.5
12	Oklahoma	18.5

Rank	State	Years
12	South Dakota	18.5
16	Texas	18.4
17	Iowa	18.3
18	Arkansas	18.2
18	Kansas	18.2
18	Wisconsin	18.2
21	California	18.1
21	Connecticut	18.1
21	New York	18.1
21	Washington	18.1
21	Wyoming	18.1
26	Massachusetts	18.0
26	Montana	18.0
26	New Mexico	18.0
26	Virginia	18.0
30	South Carolina	17.9
30	Tennessee	17.9
32	Alabama	17.8
32	Nevada	17.8
34	Illinois	17.7
34	New Hampshire	17.7
34	New Jersey	17.7
34	Virginia	17.7
38	Indiana	17.6
38	Louisiana	17.6
40	Delaware	17.5
40	Kentucky	17.5
40	Maryland	17.5
40	Michigan	17.5
44	Maine	17.4
44	Pennsylvania	17.4
46	Mississippi	17.3
46	Ohio	17.3
46	Rhode Island	17.3
49	West Virginia	17.2
50	Vermont	17.1

79. The Elderly in the Work Force

The representation of elderly persons in the work force has declined over the past two decades, from 4.4% in 1960 to 3.7% in 1970 and 2.8% in 1980. The trend toward earlier retirement has now probably run its course and increasing representation of older people in the work force will certainly be the rule in the future. Rates for the states vary between 5.0% and 1.0%, with the highest rates generally observed in the center of the country, often in precisely the same states where the elderly make up a relatively large share of the general population. Where there are fewer young hands about, opportunities for older people remain open.

Table: Elderly in the Work Force
Date: 1980
Source: Bureau of Labor Statistics

Description: Percentage of the civilian labor force 65 years of age and over.
United States average: 2.8%
State median: 3.0%

ELDERLY IN THE WORK FORCE

Rank	State	Percent of civilian labor force	Civilian labor force aged 65 and over (in thousands)
1	Nebraska	5.0	39
2	South Dakota	4.7	16
3	Oklahoma	4.4	58
4	Mississippi	4.1	42
5	Arkansas	3.9	38
5	North Dakota	3.9	12
7	Kansas	3.7	54
8	Montana	3.5	13
8	Rhode Island	3.5	16
8	Texas	3.5	223
11	Florida	3.4	132
11	Iowa	3.4	49
11	Missouri	3.4	77
14	Vermont	3.3	8
15	Minnesota	3.2	67
15	New York	3.2	257
17	Idaho	3.1	13
18	Alabama	3.0	50
18	Connecticut	3.0	49
18	Illinois	3.0	163
18	Indiana	3.0	78
18	Louisiana	3.0	51
18	North Carolina	3.0	83
18	Utah	3.0	18
18	Virginia	3.0	77
26	Georgia	2.9	68
26	Massachusetts	2.9	83
26	Pennsylvania	2.9	157
29	Hawaii	2.8	11
29	Kentucky	2.8	46
29	Maine	2.8	14
29	New Hampshire	2.8	13
29	Oregon	2.8	35
34	Nevada	2.7	10
34	New Jersey	2.7	97
34	Tennessee	2.7	55
34	Wisconsin	2.7	66
38	New Mexico	2.6	14
38	Wyoming	2.6	6
40	California	2.4	266
41	Maryland	2.3	49
41	West Virginia	2.3	18
43	Ohio	2.2	112
44	Colorado	2.1	31
44	Delaware	2.1	6
44	South Carolina	2.1	27
47	Arizona	2.0	23
47	Michigan	2.0	88
49	Washington	1.9	36
50	Alaska	1.0	2

80. The Elderly Poor

Poverty is significantly more prevalent among older Americans than among the general population. A comparison with overall state poverty levels (presented in the next section) indicates that the rankings are generally similar (but compare the relative positions of Arizona and Florida in Tables 80 and 83). Poverty rates among the elderly in the South are three to four times as high as among the elderly in the most affluent states.

Table: Poverty among the Elderly
Date: 1979
Source: Census Bureau
Description: Percentage of population 65 years and older that have incomes under the federal poverty line.
United States average: 14.7%
State median: 14.0%

POVERTY AMONG THE ELDERLY

Rank	State	Percent
1	Mississippi	34.9
2	Alabama	28.6
3	Arkansas	27.6
4	Louisiana	26.0
5	Georgia	24.9
5	South Carolina	24.9
7	Tennessee	24.7
8	North Carolina	24.0
9	New Mexico	22.5
10	Kentucky	22.0
11	Oklahoma	20.9
12	Texas	20.0
13	South Dakota	19.9
14	Missouri	18.0
15	West Virginia	17.7
16	North Dakota	17.6
17	Virginia	17.3
18	Idaho	16.5
18	Maine	16.5
20	Wyoming	16.0
21	Montana	14.8
22	Kansas	14.4
23	Minnesota	14.3
24	Iowa	14.2
25	Nebraska	14.0
26	Delaware	13.9
27	Michigan	13.5
27	Ohio	13.5
29	New Hampshire	13.3
30	Colorado	13.1
31	Maryland	12.9
32	Vermont	12.7
33	Rhode Island	12.6
34	Alaska	12.5
34	Indiana	12.5
36	Florida	12.3
37	Washington	12.2

Rank	State	Percent
38	Hawaii	11.9
39	Oregon	11.8
40	Illinois	11.7
41	New York	11.2
41	Pennsylvania	11.2
43	Nevada	11.1
44	Arizona	10.8
44	New Jersey	10.8
46	Utah	10.3
47	Massachusetts	9.6
48	Connecticut	9.2
49	Wisconsin	8.7
50	California	8.3

81. Social Security Benefit Levels

Single individuals who received Social Security survivors' benefits in 1979, almost all of them women, were granted about $270.00 per month on average. Typical monthly payment levels in the states varied between about $200 and $300, with higher payments in the Northeast and Midwest and low benefit levels in the South. In view of the rising levels of claims on Social Security, future increases in benefit levels and movement toward equality across the states will be intensely debated in the nation's capital.

Table: Widow and Widower Benefits
Date: 1979
Source: Social Security Administration
Description: Median monthly benefits for aged widows and widowers and number of beneficiaries.
United States average: $269.54
State median: $275.58
Total United States beneficiaries: 4,191,699

WIDOW AND WIDOWER BENEFITS

Rank	State	Median monthly benefit	Number of beneficiaries
1	Connecticut	$305.89	54,027
2	New Jersey	302.81	135,355
3	Michigan	301.53	169,340
4	New York	299.10	328,789
5	Illinois	297.59	204,074
6	Ohio	296.41	221,899
7	Massachusetts	294.31	108,987
8	Delaware	292.88	10,069
9	Pennsylvania	292.65	281,519
10	Washington	292.35	62,598
11	Wisconsin	291.93	92,600
12	Indiana	290.89	101,370
13	Utah	289.77	15,235
14	California	289.53	331,963
15	Oregon	288.98	41,953

Rank	State	Median monthly benefit	Number of beneficiaries
16	Arizona	$288.75	37,737
17	Florida	287.42	206,030
18	Rhode Island	286.49	18,477
19	New Hampshire	284.61	14,406
20	Nevada	284.60	7,754
21	Maryland	283.11	64,855
22	Montana	279.08	13,546
23	Colorado	277.88	38,324
24	Iowa	275.68	67,282
25	Minnesota	275.67	77,051
26	Wyoming	275.48	5,579
27	Kansas	275.38	49,718
28	Idaho	273.10	13,391
29	Vermont	271.04	9,425
30	Missouri	270.77	105,539
31	Nebraska	267.46	32,666
32	Maine	264.12	23,006
33	West Virginia	263.02	51,849
34	Hawaii	261.71	8,867
35	Alaska	258.18	1,318
36	North Dakota	256.54	13,722
37	Texas	253.74	231,610
38	South Dakota	252.90	15,878
39	New Mexico	252.20	16,682
40	Oklahoma	251.58	62,131
41	Virginia	247.28	86,971
42	Louisiana	239.91	77,507
43	Kentucky	235.74	78,323
44	Tennessee	226.17	89,947
45	Georgia	225.35	85,521
46	Alabama	223.04	83,172
47	North Carolina	219.80	101,618
48	South Carolina	219.74	47,658
49	Arkansas	215.44	51,810
50	Mississippi	195.07	49,549

82. Membership in the American Association of Retired Persons

The elderly are beginning to organize as an interest group (and none too soon, given Social Security funding problems). The major organization is the American Association of Retired Persons (AARP), with its affiliate, the National Retired Teachers' Association. The AARP coordinates lobbying efforts on behalf of the elderly and serves as a clearing house for several special services and benefits. The 1982 membership figures for each state, as reported by the AARP, are presented below.

To give a rough idea of the scope of the organization, the relation of the 1982 membership figures to the 1980 state populations of persons 65 and over is also presented. Leaving aside Alaska (100% membership), the highest levels are observed for New Hampshire and Vermont (over 80%), the lowest levels for Alabama and Mississippi

(25% each). The impressive range of AARP influence throughout the country is readily apparent.

Table: Membership in the American Association of Retired Persons
Date: 1982
Source: Unpublished figures supplied by the American Association of Retired Persons
Description: Total 1982 membership in the American Association of Retired Persons and in the National Retired Teachers' Association, and percentage of the 1980 elderly population.
United States total: 13,550,000
State median: 164,000
United States average: 271,000

MEMBERSHIP IN THE AMERICAN ASSOCIATION OF RETIRED PERSONS

Rank	State	Total membership (in thousands)	1982 membership as a percentage of the 1980 elderly population
1	California	1400	58
2	New York	1250	58
3	Florida	1100	65
4	Pennsylvania	960	63
5	Illinois	720	57
6	Texas	615	45
7	New Jersey	600	70
7	Ohio	600	51
9	Michigan	495	54
10	Massachusetts	460	63
11	Wisconsin	305	54
12	Missouri	295	46
13	Connecticut	290	79
14	Virginia	280	55
15	Indiana	275	47
16	Maryland	250	63
17	Washington	246	57
18	Minnesota	235	49
19	North Carolina	210	35
20	Arizona	205	67
21	Oregon	187	62
22	Kansas	180	59
23	Georgia	175	34
23	Iowa	175	45
25	Colorado	171	69
26	Tennessee	158	31
27	Oklahoma	141	38
28	Louisiana	135	33
29	Kentucky	111	27
30	Alabama	110	25
31	Arkansas	105	34
31	South Carolina	105	37
33	West Virginia	100	42
34	Maine	90	64
35	New Hampshire	89	86
36	Nebraska	88	43
37	Rhode Island	73	57
38	Mississippi	71	25
39	New Mexico	69	59
40	Idaho	54	57
41	Utah	49	45
42	Nevada	48	73
43	Montana	47	55
43	Vermont	47	81
45	Delaware	43	73
46	South Dakota	40	44
47	North Dakota	32	40
48	Hawaii	28	37
49	Wyoming	26	68
50	Alaska	12	100

POVERTY AND WELFARE

The problem of poverty was at the center of American political discussion during the 1960s, the decade in which the present structure of antipoverty programs was established. We have been discussing the effectiveness and the proper scope of federal government effort ever since. Poor persons or families are those that do not have the means to live in an adequate way. The standards used to identify poverty can be set down in a definition when, for example, it must be decided who should benefit from certain welfare services; but the political concept of poverty is variable and relative to shifting standards of evaluation. As Americans became aware of the great affluence that had been widely attained in the 1950s and 1960s, so too they became aware of the fact that many Americans had been left behind in this march of progress. Social legislation concerning incomes, health, education, housing and other areas was subsequently drafted with the problem of poverty in mind.

This legislation clearly provided some relief for the distress of millions, but questions arose regarding the overall effects of the programs and, especially, their cost. "Tax revolts" in the late 1970s and budget restrictions carried through by the Reagan administration in 1981 have changed the pattern of increases in welfare expenditures. The issue of future economic growth has replaced the issue of poverty as the focus of domestic politics, but the two issues may be more closely linked in the future. Permanently high "structural unemployment" (a basic level of unemployment not affected by recession and recovery cycles) is a likely outcome of the economic growth policies now envisioned by both major political parties; and welfare expenditures under existing basic commitments will lead to ever higher federal deficits as economically displaced persons appear increasingly on the welfare rolls. A new, coordinated strategy for fighting poverty will have to be worked out in response to these conditions.

This section covers selected aspects of poverty and welfare using the most recent available data. These data document the situation prior to the 1981 federal budget cuts. Ironically, some of these cuts have delayed publication of data that show the effects of other cuts. It is safe to assume, given the long recession and the new federal posture, that there is now somewhat more poverty and somewhat less welfare than a few years ago.

83. Pecentage of Poor Families

Over five million American families, 9.1% of all families, were living in poverty in 1979. The poverty rate for white families was 6.8%, for black families 27.6%. The annual income level defined as the poverty threshold varies according to the size of a family and the ages of its members. The poverty level income figure is about one-third of the median income for all families of a given type and is updated each year to reflect inflation. Average poverty level thresholds in 1979 were set at an annual income of $7,412 for a family of four and $4,876 for a nonelderly family of two. The poverty level was first defined in 1964 as a tool for measuring the success of the Johnson administration's War on Poverty. This federal effort did help to reduce the extent of poverty; by 1969 the precentage of American families that were poor had fallen from the 1959 rate of 18.5% to 9.7%. This figure has not changed very much since 1969. Many experts believe, however, that poverty has increased to higher levels in the last few years as a result of joblessness and reduced federal income support.

In Mississippi, one family in five is poor. Proportions of poor families exceed the national average in all the southern states except Virginia and Florida. The poverty threshold is the same for all the states, so it is not surprising that the South, with its generally low income levels, appears in this table as the poorest region. Another group of states with high poverty levels extends westward from this region through Missouri, Oklahoma, Texas and New Mexico. States in other areas with above average poverty levels are New York, Idaho and Maine. Lower price levels help to absorb some of the impact of poverty in the South, but this is not the case in New York, where prices are relatively high.

Table: Percentage of Poor Families
Date: 1979
Source: Census Bureau
Description: Percentage of families with income less than the federal poverty level.
United States average: 9.1%
State median: 8.6%

PERCENTAGE OF POOR FAMILIES

Rank	State	Percent
1	Mississippi	19.5
2	Louisiana	15.3
3	Kentucky	14.9
4	Arkansas	14.7
5	Alabama	13.9
6	New Mexico	13.8
7	Tennessee	13.5
8	Georgia	13.4
9	South Carolina	12.4
10	South Dakota	12.0
11	Texas	11.3
12	North Carolina	11.2
12	West Virginia	11.2
14	New York	10.9
15	Oklahoma	10.4
16	Idaho	9.9
17	Maine	9.7
18	North Dakota	9.6
19	Florida	9.5
20	Missouri	9.2
21	Montana	9.1
22	Delaware	8.8
22	Virginia	8.8
24	Arizona	8.7
25	California	8.6
25	Illinois	8.6
27	Michigan	8.5
28	Vermont	8.3
29	Ohio	8.2
30	Oregon	8.1
31	Rhode Island	7.9
32	Hawaii	7.8
32	New Jersey	7.8
34	Alaska	7.7
34	Massachusetts	7.7
34	Nebraska	7.7
37	Kansas	7.6
37	Pennsylvania	7.6
37	Utah	7.6
40	Colorado	7.5
41	Indiana	7.4
42	Maryland	7.3
42	Washington	7.3
44	Minnesota	7.0
45	Iowa	6.9
46	Connecticut	6.6

Rank	State	Percent
47	Wisconsin	6.4
48	New Hampshire	6.2
49	Nevada	5.9
49	Wyoming	5.9

84. Percentage of Poor Families in Selected SMSAs

Because SMSAs include both central cities and relatively affluent suburban areas, the degree of poverty observed in this listing of 20 large SMSAs is relatively low. Central city poverty rates in these areas are generally more than twice as high as the figures given here. There are only three SMSAs on this list in which the percentage of poor families is higher than the overall national average: New York, Atlanta and Newark. The relatively high rates of poverty in Houston and Los Angeles show that prosperous, growing cities are not automatically free of poverty. Income distribution plays a more important part here than general income level.

Table: Percentage of Poor Families in Selected SMSAs
Date: 1979
Source: Census Bureau
Description: Percentage of families with income less than the federal poverty level in 20 large SMSAs.

PERCENTAGE OF POOR FAMILIES IN SELECTED SMSAs

Rank	Metropolitan area	Percent
1	New York	12.4
2	Atlanta	10.7
3	Newark	9.3
4	Houston	9.0
5	Los Angeles-Long Beach	8.9
6	Philadelphia	8.8
7	Chicago	8.7
8	Boston	8.6
9	Cleveland	7.5
10	St. Louis	7.4
11	Detroit	7.0
12	San Francisco-Oakland	6.9
13	Dallas	6.4
14	Baltimore	6.3
15	Minneapolis-St. Paul	5.7
16	Anaheim-Santa Ana-Garden Grove, Calif.	5.6
16	Washington, D.C.	5.6
18	Milwaukee	5.0
19	Seattle-Everett	4.7
20	Pittsburgh	3.9

85. State and Local Welfare Expenditures Per Capita

State and local governments spent a total of over $45 billion for public welfare in 1980. The state portions of Aid to Families with Dependent Children (AFDC) and Medicaid account for most of this money, but a host of other income support programs and services are also involved. There are astonishing differences in the degree to which states provide welfare support for their citizens. The figures in this table use spending per citizen as a general yardstick of welfare effort in each state. The observed levels of effort result from a combination of the extent of welfare needs in a given state—which depends basically on the average level and distribution of income—and the willingness of the state government to recognize a responsibility to meet those needs.

The table splits the states of the Union rather neatly into regional groupings. In the upper half of the table are found the five states that touch the Pacific and the states of the Northeast and the industrial Midwest. In the lower half are the states of the South, the Southwest and the western interior. The breaking point between these two large groupings is in the $160 – $190 range. The welfare provided in Indiana is notably lower than in its neighboring states. It is the state that clearly differs from the overall regional pattern.

Although it is sometimes argued that poor families and individuals tend to relocate in states with high welfare benefit levels, recent studies by the Census Bureau have shown that the poor, like everyone else, are more likely to follow the trail of job opportunities. Low levels of welfare support in the Sunbelt have not deterred poor people from moving in recent years to these states with job opportunities, and rates of migration from the South to the high-welfare areas identified above have been reduced to near zero or even negative levels. The difficulties faced by people out of work for extended periods who migrated to the Houston area—indeed the unfriendly reception they received—has been news of nationwide interest in the past few years.

Table: State and Local Public Welfare Expenditures Per Capita
Date: 1980
Source: Census Bureau
Description: Annual per capita direct general expenditure of state and local governments for public welfare.
United States average: $201
State median: $157

STATE AND LOCAL PUBLIC WELFARE EXPENDITURES PER CAPITA

Rank	State	Annual per capita welfare expenditure
1	New York	358
2	Rhode Island	315
3	Massachusetts	314
4	Michigan	292
5	Alaska	288
6	California	286
7	Wisconsin	261
8	Minnesota	254
9	Hawaii	240
10	Pennsylvania	236
11	Maine	235
12	Illinois	223
13	Connecticut	212
14	New Jersey	208
15	Washington	191
16	Iowa	189
17	Vermont	187
18	New Hampshire	182
19	Oklahoma	181
19	Oregon	181
21	Maryland	179
22	Kentucky	177
23	Ohio	167
24	Delaware	165
25	Kansas	158
26	Mississippi	156
27	Louisiana	154
28	South Dakota	152
29	Virginia	144
30	Alabama	141
30	Arkansas	141
32	North Dakota	140
33	Colorado	139
34	Montana	137
35	Missouri	134
36	North Carolina	131
37	Tennessee	130
37	West Virginia	130
39	Georgia	129
39	Utah	129
41	New Mexico	128
42	Idaho	123
43	Nebraska	122
44	Indiana	121
45	South Carolina	116
46	Texas	105
47	Nevada	96
48	Wyoming	91
49	Florida	78
50	Arizona	68

36. Persons Receiving Public Aid as a Percentage of Population

Aid to Families of Dependent children (AFDC) and

Supplemental Security Income (SSI) are the two most important government programs providing direct cash relief to poor people in the United States. Two other programs that are important to the poor, Food Stamps and Medicaid, do not provide cash directly. The AFDC program provides assistance to children under 18 years of age who are being raised by a single parent with a low income. The states organize the program and set the eligibility requirements; federal grants to the states cover more than half of the total costs. SSI provides assistance to elderly, blind or disabled people who qualify on the grounds of low income. It is a federal program, but most states operate parallel programs to supplement federal payments. Over 11 million individuals received AFDC benefits in 1980; 68% were children and the rest were the adults who care for them. Over 4 million individuals received SSI benefits in 1980. Total state and federal payments amounted to $12.5 billion for AFDC and $7.9 billion for SSI. Monthly payments per recipient averaged $100 for AFDC and $168 for SSI.

Persons receiving AFDC or SSI support made up 6.5% of the population in 1980. Contrary to popular assumptions, the percentage of persons who received payments actually declined slightly throughout the 1970s. In 1975 the comparable figure was 7.2%. The data given here represent the situation before the welfare reductions and changes in program operations introduced in October 1981. Complete data on the extent of reductions are not yet available, but estimates indicate that over 230,000 families lost all AFDC benefits. It is estimated that 15% of families that were receiving AFDC either lost all benefits or began to receive smaller payments.

Variations in the percentage of state populations receiving these forms of support depend on several factors, including the extent of poverty, the willingness of qualified poor persons to seek support, and the eligibilty requirements set in each state. Mississippi, the poorest state in the nation, also has the highest percentage of residents receiving benefits, but many of the other states where poverty is high are not among the leaders in this table. New Mexico, Tennessee and South Dakota are examples. In Michigan, California, New York and Massachusetts a larger fraction of the population is supported than might be expected on the basis of the extent of poverty.

Table: Persons Receiving Public Aid as a Percentage of Population
Date: 1980
Source: Social Security Administration
Description: Aid to Families with Dependent Children

(AFDC) and Supplemental Security Income (SSI) Recipients as a Percentage of Population.
United States average: 6.5%
State median: 6.0%

PERSONS RECEIVING PUBLIC AID AS A PERCENTAGE OF POPULATION

Rank	State	Percent receiving AFDC or SSI
1	Mississippi	11.4
2	Michigan	8.9
3	California	8.8
4	New York	8.4
5	Louisiana	8.3
5	Massachusetts	8.3
7	Alabama	8.1
8	South Carolina	7.6
9	Maine	7.4
9	New Jersey	7.4
11	Hawaii	7.3
12	Arkansas	7.2
12	Kentucky	7.2
12	Rhode Island	7.2
15	Illinois	7.0
16	Georgia	6.9
17	Pennsylvania	6.7
18	Delaware	6.6
19	Tennessee	6.4
19	Vermont	6.4
21	Maryland	6.1
21	New Mexico	6.1
21	Wisconsin	6.1
24	Ohio	6.0
24	West Virginia	6.0
26	Missouri	5.9
27	North Carolina	5.8
28	Connecticut	5.2
28	Oklahoma	5.2
30	Oregon	4.9
30	Washington	4.9
32	Alaska	4.6
32	Iowa	4.6
32	Virginia	4.6
35	Florida	4.4
36	Minnesota	4.2
36	South Dakota	4.2
38	Texas	4.0
39	Kansas	3.8
40	Colorado	3.7
40	Indiana	3.7
42	Montana	3.4
43	Utah	3.2
44	Nebraska	3.1
45	Arizona	3.0
45	Idaho	3.0
45	New Hampshire	3.0
45	North Dakota	3.0
49	Nevada	2.3
50	Wyoming	1.9

87. Average Monthly AFDC Payment per Family

Average AFDC payment reflects the assessment of need that prevails in the welfare department in each state. Need for cash varies to some extent according to price levels, but price levels clearly do not vary enough to explain the striking differences shown in this table. California provides 4.5 times as much assistance per family as Mississippi. The very low levels of support provided by states in the South is the most remarkable feature in this table. Arizona is the only nonsouthern state that provides comparably meager payments. The highest levels of support are observed in the three West Coast states, states in the Northeast and Upper Midwest, and the high-price states of Alaska and Hawaii. In many other respects Maryland and Delaware are similar to northeastern states, but they apparently adhere to the welfare philosophies that are dominant in the South.

Differences of this magnitude in welfare benefits are one reason why reformers interested in fair and equable treatment of the poor in all parts of the country favor a national welfare system. Repeated efforts of the Reagan administration to move in the opposite direction—to turn AFDC over entirely to the states in exchange for assuming full federal responsibility for Medicaid—have been repeatedly rebuffed by the National Governors Association. Another view of the relative expenditures of state and local government for public welfare is presented in the final table in this section.

Table: Average Monthly AFDC Payment per Family
Date: 1980
Source: Social Security Administration
Description: Average monthly payments per family under AFDC.
United States average: $280
State median: $250

AVERAGE MONTHLY AFDC PAYMENT PER FAMILY

Rank	State	Average monthly payment per family
1	California	$399
2	Hawaii	386
3	Michigan	379
4	New York	371
5	Wisconsin	366
6	Washington	365
7	Alaska	359
8	Connecticut	358
9	Massachusetts	341
10	Vermont	$340
11	Minnesota	336
12	Rhode Island	325
13	Oregon	318
14	Utah	314
15	New Jersey	312
16	Iowa	307
17	Pennsylvania	297
18	Illinois	277
18	North Dakota	277
20	Nebraska	274
21	Kansas	271
21	New Hampshire	271
23	Wyoming	262
24	Idaho	258
25	Ohio	250
25	Oklahoma	250
27	Colorado	239
28	Maine	232
29	Maryland	228
29	Montana	228
31	Delaware	227
32	South Dakota	218
33	Missouri	217
34	Virginia	214
35	Nevada	207
36	Indiana	203
37	New Mexico	185
38	West Virginia	182
39	Kentucky	176
40	Florida	175
41	Arizona	174
42	North Carolina	164
43	Louisiana	147
44	Arkansas	145
45	Georgia	133
46	Tennessee	113
47	Alabama	110
48	Texas	109
49	South Carolina	107
50	Mississippi	88

88. Percentage of Single Mothers Receiving AFDC Benefits

The AFDC program is designed to benefit children who are being raised in a single-parent family. In general, this almost always means that the child's father does not live with the family. The rising rate of marriages that fail means that a program of this type will be important for an ever larger group of children and their mothers in the future. AFDC benefits go to more than half of the American families where a mother is raising children on her own. In Hawaii, California and many of the states in the Northeast and upper Midwest at least two of three single mothers receive AFDC payments. The percentage of single mothers who need assistance varies from state to state, and there are surely some states in which a large percentage of single mothers who do need assistance refuse to apply for welfare; but the extremely low percentages observed for states near the bottom of the list are primarily due to strict eligibility requirements and other program practices in these states.

Table: Single Mothers Receiving AFDC Benefits
Date: 1980
Source: Social Security Administration
Description: Percentage of single mothers receiving AFDC benefits.
United States average: 53.3%
State median: 44.6%

SINGLE MOTHERS RECEIVING AFDC BENEFITS

Rank	State	Percent
1	Hawaii	90.8
2	Pennsylvania	80.3
3	Massachusetts	79.4
4	New Jersey	78.4
5	Michigan	78.3
6	Wisconsin	74.1
7	Maine	71.7
8	Rhode Island	66.6
9	California	66.0
10	Iowa	64.6
11	Minnesota	64.4
12	New York	64.2
13	Illinois	59.9
14	Vermont	58.7
15	Connecticut	57.3
16	Alaska	55.8
17	Maryland	54.8
18	Ohio	54.2
19	Washington	53.8
20	Missouri	50.6
21	Delaware	50.0
22	New Hampshire	46.2
23	New Mexico	46.1
24	West Virginia	45.5
25	Kansas	44.8
26	Nebraska	44.3
27	South Dakota	44.1
28	Kentucky	42.0
29	North Dakota	41.8
30	Louisiana	40.4
31	Oregon	39.2
32	Idaho	38.9
33	Mississippi	38.4
34	South Carolina	37.6
35	Arkansas	36.5
36	Oklahoma	35.6

Rank	State	Percent
37	Colorado	35.0
38	Indiana	34.5
39	Utah	34.0
40	Tennessee	33.8
41	Virginia	32.7
42	Montana	31.4
43	Alabama	30.9
44	North Carolina	30.1
45	Wyoming	27.5
46	Georgia	27.3
47	Florida	27.2
48	Arizona	26.4
49	Texas	20.2
50	Nevada	18.2

89. Percentage of Public Housing Occupied by Nonminority Tenants

Low-income public housing units make up a small fraction of the housing stock in the United States. In 1978 only about one of every 77 occupied housing units fell into this category. Such houses and apartments are meant to supply housing of decent quality for lower-income families. In most places, however, public housing units are not the cheapest accommodations on the market and poor people are more likely to live in substandard units in the private rental market.

Members of minority-group families make up the majority of tenants in public housing, but the distribution among racial/ethnic groups is more balanced than many people think it is. Nationwide, blacks make up 47.1% of residents in low-income public housing, whites 38.4%, Hispanics 12.2%, and other minority groups 2.5%. (The data from which these percentages are calculated include Guam, the Virgin Islands and Puerto Rico, which has a large public housing sector occupied almost entirely by Hispanics). The ranking of the states shows wide variation in the proportion of nonminority residents. In states near the top of the list, there are simply very few members of minority groups in the state population. States near the bottom of the list tend to have large black populations and thus what appears to be overrepresentation of blacks in public housing. Hispanics are strongly represented among tenants in Arizona, Colorado, New Mexico and Texas. In Alaska, Arizona, Montana, New Mexico, Oklahoma and South Dakota large numbers of native Americans, and in Hawaii many peoples of Asian and Pacific ethnicity, are occupants of public housing units.

Table: Percentage of Public Housing Occupied by Nonminority Tenants

Date: 1978
Source: Department of Housing and Urban Development
Description: Percentage of low-income public housing occupied by nonminority tenants.
United States average: 38.4%
State median: 44.8%

PERCENTAGE OF PUBLIC HOUSING OCCUPIED BY NONMINORITY TENANTS

Rank	State	Percent
1	Vermont	99.5
2	Maine	98.8
3	New Hampshire	98.1
4	Iowa	88.1
5	Idaho	87.6
6	Minnesota	85.4
7	Rhode Island	83.6
8	Oregon	83.1
9	North Dakota	82.3
10	West Virginia	79.4
11	Washington	78.3
12	Wisconsin	77.7
13	Utah	76.1
14	Nebraska	73.9
14	Wyoming	73.9
16	Massachusetts	70.8
17	Kansas	68.2
18	Kentucky	60.9
19	Montana	59.4
20	Arkansas	57.7
21	Oklahoma	49.9
22	South Dakota	48.1
23	Missouri	47.6
24	Indiana	46.1
25	Pennsylvania	45.9
26	New Jersey	43.7
27	Connecticut	43.5
28	Tennessee	43.3
29	Michigan	41.6
30	Ohio	41.3
31	Colorado	40.4
32	Nevada	38.4
33	Alabama	36.5
34	Illinois	36.4
35	Mississippi	32.9
36	California	32.3
37	Texas	31.3
38	Georgia	29.2
39	New York	28.7
40	Alaska	28.1
41	Florida	26.1
42	Maryland	25.3
43	South Carolina	24.7
44	Delaware	24.2
45	North Carolina	21.5
46	Louisiana	18.0
47	Hawaii	14.6
48	Arizona	14.1
49	Virginia	13.4
50	New Mexico	13.1

90. Federal Contribution to the School Lunch Program

The present version of the National School Lunch Program was established in 1970, during the Nixon administration, but its roots reach deeper into our history. Charity organizations and local school boards began serving meals to school children over 100 years ago. They reasoned that it did not make sense to provide public education if children were too hungry or undernourished to concentrate on their schoolwork. When the pressures of the Great Depression threatened to close thousands of local programs, the federal government offered emergency relief. About one quarter of all school children were receiving free or reduced-cost meals during World War II. The program was popular and in 1946, when Congress considered the surprising degree of malnutrition among men who had been drafted to fight the war, it was decided to set up a permanent federal program. This program was expanded and restructured in 1970.

Children from families with incomes below the poverty level qualify for free lunches if they attend a school that participates in the program. Children from families with somewhat higher incomes qualify for lunches at reduced cost. Over 26 million children, about 57% of all pupils in grades K through 12, received some benefit from the program in 1980. A 29% reduction in federal outlays for the School Lunch Program went into effect in 1981. An effort to save even more money by reducing the amount and nutritional value of food that schools must supply if they are in the program was sidetracked when it was discovered that the new regulations would have allowed catsup to be counted as a vegetable.

The state rankings show how the $2.2 billion in federal support for the program were distributed in fiscal year 1980. The rankings depend both on the number of pupils in participating schools and on the percentage of pupils who qualified for support because of low family income. The most populous states are at the head of the list, followed closely by a group of relatively poor southern states.

Table: Federal Contribution to the School Lunch Program
Date: 1980
Source: Department of Agriculture
Description: Federal share of school lunch program costs.
United States total: $2.2 billion

FEDERAL CONTRIBUTION TO THE SCHOOL LUNCH PROGRAM

Rank	State	Federal share (in millions of dollars)
1	California	$199.3
2	New York	186.7
3	Texas	164.1
4	Florida	99.4
5	Pennsylvania	94.1
6	Illinois	90.7
7	North Carolina	89.6
8	Ohio	82.6
9	Georgia	80.1
10	Louisiana	67.4
11	Michigan	67.3
12	New Jersey	63.1
13	Alabama	60.6
14	Tennessee	54.9
15	Virginia	53.5
16	Massachusetts	50.8
17	South Carolina	50.4
18	Mississippi	49.6
19	Kentucky	47.4
20	Missouri	45.2
21	Indiana	38.1
22	Maryland	35.3
23	Minnesota	31.8
24	Wisconsin	31.6
25	Arkansas	30.1
26	Oklahoma	$ 29.5
27	Washington	25.7
28	Iowa	23.8
29	Connecticut	23.4
30	West Virginia	23.0
31	Arizona	22.9
32	Colorado	21.5
33	New Mexico	19.3
34	Kansas	18.9
35	Oregon	17.7
36	Utah	14.2
37	Maine	13.4
38	Nebraska	12.1
39	Hawaii	9.2
40	New Hampshire	7.6
41	South Dakota	7.5
42	Idaho	7.4
43	Rhode Island	7.3
44	Montana	6.2
45	North Dakota	5.4
46	Delaware	5.3
47	Nevada	5.0
48	Vermont	4.6
49	Alaska	4.4
50	Wyoming	2.8

THE LABOR FORCE

This section reviews work and occupations in America under four general headings—the type of work, the distribution of professionals (doctors, dentists, lawyers), the dimensions of unemployment and the level of union organization and strike activity. The positions of the 50 states are established with respect to each of these areas.

The first group of tables documents a moment in the ongoing transformation of working life. The mechanization of agriculture and industry has completely overhauled the job market within the living memory of many among us today. The mechanization or computerization of office work is following close on the heels of these changes, although federal statistics for the states do not yet fully reflect this development. One signpost of the future, the growth of professional employment, is only partly reflected in available data. The second group of tables focuses on the distribution of three traditional professional groups among the states. The third group of tables shows the shape of unemployment and unemployment relief in the states, including information on joblessness among selected groups in the populations of the states. An unwelcome omen of things to come may be found in the data on high and persistent unemployment, which baffles economists and politicians alike. The final group of tables deals with the traditional forms of labor organization among workers and labor protest, that is, unions and strikes. The decline of these forms of labor activity has been evident in recent years. Leaving aside the enthusiasts who imagine wholesale imports of the Japanese style of working (Japanese managements are trying this out in their new subsidiary auto plants in Ohio and Tennessee), few people seem to have a sense of how our working life will be organized in the future. Will new forms of organization arise within the labor movement, or be invented at the business schools or learned from foreign examples? No one knows as yet. The data in this section offer in condensed form an introduction to an area of American life in the midst of profound changes.

Composition of the Labor Force

In 1980 there were 97 million Americans in the work force. Thousands of different kinds of jobs were performed, some as old as human life itself, others undreamed of only a few years ago. Changes in technology and in the division of labor among the nations of the world continue to cause major shifts in the kind of work that is available to be done. The redistribution of effort among four large groupings of occupational types in the past two decades illustrates the changes that are taking place. White-collar workers (professionals, technicians, managers, salespeople and clerks, i.e. secretaries, typists, etc.) now constitute an absolute majority of the labor force: 52.2% in 1980 as against 43.4% in 1960. The percentage of blue-collar workers (craft workers, operators of machines and vehicles, laborers) declined from 36.6% to 31.7% during the same period. The percentage of service workers (including a wide range of occupations from food service workers to fire fighters) increased slightly in these years from 12.2% to 13.3%. The most dramatic change, however, occurred in the category of farm workers (cowboys are included here). In 1960, 7.9% of the labor force was working to provide food and other agricultural products for America and the world. In 1980, just 2.8% of the labor force accomplished the same work.

The five tables below present state by state breakdowns of the percentage of the labor force in each of these four groupings, and the percentage of the work force in each state that does not have to leave home to be on the job.

91. White-Collar Workers

White-collar workers make decisions, keep records, teach children, tend computers, type letters and do a host of other things that generally do not result in working up a sweat. High proportions of white-collar workers are found in states along the Boston–Washington, D.C. corridor in the Northeast (but not in Pennsylvania or Rhode Island), along the Seattle–San Diego ribbon on the West Coast, in the southern end of the Rockies, in Hawaii and, surprisingly, in Alaska. The industrial states of the Midwest, which apparently begin in Pennsylvania in this respect, cluster in the middle of the table. The more rural states in the Midwest and most states in the South are found close to the bottom. Florida and Georgia are the white-collar states in the South.

Table: White-Collar Workers
Date: 1980
Source: Bureau of Labor Statistics
Description: White-collar workers as a percentage of the state's work force.
United States average: 52.2%
State median: 50.3%

WHITE-COLLAR WORKERS

Rank	State	Percent
1	Maryland	61.1
2	Alaska	58.4
2	Connecticut	58.4
4	California	58.1
5	Colorado	57.9
6	Arizona	57.8
6	New Jersey	57.8
8	New York	57.6
9	Utah	55.3
9	Virginia	55.3
11	Massachusetts	55.1
12	Hawaii	54.9
13	Washington	54.8
14	New Mexico	54.6
15	Delaware	54.2
16	Oregon	54.1
17	New Hampshire	53.9
18	Illinois	52.6
19	Florida	52.5
20	Texas	51.7
21	Oklahoma	51.5
22	Missouri	51.1
23	Georgia	51.0
24	Minnesota	50.6
25	Kansas	50.4
26	Louisiana	50.2
27	Ohio	50.1
28	Pennsylvania	50.0
29	Michigan	49.6
30	Vermont	49.3
31	Nevada	48.7
31	Rhode Island	48.7
33	Idaho	47.8
34	Wisconsin	46.4
34	Wyoming	46.4
36	Montana	45.9

Rank	State	Percent
36	Nebraska	45.9
38	North Carolina	45.8
39	Iowa	45.6
40	South Carolina	45.4
40	Tennessee	45.4
42	Maine	44.7
43	Mississippi	44.1
43	South Dakota	44.1
45	Kentucky	44.0
46	Indiana	43.6
47	North Dakota	43.5
48	Arkansas	42.8
49	Alabama	42.5
50	West Virginia	41.2

92. Blue-Collar Workers

Blue-collar workers are found in machine shops, factories, mines, oil refineries and other industrial establishments. They also drive trucks and build airplanes, ships and buildings, among other things. High proportions of blue-collar workers are found in the coal and steel country astride the Appalachians, in Alabama and Mississippi on the Gulf coast, and in Maine and Rhode Island in New England. On a proportional basis, the South is the most blue-collar region in the nation, with many southern states ranking ahead of states like Ohio and Michigan in the proverbial industrial heartland. States near the bottom of the list are highly varied. Some specialize in white-collar work (Maryland), some in agricultural occupations (the Dakotas), and some in services (Hawaii, Nevada). The range of proportions of blue-collar workers from the top to the bottom of the list is very wide. People in West Virginia are twice as likely to be engaged in blue-collar work as people in Nevada.

Table: Blue-Collar Workers
Date: 1980
Source: Bureau of Labor Statistics
Description: Blue-collar workers as a percentage of the work force.
United States average: 31.7%
State median: 30.8%

BLUE-COLLAR WORKERS

Rank	State	Percent
1	West Virginia	44.5
2	Alabama	41.4
3	Maine	39.6
4	North Carolina	39.5

Rank	State	Percent
5	Tennessee	39.2
6	Mississippi	39.1
7	South Carolina	39.0
8	Indiana	38.6
9	Rhode Island	38.0
10	Arkansas	37.5
11	Pennsylvania	35.7
12	Kentucky	35.4
13	Michigan	34.5
13	Ohio	34.5
15	Georgia	33.8
16	Louisiana	33.7
16	Wyoming	33.7
18	Wisconsin	33.4
19	Texas	33.0
20	Illinois	32.4
21	New Hampshire	32.3
22	Idaho	31.9
23	Utah	31.3
24	Oklahoma	31.1
25	Vermont	30.8
26	Virginia	30.7
27	Massachusetts	30.6
28	Missouri	30.5
28	Oregon	30.5
30	Iowa	30.3
31	Washington	29.9
32	Florida	29.8
33	Connecticut	29.6
33	Delaware	29.6
35	New Jersey	29.5
36	Kansas	29.0
37	Nebraska	27.9
38	Arizona	27.6
38	New Mexico	27.6
40	Alaska	27.5
40	California	27.5
42	Colorado	26.9
43	Montana	26.8
43	New York	26.8
45	Minnesota	26.3
46	Maryland	25.5
47	North Dakota	24.0
48	South Dakota	23.9
49	Hawaii	23.6
50	Nevada	22.3

93. Service Workers

Over one quarter of all workers in Nevada are employed in service occupations. This is about twice the national average, so it would seem that about half of this employment (or one-eighth of all jobs) must be attributed to the industry that makes Nevada different from the rest of the Union: the gambling business, with its associated hotels, restaurants and casinos. Hawaii and Minnesota, both favorite areas for vacations (high-budget and low-budget, respectively), are the only other states where the percentage of service workers varies from the national norm by more than two percentage points.

Table: Service Workers
Date: 1980
Source: Bureau of Labor Statistics
Description: Service workers as a percentage of the work force.
United States average: 13.3%
State median: 13.2%

SERVICE WORKERS

Rank	State	Percent
1	Nevada	26.5
2	Hawaii	18.0
3	Minnesota	16.1
4	Florida	15.2
5	South Dakota	14.9
6	New York	14.7
7	Indiana	14.6
7	Michigan	14.6
7	Wisconsin	14.6
10	Montana	14.5
10	Nebraska	14.5
12	Delaware	14.1
13	Kentucky	14.0
13	Vermont	14.0
15	Massachusetts	13.9
15	North Dakota	13.9
17	South Carolina	13.8
18	Alaska	13.7
19	Missouri	13.6
19	Washington	13.6
21	Ohio	13.5
22	Maine	13.4
23	Louisiana	13.3
23	Pennsylvania	13.3
25	Alabama	13.2
25	Wyoming	13.2
27	Arizona	13.1
27	Illinois	13.1
27	Rhode Island	13.1
30	Kansas	13.0
31	New Mexico	12.9
32	Iowa	12.8
32	New Hampshire	12.8
34	Colorado	12.6
34	Georgia	12.6
34	West Virginia	12.6
37	Arkansas	12.4
37	Maryland	12.4
39	California	12.3
39	Mississippi	12.3
39	Virginia	12.3
42	Oregon	12.2
42	Tennessee	12.2
44	New Jersey	12.0

Rank	State	Percent
44	Oklahoma	12.0
44	Texas	12.0
47	Idaho	11.9
48	Connecticut	11.7
49	North Carolina	11.3
50	Utah	11.2

94. Farm Workers

About 1.5 million farmers and farm managers plus 1.2 million farm laborers and supervisors are the basis of the enormous productivity of American farms. This productivity is so great that hundreds of thousands of farm jobs are lost each year, and the average farm employee is ever more likely to be using ever more powerful machinery and technology to accomplish the day's work. Farm employment is especially significant in states between the Mississippi River and the Rockies, and in Vermont. The states of the South fill the middle of the table. Very few farmers remain in the northern states east of the Mississippi or if they do, as in Ohio and Illinois, they form a relatively small complement to large urban populations. Indiana is the regional exception here.

Table: Farm Workers
Date: 1980
Source: Bureau of Labor Statistics
Description: Farm workers as a percentage of the work force.
United States average: 2.8%
United States median: 2.8%

FARM WORKERS

Rank	State	Percent
1	North Dakota	18.6
2	South Dakota	17.1
3	Montana	12.8
4	Nebraska	11.7
5	Iowa	11.3
6	Idaho	8.5
7	Kansas	7.6
8	Arkansas	7.3
9	Minnesota	6.9
10	Wyoming	6.7
11	Kentucky	6.6
12	Vermont	5.9
13	Wisconsin	5.6
14	Oklahoma	5.3
15	New Mexico	4.9
16	Missouri	4.8
17	Mississippi	4.5

Rank	State	Percent
18	Hawaii	3.5
19	North Carolina	3.3
20	Indiana	3.2
20	Tennessee	3.2
20	Texas	3.2
23	Oregon	3.1
24	Alabama	2.9
25	Louisiana	2.8
26	Colorado	2.7
26	Georgia	2.7
28	Nevada	2.5
29	Florida	2.4
30	Maine	2.3
31	Utah	2.2
32	Delaware	2.1
33	California	2.0
34	Illinois	1.8
34	Ohio	1.8
34	South Carolina	1.8
37	Virginia	1.7
37	Washington	1.7
37	West Virginia	1.7
40	Arizona	1.4
41	Michigan	1.3
42	New Hampshire	1.0
42	New York	1.0
44	Maryland	.9
44	Pennsylvania	.9
46	New Jersey	.7
47	Alaska	.3
47	Connecticut	.3
47	Massachusetts	.3
50	Rhode Island	.2

95. Working at Home

Comparing the rankings in this table to those in the table above, it is clear that farmers are the only group that works "at home" in significant numbers. For almost all other American workers, being on the job means a drive, a ride or a walk to a place of business. The practice of separating the home and the workplace was virtually unknown before the industrial transformation that began some 150 years ago in America. Within 50 years from that beginning, the pattern that we know today had been firmly established. This pattern has been augmented by highway, rail and air transportation systems. Commuting to work has become a fixture in American life. If the computer transformation of society is destined to reduce the amount of physical commuting that must be done by working people, as some technological prophets declare, there is as yet no evidence of this change in the present data.

Table: Working at Home
Date: 1980
Source: Census Bureau
Description: Percentage of workers working at home.
State median: 2.0%

WORKING AT HOME

Rank	State	Percent
1	South Dakota	11.1
2	North Dakota	8.9
3	Nebraska	7.1
4	Iowa	6.7
5	Idaho	5.8
6	Minnesota	5.6
7	Montana	4.9
8	Vermont	4.8
9	Kansas	4.3
10	Wisconsin	4.2
11	Colorado	3.6
11	Missouri	3.6
13	Wyoming	3.5
14	Maine	3.2
15	Oregon	3.0
16	Oklahoma	2.7
17	Idaho	2.6
17	New Hampshire	2.6
19	Kentucky	2.5
20	Arkansas	2.4

Rank	State	Percent
20	Washington	2.4
22	Alaska	2.2
22	Utah	2.2
24	Illinois	2.1
25	Delaware	2.0
25	Hawaii	2.0
25	Michigan	2.0
25	New York	2.0
25	Pennsylvania	2.0
30	New Mexico	1.9
30	Virginia	1.9
30	West Virginia	1.9
33	California	1.8
33	Texas	1.8
35	Arizona	1.7
36	Maryland	1.6
36	North Carolina	1.6
36	Tennessee	1.6
39	Alabama	1.5
39	Connecticut	1.5
39	Louisiana	1.5
39	Massachusetts	1.5
39	Mississippi	1.5
39	New Jersey	1.5
45	Nevada	1.4
46	Florida	1.3
46	Georgia	1.3
48	Ohio	1.2
48	Rhode Island	1.2
50	South Carolina	1.0

THE PROFESSIONS

The professions have enjoyed above average employment growth in the recent past. While the entire labor force was growing by 17% between 1972 and 1980, the group of "professional, technical and kindred workers" as reported by the Census Bureau expanded by 35%. The three tables below trace the distribution of doctors, dentists and lawyers among the states. This not only provides a summary of the preferred locations for members of these professions, but a rough guide to the average availability of their services in different parts of the country.

96. Physicians

There were 486,000 physicians in the United States in 1980; the group had increased in size by 40% from 1970 to 1980. About 12% were women. Only 13% of physicians are general practitioners. Other doctors describe themselves as specialists, including about 24% of all doctors identified as surgeons.

The state by state breakdown for 1979 shows that doctors in private practice are more than twice as well represented in certain states than they are in certain others. The concentration of medical talent is relatively high in states associated with large metropolitan areas or possessing especially attractive lifestyles (Vermont, Hawaii, Colorado, Florida, Arizona). Some of the physicians in these five states may be more or less retired, of course, but as a group doctors have a relatively unconstrained range of choice about where to settle down. States remote from the great centers, where incomes are low and lifestyles are unlikely to appeal to the average doctor, number far fewer doctors among their citizens on a proportional basis.

Table: Physicians
Date: 1979
Source: National Center for Health Statistics
Description: Active, nonfederally employed physicians per 100,000 civilian population.

United States average: 181 per 100,000 population
State median: 153 per 100,000 population

PHYSICIANS

Rank	State	Number of physicians per 100,000 population
1	New York	261
2	Massachusetts	258
3	Maryland	257
4	Connecticut	242
5	California	226
6	Vermont	211
7	Rhode Island	206
8	Hawaii	203
9	Colorado	199
10	Florida	188
11	Arizona	187
12	Minnesota	185
13	New Jersey	184
14	Pennsylvania	183
15	Illinois	182
16	Washington	178
17	Oregon	177
18	Virginia	170
19	Utah	164
20	Delaware	160
21	New Hampshire	159
22	Missouri	158
22	Tennessee	158
24	Ohio	157
25	Michigan	154
26	Texas	152
27	Wisconsin	151
28	Kansas	150
28	North Carolina	150
30	Louisiana	149
31	New Mexico	147
32	Maine	146
33	Nebraska	145
34	Georgia	144
35	Nevada	138
36	Kentucky	134
36	South Carolina	134
38	West Virginia	133

Rank	State	Number of physicians per 100,000 population
39	Oklahoma	128
40	Montana	127
41	Indiana	126
41	North Dakota	126
43	Alabama	124
44	Iowa	122
45	Arkansas	119
46	Alaska	118
47	Idaho	108
48	Wyoming	107
49	Mississippi	106
50	South Dakota	102

97. Dentists

The number of dentists in private practice increased by 31% from 1972 to 1980, forming a group of 104,000 practitioners in the latest census year. Only 4% were women, only 5% members of minority groups. The distribution by states for 1979 is generally equal to the distribution of doctors. The overall ratio between the level of available dental expertise in states at the top and at the bottom of the list is also about two to one. The states of Washington, Oregon and Utah enjoy rather high proportional representation of doctors, but for some reason they are even better at attracting and holding dentists.

Table: Dentists per 100,000 population
Date: 1979
Source: National Center for Health Statistics
Description: Active, nonfederally employed dentists per 100,000 civilian population.
United States average: 54 per 100,000 population
State median: 50 per 100,000 population

DENTISTS PER 100,000 POPULATION

Rank	State	Number of dentists per 100,000 population
1	New York	74
2	Connecticut	73
3	Massachusetts	71
4	Oregon	69
5	Hawaii	68
5	Washington	68
7	New Jersey	66
8	Utah	64
9	California	63
10	Minnesota	62
11	Colorado	61

Rank	State	Number of dentists per 100,000 population
11	Nebraska	61
13	Maryland	59
14	Vermont	58
14	Wisconsin	58
16	Montana	57
17	Alaska	56
17	Rhode Island	56
19	Idaho	55
19	Pennsylvania	55
21	Illinois	54
22	Michigan	53
22	New Hampshire	53
24	Florida	50
24	Iowa	50
26	Arizona	49
26	Nevada	49
26	Ohio	49
26	Virginia	49
26	Wyoming	49
31	Missouri	48
31	Tennessee	48
33	North Dakota	47
34	Delaware	46
34	Kansas	46
36	Maine	45
37	Indiana	43
37	South Dakota	43
39	Georgia	42
39	Kentucky	42
39	Oklahoma	42
39	Texas	42
43	New Mexico	41
44	Louisiana	40
45	West Virginia	39
46	North Carolina	38
47	South Carolina	36
48	Alabama	35
49	Arkansas	33
50	Mississippi	32

98. Lawyers

The legal profession exploded during the 1970s, as the number of lawyers and judges rose by 71% between 1972 and 1980. There were 547,000 lawyers in the United States in 1980. Significant advances were made in the inclusion of women and members of minority groups during the 1972–1980 period. The proportion of women rose from 3.8% to 12.8% and the proportion of minority group members rose from 1.9% to 4.7%. Like doctors and dentists, lawyers are most often found in the vicinity of large metropolitan areas. High concentrations in Alaska, Colorado and some other states show that there is also plenty of legal work involved in the development of wide open spaces.

Table: Lawyers
Date: 1981
Source: American Bar Association
Description: Number of lawyers.
United States total: 617,320

LAWYERS

Rank	State	Number
1	California	79,420
2	New York	64,450
3	Illinois	35,245
4	Texas	30,536
5	Pennsylvania	28,342
6	Florida	27,498
7	Ohio	26,558
8	New Jersey	22,002
9	Michigan	19,237
10	Massachusetts	18,525
11	Georgia	13,205
12	Missouri	12,053
13	Wisconsin	11,655
14	Maryland	11,465
15	Minnesota	11,400
16	Virginia	11,327
17	Colorado	10,542

Rank	State	Number
18	Washington	10,450
19	Louisiana	10,070
20	Oklahoma	9,382
21	Tennessee	8,525
22	North Carolina	8,352
23	Connecticut	8,075
24	Indiana	7,990
25	Kentucky	7,105
26	Oregon	6,976
27	Arizona	6,488
28	Alabama	5,893
29	Iowa	5,847
30	South Carolina	4,576
31	Kansas	4,275
32	Mississippi	3,914
33	Nebraska	3,838
34	Arkansas	3,325
35	Utah	3,240
36	New Mexico	2,950
37	West Virginia	2,577
38	Rhode Island	2,287
39	Hawaii	2,172
40	Maine	1,905
41	Montana	1,888
42	New Hampshire	1,805
43	Nevada	1,748
44	Alaska	1,551
45	Idaho	1,445
46	South Dakota	1,430
47	North Dakota	1,154
48	Wyoming	1,149
49	Vermont	1,103
50	Delaware	934

UNEMPLOYMENT

The seven tables below present a glimpse of the unemployment situation in the states from various angles. There is a "snapshot" of general unemployment levels in December 1982, followed by breakdowns according to the duration of joblessness and according to various special groups in the work force (women, nonwhites, teenagers, American Indians) for the years 1980 or 1979. The last table shows average unemployment benefits paid in 1980.

Data on unemployment are compiled by means of a survey of the adult population. Individuals are interviewed at length for several consecutive months. They discuss their employment situation or, if they have no job at the time of the interview, they indicate whether or not they are seeking work. To be counted as unemployed, you must be out of work, must be willing and able to work, and must also report having definitely looked for work within the month preceding the interview. People who are out of work but do not report looking for a job are called "discouraged" workers. They are not counted as part of the labor force and not counted as unemployed, but are placed in a separate category. When monthly surveys have been completed, the data are analyzed and estimates of the actual national (or state or local) unemployment rate are created using standard statistical procedures. The estimates for the whole labor force are probably very close to the true figure that they are trying to estimate. Estimates for subgroups or subsets are liable to a wider margin of error as the group for which the estimate is being made decreases in size. Such errors tend to balance out when averages of monthly figures are calculated for a 12-month period, so the data for even the smallest states are probably very close to accuracy.

Unemployment has become a central issue in political discussion in recent years, in some ways taking the place of poverty as a focus of concern. Joblessness and the issue of joblessness are likely to be with us for years to come, so these data provide an initial orientation for problems that we are going to be discussing more often than we might like to.

99. Unemployment in December 1982

The data in this table depict the national unemployment situation at a point close to the depth of the most serious recession since the 1930s. The data are not seasonally adjusted, so they show how things actually stood during the Christmas season in 1982 (when, as in every year, some degree of unemployment was temporarily absorbed into the seasonal sales force). One of every 10 people seeking a job was without a job. In Michigan and West Virginia the figure was closer to one in five. Over 6% of the work force in every state was idle. Plant closings and reduced production had driven the unemployment rate above 20% in the metropolitan areas of Johnstown, Pennsylvania; Flint, Michigan (near Detroit); Youngstown, Ohio; and Duluth, Minnesota.

Some reduction from these levels will certainly occur as the long awaited recovery begins, but changes in labor force participation, technology and the position of the United States in the world economy seem to point toward generally higher levels of unemployment in the future. Many economists now argue that the level of "structural unemployment" (a basic level not affected by recession and recovery cycles) has increased. More women enter the labor force every day. Older Americans are becoming increasingly reluctant to accept the income changes that accompany early retirement. This means more competition for the jobs that exist. Workers shifting from one job to another are more likely to move from one part of the country to another, increasing the duration of unemployment between jobs. Changes in technology mean that old job skills become obsolete more rapidly, increasing the costs and the time that it takes to find a new position. Some economists also argue that joblessness is less "serious" now than it was in the past, since there are more two-income families and a lower probability that losing a job means zero income for a family. This is not very convincing, since difficulty in making ends meet is often the reason that families sought a second income in the first place. New studies have shown that emotional stress, health problems, family troubles and heavy drinking are often linked to unemployment. Losing a job often means the loss of medical insurance coverage, so that many people avoid visiting a doctor at precisely the time when this would do the most good. This lack of medical coverage is coming to be recognized as a widespread problem.

The highest levels of unemployment at the end of 1982 were recorded in two areas—in the Far West and in states that lie between the Appalachians and the Mississippi River. States in this latter group have been shown above, in Table 92 to have high percentages of blue-collar workers in the labor force. The lowest levels of unemployment appear in the white-collar states of the Northeast and in several of the states with relatively high farm employment levels. When a small farm fails, as many have in the past few years, the farmer may be bankrupt and out of business but is not necessarily "unemployed" under the system now used to estimate joblessness.

Table: Unemployment in December 1982
Date: 1982
Source: Bureau of Labor Statistics
Description: Percentage of the civilian labor force, not in the Armed Forces, unemployed in December 1982.
United States average: 10.8%
State median: 9.4%

UNEMPLOYMENT IN DECEMBER 1982

Rank	State	Percent of labor force unemployed
1	West Virginia	17.8
2	Michigan	17.3
3	Alabama	15.9
4	Ohio	14.1
5	Tennessee	13.3
6	Indiana	12.9
7	Illinois	12.6
8	Pennsylvania	12.5
8	Washington	12.5
10	Nevada	12.2
10	Oregon	12.2
10	Wisconsin	12.2
13	Mississippi	11.4
14	Kentucky	11.3
15	South Carolina	11.1
16	California	11.0
17	Rhode Island	10.9
18	Louisiana	10.7
19	Arkansas	10.6
20	Arizona	10.4

Rank	State	Percent of labor force unemployed
21	Idaho	10.2
22	Alaska	10.0
23	Missouri	9.8
24	Florida	9.5
25	New Mexico	9.4
26	Minnesota	9.3
27	Montana	9.2
28	Colorado	9.0
28	North Carolina	9.0
30	Iowa	8.9
30	Utah	8.9
32	New Jersey	8.8
33	New York	8.6
34	Virginia	8.4
35	Maine	8.0
35	Wyoming	8.0
37	Georgia	7.9
37	Maryland	7.9
37	North Dakota	7.9
40	Delaware	7.4
40	Texas	7.4
42	Connecticut	7.1
42	Kansas	7.1
42	Massachusetts	7.1
42	New Hampshire	7.1
46	Nebraska	7.0
47	Oklahoma	6.8
47	Vermont	6.8
49	South Dakota	6.6
50	Hawaii	6.3

100. Long-Term Unemployment

The personal and family problems that accompany unemployment can in many cases become accentuated when joblessness continues for an extended period. During the long recession there have been numerous sad instances of suicide and violence in which prolonged unemployment has apparently played a part. People who are out of work for a long time often have special problems in getting back to work. They may be older workers who have trouble finding job offers, individuals who face problems of discrimination, or workers whose education and training are not well matched to the job market. People in this position stand at the crossroad between returning to "business as usual" and entering a life of chronic poverty. States where such people are relatively numerous face special problems in supplying welfare services.

The average duration of unemployment in 1980 was 11.9 weeks, rising to 13.9 weeks in the early months of 1981. The figures in this table show the group of in dividuals out of work for over 52 weeks (over a year) as a percentage of all unemployed individuals. The numbers are annual averages of monthly figures for 1980. A cautious interpretation of the table is necessary. Since only active job hunters were counted as the unemployed, it would not be surprising if many of the long-term unemployed were omitted because they gave up the active approach after 52 weeks of no luck. Further, the percentage of the long-term unemployed among all unemployed may be deceptively low if large numbers of people have only recently lost their jobs. There were many new layoffs in 1980, so that the combination of new and long-standing unemployment would tend to make the problem of long-term unemployment less serious than it is in states with high numbers of recent layoffs.

The data for the states are spread out, ranging from under 1% in North Dakota to over 7% in Michigan, where the decline in auto production began well before 1980. The Middle Atlantic states, extending down to Maryland and Delaware and west into Ohio, are all among the 10 states at the top. The regional picture in the rest of the table is mixed—an unusual finding given the strong regional patterns that appear in other economic data.

Table: Long-Term Unemployment
Date: 1980
Source: Bureau of Labor Statistics
Description: Annual average percentage of the unemployed who have been out of work for 52 weeks or more.
United States average: 3.4%
State median: 3.4%

LONG-TERM UNEMPLOYMENT

Rank	State	Percent of those unemployed one year or longer
1	Michigan	7.2
2	New York	6.5
3	Pennsylvania	6.4
4	Maryland	5.8
4	New Jersey	5.8
6	Ohio	5.5
7	Oregon	5.4
8	Illinois	5.2
9	Delaware	4.9
10	Hawaii	4.8
11	Maine	4.7
12	Indiana	4.6
13	Alaska	4.5
14	Mississippi	4.4
15	South Dakota	4.2
15	West Virginia	4.2
17	Alabama	4.1
18	Georgia	3.9

Rank	State	Percent of those unemployed one year or longer
19	Kentucky	3.8
19	Tennessee	3.8
19	Vermont	3.8
22	Louisiana	3.7
22	Rhode Island	3.7
22	Wisconsin	3.7
25	Missouri	3.5
26	California	3.4
27	New Hampshire	3.3
28	Florida	3.2
29	Massachusetts	3.1
30	Nevada	2.8
31	Arizona	2.5
31	North Carolina	2.5
33	New Mexico	2.4
33	Texas	2.4
35	Connecticut	2.2
35	Minnesota	2.2
35	Oklahoma	2.2
38	Arkansas	2.1
38	Idaho	2.1
40	Nebraska	2.0
41	Kansas	1.9
41	Montana	1.9
43	Virginia	1.8
43	Wyoming	1.8
45	Utah	1.7
46	Colorado	1.6
47	South Carolina	1.4
48	Iowa	1.2
49	Washington	1.0
50	North Dakota	.7

101. Unemployment Among Teenagers

The teenagers represented here are persons 16 to 19 years old, not in school, who generally satisfy the conditions of the definition of unemployment outlined above. The unemployment rates for these youths are generally two or three times as high as rates for adults, and the same is true when the figures are broken down by sex and race. For nonwhite teenagers in 1980, the rates were about 35% to 37% for both boys and girls. The states that seem to do best in getting teenagers into the labor market—the 10 states with rates below 13% for example—include New Hampshire, Vermont and eight states scattered across the center of the country where there is plenty of physical, outdoor work to be done.

Table: Unemployment among Teenagers
Date: 1980
Source: Bureau of Labor Statistics
Description: Annual average percentage of unemployed

teenagers among teenagers in the work force.
United States average: 17.7%
State median: 17.4%

UNEMPLOYMENT AMONG TEENAGERS

Rank	State	Percent of unemployed teenagers
1	Alabama	25.0
2	West Virginia	23.2
3	Arkansas	22.8
4	Mississippi	22.2
5	Indiana	21.8
6	New Mexico	21.2
7	Alaska	21.0
8	Michigan	20.9
9	Tennessee	20.8
10	Kentucky	20.2
10	New Jersey	20.2
12	New York	20.1
13	Delaware	20.0
14	Pennsylvania	19.8
15	Louisiana	19.5
16	Illinois	19.3
17	North Carolina	18.6
18	Virginia	18.3
19	Arizona	18.2
19	California	18.2
21	Florida	18.1
22	Maine	17.9
23	Oregon	17.7
24	Connecticut	17.5
25	Wisconsin	17.4
26	Idaho	17.3
26	Maryland	17.3
28	Rhode Island	17.1
29	Missouri	16.2
29	Montana	16.2
31	Georgia	16.1
32	Colorado	15.8
33	Texas	15.7
34	Nevada	15.2
34	Washington	15.2
36	Iowa	14.9
37	Hawaii	14.6
38	Massachusetts	14.0
39	South Carolina	13.5
40	Utah	13.4
41	North Dakota	12.9
41	Ohio	12.9
41	Oklahoma	12.9
44	New Hampshire	12.4
45	Vermont	12.3
46	Minnesota	11.7
47	Kansas	11.6
48	Nebraska	10.3
49	Wyoming	9.4
50	South Dakota	8.5

102. Unemployment Among Nonwhites

Blacks make up the largest portion of the nonwhite group considered in this table, although people of other races are also part of the group, including Hispanics who do not choose to classify themselves as white. The ratio of nonwhite to white unemployment has been about 2 to 1 since 1970. In 1980, the national unemployment rate average of 7.1% combined a rate of 6.3% for whites and 13.2% for nonwhites. Among 16- to 19-year-olds, the respective unemployment rates for individuals in these two groups were 15.5% and 35.8%. The 2 to 1 ratio for all workers holds true, unfortunately, even when recessions deepen. During the last quarter of 1982, when (seasonally adjusted) unemployment stood at 10.7%, the rate for whites was 9.5%. For blacks specifically, the corresponding figure was at a depression level of 20.4%.

Back in 1980 nonwhite unemployment rates were 10% or higher in at least 40 states. The data for states where there are relatively few nonwhites (compare the section on Race and Ethnicity) are not particularly reliable or significant. For blacks, the states to examine are those in the South, plus California and the major industrial states—Michigan, Ohio, Pennsylvania, Illinois and New York.

Table: Unemployment among Nonwhites
Date: 1980
Source: Bureau of Labor Statistics
Description: Annual average percentage of unemployed nonwhites among nonwhites in the work force.
United States average: 13.3%
State median: 14.0%

UNEMPLOYMENT AMONG NONWHITES

Rank	State	Percent of unemployed nonwhites
1	Michigan	23.4
2	North Dakota	22.6
3	Montana	20.7
4	Indiana	19.3
5	Ohio	19.2
6	South Dakota	18.0
7	Pennsylvania	17.4
8	Wisconsin	17.1
9	Tennessee	15.8
10	Alabama	15.6
11	Illinois	15.5
12	Alaska	15.4
13	Oregon	15.3
14	Nebraska	15.2
15	New Jersey	15.0

Rank	State	Percent of unemployed nonwhites
16	Arkansas	14.9
17	Arizona	14.8
18	Missouri	14.6
19	Kansas	14.4
19	Kentucky	14.4
21	Delaware	14.0
21	Mississippi	14.0
21	New Mexico	14.0
24	Georgia	13.1
25	Minnesota	12.9
26	Colorado	12.8
27	Oklahoma	12.4
28	Louisiana	12.2
29	North Carolina	12.1
30	South Carolina	11.9
31	California	11.6
32	New York	11.5
33	Nevada	11.4
33	Washington	11.4
35	Connecticut	11.3
36	Texas	11.1
36	Virginia	11.1
38	Maine	10.3
38	Maryland	10.3
40	Florida	10.0
40	Utah	10.0
42	Rhode Island	8.2
43	Massachusetts	5.3
44	Hawaii	4.5
45	West Virginia	N.A.
45	Wyoming	N.A.
	Vermont	N.A.
	New Hampshire	N.A.
	Iowa	N.A.
	Idaho	N.A.

103. Unemployment Among Women

The national unemployment rate for all workers averaged 7.1% in 1980: 6.9% for men and 7.4% for women. Women are an increasingly important part of the labor force. Between 1960 and 1980 the proportion of women among all workers rose from 32.2% to 42.6%. Only 37.7% of women 16 years of age or over were in the job market in 1960; by 1980 over half of all women were working or looking for work. The labor market participation rate of men 16 years of age or over actually declined, from 83.3% to 77.4%, during the same period. Women participate in the labor market at especially high levels in three states noted for rugged outdoors lifestyles—Alaska (60.4%), Colorado (59.5%), Minnesota (59.1%)—and one state noted for the complete irrelevance of the outdoors—Nevada (59.1%). The very lowest level of participation,

far below that for any other state, is found in West Virginia (39.1%).

In general, rates for unemployment among women are parallel to the rates for men in a given state, but they run a fraction of a percentage point higher. There are three states where women's unemployment is notably higher than unemployment among men—Alabama (10.4% v. 7.6%), Georgia (8.4% v. 4.8%) and Mississippi (9.5% v. 5.8%). There are 12 states, however, where unemployment is lower among women than among men, notably Alaska (8.8% v. 10.1%) and Michigan (11.1% v. 13.6%), but also (by smaller ratios) Arizona, Illinois, Kentucky, Massachusetts, Minnesota, Ohio, South Dakota, Washington, West Virginia and Wisconsin. Several of these states have been hit hard by recession in manufacturing, which has displaced men in blue-collar jobs.

Table: Unemployment among Women
Date: 1980
Source: Bureau of Labor Statistics
Description: Annual average percentage of unemployed women among women in the work force.
United States average: 7.4%
State median: 7.1%

UNEMPLOYMENT AMONG WOMEN

Rank	State	Percent of unemployed women
1	Michigan	11.1
2	Alabama	10.4
3	Indiana	9.7
4	Mississippi	9.5
5	Oregon	9.0
6	Delaware	8.9
7	Alaska	8.8
8	West Virginia	8.6
9	Georgia	8.5
9	Idaho	8.5
11	Maine	8.4
12	Ohio	8.3
13	Arkansas	8.2
14	Illinois	8.1
14	New Jersey	8.1
16	New Mexico	7.9
16	Rhode Island	7.9
18	Pennsylvania	7.8
19	Kentucky	7.7
19	New York	7.7
19	South Carolina	7.7
19	Tennessee	7.7
23	Vermont	7.5
24	Washington	7.4
25	Louisiana	7.1
25	Missouri	7.1

Rank	State	Percent of unemployed women
25	North Carolina	7.1
25	Utah	7.1
29	Maryland	6.9
30	California	6.8
30	Connecticut	6.8
30	Florida	6.8
33	Wisconsin	6.6
34	Montana	6.5
35	Colorado	6.4
35	Nevada	6.4
37	Arizona	6.3
37	Texas	6.3
39	Virginia	6.1
40	Iowa	5.9
41	Massachusetts	5.6
42	Hawaii	5.4
43	North Dakota	5.2
44	Minnesota	5.1
44	New Hampshire	5.1
44	Wyoming	5.1
47	Oklahoma	5.0
48	Kansas	4.8
49	Nebraska	4.6
49	South Dakota	4.6

Rank	State	Percent of unemployed	Number of persons living on or near Indian lands
3	Minnesota	50	16,476
5	Nebraska	42	3,318
6	Wyoming	37	6,926
7	California	35	11,608
7	Washington	35	34,940
9	Iowa	34	649
9	South Dakota	34	42,439
9	Wisconsin	34	16,544
12	Florida	31	1,567
12	North Dakota	31	18,336
14	Idaho	30	5,847
14	Nevada	30	6,281
16	Montana	27	16,483
17	New York	23	8,753
18	Arizona	21	145,258
19	Maine	20	1,247
19	New Mexico	20	104,153
19	Oregon	20	3,873
19	Utah	20	8,755
23	Mississippi	18	4,490
24	Kansas	17	2,225
24	North Carolina	17	5,925
26	Oklahoma	15	126,213
27	Louisiana	7	554

104. Unemployment Among American Indians

The unemployment rates reviewed above, disturbing though they may be, are less drastic in comparison to the rates prevailing among American Indians who live on or near Indian lands. Considering only the 27 states where large groups of native Americans are found, it is clear that outside of Arizona, Oklahoma and New Mexico the situation is truly miserable.

Table: Unemployment among American Indians
Date: 1979
Source: Bureau of Indian Affairs
Description: Annual average percentage of unemployed American Indians and number of American Indians living on or adjacent to federally recognized reservations in 27 states.

UNEMPLOYMENT AMONG AMERICAN INDIANS

Rank	State	Percent of unemployed	Number of persons living on or near Indian lands
1	Colorado	57	2,285
2	Alaska	51	72,664
3	Michigan	50	3,354

105. Average Weekly Unemployment Benefits

The surveys used to estimate the amount of unemployment are not connected in any way to the unemployment insurance programs operated jointly by the federal government and the states. In order to qualify for unemployment benefits it is necessary to have worked in a job covered by the program for a certain amount of time. Simply reporting that you are out of work will not do the trick. Among an estimated 7.5 million individuals who were jobless at some time during 1980, only about 45% qualified for unemployment insurance benefits. Persons who did qualify received benefits for an average of 15 weeks; 31% of this group exhausted their payment eligibility period (26 weeks, or 39 weeks in some cases) without having found work.

The amount of the average benefits paid by a given state depends on several factors, including specific state formulas used to calculate maximum payments, as well as the average wages earned by workers before being laid off. This would depend, in turn, on average wage levels in the state and the particular types of workers (well or poorly paid) who are being laid off. It is clear from the table that rankings do not reflect average income levels very well, although low-income states in the South do cluster at the bottom, with benefit rates 20% to 30% below the median value for all states. Many of the states near the top are strong labor union states (see the following table), but this does not seem to have improved benefits much for workers in New York and Michigan. States with strong social welfare orientations like Minnesota and Wisconsin also make payments well above the national median.

Table: Average Weekly Unemployment Benefits
Date: 1980
Source: *World Almanac*
Description: Average weekly unemployment benefits.
United States average: $98.85
State median: $97.42

Rank	State	Weekly benefits paid
39	Maine	$85.55
40	Alaska	85.13
41	Indiana	84.96
42	New Hampshire	84.82
43	Arizona	83.44
44	New Mexico	82.74
45	South Carolina	82.19
46	Georgia	78.68
47	Tennessee	78.04
48	Alabama	76.76
49	Florida	74.49
50	Mississippi	69.26

AVERAGE WEEKLY UNEMPLOYMENT BENEFITS

Rank	State	Weekly benefits paid
1	Ohio	$124.95
2	Minnesota	117.72
3	Wisconsin	117.47
4	Iowa	117.02
5	Pennsylvania	115.56
6	Illinois	114.60
7	Colorado	110.99
8	Washington	110.43
9	Louisiana	108.52
10	Delaware	108.47
11	Wyoming	107.51
12	Hawaii	106.11
13	North Dakota	105.94
14	West Virginia	105.92
15	Kansas	105.84
16	Utah	105.70
17	Connecticut	102.73
18	Michigan	101.87
19	Kentucky	101.33
20	New Jersey	100.69
21	Nevada	100.09
22	Oklahoma	99.75
23	Oregon	98.86
24	Montana	98.11
25	Idaho	97.46
26	Massachusetts	97.38
27	South Dakota	96.87
28	Virginia	95.54
29	Nebraska	93.78
30	New York	93.07
31	Maryland	91.72
32	Vermont	90.13
33	Rhode Island	89.04
34	Arkansas	88.95
35	Missouri	88.41
36	North Carolina	87.09
37	California	86.41
38	Texas	86.22

106. Union Membership

In four of the six most highly organized states a single union is the dominant voice of labor: West Virginia (United Mine Workers), Michigan (United Auto Workers), Pennsylvania (United Steelworkers), Hawaii (Longshoremen). A variety of unions may be found in New York, including several unions of white-collar employees in schools, hospitals and government, and in Washington, which was once a stronghold of the International Workers of the World (IWW) and still figures as a center of labor militancy. Unions are very weak in the South, the Southwest and most of the territory between the Mississippi River and the Rockies, with New Hampshire as the chief regional anomaly. Corporations relocating or starting up new plants have increasingly chosen to take advantage of the lower wage levels and absence of restrictions characteristic of nonunion states. New patterns of industrial location together with the declining fraction of blue-collar workers in the labor force have driven levels of union organization to new postwar lows. In 1960, 1970 and 1978, the percentages of unionized nonagricultural workers were 31.4%, 27.5% and 23.6% respectively.

Table: Union Membership
Date: 1978
Source: Bureau of Labor Statistics
Description: Total union and employee association membership as a percentage of employees in nonagricultural establishments.
United States average: 26.9%
State median: 23.3%

UNION MEMBERSHIP

Rank	State	Percent of union members among nonagricultural employees
1	New York	41.0
2	West Virginia	40.4
3	Michigan	38.5
4	Pennsylvania	37.3
5	Washington	36.5
6	Hawaii	35.8
7	Ohio	33.6
8	Illinois	33.4
9	Alaska	32.3
10	Indiana	31.9
11	Missouri	31.0
12	Wisconsin	30.5
13	Montana	29.9
13	Rhode Island	29.9
15	Oregon	29.5
16	California	28.8
17	Massachusetts	27.7
18	Minnesota	27.6
19	New Jersey	27.3
20	Nevada	27.1
21	Connecticut	26.4
22	Kentucky	25.4
23	Maryland	25.0
24	Maine	24.7
25	Alabama	24.6
26	Delaware	23.9
27	Vermont	22.8
28	Iowa	22.6
29	Tennessee	21.0
30	Wyoming	19.7
31	Utah	19.6
32	North Dakota	19.4
33	Nebraska	19.3
34	Idaho	19.1
35	Colorado	18.1
36	Arizona	18.0
37	Arkansas	17.6
38	Oklahoma	17.3
39	Louisiana	16.9
39	New Hampshire	16.9
41	Georgia	15.8
41	Kansas	15.8
43	Virginia	15.3
44	Mississippi	15.0
45	New Mexico	14.8
46	South Dakota	14.7
47	Texas	13.3
48	Florida	13.2
49	North Carolina	10.7
50	South Carolina	8.9

107. Strikes

Periods of recession generally find workers on the defensive and strike activity at a low ebb. The declining economy in 1980 presented just such a situation. The continuing recession was characterized by such high unemployment in industries where unions are strong that concessions rather than demands were the order of the day for several years. The recovery in 1983 encouraged unions to make up for lost ground; higher levels of militancy seemed likely to prevail in the next year or two. There is only a very weak relation between the amount of time lost because of strikes (or "work stoppages," as the Labor Department prefers to call them) and the level of unionization. Where experience is lacking in establishing relationships between unions and management, or where unions are just getting organized, struggles to the bitter end are more common. The top three states on this list are all characterized by relatively low levels of union organization.

Table: Strikes
Date: 1980
Source: Bureau of Labor Statistics
Description: Total number of days idle (in thousands) due to work stoppages, and percent of estimated nonagricultural total working time lost to stoppage.
United States average: 14
State median: 12

STRIKES

Rank	State	Working days lost per 10,000 working days	Total work days lost
1	Arizona	46	1,164
2	Indiana	38	2,081
3	California	27	6,775
3	Utah	27	383
5	Washington	24	959
6	Ohio	22	2,430
6	West Virginia	22	353
8	Illinois	20	2,443
8	Michigan	20	1,779
10	Colorado	19	594
10	Wisconsin	19	925
12	Alaska	18	77
12	Kentucky	18	564
12	Pennsylvania	18	2,216
15	Texas	15	2,203
16	Alabama	14	487
16	Connecticut	14	514
16	Hawaii	14	138
16	Missouri	14	682
16	Montana	14	96
21	Minnesota	13	580
21	Rhode Island	13	131

Rank	State	Working days lost per 10,000 working days	Total work days lost
23	Idaho	12	99
23	Nevada	12	125
23	Tennessee	12	529
26	Maine	11	111
27	New Jersey	10	809
28	Louisiana	9	360
28	Wyoming	9	47
30	New York	8	1,371
30	Oklahoma	8	236
30	Oregon	8	209
33	New Mexico	7	83
34	Massachusetts	6	413
34	New Hampshire	6	59
34	Vermont	6	28

Rank	State	Working days lost per 10,000 working days	Total work days lost
37	Delaware	5	35
37	Mississippi	5	115
39	Arkansas	4	73
39	Kansas	4	97
39	Virginia	4	196
42	Iowa	3	81
42	Maryland	3	119
44	Florida	2	201
44	Georgia	2	123
44	North Dakota	2	15
44	South Carolina	2	51
48	Nebraska	1	18
48	North Carolina	1	63
50	South Dakota	.5	1

AGRICULTURE

Once a nation of small subsistence farmers, America has become an urban civilization with a mixture of large- and small-scale agricultural production for national and international markets. The average farm enterprise is still small enterprise, but the agricultural sector includes businesses run on the most advanced technical and managerial principles. The number of farms and farmers has been declining steadily since the 1930s, although the United States has become an ever more productive supplier of food and natural products in the world marketplace.

The great success of American agriculture has, paradoxically, led to hard times for many people who work in this sector. Small farmers find themselves squeezed between rising costs and declining prices, as corporate competitors and the commodity markets combine to make production and distribution so efficient that large investments are the only ones that can make a reasonable profit. Federal encouragement of increased agricultural production for export to offset oil deficits in the balance of trade have led to overproduction, falling prices and a sharp increase in the rate of farm failures and foreclosures. Parades of tractors in Washington and the state capitals, and assemblies of angry farm neighbors at bank foreclosure sales now offer constant reminders of the crisis in agriculture.

This section reviews basic data on farms and farm products in the states. An overview of the types of farms in the United States in 1978 is contained in the following figures (only farms with over $2,500 in income are included). The distribution of farms according to the product from which a majority of their income was derived was: livestock 37.8%, grain 28.2%, dairy products 9.0%, tobacco 5.8%, fruits and nuts 3.1%, poultry and eggs 2.3%, cotton 1.6%, vegetables 1.4%, all other products (includes farms with less than half of income from one type of product) 10.9%. Additional basic data on farms are presented in the discussion of the first table below.

108. Number of Farms

A rough, and rather romantic, idea of what we think of as a farm suits most of us just fine most of the time; the Bureau of the Census, which is in the business of counting farms among other things, needs a much sharper definition in order to get on with its work. Since 1974, a farm has been defined as all land under the day-to-day control of a single management, on which agricultural products with a market value of at least $1,000 were produced in a given year, whether or not the goods or services actually went to market. The control in question may be exercised by virtue of ownership, management for an owner, lease, rental or sharecropping arrangement. This means that each tenant farmer renting land from an owner of several properties is counted as a farmer on a separate farm. Other definitions involving lower market value figures and acreage specifications were used prior to 1974. The net effect of the new definition was to remove some 250,000 properties from the roster of farms and perhaps 1.5 million people from the ranks of the farm population.

Some of the operations included under the revised definition are organized as corporations (2.1% of farms, but 12.3% of farmland in 1978) and some are organized as partnerships (9.7% of farms and 16.3% of farmland in 1978), but "agri" remains primarily a "-culture" rather than a "-business" in the United States. Family-operated farms accounted for 87.8% of farms and 70.5% of farmland in 1978. There are of course great variations in the scale of family farming. "Farms" include such diverse operations as cattle ranches, mushroom farms, cranberry bogs, cotton plantations, greenhouses, stables, kennels, orchards and fish hatcheries, along with more typical farms specializing in dairy, poultry, grain, pork or vegetable production. Enterprises specializing in forest or fishing products are not classified as farms.

Under the definition of a farm that prevailed in 1930, 6.5 million farms were identified, averaging 151 acres in area. For 1950 the corresponding figures were 5.6 million farms and 213 acres, and for 1970 the numbers read 2.9 million farms and 374 acres. The 1981 figures are 2.4 million farms and 430 acres. Total land in farms is almost exactly the same today as it was in 1930, but now there are four million fewer separate farms and 24 million fewer people living on the same amount of farmland (although not exactly the same physical territory, of course).

There are over 1,000 farms in 48 of the 50 states. The states near the top of this list are those in which almost all farms are small-scale enterprises. Despite the tremendous concentration in the farming sector over the past 50 years it remains one of the *least* concentrated industries in the economy, with high proportions of small enterprises in every state and every area of agricultural production. In general, the larger the average farm in a given state the less room there is for a large number of farms. Texas is at the top of the list, however, even though there are many gigantic cattle ranches among the farms in the state. Texas is so big that numerous farms of relatively high average size fit right in. The states in the 10 positions following Texas form a single geographical block sweeping across the Appalachians from North Carolina and wrapping up around the southwestern corner of the Great Lakes. Except for New York and Pennsylvania, there are relatively few farms in the Northeast.

Table: Number of Farms
Date: 1981
Source: Department of Agriculture
Description: Number of farms.
United States total: 2.4 million
State average: 48,000
State median: 39,000

NUMBER OF FARMS

Rank	State	Number of farms (in thousands)
1	Texas	186
2	Missouri	120
3	Iowa	118
4	Illinois	107
5	Minnesota	105
6	Kentucky	103
7	Tennessee	95
8	Ohio	94
9	Wisconsin	93
10	North Carolina	91
11	Indiana	89
12	California	82
13	Kansas	76
14	Oklahoma	71
15	Michigan	66

Rank	State	Number of farms (in thousands)
16	Nebraska	65
17	Pennsylvania	61
18	Georgia	60
19	Virginia	59
20	Arkansas	58
21	Alabama	57
22	Mississippi	56
23	New York	49
24	Florida	40
24	Washington	40
26	North Dakota	39
27	Louisiana	38
27	South Dakota	38
29	Oregon	36
30	South Carolina	34
31	Colorado	26
32	Idaho	24
32	Montana	24
34	West Virginia	20
35	Maryland	18
36	New Mexico	14
37	Utah	13
38	New Jersey	10
39	Wyoming	9
40	Arizona	8
40	Maine	8
40	Vermont	8
43	Massachusetts	6
44	Connecticut	4
44	Delaware	4
44	Hawaii	4
47	Nevada	3
47	New Hampshire	3
49	Rhode Island	.8
50	Alaska	.4

109. Land in Farms

About one billion acres, 46% of the total land area in the United States, is devoted to farm uses. There are vast differences among the states in amount of farm area—from 80,000 acres in Rhode Island to 138 million acres in Texas. In Nebraska, Iowa, Kansas and the Dakotas over 90% of all land area is in farms. Texas and Montana are enormously spacious states, so the vast farm areas shown here account for only about 80% and 65% of their respective surface areas. States in which less than 20% of surface area is in farms are Rhode Island, Alaska, Maine, New Hampshire, Massachusetts, Nevada and Connecticut. You can carry out your own calculations of the percentage of state area in farms using the data in the section on geography, a pocket calculator, and the knowledge that 640 acres is equal to 1 square mile.

In 1978 about 35% of farmland was used to grow crops.

The remainder consisted primarily of grassland or semiforested areas used as pasture for livestock. Iowa is the best example of a state where almost all farmland is devoted to crops. Arizona, New Mexico and Wyoming offer good examples of states where grazing land makes up the bulk of farm area. Texas has the most rangeland, but also the most cropland in the nation.

Table: Land in Farms
Date: 1981
Source: Department of Agriculture
Description: Farm acreage.
United States total: 104 billion acres
United States average: 20.8 million acres
United States median: 13.9 million acres

LAND IN FARMS

Rank	State	Farmland (in thousands of acres)
1	Texas	138,500
2	Montana	62,100
3	Kansas	48,500
4	Nebraska	47,700
5	New Mexico	47,400
6	South Dakota	44,700
7	North Dakota	41,700
8	Arizona	39,000
9	Colorado	36,500
10	Wyoming	35,300
11	Oklahoma	34,300
12	California	34,000
13	Iowa	33,800
14	Missouri	31,500
15	Minnesota	30,400
16	Illinois	28,800
17	Wisconsin	18,600
18	Oregon	18,200
19	Indiana	16,900
20	Arkansas	16,300
20	Ohio	16,300
22	Georgia	15,500
23	Idaho	15,100
24	Kentucky	14,600
24	Mississippi	14,600
26	Tennessee	13,500
27	Florida	13,200
28	Alabama	12,400
28	Utah	12,400
30	Michigan	11,500
31	North Carolina	11,400
32	Louisiana	10,000
33	Virginia	9,800
33	Washington	9,800
35	New York	9,700
36	Nevada	8,900
36	Pennsylvania	8,900

Rank	State	Farmland (in thousands of acres)
38	South Carolina	6,300
39	West Virginia	4,250
40	Maryland	2,800
41	Hawaii	1,965
42	Vermont	1,800
43	Maine	1,600
44	Alaska	1,520
45	New Jersey	1,030
46	Massachusetts	660
47	Delaware	650
48	New Hampshire	545
49	Connecticut	500
50	Rhode Island	80

110. Average Farm Acreage

The data in this table are based on source data for the two preceding tables. The states at the head of the list are the ones in which large tracts of grazing land account for most of the farm acreage. The states that concentrate on growing grain, citrus fruits and, in one case, pineapples are found in the center of the list. In the states bordering on the Great Lakes, in the South and in the Northeast farms tend to be relatively small. Many farms specializing in dairy, poultry, fruit and vegetable production for regional markets are found in these areas.

Table: Average Farm Acreage
Date: 1981
Source: Department of Agriculture
Description: Average number of acres per farm.
United States average: 428 acres
United States median: 264 acres

AVERAGE FARM ACREAGE

Rank	State	Average number of acres per farm
1	Arizona	5,200
2	Alaska	3,897
3	Wyoming	3,796
4	New Mexico	3,386
5	Nevada	2,871
6	Montana	2,598
7	Colorado	1,377
8	South Dakota	1,176
9	North Dakota	1,069
10	Utah	954
11	Texas	745
12	Nebraska	734
13	Kansas	638

Rank	State	Average number of acres per farm
14	Idaho	629
15	Oregon	499
16	Oklahoma	483
17	Hawaii	457
18	California	415
19	Washington	413
20	Florida	330
21	Minnesota	290
22	Iowa	286
23	Arkansas	281
24	Illinois	269
25	Louisiana	266
26	Missouri	262
27	Mississippi	261
28	Georgia	258
29	Vermont	220
30	Alabama	218
31	West Virginia	208
32	Wisconsin	200
33	Maine	198
33	New York	198
35	Indiana	190
36	Delaware	186
37	South Carolina	185
38	Michigan	174
39	Ohio	173
40	Virginia	166
41	New Hampshire	160
42	Maryland	154
43	Pennsylvania	146
44	Tennessee	142
45	Kentucky	141
46	North Carolina	125
47	Massachusetts	118
48	Connecticut	116
49	New Jersey	108
50	Rhode Island	98

111. Average Value of Farm Real Estate

The value of farm real estate depends on the productivity of the land and the scarcity of that type of land in a given area. The values in this table also reflect the average size of farms, since the high value of buildings and facilities found on any farm is distributed over fewer acres if average farm size is small. The states with large tracts of grazing land are at the bottom of the table, while the five states at the top are all located in areas where urban expansion has produced new kinds of buyers for farm properties.

Table: Average Dollar Value of Farm Real Estate (Land and Buildings)

Date: 1981
Source: Department of Agriculture
Description: Average dollar value of farm land and buildings per acre for the 48 contiguous states.
United States average: $796

AVERAGE DOLLAR VALUE OF FARM REAL ESTATE (LAND AND BUILDINGS)

Rank	State	Average dollar value per acre
1	New Jersey	$2,998
2	Rhode Island	2,693
3	Maryland	2,556
4	Connecticut	2,533
5	Illinois	2,133
6	Indiana	1,972
7	Iowa	1,947
8	Delaware	1,931
9	California	1,735
10	Ohio	1,727
11	Massachusetts	1,641
12	Louisiana	1,519
13	Florida	1,507
14	Pennsylvania	1,447
15	North Carolina	1,331
16	Michigan	1,232
17	Minnesota	1,231
18	Wisconsin	1,105
19	Virginia	1,080
20	Arkansas	1,061
21	Mississippi	1,047
22	New Hampshire	1,046
23	Tennessee	1,024
24	Kentucky	991
25	Missouri	941
26	Alabama	935
27	South Carolina	930
28	Georgia	915
29	Washington	854
30	Vermont	751
30	West Virginia	751
32	New York	749
33	Idaho	717
34	Oklahoma	662
35	Nebraska	660
36	Maine	612
37	Oregon	605
38	Kansas	590
39	Utah	567
40	Texas	492
41	North Dakota	423
42	Colorado	412
43	South Dakota	297
44	Arizona	282
45	Nevada	271
46	Montana	239
47	New Mexico	203
48	Wyoming	164

112. Average Increase in the Value of Farm Real Estate from 1967 to 1981

The value of farm real estate has appreciated considerably in recent decades. In a typical state, an acre that was worth $100 (the index value) in 1967 had a value of $432 in 1981. Index values for the states vary across a wide range, from $275 to $668.

Table: Average Increase in the Value of Farm Real Estate
Date: 1981
Source: Department of Agriculture, Economic Research Service
Description: Indexes of average value per acre (based on an index value of $100 in 1967) for the 48 contiguous states.
United States average: $448
State median: $432

AVERAGE INCREASE IN THE VALUE OF FARM REAL ESTATE

Rank	State	Indexes of average value per acre
1	West Virginia	$668
2	Minnesota	660
3	Pennsylvania	607
4	Maryland	595
5	Iowa	593
6	Nevada	584
7	Wisconsin	577
8	Delaware	555
9	Ohio	531
10	Utah	522
11	Indiana	516
12	Illinois	507
13	North Dakota	504
14	New Hampshire	499
15	Vermont	494
16	Alabama	484
17	Montana	474
18	Missouri	469
19	New Jersey	464
20	Nebraska	463
21	Colorado	461
22	Virginia	449
23	Arkansas	448
24	Georgia	447
25	Louisiana	435
26	Kentucky	430
26	Mississippi	430
28	South Dakota	429
29	South Carolina	427
30	Idaho	425
31	Connecticut	416
32	Maine	408
33	Arizona	407
34	Rhode Island	406

Rank	State	Indexes of average value per acre
35	New Mexico	$404
36	Oklahoma	403
37	Michigan	402
38	Tennessee	400
39	Florida	398
40	New York	394
41	Massachusetts	390
42	North Carolina	380
43	Wyoming	367
44	Oregon	366
45	Washington	364
46	Kansas	363
47	Texas	361
48	California	275

113. Gross Farm Marketing Income

Gross farm marketing income amounted to $15,015 billion in 1980. Comparable figures (not adjusted for inflation, however) were $38.9 billion in 1960 and $58.6 billion in 1970. About 91% of the 1980 gross income, or $136.4 billion, was derived from the sale of farm products (crops, livestock and livestock products such as milk and eggs). In 1960, outstanding farm debt equaled about 64% of gross income, rising to 90% of gross income in 1970 and 116% in 1980. Clearly, the financial condition of the farms is deteriorating. Net income of farms (using constant 1967 dollars) was $13.0 billion in 1960, $12.2 billion in 1970, but just $8.0 billion in 1980 and on a declining trend.

The major agricultural states are at the top of this list. The first four states produced more than 30% of all farm products that were sold in 1980. From about the 11th position downward the decline from state to state becomes more gradual, indicating the widespread distribution of certain farming activities throughout the nation.

Table: Farm Income
Date: 1980
Source: Department of Agriculture, Economic Research Service
Description: Total revenues from farm marketing of crops, livestock and products.
United States total: $136.4 billion
State average: $2.7 billion
State median: $2.1 billion

FARM INCOME

Rank	State	Revenues (in millions of dollars)
1	California	$13,539
2	Iowa	10,040

Rank	State	Revenues (in millions of dollars)
3	Texas	$8,954
4	Illinois	7,891
5	Minnesota	6,292
6	Nebraska	6,075
7	Kansas	5,887
8	Wisconsin	4,712
9	Indiana	4,508
10	Missouri	4,105
11	Florida	3,804
12	Ohio	3,737
13	North Carolina	3,621
14	Oklahoma	3,231
15	Colorado	3,185
16	Arkansas	2,988
17	Washington	2,705
18	Michigan	2,694
19	Georgia	2,677
19	Kentucky	2,677
21	Pennsylvania	2,666
22	South Dakota	2,546
23	New York	2,418
24	North Dakota	2,386
25	Mississippi	2,145
26	Idaho	2,007
27	Alabama	1,836
28	Tennessee	1,737
29	Arizona	1,720
30	Louisiana	1,653
31	Oregon	1,612
32	Virginia	1,459
33	Montana	1,407
34	New Mexico	1,145
35	South Carolina	1,069
36	Maryland	903
37	Wyoming	651
38	Utah	524
39	Hawaii	439
40	New Jersey	432
41	Maine	425
42	Vermont	378
43	Delaware	333
44	Massachusetts	309
45	Connecticut	296
46	West Virginia	237
47	Nevada	233
48	New Hampshire	98
49	Rhode Island	33
50	Alaska	12

114. Corn Production

Iowa and Illinois are the heart of the American corn belt, producing nearly 40% of all corn between them. Seven other states in the top 10 producers are clustered around these states, mainly extending east and north to circle the Great Lakes. Texas, large enough to be a leader in almost anything that it does, rounds out the top 10.

Corn production is geographically concentrated to a high degree, with 85% of the total yield coming from these 10 states alone.

Table: Corn Production
Date: 1980
Source: Department of Agriculture
Description: Corn production and percentage of total United States yield for the top 10 producer states.
United States total: 6.6 million bushels

CORN PRODUCTION

Rank	State	Millions of bushels	Percent of United States yield
1	Iowa	1,463	22.3
2	Illinois	1,066	16.0
3	Minnesota	610	9.2
4	Indiana	603	9.1
4	Nebraska	603	9.1
6	Ohio	441	6.6
7	Wisconsin	348	5.2
8	Michigan	247	3.7
9	South Dakota	122	1.8
10	Texas	117	1.7

115. Corn Yield per Acre

Corn yields vary according to the general quality of land, the style of farming and weather conditions in a given year. Changes in the weather make shifts of 25% or more in average yield from one year to the next not unusual. In 1980 Iowa had high average yield in comparison to other states, even though yield per acre had declined by more than 10% from 1979. South Dakota always has lower productivity figures than the other states on the list of 10 top producers, but 1980 was a particularly bad year for the state, with yield per acre down almost 30% from 1979.

Table: Corn Yield per Acre
Date: 1980
Source: Department of Agriculture
Description: Corn yield per acre for the top 10 producer states.
United States average: 91 bushels per acre

CORN YIELD PER ACRE

Rank	State	Bushels per acre
1	Ohio	113
2	Iowa	110

Rank	State	Bushels per acre
3	Wisconsin	104
4	Minnesota	97
5	Indiana	96
6	Michigan	95
7	Illinois	93
8	Texas	90
9	Nebraska	85
10	South Dakota	53

116. Wheat Production

Wheat producing country opens out to the west of the corn belt and the Mississippi Valley, extending all along the Canadian border from Minnesota to Washington. The cultivation of wheat and corn are relatively distinct activities; only three states on this list—Texas, Nebraska and Minnesota—are also among the top 10 corn producers. Most of the American wheat crop is winter wheat, planted in the late fall for spring harvesting. Wheat is a vital commodity in international trade, and sales to the Soviet Union have become a factor in the relations between the superpowers during the past decade. The top 10 wheat producing states accounted for 68.4% of the total crop in 1980, with Kansas leading the way by a large margin. Wheat production is more widely distributed among the states than the production of most other major crops.

Table: Wheat Production
Date: 1980
Source: Department of Agriculture
Description: Wheat production and percentage of total United States yield for the top 10 producer states.
United States total: 2.4 billion bushels

WHEAT PRODUCTION

Rank	State	Millions of bushels	Percent of United States yield
1	Kansas	420.0	17.7
2	Oklahoma	195.0	8.2
3	North Dakota	179.7	7.6
4	Washington	160.2	6.8
5	Texas	130.0	5.5
6	Montana	119.8	5.0
7	Nebraska	112.1	4.7
8	Colorado	109.9	4.6
9	Minnesota	102.6	4.3
10	Idaho	96.0	4.0

117. Wheat Yield per Acre

Among the 10 usual leading wheat producers, yield per acre figures in 1980 were most impressive for Idaho and Washington. The wheat country of North Dakota was less than one-third as productive as that in Idaho. California, however, which as the 12th-place producer of wheat, is not included in the list, was even more productive than Idaho in 1980 (74 bushels per acre).

Table: Wheat Yield per Acre
Date: 1980
Source: Department of Agriculture
Description: Wheat yield per acre for the top 10 producer states.
United States average: 33 bushels per acre

WHEAT YIELD PER ACRE

Rank	State	Bushels per acre
1	Idaho	62
2	Washington	51
3	Nebraska	38
4	Kansas	35
5	Colorado	32
5	Minnesota	32
7	Oklahoma	30
8	Texas	25
9	Montana	24
10	North Dakota	19

118. Oat Production

Six states in the upper Midwest produce about two-thirds of the oats grown in the United States. Ohio, Pennsylvania and New York complete the circle of major oat producers that rings the Great Lakes, and Texas fills out the list of the top 10. Oats are primarily used on farms, as feed for animals. Only about 5% of all oats wind up in cereal bowls.

Table: Oat Production
Date: 1980
Source: Department of Agriculture
Description: Oat production and percentage of total United States yield for the top 10 producer states.
United States total: 508 million bushels

OAT PRODUCTION

Rank	State	Millions of bushels	Percent of United States yield
1	Minnesota	90	17.7
2	South Dakota	71	13.9

Rank	State	Millions of bushels	Percent of United States yield
3	Iowa	60	11.7
4	Wisconsin	53	10.4
5	North Dakota	44	8.7
6	Michigan	21	4.1
7	Pennsylvania	20	3.9
8	Texas	19	3.7
9	New York	18	3.5
10	Ohio	17	3.3

119. Oat Yield per Acre

There are five high-yield states among the top 10 oat producers. Yields in Pennsylvania and Wisconsin are about average, while productivity per acre is much lower in Texas and the Dakotas.

Table: Oat Yield per Acre
Date: 1980
Source: Department of Agriculture
Description: Oat yield per acre for the top 10 producer states.
United States average: 54 bushels per acre

OAT YIELD PER ACRE

Rank	State	Bushels per acre
1	New York	64
2	Minnesota	63
2	Ohio	63
4	Iowa	62
4	Michigan	62
6	Pennsylvania	58
6	Wisconsin	58
8	North Dakota	46
8	Texas	46
10	South Dakota	43

120. Potato Production

The Idaho-Washington-Oregon area is the center of potato production in the United States. Over 45% of the national output in 1980 came from this area. The largest individual farm proprietor in the country, J. R. Simplot, grows potatoes in Idaho. Maine is the only other major potato producing area.

Table: Potato Production
Date: 1980
Source: Department of Agriculture

Description: Potato production and percentage of total United States yield for the top 10 producer states.
United States total: 301 million hundredweight

POTATO PRODUCTION

Rank	State	Million hundredweight	Percent of United States yield
1	Idaho	78	26.0
2	Washington	44	15.0
3	Maine	25	8.3
4	Oregon	20	6.6
5	California	19	6.3
6	North Dakota	16	5.3
6	Wisconsin	16	5.3
8	Colorado	13	4.3
9	Minnesota	11	3.7
9	New York	11	3.7

121. Potato Yield per Acre

Idaho potato productivity is right at the national average level. Much higher yields were obtained in the three far western states in 1980, while average yield per acre among the major producers in the upper Midwest lagged far behind.

Table: Potato Yield per Acre
Date: 1980
Source: Department of Agriculture
Description: Potato yield per acre for the top 10 producer states.
United States average: 261 hundredweight per acre

POTATO YIELD PER ACRE

Rank	State	Hundredweight per acre
1	Washington	505
2	Oregon	420
3	California	370
4	Wisconsin	320
5	Colorado	288
6	Idaho	262
7	New York	244
8	Maine	240
9	Minnesota	166
10	North Dakota	140

122. Cotton Production

The 10 states listed here produced 97% of the American cotton crop in 1980. Some cotton country remains in the old South, but the center of production is now found in Texas, California and Arizona.

Table: Cotton Production
Date: 1980
Source: Department of Agriculture
Description: Cotton production and percentage of total United States yield for the top 10 producer states.
United States total: 11.1 million bales

COTTON PRODUCTION

Rank	State	Thousands of bales	Percent of United States yield
1	Texas	3,345	30.0
2	California	3,109	28.0
3	Arizona	1,426	12.9
4	Mississippi	1,143	10.3
5	Louisiana	460	4.1
6	Arkansas	444	4.0
7	Alabama	275	2.5
8	Oklahoma	205	1.9
9	Tennessee	200	1.8
10	Missouri	177	1.6

123. Cotton Yield per Acre

Except for Arizona and California, 1980 was a very poor year for the major cotton growing states. Average yields were off 25% to 40% from 1979 levels. In Texas and Oklahoma, where small sharecroppers are prevalent, average yields were well below the national average.

Table: Cotton Yield per Acre
Date: 1980
Source: Department of Agriculture
Description: Cotton yield per acre for the top 10 producer states.
United States average: 404 pounds per acre

COTTON YIELD PER ACRE

Rank	State	Pounds per acre
1	Arizona	1,085
2	California	995
3	Mississippi	488
4	Alabama	411
5	Louisiana	390
6	Missouri	353
7	Tennessee	349
8	Arkansas	330
9	Texas	234
10	Oklahoma	174

124. Tobacco Production

Two-thirds of the tobacco grown in the United States is raised in North Carolina and Kentucky. Other states in the same region produce all but a tiny percentage of the total tobacco yield. The regional concentration of the growing area is thus completely distinct from that of other major agricultural commodities. Tobacco, believed to be native to the Western hemisphere, has been grown for marketing in the South since colonial times. Due to a tie at the 10th position, data for 11 states are presented here.

Table: Tobacco Production
Date: 1980
Source: Department of Agriculture
Description: Tobacco production and percentage of total United States yield for the top 11 producer states.
United States total: 1.8 billion pounds

TOBACCO PRODUCTION

Rank	State	Millions of pounds	Percent of United States yield
1	North Carolina	762	43.0
2	Kentucky	417	23.4
3	South Carolina	125	7.0
4	Tennessee	112	6.3
5	Georgia	111	6.2
6	Virginia	107	6.0
7	Pennsylvania	25	1.4
7	Wisconsin	25	1.4
9	Maryland	23	1.3
10	Florida	20	1.1
10	Ohio	20	1.1

125. Tobacco Yield per Acre

North Carolina and Kentucky, which produce the lion's share of all tobacco in the United States, are also the leaders on a yield per acre basis. Maryland is only about half as productive as these leading states.

Table: Tobacco Yield per Acre
Date: 1980
Source: Department of Agriculture
Description: Tobacco yield per acre for the top 10 producer states.
United States average: 1945 pounds per acre

TOBACCO YIELD PER ACRE

Rank	State	Pounds per acre
1	Kentucky	2,075
2	North Carolina	2,011

Rank	State	Pounds per acre
3	Georgia	2,010
4	Wisconsin	1,978
5	Florida	1,975
6	South Carolina	1,930
7	Pennsylvania	1,900
8	Ohio	1,788
9	Tennessee	1,728
10	Virginia	1,636

126. Cattle

This table presents a roundup of data on the location of cattle in the 38 states with the largest herds in 1981. The states that supply cattle for beef occupy the top half of the table; herds in the remaining states consist largely of dairy cows. Wisconsin and Minnesota are dairy states that sell widely in national markets, so they appear in relatively high positions. For every two American citizens there is one cow. Texas is the great metropolis of the cow population, the home of better than one cow in ten in the nation.

Table: Cattle
Date: 1981
Source: Department of Agriculture
Description: Number of cattle on farms in the 38 leading cattle raising states
United States total: 115 million

CATTLE

Rank	State	Number of cattle (in thousands)
1	Texas	13.700
2	Iowa	7,450
3	Nebraska	6,950
4	Kansas	6,450
5	Missouri	5,550
6	Oklahoma	5,400
7	California	4,760
8	Wisconsin	4,550
9	South Dakota	4,190
10	Minnesota	3,800
11	Colorado	3,125
12	Montana	2,675
13	Illinois	2,650
14	Kentucky	2,600
15	Florida	2,480
16	Tennessee	2,400
17	Arkansas	2,300
18	Pennsylvania	2,050
19	Idaho	1,990
20	Alabama	1,925
21	Georgia	1,910

Rank	State	Number of cattle (in thousands)
22	North Dakota	1,850
23	New York	1,831
24	Ohio	1,815
25	Indiana	1,800
25	Mississippi	1,800
25	Virginia	1,800
28	Oregon	1,750
29	New Mexico	1,450
29	Washington	1,450
31	Michigan	1,380
32	Louisiana	1,360
33	Wyoming	1,350
34	North Carolina	1,160
35	Arizona	1,075
36	Utah	875
37	Nevada	640
38	South Carolina	625

127. Pigs and Hogs

Cattle outnumber pigs and hogs in the nation by about two to one, but swine are more concentrated than cattle in terms of state production. Iowa is the great center, accounting for one quarter of the national total. With the exception of North Carolina and Georgia, the major producers of ham, bacon and pork products are near neighbors of Iowa. This table covers the 30 states with the largest herds—actually 31 states because of a tie for the final spot.

Table: Pigs and Hogs
Date: 1980
Source: Department of Agriculture
Description: Number of pigs and hogs on farms in the 31 leading producer states.
United States total: 64.5 million

PIGS AND HOGS

Rank	State	Number of pigs and hogs (in thousands)
1	Iowa	16,100
2	Illinois	6,600
3	Minnesota	5,100
4	Indiana	4,600
5	Missouri	3,980
5	Nebraska	3,980
7	North Carolina	2,460
8	Georgia	2,300
9	Ohio	2,150
10	Kansas	1,900
11	South Dakota	1,860
12	Wisconsin	1,680

Rank	State	Number of pigs and hogs (in thousands)
13	Kentucky	1,220
14	Tennessee	1,140
15	Pennsylvania	980
16	Texas	930
17	Michigan	830
18	Alabama	800
19	Virginia	750
20	Arkansas	720
21	South Carolina	700
22	Mississippi	410
23	Florida	370
24	Oklahoma	350
25	Colorado	310
26	North Dakota	265
27	Montana	250
28	Arizona	180
28	California	180
30	Idaho	175
30	New York	175

Rank	State	Number of sheep (in thousands)
16	Nebraska	250
17	Kansas	200
18	Illinois	184
19	Virginia	160
20	Missouri	138
21	Indiana	135
22	Nevada	134
23	Wisconsin	127
24	Michigan	124
25	Pennsylvania	105
26	Oklahoma	95
27	Washington	80
28	New York	69
29	Kentucky	22
30	Louisiana	12

128. Sheep

Sheepherding is an important industry in Texas, California and the Rocky Mountain states. The 30 states with the largest herds in 1981 are included in this table. The top five states account for just about half of all the sheep in the country.

Table: Sheep
Date: 1981
Source: Department of Agriculture
Description: Number of sheep and lambs on farms in the 30 leading producer states.
United States total: 12.9 million

SHEEP

Rank	State	Number of sheep (in thousands)
1	Texas	2,360
2	California	1,205
3	Wyoming	1,110
4	Colorado	810
4	South Dakota	810
6	Utah	660
7	New Mexico	650
8	Montana	595
9	Oregon	520
10	Idaho	512
11	Iowa	437
12	Arizona	372
13	Ohio	310
14	Minnesota	295
15	North Dakota	262

129. Turkeys

The first Thanksgiving was celebrated in New England, but the chances are that your bird this year will have been raised in one of the 10 leading producer states listed in this table. Since turkeys are raised to be eaten, and not for their eggs, centers of turkey production are much more concentrated than the areas where chickens are kept. Over 80% of all turkeys are raised in just 10 states, with Minnesota and North Carolina leading the way.

Table: Turkeys Raised
Date: 1980
Source: Department of Agriculture
Description: Number of turkeys raised in the top 10 producer states.
United States total: 164.7 million

TURKEYS RAISED

Rank	State	Millions of turkeys	Percent of United States total
1	Minnesota	25.5	15.5
2	North Carolina	23.8	14.5
3	California	20.8	12.6
4	Arkansas	14.5	8.8
5	Missouri	12.4	7.5
6	Virginia	10.1	6.1
7	Texas	7.8	4.7
8	Iowa	6.6	4.0
9	Indiana	6.2	3.8
10	Pennsylvania	5.5	3.3

130. Chickens

Chickens are raised everywhere in the United States, so this complete chicken census of the 50 states seems to be in order. Arkansas, with over two billion pounds of chickens and broilers sold, is the leader. The chicken to citizen ratio in Arkansas is the highest in the nation. Centers of poultry and egg production are found in several regions, but notably the South.

Table: Chickens
Date: 1981
Source: Department of Agriculture
Description: Thousands of pounds of chickens sold.
United States total: 17,699,085 pounds

CHICKENS

Rank	State	Pounds of chickens sold (in thousands)
1	Arkansas	2,620,432
2	Georgia	2,510,994
3	Alabama	2,044,794
4	North Carolina	1,822,356
5	Mississippi	1,170,460
6	Maryland	1,097,946
7	Texas	966,400
8	California	827,932
9	Delaware	767,150
10	Virginia	580,256
11	Pennsylvania	549,580
12	Louisiana	418,349
13	Florida	413,556
14	Tennessee	246,276
15	Maine	229,162
16	Oklahoma	201,841
17	South Carolina	189,160
18	Missouri	138,720
19	Minnesota	122,350
20	Indiana	114,530
21	Washington	113,014
22	West Virginia	91,065
23	Oregon	86,415
24	Ohio	85,370
25	Wisconsin	64,900
26	Iowa	37,575
27	New York	32,805
28	Michigan	27,106
29	Kentucky	16,924
30	Illinois	16,206
31	Connecticut	14,410
32	Nebraska	12,741
33	Hawaii	12,192
34	Massachusetts	9,075
35	Kansas	7,670
36	New Mexico	6,042
37	Colorado	5,400
38	New Hampshire	5,040
39	South Dakota	3,980
40	Utah	3,648
41	New Jersey	3,360
42	North Dakota	3,087
43	Montana	2,900
44	Idaho	1,794
45	Rhode Island	1,650
46	Vermont	1,456
47	Arizona	832
48	Wyoming	96
49	Alaska	72
50	Nevada	16

INCOME AND COST OF LIVING

This section surveys basic economic data for the states and selected SMSAs. Average income levels, which vary by a wide margin from state to state, clearly influence the degree to which people in different parts of the country are able to satisfy their economic needs and desires. Other factors, however, compensate for inequalities or reduce sensitivity to their effects. The cost of living varies to some extent according to income level. Compare the partial but representative data on variation in the costs of housing and other goods before making judgments on differences in the standard of living in different parts of the country. The data for Alaska and Hawaii show that both income and price levels in these states are unusually high. Alaskan workers in government and the corporate extractive industries receive premium salaries that compensate for the high cost of many types of goods that must be "imported." This is also true in Hawaii, but a more important factor there is a special form of price inflation resulting from the luxury prices that prevail in the tourist economy.

Beyond variations in the cost of living, the fact that people in different parts of the country generally prefer the things that are readily available to them also helps to overcome the feeling that lower income levels mean a lower quality of life. Economic success and satisfaction in life are two different things, and many residents of lower-income states would not trade life in their particular community or environment "for all the money in the world."

The state by state tables below cover total income and per capita income in 1981, including percentage growth in per capita income from 1971 to 1981, and the percentages of high-income and below-average income households in 1979. Lists of the 25 richest and poorest SMSAs in 1980 are presented, followed by cost-of-living data for selected SMSAs.

131. Per Capita Personal Income and Percentage of Increase from 1971 to 1981

The relatively low level of personal income in the South

is still the most striking feature of American income distribution in the 1980s. Virginia, with its affluent suburbs of the nation's capital, and Florida, with its wealthy retirement colonies, are the only states in the southern region where per capita personal income is greater than $10,000. Alaska, operating on an income and price level all its own, tops the list with a figure more than $3,000 above the national average and nearly $1,000 above second place Connecticut. Several of the high-income states are located in the East, but all parts of the country except the South are found in the group of 20 states where per capita personal income is above the national average. The high-income suburbs of New York City help to account for the high rankings of Connecticut and New Jersey.

Some differences among states are very great. Per capita income in fourth place California is 38% higher than in 40th place North Carolina and 61% higher than in 50th place Mississippi. Costs of living vary to some degree according to how much money is available for spending, so it would be wrong to conclude that the standard of living in California is fully 61% higher than it is in Mississippi. Some costs, however, are either fairly uniform or balanced out across the country, and this means that there are real regional and state differences in the degree to which people are able to attain given economic objectives.

The entry of more married women into the labor force and the trend toward smaller families helped to raise per capita personal income during the 1970s (because people at work now accounted for a larger percentage of the population); but the 152% increase in the national average between 1971 and 1981 is primarily a measure of inflation. Per capita personal income measured in constant (1972) dollars increased only 25% from 1970 to 1980. State figures should be compared to the national average and to one another as indicators of relative advance or decline in income in the recent past. Relative advances in Wyoming, Louisiana, Oklahoma and Texas were outstanding, all of them more than 25% above the national average.

Old and new residents of these energy-producing states appear to have been the principal beneficiaries of economic shifts caused by the oil crisis. Energy-related development also played a part in the performance of four additional states where income increased at a rate more than 10% higher than the national average: North Dakota, Alaska, Washington and Mississippi. Relatively poor performances (per capita income growth lagging behind the national average by more than 10%) were turned in by Hawaii, New York, Delaware, Vermont and Nevada. The income of an average resident in these states declined sharply in relative terms during this 10-year period.

Table: Per Capita Personal Income
Date: 1981
Source: *Survey of Current Business*
Description: Per capita personal income and percentage of increase from 1971 to 1981.
United States average: $10,491
United States average percentage of increase 1971–1981: 152%

Rank	State	Per capita personal income	Percent of increase 1971-1981
32	Indiana	$9,720	143
33	Missouri	9,651	145
34	Louisiana	9,518	195
35	Montana	9,410	166
36	Idaho	8,937	154
37	Georgia	8,934	151
38	South Dakota	8,833	160
39	Vermont	8,723	134
40	North Carolina	8,649	154
41	Maine	8,535	148
42	New Mexico	8,529	160
43	Tennessee	8,447	154
44	Kentucky	8,420	157
45	West Virginia	8,377	156
46	Utah	8,313	142
47	Alabama	8,219	164
48	Arkansas	8,044	170
49	South Carolina	8,039	154
50	Mississippi	7,408	169

PER CAPITA PERSONAL INCOME

Rank	State	Per capita personal income	Percent of increase 1971-1981
1	Alaska	$13,763	176
2	Connecticut	12,816	151
3	New Jersey	12,127	139
4	California	11,923	154
5	Wyoming	11,665	196
6	Illinois	11,576	142
6	Nevada	11,576	136
8	Maryland	11,477	151
9	New York	11,466	132
10	Washington	11,277	169
11	Colorado	11,215	166
12	Massachusetts	11,128	142
13	Delaware	11,095	133
14	Hawaii	11,036	129
15	Kansas	10,813	166
16	Michigan	10,790	148
17	Minnesota	10,768	164
18	Texas	10,729	191
19	Iowa	10,474	167
20	Pennsylvania	10,370	152
21	Nebraska	10,366	161
22	Virginia	10,349	159
23	Ohio	10,313	148
24	Oklahoma	10,247	193
25	North Dakota	10,213	180
26	Florida	10,165	152
27	Rhode Island	10,153	148
28	Wisconsin	10,035	151
29	Oregon	10,008	153
30	New Hampshire	9,994	153
31	Arizona	9,754	146

132. Total Personal Income

This table shows the state by state breakdown of more than two trillion dollars received by Americans as personal income in 1981. The ranking depends a great deal on the number of persons in each state, but differences in average income level (shown in table 131) are large enough to shift many states a few positions away from their population ranking. Californians received nearly 290 billion dollars in personal income during 1981, almost half again as much as New Yorkers. There is plainly a vast gap in the revenues that could potentially be collected in state taxes between these states and the 20 states where total personal income is less than ten billion dollars. About two-thirds of all personal income is received in the form of wages, salaries and other forms of compensation for labor: one-eighth as interest or dividend income, one-eighth in transfer payments (Social Security and other government programs), and smaller fractions as rent or income from business.

Table: Total Personal Income
Date: 1981
Source: *Survey of Current Business*
Description: Total personal Income for the 50 states in millions of dollars.
United States Total Personal Income: $2415.8 billion

TOTAL PERSONAL INCOME

Rank	State	Total personal income (in millions)
1	California	$288,481
2	New York	201,823
3	Texas	158,431
4	Illinois	132,675
5	Pennsylvania	123,096
6	Ohio	111,179
7	Florida	103,502
8	Michigan	99,314
9	New Jersey	89,788
10	Massachusetts	64,248
11	Virginia	56,191
12	Indiana	53,147
13	North Carolina	51,494
14	Georgia	49,797
15	Maryland	48,929
16	Missouri	47,682
17	Wisconsin	47,579
18	Washington	47,557
19	Minnesota	44,087
20	Louisiana	41,001
21	Connecticut	40,164
22	Tennessee	38,957
23	Colorado	33,256
24	Alabama	32,198
25	Oklahoma	31,771
26	Kentucky	30,836
27	Iowa	30,362
28	Arizona	27,256
29	Oregon	26,526
30	Kansas	25,762
31	South Carolina	25,457
32	Mississippi	18,749
33	Arkansas	18,467
34	West Virginia	16,352
35	Nebraska	16,346
36	Utah	12,619
37	New Mexico	11,324
38	Hawaii	10,823
39	Nevada	9,782
40	Rhode Island	9,676
41	Maine	9,669
42	New Hampshire	9,350
43	Idaho	8,574
44	Montana	7,458
45	North Dakota	6,725
46	Delaware	6,640
47	South Dakota	6,056
48	Wyoming	5,738
49	Alabama	5,667
50	Vermont	4,497

133. Percentage of Households with Annual Money Income above $50,000

The figures in this table are based on annual household incomes. Households include persons living alone and groups of persons, mostly families, who live together under one roof. Persons who live in institutions (dormitories, nursing homes, etc.) are not included. The states are ranked according to the percentage of households in which the total personal income of all household members was greater than $50,000 a year. Only about one American household in 20 made this much money in 1979, so this table provides a fairly good picture of the distribution of the economic elite.

Since these high incomes are figured into average incomes for each state, it is not surprising that this ranking is similar to the ranking by per capita personal income presented in Table 131. Hawaii and especially Alaska lead the field by a wide margin. States with large metropolitan centers or close to such centers (states such as New Jersey, Connecticut, Maryland, Virginia and Delaware) crowd close to the top of the list. Wealthy households tend to be metropolitan households, and the common characteristic of states at the bottom of the list, with a few exceptions, is remoteness from the great centers. Many of these states are in the South, but upper New England and other areas are also represented.

There are several reasons why this ranking by percentage of high-income households fails to correspond to the ranking by per capita income for certain states. Changes that occurred between the year to which these data refer (1979) and the year to which per capita data refer (1981) may have some effect, but two other reasons are far more important. The first concerns average household size. If households in a state are comparatively large on the average, then more of the income measured on a per capita basis will fall to each household and the state will have a higher ranking in this table. In Utah and Hawaii average household size is far above the national average (3.20 and 3.15 persons respectively, compared to 2.75 for the nation as a whole in 1980), both states therefore have much higher rankings here than in the per capita income table. The effect is reversed if households tend to be small. Nevada and Kansas exemplify this effect, with lower rankings in the present table.

The second reason for discrepancies between high-income and per capita income percentages is more complex and has to do with the distribution of income in itself. If the overall income distribution within a given state is relatively even, high per capita income may be combined with a fairly small group of high-income households. States like this will have lower rankings here than in the per capita income table. Illinois and Pennsylvania seem to fit this pattern. If, on the other hand, incomes tend to be either high or low, with a gap at the middle level of the income distribution, low per capita income may be combined with a larger group of high-income households. Such states would have higher rankings here. Virginia, Georgia and Florida seem to fit this pattern. Since average household size in Florida is the smallest in the nation (2.55 persons in 1980), and this would lead us to expect a lower ranking here, the fact that Florida actually moves up seven positions (from 26 to 19) is evidently a sign of a very severe contrast in economic groups in the state economy. Although all the factors noted above work together to determine differences in rankings between the two tables, it appears that the economies of Virginia, Georgia and Florida are really more like two economies operating side by side, one with high income levels and one with lower levels.

Table: Annual Household Income above $50,000
Date: 1979
Source: Census Bureau
Description: Percentage of households with annual money income above $50,000.
United States average: 4.6%
State median: 3.8%

ANNUAL HOUSEHOLD INCOME ABOVE $50,000

Rank	State	Percent over $50,000
1	Alaska	15.6
2	Hawaii	8.3
3	New Jersey	6.9
4	Connecticut	6.6
5	Maryland	6.5
6	California	6.3
7	Delaware	5.4
7	Michigan	5.4
7	Virginia	5.4
10	Colorado	5.3
10	New York	5.3
12	Nevada	5.2
12	Wyoming	5.2
14	Illinois	5.1
15	Texas	4.9
16	Minnesota	4.6
16	Washington	4.6
18	Massachusetts	4.4
19	Florida	4.3
20	Georgia	4.2
21	Utah	4.1
22	Arizona	4.0
22	Iowa	4.0
22	Wisconsin	4.0
25	Kansas	3.8
25	Nebraska	3.8
25	Ohio	3.8
28	Oregon	3.7
28	Pennsylvania	3.7
30	Louisiana	3.6
30	Oklahoma	3.6
32	Indiana	3.4

Rank	State	Percent over $50,000
32	New Hampshire	3.4
32	North Dakota	3.4
35	Missouri	3.3
35	Tennessee	3.3
37	New Mexico	3.2
37	Rhode Island	3.2
37	South Carolina	3.2
40	Idaho	2.9
40	West Virginia	2.9
42	Alabama	2.8
42	Montana	2.8
44	Vermont	2.7
45	Mississippi	2.6
45	North Carolina	2.6
47	Kentucky	2.5
48	South Dakota	2.4
49	Maine	2.0
50	Arkansas	1.9

134. Percentage of Households with Annual Money Income below $15,000

The median household income in the United States was $16,830 in 1979. About 45% of all households received less than $15,000 in money income. Except for Alaska, the proportion of households in this category ranged between 35% and 60% in the various states. All of the southern states except Virginia will be found in the upper half of the table. More than half of all households in eight southern states plus South Dakota, Maine and New Mexico received less than $15,000. Generally speaking, wealthier states have many high-income households and relatively few households with below-average incomes, so this table naturally looks a lot like the previous table turned upside down. Florida and Georgia are the only two states in the top 20 in both tables. Indiana is the only state in the lower 20 in both tables. The first case suggests, as discussed above, the presence of a relatively large economic elite of affluent households in an economy where the basic income structure is rather depressed. The second case presents a situation where there are fairly good chances of making an above-average income, but few opportunities to really strike it rich.

Table: Annual Household Income below $15,000
Date: 1979
Source: Census Bureau
Description: Percentage of households with annual money income below $15,000.
United States average: 44.5%
State median: 45.5%

ANNUAL HOUSEHOLD INCOME BELOW $15,000

Rank	State	Percent below $15,000
1	Arkansas	59.9
2	Mississippi	57.7
3	South Dakota	54.7
4	Maine	54.1
5	Alabama	53.0
5	Kentucky	53.0
7	Tennessee	52.9
8	New Mexico	50.7
9	North Carolina	50.4
9	West Virginia	50.4
11	Florida	50.2
12	Oklahoma	49.9
13	Vermont	49.8
14	Louisiana	49.6
14	South Carolina	49.6
16	Georgia	49.3
17	North Dakota	49.1
18	Idaho	48.9
19	Montana	47.9
20	Missouri	47.5
21	Nebraska	46.6
22	Rhode Island	46.2
23	Kansas	46.0
24	Texas	45.7
25	Arizona	45.6
26	New York	45.4
27	Oregon	45.2
28	Iowa	43.6
29	Pennsylvania	43.4
30	New Hampshire	43.0
31	Delaware	42.3
32	Massachusetts	42.0
33	Indiana	41.9
34	Ohio	41.7
34	Virginia	41.7
36	California	41.2
37	Wisconsin	41.0
38	Washington	40.9
39	Utah	40.8
40	Colorado	40.7
41	Illinois	39.9
42	Minnesota	39.8
43	Michigan	39.3
43	Nevada	39.3
45	New Jersey	37.5
46	Wyoming	36.4
47	Maryland	36.3
48	Connecticut	35.6
49	Hawaii	35.3
50	Alaska	29.1

135. The 25 Richest SMSAs

Among the 318 SMSAs introduced in the section on population, these are the 25 with the highest levels of annual per capita personal income. The fact that most of the very large SMSAs are found on this list indicates that high income levels and large agglomerations of population are closely related in the United States. High-paying jobs, especially managerial jobs in large business and government organizations, tend to be concentrated in these areas. Most of the smaller SMSAs on this list are actually satellites of the great centers, especially New York City. Anchorage stands at the head of the list because of the peculiar Alaskan price level. Casper, Wyo. is here because of new technical and skilled jobs in the energy sector. Reno, Palm Beach and Sarasota stand as a testament to the settlement choices made by affluent retired persons and seekers after the good life. Income levels for all 25 of these SMSAs are more than 16% higher than the 1980 U.S. average annual per capita income of $9,521.

Table: The 25 Richest SMSAs in the United States
Date: 1980
Source: Department of Commerce
Description: The 25 SMSAs with the highest annual per capita personal income.

THE 25 RICHEST SMSAs IN THE UNITED STATES

Rank	SMSA	Annual per capita personal income
1	Anchorage	$14,266
2	Bridgeport-Stamford-Norwalk-Danbury	14,197
3	Casper, Wyo.	14,072
4	Midland, Tex.	13,761
5	San Francisco-Oakland	12,998
6	Washington, D.C.	12,871
7	Reno	12,371
8	San Jose	12,297
9	Nassau-Suffolk, (Long Island)	12,258
10	Seattle-Everett	11,882
11	Houston	11,861
12	Anaheim-Santa Ana-Garden Grove	11,857
13	Newark	11,689
14	West Palm Beach-Boca Raton	11,554
15	Hartford-New Britain-Bristol	11,395
16	Chicago	11,394
17	Los Angeles-Long Beach	11,350
18	Minneapolis-St Paul	11,329
19	Denver-Boulder	11,301
20	Sarasota	11,287
21	Cleveland	11,236
22	Detroit	11,208
23	New Brunswick-Perth Amboy-Sayreville, N.J.	11,174
24	New York	11,087
25	Dallas-Fort Worth	11,041

136. The 25 Poorest SMSAs

The 25 richest SMSAs tend to have large populations and are scattered around the country. The 25 poorest SMSAs tend to be small in comparison to other SMSAs and are concentrated in the South. Many of these areas are simply population centers built up around large universities, including all four of the outstanding exceptions to the southern regional pattern: Provo (Brigham Young), Las Cruces (New Mexico State), Bloomington (Indiana) and State College (Penn State). Students with low earnings of their own swell the populations of these areas. Annual personal income levels for all 25 of these SMSAs are more than 24% lower than the 1980 U.S. average annual per capita income.

Table: The 25 Poorest SMSAs in the United States
Date: 1980
Source: Department of Commerce
Description: The 25 SMSAs with the lowest annual per capita personal income.

THE 25 POOREST SMSAs IN THE UNITED STATES

Rank	SMSA	Annual per capita personal income
1	McAllen-Pharr-Edinburg (Tex.)	$4,808
2	Laredo (Tex.)	5,439
3	Brownsville-Haringen-San Benito (Tex.)	5,444
4	Jacksonville (N.C.)	5,876
5	Provo-Orem (Utah)	5,888
6	Las Cruces (N. Mex.)	6,328
7	Alexandria (La.)	6,643
8	Bloomington (Ind.)	6,647
9	El Paso (Tex.)	6,677
10	Fayetteville (N.C.)	6,697
11	Bryan-College Station (Tex.)	6,703
12	Florence (S.C.)	6,811
13	Biloxi-Gulfport (Miss.)	6,903
13	Clarksville-Hopkinsville (Tenn., Ky.)	6,903
15	Pascagoula-Moss Point (Miss.)	6,911
16	Lawton (Okla.)	6,962
17	Athens (Ga.)	6,963
18	Ocala (Fl.)	6,966
19	Tuscaloosa (Ala.)	7,052
20	Gainesville (Fl.)	7,055
21	Fort Smith (Ark., Okla.)	7,058
22	Danville (Va.)	7,074
23	Anniston (Ala.)	7,090
24	Johnson City-Kingsport-Bristol (Tenn., Va.)	7,147
25	State College (Pa.)	7,153

137. Median Purchase Price for Single-Family Homes in Selected SMSAs

The prices of single-family homes are a bellwether of general housing costs in a given area. Since expenses for housing and for food each account for about one quarter of all money spent by households, the prices of single-family homes provide a good starting point for comparing the costs of living in different places.

Homeowners have been more fortunate than non-homeowners during the Great Inflation of the 1970s. Their assets have appreciated in value, often at a higher rate than inflation in general. Single-family homes are no longer affordable for many people who want to buy them and who would have been able to do so in the past. High interest rates and high building costs have increased the value of existing homes and reduced demand for new homes so much that the construction industry has been depressed for many years.

This table shows that homes in California and the West are presently far more costly than homes elsewhere in the nation. Only the Washington, D.C. area has prices anything like those in the West. People in the East and the Midwest may not think of single-family homes as a bargain at current prices, but these prices are moderate by California standards. There are two main reasons why prices are so high in the West. First, rapid population growth means that the demand for housing is high relative to other parts of the country. Second, there is more new housing in the West and the overall housing stock is not as old as it is elsewhere. Buyers in other parts of the country may enjoy lower purchase prices, but they can expect to spend more on repairs and upkeep. Since the populations in the eastern part of the country are fairly stable or declining, there are already enough buildings in place to house everyone. The key problem is renovation or restoration of these buildings so that they remain habitable.

Table: Median Home Prices
Date: 1980
Source: Census Bureau
Description: Median purchase prices of single-family houses in 28 selected SMSAs.

MEDIAN HOME PRICES

Rank	SMSA	Price
1	San-Francisco-Oakland	$109,500
2	Las Vegas	97,900
3	Anchorage	90,000
3	Los Angeles-Long Beach	90,000
5	Honolulu	88,500

Rank	SMSA	Price
6	Washington, D.C.	$87,500
7	San Diego	85,500
8	Phoenix	79,500
9	New York	73,500
10	Seattle-Everett	70,500
11	Milwaukee	70,000
12	Baton Rouge	69,900
13	Denver-Boulder	68,900
14	Atlanta	68,800
15	Houston	67,900
16	Portland (Oreg.-Wash.)	65,000
17	Chicago	63,000
18	Burlington (N.C.)	62,500
19	Kansas City	61,500
20	Oklahoma City	59,000
21	Cleveland	58,000
22	Nashville-Davidson	55,500
23	Pittsburgh	54,000
24	St. Louis	50,200
25	Buffalo	50,000
26	Omaha	48,000
27	Orlando (Fla.)	45,000
27	Portland (Maine)	45,000

138. Annual Intermediate Family Food Budget in Selected SMSAs

On the average, about one-quarter of annual household expenditures in the United States goes toward food purchases. This fraction varies somewhat from place to place, and this variation accounts for the fact that the ranking of the SMSAs is slightly different here than in the table above. The data in this table are taken from the same estimates used for the total intermediate budget*.

Since the most costly items of consumption other than food are housing and energy, variations in the prices of these items combine with regional variations in food costs to change the percentage of expenditure that goes for food. The lowest percentage of expenditure for food is observed in Boston (20.3%), Anchorage, Milwaukee and Minneapolis. High winter heating costs that eat into the food budget are the major factor in these SMSAs. Three of the four SMSAs have lower rankings here than in the previous table; and in Anchorage, where total family budget is

*The Bureau of Labor Statistics computes budgets at three levels representing upper, intermediate and lower levels of the middle class. These figures do not represent actual spending, but rather what the hypothetical family of four might spend for a given list of commodities appropriate for its socioeconomic level. The figures for the intermediate level reveal the cost of living at a decent but not excessive level.

nearly $2,000 higher on the average than it is in New York, families spend only about $70 more per year for food than New York families. High fractions of expenditure go for food in Atlanta, Dallas, Houston, Philadelphia and Pittsburgh. Low energy usage and cost in the Sunbelt cities and low housing costs in the Pennsylvania cities account for this pattern and, accordingly, for their relatively higher rankings in the present table.

Food costs in New York and Philadelphia are about 19% higher than food costs in Denver. In Honolulu, however, food costs are 17% higher than they are in New York and Philadelphia.

Table: Annual Intermediate Family Food Budget
Date: 1981
Source: Bureau of Labor Statistics
Description: Dollars annually spent for food by a four-person family in 20 selected SMSAs.

FAMILY FOOD BUDGET

Rank	SMSA	Dollars spent on food per year
1	Honolulu	$7,626
2	Anchorage	6,586
3	New York	6,516
3	Philadelphia	6,516
5	Pittsburgh	6,040
6	Cincinnati	5,939
7	Boston	5,918
8	Buffalo	5,890
9	Detroit	5,886
10	Cleveland	5,859
11	Houston	5,816
12	Chicago	5,779
13	Kansas City	5,727
14	Los Angeles, Long Beach	5,700
15	Milwaukee	5,660
16	Atlanta	5,614
17	Minneapolis-St. Paul	5,607
18	Dallas	5,568
19	Baltimore	5,526
20	Denver	5,480

139. Intermediate Family Budget in Selected SMSAs

The figures in this table are estimates made by the Bureau of Labor Statistics on the basis of consumer surveys. Publications of the bureau should be consulted for the complex technical details. The numbers are meant to represent the cost of maintaining a moderate standard of living for a four-person family in the designated SMSAs.

Honolulu and Anchorage stand out as special cases, indicating the price aspect of conditions that have been noted above. There are sharp differences in price levels among the other 18 SMSAs included here. Costs in Atlanta and the Texas SMSAs are well below the rest. The cost of living in New York City is 30% higher than the cost of living in Dallas. Different levels of energy consumption and very different energy costs explain much of this difference.

Table: A Four-person Annual Intermediate Family Budget
Date: 1981
Source: Bureau of Labor Statistics
Description: Annual intermediate budget for a four-person family for all items in 20 selected SMSAs.

FAMILY BUDGET

Rank	SMSA	Dollars spent for all items per year
1	Honolulu	$31,893
2	Anchorage	31,390
3	New York	29,540
4	Boston	29,213
5	Milwaukee	26,875
6	Philadelphia	26,567
7	Buffalo	26,473
8	Minneapolis-St. Paul	25,799
9	Cleveland	25,598
10	Cincinnati	25,475
11	Chicago	25,358
12	Detroit	25,208
13	Baltimore	25,114
14	Los Angeles-Long Beach	25,025
15	Denver	24,820
16	Pittsburgh	24,717
17	Kansas City	24,528
18	Houston	23,601
19	Atlanta	23,273
20	Dallas	22,678

TAXES

"In this world," wrote Benjamin Franklin in 1789, "nothing is certain but death and taxes." For generations Americans have gladly (or grudgingly) made their contributions to the lifeblood of our federal, state and local governments. But in a generation when the hope of cheating death has inspired some people (consider the growth of life-support technology and the practice of freezing dead bodies to await future medical invention), the practice of cheating the tax collector has become more inspired than ever before. The Internal Revenue Service (IRS) estimated that taxpayers would fail to pay about $100 billion of the $750 billion that they owed to Uncle Sam for the year 1982. Fraudulent underpayment of state taxes is presently estimated at about $50 billion per year, an amount equal to one-third of the state taxes actually paid. The incidence of cheating appears to have increased rapidly during the past decade, and surveys have disclosed that social acceptance of cheating and even a certain pride in cheating is more widespread than ever before. While debates about taxes focused in the past on the fairness of progressive taxation and the extent to which the wealthiest individuals and corporations evade or subvert this system, the new issue concerns the extent to which average Americans have taken to emulating the rich.

Some students of the problem blame the inflation of the 1970s, which caused incomes that had remained about the same in purchasing power to be taxed at higher rates because of increased dollar amounts. Average Americans, with a sense of paying more than their "fair share," began to take the matter of tax relief into their own hands. A political manifestation of this discontent appeared in the mid-1970s with the "tax revolt" and the budget-limiting referenda in California, Massachusetts and other states.

Other students of the problem point to the fact that general respect for the government has declined (especially since Vietnam and Watergate), or that the highly complex tax system, with thousands of special exemptions and advantages, have angered those without access to special breaks and encouraged those with access to go one step further. It is clear, at any rate, that wealthier taxpayers often take pride in employing specialists to find complex legal or semilegal loopholes and shelters, or to find ways to conceal income. The "bartering" of services—exchanges not involving money—has become more common among professionals. A final, important cause of the rise of tax fraud is the growth of the "underground economy." All transactions that occur without the keeping of records for the tax authorities are criminal by that token alone, but the heart of the underground economy is organized crime. Standard rackets and the fencing of stolen goods go on as before, but illegal drug traffic involving billions of dollars in cash transactions are now the major problem.

To save money the Carter and Reagan administrations both cut back on the enforcement activities of the IRS. The percentage of audited tax returns dropped from 2.59% in 1976 to 1.55% in 1982, despite the finding that the IRS realizes an average $10 return for each $1 spent on enforcement. New IRS computer systems were used to compare returns with information from other sources in 1983. This may help to bring the problem under control, but prosecutions of prominent tax evaders may be of even more use. The successful prosecution of Al Capone is probably the most famous case in IRS history, but recent attention-focusing judgments have also been won against the likes of Billy Carter, Spiro T. Agnew and the Rev. Sun Myung Moon. The most promising reform ideas call for a drastic simplification of the tax codes. A restoration of the sense of a civic responsibility to pay taxes will also be needed, and a motto for efforts with this aim might well be drawn from the French philosopher Montesquieu, who in 1748 wrote: "In constitutional states liberty is compensation for heavy taxation; in despotic states the equivalent of liberty is light taxation." When individuals become accustomed to lightening their own taxes by devious methods, the grounds for a more devious and despotic political system are being prepared.

While the morality of tax paying and tax collecting for purposes such as building nuclear weapons is the major contemporary issue in this area, an absence of relevant data for the states prohibits a focus on this issue in this section. The data presented here provide instead some basic facts about the volume of taxes successfully collected and their distribution across the states. The first four tables cover the burden of federal taxes in the states and the extent to which taxes raised by the federal government return in the form of services and payments to the states from which they originate. The issue of equity among the states in financial dealings with Washington is a perennial concern of the Congress. The remaining tables in this section survey the variety of taxing systems found in the 50 states. The level of state tax revenue per capita is examined and these revenues are then broken down according to the types of taxes from which they derive. General sales tax rates and rates of excise taxes on gasoline and cigarettes are compared across the states. The final table examines the state lotteries, which make a small but morally controversial contribution to public finances in certain states.

140. Federal Tax Revenue

The federal government collected $500 billion in all forms of taxes during fiscal year 1980 (ending Sept. 30, 1980). This comes to $2,212 for every person in the country on census day. The major federal sources were individual income taxes ($244 billion), social insurance taxes ($161 billion) and corporate income taxes ($65 billion). State governments collected $137 billion in taxes during their 1980 fiscal years, while local governments collected $86 billion.

Although Americans complain of high overall taxation, the burden is light in comparison to most of the major industrial nations. Taxes collected by all levels of the U.S. government came to 30.7% of the gross domestic product in 1980. Comparable figures for other countries are: Sweden 49.6%, France 42.6%, West Germany 37.4% and Britain 36.1%. Japan (26.1%) is the only technologically advanced noncommunist country with a lower quotient.

The data in this table show the per capita burden of all federal taxes for the states. The figures are estimates prepared by the Tax Foundation Incorporated. The estimation involves an adjustment that assigns tax revenue to the state where it originates instead of the state where the tax money is actually collected—for example, in the very important matter of corporate taxes, which may be paid in a headquarters state far from the main areas of productive activity.

The federal tax burden in Alaska is unusually high, but this mainly reflects high corporate tax revenues. Since Alaskans also happen to have high per capita incomes, however, it is possible that the progressive tax rate structure would cause the state to be at the top of the list

even if this factor were removed. In general, the ranking of states by tax burden is close to the ranking by average income, with some position shifts due to higher or lower levels of business activity. The wealthier industrial states of the East, the Midwest and the Far West dominate the top of the table, while states in the South are heavily represented at the bottom.

Table: Per Capita Federal Tax Burden
Date: 1980
Source: Office of Management and Budget and the Tax Foundation Incorporated
Description: Estimated per capita federal tax burden and tax collected.
United States average: $2,212
State median: $2,138
Total collections: $500.9 billion

PER CAPITA FEDERAL TAX BURDEN

Rank	State	Per capita federal tax	Total tax collected (in billions)
1	Alaska	$3,628	$1.5
2	Connecticut	2,821	8.8
3	Illinois	2,703	30.9
4	New Jersey	2,680	19.7
5	Maryland	2,531	10.7
6	Michigan	2,527	23.4
7	Delaware	2,525	1.5
8	California	2,457	58.2
9	Wyoming	2,447	1.2
10	Nevada	2,445	2.0
11	New York	2,397	42.1
12	Washington	2,365	9.8
13	Ohio	2,338	25.2
14	Massachusetts	2,288	13.1
15	Minnesota	2,285	9.3
16	Hawaii	2,284	2.2
17	Iowa	2,270	6.6
18	Kansas	2,268	5.4
19	Oregon	2,264	6.0
20	Indiana	2,235	12.3
21	Pennsylvania	2,225	26.4
22	Colorado	2,202	6.4
23	Nebraska	2,170	3.4
24	Virginia	2,164	11.6
25	Texas	2,155	30.7
26	New Hampshire	2,122	2.0
27	Wisconsin	2,119	10.0
28	Rhode Island	2,116	2.0
29	Missouri	2,099	10.3
30	Montana	2,038	1.6
31	North Dakota	1,996	1.3
32	Florida	1,970	19.2
33	Oklahoma	1,937	5.9
34	Louisiana	1,835	7.7
35	Arizona	1,825	5.0
36	West Virginia	1,773	3.5

Rank	State	Per capita federal tax	Total tax collected (in billions)
37	Tennessee	$1,768	$8.1
38	Idaho	1,751	1.7
38	Kentucky	1,751	6.4
40	South Dakota	1,742	1.2
41	Georgia	1,733	9.5
42	North Carolina	1,714	10.1
43	New Mexico	1,698	2.2
44	Alabama	1,674	6.5
45	Vermont	1,665	0.9
46	Maine	1,648	1.9
47	Utah	1,646	2.4
48	South Carolina	1,606	5.0
49	Arkansas	1,512	3.5
50	Mississippi	1,371	3.5

141. Federal Aid to State and Local Governments

The figures in this table, reported on a per capita basis, cover funds transferred by the federal government for spending by the state government and all local governments in each state. A total of about $94 billion was transferred during the federal fiscal year ending Sept. 30, 1981. Most of these funds were targeted for specific grant-in-aid programs in such areas as education (including job training), health (especially Medicaid), highways, public assistance (including direct grants to individual state residents), housing and environmental protection. General revenue-sharing funds, with fewer strings attached, are also included here (see Table 142).

Wyoming and especially Alaska are the unusual states in this table. Federal efforts to develop highways and other "infrastructure" facilities in these thinly settled states lead to very high levels of transfers per capita. For the other 48 states a ratio of about 2 to 1 is found between the highest and lowest levels of transfers. Geographical patterns are mixed, with neighboring states like Vermont and New Hampshire or New Mexico and Arizona at opposite ends of the table. More detailed information on federal aid to schools can be found in the section on education.

Table: Federal Aid Per Capita
Date: 1981
Source: Department of the Treasury
Description: Federal aid per capita to state and local governments.
United States average: $432
State median: $406

FEDERAL AID PER CAPITA

Rank	State	Per capita federal aid
1	Alaska	$1,087
2	Wyoming	652
3	New York	589
4	Montana	566
5	Vermont	541
6	New Mexico	539
7	Delaware	524
8	South Dakota	518
9	Rhode Island	506
10	Massachusetts	500
11	Wisconsin	485
12	North Dakota	483
13	West Virginia	482
14	Maine	473
15	Hawaii	452
16	Michigan	446
17	Maryland	443
17	Oregon	443
19	Mississippi	434
20	Minnesota	433
21	Washington	420
22	Nevada	415
23	California	414
23	Tennessee	414
25	Pennsylvania	412
26	Illinois	402
27	Louisiana	401
28	Kentucky	391
28	Utah	391
30	New Jersey	390
31	Georgia	389
32	Arkansas	386
33	Alabama	381
34	Connecticut	377
34	Idaho	377
36	Ohio	346
37	Colorado	345
38	Virginia	343
39	Missouri	337
39	Oklahoma	337
41	Iowa	331
42	Nebraska	328
43	New Hampshire	327
44	Kansas	325
45	North Carolina	321
46	South Carolina	319
47	Indiana	316
48	Arizona	309
49	Florida	282
50	Texas	281

142. Revenue Sharing

State and local governments are fond of general revenue-sharing assistance because there are so few federal restrictions on how these funds may be spent. At present, however, general revenue sharing accounts for only about 6% of all transfers from Washington to the state and local governments. The principle that the level of government where tax funds are raised should be the level at which the decisions on how to spend it are made remains largely intact. Over 80% of these funds went directly to county, city and town governments in 1981. The funds are distributed according to a formula that considers the population, the average income level and the present level of taxation in each unit of government. Larger units with lower average income levels and citizens who are already up to their ears in taxes get the largest payments. New York City, which fits this description perfectly, receives the largest individual revenue-sharing grants. The aim is to give assistance to the "most deserving" units of government, but Congress tinkers with the formula from time to time in order to remove inequities that become apparent and to adjust to shifting patterns of political power (such as the migration of many voters to the West and to the suburbs in the past decade). Data in this table are for fiscal year 1981 for all states except Vermont, Alabama and Texas (fiscal year 1980).

Alaska and New York receive exceptionally high levels of support. The ratio between the extreme high and low per capita levels for the other states is about 2 to 1, with Florida and Texas at the bottom of the heap. Since the population factor in the formula is accounted for in this table (per capita rates), the position of these two states may be ascribed to their relatively abundant wealth and low levels of present tax effort. The regional pattern is so well mixed that it can only be explained as the result of a very complex process of bargaining among the members of Congress who agreed on the allocation formula.

Table: Federal Revenue Sharing
Date: 1981
Source: Department of Commerce
Description: Per capita federal revenue sharing by local and state governments.
United States average: $24.93
State median: $24.56

Rank	State	Per capita federal revenue sharing
7	Maine	$29.15
8	Wisconsin	28.20
9	Hawaii	27.81
10	Minnesota	27.71
11	Louisiana	27.46
12	Montana	27.11
13	California	27.09
14	South Dakota	26.86
15	West Virginia	26.60
16	Maryland	26.36
17	Michigan	26.21
18	Rhode Island	26.14
19	Kentucky	25.57
20	New Mexico	25.46
21	Arkansas	25.05
22	Utah	24.99
23	Iowa	24.88
24	Wyoming	24.73
25	North Dakota	24.58
26	Illinois	24.55
27	Oregon	24.50
28	North Carolina	24.38
29	Arizona	24.20
30	Nebraska	23.57
31	Tennessee	23.46
32	Pennsylvania	23.41
33	Georgia	23.14
34	New Jersey	23.09
35	Connecticut	23.03
36	Idaho	22.82
37	South Carolina	22.46
38	Colorado	22.26
39	Virginia	22.18
40	Ohio	21.57
41	Kansas	21.37
42	New Hampshire	21.02
43	Oklahoma	20.98
44	Alabama	20.48
45	Indiana	20.25
46	Washington	19.96
47	Missouri	18.72
48	Nevada	18.69
49	Florida	17.65
50	Texas	17.50

FEDERAL REVENUE SHARING

Rank	State	Per capita federal revenue sharing
1	Alaska	$44.80
2	New York	38.50
3	Vermont	33.46
4	Massachusetts	31.71
5	Mississippi	31.37
6	Delaware	29.23

143. Federal Taxes per Dollar of Federal Aid

The figures in this table capture the essence of ongoing controversies in Washington. They were computed by the Tax Foundation for fiscal year 1980. The estimated federal tax contributions presented in the first table above (Table 140) were used to calculate the percentage of total federal tax revenue from each state, and therefore presumably the percentage contribution of each state to the pool of federal funds that was ultimately transferred back to the states and local governments in federal aid. These figures were then compared with state percentages of actual federal grants to states and localities in fiscal year 1980 (similar data for the following year were reported in the second table above). If the percentages from the two series are the same for a given state it means that the state actually received one dollar in aid for every tax dollar paid into the pool of transferred funds. But this is never quite the case. The ratio displayed below shows the amount paid into the pool by each state for every dollar actually received from the pool; for the nation as a whole the average is $1 for each $1 by definition.

The top 23 states gave more than they received from the federal government—Texas, Connecticut and Indiana above all. Revenue was in effect transferred from these states to the 27 states that received more than they gave. Mississippi, Alaska, South Dakota and Vermont each received about twice as much as they paid.

Congressional representatives never tire of arguing over numbers like these. Two points should be kept in mind in judging these discussions. First, there are many different ways to calculate such figures. The assumptions used in the calculation help to determine the outcome. Note, for example, that direct federal spending in the states (say for defense) is not considered in this particular calculation. Second, any such comparison is artificial in the sense that it considers only a particular moment in time. The contributions of certain states in the past, or their potential contributions in the future may be sufficient to justify large short-term imbalances. This is a matter of political judgment in a democratic nation.

Table: Federal Tax Burden
Date: 1980
Source: Tax Foundation Incorporated, Department of the Treasury and Office of Management and Budget
Description: Estimated federal tax burden for grants.
United States average: $1.00
State median: $0.94

FEDERAL TAX BURDEN

Rank	State	Amount
1	Texas	$1.40
2	Connecticut	1.35
3	Indiana	1.34
4	Ohio	1.27
5	Florida	1.23
6	New Jersey	1.21
7	California	1.20

Rank	State	Amount
7	Colorado	$1.20
7	Kansas	1.20
10	Illinois	1.18
11	Virginia	1.14
12	Arizona	1.13
12	Iowa	1.13
14	Wyoming	1.11
15	Nebraska	1.10
15	Nevada	1.10
15	Washington	1.10
18	Missouri	1.09
19	Oklahoma	1.05
20	Michigan	1.03
20	New Hampshire	1.03
22	Oregon	1.02
22	Pennsylvania	1.02
24	Maryland	.98
25	Minnesota	.96
26	Delaware	.93
27	North Carolina	.92
28	Louisiana	.91
29	Tennessee	.90
30	Wisconsin	.89
31	Hawaii	.84
32	South Carolina	.82
33	Massachusetts	.80
34	Idaho	.79
34	Utah	.79
36	Kentucky	.78
37	New York	.76
37	Rhode Island	.76
39	New Mexico	.74
40	Alabama	.73
41	Georgia	.72
42	Arkansas	.67
42	North Dakota	.67
44	Maine	.63
44	West Virginia	.63
46	Montana	.60
47	Mississippi	.53
48	Alaska	.52
49	South Dakota	.48
50	Vermont	.45

144. State Tax Revenue

The 50 states collected $162.7 billion in taxes from all sources during fiscal year 1982. Sales taxes (48%) and personal income taxes (28%) were the major components. Sales taxes in general include special excise taxes on items such as gasoline, alcohol and tobacco. Smaller percentages of the national total tax revenue for the states were produced by corporate income taxes (9%), license taxes (6%), severance taxes (5%) and miscellaneous taxes on estates, property, and certain kinds of transactions.

The severance taxes—charges imposed on the production of nonrenewable resources, such as oil, coal, minerals and some agricultural and forest products intended for consumption in other states—account for a small portion of overall revenue but a large portion of the disagreements among state governments about forms of taxation. States with high severance-tax income are able to enjoy levels of state services that are high in relation to the tax burden imposed on resident individuals and most resident businesses. Consumers in other states who pay tax-inflated rates for raw materials are in effect footing the bill for government services in the resource-rich states. Ten states may be singled out as the chief beneficiaries of this process. Listed in the order of the percentage of total state revenue that comes from severance taxes, they are: Alaska (68%), Wyoming (56%), Montana (36%), North Dakota (36%), Louisiana (32%), Oklahoma (29%), Texas (27%), Washington (22%), Kentucky (19%) and Florida (11%).

Severance taxes also account for several of the extreme values found in this table. Oil and gas severance taxes, combined with corporate income taxes paid largely by the oil and gas companies, account for over 95% of all taxes collected in the state of Alaska. The sharp revenue increase reported for Wyoming is due to a jump in coal and mineral severance taxes. Leaving aside Alaska and Wyoming, there is a ratio of about 3 to 1 between the states with the highest and the lowest per capita tax revenues. New Hampshire, where state services are held to a minimum and a volunteer spirit prevails in state government, manages to conduct its business with a level of revenue far below that of any other state in the nation. A gasoline tax increase from 11 to 14 cents per gallon in New Hampshire during 1981 did, however, contribute to one of the largest gains in state tax revenue from fiscal 1981 to fiscal 1982. Tax revenues increased in all states except Hawaii and Oregon during fiscal 1982.

Figures in the third column of this table show the state share of all tax revenues raised by the state plus its local governments during fiscal 1981. (Data for 1982 are not yet available.) High-ranking states generally take larger shares of this total. This means that the combined state and local tax revenues per capita are somewhat more closely grouped than the figures for state tax revenue. Many states with low rankings in this table simply forgo tax collections in favor of their local governments. A good estimate of combined per capita revenues for state and local governments in 1982 can be calculated by dividing the figure in column one by the figure in column three. For New York, this calculation is $879÷.49 = $1,794 in combined taxes per capita. For Oklahoma, which ranks just ahead of New York in the table but which does not have such heavy local taxation, the result is $1,229 in combined taxes. Similar calculations show that the combined tax rate in New Hampshire, where local

government is strong financially, turns out to be higher than that of several other states, including Kentucky (rank 24).

Table: Per Capita State Taxes
Date: 1982
Source: Department of Commerce and Census Bureau
Description: Per capita state taxes and percent of change from 1981 to 1982.
United States average: $720
State median: $676
Average percent of change from 1981 to 1982: 8.6%
Average state share of state and local taxes 1980–81: 61.2%

PER CAPITA STATE TAXES

Rank	State	Per capita state tax	Percent of change 1981–1982	State share (%) of combined state and local tax revenues in 1981
1	Alaska	$6,316	10	90
2	Wyoming	1,622	63	59
3	Hawaii	1,105	−2	81
4	Delaware	1,001	8	82
5	New Mexico	942	4	82
6	Nevada	932	45	58
6	Minnesota	932	13	71
8	California	922	6	69
9	Oklahoma	897	22	73
10	New York	879	11	49
11	Washington	854	13	73
12	Massachusetts	837	11	56
13	Wisconsin	836	8	67
14	North Dakota	816	18	70
15	Maryland	757	8	60
15	New Jersey	757	11	56
17	Connecticut	753	13	56
17	West Virginia	753	16	78
19	Louisiana	744	12	68
20	Rhode Island	713	11	59
21	Pennsylvania	690	8	62
22	Iowa	685	9	61
23	Arizona	683	4	65
24	Kentucky	681	9	79
24	Michigan	681	2	58
26	Montana	672	13	54
27	Utah	651	12	64
28	Illinois	650	2	55
28	Maine	650	8	63
28	Vermont	650	13	58
31	North Carolina	644	11	72
32	Texas	640	11	60
33	South Carolina	628	7	75
34	Idaho	613	8	70
35	Kansas	610	4	59
36	Virginia	605	7	60
37	Georgia	601	9	65

Rank	State	Per capita state tax	Percent of change 1981–1982	State share (%) of combined state and local tax revenues in 1981
38	Oregon	$590	−4	55
39	Colorado	585	17	49
40	Mississippi	580	5	78
41	Florida	570	4	64
42	Alabama	564	2	75
43	Indiana	558	9	62
44	Arkansas	553	6	77
45	Nebraska	548	7	53
46	Ohio	539	11	56
47	South Dakota	476	10	51
48	Missouri	470	8	55
49	Tennessee	468	10	58
50	New Hampshire	353	21	37

145. Sales Tax as a Share of State Tax Revenue

The distribution of revenues from different types of taxes shows remarkable variation from one state to another. No two states accumulate their funds in quite the same way. This table and the three succeeding tables show the percentages (not the revenues) of state tax revenues that come from four major sources. Rates of a few special taxes are presented in separate tables following.

This first table indicates the shares of revenue from general state sales taxes, the leading source. Revenues from selective taxes on gasoline, alcohol, tobacco, racetrack receipts, public utility bills and a variety of other items are not included here. These selective taxes account for 17.5% of all state tax revenues, as compared to the 30.9% share for general sales taxes. Information on revenue from gasoline taxes is included in the table on motor vehicle taxes below.

Five states have no general sales tax: Alaska, Delaware, Montana, New Hampshire and Oregon. Sales tax accounts for between 14% and 54% of the revenue in the other 45 states. Prescription drugs are exempt from the general sales tax in most states. The four exceptions are Georgia, Hawaii, Illinois and New Mexico. Food products are exempt from the general sales tax in 25 states. These states are indicated in the table on sales-tax rates below.

Sales tax is not progressive; that is, equal shares are paid by all consumers regardless of their income level. States near the top of the list, therefore, impose relatively heavy burdens on residents with lower incomes. Such states tend to be located in the West (Oregon is the main exception, but also Alaska, Montana and Oklahoma, with their high severance taxes) and parts of the South. Connecticut is the major exception to a pattern of lower sales tax shares in states on the East Coast and in the upper Midwest.

Table: General State Sales Tax
Date: 1982
Source: Department of Commerce
Description: Percentage of general sale tax as a share of state tax revenue.
United States average: 30.9%
State median: 30.6%

GENERAL STATE SALES TAX

Rank	State	Percent
1	South Dakota	54.3
2	Hawaii	54.1
3	Washington	53.6
4	West Virginia	53.2
5	Mississippi	52.5
6	Tennessee	52.1
7	Nevada	50.4
8	Florida	50.1
9	Indiana	49.3
10	New Mexico	43.5
11	Arizona	43.2
12	Connecticut	42.9
13	Utah	40.8
14	Texas	38.3
15	Colorado	36.3
15	Missouri	36.3
17	California	35.4
18	Maine	34.1
19	Nebraska	33.5
20	Arkansas	33.2
20	Georgia	33.2
22	South Carolina	33.0
23	Kansas	32.6
24	Illinois	31.4
25	Ohio	31.3
26	Wyoming	29.9
27	Louisiana	29.6
27	Rhode Island	29.6
29	Michigan	29.2
30	Alabama	28.7
31	North Dakota	27.6
32	Kentucky	27.4
33	Pennsylvania	27.2
34	Iowa	26.2
35	Idaho	25.3
36	Maryland	25.0
37	New Jersey	24.7
38	Wisconsin	24.4
39	Minnesota	23.0
40	New York	20.7
40	Virginia	20.7
42	North Carolina	20.6
43	Massachusetts	19.1
44	Oklahoma	17.8
45	Vermont	14.6
46	Alaska	0

Rank	State	Percent
46	Delaware	0
46	Montana	0
46	New Hampshire	0
46	Oregon	0

146. Individual Income Tax as a Share of State Tax Revenue

Taxes on personal income make up a share of state tax revenues only slightly smaller than the share from general sales taxes. There were 44 states with taxes on individual income in fiscal year 1982. The six exceptions are Florida, Nevada, South Dakota, Texas, Washington and Wyoming. In eight states the share of revenue from the income tax was less than 12%: Mississippi, Louisiana, North Dakota, Connecticut, New Hampshire, Tennessee, New Mexico and Alaska. It is interesting to note that seven of these 14 states at the bottom of the table were cited above as states with high revenue shares from severance taxes. The other three states with high severance-tax revenues (Montana, Kentucky and Oklahoma) also have relatively low positions in this table (25, 30 and 32 respectively). Severance taxes are apparently used as a substitute for personal income taxes in these fortunate states.

In Oregon and New York the personal income tax is the largest single source of state revenue. Generally speaking, states with high revenue from income taxes have low revenues from sales taxes. They tend to be near the bottom of the previous table. Although tax *rates* in these states are not necessarily higher for individuals with larger incomes, the tax structures tend to be more progressive than those in states which rely heavily on sales taxes. This is because low-income individuals generally have to spend a larger fraction of their earnings for standard items like food, clothing and housing. This means that a larger part of their earnings will eventually be paid in taxes when the sales tax is predominant.

Table: State Individual Income Tax
Date: 1982
Source: Department of Commerce
Description: Percentage of individual income tax as a share of state tax revenue.
United States average: 28.1%
State median: 26.8%

STATE INDIVIDUAL INCOME TAX

Rank	State	Percent
1	Oregon	62.4
2	New York	52.0
3	Massachusetts	48.3
4	Delaware	48.1
5	Virginia	44.7
6	Wisconsin	42.7
7	Maryland	42.4
8	Minnesota	40.8
9	North Carolina	38.2
10	Idaho	38.0
11	Iowa	36.1
12	Georgia	36.0
13	Utah	34.8
14	California	34.2
15	Vermont	33.9
16	Michigan	33.7
17	Missouri	32.9
18	South Carolina	32.8
19	Colorado	32.4
20	Kansas	31.9
20	Rhode Island	31.9
22	Illinois	29.9
23	Maine	28.7
24	Arkansas	28.0
25	Montana	27.2
26	Hawaii	26.5
27	Nebraska	26.3
28	Indiana	24.4
29	Pennsylvania	24.3
30	Kentucky	24.1
31	Arizona	23.7
32	Oklahoma	23.6
33	New Jersey	23.4
34	Alabama	21.9
35	Ohio	21.4
36	West Virginia	20.8
37	Mississippi	11.5
38	Louisiana	7.0
39	North Dakota	6.6
40	Connecticut	5.8
41	New Hampshire	4.6
42	Tennessee	2.1
43	New Mexico	1.3
44	Alaska	.1
45	Florida	0
45	Nevada	0
45	South Dakota	0
45	Texas	0
45	Washington	0
45	Wyoming	0

147. Motor Vehicle Taxes as a Share of State Tax Revenue

The data in this table combine revenues from two distinct types of taxes: the fees for registration of motor vehicles (including both title registration and annual vehicle registration fees) and selective sales tax on motor vehicle fuel (mainly gasoline). These forms of taxation account for an average of 9.8% of state tax revenues: 3.4% from registrations and 6.4% from fuel taxes. The state median value (11.2%) is significantly higher than the national average, indicating that motor vehicle tax revenues tend to be low in states with large populations like California (rank 47), New York (48) and Texas (43).

Revenue from sale of drivers' licenses are not included here, except for the states of Indiana, Rhode Island and West Virginia. This is not a major revenue source for the states. For the nation as a whole, drivers' license fees raise only 8.7% of the amount that is collected in vehicle registration fees. The only states in which drivers' licenses are especially expensive in relation to vehicle registrations are Alabama and Massachusetts, where they raise about 25% of the amounts realized from vehicle registrations. Other states with above average drivers' license fees (producing 15% to 17% of the amount from vehicle registrations) are Connecticut, Pennsylvania, Washington, Georgia, Kentucky, Louisiana, Mississippi and North Carolina.

Returning to the data presented below, New Hampshire is clearly the leader in using motor vehicle taxes as a source of state revenue. These taxes are really users' fees, paid by persons (and enterprises that operate motor vehicles) only to the extent that they engage in a certain activity. Other states in the top 10 include New Hampshire's neighbor Vermont and a set of states scattered across the center of the country from Tennessee to Montana. Motor vehicle taxes are negligible in Alaska and Hawaii.

Table: State Motor Vehicle Use Taxes
Date: 1982
Source: Census bureau
Description: Percentage of motor vehicle fuel and registration license taxes as a share of state tax revenue.
United States average: 9.8%
State median: 11.2%

STATE MOTOR VEHICLE USE TAXES

Rank	State	Percent
1	New Hampshire	27.3
2	South Dakota	21.3
3	Nebraska	19.7
4	Tennessee	18.1
5	Kansas	18.0
6	Idaho	16.6
7	Iowa	16.3

Rank	State	Percent
8	Vermont	16.0
9	Arkansas	15.7
10	Ohio	14.1
11	Montana	13.7
12	North Carolina	13.5
13	Virginia	13.3
14	Missouri	13.2
15	South Carolina	13.0
16	Indiana	12.9
17	Oregon	12.6
18	Alabama	12.3
19	Florida	12.2
19	Georgia	12.2
21	North Dakota	11.9
22	Arizona	11.4
22	Colorado	11.4
24	Oklahoma	11.3
24	Pennsylvania	11.3
26	Nevada	11.2
27	Maine	11.1
27	Utah	11.1
29	Minnesota	11.0
30	Michigan	10.4
31	New Mexico	10.3
31	West Virginia	10.3
31	Wisconsin	10.3
34	Kentucky	10.2
34	Washington	10.2
36	Wyoming	10.0
37	Mississippi	9.9
38	Delaware	9.8
38	Rhode Island	9.8
40	Connecticut	9.7
40	New Jersey	9.7
42	Illinois	9.4
43	Texas	9.0
44	Maryland	8.6
45	Louisiana	8.5
46	Massachusetts	7.6
47	California	6.4
48	New York	5.0
49	Hawaii	3.9
50	Alaska	1.7

148. Corporate Income Tax as a Share of State Tax Revenue

Alaska and New Hampshire stand out as the leaders in raising revenue from corporations that operate within their boundaries. California and a number of states in the East and the Midwest are the other major users of this form of taxation. The states of Nevada, Texas, Wyoming and Washington have no corporate income taxes as such. They do, however, derive income from business enterprises through severance taxes or, in the case of Nevada, through taxes on gambling and amusements. Lower shares in this table are generally found in the Sunbelt states, an indicator of the incentives that have helped to bring about the great business migration of the past decade.

Table: State Corporate Income Tax
Date: 1982
Source: Department of Commerce
Description: Percentage of corporate income tax as a share of state tax revenue.
United States average: 8.6%
State median: 7.2%

STATE CORPORATE INCOME TAX

Rank	State	Percent
1	Alaska	27.7
2	New Hampshire	24.5
3	Michigan	15.1
4	Connecticut	14.9
5	New Jersey	13.0
6	Massachusetts	12.5
7	California	12.1
8	Pennsylvania	10.6
9	Illinois	9.6
9	Tennessee	9.6
11	Ohio	9.4
12	Louisiana	9.3
13	New York	8.7
14	Minnesota	8.6
15	Kansas	8.5
16	Montana	8.4
17	Georgia	8.2
17	Wisconsin	8.2
19	Oregon	8.0
20	Idaho	7.9
21	Rhode Island	7.8
22	Vermont	7.5
23	Iowa	7.4
24	Arkansas	7.3
24	North Carolina	7.3
26	North Dakota	7.1
27	Florida	6.9
28	Kentucky	6.7
28	South Carolina	6.7
30	Arizona	6.2
31	Delaware	6.1
32	Alabama	5.6
32	Nebraska	5.6
34	Virginia	5.5
35	Colorado	5.4
36	Missouri	5.3
37	Oklahoma	5.1
38	Maine	4.9
38	Mississippi	4.9
38	New Mexico	4.9
41	Maryland	4.7
42	Utah	4.3
43	Hawaii	4.1
43	Indiana	4.1

Rank	State	Percent
45	West Virginia	2.3
46	South Dakota	0.3
47	Nevada	0
47	Texas	0
47	Washington	0
47	Wyoming	0

149. General State Sales Tax Rates

Among the 45 states with general sales taxes, the effective rates range from 2% in Oklahoma to 7.5% in Connecticut. The 25 states in which the general sales tax does not apply to food products are noted with an asterisk. In general, it seems that this exemption is important in explaining how certain states come to have high general sales tax rates. Since food purchases make up roughly one-quarter of consumer spending on the average, the effective sales tax rates in the indicated states are about 25% (or more than 1 percentage point) lower than the stated figure. Data presented here do not include the local sales taxes found in many states. There are only three states among those with rates above 4% that do not exempt food products from taxation: Washington, Mississippi and Tennessee.

Table: General State Sales Tax Rates
Date: 1982
Source: Department of Commerce
Description: General sales tax rates as a percentage of state tax revenue.
State median: 4.0%

GENERAL STATE SALES TAX RATES

Rank	State	General sales tax rate (%)
1	Connecticut*	7.5
2	Pennsylvania*	6.0
2	Rhode Island*	6.0
4	Nevada*	5.75
5	Washington	5.4
6	Florida*	5.0
6	Kentucky*	5.0
6	Maine*	5.0
6	Maryland*	5.0
6	Massachusetts*	5.0
6	Minnesota*	5.0
6	Mississippi	5.0
6	New Jersey*	5.0
6	Ohio*	5.0
6	West Virginia*	5.0
6	Wisconsin*	5.0
17	California*	4.75

Rank	State	General sales tax rate (%)
18	Tennessee	4.5
19	Alabama	4.0
19	Arizona*	4.0
19	Hawaii	4.0
19	Illinois	4.0
19	Indiana*	4.0
19	Michigan*	4.0
19	New York*	4.0
19	South Carolina	4.0
19	South Dakota	4.0
19	Texas*	4.0
19	Utah	4.0
19	Vermont*	4.0
31	Nebraska	3.5
31	New Mexico	3.5
33	Missouri	3.13
34	Arkansas	3.0
34	Colorado*	3.0
34	Georgia	3.0
34	Idaho	3.0
34	Iowa*	3.0
34	Kansas	3.0
34	Louisiana*	3.0
34	North Carolina	3.0
34	North Dakota*	3.0
34	Virginia	3.0
34	Wyoming	3.0
45	Oklahoma	.2
46	Alaska	0
46	Delaware	0
46	Montana	0
46	New Hampshire	0
46	Oregon	0

150. Gasoline Tax Rates

New Hampshire and Nebraska lead the nation in taxation of motor vehicle fuels. These rates account for their high rankings in Table 147 dealing with percentage of state tax revenue from motor vehicle taxes. There is generally a close relationship between the ranking in that table and the ranking by tax rate presented here. The oil-producing state of Texas has a tax rate two percentage points below that of any other state. In California, where automobile use is, in effect, the only significant form of mass transportation, legislators have not seen fit to displease their hard-driving constituents by imposing high gasoline taxes.

Table: Gasoline Tax Rates
Date: 1982
Source: Department of Commerce
Description: Gasoline tax rates in cents per gallon.
State median: 10 cents per gallon

GASOLINE TAX RATES

Rank	State	Cents per gallon
1	New Hampshire	14
2	Nebraska	13.7
3	Iowa	13
3	South Carolina	13
3	South Dakota	13
3	Minnesota	13
3	Wisconsin	13
8	Idaho	12.5
9	North Carolina	12
9	Washington	12
11	Ohio	11.7
12	Indiana	11.1
13	Alabama	11
13	Connecticut	11
13	Delaware	11
13	Maryland	11
13	Michigan	11
13	Pennsylvania	11
13	Utah	11
13	Vermont	11
13	Virginia	11
22	West Virginia	10.5
23	Massachusetts	10.4
24	Nevada	10.25
25	Arizona	10
25	New Mexico	10
25	Rhode Island	10
28	Kentucky	9.8
29	Arkansas	9.5
30	Colorado	9
30	Maine	9
30	Mississippi	9
30	Montana	9
30	Tennessee	9
35	Oklahoma	8.58
36	Hawaii	8.5
37	Alaska	8
37	Florida	8
37	Kansas	8
37	Louisiana	8
37	New Jersey	8
37	New York	8
37	North Dakota	8
37	Oregon	8
37	Wyoming	8
46	Georgia	7.5
46	Illinois	7.5
48	California	7
48	Missouri	7
50	Texas	5

151. Cigarette Tax Rates

State tax per package of cigarettes shows wide variation across the country. The three major cigarette producing states, which keep taxes low to encourage consumption, form a special group at the bottom of the table. Rates in other states vary between seven and 25 cents per pack. The states at the top of the table have such high tax rates that consumers who cut back on smoking (or cross state lines to buy smokes) in order to save money may actually be producing less tax revenue for the state than would be produced with lower rates. But causing a reduction in smoking (not the crossing of state lines) may in fact be the real purpose of such high rates.

Table: Cigarette Taxes
Date: 1982
Source: Department of Commerce
Description: Cigarette tax rates in cents per pack (20 cigarettes).
State median: 13 cents per pack

CIGARETTE TAXES

Rank	State	Cents per pack
1	Wisconsin	25
2	New Jersey	24
3	Rhode Island	23
3	Washington	23
5	Connecticut	21
5	Florida	21
5	Massachusetts	21
5	Michigan	21
9	Oregon	19
10	Texas	18.5
11	Iowa	18
11	Minnesota	18
11	Nebraska	18
11	Oklahoma	18
11	Pennsylvania	18
16	Arkansas	17.75
17	West Virginia	17
18	Alabama	16
18	Maine	16
20	New York	15
20	South Dakota	15
22	Delaware	14
22	Ohio	14
24	Arizona	13
24	Maryland	13
24	Missouri	13
24	Tennessee	13
28	Georgia	12
28	Illinois	12
28	Montana	12
28	New Hampshire	12
28	New Mexico	12
28	North Dakota	12
28	Utah	12
28	Vermont	12
36	Kansas	11
36	Louisiana	11
36	Mississippi	11
39	Indiana	10.5

Rank	State	Cents per pack
40	California	10
40	Colorado	10
40	Nevada	10
43	Idaho	9.1
44	Alaska	8
44	Wyoming	8
46	South Carolina	7
47	Kentucky	3
48	Virginia	2.5
49	North Carolina	2
No rank	Hawaii	40% of wholesale price

152. State Lotteries

There were 14 state lotteries in operation during the year 1980. The largest was in Michigan, where $237 million in prize money was returned to the players and $195 million remained as state revenue after prize money had been returned and administrative costs accounted for. Nationwide, lottery proceeds amounted to about $1 billion, or less than 1% of the amount collected in taxes by the states. Even in Michigan the profit to the state ($195 million) was very small in comparison to 1980 tax revenues of nearly $6 billion. The larger lotteries generally clear over 40% of total revenue as net profit. The smaller lotteries, with relatively higher administrative expenses, tend to clear smaller shares of the take as profit.

Table: State Lotteries
Date: 1980
Source: Council of State Governments
Description: Gross revenues and proceeds available for other purposes from state lotteries, by state, for 14 states.

STATE LOTTERIES

Rank	State	Gross revenue (millions)	Prizes (millions)	Net revenue (millions)	Net revenue as a percentage of gross
1	Michigan	$444	$237	$195	44
2	Pennsylvania	357	190	151	42
3	Maryland	354	174	167	47
4	New Jersey	320	174	141	44
5	New York	166	73	80	48
6	Massachusetts	152	90	49	32
7	Connecticut	123	67	46	38
8	Ohio	118	61	45	38
9	Illinois	90	46	35	39
10	Rhode Island	29	15	12	41
11	Delaware	15	8	6	37
12	New Hampshire	11	6	4	11
13	Maine	5	3	3	16
14	Vermont	3	1	1	31

HEALTH

Health and health care have improved greatly in this country during the 20th century. The annual death rate has been cut in half since 1900 and diseases such as typhoid, diphtheria and tuberculosis, which once killed thousands of persons every year, have been all but eradicated. Our health care and hospital system is one of the most extensive and technically advanced in the world. High-quality health care is available to everyone potentially; in actuality, there is still a good deal of variation in the amount and quality of care received by individuals.

Despite this tangible progress, the health care system has become one of the most criticized institutions in American life. Costs have been increasing rapidly. It is not at all uncommon for people to go into debt or lose their life savings in the course of obtaining treatment for emergency conditions or chronic illnesses. As the population grows older the severity of the problem of health care cost can only increase. Cost problems have been acute for middle-class Americans who are not wealthy enough to absorb recent increases easily, but not poor enough to qualify for public medical assistance. These difficulties have been aggravated as many people in this group have lost health benefits along with jobs in the Great Recession. Criticism has also focused on the deteriorating quality of hospital care and the high-speed, impersonal practices of increasingly specialized physicians. The medical care system may be keeping us healthy, but we seem to be less satisfied with the way that this is done.

The overview of health conditions in this section begins, somewhat ironically, with a review of the major causes of death among Americans. These data provide indications of the seriousness of various types of illness and disease in the population, highlighting the central importance of a few major causes of death among older Americans. A table on the incidence of gonorrhea, the most widespread communicable disease in the United States save for the common cold, provides a transition to a set of tables on the hospital system and levels of life insurance protection.

153. Death Rate

The average life expectancy of a newborn baby increased from 54.1 years in 1920 to 73.3 years in 1978. On the average, the babies of 1978 will be granted 19.2 more years of life than the babies of 1920. This change testifies to the remarkable improvement in general conditions of health during this century.

There is now a greater divergence than ever before between the life expectancies of men and women. From a difference of one year in 1920 (53.6 years for males, 54.6 years for females), the gap increased to almost eight years in 1978 (69.5 years for males, 77.2 years for females). Life expectancy differences between whites and members of other races remain significant, but there has been some convergence in recent decades. In 1920 the figures were 54.9 years for whites and 45.3 years for blacks and others. The corresponding figures in 1978 were 74.0 years and 69.2 years.

The data for the states in this table represent overall (or "crude") death rates: the number of deaths per 1,000 persons in the population. These data are not as refined as the life expectancy measures, which are derived by examining death rates at specific ages. Since the highest death rates are found among older persons and infants, the states with greater numbers of elderly people in the population or relatively high numbers of births combined with high infant mortality have higher death rates. There is a strong relationship between the death rate and the average age of a state population. This table is useful as a baseline for evaluating the rates of death attributed to specific causes that appear in the tables that follow. When rankings in these tables vary significantly from the rankings given in the first table, the relatively high or low incidence of specific threats to health in a given state is indicated.

For the nation as a whole there were about 1.9 million deaths in 1978, or about nine deaths for every 1,000 persons in the population. Since death rates change very slowly over time, the state-specific rates for 1978 are still extremely close to the rates prevailing at present. This is also true for the rates of death from specific causes presented further on.

The highest crude death rates are found in Florida, with its large population of retired persons, and in a number of states where there has been no net inflow of younger migrants in recent years. The high rate for Mississippi is also related to a relatively high incidence of infant mortality. Low crude death rates are observed in a number of states in the West, where high rates of birth and in-migration have produced populations in which younger people are heavily represented.

Table: Death Rate
Date: 1978
Source: National Center for Health Statistics
Description: Rate of deaths per 1,000 population.
United States average: 8.8 per 1,000 population
State median: 8.7 per 1,000 population

DEATH RATE

Rank	State	Death rate per 1,000 population
1	Florida	11.0
2	West Virginia	10.6
3	Missouri	10.2
3	Pennsylvania	10.2
5	Arkansas	10.1
6	Oklahoma	9.8
7	Mississippi	9.7
8	Kentucky	9.6
9	Rhode Island	9.5
10	Iowa	9.4
10	New York	9.4
10	South Dakota	9.4
13	Alabama	9.3
13	Maine	9.3
15	Illinois	9.2
15	Kansas	9.2
15	Nebraska	9.2
18	Massachusetts	9.1
18	Vermont	9.1
20	New Jersey	9.0
20	Ohio	9.0
22	Louisiana	8.9
22	Tennessee	8.9
24	Indiana	8.8
25	Wisconsin	8.6
26	Delaware	8.5
26	Georgia	8.5
26	New Hampshire	8.5
26	North Carolina	8.5
26	Oregon	8.5

Rank	State	Death rate per 1,000 population
31	Connecticut	8.4
31	North Dakota	8.4
33	Minnesota	8.3
33	Montana	8.3
33	South Carolina	8.3
36	Michigan	8.2
37	Arizona	8.1
38	Maryland	8.0
38	Texas	8.0
38	Washington	8.0
41	California	7.9
41	Virginia	7.9
43	Nevada	7.6
44	Idaho	7.4
45	Wyoming	7.3
46	New Mexico	7.0
47	Colorado	6.8
48	Utah	6.0
49	Hawaii	5.1
50	Alaska	4.1

154. Death Rate—Heart Disease

Except for combat wounds during the first and second world wars, heart disease has been the leading cause of death among Americans in this century. About 38% of all deaths in 1978 were caused by some form of heart disease, including various forms of heart attacks, rheumatic fever and hypertensive heart disease. As infant deaths and deaths due to specific illnesses have declined in importance over the years, the leading position of heart disease as a cause of death, especially among older persons, has been strengthened. This helps to account for the high concentration of medical research in the area of heart ailments. As heart-stimulating drugs, pacemakers and even the potentiality of transplants have become available, many additional years of life have been granted to persons with heart disease. Dr. Barney Clark, who in 1982 became the first person to receive an artificial heart, survived for a few painful months following the implant.

For the nation as a whole, about three of every 1,000 persons in 1978 died of heart disease. The highest rates in the table appear in West Virginia and Pennsylvania. Compared to their positions in the previous table, they have slipped ahead of Florida in the rankings. This indicates that heart disease accounts for a slightly smaller fraction of all deaths in the Sunshine State. Rhode Island advances from 10th position in the previous table to fourth position here, indicating a relatively high incidence of heart disease. Further comparison of the two tables shows that the incidence of deaths related to heart disease is relatively low in Oklahoma, Arkansas and Mississippi.

Since heart disease rarely strikes individuals who have not reached middle age (say age 40), deaths due to heart disease make up a larger fraction of all deaths in states with older populations. In Rhode Island, for example, over 42% of all deaths are due to heart disease, in Alaska only about 18%. To work out the percentage of all deaths due to specific causes, you can divide state figures in these tables for specific causes by 100 times the general state death rate given in Table 153.

Table: Deaths From Heart Disease
Date: 1978
Source: National Center for Health Statistics
Description: Deaths from heart disease per 100,000 population.
United States average: 334.3 per 100,000 population
State median: 321.4 per 100,000 population

DEATH RATE—HEART DISEASE

Rank	State	Deaths per 100,000 population
1	West Virginia	431.0
2	Pennsylvania	414.9
3	Florida	410.9
4	Rhode Island	402.5
5	New York	396.2
6	Iowa	380.5
7	Missouri	380.2
8	Illinois	379.6
9	Kentucky	379.1
10	New Jersey	377.4
11	Arkansas	364.3
11	Oklahoma	364.3
13	Maine	358.9
14	Massachusetts	357.3
15	Ohio	356.7
16	South Dakota	354.8
17	Wisconsin	349.0
18	Nebraska	348.4
19	Kansas	345.3
20	Vermont	341.3
21	Delaware	334.6
22	Indiana	334.2
23	Tennessee	324.3
24	Connecticut	321.9
25	Michigan	321.0
26	Mississippi	320.8
27	Louisiana	317.9
28	North Dakota	313.6
29	North Carolina	313.1
30	Maryland	308.5
31	Minnesota	307.2
32	New Hampshire	306.9
33	Alabama	304.2
34	Georgia	301.9

Rank	State	Deaths per 100,000 population
35	Oregon	296.9
36	Virginia	295.5
37	South Carolina	295.4
38	Washington	284.5
39	Montana	279.6
40	California	278.8
41	Texas	267.5
42	Arizona	265.1
43	Nevada	246.7
44	Idaho	241.8
45	Wyoming	233.2
46	Colorado	229.1
47	Utah	198.9
48	New Mexico	168.6
49	Hawaii	156.7
50	Alaska	75.7

155. Death Rate—Malignant Neoplasms

Malignant neoplasms caused 21% of all deaths in 1978, ranking second behind heart disease in this respect. Nine classes of malignant neoplasms are defined in official mortality statistics; seven of these are generally known as cancers. There are six specific categories for cancer in the official statistical record, divided according to the organ of the body in which the cancer is found, and one category for cancers in all other parts of the body. Leukemia is treated as a separate class of malignant neoplasm, and the ninth category in the classification system is for neoplasms appearing in the blood or the lymphatic system.

In 1978 there were about 397,000 deaths resulting from malignant neoplasms. The cancers account for over 90% of the deaths falling within this general group, since leukemia and other neoplasms of the blood and lymphatic systems were responsible for only about 37,000 deaths. Lung cancer and cancer of the digestive system (the stomach, etc.) each accounted for about one-quarter of all deaths assigned to the entire group.

The highest rates of death attributed to causes in this group are found in states of the Northeast, together with Florida and Missouri. In the northeastern states, deaths from these causes generally make up percentages of all deaths slightly higher than the national average of 21%. Five of the 10 states at the top of the table for overall death rates do not appear among the top 10 here: Arkansas (rank 14), Oklahoma (17), Kentucky (20), South Dakota (26) and Mississippi (30). Deaths caused by cancer/leukemia in these states make up a share of all deaths that is below the national average level.

Table: Deaths From Malignant Neoplasms
Date: 1978
Source: National Center for Health Statistics
Description: Death rate from malignant neoplasms per 100,000 population.
United States average: 181.9 per 100,000 population
State median: 176.9 per 100,000 population

DEATH RATE—MALIGNANT NEOPLASMS

Rank	State	Deaths per 100,000 population
1	Florida	248.7
2	Rhode Island	229.1
3	Pennsylvania	215.2
4	New Jersey	207.8
5	Massachusetts	206.8
6	New York	205.2
7	Maine	202.4
8	Missouri	200.5
9	West Virginia	197.8
10	New Hampshire	196.1
11	Delaware	194.5
12	Vermont	194.0
13	Connecticut	192.7
14	Arkansas	190.7
15	Nebraska	188.1
16	Iowa	187.5
17	Oklahoma	186.9
18	Illinois	186.8
19	Ohio	185.8
20	Kentucky	183.4
21	Maryland	182.3
22	Kansas	180.1
23	Indiana	179.3
24	Oregon	178.9
25	Wisconsin	177.0
26	South Dakota	176.8
27	Alabama	174.2
28	Tennessee	172.7
29	California	171.6
30	Mississippi	169.6
31	Washington	169.3
32	Louisiana	168.8
33	Minnesota	167.8
34	Michigan	166.5
35	North Dakota	164.5
36	Arizona	162.9
37	North Carolina	159.9
38	Nevada	158.6
39	Virginia	157.4
40	Montana	157.3
41	Georgia	154.5
42	Texas	152.0
43	South Carolina	146.4
44	Idaho	133.7
45	Wyoming	130.1
46	New Mexico	126.1
47	Colorado	125.1
48	Hawaii	113.7
49	Utah	97.8
50	Alaska	68.4

156. Death Rate—Cerebrovascular Diseases

Cerebrovascular diseases—disorders in the delivery of blood to the brain that characteristically result in strokes—make up the third major group of fatal organic diseases. About 9% of all deaths in 1978 were traced to this cause. Like heart disease and malignant neoplasms, cerebrovascular disease usually results from wear and tear absorbed by the body over many years and therefore typically appears among older Americans. As deaths from specific infectious diseases have declined during this century, these three diseases of old age (sometimes an old age hastened by chronic abuse of the body, such as smoking and drinking) have consolidated their positions as the principal causes of death. Taken together, these three causes account for over two-thirds of all deaths.

Six of the 10 states with the highest overall death rates also appear among the top 10 here. Alabama, Tennessee, Iowa and Nebraska are the states added to the top 10. These four states and the six others owe their positions here to relatively high proportions of elderly individuals—persons who have already survived the period of middle age when heart disease or cancer claim many victims. The states that drop from the top 10 here are Missouri (but only to rank 11) and three states where heart attacks and cancer claim the lives of many persons who would otherwise live long enough to die of strokes: West Virginia, Pennsylvania and especially Rhode Island. The set of states with youthful populations—found in the lower part of the table for overall death rates—appears more or less intact at the bottom of this table, as in the two previous tables dealing with causes of death for the most part in old age.

Table: Deaths From Cerebrovascular Diseases
Date: 1978
Source: National Center for Health Statistics
Description: Deaths from cerebrovascular diseases per 100,000 population.
United States average: 80.5 per 100,000 population
State median: 79.8 per 100,000 population

DEATH RATE—CEREBROVASCULAR DISEASES

Rank	State	Deaths per 100,000 population
1	Arkansas	114.2
2	Alabama	102.8
3	Mississippi	102.1
4	South Dakota	100.4
5	Florida	100.1
6	Oklahoma	100.0

Rank	State	Deaths per 100,000 population
7	Tennessee	98.4
8	Kentucky	98.0
9	Iowa	97.8
10	Nebraska	97.6
11	Missouri	97.3
12	Georgia	96.7
13	Indiana	91.8
14	Kansas	90.8
15	West Virginia	88.7
16	Minnesota	87.9
17	South Carolina	87.3
18	North Carolina	84.3
19	Louisiana	83.9
20	Oregon	83.6
21	North Dakota	83.5
22	Maine	82.6
23	Pennsylvania	82.1
24	Ohio	80.9
25	Wisconsin	80.0
26	Illinois	79.7
27	Washington	79.4
28	Texas	77.9
29	Massachusetts	76.3
30	Connecticut	76.2
31	Rhode Island	74.1
32	New Jersey	73.1
33	Virginia	72.6
34	California	72.5
35	Montana	71.7
36	Michigan	71.3
36	Vermont	71.3
38	New Hampshire	70.2
39	New York	69.2
40	Idaho	68.4
41	Wyoming	61.4
42	Arizona	59.3
43	Nevada	56.5
44	Delaware	54.6
45	Colorado	54.0
46	Maryland	53.3
47	Utah	52.7
48	New Mexico	50.0
49	Hawaii	49.3
50	Alaska	16.8

157. Death Rate—Accidents

Accidental death struck about one of every 2,000 persons in the American population during 1978, accounting for 5.5% of all deaths. For persons in the age groups 1–4, 5–14, 15–24 and 25–44, accidents are the leading cause of death. Motor vehicle accidents alone claimed 52,411 lives in 1978. All other accidents claimed 53,150 lives in the same year. About 46 of every 100,000 persons in the age range 15–24 died in a motor vehicle accident, compared to 24 of every 100,000 persons in the population as a whole.

The highest rates of accidental death are found in the West and the South. Alaska, where an extraordinary 27% of all deaths are accidental, is considerably more dangerous than any other state. High rates of accidental death are apparently related to closer direct contact between people and the natural environment, especially in their occupations. Since younger people are more likely to die in accidents than senior citizens, there is a tendency for states with low average ages to move toward the top of the table. The lowest rates of accidental death are found in states along the East Coast and in Hawaii (probably because the youthful population of Hawaii has low access to automobiles and freeways to speed on). The relatively mature population of West Virginia should make for a very low rate of accidental death, but a combination of treacherous highways and mining accidents holds the rate at a fairly high level.

Table: Accidental Deaths
Date: 1978
Source: National Center for Health Statistics
Description: Deaths from accidents, per 100,000 population.
United States average: 48.4 per 100,000 population
State median: 53.8 per 100,000 population

DEATH RATE—ACCIDENTS

Rank	State	Deaths per 100,000 population
1	Alaska	111.4
2	New Mexico	80.7
3	Wyoming	79.8
4	Nevada	73.4
5	Mississippi	72.3
6	Montana	69.7
7	Arizona	69.3
7	Idaho	69.3
9	Alabama	66.1
10	Oklahoma	63.3
11	Arkansas	60.6
12	Louisiana	59.9
13	South Carolina	59.5
14	North Dakota	59.3
15	Georgia	58.6
16	Oregon	58.3
17	Maryland	58.1
18	South Dakota	57.8
19	Tennessee	57.4
20	West Virginia	57.2
21	North Carolina	56.5
22	Utah	56.0
23	Texas	55.5

Rank	State	Deaths per 100,000 population
24	Kansas	54.0
25	Washington	53.9
26	Missouri	53.6
27	Kentucky	52.6
28	Colorado	51.6
29	Vermont	50.7
30	Florida	50.2
31	California	50.0
32	Minnesota	48.5
33	Nebraska	47.9
34	Iowa	47.8
35	Indiana	47.6
36	Virginia	46.6
37	Maine	46.1
38	Michigan	43.3
39	Illinois	42.9
40	Wisconsin	42.6
41	Ohio	41.6
42	Delaware	41.4
43	Massachusetts	40.0
43	Pennsylvania	40.0
45	New Hampshire	38.2
46	Hawaii	35.5
47	Connecticut	33.9
48	New York	33.5
49	New Jersey	33.4
50	Rhode Island	29.7

158. Death Rate—Cirrhosis of the Liver

Cirrhosis of the liver claimed 30,066 lives in 1978. Chronic alcohol abuse was definitely established as the major factor in 12,828, or 43%, of these cases, although excessive alcohol use figures to some extent in almost all cases. The ratio between the highest and the lowest death rates in this table is about 3 to 1. There is a break in the distribution between the fourth and fifth positions. New York, Nevada, California and Florida have rates notably higher than those in the rest of the nation. Differences between neighboring states are often sharp as, for example, between Maine and New Hampshire (ranks seven and ten) and Vermont (37 rank). States in the Midwest and the South tend to have low rankings.

Table: Deaths From Cirrhosis Of The Liver
Date: 1978
Source: National Center for Health Statistics
Description: Deaths from cirrhosis of the liver per 100,000 population.
United States average: 13.8 per 100,000 population
State median: 11.8 per 100,000 population

DEATH RATE—CIRRHOSIS OF THE LIVER

Rank	State	Deaths per 100,000 population
1	New York	19.9
2	Nevada	19.1
3	California	19.0
4	Florida	18.9
5	New Jersey	16.6
6	Arizona	16.3
7	Maine	15.8
7	Massachusetts	15.8
9	Delaware	15.4
10	New Hampshire	15.3
11	New Mexico	15.2
12	Connecticut	14.8
12	Illinois	14.8
12	Michigan	14.8
15	Pennsylvania	13.9
15	South Dakota	13.9
17	Rhode Island	13.6
18	Montana	13.5
19	Maryland	13.1
20	West Virginia	12.8
21	Wyoming	12.5
22	Ohio	12.2
22	Oregon	12.2
24	Washington	12.1
25	North Carolina	11.9
26	Oklahoma	11.6
27	Georgia	11.4
28	Missouri	10.7
28	North Dakota	10.7
28	South Carolina	10.7
31	Virginia	10.6
32	Texas	10.5
33	Kentucky	10.4
34	Louisiana	10.3
34	Wisconsin	10.3
36	Colorado	10.2
37	Vermont	9.9
38	Indiana	9.6
39	Alabama	9.5
40	Tennessee	9.3
41	Alaska	9.2
41	Nebraska	9.2
43	Idaho	8.7
44	Minnesota	8.6
45	Utah	8.4
46	Iowa	8.3
47	Mississippi	8.0
48	Kansas	7.8
49	Arkansas	7.6
50	Hawaii	6.7

159. Alcohol-Related Deaths

Cirrhosis of the liver is only one of several potential fatal results of alcohol abuse. The data in this table (for the year 1979) express the number of alcohol-related deaths as a share of all deaths in the nation. The four direct causes covered here are alcoholic cirrhosis of the liver (about 70% of the total), alcoholism (about 26%), and (in smaller percentages) alcoholic psychosis and alcohol poisoning. About one death in 100 results from alcohol abuse according to this definition. Alaska, Nevada and New Mexico, where tragic levels of alcohol abuse prevail among native Americans or among those addicted to life in the fast lane, have rates far above the national average.

These data do not include uncertain diagnoses, as in the case of cirrhosis of the liver, or deaths indirectly related to the use of alcohol. Experts estimate that alcohol is involved in 30% to 50% of all motor vehicle deaths, 45% of deaths due to accidental falls, 25% of deaths in fires, 50% to 70% of all homicides and 25% to 35% of all suicides.

Table: Alcohol-Related Deaths
Date: 1979
Source: National Institute on Alcohol Abuse and Alcoholism
Description: Verified deaths due to selected alcohol-related causes per 10,000 deaths.
United States average: 99 per 10,000 deaths
State median: 94 per 10,000 deaths

ALCOHOL-RELATED DEATHS

Rank	State	Death rate per 10,000 deaths
1	Alaska	353
2	Nevada	287
3	New Mexico	256
4	California	180
5	North Carolina	160
6	New York	152
7	Wyoming	148
8	Oregon	135
9	Delaware	133
9	Rhode Island	133
11	North Dakota	131
12	Arizona	130
13	Utah	129
14	Colorado	121
15	Connecticut	119
16	Montana	116
17	New Hampshire	111
17	Virginia	111
19	Florida	109
20	Idaho	108
21	Oklahoma	107
22	Maryland	106
23	Georgia	104
24	Washington	101
25	South Carolina	95

Rank	State	Death rate per 10,000 deaths
26	South Dakota	92
27	Minnesota	88
28	Nebraska	87
29	Maine	85
30	West Virginia	81
30	Wisconsin	81
32	Michigan	80
33	Vermont	76
34	Hawaii	72
35	Illinois	67
35	Kentucky	67
35	New Jersey	67
38	Kansas	66
38	Tennessee	66
40	Massachusetts	65
41	Pennsylvania	63
42	Ohio	62
43	Texas	60
44	Missouri	59
45	Alabama	55
45	Indiana	55
47	Louisiana	53
48	Mississippi	50
49	Iowa	47
50	Arkansas	40

160. Death Rate—Suicide

There were 27,294 identified suicides in 1978, as compared to 20,432 homicides in the same year. The number of Americans who took their own lives was 34% larger than the group whose lives were taken by others. About 65% of all suicides were committed by men. Among men the suicide rate was 19.0 per 100,000, among women 6.3 per 100,000. The news media tend to devote attention to suicides among younger persons, particularly teenagers. The suicide rate among teenagers is in fact rather low—12.4 suicides per 100,000 persons in the age group 15–24 in 1978. Suicide rates increase with age up to age 85, with a peak of 22.6 suicides per 100,000 persons in the age group 75–84 in 1978.

Risky lifestyles in Nevada contribute to a suicide rate twice the national average and well above the rates in other states. Florida joins a number of states in the West with rates bove 15 per 100,000 population. Suicide rates in the East (except for upper New England) and in selected states in the South and the Midwest are relatively low. About 64% of the suicides in 1978 were accomplished by means of firearms, up from 54% among the suicides in 1960.

Table: Deaths By Suicide
Date: 1978
Source: National Center for Health Statistics
Description: Deaths by suicide per 100,000 population.
United States average: 12.5 per 100,000 population
State median: 12.4 per 100,000 population

DEATHS BY SUICIDE

Rank	State	Deaths per 100,000 population
1	Nevada	24.8
2	Arizona	19.3
3	Colorado	17.8
4	Florida	17.7
5	Wyoming	17.6
6	New Mexico	17.1
7	California	16.3
8	Montana	15.5
8	Oregon	15.5
10	New Hampshire	15.0
11	Alaska	14.8
11	Vermont	14.8
13	Delaware	14.6
14	Washington	14.2
15	Virginia	14.1
16	West Virginia	14.0
17	Maine	13.9
18	Georgia	13.6
19	Oklahoma	13.5
20	Idaho	13.4
21	Utah	12.8
22	Texas	12.7
23	Ohio	12.6
23	Tennessee	12.6
25	Kentucky	12.5
26	Wisconsin	12.4
27	Michigan	12.3
28	Missouri	12.2
29	Indiana	11.9
29	Pennsylvania	11.9
31	Hawaii	11.8
31	Iowa	11.8
31	Louisiana	11.8
34	North Carolina	11.7
34	South Dakota	11.7
36	Rhode Island	11.5
37	South Carolina	11.3
38	Maryland	10.9
39	Kansas	10.8
40	Alabama	10.5
40	Arkansas	10.5
42	Connecticut	10.3
43	Minnesota	10.2
44	Illinois	10.0
45	North Dakota	9.8
46	Mississippi	9.6
46	New York	9.6
48	Nebraska	9.2
49	Massachusetts	8.9
50	New Jersey	7.2

161. Infant Mortality

Medical experts consider the rate of infant mortality—computed as the number of deaths among infants under one year of age divided by the number of live births in a given year—as the most reliable general indicator of health and health care conditions in a population. The infant mortality rate of 11.2 deaths per 1,000 live births in 1982 was the lowest in American history, down from 47.0 in 1940, 29.2 in 1950, 26.0 in 1960 and 20.0 in 1970. The controversy over stable or slightly higher rates for certain states in 1982 as compared to 1981—developments attributed by critics to federal welfare cutbacks—is concerned with extremely small shifts in rates that are much lower than those of a generation ago. It is nevertheless true that there are 14 nations in the world with rates of infant mortality lower than in the United States. Sweden leads the way with a rate of 6.7 per 1,000 live births. It is also true that death rates for nonwhite infants in the United States remain about twice as high as rates for white infants.

Differences in rates between whites and nonwhites, which correspond in part to differences between groups with relatively high and low average incomes, are a key factor in explaining the distribution of states in this table. Blacks make up a large share of the populations of all states near the top of the list except North Dakota. Figures for percentage of decline in rates over the past decade indicate that the states of North Dakota and Utah (ranked nine and fourteen, respectively) have shown the least improvement. The greatest improvements have occurred in Wyoming, Montana and South Dakota (fifty, forty-eight and forty-six in the ranking).

Table: Infant Mortality
Date: 1982
Source: Public Health Service
Description: Deaths under one year of age per 1,000 live births in 1982 and percentage of decline from 1972.
United States average: 11.2 per 1,000 live births
State median: 10.9 per 1,000 live births

INFANT MORTALITY

Rank	State	Deaths per 1,000 live births	Percent of decline 1972–1982
1	Mississippi	15.2	−42
2	South Carolina	14.4	−32
3	Alabama	14.1	−38
4	North Carolina	13.8	−41
5	Tennessee	13.5	−36

Rank	State	Deaths per 1,000 live births	Percent of decline 1972–1982
6	Illinois	13.3	−34
7	Louisiana	13.0	−41
8	Florida	12.8	−30
9	North Dakota	12.7	−14
10	New York	12.6	−28
11	Georgia	12.5	−36
11	Missouri	12.5	−32
13	Virginia	12.1	−41
14	Nevada	11.9	−27
14	Utah	11.9	−15
16	Delaware	11.8	−38
17	Alaska	11.7	−36
17	Michigan	11.7	−36
19	Kentucky	11.4	−36
19	Oklahoma	11.4	−40
21	Indiana	11.3	−40
21	New Jersey	11.3	−35
23	Texas	11.1	−46
24	Rhode Island	11.0	−43
24	West Virginia	11.0	−43
26	Oregon	10.8	−35
27	Massachusetts	10.6	−28
28	Ohio	10.5	−43
29	Nebraska	10.4	−38
30	Maryland	10.3	−36
31	Arizona	10.0	−42
31	Colorado	10.0	−42
33	Arkansas	9.9	−44
33	Colorado	9.9	−37
33	New Mexico	9.9	−46
36	Kansas	9.7	−45
37	Washington	9.5	−44
38	Connecticut	9.4	−44
38	Minnesota	9.4	−47
40	Pennsylvania	9.3	−47
41	Maine	9.2	−50
42	Hawaii	8.9	−37
42	Iowa	8.9	−49
44	Idaho	8.6	−49
44	New Hampshire	8.6	−48
46	South Dakota	8.4	−58
47	Vermont	7.8	−43
48	Montana	7.4	−65
49	Wisconsin	7.3	−48
50	Wyoming	6.3	−75

162. Gonorrhea

There are 46 different communicable diseases that physicians are legally obliged to report to the Public Health Service. The venereal disease gonorrhea is far and away the most common of these diseases, with over one million new cases reported in 1980—about 60% among men and 40% among women. (Chicken pox was a distant second, with 191 thousand cases, and all other diseases in

this group had much lower rates of incidence—48,000 cases of hepatitis and 14,000 cases of measles, for example.) The overall incidence of gonorrhea in 1980 was 443 cases per 100,000 population. After a period of steady and sharp increase between 1964 and 1975, the incidence of gonorrhea has been receding slightly in recent years. Federally sponsored public health programs created in 1973 to deal with the problem are thought to be responsible for this leveling off. In 1982 reported cases dropped to 962,000. The fear of contracting genital herpes—a recently identified chronic health problem that may affect over 10 million Americans—has also apparently led to greater caution in selecting sexual partners and therefore to lower transmission rates for all venereal diseases.

Gonorrhea is especially prevalent in Alaska, Nevada and Georgia. Rates of incidence in Maryland, Delaware, Texas, California and throughout the South are also relatively high. The lowest levels are observed in New England and across the North Central section of the country. The differences among the states are significant, with a high ratio between the most extreme rates in the distribution.

Table: Gonorrhea
Date: 1980
Source: Center for Disease Control
Description: Reported cases of gonorrhea per 100,000 population.
United States average: 443.3 per 100,000 population

GONORRHEA

Rank	State	Cases per 100,000 population
1	Alaska	1,016.5
2	Nevada	886.6
3	Georgia	866.7
4	South Carolina	754.3
5	Florida	671.9
6	North Carolina	651.9
7	Tennessee	646.2
8	Maryland	640.0
9	Alabama	617.5
10	Mississippi	613.6
11	Delaware	608.6
12	Texas	564.4
13	California	554.7
14	Louisiana	537.2
15	Missouri	447.9
16	Arkansas	443.1
17	Virginia	434.9
18	Oregon	423.8
19	Oklahoma	420.6
20	Illinois	410.8
21	Ohio	400.1

Rank	State	Cases per 100,000 population
22	Arizona	389.1
23	Michigan	377.5
24	New York	372.3
25	Colorado	366.4
26	New Mexico	350.9
27	Kansas	348.1
28	Washington	344.2
29	Hawaii	338.6
30	Connecticut	333.5
31	Kentucky	323.4
32	Indiana	317.2
33	Wisconsin	305.7
34	New Jersey	278.6
35	Nebraska	236.9
36	Wyoming	232.7
37	Pennsylvania	232.5
38	South Dakota	197.3
39	Minnesota	194.5
40	Massachusetts	188.2
41	Montana	186.7
42	Idaho	183.7
43	Iowa	174.8
44	West Virginia	171.5
45	Rhode Island	171.1
46	Utah	134.3
47	Maine	129.8
48	Vermont	104.3
49	North Dakota	104.1
50	New Hampshire	96.4

163. Hospital Beds

According to the American Hospital Association, there were 1.37 million hospital beds (that is, places for patients in hospitals) during the year 1979. The number of beds had declined 15% from the level of 1970. During the same 1970–1979 period the number of inpatients in hospitals on an average day declined by 20%. High costs of hospital care and changes in the practices of physicians have led to lower rates of hospitalization. The number of hospital beds has been declining in response to the lower demand for patient placement, but not fast enough to keep the average occupancy rate in hospitals from dipping to 76.1% in 1979 from the level of 80.3% in 1970.

Community leaders and local politicians who once had no difficulty in getting support for hospital construction no longer find investors and taxpayers eagerly backing their plans. Expansion of the hospital system has given way to consolidation and rationalization. Many long-term care hospitals for tuberculosis and for the mentally ill have been closed down. The average daily population of short-stay general hospitals, which grew somewhat more rapidly than the general population from 1960 to 1975, is now edging toward stability or decline. Treatment options such as outpatient care, outpatient surgery in doctors' offices and emphasis on preventive medicine—especially in the new health maintenance organizations (HMOs) that combine prevention and treatment functions—are now chosen more frequently. Rising costs probably also cause people to delay or do without treatments that they might have undergone in hospitals in the past. Higher levels of medication are used to support these options.

Rates of hospital bed availability in states near the top of the list are about twice as high as rates for states at the bottom, with one extreme exception at the top for North Dakota. The rate in Utah, with its relatively young and healthy population and a religious structure that fosters coordinated charities and little competitive overbuilding of hospitals, is the lowest in the nation.

Table: Hospital Beds
Date: 1979
Source: American Hospital Association
Description: Number of hospital beds available per 100,000 population.
United States average: 611 per 100,000 population
State median: 594 per 100,000 population

HOSPITAL BEDS

Rank	State	Number of beds per 100,000 residents
1	North Dakota	908
2	South Dakota	812
3	Kansas	784
4	Massachusetts	774
5	Nebraska	761
6	Minnesota	759
7	New York	745
8	Iowa	736
9	Pennsylvania	727
9	West Virginia	727
11	Missouri	711
12	Delaware	705
13	Tennessee	692
14	Montana	674
15	Mississippi	657
16	Alabama	655
17	Illinois	644
17	Rhode Island	644
19	Maine	630
20	Wisconsin	615
21	Louisiana	608
22	Virginia	598
23	Florida	597
24	Maryland	596
25	Connecticut	595
26	New Jersey	593
27	Oklahoma	592

Rank	State	Number of beds per 100,000 residents
28	Indiana	591
29	Ohio	589
30	Vermont	582
31	Georgia	577
31	Texas	577
33	North Carolina	575
34	Arkansas	562
35	Wyoming	560
36	South Carolina	547
37	Michigan	543
38	Colorado	527
39	New Hampshire	513
40	Kentucky	510
41	California	492
42	New Mexico	477
43	Oregon	451
44	Arizona	444
45	Nevada	425
46	Alaska	419
47	Hawaii	409
48	Idaho	402
49	Washington	398
50	Utah	362

164. Hospital Occupancy Rate

During 1979 about three-quarters of available hospital inpatient capacity was actually used. The national rate has been higher in the past—84.6% in 1960 and 80.3% in 1970—but deciding whether the present rate is too low is really a matter of judgment. Excessive capacity is often cited as a cause of rising hospital costs. The business judgments of hospital administrators and the thinking of public health officials and health insurance administrators now seem to be converging on the idea that there are too many available hospital beds. The present occupancy rate compares rather closely, however, with rates of use of available capacity in other sectors of the economy, such as the manufacturing sector.

States with high levels of hospital inpatient capacity, presented in the previous table, do not necessarily have low occupancy rates. Among the top 12 in that table only four (the Dakotas, Nebraska and Iowa) turn up here among the 12 with the lowest occupancy rates. Four of those 12 states with high capacity (New York, Delaware, Massachusetts and Pennsylvania) actually appear in this table among states with the highest occupancy rates.

Table: Hospital Occupancy Rate
Date: 1979

Source: American Hospital Association
Description: Number of average daily inpatients for every 100 beds.
United States average: 76.1%
State median: 73.8%

HOSPITAL OCCUPANCY RATE

Rank	State	Occupancy rate
1	New York	86.3
2	Rhode Island	86.2
3	Delaware	83.9
4	New Jersey	82.3
5	Maryland	81.8
6	Massachusetts	81.3
7	Connecticut	79.3
7	Pennsylvania	79.3
9	Indiana	78.4
9	Michigan	78.4
11	Ohio	78.3
12	Virginia	77.5
13	Hawaii	77.3
14	Tennessee	77.2
14	West Virginia	77.2
16	Kentucky	76.9
17	North Carolina	76.7
18	Illinois	76.4
19	South Carolina	76.1
20	Alabama	75.6
21	Maine	75.4
21	Mississippi	75.4
23	Vermont	74.8
24	Missouri	74.6
25	New Hampshire	74.1
26	Wisconsin	73.5
27	Florida	72.9
27	Utah	72.9
29	Arizona	72.7
29	Minnesota	72.7
31	Georgia	71.7
32	Texas	71.3
33	Kansas	71.2
34	New Mexico	70.8
34	Washington	70.8
36	Arkansas	70.5
37	Oregon	70.4
38	California	70.0
38	Louisiana	70.0
40	Colorado	69.0
40	Oklahoma	69.0
42	Iowa	68.4
43	Nevada	68.2
44	Nebraska	67.6
45	North Dakota	67.5
46	Idaho	66.4
47	Montana	64.1
47	South Dakota	64.1
49	Wyoming	62.2
50	Alaska	57.4

165. Hospital Room Costs

The costs of hospitalization have skyrocketed in recent years, rising at rates well above the general rate of inflation. The average charge for a semiprivate room in a nongovernment general hospital increased 53% between 1976 and 1980—from $83 per day to the $127 level displayed as the national average for data in this table. A 12.6% increase to $143 per day followed in 1981. Persons with medical insurance coverage, especially coverage received as a job benefit, have been protected from the effects of these startling shifts. Rising costs of insurance have been absorbed gradually. Persons without coverage have been priced out of private hospitals altogether.

Hospitals collected about 41 cents on every dollar spent on health care in 1981. This is a significant amount of money, since per capita health care spending in 1981 came to about $1,225. With general inflation running at 8.9% in 1981, overall health care costs rose 15.1%.

Alaska has extremely high hospital costs, related to the costs of construction and of supplying medical facilities where materials must be transported over long distances. For the remaining states, there is a ratio of about 2 to 1 between the high and low ends of the distribution. Charges on the East Coast, the West Coast and around the Great Lakes are generally high. The lowest charges appear in the South, with somewhat higher rates in the Plains states.

Table: Hospital Room Charges
Date: 1980
Source: American Hospital Association
Description: Average daily hospital room charge.
United States average: $127
State median: $110

HOSPITAL ROOM CHARGES

Rank	State	Average daily charge
1	Alaska	$189
2	California	161
3	New York	157
4	Massachusetts	151
4	Michigan	151
6	New Jersey	146
7	Illinois	144
8	Ohio	139
9	Rhode Island	138
10	Oregon	133
11	Pennsylvania	132
12	Connecticut	127
12	Hawaii	127

Rank	State	Average daily charge
14	Delaware	$125
14	Nevada	125
14	New Hampshire	125
14	Washington	125
18	Colorado	124
18	Maine	124
20	Maryland	119
21	Vermont	116
22	New Mexico	115
23	Montana	113
24	Utah	112
25	Idaho	110
25	West Virginia	110
27	Florida	109
28	Indiana	107
28	Iowa	107
28	Missouri	107
31	Arizona	106
32	Kansas	104
32	Minnesota	104
32	Wisconsin	104
35	Oklahoma	101
35	Virginia	101
37	Nebraska	100
38	Wyoming	98
39	Alabama	96
39	South Dakota	96
41	North Dakota	93
42	Georgia	92
42	Kentucky	92
44	Tennessee	91
44	Texas	91
46	Louisiana	89
47	North Carolina	87
48	Arkansas	86
49	South Carolina	80
50	Mississippi	67

166. State and Local Spending on Health and Hospitals

State and local governments spent $32.2 billion on health and hospital functions in 1980. About 45% of this amount was federal money passed along to and spent by the states. The spending covered in this table includes nearly $14 billion of federal money for Medicaid assistance to low-income individuals that is paid out by the states, but not the $29 billion in Medicare assistance to older individuals that is paid out directly by the federal government.

States at the top of the list are a mixed group, including several states in the South, Wyoming and Nevada, and the state of New York, which maintains a vast system of public hospitals. Rates at the top are about twice as high as rates at the bottom, with very low levels of spending in the Dakotas, Delaware and upper New England.

Table: State And Local Government Expenditures On Health And Hospitals
Date: 1980
Source: Census Bureau
Description: Per capita state and local government expenditures on health and hospitals.
United States average: $142
State Median: $133

STATE AND LOCAL GOVERNMENT EXPENDITURES ON HEALTH AND HOSPITALS

Rank	State	Per capita health and hospital expenditure
1	Georgia	$215.87
2	Wyoming	204.25
3	New York	197.02
4	South Carolina	181.05
5	Alabama	179.28
6	Louisiana	178.19
7	Nevada	177.78
8	Michigan	174.99
9	Iowa	173.75
10	Mississippi	172.09
11	Tennessee	165.99
12	Minnesota	157.09
13	Florida	155.24
14	California	153.84
15	Ohio	150.46
16	Alaska	150.16
17	Massachusetts	147.83
18	Rhode Island	147.73
19	Maryland	144.15
20	Nebraska	143.05
21	Hawaii	141.70
22	Wisconsin	139.55
23	New Mexico	136.31
24	Missouri	136.22
25	Indiana	133.49
26	Colorado	132.73
27	Kansas	128.26
28	Virginia	127.67
29	Texas	125.09
30	Idaho	124.54
31	North Carolina	123.89
32	Oklahoma	116.94
33	Arkansas	116.46
34	Arizona	110.12
35	Washington	109.08
36	Oregon	108.87
37	New Jersey	108.09
38	West Virginia	107.92
39	Utah	101.59
40	Illinois	100.91
41	Connecticut	98.51

Rank	State	Per capita health and hospital expenditure
42	Montana	$96.27
43	Pennsylvania	93.76
44	Kentucky	91.26
45	Vermont	86.81
46	Delaware	82.76
47	North Dakota	80.69
48	South Dakota	71.96
49	New Hampshire	64.45
50	Maine	63.87

167. Life Insurance

According to the American Council of Life Insurance, there were 402 million life policies in force during 1980, providing $3.5 trillion in coverage. There were 1,948 companies offering life insurance coverage, but 47% of the dollar value of all coverage was written by the top 10 companies, and 70% by the top 50 companies.

The average insured family held coverage worth $41,500, with state average figures varying between $28,300 and $59,600, a ratio of about 2 to 1 between the extremes of a smooth distribution of values. There are no clear regional patterns. Many states with a more rural orientation are found near the bottom of the table, but Florida and California are also in this lower group. Perhaps the insurance industry has simply not yet caught up with population growth in the major Sunbelt states.

LIFE INSURANCE

Rank	State	Average amount of life insurance per family
1	Delaware	$59,600
2	Connecticut	55,100
3	Hawaii	53,100
4	Alaska	50,000
5	Michigan	49,400
6	New Jersey	49,300
7	Illinois	48,500
8	Colorado	46,700
9	Minnesota	45,900
10	Ohio	45,800
11	Nebraska	45,500
12	North Dakota	45,200
13	Rhode Island	44,900
14	Georgia	44,200
14	Iowa	44,200
16	Indiana	43,800
17	Nevada	43,600
18	Texas	43,200
19	Louisiana	43,100
20	Wisconsin	43,000

Rank	State	Average amount of life insurance per family	Rank	State	Average amount of life insurance per family
21	Kansas	$42,600	36	Utah	$38,400
22	Maryland	42,300	37	Arizona	38,200
23	New Hampshire	42,100	38	California	37,000
24	Massachusetts	42,000	38	Idaho	37,000
25	Pennsylvania	41,500	40	Oregon	36,700
26	Virginia	41,300	41	Washington	36,300
27	New York	41,200	42	Oklahoma	36,100
28	Wyoming	39,900	43	Vermont	35,800
29	South Carolina	39,600	44	Montana	34,900
30	Alabama	39,500	45	Kentucky	33,000
30	Missouri	39,500	46	Maine	32,400
30	Tennessee	39,500	47	Florida	32,100
33	South Dakota	39,100	48	Mississippi	31,800
34	New Mexico	38,500	49	West Virginia	31,500
34	North Carolina	38,500	50	Arkansas	28,300

EDUCATION

One of every four Americans is looking forward to a graduation day. This is the ratio that emerges from a count of all those enrolled in institutions ranging from preschools to graduate schools offering PhD programs. The ratio would be even higher if the count included all those who take occasional courses for pleasure or to upgrade their job skills. As our world has become more complex and changeable, education has come to be viewed as a lifelong process. All Americans must spend some time in school—it's the law—but more and more people now voluntarily go far beyond what the law requires. The percentage of gross national product (GNP) spent for all types of education has been rising throughout this century. Consider these postwar data:

School Year	Percentage of GNP spent on education
1949–50	3.4
1955–56	4.2
1959–60	5.1
1965–66	6.6
1969–70	7.5
1975–76	8.0
1979–80	6.9
1980–81	6.9

Growth peaked in 1975–76; five years later the figure slipped back close to a 7% level because the bulk of the baby-boom generation finally moved out of the educational system and into the job market. It is clear, however, that education has carved out a larger and more permanent position in our national life.

Several major studies of American schools have been released during the past two years. The news has not been good. Political interest in education is now heating up to a degree not equaled since the days when the Supreme Court (*Brown* vs. *The Board of Education* of Topeka, 1954) and Sputnik spurred efforts to provide equal access to education for all Americans and to upgrade math and science education. A debate on busing dragged on during the late 1970s without offering much in the way of inspired thinking about the quality of education. The new round of reports focus on this issue. The National Commission on Excellence in Education has concluded, for example, that there is a "rising tide of mediocrity" in the public schools. The Carnegie Foundation for the Advancement of Teaching released a report in which the "crisis" in the schools was related to relative decline in public spending for education, with resulting loss of purchasing power and morale among teachers. Then there are the reports that compare our schools to schools in Japan and other advanced countries. These reports are concerned about our ability to compete in world markets. It seems that brainpower has become a valuable commodity. A recent study by a former dean of the Harvard Graduate School of Education has proposed radical changes in the organization of high schools, such as requiring students to progress through grade levels at whatever rate they are able to go, instead of moving in unison with a particular entering class or age-group. President Reagan even entered the debate with a call for more discipline in the schools. It appears that we will all be talking about education more frequently during the next few years.

The tables in this section sketch the basic dimensions of education in the states, beginning with information on educational attainment, as indicated by the percentages of high-school and college graduates in the adult populations of the states. A table on public school enrollment as a percentage of population provides a sense of the constituency for public education throughout the nation. Studies have shown that the percentage of all adults with children in public schools fell rapidly from 40% in 1975 to 26% in 1982. There is some fear that the decline of this natural constituency for public school spending could lead to funding problems in the future. Another set of tables explores various dimensions of state public school systems—spending per pupil, level of federal aid, teachers' salaries, pupil/teacher ratio and the use of computers in the classroom. Data on teachers' salaries may be especially important in accounting for the declining quality of schools that so many trained observers have noted. These data show that teachers have fallen on hard times in the past decade. Many talented teachers have left our school systems not willingly but reluctantly, having realized that they could simply no longer afford to remain in the profession at current salary levels. The remaining tables in this section focus on two topics: state by state Scholastic Aptitude Test (SAT) scores—where a remarkable disparity among the states is revealed, and levels of enrollment in institutions of higher education and advanced vocational training.

168. Public School Enrollment

Nearly one of every five Americans is a child enrolled in a public elementary or secondary school. Although this proportion has declined slightly as baby-boom children have moved through high school, our schoolchildren remain a significant segment of the present population as well as the hope of the future. California has the largest public school system, with over four million pupils enrolled. The Alaskan system, with 86,000 pupils, is the smallest.

The percentage of state populations in the public schools varies within a fairly narrow range between 15.4% and 23.5%. The age structure of state populations is the decisive factor in determining the rankings here, since 87.7% of all American children in the age range 5–17 were enrolled in the public systems during the school year 1980/81. State figures varied between 97.8% (Alaska) and 82.5% (Delaware). This range of variation indicates the second main factor behind this set of rankings—the percentage of the school-age population enrolled in private schools, especially Catholic schools. States that have the highest positions in this table have both large percentages of children in the general population and relatively low enrollments in Catholic schools. The reverse is true for states with the lowest positions.

Table: Public School Enrollment
Date: 1980/1
Source: National Center for Education Statistics and the Census Bureau.
Description: Enrollment in public schools and percentage of state population enrolled.

United States average: 18.1%
State median: 18.6%

PUBLIC SCHOOL ENROLLMENT

Rank	State	Percent of state population in public schools	Enrollment (in thousands)
1	Utah	23.5	344
2	Alaska	21.5	86
2	Idaho	21.5	203
4	Wyoming	21.0	98
5	New Mexico	20.8	271
6	Texas	20.4	2,900
7	Michigan	20.1	1,863
8	Maine	19.8	222
9	Montana	19.7	155
9	West Virginia	19.7	384
11	Arkansas	19.6	448
11	Georgia	19.6	1,069
13	Alabama	19.5	759
14	Indiana	19.2	1,056
14	North Carolina	19.2	1,129
16	Oklahoma	19.1	578
17	Arizona	19.0	514
17	Mississippi	19.0	477
19	Colorado	18.9	546
19	Virginia	18.9	1,010
21	Nevada	18.7	149
21	Vermont	18.7	96
23	South Dakota	18.6	129
23	Tennessee	18.6	854
25	Louisiana	18.5	778
25	Minnesota	18.5	754
27	Ohio	18.4	1,957
28	Iowa	18.3	534
28	Kentucky	18.3	670
28	Washington	18.3	758
31	New Hampshire	18.2	167
32	Nebraska	17.9	280
32	North Dakota	17.9	117
34	Maryland	17.8	751
34	Massachusetts	17.8	1,022
36	Kansas	17.6	415
36	Oregon	17.6	465
36	Wisconsin	17.6	830
39	California	17.4	4,118
39	Illinois	17.4	1,983
41	Missouri	17.2	845
42	Connecticut	17.1	531
42	Hawaii	17.1	165
44	South Carolina	17.0	619
45	New Jersey	16.9	1,246
46	Delaware	16.7	99
47	New York	16.4	2,871
48	Pennsylvania	16.1	1,909
49	Rhode Island	15.7	148
50	Florida	15.4	1,510

169. Higher Education Enrollment

Figures presented above indicate that about 18% of all Americans are pupils in public elementary and secondary schools. Allowing another 2% for pupils in nonpublic schools and adding the 5.3% of the population identified in this table as students in postsecondary institutions, it can be concluded that a solid 25% of all Americans are engaged in some program of formal education and looking forward to a graduation day.

There were 12.1 million individuals enrolled in postsecondary institutions in the fall of 1980. About 59% of these were full-time students, 78% were enrolled in public institutions, and 51% were women. There are only 13 states in which men outnumber women among those engaged in higher education; and the differences in numbers are very small in every state except Utah (56% male). Full-time students are in the majority in 45 states. The states where part-time students predominate are Alaska (73%), Nevada (67%), California (58%), Arizona (55%), and Maryland (51%). Part-time pursuit of studies seems to be particularly characteristic of the Southwest. Most individuals included in this table were studying for bachelors degrees or higher degrees at colleges and universities, but the figures also include 2.4 million people pursuing degrees in vocational training schools (covered in the following table).

Over 7% of all state residents are engaged in higher education in California, Arizona, Washington, Massachusetts and Rhode Island. California has nearly 1.8 million such students, or about 15% of all students in the nation. About 89% of California students are enrolled in public institutions of higher education, most of them in the vast state system of universities and colleges. Massachusetts and Rhode Island are exceptional because the proportions of students in private institutions are very high—56% of students in private colleges and universities for Massachusetts, 48% for Rhode Island. Public institutions are generally predominant in the Far West. Other states in which private institutions account for over 40% of the student body are Idaho, New Hampshire, New York, Pennsylvania and Vermont.

Table: Higher Education Enrollment
Date: 1980
Source: National Center for Education Statistics and Census Bureau
Description: Enrollment in institutions of higher education and percentage of state population enrolled.
United States average: 5.3%
State median: 5.0%
United States total: 12.1 million

HIGHER EDUCATION ENROLLMENT

Rank	State	Enrollment as a percentage of state population	Enrollment (in thousands)
1	California	7.6	1,791
2	Arizona	7.5	203
3	Massachusetts	7.3	418
3	Washington	7.3	304
5	Rhode Island	7.1	67
6	Utah	6.4	94
7	Oregon	6.0	157
7	Vermont	6.0	31
9	Kansas	5.8	137
10	Nebraska	5.7	89
10	New York	5.7	992
10	Wisconsin	5.7	269
13	Colorado	5.6	163
13	Illinois	5.6	644
13	Michigan	5.6	520
16	Delaware	5.5	33
17	Alaska	5.3	21
17	Maryland	5.3	226
17	Oklahoma	5.3	160
20	North Dakota	5.2	34
20	Virginia	5.2	281
22	Connecticut	5.1	160
22	Minnesota	5.1	207
22	Nevada	5.1	40
22	New Hampshire	5.1	47
26	Texas	5.0	701
27	Hawaii	4.9	47
27	North Carolina	4.9	288
29	Iowa	4.8	140
29	Missouri	4.8	234
31	South Dakota	4.7	33
32	Idaho	4.6	43
33	Indiana	4.5	247
33	Montana	4.5	35
33	New Mexico	4.5	58
33	Ohio	4.5	489
33	Tennessee	4.5	205
33	Wyoming	4.5	21
39	New Jersey	4.4	322
40	Pennsylvania	4.3	508
41	Alabama	4.2	164
41	Florida	4.2	412
41	South Carolina	4.2	132
41	West Virginia	4.2	82
45	Mississippi	4.1	102
46	Kentucky	3.9	143
47	Louisiana	3.8	160
47	Maine	3.8	43
49	Arkansas	3.4	78
49	Georgia	3.4	184

170. Enrollment in Vocational Schools

There are about 9,500 postsecondary schools in the

United States that prepare students for specific careers. Colleges and universities with vocational programs are included in the total, but the principal special types are barber/cosmetology schools (about 2,100), business and commercial colleges (1,400), health care schools (1,200), community colleges (1,100), flight training schools for airline careers (900), vocational and technical institutes (800), trade schools (800) and schools of arts and design (250). About 78% of these schools are private institutions. Vocational and technical institutes and community colleges are the only types in which public institutions are predominant.

Enrollment in all schools included here was 2.4 million in 1980. Private institutions accounted for 61% of enrollment. About 53% of the students were women. California has the largest enrollment, with more than twice as many students as second place New York.

Table: Vocational Schools
Date: 1980
Source: National Center for Education Statistics
Description: Enrollment in postsecondary public schools with occupational programs and percentage enrolled.
United States Average % public: 61
U.S. total enrollment: 2.4 million

VOCATIONAL SCHOOLS

Rank	State	Enrollment (in thousands)	Percentage of state population enrolled
1	California	397	28
2	New York	178	24
3	Florida	162	78
4	Michigan	152	16
5	Illinois	144	21
6	Pennsylvania	141	34
7	Ohio	93	38
8	New Jersey	92	28
9	Texas	82	36
10	Minnesota	66	68
11	Georgia	64	65
12	Arizona	57	16
13	Missouri	52	22
14	Louisiana	51	67
15	Massachusetts	49	29
16	Alabama	44	78
17	Colorado	41	45
18	Virginia	40	22
19	Oregon	38	14
20	Washington	37	63
21	Kentucky	36	66
22	Indiana	35	40
23	Tennessee	34	67
24	Connecticut	32	21
25	Oklahoma	31	57

Rank	State	Enrollment (in thousands)	Percentage of state population enrolled
26	Maryland	24	32
26	Wisconsin	24	61
28	North Carolina	23	65
29	Kansas	21	66
30	Iowa	18	64
31	Arkansas	15	59
32	New Mexico	13	65
33	Nevada	12	7
33	South Carolina	12	58
33	West Virginia	12	59
36	Idaho	10	68
36	Mississippi	10	69
36	Nebraska	10	42
39	Utah	9	68
40	Hawaii	8	36
40	Maine	8	62
42	Rhode Island	7	19
43	Montana	5	62
43	New Hampshire	5	28
43	South Dakota	5	56
46	Delaware	4	19
46	North Dakota	4	68
48	Alaska	3	58
48	Vermont	3	29
50	Wyoming	2	52

171. Federal Aid to Public Schools

About 43% of the revenue for public elementary and secondary schools is raised by local school districts. Another 47% is provided by state governments. Federal aid to education programs accounts for the remaining 10%. Over two-thirds of this federal aid is provided under programs for the educationally or economically deprived, including the Title 1 program under the Education Act, the Head Start and Follow Through programs, and programs for handicapped and bilingual students. Lesser amounts of federal aid go to districts affected by the presence of federal facilities such as military bases, and for a variety of purposes such as support of planning and evaluation or the purchase of library materials or special equipment.

Federal assistance accounted for an extraordinary 25.1% of school revenues in Mississippi during the school year 1980/81. Without this federal aid the level of per pupil spending in Mississippi (given in Table 172) would have been just $1,150—by far the lowest in the nation. Levels of federal support are also fairly high in Tennessee and Alabama (which rank below Mississippi in Table 172), but without this aid their spending levels would still have been $1,233 and $1,215 respectively. In general, federal support shares are high in most states in the South, in Hawaii, and in the states of New Mexico and South Dakota, where assistance to American Indian children is significant.

Table: Federal Aid to Public Schools
Date: 1980/81
Source: National Center for Education Statistics
Description: Federal aid to education as a percentage of total education expenditures for primary and secondary level schools.
U.S. Average: 10.6%
State median: 9.8%

FEDERAL AID TO PUBLIC SCHOOLS

Rank	State	Percent of total education expenditures
1	Mississippi	25.1
2	South Carolina	17.8
3	Arkansas	16.6
3	New Mexico	16.6
5	Kentucky	16.0
6	South Dakota	15.4
6	Tennessee	15.4
8	Hawaii	15.3
9	Louisiana	14.6
10	Georgia	14.1
10	Oklahoma	14.1
12	North Carolina	13.8
13	Delaware	12.5
14	Alabama	12.2
14	Arizona	12.2
16	Texas	11.6
17	Florida	11.3
18	North Dakota	11.2
19	West Virginia	11.1
20	Virginia	11.0
21	California	10.7
22	Missouri	10.6
23	Rhode Island	10.3
24	Maine	9.9
24	Pennsylvania	9.9
26	Idaho	9.6
26	Oregon	9.6
28	Montana	9.4
29	Alaska	9.3
30	Washington	9.0
31	Vermont	8.8
32	Maryland	8.5
32	Utah	8.5
34	Illinois	8.3
34	Indiana	8.3
36	New York	8.2
37	Ohio	7.7
38	Nebraska	7.6
39	Michigan	7.2
40	Connecticut	7.0
41	Kansas	6.9
42	Nevada	6.7

Rank	State	Percent of total education expenditures
43	New Hampshire	6.6
43	New Jersey	6.6
45	Colorado	6.5
45	Massachusetts	6.5
47	Iowa	6.4
48	Minnesota	5.9
49	Wisconsin	5.6
49	Wyoming	5.6

172. Public School Spending

The data in this table cover spending by all public school districts in each state for the school year 1980/81. The figures are computed on a per pupil basis, using average number of pupils in attendance throughout the school year (rather than enrollment) as the divisor in the calculation.

The table shows that there are great differences among the states in the level of spending for public schools. Some of these differences are simply related to different general price levels in the states, which lead to lower salaries for teachers and lower costs of constructing and operating schools. Price levels help to explain the extreme value for Alaska, although special problems of geography and climate also figure in here. Lower price levels also partly explain the position of southern states at the bottom of the table, though it should be noted, as described two tables below, that teachers' salaries in the South are no lower than salaries in upper New England. The differences in this table between Maine, New Hampshire and Vermont as compared to the southern states may simply have to do with the high costs of heating New England classrooms in the winter.

These data are really too rough to be used as a measure of the commitment to quality schooling in a given state. They simply indicate that there is a great deal of variability in what it costs to educate a child in the public schools. If we multiply the national average figure by 13 (for one year of kindergarten and the 12 graded years), we find that (if things stay just as they are today) the average cost to the public of educating each child who finishes high school comes to $30,500. The state extremes are Alaska ($65,140) and Alabama ($17,992).

Table: Per Pupil Expenditure
Date: 1980/81
Source: National Center for Education Statistics
Description: Annual current expenditure per pupil (based on average daily attendance).

United States average: $2,350
State median: $2,161

PER PUPIL EXPENDITURE

Rank	State	Expenditure
1	Alaska	$5,010
2	New York	3,358
3	Massachusetts	3,174
4	Oregon	3,049
5	Montana	2,948
6	Pennsylvania	2,798
7	New Jersey	2,791
8	Delaware	2,781
9	Wisconsin	2,769
10	Kansas	2,714
11	Connecticut	2,697
12	Colorado	2,656
13	Washington	2,653
14	Wyoming	2,596
15	California	2,594
16	Iowa	2,560
17	Rhode Island	2,559
18	Maryland	2,541
19	Minnesota	2,484
20	Michigan	2,461
21	Illinois	2,441
22	Florida	2,262
23	Virginia	2,223
24	New Mexico	2,219
25	Nevada	2,179
26	Ohio	2,143
27	Hawaii	2,121
28	Nebraska	2,105
29	Missouri	2,079
30	North Dakota	2,062
31	Maine	2,055
32	New Hampshire	2,033
33	Vermont	2,017
34	Oklahoma	2,007
35	South Dakota	1,995
36	North Carolina	1,992
37	Louisiana	1,972
38	Texas	1,955
39	Arizona	1,914
40	West Virginia	1,816
41	Indiana	1,793
42	Idaho	1,780
43	Utah	1,742
44	Georgia	1,652
45	Arkansas	1,571
46	Kentucky	1,569
47	South Carolina	1,560
48	Mississippi	1,536
49	Tennessee	1,458
50	Alabama	1,384

173. Teachers' Salaries

The average public school classroom teacher earned $20,531 for the school year 1982/83. The value for Alaska, as shown in this table, is extreme, reflecting both the high cost of living and the difficulty in attracting qualified teachers to work in an area remote from the rest of the nation. The main sequence of values begins with New York ($25,100) and declines some 40% before reaching Mississippi ($14,285). Higher levels are found in most of the East, the Midwest and the Far West. Low levels characterize states on the Plains, in the South and in upper New England. Given prevailing price levels, teachers' salary levels for Vermont, New Hampshire and Maine appear to be depressingly low.

National Education Association figures on change in the purchasing power of the average classroom teacher's salary from 1972/73 to 1982/83 confirm the bleak situation of teachers in New England. New Hampshire, Vermont, Maine and Massachusetts are the states in which the average teacher today has less than 80% of the purchasing power of the average teacher ten years ago. New Jersey is the only state with a comparable level of deterioration in the position of teachers. An oversupply of qualified teachers in this area of the country may be the basic reason for this rapid change. Data for the nation as a whole show, however, that this has been a bad decade for teachers throughout America; purchasing power declined by 12%. Although seven states showed some improvement in this respect, the only significant advance was registered in Wyoming.

Table: Teachers' Salaries
Date: 1982/83
Source: National Education Association
Description: Average salary for classroom teachers and percentage of change in purchasing power from 1972/73 to 1982/83.
United States average: $20,531
State median: $19,134
United States average purchasing power change: 1972/73 to 1982/83: −12%

TEACHERS' SALARIES

Rank	State	Average salary	Percentage of change in purchasing power
1	Alaska	$33,953	.6
2	New York	25,100	−12.0
3	Hawaii	24,796	12.4
4	Wyoming	24,000	12.3
5	Michigan	23,965	−12.8
6	California	23,555	−15.2
7	Washington	23,413	−3.9
8	Rhode Island	23,175	−5.0

Rank	State	Average salary	Percentage of change in purchasing power
9	Maryland	$22,786	−11.2
10	Illinois	22,618	−12.2
11	Oregon	22,334	1.2
12	Minnesota	22,296	−7.0
13	New Jersey	21,642	−19.8
14	Colorado	21,500	−3.3
15	Pennsylvania	21,000	−12.1
16	Nevada	20,944	−16.3
17	Wisconsin	20,940	−12.6
18	Delaware	20,665	−15.2
19	New Mexico	20,600	2.9
20	Ohio	20,360	−8.0
21	Connecticut	20,300	−16.7
22	Indiana	20,067	−13.2
23	Utah	19,677	.6
24	Texas	19,500	−2.4
25	Louisiana	19,269	−5.2
26	Massachusetts	19,000	−21.5
27	Arizona	18,849	−18.4
28	Iowa	18,709	−15.2
29	Virginia	18,707	−15.5
30	Florida	18,538	−13.0
31	Kentucky	18,400	2.6
32	North Dakota	18,390	−1.0
33	Kansas	18,299	−6.5
34	Oklahoma	18,110	.9
35	Alabama	17,850	−4.2
36	North Carolina	17,836	−15.4
37	Missouri	17,726	−15.0
38	Idaho	17,549	−.4
39	Montana	17,463	−5.0
40	Tennessee	17,425	−8.7
41	Georgia	17,412	−7.7
41	Nebraska	17,412	−13.3
43	West Virginia	17,370	−7.0
44	South Carolina	16,380	−11.6
45	Maine	15,772	−23.4
46	South Dakota	15,595	−14.2
47	New Hampshire	15,353	−27.1
48	Vermont	15,338	−25.0
49	Arkansas	15,176	−9.9
50	Mississippi	14,285	−10.1

174. Pupil-Teacher Ratio

During the school year 1980/81 there were 18.8 pupils for every teacher employed by the nation's elementary and secondary schools. These figures are based on enrollment of pupils. A similar figure based on average daily attendance suggests that there were 17.3 pupils per classroom on a typical school day. All other things being equal, such as quality of instruction and school facilities, smaller classes are thought to be better for pupils because each child receives a larger share of attention from teachers. States at the bottom of the list approach this ideal most closely. The 10 states at the bottom include four from New England, five from the Plains and New Jersey. Utah and Hawaii have the largest classes. The 14 states in which the pupil-teacher ratio is 20 to 1 or higher are all found in the West and the South.

Table: Pupil-Teacher Ratio
Date: 1980/81
Source: National Center for Educational Statistics
Description: Pupils per teacher based on enrollment in public elementary and secondary schools.
United States average: 18.8 pupils
State median: 18.4 pupils

PUPIL-TEACHER RATIO

Rank	State	Ratio
1	Utah	25.1
2	Hawaii	23.0
3	Michigan	22.1
4	Washington	21.3
5	California	21.2
6	Alabama	21.0
6	Nevada	21.0
8	Tennessee	20.7
9	Oregon	20.6
10	Idaho	20.5
11	Florida	20.4
11	Kentucky	20.4
13	North Carolina	20.1
14	Arizona	20.0
15	Indiana	19.9
16	New Hampshire	19.8
17	Ohio	19.5
18	New Mexico	19.2
18	South Carolina	19.2
20	Georgia	18.9
20	Maine	18.9
22	Arkansas	18.6
23	New York	18.5
24	Illinois	18.4
24	Maryland	18.4
24	Mississippi	18.4
27	Colorado	18.3
28	Texas	18.2
29	Delaware	17.7
29	Louisiana	17.7
29	West Virginia	17.7
29	Virginia	17.7
33	Pennsylvania	17.4
34	Missouri	17.3
35	Minnesota	17.1
35	Wisconsin	17.1
37	Oklahoma	17.0
38	Nebraska	16.7
39	Alaska	16.6
39	Montana	16.6

Rank	State	Ratio
41	Iowa	16.3
41	New Jersey	16.3
43	Rhode Island	16.1
43	South Dakota	16.1
45	Kansas	15.8
45	North Dakota	15.8
47	Massachusetts	15.7
48	Wyoming	15.5
49	Connecticut	15.4
50	Vermont	14.8

175: High-school Graduates

The average number of years that Americans spend in schools has been increasing steadily during the past century, with a rapid upward shift since World War II. In 1940, only 25% of the population above age 24 had completed four years of high school. This figure rose to 34% in 1950, 41% in 1960 and 55% in 1970. By 1980 fully two-thirds of Americans aged 25 and over had graduated from high school and many of them had gone on to college.

This table shows that over half of the 25-plus age group in all 50 states now consists of high-school graduates. The states in which such graduates make up over three-fourths of the adult population are all found in the Far West. The 10 states with under 60% high-school graduates are all located in the South. The pattern in Texas resembles that of the South rather than the West.

It is important to take the age structure of a state population into account before rushing to praise or blame the educational diligence of state residents. Where younger persons are well represented, as in the western states, the overall average of high-school graduates will be higher. This is due to the higher graduation rates of recent decades. (For the 25 to 29 age group in 1980, 86% of whites and 80% of blacks had finished high school. For the 55-plus age group, the corresponding figures were 50% for whites and 24% for blacks.) The rates for western states also tend to be higher because the stream of migrants into this area since 1950 has included an above average share of persons who were well educated—in other states.

Table: High-school Graduates
Date: 1980
Source: Census Bureau
Description: Percentage of people 25 and over who have completed four years of of high school or more.
U.S. average: 66.3%
State median: 68%

HIGH-SCHOOL GRADUATES

Rank	State	Percent of high school graduates
1	Alaska	82.8
2	Utah	80.3
3	Colorado	78.1
4	Wyoming	77.8
5	Washington	77.0
6	Nevada	75.5
7	Montana	75.4
8	Oregon	74.7
9	Nebraska	73.8
10	California	73.6
11	Hawaii	73.4
12	Idaho	72.8
13	Massachusetts	72.7
14	Minnesota	72.4
15	Arizona	72.3
15	Kansas	72.3
17	New Hampshire	72.0
18	Iowa	71.2
19	Connecticut	70.5
19	Vermont	70.5
21	Wisconsin	70.0
22	Maine	68.5
22	South Dakota	68.5
24	Michigan	68.2
24	New Mexico	68.2
26	Delaware	67.8
26	New Jersey	67.8
28	Ohio	67.4
29	Florida	67.2
30	Maryland	66.7
30	Oklahoma	66.7
32	North Dakota	66.5
33	New York	66.2
34	Indiana	65.9
35	Illinois	65.0
36	Pennsylvania	64.5
37	Missouri	63.7
38	Virginia	62.5
39	Texas	61.4
40	Rhode Island	60.7
41	Louisiana	58.0
42	Alabama	56.7
43	West Virginia	56.6
44	Georgia	56.5
45	Tennessee	55.4
46	North Carolina	55.3
47	Mississippi	55.1
48	Arkansas	54.9
49	South Carolina	54.0
50	Kentucky	51.9

176: College Graduates

About one of every six Americans 25 years old or older is a college graduate. The average percentage of college graduates in this age range has increased rapidly over the past 30 years, from 6% in 1950, 8% in 1960 and 11% in

1970 to the present level. There is still a significant gap in college graduation rates between men (21%) and women (13%), but this gap is gradually narrowing. The state age structure effect noted for the preceding table is also a factor here. States with younger populations tend to have more college graduates. In the 25 to 29 age group, in 1980, the percentages of college graduates were 22% for whites and 12% for blacks. In the 55-plus age group, the figures were 10% for whites and 3% for blacks. While blacks have pulled very close to the white majority in rates of completing high school, there is still a broad gap between rates of college graduation.

A few of the western states with high rankings in the previous table are also near the top here, but the standing of a number of states in the East is a good deal higher. Indiana and Pennsylvania join eight southern states with fewer than 14 college graduates per 100 adults. The states of Virginia and Georgia, with their highly educated (political and southern business) elites, have very high ranks here as compared to the rankings in the last table.

Table: College Graduates
Date: 1980
Source: National Center for Education Statistics
Description: Percentage of the population who completed their college education.
United States average: 16.3%
State median: 15.7%

COLLEGE GRADUATES

Rank	State	Percent of college graduates in state population
1	Colorado	23.0
2	Alaska	22.4
3	Connecticut	21.2
4	Hawaii	20.4
5	Utah	20.3
6	Massachusetts	20.0
7	California	19.8
7	Maryland	19.8
9	Vermont	19.5
10	Virginia	19.2
11	Washington	18.8
12	New York	18.7
13	New Jersey	18.6
14	New Hampshire	18.4
15	Montana	17.3
15	New Mexico	17.3
17	Oregon	17.2
17	Wyoming	17.2
19	Arizona	16.8
20	Minnesota	16.7
21	Delaware	16.3
22	Idaho	16.1

Rank	State	Percent of college graduates in state population
22	Nebraska	16.1
24	Texas	16.0
25	Kansas	15.7
25	Oklahoma	15.7
27	Georgia	15.3
27	Rhode Island	15.3
29	Michigan	15.2
29	North Dakota	15.2
31	Nevada	15.1
32	Wisconsin	14.9
33	Ohio	14.8
34	Florida	14.7
35	Illinois	14.5
36	South Carolina	14.2
36	South Dakota	14.2
38	Iowa	14.1
39	Maine	14.0
39	Missouri	14.0
41	Louisiana	13.4
41	North Carolina	13.4
43	Pennsylvania	13.3
44	Mississippi	13.0
45	Alabama	12.6
46	Indiana	12.4
47	Tennessee	11.9
48	Kentucky	11.0
49	West Virginia	10.5
50	Arkansas	9.7

177: Scholastic Aptitude Test Scores

The Scholastic Aptitude Test (SAT), which almost all college-bound students are obliged to take, has become a rite of passage in modern American society. The degree of controversy that always surrounds the tests is proof that the SATs have taken their place among our key institutions. How could it be otherwise, given the power of test results to open or close the doors of institutions of higher education, the springboards to success? Controversy has always centered on the degree to which these standardized tests successfully measure true academic ability. New issues are always arising. The fairness of the tests in measuring the overall talents and especially the language skills of minority students is a topic of special concern. With the establishment of "coaching academies" and computer software packages a new question has been raised about unfair advantages for students who can afford such special training and equipment.

The SAT scores for high-school seniors in the class of 1982 were slightly higher than those for seniors in the class of 1981, reversing a steady and disturbing downward trend in average scores that had persisted for 18 years in a row. How were average scores distributed across the states for the class of 1982? This table gives the answer. The pattern seems simple enough at first glance. At the top of the list we find states scattered across the Great Plains with average combined scores above 1000. At the bottom we find states from the East and a few from the South with scores below 900. This appears to settle the question of where American brainpower is coming from—but appearances are deceiving.

A closer look at the data reveals a remarkable pattern. The top 27 states (plus Nevada at rank 30) happen to be the ones in which very few high-school seniors take the SAT. Using data for the seniors of 1980—which cannot be very much different than the data for the seniors of 1982—it turns out that in these 28 states the percentage of graduating seniors who took the test is 18% or less (column 4). In the top three states the state "averages" are really averages for only 2% or 3% of all high-school seniors. The other 22 states have much higher test-taking rates, from 31% of seniors in Alaska to 69% in Connecticut. Is it really a surprise that average scores in these states are lower? If only 3% of the seniors in Connecticut were to take the SAT, it is likely that they would be drawn from the group of the very brightest students in the state, and that their average combined score would be well above the 1088 level recorded for Iowa.

The most revealing information in this table is therefore found in the last column. It appears that states can be broken into two very distinct groups according to the percentage of high-school students who are bound for college. The figure given in this column can be taken as an approximation of that percentage. This is a far better indicator of the contribution of each state to the pool of highly educated Americans than the average SAT scores.

It is interesting to note that differences between average math and verbal scores are somewhat larger near the very top of the table. Below rank 15 or so the difference values do not stray far from the national average differential of 41 points (favoring mathematics). Louisiana has the smallest difference (25 points) and the largest difference is found in Hawaii (73 points), where many test-takers apparently have unusual difficulty with the subtleties of the English language.

Table: Scholastic Aptitude Test Scores
Date: 1981/82
Source: College board
Description: Scholastic aptitude test scores (combined math and verbal) and percentage of 1980 high-school graduates who took the SAT prior to graduation.

U.S. average combined score: 893
U.S. average math: 467
U.S. average verbal: 426

SAT SCORES

Rank	State	SAT combined score	Percent taking test
1	Iowa	1,088	3
2	South Dakota	1,075	2
3	North Dakota	1,068	3
4	Kansas	1,045	5
4	Nebraska	1,045	5
6	Montana	1,033	8
7	Minnesota	1,028	7
8	Utah	1,022	4
9	Wyoming	1,017	5
10	Wisconsin	1,011	10
11	Oklahoma	1,001	5
12	Arkansas	999	4
12	Tennessee	999	9
14	New Mexico	997	8
15	Idaho	995	7
16	Mississippi	988	3
17	Kentucky	985	6
18	Colorado	983	16
19	Washington	982	19
20	Arizona	981	11
21	Illinois	977	14
22	Louisiana	975	5
22	Missouri	975	10
24	Michigan	973	10
25	West Virginia	968	7
26	Alabama	964	6
27	Ohio	958	16
28	New Hampshire	925	56
29	Alaska	923	31
30	Nevada	917	18
31	Oregon	908	40
32	Vermont	904	54
33	California	899	36
34	Delaware	897	42
35	Connecticut	896	69
35	New York	896	59
37	Maine	890	46
38	Florida	889	39
38	Maryland	889	50
40	Massachusetts	888	65
40	Virginia	888	52
42	Pennsylvania	885	50
43	Rhode Island	877	59
44	New Jersey	869	64
45	Texas	868	32
46	Indiana	860	48
47	Hawaii	857	47
48	North Carolina	827	47
49	Georgia	823	51
50	South Carolina	790	48

Table: Scholastic Aptitude Test Scores—Math
Date: 1980
Source: College Board
Description: Scholastic Aptitude Test Mean Math Scores of 1980 college-bound high-school seniors.
United States average: 467
United States mean: 505

SAT MATH SCORES

Rank	State	Scores
1	Iowa	572
2	North Dakota	563
3	South Dakota	553
4	Nebraska	552
5	Montana	546
6	Kansas	545
7	Minnesota	543
8	Wisconsin	535
9	Wyoming	533
10	Utah	528
11	Arkansas	519
11	Tennessee	519
13	Oklahoma	518
14	New Mexico	517
15	Colorado	515
15	Illinois	515
17	Michigan	514
17	Washington	514
19	Idaho	513
20	Arizona	511
21	Kentucky	510
21	Missouri	510
23	Mississippi	509
24	West Virginia	506
25	Louisiana	505
26	Ohio	502
27	Alabama	501
28	New Hampshire	482
29	Nevada	481
30	Alaska	477
31	California	474
32	Oregon	473
33	Vermont	471
34	New York	467
35	Delaware	465
35	Hawaii	465
37	Connecticut	464
37	Maryland	464
39	Florida	463
39	Maine	463
39	Massachusetts	463
42	Virginia	462
43	Pennsylvania	461
44	Rhode Island	457
45	Indiana	453
45	New Jersey	453
45	Texas	453
48	North Carolina	431
49	Georgia	429
50	South Carolina	412

Table: Scholastic Aptitude Test Scores—Verbal
Date: 1980
Source: College Board
Description: Scholastic Aptitude Test Mean Verbal Scores of 1980 college-bound high-school seniors.
United States average: 426
United States mean: 462

SAT VERBAL SCORES

Rank	State	Scores
1	South Dakota	522
2	Iowa	516
3	North Dakota	505
4	Kansas	500
5	Utah	494
6	Nebraska	493
7	Montana	487
8	Minnesota	485
9	Wyoming	484
10	Oklahoma	483
11	Idaho	482
12	Arkansas	480
12	New Mexico	480
12	Tennessee	480
15	Mississippi	479
16	Wisconsin	476
17	Kentucky	475
18	Arizona	470
18	Louisiana	470
20	Colorado	468
20	Washington	468
22	Missouri	465
23	Alabama	463
24	Illinois	462
24	West Virginia	462
26	Michigan	459
27	Ohio	456
28	Alaska	446
29	New Hampshire	443
30	Nevada	436
31	Oregon	435
32	Vermont	433
33	Connecticut	432
33	Delaware	432
35	New York	429
36	Maine	427
37	Florida	426
37	Virginia	426
39	California	425
39	Maryland	425
39	Massachusetts	425
39	Pennsylvania	425
43	Rhode Island	420
44	New Jersey	416
45	Texas	415
46	Indiana	407
47	North Carolina	396
48	Georgia	394
49	Hawaii	392
50	South Carolina	378

178: Computers in the Classroom

With the boom in home computers and the prospect that computer skills may be a kind of "basic literacy" skill in a generation or so, it is interesting to see how far schools in different parts of the country have gone in providing access to computers. The data in this table indicate the percentage of schools in each state that own or have access to small computers for instructional purposes. The median value for the states is 18.2%. Classroom computers are present in at least a few schools in every state except Alaska and Hawaii. Rhode Island and Minnesota hold a large lead over the other states. The states at the bottom of the table are generally those that have low levels of overall spending on public education, including most states in the South.

Table: Computers in the classroom
Date: 1982
Source: *U.S. News & World Report*
Description: Percentage of schools using small computers for instruction.
U. S. average: 19.3%
State median: 10.1%

COMPUTERS IN THE CLASSROOM

Rank	State	Percentage of schools using computers
1	Rhode Island	53.3
2	Minnesota	50.4
3	Delaware	42.9
4	Iowa	34.4
5	Oregon	30.8
6	New York	28.7
7	North Dakota	27.2
8	Florida	26.5
9	Colorado	26.3
10	Utah	25.6
11	Wisconsin	23.6
12	Kansas	23.3
13	Maryland	23.0
14	Wyoming	22.9
15	Michigan	22.7
16	Arizona	21.6
17	Connecticut	21.3
18	Nebraska	21.1
19	Massachusetts	21.0
20	Montana	20.7
21	South Dakota	20.3
22	New Jersey	20.1
23	Illinois	19.9
24	Washington	18.5
25	Mississippi	18.3
26	New Mexico	18.1
27	Indiana	17.9
28	Pennsylvania	17.3
29	Vermont	17.1
30	Ohio	16.4
30	Texas	16.4
32	Georgia	15.2
33	California	14.8
34	Nevada	14.2
35	Maine	13.5
36	Missouri	13.4
37	Oklahoma	13.2
38	Arkansas	12.7
39	North Carolina	12.6
40	Virginia	12.5
41	Kentucky	12.2
42	Idaho	11.7
43	South Carolina	10.9
44	New Hampshire	10.5
45	Tennessee	8.7
46	Louisiana	7.7
47	Alabama	6.3
48	West Virginia	5.5
49	Alaska	0
49	Hawaii	0

CRIME

Crime and the fear of crime have been rising steadily during the past decade. Justice Department statistics show that between 1971 and 1980 the number of reported major crimes against property (burglary, larceny, motor vehicle theft) increased by 41%. During the same period the number of reported major violent crimes against persons (murder/manslaughter, rape, robbery, assault) increased by 47%. Public opinion polls since the mid-1970s have consistently shown that fear of victimization is high, and stable or rising. Spectacular cases of mass murder, assassination and attempted assassination, and kidnapping have guided the attention of the nation to the issue of public safety. Americans, who already own over 50 million handguns, are now adding to their private armories at the rate of over 50 handguns per hour. Public doubts about the effectiveness of police protection have led to the proliferation of private police forces, neighborhood patrol organizations, and a boom in the sales of sophisticated security equipment.

The American criminal justice system has been heavily criticized in recent years for its lack of success in stemming the rise of crime. There is widespread agreement that basic causes of crime include lack of economic opportunity, the failure of families and other agencies to carry out effective moral training, and the absence of institutions providing guidance at the community level, but there is also a strong sense that police, courts and prisons are not performing very well. Political debate on the rise of crime often focuses on the issue of punishment—especially the possibility that a more rigorously enforced death penalty might serve to discourage criminals—instead of facing the more difficult issues of judicial reform, prison reform and the need for more funding in the area of criminal justice.

The first eight tables in this section focus on rates of major crimes reported in the states and major cities. A table on state and local spending for police protection is then presented, followed by two tables on the police forces of the larger cities: size of the police force and representation of women on the force. The last three tables deal with the penal system, showing the relative size of prison populations in the states and the past and present status of the death penalty.

179: Major Crimes—Crime Index Rates

The data in this table represent reported crimes included in the Crime Index compiled each year by the Department of Justice. Seven types of crimes are included in the index: the four violent crimes of murder/manslaughter, forcible rape, robbery and aggravated assault and the three property crimes of burglary, larceny and motor vehicle theft.

There were over 13 million crimes falling into these seven categories during 1980. This works out to a rate of nearly 6 reported major crimes per 100 persons in the general population. Generally rising trends were observed in each one of the index categories during the decade 1971-1980. The Crime Index value stood at 4,165 in 1971, 5,266 in 1976 and 5,900 in 1980. Crime Index values continued to rise steadily in six-month reporting periods from 1978 to 1981 before declining slightly in the first half of 1982.

The highest crime rates are found in a number of Sunbelt states: Nevada, Florida, Arizona, California, Hawaii and Colorado. The safest states are found in certain areas of the South, the northern Plains and upper New England.

Table: Total Crime Rate
Date: 1980
Source: Federal Bureau of Investigation
Description: Rate of crimes per 100,000 population and number of crimes.
U.S. total: 13.3 million crimes
U.S. average: 5,900 per 100,000 population
State median: 5,405 per 100,000 population.

TOTAL CRIME RATE

Rank	State	Crimes per 100,000 population	Number of crimes
1	Nevada	8,854	70,860
2	Florida	8,402	803,825

Rank	State	Crimes per 100,000 population	Number of crimes
3	Arizona	8,171	221,866
4	California	7,833	1,843,332
5	Hawaii	7,482	72,180
6	Colorado	7,334	211,087
7	Washington	6,915	284,436
8	New York	6,912	1,209,984
9	Delaware	6,777	40,306
10	Oregon	6,687	174,561
11	Michigan	6,676	616,065
12	Maryland	6,630	277,949
13	New Jersey	6,401	469,996
14	Alaska	6,210	24,849
15	Texas	6,143	870,458
16	Massachusetts	6,079	348,231
17	New Mexico	5,979	77,457
18	Rhode Island	5,933	56,113
19	Connecticut	5,882	182,051
20	Utah	5,881	85,782
21	Georgia	5,604	302,645
22	Louisiana	5,454	229,032
23	South Carolina	5,439	166,686
24	Missouri	5,433	266,292
25	Ohio	5,431	584,787
26	Kansas	5,379	126,660
27	Illinois	5,275	599,009
28	Oklahoma	5,053	151,650
29	Montana	5,024	39,271
30	Vermont	4,988	25,506
31	Wyoming	4,986	25,384
32	Alabama	4,934	190,511
33	Indiana	4,930	269,252
34	Minnesota	4,800	194,918
35	Wisconsin	4,799	224,619
36	Idaho	4,782	45,126
37	Iowa	4,747	138,026
38	New Hampshire	4,680	43,011
39	North Carolina	4,640	271,174
40	Virginia	4,620	245,942
41	Tennessee	4,498	204,456
42	Maine	4,368	49,077
43	Nebraska	4,305	67,330
44	Arkansas	3,811	87,046
45	Pennsylvania	3,736	441,793
46	Kentucky	3,434	125,039
47	Mississippi	3,417	85,822
48	South Dakota	3,243	22,320
49	North Dakota	2,964	19,336
50	West Virginia	2,552	49,266

180: Crime Index Rates in Selected Large Cities

As a rule, the relative frequency of crime is related to the size of a concentrated population. This can be illustrated by a simple chart using Crime Index data for all American cities in 1980:

CRIME INDEX BY SIZE OF CITY

Cities by population size groups	Crime index values		
	Total crimes	Violent crimes	Property crimes
250,000 or more	9,402	1,414	7,988
100,000–249,999	8,742	812	7,930
50,000–99,999	7,137	602	6,535
25,000–49,999	6,508	455	6,053
10,000–24,999	5,411	352	5,059
Fewer than 10,000	4,859	298	4,562

The likelihood of both violent crime and property crime increases uniformly with city population. The high concentration of violent crime in the largeest cities is the most notable pattern here.

Among the 25 large cities included in the table, the general crime rate is above the national average of 5,900 per 100,000 population in all but Indianapolis. Rates in St. Louis, Boston and Denver are more than twice the national average. An extremely high rate of auto theft in the city of Boston—more than seven times the national average—is a major reason for the position of the Yankee metropolis in this table. Cities with high crime rates are found in all parts of the country, but data for the entire SMSAs of which they are a part show that with the exception of New York, the highest metropolitan crime rates tend to be found in the West. Sharp differences between city and metropolitan rates—in St. Louis, for example—indicate a wide gulf in relative safety between a city and its suburbs, with highly concentrated criminal activity.

Table: Crime Rate in Selected Large Cities
Date: 1980
Source: Federal Bureau of Investigation
Description: Total crimes per 100,000 population in 25 large cities and in the SMSAs of which they are part.

CRIME RATE IN SELECTED LARGE CITIES

Rank	City	Crimes per 100,000 population	SMSA
1	St. Louis	14,332	6,488
2	Boston	13,465	6,493
3	Denver	12,013	8,357
4	Dallas	11,778	8,271
5	Phoenix	11,454	9,308
6	Seattle	10,834	7,862
7	Detroit	10,624	7,582
8	San Francisco	10,446	8,541
9	New York	10,094	8,953
10	Cleveland	10,059	5,634
11	Washington, D.C.	10,023	6,939

Rank	City	Crimes per 100,000 population	SMSA
12	Los Angeles	9,952	8,419
13	Baltimore	9,777	7,473
14	New Orleans	9,605	7,890
15	Columbus, Ohio	9,488	7,541
16	Houston	8,886	6,900
17	San Jose	8,252	7,612
18	San Diego	8,059	7,038
19	Jacksonville	7,902	7,137
20	Memphis	7,895	6,492
21	San Antonio	7,344	6,411
22	Chicago	6,583	5,722
23	Milwaukee	6,539	5,364
24	Philadelphia	6,016	5,358
25	Indianapolis	5,327	6,009

181: Property Crime

Property crimes (burglary, larceny, motor vehicle theft) are about 12 times as frequent as violent crimes. For this reason, the ranking in the present table is nearly identical to the ranking in the table with overall Crime Index values. The same six Sunbelt states are found at the top of both lists. Property remains relatively safe in the Dakotas, in several states in the South and in Pennsylvania.

Table: Property Crime Rate
Date: 1980
Source: Federal Bureau of Investigation
Description: Rate of property crime per 100,000 population and number of property crimes.
U.S. total: 11,986,501
U.S. average: 5,319.1 per 100,000 population
State median: 4,844 per 100,000 population

PROPERTY CRIME RATE

Rank	State	Property crimes per 100,000 population	Number of property crimes
1	Nevada	7,941.4	63,556
2	Arizona	7,519.9	204,193
3	Florida	7,418.4	709,730
4	Hawaii	7,182.8	69,291
5	California	6,939.5	1,633,042
6	Colorado	6,804.9	195,872
7	Washington	6,450.7	265,338
8	Delaware	6,301.8	37,482
9	Oregon	6,196.5	161,759
10	Michigan	6,036.4	557,051
11	New York	5,882.0	1,029,749
12	New Jersey	5,797.0	425,623
13	Maryland	5,777.7	242,214
14	Alaska	5,730.5	22,930

Rank	State	Property crimes per 100,000 population	Number of property crimes
15	Texas	5,592.7	792,480
16	Utah	5,577.3	81,357
17	Rhode Island	5,524.1	52,249
18	Massachusetts	5,477.8	313,787
19	Connecticut	5,469.2	169,283
20	New Mexico	5,364.1	69,490
21	Georgia	5,048.3	272,652
22	Kansas	4,989.5	117,492
23	Wyoming	4,953.8	21,543
24	Ohio	4,933.1	531,141
25	Missouri	4,878.6	239,115
26	Vermont	4,809.7	24,592
27	Montana	4,801.9	37,531
28	Louisiana	4,788.8	201,106
29	Illinois	4,781.0	542,881
30	South Carolina	4,779.2	146,461
31	Oklahoma	4,633.4	139,061
32	Wisconsin	4,616.0	216,073
33	Minnesota	4,571.7	185,668
34	Indiana	4,552.5	248,619
35	Iowa	4,546.4	132,200
36	New Hampshire	4,499.8	41,358
37	Alabama	4,485.1	173,191
38	Idaho	4,468.8	42,169
39	Virginia	4,312.8	229,587
40	North Carolina	4,185.5	244,585
41	Maine	4,174.2	46,904
42	Nebraska	4,080.6	63,818
43	Tennessee	4,039.8	183,632
44	Arkansas	3,475.9	79,390
45	Pennsylvania	3,372.4	398,761
46	Kentucky	3,167.1	115,328
47	South Dakota	3,116.3	21,447
48	Mississippi	3,075.2	77,234
49	North Dakota	2,909.7	18,984
50	West Virginia	2,367.9	45,719

182: Motor Vehicle Theft

Lower New England, particularly the Boston-Providence area, is the auto theft center of the United States. Massachusetts and Rhode Island are well ahead of the other states in the incidence of crime. The three states surrounding the New York City area make up a second region where vehicle theft rates are high, while California and Nevada form a western high-risk zone. These seven states stand somewhat apart from the rest of the nation in this table. The main smooth sequence of descending rates begins with Alaska and Hawaii and ends with the Dakotas and Mississippi. Residents of Massachusetts are about six times more likely to lose their cars than residents of South Dakota. From 1971 to 1978 the national rate of motor vehicle theft moved up and down in the area of 450 thefts per 100,000 population before rising by about 10% to levels of 498 and 495 per 100,000 population in 1979 and 1980, respectively.

Table: Motor Vehicle Theft Rate
Date: 1980
Source: Federal Bureau of Investigation
Description: Motor vehicle theft rate per 100,000 population and number of thefts.
United States total: 1.1 million
United States average: 495 per 100,000 population
State median: 368 per 100,000 population

MOTOR VEHICLE THEFT RATE

Rank	State	Motor vehicle thefts per 100,000 population	Number of thefts
1	Massachusetts	1,052	60,241
2	Rhode Island	844	7,979
3	New York	760	133,041
4	California	742	174,834
5	New Jersey	730	53,563
6	Connecticut	679	21,014
7	Nevada	678	5,429
8	Alaska	617	2,469
9	Hawaii	612	5,905
10	Michigan	585	53,979
11	Texas	558	79,088
12	Illinois	499	56,652
13	Florida	478	45,682
14	Arizona	473	12,852
15	Delaware	455	2,707
16	Maryland	450	18,887
17	Colorado	448	12,903
18	Indiana	432	23,602
19	Ohio	427	25,945
20	Oklahoma	420	12,610
21	Pennsylvania	418	49,465
22	Missouri	415	20,319
23	Washington	396	16,272
24	Louisiana	376	15,811
25	Georgia	372	20,115
26	Tennessee	363	16,505
27	Oregon	360	9,406
28	New Mexico	351	4,542
29	Wyoming	345	1,619
30	Utah	324	4,720
31	Montana	322	2,514
32	Alabama	316	12,210
33	New Hampshire	310	2,848
34	South Carolina	306	9,379
35	Minnesota	296	12,016
36	Vermont	295	1,508
37	Kansas	272	6,398
38	Kentucky	251	9,131
39	Iowa	248	7,205
40	Wisconsin	245	11,479
41	Nebraska	244	3,810
42	Idaho	237	2,235

Rank	State	Motor vehicle thefts per 100,000 population	Number of thefts
43	Virginia	228	12,130
44	Maine	219	2,462
45	North Carolina	216	12,631
46	West Virginia	200	3,855
47	Arkansas	187	4,273
48	North Dakota	179	1,169
49	Mississippi	178	4,480
50	South Dakota	169	1,160

183: Violent Crime

During the year 1980 there were 1.3 million reported acts of murder/manslaughter, forcible rape, robbery and aggravated assault. The lowest levels of violent crime are observed in the Dakotas. Northern New England, West Virginia and the upper Midwest are also areas where violent crime is not often reported (which probably means that it does not often occur). New York is the most violent state, with a rate about five times higher than the rates prevailing at the bottom of the list. Florida is a close second in violence, with California, Nevada and Maryland completing a group of five states that stands out at the top of the list. Rates in this group are all more than 25% higher than the rates in Louisiana and South Carolina, the most violent states in the South. The national rate of violent crime moved more or less steadily upward from 1970 (363 per 100,000 population) to 1980 (581 per 100,000 population).

Table: Violent Crime Rate
Date: 1980
Source: Federal Bureau of Investigation
Description: Rate of violent crime reported per 100,000 population and number of violent crimes.
United states total: 1.3 million
United states average: 581 per 100,000 population
State median: 434 per 100,000 population

VIOLENT CRIME RATE

Rank	State	Violent crimes per 100,000 population	Number of violent crimes
1	New York	1,030	180,235
2	Florida	984	94,095
3	Nevada	913	7,304
4	California	894	210,290
5	Maryland	852	35,735
6	Louisiana	665	27,926

Rank	State	Violent crimes per 100,000 population	Number of violent crimes
7	South Carolina	660	20,225
8	Arizona	651	17,673
9	Michigan	640	59,014
10	New Mexico	615	7,967
11	New Jersey	604	44,373
12	Massachusetts	601	34,444
13	Georgia	555	29,993
14	Missouri	554	27,177
15	Texas	550	77,978
16	Colorado	529	15,215
17	Ohio	498	53,646
18	Illinois	494	56,128
19	Oregon	490	12,802
20	Alaska	480	1,919
21	Delaware	475	2,824
22	Washington	464	19,098
23	Tennessee	458	20,824
24	North Carolina	455	26,589
25	Alabama	448	17,320
26	Oklahoma	420	12,589
27	Connecticut	412	12,768
28	Rhode Island	408	3,864
29	Wyoming	393	1,841
30	Kansas	389	9,168
31	Indiana	378	20,633
32	Pennsylvania	364	43,032
33	Mississippi	342	8,588
34	Arkansas	335	7,656
35	Idaho	313	2,957
36	Virginia	307	16,355
37	Utah	303	4,425
38	Hawaii	300	2,889
39	Kentucky	267	9,711
40	Minnesota	228	9,250
41	Nebraska	225	3,512
42	Montana	223	1,740
43	Iowa	200	5,826
44	Maine	193	2,173
45	West Virginia	184	3,547
46	Wisconsin	183	8,546
47	New Hampshire	180	1,653
48	Vermont	179	914
49	South Dakota	127	873
50	North Dakota	54	352

184: Murder and Manslaughter

There were over 23,000 reported acts of murder and nonnegligent (i.e., more or less intentional) manslaughter during 1980. Over one-third of these acts occurred in just three states: California, Texas and New York. The rates of murder/manslaughter are also relatively high in these states, but Nevada is the deadliest state of all on a relative basis. The national rate of murderous acts per 100,000 population varied between 8.6 and 9.8 from 1971 to 1979 before rising to 10.2 in 1980. The nine states with the highest rates are very neatly laid out along the southern rim of the United States, from California to Texas and along the Gulf Coast to Florida. States in the South, many of which are near the bottom of lists for other major crimes, all have fairly high positions in this table.

Table: Murder and Manslaughter Rate
Date: 1980
Source: Federal Bureau of Investigation
Description: Rate of reported incidents of murder and nonnegligent manslaughter per 100,000 population and number of murders/manslaughters.
United States total: 23,040
United States average: 10.2 per 100,000 population
State median: 8.4 per 100,000 population

MURDER AND MANSLAUGHTER RATE

Rank	State	Murders/ manslaughters per 100,000 population	Number of murders/ manslaughters
1	Nevada	20.0	160
2	Texas	16.9	2,392
3	Louisiana	15.7	661
4	California	14.5	3,411
4	Florida	14.5	1,387
4	Mississippi	14.5	365
7	Georgia	13.8	743
8	Alabama	13.2	509
9	New Mexico	13.1	170
10	New York	12.7	2,228
11	South Carolinia	11.4	348
12	Missouri	11.1	544
13	Tennessee	10.8	489
14	Illinois	10.6	1,205
14	North Carolina	10.6	619
16	Arizona	10.3	279
17	Michigan	10.2	940
18	Oklahoma	10.0	299
19	Alaska	9.7	39
20	Maryland	9.5	399
21	Arkansas	9.2	210
22	Indiana	8.9	485
23	Kentucky	8.8	321
24	Hawaii	8.7	84
25	Virginia	8.6	459
26	Ohio	8.1	871
27	West Virginia	7.1	138
28	Colorado	6.9	198
28	Delaware	6.9	41
28	Kansas	6.9	163
28	New Jersey	6.9	504
32	Pennsylvania	6.8	809
33	Wyoming	6.2	29
34	Washington	5.5	225

Rank	State	Murders/ manslaughters per 100,000 population	Number of murders/ manslaughters
35	Oregon	5.1	132
36	Nebraska	4.4	69
36	Rhode Island	4.4	42
38	Connecticut	4.2	181
39	Massachusetts	4.1	232
40	Montana	4.0	31
41	Utah	3.8	55
42	Idaho	3.1	29
43	Wisconsin	2.9	136
44	Maine	2.8	32
45	Minnesota	2.6	106
46	New Hampshire	2.5	23
47	Iowa	2.2	63
47	Vermont	2.2	11
49	North Dakota	1.2	8
50	South Dakota	0.7	5

185: Murder and Manslaughter in Selected Large Cities

Every six months or so the FBI issues a report on murderous acts. Newspapers use these reports as the basis for identifying the new "murder capitals" of the nation. Detroit, Houston and New Orleans, along with St. Louis, have all held this dubious distinction at some point in recent years. Since rates for cities are figured on the basis of a relatively small number of criminal acts, they fluctuate a good bit from one period to the next. Instead of focusing on precise annual figures, it makes more sense to examine the general range in which a city falls. It appears that any of the top seven or eight cities on this list is murderous enough to be the "murder capital" in any given period. Cities in the center of the list, say from Chicago to Denver, are moderately deadly while the 10 cities at the bottom are zones of relative safety from murder.

At the level of metropolitan areas, Houston, Los Angeles, New Orleans and New York stand out above the remaining SMSAs. City rates are about three times higher than SMSA rates for the top three cities on the list, an indicator that murder is concentrated in downtown areas. The drop is much less steep in New Orleans, Houston and Los Angeles, where suburban murders are not uncommon, and in New York, where the city accounts for much of the overall SMSA. In Memphis, San Antonio and Jacksonville there is little difference between the central city and suburban rates.

Table: Murder and Manslaughter Rate in Selected Large Cities
Date: 1980
Source: Federal Bureau of Investigation
Description: Murder and manslaughter rates per 100,000 population in 25 large cities and in the SMSAs of which they are part.

MURDER AND MANSLAUGHTER RATE IN SELECTED LARGE CITIES

Rank	City	Murder/manslaughter rate per 100,000 population City	SMSA
1	St. Louis	49.9	15.2
2	Cleveland	46.3	15.9
3	Detroit	45.7	16.1
4	Houston	39.1	27.6
4	New Orleans	39.1	22.3
6	Dallas	35.4	18.1
7	Los Angeles	34.2	23.3
8	Washington, D.C.	31.5	10.7
9	Chicago	28.9	14.5
10	Baltimore	27.5	12.5
11	Philadelphia	25.9	12.1
12	New York	25.8	21.0
13	Memphis	23.6	19.5
14	San Antonio	20.8	17.5
15	Denver	20.2	9.4
16	Boston	16.3	5.2
16	San Francisco	16.3	11.7
18	Columbus, Ohio	15.5	9.9
19	Indianapolis	15.3	11.9
20	Phoenix	13.3	10.5
21	Jacksonville	12.9	12.4
22	Seattle	12.8	6.7
23	San Diego	11.8	9.9
24	Milwaukee	11.7	5.7
25	San Jose	9.9	7.6

186: Forcible Rape

The incidence of rape increased dramatically during the 1970s, from 42,260 reported cases (20.5 per 100,000 population) in 1971 to 82,090 cases (36.4 per 100,000 population) in 1980. It is not possible to say how much of this change was due to an actual increase in the incidence of rape and how much was due to the increasing likelihood that women victimized by rapists will report the crime. To report an act of rape requires considerable courage and fortitude on the part of the victim. Standard police and court procedures do not offer very much personal protection and support for the victim, and convictions are difficult to obtain. As a consequence, many women simply suffer the pain and humiliation of rape alone and the percentage of forcible rapes reported to the police remains relatively low.

There are strong state to state variations in the frequency of rape, with a ratio of about 5 to 1 between values for states at the extremes of the distribution. There are general similarities between this ranking and the position of the states in the murder/manslaughter table. Seven states appear among the 12 most dangerous states in both tables: Nevada, California, New Mexico, Texas, Louisiana, Georgia and Florida. There are eight states that appear among the 12 safest in both tables: North Dakota, South Dakota, Iowa, Wisconsin, Montana, Idaho, New Hampshire and Maine. Three states in which ranking by incidence of rape is much higher than ranking by incidence of murder/manslaughter are Colorado, Washington and Alaska. The reverse is true (lower ranking in this table) for the states of West Virginia, Kentucky and North Carolina.

Table: Rate of Forcible Rape
Date: 1980
Source: Federal Bureau of Investigation
Description: Rate of reported rapes per 100,000 population and number of reported rapes.
United States total: 82,090
United States average: 36.4 per 100,000 population
State median: 29.6 per 100,000 population

RATE OF FORCIBLE RAPE

Rank	State	Reported rapes per 100,000 population	Number of reported rapes
1	Nevada	67.2	538
2	Alaska	62.5	250
3	California	58.2	13,693
4	Florida	56.9	5,439
5	Washington	52.7	2,169
6	Colorado	52.5	1,510
7	Texas	47.3	6,700
8	Michigan	46.6	4,304
9	Arizona	45.2	1,227
10	Louisiana	44.5	1,867
11	Georgia	44.3	2,391
12	New Mexico	43.3	561
13	Oregon	41.5	1,084
14	Maryland	40.1	1,681
15	South Carolina	37.5	1,148
16	Tennessee	37.4	1,700
17	Oklahoma	36.3	1,088
18	Hawaii	34.7	335
19	Ohio	34.3	3,696
20	Indiana	33.1	1,808
21	Missouri	32.6	1,600
22	Kansas	31.5	742
23	New York	30.9	5,405
24	New Jersey	30.7	2,257
25	Alabama	30.0	1,158
26	Vermont	29.1	149
27	Wyoming	28.6	134
28	Utah	27.7	404
29	Virginia	27.4	1,458

Rank	State	Reported rapes per 100,000 population	Number of reported rapes
30	Massachusetts	27.3	1,562
31	Illinois	26.9	3,051
32	Arkansas	26.7	609
33	Mississippi	24.6	619
34	Delaware	24.2	144
35	Minnesota	23.2	942
35	Nebraska	23.2	363
37	Pennsylvania	23.0	2,722
38	North Carolina	22.7	1,324
39	Idaho	22.4	211
40	Connecticut	21.6	670
41	Montana	21.0	164
42	Kentucky	19.2	698
43	New Hampshire	17.3	159
44	Rhode Island	17.1	162
45	West Virginia	15.8	306
46	Wisconsin	14.9	697
47	Iowa	14.3	416
48	Maine	12.9	145
49	South Dakota	12.5	86
50	North Dakota	9.5	62

187: State and Local Spending for Police Protection

About 80 of the total spending recorded here is made by local governments for local police forces. There are only a few states in which expenditures for state police make up more than 30% of the total. Alaska is the only state in which spending on state forces is greater than spending on local police. Relatively strong state police forces are also found in Vermont, Delaware, Mississippi and West Virginia.

Alaska is also the unusual state in terms of total spending for police protection. This is just one aspect of the generally high costs of administration in a large, sparsely populated territory that turn up in data presented in the section on state and local government. Something of the frontier, with its peculiar problems of maintaining law and order in the wide open spaces, is still a reality in Alaska. For the remaining 49 states there is a ratio of about 3 to 1 between extreme cases in the range of spending levels. Since law enforcement problems are greater in areas of high population concentration, it is not surprising that police spending is high in states with big metropolitan areas and low in states with a more rural character.

Table: Per Capita Expenditures on Police Protection
Date: 1981
Source: Census Bureau

Description: Per capita expenditures by state and local governments on police protection.
State median: $55.40
United States average: $61.13

PER CAPITA EXPENDITURES ON POLICE PROTECTION

Rank	State	Per capita expenditure
1	Alaska	$167.05
2	Arizona	96.51
3	New York	92.60
4	Nevada	92.13
5	Wyoming	90.09
6	California	89.86
7	Illinois	80.85
8	New Jersey	78.93
9	Michigan	76.47
10	Florida	75.65
11	Maryland	75.16
12	Delaware	71.51
13	Massachusetts	70.78
14	Colorado	70.03
15	Wisconsin	69.00
16	Louisiana	67.78
17	Oregon	66.91
18	Hawaii	66.79
19	New Mexico	61.75
20	Rhode Island	61.50
21	Connecticut	61.41
22	Missouri	60.75
23	Washington	60.74
24	Utah	55.56
25	Ohio	55.25
26	Minnesota	54.90
27	Pennsylvania	53.95
28	Virginia	53.93
29	Montana	52.49
30	Texas	50.82
31	New Hampshire	50.29
32	North Carolina	49.63
33	Georgia	48.99
34	Idaho	48.42
35	Oklahoma	48.09
36	Nebraska	46.79
37	Alabama	46.42
38	Kansas	46.22
39	Tennessee	46.20
40	Iowa	44.74
41	Kentucky	44.50
42	South Carolina	43.51
43	South Dakota	42.70
44	Indiana	41.65
45	North Dakota	41.52
46	Vermont	40.61
47	Maine	40.18
48	Mississippi	38.26
49	Arkansas	33.83
50	West Virginia	32.92

188: The Police Force in Selected Large Cities

Washington, D.C. is the most heavily policed large city in the nation. The ratio of officers to population there is a good bit higher than that in the other towns in the leading group: Philadelphia, St. Louis, Chicago and Baltimore. The preeminence of Washington as a well-policed town derives from a special interest in maintaining order in a politically sensitive place with hosts of domestic and foreign visitors who make inviting targets for street crime. Crowds and demonstrations with their special problems of control are also relatively frequent in the nation's capital.

Among the other cities on the list there is a clear regional break between positions nine and 10. Except for Columbus and Indianapolis, all 15 cities in the lower part of the list are in the expanding regions of the West and South. While the large centers of the East and the Midwest, found near the top of the list, are losing population at a faster rate than they are cutting police forces, the Sunbelt cities have only begun to gear up their police departments to reflect recent population gains. The large differences in levels of policing will gradually even out over time. Comparison of this table to the tables for the Crime Index and for rates of murder/manslaughter in the same set of cities reveals very little relation between levels of policing and levels of crime.

Table: Size of Police Force
Date: 1980
Source: Federal Bureau of Investigation
Description: Size of police force and number of police per 10,000 people for the 25 largest cities.

SIZE OF POLICE FORCE

Rank	City	Number of police per 10,000 population	Size of police force
1	Washington, D.C.	57.3	3,652
2	Philadelphia	44.4	7,454
3	St. Louis	43.5	1,950
4	Chicago	41.7	12,392
5	Baltimore	40.4	3,171
6	Boston	37.5	2,108
7	Detroit	34.9	4,166
8	Cleveland	32.8	1,877
9	Milwaukee	32.2	2,039
9	New York	32.2	22,590
11	Denver	28.5	1,393
12	San Francisco	25.8	1,738
13	New Orleans	25.1	1,397
14	Los Angeles	22.3	6,587
15	Dallas	22.1	1,990
16	Seattle	21.1	1,036

Rank	City	Number of police per 10,000 population	Size of police force
17	Phoenix	20.8	1,622
18	Houston	19.7	3,070
19	Memphis	18.8	1,210
20	Jacksonville	17.6	951
21	Columbus, Ohio	17.2	968
22	San Diego	15.9	1,380
23	San Antonio	14.5	1,137
24	Indianapolis	13.9	969
25	San Jose	12.5	796

189: Women Police Officers in Selected Large Cities

The progress of women in attaining positions in municipal police departments has been relatively slow and rather uneven. Thus far there is no major city in which women make up more than 10% of the police force. The median value for this list of 25 cities is just 4.8%. San Diego, Indianapolis and Washington have been the most receptive departments. Women police officers are very rare in San Antonio, Jacksonville and Los Angeles.

Table: Women Police Officers
Date: 1980
Source: Federal Bureau of Investigation
Description: Women police officers as a percentage of all police officers for the 25 largest cities.

WOMEN POLICE OFFICERS

Rank	City	Percentage of women police officers
1	San Diego	9.5
2	Indianapolis	8.9
3	Washington, D.C.	8.7
4	San Francisco	7.9
5	Detroit	7.4
6	Cleveland	7.2
6	Dallas	7.2
8	Denver	6.5
9	Houston	6.4
10	Columbus, Ohio	6.2
11	Seattle	6.1
12	Memphis	6.0
13	New Orleans	4.8
14	Baltimore	4.3
15	Milwaukee	4.1
16	Chicago	3.9
17	Boston	3.8
18	St. Louis	3.4
19	Philadelphia	3.3
20	New York	3.1
20	Phoenix	3.1
20	San Jose	3.1
23	Los Angeles	2.7
24	Jacksonville	2.2
25	San Antonio	.2

190: Prison Populations

Higher crime rates and tougher sentencing laws have led to recent sharp upturns in the numbers of inmates in state and federal prisons. The figures presented here are based on counts of prisoners sentenced to terms of one year or more. Inmates of local jails are not counted. Using this measure, there were about 369,000 inmates in 1981, or about 154 per 100,000 members of the general population. Comparable figures (number of prisoners in thousands and rate per 100,000 population) were 196 and 97 in 1970, 241 and 113 in 1975, 314 and 139 in 1979. The number of inmates increased by 12 from 1980 to 1981, with increases in every state except Michigan.

There are large variations in rates of prisoners per 100,000 population in the states. Delaware and Maryland round out a group of 10 states otherwise found farther South and in the Southwest where rates are over 200. The 17 states with rates below 100 include all the states in the Northeast except New York, and a scattering of states in other parts of the country, most of them in the North Central section.

Table: Rate of Incarceration in Federal and State Prisons
Date: 1981
Source: Bureau of Justice statistics
Description: Rate of incarceration per 100,000 general population in federal and state prisons.
United States average: 154
State median: 117

RATE OF INCARCERATION IN FEDERAL AND STATE PRISONS

Rank	State	Prison inmates per 100,000 population
1	Nevada	253
1	South Carolina	253
3	North Carolina	250
4	Georgia	246
5	Florida	222
6	Louisiana	218
7	Delaware	214
7	Texas	214
9	Maryland	209
10	Alabama	186

Rank	State	Prison inmates per 100,000 population
10	Arizona	186
12	Mississippi	178
13	Alaska	172
14	Tennessee	171
15	Oklahoma	169
16	Virginia	166
17	Michigan	163
18	New York	145
19	Arkansas	142
20	Ohio	139
21	Indiana	138
22	Washington	127
23	Missouri	125
24	Oregon	124
25	Kansas	118
26	California	116
27	Illinois	114
28	Wyoming	113
29	Kentucky	109
30	New Mexico	107
31	Idaho	104
32	Montana	101
33	Nebraska	97
33	South Dakota	97
35	Connecticut	96
36	Iowa	94
37	Colorado	93
38	Wisconsin	92
39	New Jersey	90
40	Pennsylvania	78
41	Hawaii	77
41	Vermont	77
43	Utah	74
44	Rhode Island	72
45	West Virginia	67
46	Maine	65
46	Massachusetts	65
48	Minnesota	49
49	New Hampshire	41
50	North Dakota	37

unconstitutional because it was disproportionately imposed on individuals who were members of minority and lower economic groups. Four years later, however, the Court ruled that capital punishment for convicted murderers did not, as such, violate the constitutional constraint on cruel and unusual punishment. There has been no Court ruling directly concerned with the legality of the death penalty. The executions of many persons sentenced to death have been delayed for years in consideration of this lack of clarity in the law and the associated public controversy. There were no executions in the United States from 1968 through 1976. Between 1977 and 1980 there were just three executions, one each in the states of Florida, Nevada and Utah (the celebrated Gary Gilmore).

From 1930 through 1967, however, executioners were hard at work. There were a total of 3,859 executions in 42 different states and the District of Columbia. The death toll decade by decade reads as follows: 1930-1939 (1667 executions), 1940-1949 (1284), 1950-1959 (717), 1960-1967 (191). Although blacks made up only about 10% of the general population throughout this period, 55% of those executed were black; the situation in the South is evident in the table. The crimes for which people were executed included murder, sabotage and espionage (as in the case of the Rosenbergs, convicted of stealing secrets of atomic weapon production). In Alabama and North Carolina there were some executions for burglary.

Table: Prisoners Executed 1930-1976
Date: 1930-1976
Source: Law Enforcement Assistance Administration
Description: Total number of executions in the United States and executions according to race from 1930 to 1976.

191: The Death Penalty (1): Executions 1930–1967

The death penalty is a controversial issue. Some people support it as a deterrent to crime and a proper punishment for taking the life of another. Others oppose it as uncivilized and unconstitutional, since it has often been applied arbitrarily or unfairly. Blacks, for example, have historically been more likely than whites to be sentenced to death for equivalent crimes. The possibility that innocent persons may be executed is also a weighty concern.

In 1972 the Supreme Court ruled that capital punishment as then practiced in the United States was

PRISONERS EXECUTED 1930 – 1976

Rank	State	Total	Blacks	Whites
1	Georgia	366	298	68
2	New York	329	90	234
3	Texas	297	182	114
4	California	292	53	221
5	North Carolina	263	199	59
6	Ohio	172	67	104
7	Florida	170	113	57
8	South Carolina	162	127	35
9	Mississippi	154	124	30
10	Pennsylvania	152	57	95
11	Alabama	135	107	28
12	Louisiana	133	103	30
13	Arkansas	118	90	28
14	Kentucky	103	52	51

Rank	State	Total	Blacks	Whites
15	Tennessee	93	66	27
16	Virginia	92	75	17
17	Illinois	90	31	59
18	New Jersey	74	25	47
19	Maryland	68	55	13
20	Missouri	62	33	29
21	Oklahoma	60	15	42
22	Colorado	47	5	41
22	Washington	47	7	40
24	Indiana	41	10	31
25	District of Columbia	40	37	3
25	West Virginia	40	9	31
27	Arizona	38	10	28
28	Nevada	29	2	27
29	Massachusetts	27	2	25
30	Connecticut	21	3	18
31	Oregon	19	3	16
32	Iowa	18	0	18
33	Kansas	15	3	12
34	Utah	13	0	13
35	Delaware	12	7	5
36	New Mexico	8	2	6
37	Wyoming	7	1	6
38	Montana	6	2	4
39	Nebraska	4	0	3
39	Vermont	4	0	4
41	Idaho	3	0	3
42	New Hampshire	1	0	1
42	South Dakota	1	0	1
44	Alaska	0	0	0
44	Hawaii	0	0	0
44	Maine	0	0	0
44	Michigan	0	0	0
44	Minnesota	0	0	0
44	North Dakota	0	0	0
44	Rhode Island	0	0	0
44	Wisconsin	0	0	0

192: The Death Penalty (2): Prisoners on Death Row and Method of Execution

Death row populations in Florida, Texas, Georgia and California are far larger than those elsewhere in the nation. Several states that have the death penalty have no prisoners standing under sentence of death. In 18 of the 36 states where the death penalty is permitted, the electric chair is the instrument of death. The gas chamber is preferred by authorities in nine states. Nine other states provide for execution by lethal injection, hanging or firing squad.

Table: Prisoners on Death Row
Date: December 1981
Source: American Civil Liberties Union
Description: Prisoners on death row as of December 1981 and method of execution, by state, for 36 states.

PRISONERS ON DEATH ROW

Rank	State	Persons on death row	Method of execution
1	Florida	162	Electrocution
2	Texas	144	Lethal Injection
3	Georgia	109	Electrocution
4	California	80	Gas Chamber
5	Alabama	55	Electrocution
6	Illinois	40	Electrocution
7	Arizona	37	Gas Chamber
7	Oklahoma	37	Lethal Injection
9	Louisiana	30	Electrocution
10	Tennessee	26	Electrocution
11	Arkansas	23	Electrocution
11	Mississippi	23	Gas Chamber
11	Pennsylvania	23	Electrocution
14	South Carolina	21	Electrocution
15	North Carolina	17	Gas Chamber
15	Virginia	17	Electrocution
17	Missouri	14	Gas Chamber
18	Nebraska	12	Electrocution
18	Nevada	12	Gas Chamber
20	Indiana	10	Electrocution
20	Kentucky	10	Electrocution
22	Maryland	7	Gas Chamber
23	Delaware	4	Hanging
24	Montana	3	Hanging
24	New Mexico	3	Lethal Injection
24	Utah	3	Firing Squad
27	Colorado	1	Gas Chamber
27	Wyoming	1	Gas Chamber
29	Connecticut	0	Electrocution
29	Idaho	0	Lethal Injection
29	New Hampshire	0	Hanging
29	New York	0	Electrocution
29	Ohio	0	Electrocution
29	South Dakota	0	Electrocution
29	Vermont	0	Electrocution
29	Washington	0	Hanging or lethal injection

ENERGY

Although there has been some progress in energy conservation during the past decade, stimulated by the oil crisis, the United States remains a nation of energy guzzlers. Americans use vast quantities of energy of all types to run factories and offices, to operate motor vehicles, to heat and light homes, to cook food, and to power a dazzling array of consumer appliances ranging from vacuum cleaners and toasters to electric toothbrushes and home computers. The nation produces about one-fourth of the world's energy, but consumes about one-third. This imbalance requires some reliance on foreign suppliers and implies some degree of vulnerability to future energy crises. Nuclear power has been promoted as a strategy for "energy independence," but deep public misgivings following a near-disaster at the Three Mile Island plant in southeastern Pennsylvania, combined with skyrocketing costs of building such nuclear plants, have brought the development of nuclear power to a standstill. Until the public can be persuaded that safe operation of reactors and safe disposal of radioactive wastes can be guaranteed, the present distribution of fuel consumption and the present reliance on imports will stay about as they are.

The tables in this section focus on the relative importance of various energy sources in different parts of the country. Regional variation in energy needs (depending on climate and amount of industrial production) and availability of specific sources, such as oil and water power, produce patterns of consumption that are far from uniform. The first three tables compare the states in terms of the major fuels used for home heating. Consumer costs for gas and electric utilities are treated in the next three tables. The final series of tables deals with the sources of power used to generate electricity, including data on the generating power of nuclear plants in the 28 states where they are used.

193. Average Annual Residential Gas Bill and Average Increase from 1980 to 1981

The average residential gas customer paid out $434 for service in 1981, up 9.3% from $397 in 1980. Average gas bills depend, above all, on three factors: the per unit cost of gas, the proportion of households that use gas for heating and, in connection with this, how often cold weather forces gas-heat customers to burn fuel. The two states with average bills far above those of the rest of the nation are very different. Hawaii simply has an extremely high cost per unit of gas for cooking, while Vermont combines high unit cost with cold winters. Warmer states are at the bottom of the list. Changes in the average bill from 1980 to 1981 show wide variation, from $165 in extra cost for Maine to a $22 reduction in California.

Table: Average Annual Residential Gas Bill and Average Increase 1980–1981
Date: 1983
Source: Department of Energy
Description: Average annual residential gas bill and average increase from 1980 to 1981.
United States average: $434
State median: $440
United States average increase 1980–1981: $37

AVERAGE ANNUAL RESIDENTIAL GAS BILL AND AVERAGE INCREASE 1980–1981

Rank	State	Average annual residential gas bill	Amount of increase or decrease
1	Hawaii	$835	$82
2	Vermont	817	70
3	Illinois	615	52
4	Massachusetts	604	95
5	Michigan	597	61
6	Rhode Island	587	84
7	Pennsylvania	583	84
8	Ohio	578	36
9	Wisconsin	544	54
10	West Virginia	542	69
11	New Hampshire	529	87
12	New Jersey	511	68
13	Connecticut	500	97
14	Minnesota	499	63
15	New York	498	52

Rank	State	Average annual residential gas bill	Amount of increase or decrease
16	Maryland	$489	$68
17	Indiana	484	41
18	Delaware	480	97
19	North Dakota	478	2
20	Virginia	477	39
21	Washington	474	5
22	North Carolina	466	92
23	Utah	453	39
24	Missouri	452	37
25	Iowa	441	37
26	Maine	438	165
27	Oregon	409	−6
28	Kentucky	408	25
29	South Dakota	401	46
30	Wyoming	397	34
31	Idaho	394	1
32	Georgia	391	57
33	Colorado	390	16
34	Montana	389	33
35	Alaska	384	13
35	Nebraska	384	42
37	Alabama	377	43
38	Nevada	366	44
39	South Carolina	347	46
40	Kansas	326	30
41	Mississippi	312	23
41	New Mexico	312	5
41	Tennessee	312	28
44	Louisiana	299	43
45	Texas	288	27
46	Arkansas	284	30
47	Oklahoma	264	13
48	California	258	−22
49	Arizona	221	2
50	Florida	200	25

194: Gas Heat

Gas is the fuel most commonly used to heat American homes; about three of every five homes are kept warm with gas heat. States where high proportions of households heat with gas are scattered across the center of the country, including colder states with high heating bills, like Wyoming and Michigan, and warmer states where the heater is not used very often, like Louisiana and Texas.

Table: Home Heating by Gas
Date: 1980
Source: Census Bureau
Description: Percentage of homes using gas for heating.
United States average: 58.8%
State median: 58.6%

HOME HEATING BY GAS

Rank	State	Percent of homes using gas heat
1	Kansas	89.0
2	Colorado	87.1
2	Illinois	87.1
4	New Mexico	86.1
5	Nebraska	84.3
6	Wyoming	83.6
7	Utah	82.5
8	California	81.2
9	Michigan	80.0
9	Oklahoma	80.0
11	Iowa	79.5
12	Missouri	79.4
13	Louisiana	75.7
14	Ohio	73.9
15	Texas	72.8
16	Georgia	72.7
17	Arkansas	71.9
18	Montana	68.1
19	Indiana	67.9
20	Minnesota	66.9
21	Mississippi	66.2
22	Wisconsin	65.9
23	Alabama	64.6
24	West Virginia	61.1
25	Arizona	60.7
26	Kentucky	58.7
27	South Dakota	58.5
28	Nevada	53.1
29	Maryland	52.0
30	Pennsylvania	49.9
31	Maryland	48.1
32	New Jersey	45.4
33	New York	39.1
34	South Carolina	38.6
35	Alaska	36.4
36	Massachusetts	33.5
36	Rhode Island	33.5
38	Tennessee	33.3
39	Virginia	32.6
40	Idaho	30.9
41	Delaware	30.4
42	Oregon	25.4
43	Washington	24.0
44	Connecticut	23.0
45	Florida	22.5
46	North Carolina	22.0
47	New Hampshire	15.0
48	Vermont	11.1
49	Hawaii	5.8
50	Maine	2.6

195: Electric Heat

About one American home in five has electric heat. Florida is clearly the leader in this area, followed by Tennessee and three states in the Pacific Northwest. The other states with above average frequencies of use of electric power are all found in the South and the Southwest, where year-round air conditioning is a more important concern than heating. The states of the Pacific Northwest are included in this group because of the relatively high cost of gas heating in the region (see Table 197) and the absence of major oil ports.

Table: Home Heating (or air conditioning) by Electricity
Date: 1980
Source: Census Bureau
Description: Percentage of homes using electricity for heating (or air conditioning).
United States average: 18.4%
State median: 14.3%

HOME HEATING (OR AIR CONDITIONING) BY ELECTRICITY

Rank	State	Percent of homes using electricity
1	Florida	61.5
2	Washington	52.5
3	Tennessee	48.9
4	Oregon	42.0
5	Idaho	38.6
6	Nevada	36.7
7	Arizona	35.0
8	South Carolina	31.0
9	North Carolina	28.9
10	Alabama	26.2
11	Texas	25.3
11	Virginia	25.3
13	Mississippi	24.7
14	Kentucky	23.0
15	Louisiana	22.4
16	Georgia	19.4
17	West Virginia	18.7
18	North Dakota	17.2
19	Arkansas	16.9
20	Indiana	16.6
21	Montana	15.8
22	California	15.7
23	Oklahoma	15.4
23	South Dakota	15.4
25	Alaska	14.8
26	Ohio	13.8
27	Maryland	13.5
28	New Hampshire	12.8
29	Missouri	12.0
30	Delaware	11.6
31	Connecticut	11.1
32	Wyoming	10.9
33	Maine	10.6
34	Pennsylvania	10.4
35	Massachusetts	10.3
36	Utah	10.2
37	Colorado	9.6

Rank	State	Percent of homes using electricity
37	Vermont	9.6
39	Nevada	9.3
40	Iowa	8.6
41	Minnesota	8.0
42	Kansas	7.8
43	New Jersey	7.5
44	Illinois	7.1
45	New Mexico	7.0
46	Wisconsin	6.5
47	Rhode Island	6.3
48	Michigan	5.0
49	New York	4.6
50	Hawaii	4.5

196: Oil Heat

Petroleum-based products are heating fuels for about one American household in five, but the regional variation in this rate is striking. The relatively cold states in the Northeast are the most oil dependent. Residents of these states have absorbed huge increases in the cost of home heating during the past decade. Oil heat is, on the other hand, almost unknown in states stretching across the southern half of the country from Georgia to California.

Table: Home Heating by Fuel Oil and Kerosene
Date: 1980
Source: Census Bureau
Description: Percentage of homes using fuel oil and kerosene for heating.
United States average: 18.1%
State median: 10.7%

HOME HEATING BY FUEL OIL AND KEROSENE

Rank	State	Percent of homes using oil/kerosene for heating
1	Maine	71.1
2	Connecticut	63.4
3	Vermont	61.3
4	New Hampshire	60.5
5	Rhode Island	57.9
6	Delaware	55.7
7	Massachusetts	53.8
8	New York	53.7
9	New Jersey	46.0
10	North Carolina	40.1
11	Alaska	38.7
12	Maryland	35.8
13	Pennsylvania	34.3
14	Virginia	34.2

Rank	State	Percent of homes using oil/kerosene for heating
15	North Dakota	27.8
16	Wisconsin	25.0
17	South Carolina	23.4
18	South Dakota	22.8
19	Minnesota	22.2
20	Oregon	19.2
21	Washington	18.4
22	Idaho	16.8
23	Michigan	12.8
24	Indiana	12.2
25	Florida	10.9
26	West Virginia	10.5
27	Iowa	10.3
28	Ohio	9.6
29	Nevada	7.1
30	Kentucky	6.0
31	Montana	5.9
32	Illinois	4.7
32	Nebraska	4.7
34	Tennessee	3.8
35	Missouri	3.3
36	Utah	2.9
37	Georgia	2.2
38	Wyoming	1.1
39	Alabama	.5
39	Colorado	.5
41	Kansas	.4
41	New Mexico	.4
43	Hawaii	.3
44	Arizona	.2
44	California	.2
44	Mississippi	.2
47	Arkansas	.1
47	Louisiana	.1
47	Oklahoma	.1
47	Texas	.1

197: Residential Gas Rates

In the lower 48 states, residential gas rates vary from $6.43 to $2.31 per million Btu (British thermal units), with the highest rates in New England and the Pacific Northwest. The two outlying states are at the extremes in this table. Natural gas arrives in Hawaii by ship, not by pipeline, which accounts for costs per unit four times the national average. Alaska has abundant internal sources of natural gas and, consequently, costs per unit about half the national average.

Table: Residential Gas Rates
Date: 1980
Source: American Gas Association

Description: Average gas prices for residential use.
United States average: $3.61
State median: $3.66 per million Btu

RESIDENTIAL GAS RATES

Rank	State	Average rate per million Btu
1	Hawaii	$14.58
2	Vermont	6.43
3	Maine	6.34
4	Connecticut	5.73
5	Rhode Island	5.46
6	Massachusetts	5.41
7	Oregon	5.36
8	Idaho	4.94
9	Washington	4.91
10	New Jersey	4.89
11	New York	4.86
12	Florida	4.53
12	New Hampshire	4.53
14	Maryland	4.40
15	Virginia	4.24
16	Delaware	4.15
17	South Carolina	4.12
18	Alabama	4.11
19	Georgia	4.06
20	North Carolina	4.04
21	Nevada	3.97
22	North Dakota	3.83
23	Wisconsin	3.80
24	Pennsylvania	3.74
25	Arizona	3.72
26	West Virginia	3.61
27	Illinois	3.46
28	Ohio	3.45
29	California	3.38
29	Mississippi	3.38
31	Missouri	3.37
32	Texas	3.30
33	Minnesota	3.24
34	Colorado	3.22
35	New Mexico	3.21
36	Iowa	3.20
37	Michigan	3.15
38	Indiana	3.12
39	South Dakota	3.11
40	Kentucky	3.08
41	Louisiana	3.06
42	Tennessee	2.94
43	Montana	2.88
44	Nebraska	2.71
45	Wyoming	2.69
46	Utah	2.68
47	Kansas	2.38
48	Oklahoma	2.35
49	Arkansas	2.31
50	Alaska	1.73

198: Average Annual Residential Electric Bill

The $437 average household electric bill in 1980 was just a bit higher than the $397 average gas bill. Overall variation from state to state is less than that for gas bills, and the regional pattern is quite different. States with high costs for hot weather air conditioning tend to cluster near the top of this list. In general, residents of these states are compensated by lower heating costs, as suggested by their low ranking in the previous table. Residents of Hawaii, however, have very high bills for both gas and electricity.

Table: Cost of Residential Electric Utilities
Date: 1980
Source: Census Bureau
Description: Average annual bill per customer for residential electric utilities.
United States average: $437
State median: $424

COST OF RESIDENTIAL ELECTRIC UTILITIES

Rank	State	Average annual residential cost
1	Virginia	$595
2	Florida	585
3	Arizona	583
4	Texas	554
5	Hawaii	550
6	Alabama	528
7	Tennessee	517
8	Nevada	513
9	Delaware	511
9	New Jersey	511
11	South Carolina	502
12	Mississippi	$495
13	Connecticut	485
14	Louisiana	483
15	North Carolina	482
16	Maryland	469
17	Georgia	464
18	New Hampshire	459
19	Alaska	452
20	Ohio	448
21	Arkansas	444
22	Iowa	433
23	Kansas	430
24	Missouri	428
25	Oklahoma	425
26	Pennsylvania	424
27	Indiana	423
28	Massachusetts	418
29	Illinois	414
30	New York	408
31	Rhode Island	403
32	Kentucky	398
33	Vermont	391
34	Oregon	390
35	Maine	388
36	Idaho	382
37	North Dakota	381
38	Nebraska	380
39	Utah	379
40	West Virginia	378
41	South Dakota	367
42	Wisconsin	359
43	Michigan	355
44	California	343
45	New Mexico	337
46	Minnesota	330
47	Washington	291
48	Colorado	282
49	Montana	245
50	Wyoming	222

ENERGY SOURCES USED TO GENERATE ELECTRICITY

Electricity is produced in power plants which convert other forms of energy into this more transportable form. The basic energy sources used in this process vary from state to state depending on availability of sources and the past and present policies of the utility companies. The five major sources covered in the following tables were used to produce a total of 2,280 billion kilowatt-hours (kwh) of electricity in 1980. For the nation as a whole, the percentages of energy derived from the individual sources were as follows: coal 52%, natural gas 15%, hydro-electric power (dams) 12%, nuclear energy 11%, oil 11%. The states are ranked in the following tables according to the total amount of electricity produced from a given energy source. A state with high overall electrical production (California, for example) may therefore be ranked high in several tables.

199: Electricity from Gas

Natural gas is used to generate electricity in 46 states, but the pattern of regional specialization is extreme. Texas alone accounts for 40% of the national total of electricity from this source, and the top five states here account for 80% of the total. Texas and Oklahoma have extensive underground gas fields, while offshore gas is abundant in California, Texas and Louisiana. Gas from the Gulf of Mexico can be shipped to Florida at relatively low cost.

Table: Electric Generation by Gas
Date: 1980
Source: Department of Energy
Description: Electric generation by gas in billions of kwh.
United States total: 346.2 billion kwh
State avgerage: 6.9 billion kwh
State median: 0.4 billion kwh

ELECTRIC GENERATION BY GAS

Rank	State	Gas generation (billions of kwh)
1	Texas	138.9
2	California	50.3
3	Louisiana	41.0
4	Oklahoma	33.6
5	Florida	14.9
6	New York	10.8
7	Kansas	8.5
8	Mississippi	8.2
9	New Jersey	6.9
10	Arkansas	5.2
11	New Mexico	5.1
12	Arizona	4.5
13	Colorado	2.5
13	Nevada	2.5
15	Alaska	1.8
15	Michigan	1.8
17	Illinois	1.4
18	Missouri	1.2
19	Nebraska	.9
20	Wisconsin	.8
21	Delaware	.7
22	Minnesota	.6
23	Iowa	.4
23	Massachusetts	.4
23	Montana	.4
23	South Carolina	.4
23	Utah	.4
28	Georgia	.3
28	Maryland	.3
28	Ohio	.3
31	Indiana	.2
31	Kentucky	.2
31	Pennsylvania	.2
31	Virginia	.2
35	Alabama	.1
35	North Carolina	.1
35	Rhode Island	.1
35	Tennessee	.1
35	Washington	.1
40	Idaho	less than .05
40	North Dakota	less than .05
40	Oregon	less than .05
40	South Dakota	less than .05
40	Vermont	less than .05
40	West Virginia	less than .05
40	Wyoming	less than .05
47	Connecticut	0
47	Hawaii	0
47	Maine	0
47	New Hampshire	0

200: Electricity from Oil

In every state some electric power is generated by burning oil, although total output was less than 500,000 kwh in 12 states (the figure .1 in this table means one million kwh). Oil is obviously important as the source of gasoline for motor vehicles and, at least in the Northeast, as a home heating fuel, but in 1980 it was fifth in importance as a source for producing electricity. The top 10 states in this table accounted for 83% of the total activity. Several northeastern states are near the top of the list, together with the populous states of Florida, California and Illinois, and little Hawaii—where oil is the source of almost all electricity.

Table: Electric Generation by Oil
Date: 1980
Source: Department of Energy
Description: Electric generation by oil in billions of kwh.
United States total: 245.6 billion kwh
State average: 4.9 billion kwh
State median: 0.4

ELECTRIC GENERATION BY OIL

Rank	State	Electric generation (billions of kwh)
1	Florida	44.4
2	California	39.3
3	New York	37.8
4	Massachusetts	29.3
5	Connecticut	12.6
6	Pennsylvania	10.7
7	New Jersey	8.8
8	Virginia	8.4
9	Illinois	7.2
10	Hawaii	6.5
11	Michigan	5.6
12	Maryland	5.0
13	Louisiana	4.8
14	Delaware	3.6
15	Mississippi	3.3
16	New Hampshire	2.4
17	Maine	2.1
18	Arkansas	2.0
19	South Carolina	1.6
20	Nevada	1.5
21	Ohio	1.0
22	Arizona	.9
22	Texas	.9
24	Rhode Island	.8
25	Georgia	.5
26	Alaska	.4
26	Kansas	.4
26	West Virginia	.4
29	Indiana	.3
30	Colorado	.2
30	Minnesota	.2
30	Missouri	.2
30	New Mexico	.2
30	North Carolina	.2
30	Tennessee	.2
30	Wisconsin	.2
37	Kentucky	.1
37	Nebraska	.1
39	Alabama	less than .05
39	Idaho	less than .05
39	Iowa	less than .05
39	Montana	less than .05
39	North Dakota	less than .05
39	Oklahoma	less than .05
39	Oregon	less than .05
39	South Dakota	less than .05
39	Utah	less than .05
39	Vermont	less than .05
39	Washington	less than .05
39	Wyoming	less than .05

201: Electricity from Nuclear Energy and Nuclear Capacity

In 1980 nuclear energy was the fourth leading source of electrical power, generating over 250 billion kwh. There were 28 states with plants in operation. The leader was Illinois, where 11% of all nuclear-based electricity was produced. According to this table, the top 40 states combined account for 65% of the total, a lower degree of concentration among the top 10 than for any of the other four major sources of electric power. Fewer states use nuclear energy, but since the costs of producing this "natural resource" are high and about the same throughout the country, there are no "resource-rich" states which outperform the others by a wide margin. The amount of nuclear power in a given state reflects the policies of the state government and the utility companies, not local natural conditions.

The second column in this table shows nuclear capacity as of 1981. There has been very little new construction since then. Public mistrust, more cautious policies, the resistance presented by opponents of nuclear power, and rising construction costs (during the present phase of stable oil prices) have combined to bring new development to a stop. These are two main reasons why a ranking by capacity would be different than the ranking by power actually produced. First, some of the new capacity added in 1981 (in Arizona, for example) is not reflected in 1980 production figures. Second, the percentage of available capacity actually used varies between about 30% and 70% from state to state.

Table: Electric Generation by Nuclear Power Plants
Date: 1980/81
Source: Energy Department
Description: Electric generation by nuclear power in billions of kwh and capacity (thousands of kwh) of nuclear power reactors.
Production (1980) United States total: 251.1 billion kwh
State average: 5.0 billion kwh
State median: 1.4 billion kwh
Capacity (1981) United States total: 58,714 thousand kwh

ELECTRIC GENERATION BY NUCLEAR POWER PLANTS

Rank	State	1980 electric (billions of kwh)	1981 capacity (thousands of kwh)
1	Illinois	27.7	6,246
2	Alabama	23.5	4,024
3	New York	19.3	3,749
4	South Carolina	17.4	3,361
5	Florida	16.7	3,013
6	Michigan	15.9	3,031
7	Pennsylvania	12.1	4,747
8	Connecticut	11.8	2,105
9	Virginia	11.5	3,458
10	Maryland	10.9	1,690
11	Minnesota	10.0	1,605
12	Wisconsin	9.9	1,579
13	Georgia	8.4	1,571
14	Arkansas	7.8	NA
15	New Jersey	7.6	2,855
16	Nebraska	5.8	1,235
16	North Carolina	5.8	2,822
18	Oregon	5.4	1,130
19	California	4.9	2,825
20	Maine	4.4	790
21	Massachusetts	3.2	830
22	Vermont	3.0	514
23	Iowa	2.6	538
24	Ohio	2.1	906
25	Washington	2.0	850
26	Colorado	.7	330
27	Tennessee	.5	1,148
28	Arizona	0	1,762

202: Electricity from Hydroelectric Plants

There are 46 states where at least some electricity originates from plants located along waterways, but once again we find a high degree of specialization by state. The dams of Washington, Oregon and northern California account for 56% of the national output. New York (Niagara Falls!), with nine percent of the national total, is an exceptional case in the East. The flat states of New Jersey, Delaware, Louisiana and Mississippi (compare the section on geography) have no hydroelectric production at all.

Table: Electric Generation by Hydroelectric Power
Date: 1980
Source: Department of Energy
Description: Electric generation by hydroelectric power in billions of kwh.
United States total: 276.0 billion kwh
State average: 5.5 billion kwh
State median: 1.0 billion kwh

ELECTRIC GENERATION BY HYDROELECTRIC POWER

Rank	State	Electric generation (billions of kwh)
1	Washington	83.0
2	California	40.8
3	Oregon	30.2
4	New York	26.2
5	Montana	10.0
6	Arizona	9.8
7	Idaho	9.5
8	Alabama	9.4
9	Tennessee	8.8
10	South Dakota	5.8
11	North Carolina	5.5
12	Georgia	4.4
13	South Carolina	3.0
14	Kentucky	2.9
15	North Dakota	2.5
16	Nevada	2.4
17	Wisconsin	1.9
18	Arkansas	1.7
18	Colorado	1.7
20	Maine	1.4
21	Maryland	1.3
21	Nebraska	1.3
21	Oklahoma	1.3
24	Michigan	1.1
24	Wyoming	1.1
26	Texas	1.0
27	Iowa	.9
27	New Hampshire	.9
27	Virginia	.9
30	Utah	.8
31	Pennsylvania	.7
31	Vermont	.7
33	Minnesota	.6
33	Missouri	.6
35	Alaska	.5
35	Indiana	.5
37	West Virginia	.4
38	Connecticut	.2
38	Florida	.2
40	Illinois	.1
40	Massachusetts	.1
40	New Mexico	.1
43	Hawaii	less than .05
43	Kansas	less than .05
43	Ohio	less than .05
43	Rhode Island	less than .05

Rank	State	Electric generation (billions of kwh)
47	Delaware	0
47	Louisiana	0
47	Mississippi	0
47	New Jersey	0

203: Electricity from Coal

Coal is far and away the leading energy source for production of electrical power. There are 43 states in which some electricity is generated at coal-burning plants, but 70% of this activity occurs in the top 10 states on the list. Near the head of the list, Texas joins a group of states located along the Appalachians and around the Great Lakes where Appalachian coal is readily transportable by railroad and ship. States in the western half of the country are generally near the bottom of the list, with a few exceptions, and so are most states in New England and the Middle Atlantic region (but not Pennsylvania). New Englanders, who burn very little coal, are understandably upset about airborne wastes from coal burning in the Great Lakes region that contribute to the acid rain that is gradually destroying their forests and freshwater wildlife.

Table: Electric Generation by Coal
Date: 1980
Source: Department of Energy
Description: Electric generation by coal in billions of kwh.
United States total: 1,161.6 billion kwh
State average: 23.2 billion kwh
State median: 14.0 billion kwh

ELECTRIC GENERATION BY COAL

Rank	State	Electric generation (billions of kwh)
1	Ohio	106.8
2	Pennsylvania	98.6
3	West Virginia	70
4	Indiana	69.6
5	Illinois	66.9
6	Texas	62.1
7	North Carolina	60.5
8	Kentucky	53.9
9	Tennessee	50.6
10	Michigan	50.5
11	Georgia	49.7
12	Missouri	46.9
13	Alabama	45.2
14	Wisconsin	24.9
15	Arizona	21.7
16	Wyoming	21.1
17	Minnesota	20.1
18	Florida	19.7
19	South Carolina	19.5
20	New Mexico	19.3
21	Colorado	18.6
22	Iowa	17.8
23	Kansas	16.2
24	Maryland	14.6
25	New York	14.5
26	Virginia	13.4
27	North Dakota	13.3
28	Utah	10.9
29	Oklahoma	9.7
30	Nebraska	8.1
31	Nevada	7.8
32	Washington	7.1
33	Mississippi	7
34	New Jersey	6.4
35	Montana	5.1
36	Arkansas	2.9
37	South Dakota	2.8
38	New Hampshire	2.7
39	Delaware	2.2
40	Massachusetts	1.8
41	Oregon	.7
42	Alaska	.3
43	Vermont	.05
44	California	0
44	Connecticut	0
44	Hawaii	0
44	Idaho	0
44	Louisiana	0
44	Maine	0
44	Rhode Island	0

POLLUTION

National concern about the effects of environmental pollution on public health came to a head early in 1983, when the Environmental Protection Agency (EPA) urged residents of Times Beach, Missouri not to return to their town after a flood of the Meramec River. Parts of the town had become polluted over a number of years by the waste product dioxin, and hundreds of farm animals had been killed. Officials believed that spreading caused by the flood might have turned the entire area into a place too poisonous to live in. During the weeks that followed, many EPA officials, including the chief administrator Anne (Gorsuch) Burford, lost their jobs when it became apparent that they had generally been spending more time appeasing polluters than regulating them.

Attention then focused on 418 dumping sites for toxic waste around the country that the EPA had earlier designated as high priority cleanup areas. The notorious environment of Love Canal, near Niagara Falls, New York was only miserable enough to rank as the 116th most serious danger to public health included on the list of waste sites. Problem areas are found in many parts of the country. In Louisiana, which produces one-third of all fertilizer and one-fourth of all chemicals made in America, the Mississippi River from Baton Rouge to New Orleans is now widely known as "cancer corridor." When the age of victims and other factors are taken into account, the rate of cancer in Louisiana turns out to be nearly 10% above the national average. Bottled water is becoming more popular in the area. The environmental excesses of the past are now returning to haunt the present, and public opinion polls show that support for strong environmental supervision is growing.

Comparative data on pollution are relatively hard to find. The tables in this section provide only a glimpse of the overall situation. They deal with urban air pollution, one area of concern in which things are looking up; with one particular form of water pollution, solid waste disposal; and with the efforts of the states to correct environmental problems. Increased interest in the en- vironment should lead to further official publication of comparative data in the future.

204: Air Quality in Selected SMSAs

The Council on Environmental Quality measures air pollution with a Pollutant Standards Index (PSI). The index combines data from all the monitoring stations in a given SMSA on five kinds of pollutants: carbon mono- xide, sulfur dioxide, suspended particles, ozone and nitrogen dioxide. If the amount of one or more of these materials at any station exceeds a critical point—a point "judged to have adverse short-term effects on human health"—the index value for the SMSA for that day is said to be at an "unhealthful" level. There are also more intense degrees of air pollution measured by the index, called "very unhealthful" and "hazardous." The figures in this table indicate the average number of *days* on which air quality was rated "unhealthful" or worse during two overlapping three-year periods; data for 1978 are included in the averages for both 1976–1978 and 1978–1980. This ranking of 40 large SMSAs is based on the average number of unhealthful days in the 1976–1980 period.

The Los Angeles basin, with Riverside to the east, is by far the most air-polluted area in the country. A compa- rison of figures for the two time periods shows very little improvement in Los Angeles and worsening conditions in Riverside. During the 1978–1980 period Los Angeles also led the nation in the number of days rated "hazardous," with 15. There were five such days in Riverside during the period. Other SMSAs with "hazardous" days were Denver (9), Portland (9), St. Louis (7), Chicago (3), Houston (1) and Salt Lake City (1). The air is "unhealth- ful" every other day in Riverside, and two days out of three in Los Angeles. Smog alerts are a regular feature of local weather reporting.

In New York City, a distant third on this list, air quality showed remarkable improvement from a few years before.

Greater relative improvement occurred only in Cleveland. Unfortunately, one key reason for these improvements was simply the loss of population and industrial activity. The same link between economic decline and better air can also be seen in several other areas on the list. On the other hand, Houston and San Diego, two of the booming SMSAs of the 1970s, experienced sharp deterioration in air quality as more and more cars jammed their freeways.

Table: Air Quality in Selected SMSAs
Date: 1980
Source: Council on Environmental Quality
Description: Average number of days in the (overlapping) periods 1976–1978 and 1978–1980 on which air quality as measured by the PSI was rated "unhealthful" or worse, in 40 SMSAs.

AIR QUALITY IN SELECTED SMSAs

Rank	State	1976–1978 average	1978–1980 average
1	Los Angeles	242	231
2	Riverside, Calif.	167	174
3	New York	224	139
4	Denver	166	130
5	Pittsburgh	168	119
6	Houston	69	104
7	Chicago	124	93
8	St. Louis	136	89
9	Philadelphia	82	74
10	San Diego	52	72*
11	Louisville	119	70
11	Phoenix	84	70
13	Gary, Ind.	36	68
14	Portland, Oreg.	75	62
14	Washington, D.C.	97	62
16	Jersey City	65	58
16	Salt Lake City	81	58
18	Seattle	82	52
19	Birmingham	75	50
20	Cleveland	145	46
21	Detroit	65	39
22	Memphis	28	37
23	Baltimore	60	36
24	Indianapolis	36	34
25	Cincinnati	45	28
25	Kansas City	29	28
25	Milwaukee	33	28
28	Sacramento	28	22
29	Dallas	22	21
29	Allentown, Pa.	27	21
31	Buffalo	31	20
32	San Francisco	30	18
33	Dayton	45	15
33	Toledo	24	15
35	Tampa	12	8
36	Syracuse	9	7

* 1978–1979 only

Rank	State	1976–1978 average	1978–1980 average
37	Grand Rapids	5	6
37	Norfolk	9	6
39	Rochester, N.Y.	6	5
40	Akron	10	4

205: Pollution of Drinking Water in Selected Cities

The most serious problems of water pollution in the United States involve industrial wastes that endanger water supplies and make many of the lakes and rivers deadly for marine life and unsuitable for human consumption or recreation. Groundwater seepage around toxic dump sites is also a very serious problem. A few years ago the tragic abandonment of Love Canal in New York brought this problem to national attention. The Times Beach, Missouri disaster has provided a more recent reminder that the carelessness and ignorance with which toxic materials have been discarded are potentially a threat to everyone.

Systematic data on various forms of water pollution are hard to come by. This table focuses on one particular form of pollution of city drinking water supplies. Ironically, it is a form of pollution that arises from simple hygienic efforts on the part of local governments. The data concern levels of trihalomethanes (THMs) in water supplies. THMs are cancer-causing substances formed when chlorine added to the water to kill bacteria combines with certain organic materials. Levels above an index value of 100 are considered potentially dangerous.

Even here, recent uniform data are hard to find. The EPA is generally reluctant to publish such data. In 1978, however, *Good Housekeeping* magazine obtained and published closely held EPA figures on THM levels in a number of cities. The 50 cities listed below had the highest THM index values among the cities surveyed early in 1978. Several large cities appear on the list. Improvements may have occurred since that time, but there are no subsequent uniform data to show that this is the case.

Table: Trihalomethane Pollution of Drinking Water
Date: 1978
Source: *Good Housekeeping*, July 1978
Description: The 50 cities in the United States with the highest levels of trihalomethane parts per billion in drinking water.

TRIHALOMETHANE POLLUTION OF DRINKING WATER

Rank	Cities	THM parts per billion
1	Melbourne, Fla.	550
2	Huron, S. Dak.	300
3	Houston	250
3	Ilwaco, Wash.	250
5	Jackson, Miss.	240
6	Tampa	230
7	Columbus	210
8	Annandale, Va.	200
8	Charleston	200
8	Oklahoma City	200
11	Santa Fe	180
12	Newport, R.I.	160
12	Wheeling	160
14	Louisville	150
14	Norfolk	150
16	Cape Girardeau, Mo.	140
16	Terrabonne Parish, La.	140
18	Amarillo, Tex.	130
18	Cheyenne, Wyo.	130
18	Passaic Valley, N.J.	130
18	Phoenix	130
22	Camden, Ariz.	120
22	Omaha	120
24	California Aqueduct, Calif.	110
24	Concord, Calif.	110
24	Hackensack, N.J.	110
24	Huntington, W. Va.	110
24	Montgomery, Ala.	110
24	Washington, D.C.	110
24	Waterbury, Conn.	110
31	Bismarck, N. Dak.	100
31	Davenport, Iowa	100
31	Hagerstown, Md.	100
34	Chattanooga	98
35	San Diego	97
36	Burlington, Vt.	91
37	St. Paul	90
38	Elizabeth, N.J.	86
38	Yuma, Ariz.	86
40	Waterford Township, N.Y.	83
41	Indianapolis	82
42	Dallas	79
42	Rome, Ga.	79
42	Sioux Falls, S. Dak.	79
45	Poughkeepsie, N.Y.	78
45	San Francisco	78
47	Las Vegas	76
48	Atlanta	75
48	Birmingham	75
50	Charlotte	71

206: Environmental Spending by State Governments

Figures in this table indicate the 1980 level of per capita spending by state governments for all forms of environ-mental quality control. Federal funds actually spent by state governments are included. About 62% of the $1.66 billion total expenditure went for control of water quality, 19% for air quality, 14% for land quality, and 5% for general management expenses and other forms of environmental control (noise control around airports, for example).

There are large differences among the states in the level of financial effort. Some of the states near the bottom of the list are not highly industrialized or heavily populated, so they may simply have fewer environmental problems that demand attention. The states at the top, with levels of effort that far exceed the U.S. average of $7.36 per capita, all specialize to some extent in one form of environmental quality control. In Delaware, home base of DuPont chemicals, 81% of all spending went toward land quality control. No other state spent more than 37% of its environmental funds on land quality. Ohio focused 42% of its spending on air quality control (U.S. average: 19%), which may help to explain why the air in Cleveland is so much better lately (see Table 204). Alaska focuses on water quality, as do New Hampshire and Vermont (97% and 87% of their spending respectively) where acid rain has been killing off freshwater life for several years now.

The 10 states designated by an asterisk were rated by the National Wildlife Federation as having the best solid waste disposal programs for 1980. Several are clustered near the top of the table, showing that there is a link between program quality and the willingness to spend money. This is confirmed by data for the states that are further down on this list of overall spending levels, since they tend to concentrate their spending in the area of land quality control.

Table: State Government Environmental Expenditures
Date: 1980
Source: Census Bureau
Description: Per capita state government environmental quality control expenditures.
United States average: $7.36
State median: $5.54

STATE GOVERNMENT ENVIRONMENTAL EXPENDITURES

Rank	State	Per capita spending
1	* Delaware	$38.2
2	Alaska	36.16
3	* Ohio	35.28
4	New Hampshire	23.01
5	Vermont	13.83

Rank	State	Per capita spending
6	Rhode Island	$12.22
7	* Maryland	11.22
8	Massachusetts	11.10
9	Hawaii	9.85
10	New York	9.51
11	* Washington	9.24
12	* Oregon	8.78
13	Wisconsin	8.40
14	* California	8.12
15	Maine	7.89
16	Illinois	7.21
17	Idaho	6.86
18	Montana	6.57
19	West Virginia	6.11
20	Colorado	5.93
21	Michigan	5.90
22	Wyoming	5.85
23	Minnesota	5.69
24	* Connecticut	5.65
25	New Mexico	5.60
26	New Jersey	5.48
27	Missouri	4.97
28	Pennsylvania	4.94
29	Indiana	4.61
30	Georgia	4.33
31	North Carolina	4.32
32	Kentucky	4.21
33	Arizona	4.14
34	Nevada	4.07
35	South Dakota	4.01
36	* Tennessee	3.76
37	Nebraska	3.70
38	North Dakota	3.46
39	* South Carolina	3.34
40	Iowa	3.01
41	Virginia	3.00
42	Utah	2.57
43	Arkansas	2.43
44	Oklahoma	2.42
45	Louisiana	2.40
46	Texas	2.33
47	Kansas	2.03
48	* Florida	1.96
49	Alabama	1.73
49	Mississippi	1.73

* See text for explanation of this symbol

207: Landfills

The data in this table and the one following are derived from a survey of state solid waste managers conducted by *Waste Age* magazine. The data here refer, for the most part, to regular municipal waste disposal sites. Open dumps, reported separately in the next table, are included in these figures. Special sites for toxic waste disposal, on the other hand, are not included. Landfills are dis-tinguished from open dumps by more careful management, often with the intention of covering and thereby recovering a dump site for alternative uses in the future. Federal regulations of landfills, established in the mid-1970s, have encouraged this better management. About 1,600 of the 13,000 recognized landfills are now equipped with devices to monitor seepage of materials away from the site.

The figures represent more or less official dump sites. High numbers for a given state may reflect not only high population, but also relatively well-controlled solid waste management. There are many thousands of smaller, unofficial dump sites that are not covered here. Some experts contend, for example, that there are over 200,000 major and minor dumping grounds for *toxic* waste alone, and the EPA estimate that some 14,000 of these sites are potentially dangerous is thought to be conservative. The EPA also estimates that 90% of the 44 million *tons* of toxic wastes discarded each year are not being properly handled.

Table: Landfills
Date: 1982
Source: *Waste Age* Survey of Landfills
Description: Number of landfills.
United States total: 12,991
State average: 260
State median: 210

LANDFILLS

Rank	State	Number of landfills
1	Wisconsin	1,085
2	Texas	1,075
3	Pennsylvania	925
4	California	542
5	Louisiana	532
6	New York	525
7	Nebraska	400
8	Michigan	362
9	Indiana	348
10	Illinois	329
11	Ohio	318
12	Arkansas	311
13	Maine	308
14	Utah	296
15	Georgia	284
16	Massachusetts	283
17	Mississippi	253
18	Florida	248
19	New Mexico	228
20	Oregon	226
21	Oklahoma	225
21	South Carolina	225
23	Kansas	224

Rank	State	Number of landfills
24	Montana	222
25	Wyoming	210
26	Virginia	209
27	Colorado	206
28	South Dakota	200
29	Minnesota	185
29	New Jersey	185
31	North Carolina	167
32	Tennessee	161
33	Connecticut	151
34	Washington	136
35	Alabama	135
36	Idaho	132
37	North Dakota	130
38	Kentucky	128
38	Missouri	128
40	West Virginia	127
41	Arizona	116
42	New Hampshire	101
43	Nevada	99
44	Iowa	94
45	Vermont	92
46	Maryland	47
47	Delaware	35
48	Hawaii	25
49	Rhode Island	18
50	Alaska	N.A.

208: Open Dumps

Some 2,400 of the 13,000 recognized landfills in the nation are classified as open dumps. They include all of the landfills in Louisiana and over half of all landfills in Indiana, Mississippi, Nevada and South Dakota. The data should be viewed sceptically, since state solid waste managers are not all-knowing and some of them may have responded inappropriately to survey questions. Is it really possible that in all of Texas, where the total number of landfills reported to *Waste Age* once changed from 250 to 1,043 in a single year, there are now just 11 open dumps?

Table: Open Dumps
Date: 1983
Source: *Waste Age* Survey of Landfills
Description: Number of open dumps.
United States total: 2296
State average: 468

OPEN DUMPS

Rank	State	Number of open dumps
1	Louisiana	532
2	Indiana	191
3	Michigan	150
4	South Dakota	140
5	Mississippi	133
6	Pennsylvania	94
7	Masschusetts	81
8	Arkansas	78
9	Oklahoma	66
9	Wisconsin	66
11	Minnesota	60
12	New York	56
13	Florida	55
14	Ohio	54
15	Nevada	52
16	Virginia	50
17	Maine	45
18	Idaho	42
18	Illinois	42
20	West Virginia	41
21	California	40
22	Connecticut	36
22	Washington	36
24	Kentucky	34
25	Colorado	32
26	Arizona	28
26	Oregon	28
28	New Hampshire	26
28	Utah	26
30	Montana	16
31	Alabama	12
32	Texas	11
33	Hawaii	9
34	Georgia	6
34	Tennessee	6
36	New Jersey	5
37	Delaware	4
37	Rhode Island	4
37	Vermont	4
40	Missouri	2
41	Kansas	1
41	Nebraska	1
41	North Carolina	1
44	Iowa	0
44	Maryland	0
44	New Mexico	0
44	North Dakota	0
44	South Carolina	0
44	Wyoming	0
50	Alaska	N.A.

Travel

Various factors that influence vacation plans have pulled Americans in different directions in recent years. Lower air fares have encouraged more long-distance trips both within the country and abroad. At the same time, losses of income due to the recession and the permanently inflated price of gasoline have acted to persuade many Americans to cancel travel plans altogether or to take vacations close to their own backyards. A slowdown in business travel also accompanied the recession.

The tables in this section offer some indications of the extent and pattern of foreign travel and a brief survey of some key aspects of travel within the United States.

209: Passports Issued and Percentage of Change from 1979 to 1980

The number of new passports issued is a fairly good indicator of the amount of foreign traveling by the residents of a given state. The distribution of new passports among the states is related both to the total number of residents and the proportion of residents who obtain passports. These proportions can be obtained for states in which you are interested by dividing these figures by the 1980 populations presented in Chapter 3. High proportions will be found for wealthy metropolitan states, especially in the East. The actual number of new passports declined in most states from 1979 to 1980 as the recession cut into foreign travel plans. Alaska, New Mexico, Arizona and Hawaii are the outstanding exceptions to this pattern.

Table: Passports Issued
Date: 1980
Source: State Department
Description: Number of passports issued in 1980 and percentage of change from 1979 to 1980.
United States total: 3,020,468
United States percent of change 1979-1980: −5%

PASSPORTS ISSUED

Rank	State	Total number of passports Issued	Percent of change
1	California	483,710	−5
2	New York	371,988	−4
3	Florida	171,090	−7
4	Texas	153,640	3
5	Illinois	147,520	2
6	New Jersey	139,550	−11
7	Pennsylvania	125,790	−9
8	Massachusetts	112,220	−6
9	Ohio	100,440	−8
10	Michigan	89,590	−9
11	Connecticut	74,230	2
12	Virginia	72,390	−2
13	Washington	71,870	−8
14	Minnesota	64,470	1
15	Maryland	62,420	−8
16	Wisconsin	49,660	−2
17	Colorado	46,720	−2
18	Georgia	45,940	2
19	Indiana	43,290	−1
20	North Carolina	40,390	−11
21	Missouri	39,850	−5
22	Arizona	39,720	11
23	Oregon	38,870	−2
24	Louisiana	32,290	−15
25	Hawaii	28,800	10
26	Iowa	26,270	−4
27	Tennessee	26,020	−9
28	Oklahoma	25,010	−4
29	Alabama	24,350	−10
30	Kansas	22,860	−9
31	Utah	22,000	1
32	South Carolina	21,180	−2
33	Kentucky	19,070	−14
34	Rhode Island	15,880	5
35	Nebraska	15,470	−16
36	New Hampshire	14,420	−4
37	New Mexico	13,590	16
38	Mississippi	12,180	−9
39	Maine	11,220	−11
40	Arkansas	10,560	−15

Rank	State	Total number of passports Issued	Percent of change
41	Nevada	10,460	−2
42	West Virginia	9,310	2
43	Idaho	9,150	−13
44	Delaware	8,520	−3
45	Montana	8,150	−8
46	Alaska	7,970	40
47	Vermont	7,610	−1
48	South Dakota	5,510	−11
49	North Dakota	5,440	−21
50	Wyoming	4,890	4

210: Passports Issued and Percentage of Change from 1979 to 1980 in Selected SMSAs

In 1979, residents of SMSAs received 52% of all new passports issued. This figure climbed to 58% in 1980. While new passports issued to SMSA residents increased by 6% over 1979, the number of those granted to non-SMSA residents declined by 16%. The figures presented below for a subgroup of 40 SMSAs show wide variations in rates of change from 1979 to 1980. The greatest increase was registered in the SMSA just outside of Los Angeles; the sharpest reductions were in Indianapolis and Stamford.

Table: Passports Issued in Selected SMSAs
Date: 1980
Source: State Department
Description: Total number of passports issued in 1980 for 40 SMSAs with percentage change from 1979 to 1980.

PASSPORTS ISSUED IN SELECTED SMSAs

Rank	State	Passports issued	Percentage of change from 1979
1	New York	268,500	+ 9
2	Los Angeles-Long Beach	162,480	− 9
3	Chicago	110,400	− 18
4	San Francisco-Oakland	104,260	+ 11
5	Washington	78,720	− 14
6	Nassau-Suffolk (Long Island)	71,280	+ 49
7	Boston	66,430	− 16
8	Philadelphia	65,380	+ 12
9	Houston	49,040	− 1

Rank	State	Passports issued	Percentage of change from 1979
10	Miami	48,300	− 15
11	Anaheim-Santa Ana-Garden Grove, Calif.	47,760	+115
12	Detroit	46,750	− 14
13	Newark	43,740	+ 9
14	San Diego	41,210	+ 57
15	Dallas-Ft. Worth	41,060	+ 44
16	Seattle-Everett	38,730	− 10
17	Minneapolis-St. Paul	35,750	− 10
18	San Jose	34,960	+ 36
19	Denver-Boulder	27,330	− 26
20	Baltimore	25,000	+ 50
21	Atlanta	24,090	+ 14
22	St. Louis	24,060	+ 44
23	Honolulu	23,720	+ 75
24	Cleveland	23,200	+ 21
25	Pittsburgh	22,850	+ 45
26	Tampa-St. Petersburg	22,010	+ 73
27	Riverside-San Bernardino-Ontario, Calif.	20,640	+144
28	Portland, Oreg.	20,280	+ 5
29	Phoenix	18,720	− 3
30	Milwaukee	17,820	+ 15
31	Kansas City	15,350	+ 87
32	Hartford	15,220	− 11
33	New Orleans	14,900	− 14
34	Rochester, N.Y.	13,150	+ 91
35	San Antonio	13,100	+ 35
36	Buffalo	13,070	+ 61
37	Cincinnati	13,040	+ 17
38	Columbus, Ohio	11,280	+ 41
39	Stamford, Conn.	10,390	− 40
40	Indianapolis	10,320	− 58

211. Prospective Foreign Destinations of Travelers from 10 States

The travel plans reported to the State Department by individuals who apply for passports provide some indication of the areas of the world favored by Americans who travel abroad. The data in this six-table group cover the 10 states in which the most new passports were issued in 1980. For each state, persons obtaining passports are divided into six groups according to the area of the world which they intended to visit (first stop, if several areas are mentioned). States are then ranked in tables for each of these six world areas, according to the percentage of all prospective travelers from a state headed for the area in question. The scores for a given state in the six tables therefore add up to 100%.

Europe is the most favored destination, by a wide margin, for each of the states, with the Americas second in every case. Californians are far more likely than others in the United States to be headed for the Orient, Australia and the Pacific. The position of Florida as a leading center of commerce and social life in the Caribbean area is reflected in its high percentage of prospective destinations in the Americas.

Table: Destination of travelers from 10 states with high numbers of new passports issued
Date: 1980
Source: State Department
Description: Total number and percentage of persons receiving new passports who listed Europe as their first destination.
United States average: 72.6%

EUROPE

Rank	State	Percent of persons receiving new passports	Number of travelers
1	Massachusetts	82.5	92,590
2	Ohio	79.6	79,980
3	New Jersey	79.3	110,680
4	Illinois	78.9	116,370
5	Pennsylvania	78.6	98,860
6	Michigan	78.4	70,250
7	New York	76.1	283,208
8	Texas	73.4	112,740
9	Florida	69.5	118,910
10	California	59.2	286,580

Table: Destination of travelers from 10 states with high numbers of new passports issued
Date: 1980
Source: State Department
Description: Total number and percentage of persons receiving new passports who listed The Americas as their first destination.
United States average: 11.0%

THE AMERICAS

Rank	State	Percent of persons receiving new passports	Number of travelers
1	Florida	18.0	30,880
2	California	13.2	64,010
3	New York	11.9	44,320
4	Texas	11.1	17,020
5	New Jersey	9.8	13,630

Rank	State	Percent of persons receiving new passports	Number of travelers
6	Massachusetts	8.8	9,850
7	Illinois	8.5	12,540
7	Michigan	8.5	7,630
9	Ohio	8.3	8,330
9	Pennsylvania	8.3	10,410

Table: Destination of travelers from 10 states with high numbers of new passports issued
Date: 1980
Source: State Department
Description: Total number and percentage of persons receiving new passports who listed The Far East as their first destination.
United States average: 6.6%

THE FAR EAST

Rank	State	Percent of persons receiving new passports	Number of travelers
1	California	12.2	58,970
2	Texas	6.3	9,740
3	Illinois	5.1	7,530
4	Ohio	4.6	4,630
4	Pennsylvania	4.6	5,780
4	Michigan	4.6	4,100
7	New York	4.3	16,020
8	New Jersey	4.2	5,850
9	Florida	4.0	6,780
10	Massachusetts	3.4	3,800

Table: Destination of travelers from 10 states with high numbers of new passports issued
Date: 1980
Source: State Department
Description: Total number and percentage of persons receiving new passports who listed The Mideast as their first destination.
United States average: 4.3%

THE MIDEAST

Rank	State	Percent of persons receiving new passports	Number of travelers
1	New York	5.8	21,620
2	Florida	5.3	9,050
2	Pennsylvania	5.3	6,620
4	Texas	4.9	7,540

Rank	State	Percent of persons receiving new passports	Number of travelers
5	Michigan	4.7	4,220
6	Ohio	4.4	4,440
7	California	4.3	20,960
8	New Jersey	4.2	5,850
9	Illinois	3.8	5,570
10	Massachusetts	3.3	3,750

Table: Destination of travelers from 10 states with high numbers of new passports issued
Date: 1980
Source: State Department
Description: Total number and percentage of persons receiving new passports who listed Australia and Oceania as their first destination.
United States average: 4.2%

AUSTRALIA/OCEANIA

Rank	State	Percent of persons receiving new passports	Number of travelers
1	California	10.1	48,770
2	Texas	3.1	4,750
3	Illinois	2.8	4,150
4	Florida	2.5	4,360
4	Michigan	2.5	2,230
6	Ohio	2.0	2,050
6	Pennsylvania	2.0	2,550
8	New Jersey	1.9	2,610
9	Massachusetts	1.3	1,490
10	New York	1.1	4,080

Table: Destination of travelers from 10 states with high numbers of new passports issued
Date: 1980
Source: State Department
Description: Total number and percentage of persons receiving new passports who listed Africa as their first destination.
United States average: .9%

AFRICA

Rank	State	Percent of persons receiving new passports	Number of travelers
1	Michigan	1.3	1,140
2	Texas	1.2	1,790
2	Pennsylvania	1.2	1,570

Rank	State	Percent of persons receiving new passports	Number of travelers
4	Ohio	1.0	990
5	California	.9	4,260
5	Illinois	.9	1,300
7	New Jersey	.7	920
7	New York	.7	2,680
9	Florida	.6	1,080
9	Massachusetts	.6	710

212. Domestic Pleasure Trips

It is estimated that about 65 million Americans, or 42% of the population, went on domestic pleasure trips in 1979 and 1980. Florida and California were the most favored destinations for out-of-state trips, a tribute to mild winter weather and the mass appeal of the Disney theme parks. About one-quarter of all domestic trips lasting longer than a week included a stop in Florida.

Table: Domestic Pleasure Travel
Date: 1979-1980
Source: Travel Pulse Research Service
Description: The nine most popular states for domestic pleasure trips

DOMESTIC PLEASURE TRAVEL

Rank	State	Percent of trips
1	Florida	14
2	California	12
3	Georgia	9
3	Nevada	9
5	Ohio	8
6	Illinois	7
6	New York	7
6	Texas	7
6	Virginia	7

213. Travel Agencies

Californians and New Yorkers travel frequently and they seem to prefer professionally managed travel arrangements. Most states in the Northeast appear on this list of the 19 states with the greatest number of travel agencies—while the South is unrepresented save for Florida.

Table: Travel Agencies
Date: 1980
Source: *World Travel Directory*
Description: Total number of travel agencies, by state, for the top 19 states.

TRAVEL AGENCIES

Rank	State	Number of travel agencies
1	California	3,271
2	New York	2,727
3	Illinois	1,122
4	Florida	1,120
5	New Jersey	974
6	Pennsylvania	810
7	Texas	710
8	Massachusetts	654
9	Ohio	527
10	Michigan	519
11	Connecticut	478
12	Wisconsin	276
13	Colorado	269
14	Minnesota	260
15	Hawaii	242
16	Missouri	239
17	Indiana	216
18	Maryland	214
19	Arizona	213

214. Average Hotel Room Prices in Selected Cities

Travelers to Florida, Washington, D.C., New York and San Francisco would be well advised to bunk with friends. Otherwise they should leave room in their suitcases for plenty of cash. Room rates in hotels in these areas are among the highest in the nation. Rates near Disney World, however, are sharply lower than those in the luxury vacation areas on the east coast of Florida. The relatively low rates in the Tennessee cities describe the situation prior to the period of the World's Fair in Knoxville (1982), when upward pressure on rates became evident.

Table: Average Hotel Room Rates
Date: 1981
Source: Pannell Kerr Forster. "Trends in the Hotel Industry. United States"
Description: Average hotel room rate in 19 major cities.

AVERAGE HOTEL ROOM RATES

Rank	City	Average room rate
1	Miami	$70.21
2	Washington, D.C.	68.05
3	New York	66.81
4	San Francisco	66.66
5	Fort Lauderdale	61.91
6	Boston	58.01
7	Chicago	57.60
8	Phoenix	55.25
9	Dallas-Fort Worth	55.05
10	Los Angeles	54.26
11	San Diego	50.44
12	Houston	48.95
13	Philadelphia	45.47
14	Atlanta	45.35
15	Denver	45.11
16	Orlando (Disney World)	43.15
17	Nashville	38.50
18	Memphis	31.95
19	Knoxville	31.15

215. Hotel Occupancy Rates in Selected Cities and Percentage of Change from 1980 to 1981

The cost of a hotel room may be high, but so are the chances of finding a place to stay the night. This is true throughout the country. The sharp drop in the occupancy rate in Miami hotels from 1980 to 1981—the outstanding feature in this table—is an effect of the highly publicized Liberty City riots of May 1980 and increased perception that the chances of being a victim of crime in south Florida have gone up in the past few years.

Table: Hotel Room Occupancy Rate
Date: 1981
Source: Pennell Kerr Forster "Trends in the Hotel Industry. United States."
Description: Average room occupancy rate and percentage of change from 1980 to 1981 for 19 major cities

HOTEL ROOM OCCUPANCY RATE

Rank	City	Average room occupancy rate	Percent of increase or decrease 1980–1981
1	San Diego	78.1	.9
2	San Francisco	76.1	−1.4
3	Los Angeles	75.8	−4.7
4	Fort Lauderdale	74.8	−6.4

Rank	City	Average room occupancy rate	Percent of increase or decrease 1980–1981
5	Orlando (Disney World)	74.0	−6.8
6	Washington, D.C.	71.7	−.1
7	New York	71.3	−8.1
8	Boston	70.2	−3.8
9	Miami	69.9	−14.8
10	Phoenix	69.7	−3.5
11	Nashville	68.9	5.5
12	Houston	67.0	−2.2
13	Knoxville	65.7	−7.3
14	Dallas-Fort Worth	65.5	−9.2
15	Memphis	65.3	.3
16	Philadelphia	65.1	.2
17	Denver	63.9	−4.3
18	Atlanta	63.7	−4.4
19	Chicago	62.4	−5.3

216. Average Daily Automobile Rental Charges in Selected Cities

The cost of renting a car is highest in the Northeast, at medium levels in the West and in the middle of the country, and relatively low in the South. The degree of highway congestion, associated with higher accident rates and insurance overhead, is a key factor in the establishment of different rate levels.

Table: Car Rentals
Date: 1983
Source: *Sales and Marketing Management Survey of Transportation Costs*
Description: Average daily car rental rate (gas and mileage changes not included) in 15 metropolitan areas.

CAR RENTALS

Rank	City	Rental rate
1	New York	$62.35
2	Philadelphia	55.35
3	Baltimore	54.65
3	Washington D.C.	54.65
5	Chicago	52.35
6	Denver	51.35
7	Los Angeles	49.35
8	San Francisco	49.00
9	Houston	48.65
10	Portland	48.00
11	Detroit	47.65
12	Seattle	47.35
13	Minneapolis-St. Paul	45.00
14	Atlanta	43.35
15	Miami	37.35

ARTS AND ARTISTS

The 1980 civilian labor force of 104 million workers included just over one million individuals classified as artists. Though the group is broadly defined, including fashion designers and radio/TV announcers, among others, only about one worker in 100 is found in this group. Five specific occupations are examined in this section: musician/composer, dancer, actor/director, painter/sculptor and photographer. There were 468,854 members of these occupations in 1980, about 45 among every 10,000 members of the entire labor force. The first five tables below present state by state breakdowns on the residence of artists; the figures show where specific types of artists are most likely to live and work, thus identifying the states in which the specific arts flourish and those in which they are relatively neglected.

Rankings are based on the relative frequency of a given occupation in the total labor force of the state. Since artists are comparatively rare, the numbers are not expressed as percentages of the labor force (artists per hundred workers), but as the number of artists of a given type per 10,000 workers in the civilian labor force. Total numbers of artists of each type are also presented for each state.

The final table in this section traces spending by arts agencies in the states, with ranking according to per capita spending on the arts.

217. Actors/Directors

The great concentration of actors and directors in New York City and Los Angeles is immediately apparent in this table. About 54% of the 67,180 American theater professionals live in either New York or California. The size of New York City theatrical activity is also apparent in spillover residence in Connecticut and New Jersey. Nevada and Hawaii appear near the top of the list, although not in the same leading positions as in the fields of music and dance. Alaska and South Dakota are surprise states among the top 10. For Alaska, the data given below on state support for the arts may provide some clues.

New Hampshire, at the bottom of the list, seems downright unhospitable to performing artists (zero dancers, relatively few musicians). Many of the other states where performers are rare can be found in the South, although Wyoming also makes an appearance among the areas devoid of dramatic art.

Table: Where Actors and Directors Live
Date: 1980
Source: National Endowment for the Arts
Description: Number of actors and directors per 10,000 members of the labor force.
United States total: 67,180
United States average: 4.4 per 10,000 members of labor force.

WHERE ACTORS AND DIRECTORS LIVE

Rank	State	Number of actors and directors per 10,000 labor force	Total number
1	New York	18.9	15,180
2	California	18.2	20,751
3	Alaska	8.2	149
4	Nevada	7.1	301
5	Hawaii	5.9	258
6	Connecticut	5.4	832
7	South Dakota	5.3	165
7	Virginia	5.3	1,300
9	Arizona	5.1	609
9	New Jersey	5.1	1,785
11	Florida	5.0	2,103
11	Maryland	5.0	1,024
13	Massachusetts	4.9	1,377
14	Colorado	4.8	688
14	Washington	4.8	933
16	New Mexico	4.7	255
16	Wisconsin	4.7	640
18	Montana	4.5	162
19	Oregon	4.3	529
19	Rhode Island	4.3	197
21	Illinois	4.2	2,271
21	Utah	4.2	261
23	Minnesota	3.9	779

Rank	State	Number of actors and directors per 10,000 labor force	Total number
23	North Dakota	3.9	113
23	Vermont	3.9	94
26	Idaho	3.8	159
26	Nebraska	3.8	281
28	Texas	3.7	2,445
29	Georgia	3.6	889
29	Iowa	3.6	495
31	Kansas	3.3	367
32	Missouri	3.1	695
33	Delaware	3.0	85
33	Maine	3.0	148
35	Michigan	2.9	1,217
36	Louisiana	2.8	488
37	Kentucky	2.7	409
37	Pennsylvania	2.7	1,461
39	Oklahoma	2.6	350
39	Tennessee	2.6	548
39	North Carolina	2.6	712
39	Ohio	2.6	1,275
43	Arkansas	2.5	238
43	Indiana	2.5	645
43	West Virginia	2.5	189
46	South Carolina	2.4	340
47	Mississippi	2.1	208
48	Alabama	1.8	290
48	Wyoming	1.8	42
50	New Hampshire	1.1	50

218. Dancers

Members of chorus lines and hula dancers share the spotlight in this table since Nevada and Hawaii have percentages of professional dancers 8 to 10 times the national average. They are far ahead of the other states in this respect. The presence of Alaska and Arizona among the leaders seems surprising at first, but this probably reflects a less commercial form of the phenomenon that makes Hawaiians so light on their feet: the presentation of native American dance by professional performing companies. Dancers in shows and movies explain the positions of New York and California, with New York holding the edge because of the ballet and modern dance companies, and their associated training institutions, located in New York City.

Several of the top states in the previous table also appear near the top here, but not Tennessee. A good deal of Nashville music is made in the studios, and live performances are more likely to include a modest amount of professional square dancing than a chorus line of high-kicking hoofers. New Jersey enters the list in 10th place and it will surely rank higher in the future. Atlantic City, as the new Las Vegas of the East, has offered steadily expanding opportunities for dancers. Utah has few professional musicians (rank 47 on Table 219), but a relatively large contingent of professional dancers.

Dancers form a very small occupational group, with just 13,194 associated individuals nationwide. There appear to be no dancers at all in four states, including music-poor Wyoming and the Dakotas. The New England states, all near the bottom of the list, do not offer much support for professional dancers.

Table: Where Dancers Live
Date: 1980
Source: National Endowment for the Arts
Description: Number of dancers per 10,000 members of the labor force.
United States total: 13,194
United States average: 1.3 per 10,000 members of labor force

WHERE DANCERS LIVE

Rank	State	Number of dancers per 10,000 labor force	Total number
1	Nevada	13.4	568
2	Hawaii	10.1	441
3	Alaska	3.4	63
4	New York	3.2	2,600
5	California	2.0	2,279
6	Florida	1.9	818
7	Arizona	1.8	218
8	Colorado	1.4	196
8	Maryland	1.4	297
8	Utah	1.4	87
11	New Jersey	1.3	459
12	Kentucky	1.2	189
13	Connecticut	1.1	165
13	Delaware	1.1	30
13	Indiana	1.1	288
13	Texas	1.1	713
13	Washington	1.1	204
18	Oregon	1.0	118
19	Georgia	.9	220
19	Montana	.9	33
21	Massachusetts	.8	218
21	Mississippi	.8	82
21	Ohio	.8	383
21	Wisconsin	.8	172
25	Idaho	.7	30
25	Iowa	.7	103
25	Louisiana	.7	124
25	Minnesota	.7	149
25	Illinois	.7	399
25	North Carolina	.7	185
25	Tennessee	.7	152
32	Arkansas	.6	58
32	Nebraska	.6	43

Rank	State	Number of dancers per 10,000 labor force	Total number
32	Pennsylvania	.6	304
32	Virginia	.6	147
32	West Virginia	.6	47
37	Alabama	.5	74
37	New Mexico	.5	27
37	Oklahoma	.5	72
40	Maine	.4	19
40	Michigan	.4	153
42	Kansas	.3	38
42	Missouri	.3	76
42	Rhode Island	.3	13
42	South Carolina	.3	43
46	Vermont	.1	3
47	New Hampshire	0	0
47	North Dakota	0	0
47	South Dakota	0	0
47	Wyoming	0	0

219. Musicians/Composers

The 140,556 professional musicians and composers in the country account for 13.5 of every 10,000 American workers. About 30% of these artists live either in New York or California. They are represented in the work forces of these states at rates well above average; but the states with the largest percentages of musicians in the labor force are Hawaii and, especially, Nevada. Where tourists go, musicians are sure to follow. Fifth-place Tennessee, where the city of Nashville is the capital of country music, just barely edges ahead of the tourist state Florida. Washington and Massachusetts lead the rest of the field.

Wyoming lags well behind the 49 other states in this category. Other states with few professional musicians are found in the hill country of the South, the Midwest and the western interior. Amateur country music, folk music and singing cowboys may flourish in these areas, but there are few full-time professionals.

Table: Where Musicians and Composers Live
Date: 1980
Source: National Endowment for the Arts
Description: Number of musicians and composers per 10,000 members of the labor force.
United States total: 140,556
United States average: 13.5 per 10,000 members of labor force

WHERE MUSICIANS AND COMPOSERS LIVE

Rank	State	Number of musicians and composers per labor force	Total number
1	Nevada	41.3	1,750
2	Hawaii	25.2	1,097
3	New York	21.0	16,836
4	California	20.1	22,919
5	Tennessee	18.5	3,826
6	Florida	18.3	7,713
7	Washington	17.4	3,366
8	Massachusetts	15.1	4,257
9	Arizona	14.7	1,747
10	Colorado	14.0	2,014
11	Minnesota	13.7	2,736
12	Oregon	13.1	1,621
13	New Jersey	12.7	4,481
13	New Mexico	12.7	693
15	Maryland	12.5	2,589
16	Alaska	11.7	213
16	Texas	11.7	7,717
18	Connecticut	11.2	1,740
19	Georgia	11.1	2,745
20	Kentucky	11.0	1,666
20	Maine	11.0	548
20	Michigan	11.0	4,640
20	Missouri	11.0	2,493
20	Ohio	11.0	5,424
20	Pennsylvania	11.0	5,892
26	Louisiana	10.8	1,892
26	Vermont	10.8	262
28	Rhode Island	10.7	489
28	Wisconsin	10.7	2414
30	Virginia	10.5	2,592
31	Nebraska	10.3	768
32	Illinois	10.1	5,514
33	North Dakota	10.0	287
34	Oklahoma	9.8	1,314
35	South Dakota	9.7	303
36	North Carolina	9.6	2,652
37	New Hampshire	9.4	426
38	Montana	9.2	330
39	Alabama	9.0	1,468
40	Mississippi	8.9	899
41	Indiana	8.7	2,234
42	Delaware	8.5	237
43	Iowa	8.1	1,112
44	Kansas	8.0	904
44	South Carolina	8.0	1,131
46	Arkansas	7.7	728
47	Utah	7.5	462
48	Idaho	7.3	306
49	West Virginia	6.9	521
50	Wyoming	3.2	73

220. Photographers

The proportion of photographers does not vary as much from state to state as the proportions of other artistic occupations in the arts. The majority of the 94,762 photographers in America do the same kind of work everywhere. Commercial photographers record graduations and weddings and other affairs, they encourage babies to smile, and they cover the news. Nevada and Hawaii add nightclub and tourist photographers to this basic mix, thus rising to the top of the list. Fashion photography and the pursuit of images of stage and screen stars and politicians boost proportions in New York, California and Maryland; about a quarter of all photographers are found in New York or California. High values for Colorado, New Mexico and Arizona probably reflect the work of groups of professional nature photographers who document the great American landscape (the Grand Canyon, for example). Wyoming has a respectable if subpar proportion of photographers in its labor force. Lower scores appear for some states in the South and the Midwest, the Dakotas and interior New England.

Table: Where Photographers Live
Date: 1980
Source: National Endowment for the Arts
Description: Number of photographers per 10,000 members of the labor force.
United States total: 94,762
United States average: 9.1 per 10,000 members of labor force

WHERE PHOTOGRAPHERS LIVE

Rank	State	Number of photographers per 10,000 labor force	Total number
1	Hawaii	13.8.	603
2	Nevada	13.5	573
3	New York	13.2	10,539
4	California	11.5	13,060
5	Alabama	11.0	1,120
5	Alaska	11.0	200
7	Colorado	10.9	1,556
8	Maryland	10.2	2,097
9	New Mexico	10.1	554
10	Arizona	10.0	1,184
10	Massachusetts	10.0	2,818
12	Florida	9.7	4,098
12	Oregon	9.7	1,203
12	Utah	9.7	601
15	Connecticut	9.6	1,488
16	Rhode Island	9.4	430
17	Washington	9.3	1,806
18	Nebraska	9.1	675
19	Illinois	9.0	4,929
20	Minnesota	8.9	1,783
20	New Jersey	8.9	3,134
20	Virginia	8.9	2,196

Rank	State	Number of photographers per 10,000 labor force	Total number
23	Tennessee	8.8	1,816
24	Kansas	8.7	975
25	Missouri	8.6	307
25	Montana	8.6	1,934
27	Ohio	8.5	4,211
27	Texas	8.5	5,582
29	Delaware	8.0	223
29	Idaho	8.0	335
29	Michigan	8.0	3,384
29	Wyoming	8.0	183
33	Oklahoma	7.8	1,053
34	Maine	7.6	379
35	Wisconsin	7.4	1,669
36	Louisiana	7.3	1,274
37	Pennsylvania	7.2	3,849
38	Kentucky	7.0	1,054
38	North Carolina	7.0	1,928
40	Georgia	6.8	1,678
40	South Dakota	6.8	211
40	Vermont	6.8	165
43	South Carolina	6.7	936
44	North Dakota	6.6	190
45	Arkansas	6.2	581
45	Indiana	6.2	1,596
47	Iowa	5.7	790
48	Mississippi	5.3	540
49	New Hampshire	5.1	230
49	West Virginia	5.1	387

221. Painters/Sculptors

Painters and sculptors form the largest of the art groups considered in this section. Still, they account for only about 15 of every 10,000 workers in the United States. New Mexico, with its long-established artists' colony at Taos, has the highest relative proportion of members of the group. In absolute terms, the major centers are California and New York, as might be expected—with 16.1% and 13.9%, respectively, of the 153,162 professional painters and sculptors. Other states among the top 10 in this table include Hawaii and Alaska, where there are vigorous programs to support native arts, Vermont and Connecticut, where spillover from New York City plays a part, and three scenic states in the West. The Dakotas and Wyoming join a group of southern states with few painters and sculptors, at the bottom of the table.

Table: Where Painters and Sculptors Live
Date: 1980
Source: National Endowment for the Arts
Description: Number of painters and sculptors per

10,000 members of the labor force, by state, for the 50 states.

United States total: 153,162
United States average: 14.7 per 10,000 members of labor force

WHERE PAINTERS AND SCULPTORS LIVE

Rank	State	Number of painters and sculptors per 10,000 labor force	Total number
1	New Mexico	27.7	1,514
2	New York	26.5	21,274
3	Hawaii	25.3	1,101
4	California	21.7	24,657
5	Vermont	20.6	500
6	Alaska	20.0	366
7	Colorado	19.6	2,805
8	Arizona	19.2	2,284
9	Washington	18.7	3,620
10	Connecticut	18.2	2,835
11	Massachusetts	17.0	4,788
12	New Jersey	15.9	5,602
13	Virginia	15.7	3,878
14	Minnesota	15.4	3,060
14	Oregon	15.4	1,910
16	New Hampshire	15.1	687
16	Utah	15.1	936
18	Montana	14.9	534
19	Florida	14.1	5,926
20	Maryland	13.7	3,575
21	Rhode Island	13.6	626
22	Illinois	13.5	7,382
23	Missouri	13.1	2,968
24	Texas	12.8	8,419
25	Wisconsin	12.2	2,760
26	Pennsylvania	11.9	6,376
27	Nevada	11.8	502
28	Maine	11.7	583
29	Delaware	11.5	323
30	Kansas	11.4	1,280
31	Michigan	11.2	4,699
32	Ohio	10.8	5,373
32	Oklahoma	10.8	1,448
34	Tennessee	10.3	2,138
35	Georgia	10.2	2,538
36	Nebraska	9.9	737
37	Idaho	8.9	370
38	Iowa	8.8	1,210
39	Indiana	8.6	2,212
40	Louisiana	7.8	1,357
41	Wyoming	7.5	172
42	Alabama	7.4	1,213
43	North Carolina	7.2	1,987
44	Kentucky	7.0	1,060
45	South Carolina	6.7	946
46	South Dakota	5.7	178
47	Mississippi	5.6	570
48	Arkansas	5.1	478
48	North Dakota	5.1	146
50	West Virginia	4.7	355

222. State Appropriations for the Arts

Hawaii, mindful of the need for attractive tourist displays, and Alaska, with its sizable and increasingly militant native culture, are the states that are making the greatest efforts in aid of the arts. The performance of New York is the other outstanding feature in this table. The remaining states are spending much less money on the arts, though even here there are considerable differences from state to state. West Virginia and Utah, for example, are making efforts about nine times as intense as penny-pinching Texas. Low levels of support generally prevail in the West and especially the Southwest.

Table: State Appropriations for the Arts
Date: 1981
Source: National Assembly of State Arts Agencies
Description: State legislative appropriations for arts agencies ranked by per capita dollars.
United States total: $111,094
United States average: $49
State median: 26¢ per capita

STATE APPROPRIATIONS FOR THE ARTS

Rank	State	Per capita expenditure	Expenditures (in thousands)
1	Alaska	$4.76	$1,931
2	Hawaii	2.04	1,968
3	New York	1.90	33,179
4	West Virginia	.85	1,636
5	Utah	.80	1,148
6	Minnesota	.75	3,060
7	Massachusetts	.70	4,000
8	Michigan	.55	5,037
9	Missouri	.51	2,489
10	California	.48	11,281
10	Louisiana	.48	2,003
12	Rhode Island	.43	403
12	Ohio	.43	4,664
14	New Jersey	.41	2,983
15	Connecticut	.40	1,249
16	Arkansas	.39	856
17	Maryland	.37	1,564
18	South Carolina	.33	1,023
19	Delaware	.29	175
19	Oklahoma	.29	875
21	Florida	.28	2,675
21	Illinois	.28	3,168
21	Kentucky	.28	1,005
21	Nebraska	.28	434
25	Vermont	.27	137
26	Colorado	.25	730
27	Georgia	.24	1,316
27	North Carolina	.24	1,413

Rank	State	Per capita expenditure	Expenditures (in thousands)	Rank	State	Per capita expenditure	Expenditures (in thousands)
27	Pennsylvania	$.24	$2,821	38	North Dakota	$.15	$101
27	Virginia	.24	1,201	38	Wisconsin	.15	720
31	Indiana	.23	1,273	42	Alabama	.14	525
31	South Dakota	.23	157	43	Oregon	.13	349
33	Wyoming	.19	88	44	Idaho	.12	117
33	Maine	.19	217	44	Montana	.12	97
35	New Hampshire	.18	162	46	Arizona	.11	263
36	New Mexico	.17	215	46	Iowa	.11	305
37	Washington	.16	664	46	Nevada	.11	88
38	Kansas	.15	343	46	Tennessee	.11	514
38	Mississippi	.15	380	50	Texas	.09	1,225

SPORTS

This section traces patterns of participation and spectator interest in recreation and sports throughout the country. Adult participation in outdoor physical activities has increased in recent years, roughly on a parallel with increased awareness of the connection between inactivity and various health problems. The jogging craze of the Jimmy Carter years has become routine in Ronald Reagan's America. An interest in aerobics and other forms of preventive or corrective exercise, often associated with the desire to lose some weight, has become a sort of national movement, with personalities like Jane Fonda and Richard Simmons as leadership figures. In the absence of reliable statistics on the extent of these forms of activity, the first few tables below present state by state breakdowns on participation in activities selected from a wider spectrum of recreational opportunities available to Americans.

The remaining tables present data on spectator sports, including attendance figures for various professional and college teams and information on areas where certain sports enjoy particularly high television ratings. According to one recent survey funded by a major sponsor of TV sports, almost all adults of both sexes admit to at least a passing interest in playing or viewing some form of sport. High interest in watching football on TV was expressed by 39% of those surveyed in a national sample. (This is the sort of calculation that has inspired the development of the new spring professional football league, the USFL.) Football is tops in the viewer preference department, followed at a respectable distance by baseball (28% interest), basketball (19%), boxing (19%) and gymnastics (19%).

223. Major League Baseball Attendance

Over 44 million people went to major league baseball games in 1982, setting attendance records in both the American and National Leagues. The two southern California teams, both pennant contenders, were the attendance leaders. The remarkable performance of the Dodgers, with over 3.6 million fans in the stands during the year, set a major league record for an individual team. All-time high franchise attendance figures were also recorded by the Angels, Brewers, Athletics, Braves, Expos and Cardinals. A comparison of these data with the 1982 standings of the teams shows that good performances are rewarded by the fans.

Table: Attendance at Major League Baseball Games
Date: 1982
Source: Office of the Commissioner of Baseball
Description: Average home-game attendance of the 26 teams in the National and American Leagues.
Total attendance: 44.6 million

ATTENDANCE AT MAJOR LEAGUE BASEBALL GAMES

Rank	Team	Average attendance
1	Los Angeles Dodgers	45,111
2	California Angels	34,659
3	Philadelphia Phillies	30,862
4	Montreal Expos	29,722
5	Kansas City Royals	28,556
6	New York Yankees	27,216
7	St. Louis Cardinals	26,399
8	Milwaukee Brewers	25,370
9	Boston Red Sox	24,685
10	Atlanta Braves	23,102
11	Oakland Athletics	22,250
12	Baltimore Orioles	21,798
13	Detroit Tigers	21,527
14	Chicago White Sox	20,629
14	San Diego Padres	20,349
16	Houston Astros	19,482
17	New York Mets	17,601
18	Cincinnati Reds	16,791
19	Toronto Blue Jays	16,571
20	Chicago Cubs	16,016
21	San Francisco Giants	15,597

Rank	Team	Average attendance
22	Texas Rangers	14,800
23	Cleveland Indians	13,561
24	Pittsburgh Pirates	13,475
25	Seattle Mariners	13,215
26	Minnesota Twins	11,373

224. National Football League (NFL) Attendance

Over 13 million people attended 224 regular season NFL games for the third consecutive year in 1981. Average attendance per game—60,745—was at an all-time high. The attendance at 10 postseason games plus the Super Bowl totaled about 720,000. Fans in Detroit, Cleveland and Buffalo provided the strongest support for their teams, with average attendance over 75,000 per game. Figures on college football attendance given below confirm the impression that the heart of American football country lies close to the Great Lakes region (perhaps at Canton, Ohio, location of the Football Hall of Fame). The Baltimore Colts, who won only two of 16 games in 1981, suffered at the box office. Interest in professional football has gathered momentum over the years. Average per game attendance during the first NFL season in 1934 was 8,211. The corresponding figures for 1951 and 1971 were 26,570 and 55,363. More teams and more games have been added through the years, so that total attendance has multiplied enormously. The size of stadiums seems to be the most important limitation on uncontrolled growth of attendance at present.

Table: Attendance at National Football League Games
Date: 1981
Source: National Football League
Description: Attendance at the home games of the National Football League during the 1981 season.
Total regular season attendance: 13.6 million

ATTENDANCE AT NATIONAL FOOTBALL LEAGUE GAMES

Rank	Team	Attendance
1	Detroit Lions	603,679
2	Cleveland Browns	601,725
3	Buffalo Bills	601,136
4	Denver Broncos	598,402

Rank	Team	Attendance
5	New York Giants	552,626
6	Philadelphia Eagles	548,171
7	Tampa Bay Buccaneers	531,936
8	Dallas Cowboys	511,541
9	Kansas City Chiefs	506,634
10	Miami Dolphins	489,292
11	Los Angeles Rams	483,964
12	Seattle Seahawks	453,275
13	New Orleans Saints	440,708
14	Chicago Bears	436,564
15	San Francisco 49ers	435,182
16	Green Bay Packers	433,077
17	New York Jets	429,036
18	Cincinnati Bengals	422,430
19	Pittsburgh Steelers	421,234
20	Atlanta Falcons	419,281
21	New England Patriots	414,561
22	Washington Redskins	412,276
23	San Diego Chargers	411,661
24	St. Louis Cardinals	384,375
25	Oakland Raiders	368,560
26	Houston Oilers	364,259
27	Minnesota Vikings	361,210
28	Baltimore Colts	286,456

225. College Football Attendance

Attendance at college games was nearly three times greater than attendance at professional games in 1981. About 35.8 million fans turned out for the games of the 648 four-year colleges with varsity teams. Average home-game attendance for the top seven teams on this list was higher than that for any pro team. The University of Michigan extended its number of home games (to 41), with average attendance of over 100,000. At the University of Georgia, where Herschel Walker was the main attraction and where a stadium expansion had taken place, attendance increased 32% from the 1980 level. In the Big Ten Conference (Michigan, Ohio State and eight other teams), average attendance at 59 games was 64,089, or 91.1% of available stadium capacity. In the Southeastern Conference (Georgia, Alabama and eight other teams), the corresponding attendance figures for 66 games were 59,865 and 95.8%.

Table: Attendance for the 25 Best-Drawing Teams in College Football
Date: 1981
Source: National Collegiate Athletic Association
Description: Total attendance and average attendance at home games of the 25 best-drawing teams in college football during the 1981 season.

ATTENDANCE FOR THE 25 BEST-DRAWING TEAMS IN COLLEGE FOOTBALL

Rank	Teams	Total attendance	Average attendance
1	Michigan	632,990	105,499
2	Tennessee	558,996	93,166
3	Ohio State	521,760	86,960
4	Penn State	507,697	84,616
5	Georgia	492,732	82,122
6	Nebraska	457,675	76,279
7	Oklahoma	455,078	75,846
8	LSU	513,850	73,407
9	Southern Cal	432,266	72,044
10	Wisconsin	501,482	71,640
11	Purdue	419,351	69,892
12	Alabama	414,445	69,074
13	Texas	477,219	68,174
14	Stanford	386,321	64,337
15	Arizona State	449,153	64,165
16	Texas A & M	319,166	63,833
17	Michigan State	382,545	63,758
18	Illinois	311,826	62,365
19	Auburn	436,170	62,310
20	Clemson	371,128	61,855
21	Missouri	432,511	61,787
22	Florida	432,128	61,733
23	Iowa	360,381	60,064
24	Notre Dame	354,450	59,076
25	Kentucky	335,761	55,960

Total attendance: 4,718,973
Per game average: 14,045

ATTENDANCE AT THE GAMES OF THE NORTH AMERICAN SOCCER LEAGUE

Rank	City	Total attendance	Average attendance
1	New York	557,453	34,841
2	Montreal	379,263	23,704
3	Vancouver	371,893	23,243
4	Tampa Bay	360,502	22,531
5	Seattle	291,594	18,225
6	Tulsa	275,012	17,188
7	Minnesota	268,078	16,755
8	San Diego	236,824	14,802
9	Fort Lauderdale	213,178	13,324
10	Chicago	201,228	12,577
11	San Jose	195,876	12,242
12	Washington	193,701	12,106
13	Edmonton	170,110	10,632
14	Portland	168,259	10,516
15	Calgary	168,019	10,501
16	Jacksonville	151,846	9,490
17	California	132,778	8,299
18	Toronto	116,590	7,287
19	Atlanta	99,022	6,189
20	Los Angeles	93,031	5,814
21	Dallas	74,716	4,670

226. North American Soccer League (NASL) Attendance

Professional soccer is a relatively recent arrival on the American scene, but its popularity seems to be well established. Over 4.7 million fans attended games in the United States and Canada during 1981, an average of about 14,000 per game. The New York Cosmos, featuring a lineup of international stars, draw the largest crowds. NASL teams have shifted home cities frequently in their search for adequate fan support. Prior to the 1981 season there were shifts from Memphis to Calgary, Boston to Jacksonville, and Philadelphia to Montreal. Attendance improved in each case, but especially for the former Philadelphia franchise (from 4,465 per game in 1980 to 23,204 per game in 1981).

Table: Attendance at the Games of the North American Soccer League
Date: 1981
Source: North American Soccer League
Description: Total attendance and average attendance at the 16 home games of the North American Soccer League during the 1981 season.

227. National Basketball Association (NBA) Attendance

During the 1981–1982 NBA regular season, just under 10 million fans turned out for the games. That works out to an average of 434,322 fans per team or, based on a total of 41 home games per team, an average of 10,593 fans per game. The Seattle Supersonics have an enthusiastic following and play home games in a very large arena. They were the attendance leaders by a wide margin. The smaller arenas in Boston and Portland, Oregon, were almost always filled to capacity during the season. Attendance has been so low, however, in recent years at Salt Lake City, Indianapolis, Atlanta, Kansas City, Cleveland and San Diego that plans to shift the location of these franchises are often discussed.

Table: Attendance at National Basketball Association Games
Date: 1981–1982 Season
Source: National Basketball Association
Description: Attendance at the home games of the National Basketball Association during the 1981–1982 season.
Total attendance: 9,889,410

ATTENDANCE AT NATIONAL BASKETBALL ASSOCIATION GAMES

Rank	Team	Attendance
1	Seattle	750,059
2	Boston	622,711
3	Los Angeles	604,935
4	New Jersey	568,861
5	Portland	519,306
6	Philadelphia	506,847
7	Phoenix	487,215
8	Houston	480,128
9	Denver	475,708
10	New York	444,189
11	Milwaukee	443,288
12	San Antonio	434,243
13	Detroit	406,317
14	Golden State (San Francisco)	401,646
15	Dallas	390,292
16	Chicago	372,611
17	Washington	369,807
18	Utah (Salt Lake City)	318,236
19	Indiana (Indianapolis)	318,062
20	Atlanta	308,899
21	Kansas City	304,955
22	Cleveland	236,523
23	San Diego	224,572

ATTENDANCE FOR THE 35 BEST-DRAWING TEAMS IN COLLEGE BASKETBALL

Rank	Team	Total Attendance	Average Attendance
1	Kentucky	371,093	23,193
2	Brigham Young	339,586	21,224
3	Syracuse	320,461	18,851
4	New Mexico	264,748	16,547
5	Minnesota	240,588	16,039
6	Louisville	207,542	15,965
7	Indiana	231,862	15,457
8	Illinois	244,908	15,307
9	Vanderbilt	202,225	14,445
10	Louisiana State	225,905	14,119
11	DePaul	189,806	13,558
12	Iowa	173,745	13,365
13	Purdue	213,036	13,315
14	Ohio State	190,880	12,725
15	Tennessee	150,578	12,548
16	Utah	182,677	12,178
17	Notre Dame	178,617	11,164
18	UCLA	164,418	10,961
19	Marquette	174,333	10,896
20	Missouri	185,159	10,892
21	North Carolina	140,990	10,845
22	Kansas State	195,060	10,837
23	Alabama	138,540	10,657
24	West Virginia	180,740	10,632
25	Wichita State	148,828	10,631
26	Connecticut	147,058	10,504
27	Nebraska	143,819	10,273
28	Dayton	184,231	10,235
29	Texas	152,579	10,172
30	Oregon State	121,040	10,087
31	North Carolina State	150,600	10,040
32	Evansville	130,009	10,001
33	Maryland	157,275	9,830
34	Michigan	133,738	9,553
35	Kansas	152,293	9,518

228. College Basketball Attendance

Over 31 million fans attended the 1981–1982 season games of the 1,264 senior colleges with varsity basketball programs. The top 25 teams on this list all recorded average attendance figures higher than the overall average for professional basketball. Enthusiasm for the college game runs high. Since most of the teams on this list regularly fill their arenas to capacity, the ranking really depends on the number of available seats. The team conferences with the highest attendance figures are the same for college basketball as they are for college football: the Big Ten (11,810 per basketball game) and the Southeastern (10,951 per basketball game).

Table: Attendance for the 35 Best-Drawing Teams in College Basketball
Date: 1981
Source: National Collegiate Athletic Association
Description: Total attendance and average attendance at home games of the 35 best-drawing teams in college basketball during the 1981 season.

229. Television Audience for "ABC Wide World of Sports" in Leading Market Areas

The "Wide World" series presents a smorgasbord of moderately exotic sporting events, from stock-car derbies to surfing, that are not carried on a regular basis by the networks. "Seasons" or "leagues" for these sports are often either nonexistent or irregular in some way. Foreign events are covered frequently, as are major competitions in leading amateur or Olympic events like gymnastics and swimming. Judging by the areas listed in this table, appreciation of sports outside the American mainstream appears to be high all across the Sunbelt (appearing here as the states forming the western and southern rims of the country, from Orgon to Florida). None of the areas listed here support franchises in the major professional sports.

Explanations of ADI (Area of Dominant Influence) ratings and index numbers can be found in the section on television. The rating is the percentage of TV sets in a given area tuned to the program in question, while the index shows how this percentage (with certain adjustments) compares to a national average rating set at 100. Ratings and index numbers appear in several other tables in this section. The listed areas are those 10 with the highest index values among areas across the country for which detailed Arbitron viewer-survey data are available.

Table: Best Markets for "ABC Wide World of Sports"
Date: 1982
Source: Arbitron
Description: The 10 market areas with the highest total ADI ratings for ABC "Wide World of Sports".
Total ADI rating for all markets: 5

BEST MARKETS FOR "ABC WIDE WORLD OF SPORTS"

Rank	Market area	ADI rating	ADI index
1	Eureka, Calif.	16	305
2	Medford, Oreg.	11	218
3	Greenwood-Greenville, Miss.	10	185
4	Corpus Christi, Tex.	10	181
5	Las Vegas	9	179
6	El Centro-Yuma, Calif., Arizona	9	168
7	Sacramento-Stockton	8	160
8	Reno	8	158
9	Gainesville, Fla.	8	157
10	Fresno, Calif.	8	153

230. Television Audience for "Tuesday Night Baseball" in Leading Market Areas

Except for Los Angeles, where baseball fever runs high, the areas where TV baseball is highly popular tend to be those located just far enough away from major league cities that travel to games is impractical on a regular basis. The fact that the St. Louis Cardinals had a very good year and won the World Series helps to account for high levels of interest in Springfield, Missouri. Phillies fans (or Pirates fans) in "upstate" Pennsylvania follow all nationally televised games very carefully and account for four of the top 10 market areas. Nationwide, about 10% of all households watch "Tuesday Night Baseball." In the 10 areas listed here, levels of interest are 50% or more above the national norm.

Table: Best Markets for "Major League Baseball Night"
Date: 1982
Source: Arbitron
Description: The 10 market areas with the highest ADI rating for "Major League Baseball Night"
Total ADI rating for all markets: 10

BEST MARKETS FOR "MAJOR LEAGUE BASEBALL NIGHT"

Rank	Market area	ADI rating	ADI index
1	Columbus-Tupelo, Miss.	23	235
2	Sioux City, Iowa	22	222
3	Harrisburg-York-Lancaster-Lebanon, Pa.	19	198
3	Springfield, Mo.	19	195
5	Johnstown-Altoona, Pa.	17	170
5	Los Angeles	17	174
7	Wilkes Barre-Scranton, Pa.	16	169
8	Greenville-New Bern-Washington, N.C.	15	150
8	Louisville	15	155
8	Sacramento-Stockton	15	157

231. Television Audience for the Major League All-Star Baseball Game in Leading Market Areas

Close to one-quarter of all American households tuned in to the All-Star game in 1982. Areas where interest was above average included several of the major league cities. With the exceptions of Philadelphia and Los Angeles, the top audience areas were spread across the Midwest.

Table: Best Markets for Major League All-Star Baseball Game
Date: 1982
Source: Arbitron
Description: The 10 market areas with the highest ADI ratings for the major league all-star baseball game.
Total ADI rating for all markets: 23

BEST MARKETS FOR MAJOR LEAGUE ALL-STAR BASEBALL GAME

Rank	Market area	ADI rating	ADI index
1	Kansas City	38	169
2	Philadelphia	35	157
3	Erie, Pa.	34	152
4	Topeka	32	144
5	Detroit	31	136
5	Duluth-Superior	31	139
7	St. Louis	30	132
8	Cincinnati	29	128
8	Cleveland	29	128
8	Los Angeles	29	130

232. Television Audience for the U.S. Women's Open Golf Championship in Leading Market Areas

It is apparently much more fun to play golf than to watch it on television. The Women's Open attracted viewers in only 3% of American households. Viewer interest in the listed areas was two to three times greater than that in most parts of the country. These areas are strewn about the country, but most of them are located in warm-weather areas where golf is a relatively popular recreational activity.

Table: Best Markets for U.S. Women's Open Golf Championship
Date: 1982
Source: Arbitron
Description: The 10 market areas with the highest ADI ratings for the U.S. Open Women's Golf Championship.
Total ADI rating for all markets: 3

BEST MARKETS FOR U.S. WOMEN'S OPEN GOLF CHAMPIONSHIP

Rank	Market area	ADI rating	ADI index
1	Charleston	11	314
2	West Palm Beach	9	265
3	Colorado Springs-Pueblo, Colo.	8	240
4	Buffalo	7	191
4	Cincinnati	7	191
4	Louisville	7	196
4	Sacramento-Stockton	7	210
4	Tampa-St. Petersburg	7	208
4	Waco-Temple, Tex.	7	213
10	Joplin-Pittsburg, Mo., Kans.	6	181

233. Men's Bowling Leagues

A total of about 4.6 million men were registered as members of the American Bowling Congress during the year ending July 31, 1982. They were members of about 1.5 million teams competing in 138,660 leagues. Using these gross figures for calculation, there were about 33 bowlers per league, but since many individuals participate in several leagues the calculated figure is deceptively low. The American Bowling Congress recognized 5,949 perfect (300 points) games during the year, but rejected 536 other games originally reported as perfect. About one-third of all leagues affiliated with the congress were found in the four states at the top of the list. As a group, states in the Midwest show the most impressive levels of participation, but areas of strength are found throughout the country.

Table: Men's Bowling Leagues
Date: 1981
Source: American Bowling Congress
Description: Number of men's bowling leagues for the 50 states.
United States total: 138,660

MEN'S BOWLING LEAGUES

Rank	State	Number of leagues
1	California	14,042
2	New York	11,430
3	Ohio	10,591
4	Michigan	9,662
5	Illinois	7,644
6	Wisconsin	7,458
7	Pennsylvania	6,921
8	Texas	6,074
9	Florida	5,238
10	New Jersey	4,249
11	Indiana	4,156
12	Missouri	4,090
13	Minnesota	3,763
14	Iowa	2,993
15	Washington	2,901
16	Colorado	2,543
17	Kansas	2,049
18	Arizona	1,824
19	Nebraska	1,794
20	North Carolina	1,759
21	Virginia	1,602
22	Oklahoma	1,601
23	Tennessee	1,558
24	Oregon	1,521
25	Kentucky	1,520
26	Connecticut	1,519
27	Georgia	1,366
28	Maryland	1,360
29	Louisiana	1,184
30	South Carolina	1,095
31	Massachusetts	1,049
32	Alabama	863
33	Arkansas	807
34	North Dakota	790
35	West Virginia	769
36	South Dakota	743
37	Idaho	720
38	New Mexico	707
38	Utah	707
40	Hawaii	700
41	Montana	671
42	Nevada	654
43	Delaware	470
44	Wyoming	412
45	Rhode Island	353
46	Mississippi	329
47	Vermont	314
48	Alaska	292
49	Maine	139
50	New Hampshire	138

234. Women's Bowling Leagues

There were about 4 million registered members of the Women's International Bowling Congress in the United States during the year ending July 31, 1982. They were distributed among 160,139 leagues, for an average of 25 bowlers per league (discounting the many multiple-league memberships). The top 13 states on this list are identical to the ones at the top of the list for men's bowling leagues. As in the case of the men's leagues, the big four states account for about one-third of the total.

Table: Women's Bowling Leagues
Date: 1981
Source: Women's International Bowling Congress
Description: Number of women's bowling leagues for the 50 states.
United States total: 160,139

WOMEN'S BOWLING LEAGUES

Rank	State	Number of leagues
1	California	16,898
2	New York	12,564
3	Ohio	11,992
4	Michigan	10,734
5	Illinois	8,568
6	Wisconsin	8,418
7	Pennsylvania	7,097
8	Texas	6,950
9	Florida	6,252
10	New Jersey	4,970
11	Indiana	4,650
12	Missouri	4,548
13	Minnesota	4,340
14	Washington	4,030
15	Virginia	3,587
16	Iowa	3,345
17	Colorado	3,192
18	Kansas	2,392
19	Arizona	2,147
20	Oklahoma	2,103
21	Nebraska	2,019
22	Oregon	2,003
23	North Carolina	1,966
24	Tennessee	1,861
25	Connecticut	1,814
26	Kentucky	1,809
27	Georgia	1,657
28	Louisiana	1,625
29	Maryland	1,468
30	South Carolina	1,224
31	Massachusetts	1,175
32	Alabama	1,028
33	Arkansas	1,019
34	Utah	976
35	West Virginia	966
36	North Dakota	940
37	New Mexico	903
38	South Dakota	843
39	Montana	836
40	Hawaii	769
41	Idaho	763
42	Nevada	747
43	Delaware	557
44	Wyoming	535
45	Mississippi	443
46	Rhode Island	429
47	Alaska	366
48	Vermont	317
49	Maine	152
49	New Hampshire	152

235. Roller Skating Clubs

Over 40,000 Americans are registered with the U.S. Amateur Confederation of Roller Skating. The confederation organizes annual competitions in artistic, dance and speed skating as well as roller hockey (but has nothing to do with Roller Derby). American skaters have taken part in international competitions for over 30 years. There are over 1,100 skating clubs, in 49 states, that are registered with the confederation, but 908 of these clubs are found in the 17 states listed below. California is the leading roller skating state. Texas and Florida lead the rest of the pack, which, except for Washington, is made up of states in the East (extending south into Virginia and North Carolina) and the Midwest.

Table: Roller Skating Clubs
Date: 1982
Source: Amateur Confederation of Roller Skating
Description: Number of roller skating clubs for 17 states.

ROLLER SKATING CLUBS

Rank	State	Number
1	California	159
2	Texas	94
3	Florida	83
4	Pennsylvania	76
5	Ohio	66
6	Michigan	62
7	Massachusetts	45
8	Illinois	39
8	Virginia	39
10	North Carolina	35
10	Washington	35
12	New Jersey	34

Rank	State	Number
12	New York	34
14	Indiana	29
14	Wisconsin	29
16	Missouri	27
17	Connecticut	22

236. Figure Skaters

Nearly 40,000 figure skaters belong to some 440 ice-skating clubs affiliated with the U.S. Figure Skating Association. Areas of high membership are scattered across the country, but about three-quarters of all members are found in the 11 states at the head of the list, each with over 1,000 members.

Table: Membership in the U.S. Figure Skating Association
Date: 1981
Source: U.S. Figure Skating Association
Description: Membership in the U.S. Figure Skating Association.
United States total: 38,304

MEMBERSHIP IN THE U.S. FIGURE SKATING ASSOCIATION

Rank	State	Members
1	New York	5,138
2	California	4,672
3	Massachusetts	3,273
4	Michigan	2,973
5	Pennsylvania	2,581
6	Ohio	2,033
7	Minnesota	1,770
8	Colorado	1,595
9	Connecticut	1,420
10	Illinois	1,247
11	New Jersey	1,137
12	Texas	775
13	Washington	698
14	Wisconsin	688
15	Rhode Island	639
16	Maryland	580
17	Indiana	535
18	Georgia	487
19	New Hampshire	451
20	Virginia	432
21	Alaska	384
22	Missouri	361
23	Kansas	347
23	Nebraska	347
25	Oregon	340
26	Arizona	321
27	North Dakota	300
28	Delaware	292
29	Montana	290

Rank	State	Members
30	Florida	233
31	North Carolina	225
32	Vermont	174
33	Utah	172
34	Maine	169
35	Alabama	157
36	Louisiana	149
37	Oklahoma	140
38	Nevada	138
39	Idaho	136
40	West Virginia	117
41	Wyoming	108
42	New Mexico	102
43	Iowa	88
44	Tennessee	46
45	Kentucky	44
46	Arkansas	0
46	Hawaii	0
46	Mississippi	0
46	South Carolina	0
46	South Dakota	0

237. Ski Areas

A total of 641 designated ski areas are scattered across the United States. There are 39 states with one or more ski areas, but 65% of all such areas are in the 10 states at the head of this list. Five of these states are in the Northeast, three in the upper Midwest and two in the West. These figures tend to underplay the extent of skiing in the Rocky Mountain and other western states, since ski areas in this region tend to be larger than those elsewhere in the country and there is also much more skiing outside of designated ski areas.

Table: Ski Areas
Date: 1980
Source: Inter-Ski Services, Inc.
Description: Number of ski areas for 39 states.
United States total: 641

SKI AREAS

Rank	State	Number of ski areas
1	New York	75
2	Wisconsin	55
3	Michigan	53
4	California	38
4	New Hampshire	38
4	Pennsylvania	38
7	Colorado	32
8	Vermont	30

Rank	State	Number of ski areas
9	Massachusetts	29
9	Minnesota	29
11	Montana	19
12	Idaho	17
13	Maine	16
13	Washington	16
15	Utah	15
16	Iowa	12
16	New Mexico	12
18	Oregon	11
19	North Carolina	10
20	Indiana	9
20	New Jersey	9
20	Wyoming	9
23	Illinois	8
23	Ohio	8
25	North Dakota	7
26	Alaska	6
26	Connecticut	6
26	West Virginia	6
29	Nevada	5
29	Virginia	5
31	Arizona	4
31	South Dakota	4
33	Rhode Island	3
34	Maryland	2
35	Alabama	1
35	Georgia	1
35	Kansas	1
35	Missouri	1
35	Tennessee	1

Table: Registered Boats
Date: 1981
Source: National Marine Manufacturers
Description: Number of registered boats and persons per boat.
United States total: 8,881,312

REGISTERED BOATS

Rank	State	Number of boats	Persons per boat
1	Michigan	664,212	14.0
2	Minnesota	593,400	7.0
3	California	574,442	42.5
4	Texas	567,126	26.1
5	Florida	512,551	20.2
6	Wisconsin	412,067	11.6
7	New York	319,638	54.6
8	Ohio	304,880	35.5
9	Louisiana	300,000	14.4
10	Missouri	273,975	18.2
11	Illinois	259,297	44.3
12	Arkansas	255,705	9.2
13	Alabama	226,984	17.5
14	Washington	212,171	20.1
15	Georgia	201,692	27.9
16	South Carolina	196,110	16.4
17	North Carolina	193,900	31.1
18	Pennsylvania	188,185	63.1
19	Oklahoma	187,689	16.6
20	Tennessee	186,221	25.3
21	Iowa	186,073	15.8
22	Massachusetts	181,549	31.7
23	Indiana	173,325	32.0
24	Oregon	136,999	19.9
25	Maryland	134,104	31.8
26	New Jersey	129,885	57.0
27	Mississippi	117,384	21.9
28	Maine	115,090	10.0
29	Kentucky	112,855	33.2
30	Arizona	101,179	28.7
31	Kansas	78,945	30.3
32	Connecticut	74,441	41.8
33	Idaho	62,156	16.0
34	Colorado	56,592	53.3
35	Nebraska	51,640	30.8
36	Utah	45,825	33.7
37	Alaska	43,247	9.8
38	West Virginia	42,605	46.7
39	Delaware	34,184	17.6
40	South Dakota	31,818	22.0
41	Montana	30,334	26.6
42	North Dakota	28,812	23.0
43	Nevada	28,315	30.1
44	Vermont	26,851	19.5
45	New Mexico	25,361	53.6
46	Rhode Island	21,932	43.4
47	Wyoming	17,579	28.4
48	Virginia	14,903	38.8
49	Hawaii	13,372	74.7
50	New Hampshire	4,432	21.5

238. Registered Boats and Persons per Boat

Although the boats included in data for this table may be used for work or strictly for pleasure, the figures for a given state do provide some sense of the degree to which boating plays a part in recreational activities. Motorboats, which may be used in connection with fishing, hunting and water skiing as well as just for cruising, are included in the data for all states. Sailboats are also included for many states. A total of nearly 9 million motorboats and sailboats were registered in 1981, or roughly one boat for every 25 persons in the country as a whole. The figures in the second column show that Minnesota, Arkansas, Alaska and Maine are the leaders, with at least one boat for every 10 residents. Wisconsin, Michigan and Louisiana are not far behind. It is surprising that Hawaii, with just one boat per 75 persons, is at the bottom of the list. Two factors explain this. First, there is very little inland water in Hawaii and second, canoes and other boats propelled by paddles or oars are not included in the data.

239. Visitors to State Parks and Recreation Areas

According to the reports of 48 state park directors, there were close to 550 million visitors to state parks and recreation areas in the United States during the year ending June 30, 1980. Figures for visits to the national parks are not included in these totals. Although the 1980 total represented a significant drop (probably due to vacations and outings not taken because of the recession) from the level of about 610 million visits during the previous year, the total still works out to better than two visits per year by every man, woman and child in the country. Visits to state parks along the Pacific Coast accounted for 24% of the national total.

Table: Visitors to State Parks and Recreation Areas
Date: 1980
Source: National Association of State Park Directors
Description: Number of visitors to state parks and recreation areas.
United States total: 549 million

VISITORS TO STATE PARKS AND RECREATION AREAS

Rank	State	Number (in thousands)
1	California	58,024
2	New York	39,729
3	Washington	37,154
4	Oregon	34,455
5	Illinois	32,314
6	Kentucky	29,758
7	Michigan	21,426
8	Oklahoma	18,294
9	Hawaii	16,760
10	Pennsylvania	15613
11	Tennessee	14,989
12	Texas	14,022
13	Ohio	12,897
14	South Carolina	12,719
15	Wisconsin	12,306
16	Georgia	11,813
17	Florida	11,489
18	Massachusetts	9,872
19	Missouri	9,283
20	Iowa	8,823
21	Utah	8,718
22	West Virginia	8,206
23	Rhode Island	7,703
24	Indiana	7,691
25	Connecticut	7,300
26	Nebraska	7,282
27	Alabama	6,506
28	New Jersey	6,134
29	Minnesota	5,815
30	Arkansas	5,786
31	Maryland	5,240
32	North Carolina	4,852
33	South Dakota	4,573
34	Virginia	4,402
35	Kansas	4,342
36	Louisiana	4,211
37	New Mexico	4,104
38	Mississippi	4,065
39	New Hampshire	3,662
40	Nevada	3,338
41	Alaska	2,910
42	Delaware	2,801
43	Arizona	2,352
44	Idaho	2,049
45	Maine	1,846
46	Vermont	1,211
47	Montana	1,030
48	North Dakota	1,013
49	Colorado	not available
49	Wyoming	not available

PRINT MEDIA

Once a nation of readers, Americans have become enslaved to their televisions, radios and stereos. Is this a fair characterization of the situation in America today? The data in this section show that the art of reading and use of the printed media have not yet vanished like the buffalo. The first two tables cover circulation in the public libraries of the states and the support that state and local governments provide for these important institutions. The next two tables survey the daily newspapers, showing the number of papers, levels of circulation and circulation rates in the states. The remainder of the section is devoted to magazines. The information presented here—identifying the counties in which circulation rates of specific publications are especially high or low—is not exactly about reading, since many magazines really feature photography, but it does provide an indication of the countinuing strength of the printed media along with a short lesson in the geography of American taste.

240. Library Circulation

The 1982 edition of the *American Library Directory* lists about 8,700 public libraries and 4,600 academic libraries in the United States. The data in this table represent the annual total of items per capita checked out of the public libraries that reported to the *Directory* (about 90% of all public libraries). This is not a perfectly accurate indicator of how much reading is done in the various states, since most people buy most of the books that they read (in 1979 1.6 billion books worth $7.2 billion were purchased in the United States), but it provides a reasonable first estimate.

The citizens of Iowa are the most avid book borrowers in the nation. This is a truth both factual and poetic, for the most famous librarian in the history of the American theater, "Marian the Librarian," the winsome lass pursued by the salesman/professor Harold Hill in *The Music Man*—was the head of the public library in a small Iowa town. Maryland, Kansas and Utah are the other

states with very high borrowing rates. The lowest rates are found in Pennsylvania and in a block of states stretching across the South from the Carolinas to Oklahoma and Texas.

Table: Library Circulation
Date: 1982
Source: American Library Directory
Description: Pieces of material (in millions) checked out at public libraries and pieces per capita.
United States average: 4.73
State median: 4.8 per capita

LIBRARY CIRCULATION

Rank	State	Items per capita	Number of items (in millions)
1	Iowa	8.37	17
2	Maryland	7.39	31
3	Kansas	7.00	17
4	Utah	6.84	10
5	Ohio	6.60	71
6	Washington	6.48	27
7	Wyoming	6.43	3
8	New Hampshire	6.30	6
9	Massachusetts	6.23	35
10	Minnesota	6.20	24
10	Wisconsin	6.20	30
12	Maine	6.10	5
13	South Dakota	5.96	3
14	Connecticut	5.90	17
15	Nebraska	5.34	8
16	Hawaii	5.20	5
16	Oregon	5.20	15
16	Vermont	5.20	2
19	Missouri	5.12	25
20	Montana	5.10	4
20	Virginia	5.10	27
22	California	4.97	119
22	Idaho	4.97	5
24	Colorado	4.91	14
25	Arizona	4.80	13
26	New Jersey	4.79	35

Rank	State	Items per capita	Number of items (in millions)
27	Illinois	4.68	53
28	Alaska	4.61	2
29	New York	4.55	83
30	Nevada	4.50	4
31	Rhode Island	4.40	4
32	North Dakota	4.32	3
33	Georgia	4.07	22
34	West Virginia	4.03	7
35	Kentucky	3.93	14
36	Florida	3.65	36
37	Michigan	3.64	33
38	New Mexico	3.60	5
39	Delaware	3.58	2
40	North Carolina	3.57	21
41	Louisiana	3.38	14
42	Arkansas	3.34	8
43	Tennessee	3.30	15
44	Pennsylvania	3.15	37
45	Texas	3.00	43
46	Alabama	2.96	12
47	Mississippi	2.70	7
48	South Carolina	2.60	9
49	Oklahoma	2.47	7
50	Indiana	not available	not available

241. Library Spending

During fiscal year 1981 (fiscal year 1980 for Alabama, Michigan and Texas), state and local governments spent an average of just over $8 per capita for the operation of public libraries. Spending in Alaska was exceptionally high for a variety of reasons, including the high level of all prices, special long-distance freight charges for new acquisitions, and above-average costs in putting together a young library system. Spending in Arkansas is depressingly low. For the other 48 states a ratio of about 3 to 1 is found between the extreme values (registered in Massachusetts and Pennsylvania). Five of the 10 states with the highest borrowing rates also appear among the top 10 here: Massachusetts, Washington, Maryland, Wyoming and Wisconsin. Public interest in their libraries is clearly strong in these states. Most of the 10 states with the lowest circulation rates are also found near the bottom of this list. Pennsylvania appears once again among a block of southern states in which there is apparently little concern for public libraries. Curiously, the state of Kansas spends relatively little money on libraries (rank 40), although its citizens are among the most active borrowers in the nation.

Table: Library Expenditures
Date: 1981
Source: Department of Commerce per capita library expenditures
Description: Per capita library expenditures.
United States average: $8.23
State median: $7.60

LIBRARY EXPENDITURES

Rank	State	Library expenditures per capita
1	Alaska	$23.59
2	Massachusetts	13.24
3	Washington	13.23
4	Connecticut	13.02
5	Maryland	12.54
6	Wyoming	12.38
7	Minnesota	11.23
8	Wisconsin	11.14
9	Hawaii	10.69
10	New York	10.37
11	California	10.26
12	Utah	10.19
13	Iowa	9.86
13	New Jersey	9.86
15	Montana	9.65
16	Colorado	9.48
17	Nevada	9.04
18	Illinois	8.91
19	Arizona	8.70
20	Oregon	8.62
21	New Hampshire	8.53
22	Indiana	8.43
23	Virginia	8.29
24	Ohio	7.69
25	Louisiana	7.62
26	Vermont	7.58
27	Rhode Island	7.53
28	Michigan	7.43
29	Missouri	7.04
30	Nebraska	6.98
31	Florida	6.96
32	South Dakota	6.90
33	Kentucky	6.79
34	Texas	6.63
35	Delaware	6.52
36	New Mexico	6.50
37	Idaho	6.31
38	Maine	6.07
39	North Carolina	5.82
40	Kansas	5.76
41	North Dakota	5.62
42	Tennessee	5.19
43	West Virginia	5.12
44	Alabama	4.77
45	Oklahoma	4.62
46	Georgia	4.43
47	South Carolina	4.23
48	Mississippi	4.17
49	Pennsylvania	4.09
50	Arkansas	2.57

242. Newpapers

Freedom of the press is a basic constitutional right in America, and our nation is justifiably proud of the accomplishments of journalism in protecting democracy for over 200 years. A certain degree of sensationalism has always been one of the prices we have paid for freedom of expression (this is also certainly true in the case of commercial television), but it is difficult to imagine how our present freedoms could have been preserved if the government or a small economic elite had come to dominate the channels of communication. The performance of the *Washington Post* and other newspapers in disclosing the crimes of the Nixon administration has had a decisive impact on all aspects of political life in recent years. The protection against misuse of power afforded by the freedom of the press has been powerfully reaffirmed.

The position of the newspapers and other printed media has been much reduced by the growth of the electronic media. Summary data indicate, however, that it would be wrong to overemphasize the decline of the newspapers. Americans continue to appreciate the coverage in depth that only the printed media are able to provide. They also appreciate the fact that newspapers provide a greater variety of news items to choose from than radio or TV, and that a reader can absorb material in whatever order and at whatever speed seems best. As electronic technologies enter the world of newspapers—especially the use of computerized equipment to write and edit stories, lay out pages, assign advertising for select sections of the market, and direct printing operations—a new period of newspaper strength may be emerging.

There are over 1,700 daily newspapers in the United States, with a combined circulation of over 60 million copies per day. Although the closing of some major papers has made news in recent years—and there is a definite trend toward mergers, concentration of control over newspapers in the hands of a smaller number of parent companies—the actual number of papers has remained in the range of 1,700–1,800 since 1950. Circulation has actually increased during this period, up from 53.8 million copies per day in 1950; but because the population has been growing at an even faster rate, per capita circulation has declined. From 305 daily papers sold per 1,000 population in 1970, the rate declined to 275 per 1,000 in 1980. Per capita circulation figures are presented in the next table.

The largest numbers of newspapers are found in the vast states of California and Texas. Cities and towns lie scattered far from one another in these states, offering numerous separate markets. The tiny state of Delaware has only three papers, but the even tinier state of Rhode

Island boasts of seven. New York, which ranks behind California in nearly every table in this book based on actual counts instead of ratios, sits comfortably atop the list. About 13% of all daily newspapers in America are sold in the Empire State.

Table: Average Newspaper Circulation
Date: 1981, 1982
Source: *Editor & Publisher International Year Book*
Description: Average daily newspaper circulation, April – September 1981, and number of daily papers as of February 1982.
United States total circulation: 61.4 million
U. S. total papers: 1730

AVERAGE NEWSPAPER CIRCULATION

Rank	State	Average daily circulation	Number of daily papers
1	New York	8,036	78
2	California	5,968	124
3	Texas	3,451	116
4	Pennsylvania	3,298	98
5	Ohio	3,280	95
6	Illinois	2,755	76
7	Florida	2,645	52
8	Michigan	2,463	52
9	Massachusetts	2,025	46
10	New Jersey	1,687	26
11	Indiana	1,629	76
12	Missouri	1,511	49
13	North Carolina	1,366	55
14	Wisconsin	1,222	36
15	Washington	1,172	27
16	Virginia	1,155	38
17	Tennessee	1,063	30
18	Georgia	1,014	37
19	Minnesota	1,007	30
20	Colorado	921	27
21	Connecticut	896	25
22	Iowa	868	41
23	Oklahoma	843	53
24	Louisiana	794	25
25	Maryland	767	16
26	Kentucky	746	26
27	Alabama	740	28
28	Oregon	686	21
29	Arizona	620	18
30	South Carolina	607	19
31	Kansas	580	47
32	Arkansas	488	32
33	Nebraska	485	19
34	West Virginia	466	25
35	Mississippi	400	25
36	Rhode Island	314	7
37	Maine	292	9
38	Utah	283	6
39	New Mexico	281	20

Rank	State	Average daily circulation	Number of daily papers
40	Hawaii	247	6
41	Nevada	230	8
42	Idaho	213	14
43	Montana	201	11
44	New Hampshire	199	9
45	North Dakota	194	10
46	South Dakota	170	12
47	Delaware	152	3
48	Vermont	118	8
49	Alaska	116	8
50	Wyoming	102	10

243. Newspaper Circulation Per 1,000 Population

New Yorkers (state and city) are far and away the most avid newspaper readers in the nation. It must have something to do with the subways. Three other eastern states rank just below New York. States scattered across the center of the country round out the top 10. The lowest rates are found in Utah, Wyoming and a group of southern states. The low values for Maryland and Virginia should not be taken at face value. Many residents of these states read the Washington, D.C. papers. Daily circulation rates for the Washington papers (the *Post* and the *Star*) were 1,433 per 1,000 residents of the nation's capital in 1980.

Table: Newspaper Circulation Per 1,000 Population
Date: 1980
Source: *Editor & Publisher International Year Book*
Description: Daily Newspaper Circulation per 1,000 Population for the 50 states.
United States average: 275 per 1,000 population
State median: 251 per 1,000 population

NEWSPAPER CIRCULATION PER 1,000 POPULATION

Rank	State	Newspapers per 1,000 population
1	New York	449
2	Massachusetts	353
3	Rhode Island	334
4	Pennsylvania	325
5	Missouri	315
6	Colorado	312
7	Nebraska	310
8	Ohio	305
9	Iowa	303
10	North Dakota	300
11	Indiana	297
12	Connecticut	292
13	Washington	287
14	Nevada	278
15	Oklahoma	277
16	Florida	270
17	Oregon	267
18	Alaska	266
19	Michigan	264
20	Delaware	262
21	Wisconsin	260
22	Maine	258
23	California	254
24	Kansas	253
25	South Dakota	252
26	Minnesota	250
26	Montana	250
28	Illinois	249
29	Hawaii	247
30	Texas	242
30	West Virginia	242
32	North Carolina	235
32	Tennessee	235
34	Vermont	231
35	New Jersey	230
36	Arizona	228
37	Idaho	221
38	New Hampshire	213
39	Arkansas	210
39	New Mexico	210
41	Kentucky	207
42	Wyoming	206
43	Virginia	204
44	Louisiana	193
44	South Carolina	193
46	Alabama	192
47	Georgia	190
47	Utah	190
49	Maryland	167
50	Mississippi	158

Magazine Circulation

The 26 tables that make up the remainder of this section trace the circulation rates of certain well-known magazines in relation to county populations. As of January 1, 1980 there were 3,005 counties in the United States. Twenty counties are listed in each table—the counties with the 10 highest and the 10 lowest circulation rates per resident for each magazine in 1982. The data, based on a survey, were specifically produced for inclusion in this book by the Audit Bureau of Circulation in Chicago. Similar figures for 1978, appearing in the first edition of this book, were the first of this kind that the Audit Bureau had ever produced.

The magazines included here represent various genres or interests that will be familiar to the reader. They are listed in alphabetical order. The data provide entertaining insights into the reading tastes of people in different parts of the country.

Circulation rates are displayed to one decimal place on the basis of number of issues sold per 100 members of the county population. The population figures are estimates for 1982, based on census figures and rounded to the nearest hundred. Rankings are based on calculations carried out to further decimal places. If we were to assume that each copy of a magazine was read by one resident only, then *circulation* per unit of population would be equal to the number of *readers* per unit of population (i.e. the percentage of readers in the population). There are two problems with this interpretation. First, magazines are typically read by more than one person before being discarded. Many single copies are read at least by all members of a given family. Second, these data cover total sales, not just subscriptions, so areas with many magazine-buying visitors, as in the Colorado ski resort counties, have rates calculated on a population base that is too small. Use these figures, which portray *circulation* as a percentage of population, cautiously. For most counties they are very low estimates of the percentage of *readers* in the population, but for a few tourist counties the estimates are much too high.

Where there are ties among counties with zero circulation, they are ranked according to county population on the assumption that zero interest in a magazine is increasingly improbable (and therefore more interesting) as population increases. In many cases there are more than 10 counties largest among such counties are listed. The county of Loving, Texas (pop. 100, rounded) appears frequently in the tables below. It is the least populous county in the nation, so when there are no readers of a magazine in Loving, the county is always the last to be listed among those with zero circulation. If there is just *one* reader in Loving, the circulation rate jumps to 1%, which can sometimes be enough to qualify a county for a place in the top 10. Since the preferences of just a few readers in the very small counties can boost percentages dramatically, many of the counties found among the top 10 in these tables are actually those with small populations.

244. *Better Homes and Gardens*

A magazine of home improvement and design, *Better Homes and Gardens* has readers in every county in the United States. Boise County, Idaho (pop. 3,200), not the city of Boise (pop. 102,000), is apparently the home of a good many style-conscious homeowners. Other counties with high rates are found in farming country, especially in Nebraska. Low rates of interest are displayed in parts of Alaska, North Dakota and several states in the South.

Table: *Better Homes and Gardens*
Date: 1982
Source: The Audit Bureau of Circulation
Description: The 10 counties with the highest and 10 with the lowest circulation, per 100 population, of *Better Homes and Gardens*.

BETTER HOMES AND GARDENS
Counties With Highest Circulation Per 100 Population

Rank	County	Circulation
1	Boise, Idaho	14.1
2	Cheyenne, Kans.	8.2

Rank	County	Circulation
3	Clark, Kans.	7.4
4	Hardin, Iowa.	7.3
4	Thayer, Nebr.	7.3
6	Furnas, Nebr.	7.0
7	Rush, Kans.	7.1
8	Clay, Nebr.	7.0
9	Deuel, Nebr.	6.8
9	Hooker, Nebr.	6.8

Counties With Lowest Circulation Per 100 Population

Rank	County	Circulation
1	Chattahoochee, Ga.	0.2
1	Echols, Ga.	0.2
3	Miller, Ark.	0.3
3	Wade Hampton, Alaska	0.3
5	Borden, Tex.	0.4
6	Shannon, S. Dak.	0.5
7	Leslie, Ky.	0.6
7	North Slope, Alaska	0.6
7	Randall, Tex.	0.6
7	Wakulla, Fla.	0.6

Rank	County	Circulation
6	Norfolk, Mass.	0.7
6	Sierra, Calif.	0.7
8	Columbia, Wis.	0.6
8	New York, N.Y.	0.6
8	Webb, Tex.	0.6

Counties With Lowest Circulation Per 100 Population

Rank	County	Circulation
1	Limestone, Ala.	0
2	Hood, Tex.	0
3	Edgefield, S.C.	0
4	Marion, Ky.	0
5	Wayne, Ky.	0
6	Breckinbridge, Ky.	0
7	Warren, N.C.	0
8	McCreary, Ky.	0
9	McDonald, Mo.	0
10	Dent, Mo.	0

245. Bride's Magazine

The title of this magazine explains what it offers—a digest of all the things a young woman needs to know in order to arrange a tasteful wedding and to overcome difficulties early in married life. Copies floating around in the specialty bridal ship in Manhattan (New York County) explain the position of the metropolis among the circulation leaders. The rate in Republic County, Kansas, is the highest in the nation, perhaps as a direct consequence of or a kind of defensive response to the situation in Republic, portrayed below in the table for *Penthouse*.

Table: *Bride's Magazine*
Date: 1982
Source: The Audit Bureau of Circulation
Description: The 10 counties with the highest and 10 with the lowest circulation, per 100 population, of *Bride's Magazine*.

BRIDE'S MAGAZINE
Counties With Highest Circulation Per 100 Population

Rank	County	Circulation
1	Republic, Kans.	3.2
2	Arenac, Mich.	2.0
3	Edmondson, Ky.	1.3
4	Cass, Iowa	0.8
4	Holt, Mo.	0.8

246. Business Week

New York County is Manhattan, the only place in the country where two or more copies of *Business Week* circulate per 100 residents. All counties in the top 10 except Pitkin (the city of Aspen) are associated with major metropolitan areas. In most cases the figures reflect copies available at work, not at home. Arkansas is definitely not *Business Week* territory.

Table: *Business Week*
Date: 1982
Source: The Audit Bureau of Circulation
Description: The 10 counties with the highest and 10 with the lowest circulation, per 100 population, of *Business Week*.

BUSINESS WEEK
Counties With Highest Circulation Per 100 Population

Rank	County	Circulation
1	New York, N.Y.	2.3
2	Fairfield, Conn.	1.4
3	Fulton, Ga.	1.2
3	San Francisco, Calif.	1.2
3	Suffolk, Mass.	1.2
3	Washington, D.C.	1.2
7	Arlington, Va.	1.1
7	Pitkin, Colo.	1.1
7	Warren, Ill.	1.1
10	Nassau, N.Y.	1.0

Counties With Lowest Circulation Per 100 Population

1	Miller, Ark.	0
2	Russell, Ky.	0
3	Johnson, Tenn.	0
4	Caldwell, La.	0
5	Coffey, Kans.	0
6	Metcalfe, Ky.	0
7	Searcy, Ark.	0
8	Newton, Ark.	0
9	Cleveland, Ark.	0
10	Franklin, Tex.	0

247. *Catholic Digest*

High circulation areas for *Catholic Digest* are rural, predominantly Catholic counties in the upper Midwest. There are few Catholics and fewer readers of this magazine in much of the South.

Table: *Catholic Digest*
Date: 1982
Source: The Audit Bureau of Circulation
Description: The 10 counties with the highest and 10 with the lowest circulation, per 100 population, of *Catholic Digest*.

CATHOLIC DIGEST
Counties With Highest Circulation Per 100 Population

Rank	County	Circulation
1	Hettinger, N. Dak.	4.0
2	Greeley, Nebr.	3.2
3	Golden Valley, N. Dak.	3.1
4	Cedar, Nebr.	2.5
4	Mahnomen, Minn.	2.5
6	Stark, N. Dak.	2.4
7	Carroll, Iowa	2.1
7	Lyon, Minn.	2.1
7	Red Lake, Minn.	2.1
10	Faulk, S. Dak.	2.0

Counties With Lowest Circulation Per 100 Population

1	Chattahoochee, Ga.	0
2	Monroe, Ga.	0
3	Wayne, Tenn.	0
4	Cook, Ga.	0
5	Pickens, Ga.	0
6	Greene, Ga.	0
7	Haskell, Okla.	0
8	Bryan, Ga.	0
9	Green, Ky.	0
10	Pike, Ark.	0

248. *Cosmopolitan*

A monthly pep talk for the maturing, socially active single woman, *Cosmo* enjoys a truly astounding circulation rate in tiny (pop. 1,300) Alpine County, California. Men who find themselves in Alpine, a ski area that draws crowds from San Francisco, would be well advised, before venturing out on the street, to check the latest *Cosmo* schemes for managing relationships. Colorado ski areas also have high circulation rates. The rates for such areas are somewhat deceptive, since they are calculated using only the resident population as a base, but they do give a sense of what the winter sports enthusiasts are reading. The highest circulation rate for a major urban area is found in Boston (Suffolk County).

Table: *Cosmopolitan*
Date: 1982
Source: The Audit Bureau of Circulation
Description: The 10 counties with the highest and 10 with the lowest circulation, per 100 population, of *Cosmopolitan*.

COSMOPOLITAN
Counties With Highest Circulation Per 100 Population

Rank	County	Circulation
1	Alpine, Calif.	59.2
2	Pitkin, Colo.	9.2
3	Eagle, Colo.	5.8
4	Adams, Pa.	5.5
4	Summit, Colo.	5.5
6	La Plata, Colo.	5.2
7	Loving, Tex.	5.0
8	Wood, Ohio	4.9
9	Alexander, N.C.	4.7
10	Suffolk, Mass.	4.6

Counties With Lowest Circulation Per 100 Population

1	Conecuh, Ala.	0
2	George, Miss.	0
3	Casey, Ky.	0
4	Wilcox, Ala.	0
5	Grant, Ark.	0
6	Bryan, Ga.	0
7	St. Helena, La.	0
8	Perry, Miss.	0
9	Pike, Ga.	0
10	Gates, N.C.	0

249. *Ebony*

A magazine similar in format to *Life*, but oriented

toward black readers, *Ebony* achieves its highest circulation rates in the South. Washington, D.C., Atlanta (Fulton County) and Norfolk are major urban areas with high circulations.

Table: *Ebony*
Date: 1982
Source: The Audit Bureau of Circulation
Description: The 10 counties with the highest and 10 with the lowest circulation, per 100 population, of *Ebony*.

EBONY
Counties With Highest Circulation Per 100 Population

Rank	County	Circulation
1	Northampton, Va.	10.5
2	Washington, D.C.	6.7
3	Macon, Ala.	4.2
3	Montgomery, Ga.	4.2
5	Clinton, N.Y.	3.6
6	Fulton, Ga.	3.5
7	Dinwiddie, Va.	3.3
8	Peach, Ga.	2.9
9	Norfolk City, Va.	2.8
10	Edgecombe, N.C.	2.7

Counties With Lowest Circulation Per 100 Population

1	Chesapeake City, Va.	0
2	Greene, Ind.	0
3	Cumberland, Tenn.	0
4	Lincoln, W. Va.	0
5	Douglas, Wash.	0
6	Starke, Ind.	0
7	Texas, Mo.	0
8	Scott, Tenn.	0
9	Franklin, Ind.	0
10	Adair, Okla.	0

250. *Good Housekeeping*

If the folks in little Loving County, Tex. fail to read a good many other magazines, it may be because almost everyone in town is busy poring over the latest copy of *Good Housekeeping*. Household hints are also popular among the married skiers in Alpine County, unless of course some of those single women who read *Cosmo* are also boning up on the mechanics of settling down. *Good Housekeeping* is read in every county in the country. Shawnee, Kansas. (suburban Topeka) has the highest rate among large counties.

Table: *Good Housekeeping*
Date: 1982
Source: The Audit Bureau of Circulation
Description: The 10 counties with the highest and 10 with the lowest circulation, per 100 population, of *Good Housekeeping*.

GOOD HOUSEKEEPING
Counties With Highest Circulation Per 100 Population

Rank	County	Circulation
1	Loving, Tex.	26.0
2	Alpine, Calif.	17.4
3	Prince of Wales-Outer Ketchikan, Alaska	8.8
4	Thomas, Nebr.	8.1
5	Shawnee, Kans.	8.0
6	Cheboygan, Mich.	7.8
7	Sheridan, Mont.	6.9
8	Phelps, Nebr.	6.7
8	Treasure, Mont.	6.7
10	Langlade, Wis.	6.6

Counties With Lowest Circulation Per 100 Population

1	Chattahoochee, Ga.	0.1
2	Echols, Ga.	0.2
2	Issaquena, Miss.	0.2
4	Shannon, S. Dak.	0.3
4	Starr, Tex.	0.3
4	St. Helena, La.	0.3
7	Baker, Ga.	0.4
7	Hancock, Tenn.	0.4
7	Hartley, Tex.	0.4
7	Maverick, Tex.	0.4

251. *Gourmet*

People in many counties of the United States have never even heard of *Gourmet*. The list of the top 10 counties reads like a Cook's tour of the upper-crust communities and vacation spots in America—where the elite meet to eat. Cape Cod, the Rockies and the Bay Area all turn up twice on the list, joined by the suburbs of Washington, D.C., Manhattan (New York County), an island in Puget Sound and a ski resort county in Idaho.

Table: *Gourmet*
Date: 1982
Source: The Audit Bureau of Circulation
Description: The 10 counties with the highest and 10 with the lowest circulation, per 100 population, of *Gourmet*.

GOURMET
Counties With Highest Circulation Per 100 Population

Rank	County	Circulation
1	Nantucket, Mass.	3.2
2	Pitkin, Colo.	2.6
3	Dukes, Mass.	1.9
4	Marin, Calif.	1.8
5	Arlington, Va.	1.6
6	New York, N.Y.	1.4
6	San Francisco, Calif.	1.4
8	Eagle, Colo.	1.3
8	San Juan, Wash.	1.3
10	Blaine, Idaho	1.2

Counties With Lowest Circulation Per 100 Population

1	Tipton, Tenn.	0
2	Mason, W. Va.	0
3	Douglas, Wash.	0
4	Clay, Ky.	0
5	Meade, Ky.	0
6	Barrow, Ga.	0
7	Hoke, N.C.	0
8	Caswell, N.C.	0
9	Itawamba, Miss.	0
10	Clay, Ark.	0

NATIONAL GEOGRAPHIC
Counties With Highest Circulation Per 100 Population

Rank	County	Circulation
1	San Juan, Colo.	12.6
2	Pitkin, Colo.	12.4
3	Los Alamos, N. Mex.	12.1
4	San Juan, Wash.	11.5
5	Mineral, Colo.	11.0
5	Teton, Wyo.	11.0
7	Blaine, Idaho	10.9
7	Duray, Colo.	10.9
9	Hinsdale, Colo.	10.8
10	Haines, Alaska	10.2

Counties With Lowest Circulation Per 100 Population

1	Chattahoochee, Ga.	0.1
2	Elliott, Ky.	0.4
2	Issaquena, Miss.	0.4
2	Knott, Ky.	0.4
2	Magoffin, Ky.	0.4
6	Hancock, Ga.	0.5
6	Knox, Ky.	0.5
6	McCreary, Ky.	0.5
6	Starr, Tex.	0.5
6	Van Buren, Tenn.	0.5

252. *National Geographic*

National Geographic is not sold on the newstands. It comes by subscription only to members of the National Geographic Society (membership delightfully inexpensive). This means that the figures in this table give a truer indication of the distribution of interest than those in most other tables. There are members of the society in every county, with high concentrations among the lovers of the great outdoors throughout the Rockies, and among the atomic scientists of Los Alamos. This is one of the few magazines that people collect and keep. No secondhand book store is complete without a selection of *National Geographics* that goes way back.

Table: *National Geographic*
Date: 1982
Source: The Audit Bureau of Circulation
Description: The 10 counties with the highest and 10 with the lowest circulation, per 100 population, of *National Geographic*.

253. *The New Yorker*

The New Yorker is America's most sophisticated magazine, featuring cartoons, short fiction, poetry, articles on personalities and current affairs, schedules of and critical reports on cultural events in New York, book reviews and advertisements for a dazzling array of luxury products. Most American magazines are basically picture magazines, but the only photographs in *The New Yorker* are in the advertisements. The cartoons and vignette drawings supply visual enjoyment. Manhattan is, understandably, the focal point of circulation. Areas of high circulation outside of the New York County area (note that none of the other boroughs or suburbs of New York City are listed) include many of the same counties in which *Gourmet* is well favored. Orange County, N.C. is part of the Raleigh-Durham SMSA, one of the chief economic and intellectual centers in the South.

Table: *The New Yorker*
Date: 1982
Source: The Audit Bureau of Circulation
Description: The 10 counties with the highest and 10 with the lowest circulation, per 100 population, of *The New Yorker*.

THE NEW YORKER
Counties With Highest Circulation Per 100 Population

Rank	County	Circulation
1	New York, N.Y.	3.3
2	Dukes, Mass.	2.2
3	Nantucket, Mass.	2.1
4	Washington, D.C.	1.6
5	Pitkin, Colo.	1.5
5	Arlington, Va.	1.5
7	Alpine, Calif.	1.3
8	Orange, N.C.	1.2
8	San Francisco, Calif.	1.2
8	Marin, Calif.	1.2

Counties With Lowest Circulation Per 100 Population

Rank	County	Circulation
1	Bullitt, Ky.	0
2	Evangeline, La.	0
3	Chilton, Ala.	0
4	Sabine, La.	0
5	Prentiss, Miss.	0
6	Assumption, La.	0
7	McNairy, Tenn.	0
8	Winston, Ala.	0
9	Hardin, Tenn.	0
10	Union, Miss.	0

PENTHOUSE
Counties With Highest Circulation Per 100 Population

Rank	County	Circulation
1	Republic, Kans.	34.8
2	Sedgwick, Colo.	15.5
3	Summit, Colo.	11.0
4	Eagle, Colo.	10.0
5	Grand, Colo.	8.5
6	Worcester, Md.	8.0
7	Charlotte, Fla.	7.8
8	Chattahoochee, Ga.	7.6
8	Dare, N.C.	7.6
10	Crawford, Mich.	7.4

Counties With Lowest Circulation Per 100 Population

Rank	County	Circulation
1	Lamar, Miss.	0
2	Knott, Ky.	0
3	Jasper, S.C.	0
4	Walthall, Miss.	0
5	Nevada, Ark.	0
6	Green, Ky.	0
7	Webster, Miss.	0
8	Carroll, Miss.	0
9	Hancock, Tenn.	0
10	Warren, Ga.	0

254. *Penthouse*

Penthouse is a picture magazine for men about sex and other things that happen to interest men who are interested in sex. The men of Republic County are very interested in *Penthouse*. If we assume that women make up anything close to half of the county population, that women almost never buy the magazine, and that minors are not allowed to buy it, then it would seem that virtually every adult male in Republic County must have a copy. Counties in Colorado and the South fill many of the other slots in the top 10. For more on what looks like a major battle of the sexes in Republic County (pop. 7,400), see the figures for *Bride's Magazine* and *True Story*.

Table: *Penthouse*
Date: 1982
Source: The Audit Bureau of Circulation
Description: The 10 counties with the highest and 10 with the lowest circulation, per 100 population, of *Penthouse*.

255. *People*

Loving County is at the bottom of the low circulation list, so it is safe to assume that there are only 10 counties in the country where no one reads *People*. Most of these counties are in rural Tennessee. Elsewhere, Americans enjoy their weekly dose of the exploits of the famous, above all in Clarke County, (outside Athens). The major urban area which devotes the greatest attention to this celebration of the newsworthy ego is, as you might have guessed, Washington, D.C.

Table: *People*
Date: 1982
Source: The Audit Bureau of Circulation
Description: The 10 counties with the highest and 10 with the lowest circulation, per 100 population, of *People*.

PEOPLE
Counties With Highest Circulation Per 100 Population

Rank	County	Circulation
1	Clarke, Ga.	8.0
2	Adams, Iowa	7.8
3	Sierra, Calif.	7.3
4	Pitkin, Colo.	6.7

Rank	County	Circulation
5	Eagle, Colo.	5.8
6	Wood, Wis.	5.6
7	Blue Earth, Minn.	4.9
8	Washington, D.C.	4.7
9	Ness, Kans.	4.6
10	Cass, Iowa	4.4

Counties With Lowest Circulation Per 100 Population

1	Clay, Tenn.	0
2	Perry, Tenn.	0
3	Van Buren, Tenn.	0
4	Pickett, Tenn.	0
5	Robertson, Ky.	0
6	Piute, Utah	0
7	Billings, N. Dak.	0
8	Clark, Idaho	0
9	Kino, Tex.	0
10	Loving, Tex.	0

LF⅛⅛?

Counties With Lowest Circulation Per 100 Population

1	Echols, Ga.	0.1
2	Issaquena, Miss.	0.1
3	Twiggs, Ga.	0.1
4	St. Helena, La.	0.1
5	Buffalo, S. Dak.	0.1
6	Pickett, Tenn.	0.1
7	Van Buren, Tenn.	0.1
8	Bains, Tex.	0.1
9	Walthall, Miss.	0.1
10	Lincoln, W. Va.	0.1

256. *Playboy*

Playboy magazine, the longest-running floating girlie show in America, attracts readers and gawkers in all 3,000 odd counties. Those who breathe mountain air appear to be especially appreciative of its charms. The magazine is special also because a complex of enterprises has been built up around it (clubs, hotels, casinos) and because it established at least one new cultural institution, the centerfold.

Table: *Playboy*
Date: 1982
Source: The Audit Bureau of Circulation
Description: The 10 counties with the highest and 10 with the lowest circulation, per 100 population, of *Playboy*.

PLAYBOY
Counties With Highest Circulation Per 100 Population

Rank	County	Circulation
1	Summit, Colo.	19.3
2	Garfield, Colo.	13.1
3	Eagle, Colo.	10.0
3	Sierra, Calif.	10.0
5	Pitkin, Colo.	8.7
6	Douglas, Kans.	7.5
7	Geary, Kans.	7.2
7	Routt, Colo.	7.2
9	Mono, Calif.	6.9
10	Lancaster, Va.	6.8

257. *Popular Science*

The popularity of *Popular Science* is all but universal. Readers are found in all counties save two. Although the members of the scientific community at Los Almos are now engaged in building really large-scale gizmos, it is clear that they still like to stay in touch with the how-does-it-work/built-it-yourself work of scientific hobbies that inspired them in younger days. The practical spirit of Alaskans shines through in these data, which disclose three counties from Alaska among the top 10. Clay County (suburban Kansas City) is the most populous county on the list.

Table: *Popular Science*
Date: 1982
Source: The Audit Bureau of Circulation
Description: The 10 counties with the highest and 10 with the lowest circulation, per 100 population, of *Popular Science*.

POPULAR SCIENCE
Counties With Highest Circulation Per 100 Population

Rank	County	Circulation
1	Los Almos, N. Mex.	2.6
2	Levy, Fla.	2.4
3	Ketchikan Gateway, Alaska	2.3
4	Clay, Mo.	2.2
5	Camas, Idaho	2.1
5	Chouteau, Mont.	2.1
5	Fairbanks North Star, Alaska	2.1
8	Cook, Minn.	2.0
8	Hinsdale, Colo.	2.0
8	Juneau, Alaska	2.0

Counties With Lowest Circulation Per 100 Population		
1	Baker, Ga.	0
1	Kenedy, Tex.	0
3	Benton, Miss.	0.1
3	Echols, Ga.	0.1
3	Hancock, Ga.	0.1
3	Hayes, Nebr.	0.1
3	Issaquena, Miss.	0.1
3	Jefferson, Miss.	0.1
3	Perry, Miss.	0.1
3	St. Helena, La.	0.1

Counties With Lowest Circulation Per 100 Population		
1	Borden, Tex.	0
1	Buffalo, S. Dak.	0
1	Dillingham, Alaska	0
1	Glasscock, Tex.	0
1	King, Tex.	0
1	Loving, Tex.	0
1	Wheatland, Mont	0
8	Echols, Ga.	0.1
8	Jackson, Tenn.	0.1
8	Webster, Ga.	0.1

258. Psychology Today

Rural Alaskans display extraordinary interest in the well-springs of human motivation that form the prinicpal subject matter of this monthly adventure in popular psychology. Americans in all but seven counties regularly join them in this quest for answers to the riddle of who does what and why. Big cities are featured to an unusual degree in the list of high circulation areas, especially the cities of Colorado (not the ski towns, where people are perhaps less confused or curious about their intentions). Manhattan appears among the top 10, along with Marin County, just across the Golden Gate from San Francisco.

Table: *Psychology Today*
Date: 1982
Source: The Audit Bureau of Circulation
Description: The 10 counties with the highest and 10 with the lowest circulation, per 100 population, of *Psychology Today*.

PSYCHOLOGY TODAY
Counties With Highest Circulation Per 100 Population

Rank	County	Circulation
1	Wade Hampton, Alaska	6.6
2	Bristol Bay, Alaska	4.1
3	Clay, Mo.	1.5
4	Arlington, Va.	1.4
5	Pitkin, Colo.	1.3
6	Denver, Colo.	1.2
7	Marin, Calif.	1.1
7	New York, N.Y.	1.1
7	Summit, Colo.	1.1
10	Boulder, Colo.	1.0

259. Reader's Digest

Reader's Digest is a uniquely American institution, dedicated to keeping the busy citizen up to date on opinion about a wide variety of contemporary topics. Each month the magazine presents numerous short resumes of longer articles printed elsewhere. There are no photographs, just writing. The editorial tone is conservative and reassuring. Around the magazine an empire of condensed books has come into being, including a condensed Bible, published in 1983.

This is the most popular real magazine covered in this section; *TV Guide* is a special type. Although there are four counties in which there are no *Reader's Digest* readers, there are only four other counties where the circulation rate falls below two issues per 100 population. (Compare figures in the other tables to get a sense of the impressiveness of this level of distribution.) Numbers for the counties at the top of this list indicate that a copy may be found in virtually every home in these areas.

Table: *Reader's Digest*
Date: 1982
Source: The Audit Bureau of Circulation
Description: The 10 counties with the highest and 10 with the lowest circulation, per 100 population, of *Reader's Digest*.

READER'S DIGEST
Counties With Highest Circulation Per 100 Population

Rank	County	Circulation
1	Greene, N.Y.	39.2
2	Daniels, Mont.	29.2
3	Grant, Nebr.	27.0
4	Hooker, Nebr.	21.2
5	Faulk, S. Dak.	19.0

Rank	County	Circulation
6	Thomas, Nebr.	18.9
6	Camas, Idaho	18.9
8	Lewis, Idaho	18.5
8	Sherman, Oreg.	18.5
10	Custer, Idaho	18.2

Counties With Lowest Circulation Per 100 Population

1	Bristol Bay, Alaska	0
1	Haines, Alaska	0
1	Menominee, Wis	0
1	Southeast Fairbanks, Alaska	0
5	Chattahoochee, Ga.	0.5
6	Miller, Ark.	0.8
7	Issaquena, Miss.	1.5
8	Randall, Tex.	1.6
9	Echols, Ga.	2.0
9	Starr, Tex.	2.0

Counties With Lowest Circulation Per 100 Population

1	Carroll, Miss.	0
2	Bacon, Ga.	0
3	San Augustine, Tex.	0
4	Irwin, Ga.	0
5	Pickett, Tenn.	0
6	Elk, Kans.	0
7	Briscoe, Tex.	0
8	Issaquena, Miss.	0
9	Quitman, Ga.	0
10	Wheatland, Mont.	0

260. *Rolling Stone*

A magazine about the entertainment industry for the Woodstock generation, *Rolling Stone* provides the inside dope on the lifestyles and careers of musicians and actors, plus reports on politics and morals at home and abroad. Skiers in Alpine County can often be found reading the *Rolling Stone* between forays in the snow. Apart from the affluent Massachusetts counties by the ocean, which also appear among the leaders for *Gourmet* and *The New Yorker*, the rest of the top 10 counties for *Rolling Stone* are all very snowy places.

Table: *Rolling Stone*
Date: 1982
Source: The Audit Bureau of Circulation
Description: The 10 counties with the highest and 10 with the lowest circulation, per 100 population, of *Rolling Stone*.

ROLLING STONE
Counties With Highest Circulation Per 100 Population

Rank	County	Circulation
1	Alpine, Calif.	6.9
2	Summit, Colo.	1.7
3	Blaine, Idaho	1.6
3	Pitkin, Colo.	1.6
5	San Miguel, Colo.	1.4
6	Nantucket, Mass.	1.3
7	Bristol Bay, Alaska	1.2
7	Dukes, Mass.	1.2
7	Eagle, Colo.	1.2
7	North Slope, Alaska	1.2

261. *Smithsonian*

This is the magazine of the Smithsonian Institution in Washington, and it treats a wide range of subjects: science, technology, history and art—reflecting the range of interests of the many museums under the Institution's jurisdiction. Handsomely illustrated with photographs, *Smithsonian* has articles that appeal to the general informed reader. The Washington D.C. metropolitan area contributes six counties to the list of the top 10, which also includes Bristol Bay, Pitkin, (the resort town of Aspen) and the two Massachusetts seaside counties which have been noted several times in this section for their highbrow tastes in magazines. There are only five counties in the nation with no *Smithsonian* readers whatsoever.

Table: *Smithsonian*
Date: 1982
Source: The Audit Bureau of Circulation
Description: The 10 counties with the highest and 10 with the lowest circulation, per 100 population, of *Smithsonian*.

SMITHSONIAN
Counties With Highest Circulation Per 100 Population

Rank	County	Circulation
1	Arlington, Va.	10.1
2	Bristol Bay, Alaska	5.7
3	Washington, D.C.	5.3
4	Montgomery, Md.	5.2
5	Fairfax, Va.	4.6
6	Nantucket, Mass.	3.7
7	Pitkin, Colo.	3.3
8	Dukes, Mass.	3.2
8	Howard, Md.	3.2
10	Talbot, Md.	3.1

Counties With Lowest Circulation Per 100 Population

1	Borden, Tex.	0
1	Buffalo, S. Dak.	0
1	Dillingham, Alaska	0
1	Echols, Ga.	0
1	Wheeler, Nebr.	0
2	Clay, Tenn.	0.1
2	Glascock, Ga.	0.1
2	Lanier, Ga.	0.1
2	Van Buren, Tenn.	0.1
2	Wayne, Tenn.	0.1

262. *Sports Illustrated*

This is the leading American sports weekly, providing documentation in word and picture (great pictures) of happenings in all branches of athletics. Tiny Loving County is the only county that can resist the magazine. Three major counties appear among the top 10—Richmond, (Staten Island), Arlington (suburban Washington, D.C.) Fulton (suburban Atlanta). The ski resort counties are also represented at the top here.

Table: *Sports Illustrated*
Date: 1982
Source: The Audit Bureau of Circulation
Description: The 10 counties with the highest and 10 with the lowest circulation, per 100 population, of *Sports Illustrated*.

SPORTS ILLUSTRATED
Counties With Highest Circulation Per 100 Population

Rank	County	Circulation
1	Clarke, Ga.	3.8
2	Pitkin, Colo.	3.5
2	Richmond, N.Y.	3.5
4	Eagle, Colo.	3.0
5	Arlington, Va.	2.9
5	Summit, Colo.	2.9
7	Blaine, Idaho	2.8
8	Orange, N.C.	2.5
9	Scott, Minn.	2.4
9	Fulton, Ga.	2.4

Counties With Lowest Circulation Per 100 Population

1	Loving, Tex.	0
2	Cumberland, Va.	0.1
2	Echols, Ga.	0.1
2	Elliott, Ky.	0.1

Counties With Lowest Circulation Per 100 Population

2	Marion, Tex.	0.1
2	Miller, Ark.	0.1
2	Piute, Utah	0.1
8	Shannon, Mo.	0.2
8	Webster, Ga.	0.2
8	Owsley, Ky.	0.2

263. *Stereo Review*

Alaskans (most of them, anyway) plainly like to spend those long winter nights listening to or tinkering with their awesome audio systems. San Francisco and Manhatten are in the top 10 along with suburban counties near Washington, D.C. and Kansas City. There are also many stereo hobbyists among the atomic scientists.

Table: *Stereo Review*
Date: 1982
Source: The Audit Bureau of Circulation
Description: The 10 counties with the highest and 10 with the lowest circulation, per 100 population, of *Stereo Review*.

STERO REVIEW
Counties With Highest Circulation Per 100 Population

Rank	County	Circulation
1	Bristol Bay, Alaska	3.6
2	Wade Hampton, Alaska	2.4
3	Arlington, Va.	0.7
4	Clay, Mo.	0.6
4	Dawson, Mont.	0.6
4	New York, N.Y.	0.6
4	North Slope, Alaska	0.6
8	Los Alamos, N. Mex.	0.5
8	San Francisco, Calif.	0.5
8	Story, Iowa	0.5

Counties With Lowest Circulation Per 100 Population

1	Jefferson Davis, Miss.	0
2	Jackson, Tenn.	0
3	Hancock, Tenn.	0
4	Owsley, Ky.	0
5	Dillingham, Alaska	0
6	Mora, N. Mex.	0
7	Mason, Tex.	0
8	Baker, Ga.	0
9	Menominee, Wis.	0
10	Coke, Tex.	0

264. *Time*

Washington, D.C., New York, Boston and San Francisco are all areas in which many households keep abreast of the news each week with *Time*. Readers are found in every county but one.

Table: *Time*
Date: 1982
Source: The Audit Bureau of Circulation
Description: The 10 counties with the highest and 10 with the lowest circulation, per 100 population, of *Time*.

TIME
Counties With Highest Circulation Per 100 Population

Rank	County	Circulation
1	Pitkin, Colo.	12.4
2	Arlington, Va.	8.8
3	Eagle, Colo.	8.0
4	Summit, Colo.	7.4
5	Blaine, Idaho	6.9
6	Washington, D.C.	6.8
7	Nantucket, Mass.	6.4
8	New York, N.Y.	6.3
9	Suffolk, Mass.	5.7
10	Marin, Calif.	5.5

Counties With Lowest Circulation Per 100 Population

1	Loving, Tex.	0
2	Crawford, Ga.	0.1
2	Echols, Ga.	0.1
2	Miller, Ark.	0.1
2	Smith, Miss.	0.1
6	Baker, Ga.	0.2
6	Choctaw, Miss.	0.2
6	Hancock, Ga.	0.2
6	Issaquena, Miss.	0.2
6	St. Helena, La.	0.2

265. *True Story*

True Story is a magazine of fictional romance for women. Unlike romantic fiction for little girls, the genre emphasizes the emotional peaks and valleys of turbulent relationships with members of the opposite sex. Evidence of high-tension misunderstandings between the sexes in Republic County, which seems to be indicated in the data for *Penthouse* and *Bride's Magazine*, continues to accumulate. Rural counties in Nebraska and the Dakotas fill six spots in the top 10. The ladies of Loving are apparently the only group that can resist the allures of this sort of romance.

Table: *True Story*
Date: 1982
Source: The Audit Bureau of Circulation
Description: The 10 counties with the highest and 10 with the lowest circulation, per 100 population, of *True Story*.

TRUE STORY
Counties With Highest Circulation Per 100 Population

Rank	County	Circulation
1	Republic, Kans.	4.5
2	Brule, S. Dak.	3.9
3	Karnes, Tex.	3.8
4	Boyd, Nebr.	3.5
5	Jones, S. Dak.	3.2
5	Towner, N. Dak.	3.2
7	Aurora, S. Dak.	3.0
7	Grant, Nebr.	3.0
7	Harding, N. Mex.	3.0
10	Furnas, Nebr.	2.9

Counties With Lowest Circulation Per 100 Population

1	Loving, Tex.	0
2	Alpine, Calif.	0.1
2	Arapahoe, Colo.	0.1
2	Camas, Idaho	0.1
2	Chesterfield, Va.	0.1
2	Jefferson, Colo.	0.1
2	Jones, Ga.	0.1
2	Randall, Tex.	0.1
2	Storey, Nev.	0.1
2	Wayne, Utah	0.1

266. *TV Guide*

A creature of the electronic media that is more a guidebook than a magazine, *TV Guide* is the biggest selling periodical in the country, a fixture at supermarket checkout stations everywhere. High circulation rates are observed especially in West Virginia and California. In the off-season, at least, it seems that the high brows on Nantucket watch plenty of TV. Alaskans watch TV too, but the scheduling is apparently so different there that local guides dominate the market.

Table: *TV Guide*
Date: 1982
Source: The Audit Bureau of Circulation
Description: The 10 counties with the highest and 10 with the lowest circulation, per 100 population, of *TV Guide*.

TV GUIDE
Counties With Highest Circulation Per 100 Population

Rank	County	Circulation
1	Nantucket, Mass.	22.0
2	Marion, W. Va.	21.0
3	Uinta, Wyo.	20.8
4	Hancock, W. Va.	20.5
4	Lancaster, Va.	20.5
6	Lake, Calif.	19.6
7	Logan, Ohio	19.3
8	Yuba, Calif.	19.1
9	Harrison, W. Va.	18.8
10	Sutter, Calif.	18.6

Counties With Lowest Circulation Per 100 Population

1	Anchorage, Alaska	0
2	Fairbanks North Star, Alaksa	0
3	Kenai Peninsula, Alaska	0
4	Juneau, Alaska	0
5	Matanuska-Susitna, Alaska	0
6	Ketchikan Gateway, Alaska	0
7	Bethel, Alaska	0
8	Kodiak Island, Alaska	0
9	Valdez-Cordova, Alaska	0
10	Sitka, Alaska	0

267. *Vogue*

A magazine of style and fashion, *Vogue* is popular in the New York, San Francisco and Washington, D.C., metropolitan areas as well as in the ski resorts of the Rockies and Republic County, occupied though it is with the battle between the sexes.

Table: *Vogue*
Date: 1982
Source: The Audit Bureau of Circulation
Description: The 10 counties with the highest and 10 with the lowest circulation, per 100 population, of *Vogue*.

VOGUE
Counties With Highest Circulation Per 100 Population

Rank	County	Circulation
1	Pitkin, Colo.	4.7
2	Eagle, Colo.	3.3
3	New York, N.Y.	3.0
4	Republic, Kans.	2.9
5	Blaine, Idaho	2.4
6	Summit, Colo.	2.0
7	San Francisco, Calif.	1.8
8	Nassau, N.Y.	1.7
9	Arlington, Va.	1.6
9	Washington, D.C.	1.6

Counties With Lowest Circulation Per 100 Population

1	Wayne, Ky.	0
2	Jackson, Ky.	0
3	Shannon, S. Dak.	0
4	Pamlico, N.C.	0
5	Crawford, Ind.	0
6	Edmondson, Ky.	0
7	Carroll, Miss.	0
8	Forest, Wis.	0
9	Clark, Mo.	0
10	Cumberland, Va.	0

268. *Woman's Day*

Women's Day, sold in supermarkets, provides tips for the practical homemaker. The women of Ottawa County, seem to be very practical people indeed. Areas of high circulation are found in many different parts of the country. Skiers, however, apparently pay scant attention to *Women's Day*.

Table: *Woman's Day*
Date: 1982
Source: The Audit Bureau of Circulation
Description: The 10 counties with the highest and 10 with the lowest circulation, per 100 population, of *Woman's Day*.

WOMAN'S DAY
Counties With Highest Circulation Per 100 Population

Rank	County	Circulation
1	Ottawa, Ohio	48.2
2	Gilliam, Oreg.	36.6
3	Gentry, Mo.	33.3
4	Carson City, Nev.	22.6
5	Columbia, Wis.	16.6
6	Wasatch, Utah	15.8
7	Baxter, Ark.	15.6
8	Brewster, Tex.	11.7
9	Ozaukee, Wis.	11.4
10	McCracken, Ky.	10.4

Counties With Lowest Circulation Per 100 Population

1	Chattahoochee, Ga.	0
2	Bledsoe, Tenn.	0
3	Banks, Ga.	0
4	Cumberland, Va	0
5	Heard, Ga.	0

Counties With Lowest Circulation Per 100 Population		
6	Rappahannock, Va.	0
7	Rains, Tex.	0
8	Wade Hampton, Alaska	0
9	Dillingham, Alaska	0
10	Hartley, Tex.	0

269. *World Tennis*

News and features about tennis draw readers from Alaska to Washington, D.C., the suburbs of Atlanta and New York (Nassau County, on Long Island, where the U.S. Open Championship is played and Monmouth County in northern New Jersey).

Table: *World Tennis*
Date: 1982
Source: The Audit Bureau of Circulation
Description: The 10 counties with the highest and 10 with the lowest circulation, per 100 population, of *World Tennis*.

WORLD TENNIS
Counties With Highest Circulation Per 100 Population

Rank	County	Circulation
1	North Slope, Alaska	0.7
2	Chesterfield, Va.	0.6
2	Fulton, Ga.	0.6
2	Macon, Ala.	0.6
2	Nassau, N.Y.	0.6
2	Pitkin, Colo.	0.6
2	Virginia Beach City, Va.	0.6
8	Clarke, Ga.	0.5
8	Monmouth, N.J.	0.5
8	Washington, D.C.	0.5

Counties With Lowest Circulation Per 100 Population		
1	Barrow, Ga.	0
2	Crawford, Ind.	0
3	Clearwater, Minn.	0
4	Cleveland, Ark.	0
5	Conejos, Colo.	0
6	Aleutian Islands, Alaska	0
7	Hancock, Tenn.	0
8	Luce, Mich.	0
9	Trimble, Ky.	0
10	Chouteau, Mont.	0

RADIO AND TELEVISION

This section surveys regional tastes in radio and television programming. Almost everyone in America is an expert on TV and radio, so there is no need for an extensive introduction. Updates on trends, and general statistical information are given in the subsection introductions below.

RADIO

According to *American Radio Spring 1982 Report* by James Duncan, Jr. (the source of this information), over 21 million Americans in 171 metropolitan marketing areas were tuned to one of 2,904 AM or FM stations during an average 15-minute broadcasting period in the spring of 1982. The radio audience had increased some 27% in the five years between 1977 and 1982. (Duncan's figures as based on audience surveys conducted by the Arbitron Company.) Americans have come to own ever more sophisticated audio equipment, and since the summer of 1978 the share of the audience listening to FM stations has been greater than the share listening to AM. The FM share increased from 40% in 1976 to 59% in 1982.

The top 25 radio stations in the country each broadcast to an audience of 80,000 or more persons during an average quarter hour of the broadcast day. The leader is WOR-AM in New York, with over 170,000 listeners per quarter hour. Fifteen of the top 25 stations are in the New York area, three are in Chicago, two in Los Angeles, and one each in Detroit, Pittsburgh, Minneapolis, St. Louis and San Francisco (sorry WKRP, none in Cincinnati).

Broadcasters sort stations into 10 major program-format types. There are 667 stations that feature rock (top 40, albums, soft rock, oldies, etc.) and other forms of contemporary music. This is the most popular format type, capturing 27.1% of the overall radio audience. The 583 middle-of-the-road "adult contemporary" stations (Sinatra, etc.), with 18.5% of the audience, hold down second place. The other format types, with number of stations and share of audience in parentheses, are "country" (552, 12.6%), "beautiful music" (274, 11.8%), "black/urban" (244, 11.7%), "news/talk" (100, 9.4%), "nostalgia/big bands" (143, 3.6%), "Spanish" (56, 2.3%), "religion" (199, 1.4%) and "classical" (35, 1.2%). Some 51 other metropolitan stations, with a total of less than 1% of the audience, do not fit into any of these categories. The tables below list market areas in which certain of these program formats are especially popular (or unpopular).

270. Radio Audiences

During an average quarter hour between 6 a.m. and midnight on any given day, about 17% of all persons 12 years old and over in the 171 surveyed market areas can be found listening to the radio. The range of variation among areas in the percentage of listeners is really rather narrow, with a high of 20.3% in northeastern Pennsylvania and a low of 14.1% in the Waterloo area of Iowa. Higher radio use appears especially in the Northeast corridor and around the Gulf coast, with Saginaw, Michigan as a notable regional exception. Many of the areas with low levels of listening are found in the heart of the country, from Wisconsin to Texas, Kentucky to Nebraska.

Table: Radio Audience
Date: 1982
Source: *American Radio*
Description: Fifteen markets with the highest average percentage of the population 12 years of age and older using radio.
United States Mean: 17.33%

RADIO AUDIENCE: Highest

Rank	Market	Percent
1	Northeastern, Pa.	20.3
2	Miami	20.2
3	Philadelphia	20.0
4	New York	19.8

Rank	Market	Percent
5	Baltimore	19.7
6	New Orleans	19.6
6	Providence	19.6
8	Boston	19.4
8	Fayetteville, N.C.	19.4
8	Savannah	19.4
11	Saginaw, Mich.	19.3
12	Bridgeport, Conn.	19.1
12	Orlando, Fla.	19.1
12	Montgomery, Ala.	19.1
12	Tallahassee, Fla.	19.1

Table: Radio Audience
Date: 1982
Source: *American Radio*
Description: Fifteen markets with the lowest average percentage of the population 12 years of age and older using radio.
United States Mean: 17.33%

RADIO AUDIENCE: Lowest

Rank	Market	Percent
1	Waterloo-Cedar Falls, Iowa	14.1
2	Terre Haute, Ind.	14.6
3	Melbourne-Titusville-Cocoa Beach, Fla.	15.0
4	Portland, Maine	15.1
4	Waco, Tex.	15.1
6	Casper, Wyo.	15.2
6	Green Bay, Wis.	15.2
6	Topeka	15.2
9	Akron	15.4
9	Binghamton, N.Y.	15.4
9	Corpus Christi, Tex.	15.4
9	Lexington, Ky.	15.4
9	Lincoln, Nebr.	15.4
9	Modesto, Calif.	15.4
9	Peoria, Ill.	15.4

271. Audiences for News/Talk Radio

News/Talk radio appeals to more mature Americans. The percentage of its audience over 50 years of age is very high at 67.8%, and only 12.7% of listeners are under 35. The national audience-share for this program format was stable from 1977 to 1982 and the shares in markets around the country are about the same everywhere. The first seven areas listed below are the only ones with unusually high audience-shares for news/talk. They include two large markets in the middle of the country, the two largest metropolitan areas on the East Coast and three large West Coast markets. All-news stations, popular among adults who prefer to be well briefed on goings-on, and call-in stations that attract older listeners with time on their hands and few opportunities to talk with family and friends, are prominent in these areas.

Table: News/Information/Talk-Show Markets
Date: 1982
Source: *American Radio*
Description: The 15 best markets for news/information/-talk-show formats by share of total area market.
U. S. Average: 9.40%

NEWS/INFORMATION/TALK-SHOW MARKETS

Rank	Market	Market-share (percent)
1	Minneapolis-St. Paul	22.4
2	St. Louis	22.2
3	New York	20.4
4	Philadelphia	19.8
5	Los Angeles	17.5
6	Seattle	16.2
7	San Francisco	14.7
8	Davenport, R.I.	13.1
9	Boston	12.8
10	Detroit	12.1
11	Portland, Oreg.	11.2
12	Oklahoma City	11.1
13	Salinas-Seaside, Calif.	11.0
14	Fresno, Calif.	10.6
15	Bridgeport	10.4

272. Audiences for Beautiful Music

"Beautiful music for easy listening" is used as a kind of background music in many American homes, the kind of music that it is easy to forget that you are listening to. The average beautiful-music listener has the radio on for 10.6 hours per day, about two hours longer than the average rock listener. Older Americans make up the bulk of the audience (59.4% at least 50 years of age and only 15.4% under 35). The easy-listening share of the national radio audience has slipped in recent years, despite the rising proportion of older persons in the population: from 17.7% in 1977 to 11.8% in 1982. Some of this audience has apparently shifted to the country stations, while another part now listens to the big band/nostalgia stations that grew from 0.1% of the national audience in 1977 to 3.6% (and rising fast) in 1982.

High audience-shares for beautiful music are found in the retirement meccas of Florida and in a variety of relatively isolated markets, especially in upstate Pennsylvania, where the mass evacuation of younger people has left high proportions of oldsters behind. Several of the areas with low audience-shares also appeared on the list of areas with high market-shares for rock music, suggesting the predominace of young people in the age structure.

Table: Beautiful Music Markets
Date: 1982
Source: *American Radio*
Description: The 15 best and worst markets for beautiful music by share of total area market.
U. S. Average: 11.8%

BEAUTIFUL MUSIC MARKETS
Highest

Rank	Market area	Market share
1	Daytona Beach	29.3
2	Sarasota	28.2
3	Lancaster, Pa.	25.2
4	West Palm Beach	24.3
5	Grand Rapids	24.0
6	Albany-Schenectady-Troy	23.4
6	Tampa-St. Petersburg	23.4
8	Medford, Oreg.	22.3
9	Reno	21.7
10	Altoona, Pa.	21.2
11	Worcester, Mass.	20.9
12	Anchorage	20.7
13	Atlantic City	20.1
13	Canton, Ohio	20.1
15	Allentown-Bethlehem-Easton, Pa.	19.5

Lowest

Rank	Market area	Market share
1	Austin, Tex.	0
1	Evansville, Ind.	0
1	Terre Haute, Ind.	0
4	Casper, Wyo.	1.1
5	Fayetteville, N.C.	2.6
6	Wilmington, N.C.	2.9
7	Topeka	3.3
8	McAllen-Brownsville, Tex.	3.7
9	Beaumont, Tex.	5.6
9	Lafayette, La.	5.6
11	Duluth	5.8
12	Oklahoma City	6.0
12	Augusta, Ga.	6.0
14	Bloomington, Ill.	6.2
15	New Orleans	6.3

273. Audiences for Rock/Contemporary Music

Surprisingly, the audience-share claimed by stations featuring the many forms of rock music has declined sharply in recent years: from 34.8% in 1977 to 27.1% in 1982. The audience for stations classified as "black/urban" has increased from 6.6% to 11.6% during the same period. Within the broad spectrum of strongly rhythmic "rock" music, programming is becoming more specialized. The rock audience is young. About 25% is comprised of persons 12 to 17 years old, and over 85% of listeners are under 35. The markets where rock is dominant are scattered across the country, but most of them are smaller, isolated metropolitan areas, where the excitement of popular music may appear especially attractive to young people who find the local situation somewhat lacking in possibilities. Some of these markets also include universities and high concentrations of young people. The markets in which rock is relatively unpopular include several large metropolitan areas (New York), several cities in Texas and the South, and retirement areas where there are relatively few young people.

Table: Rock/Contemporary Music Markets
Date: 1982
Source: *American Radio*
Description: The 15 best and worst markets for rock/-contemporary programs by share of total area market.
U. S. Average: 27.1%

ROCK/CONTEMPORARY MUSIC MARKETS
Highest

Rank	Market area	Market-share
1	Casper, Wyo.	51.7
2	Erie, Pa.	50.3
3	Fayetteville, N.C.	49.6
4	Colorado Springs	48.7
5	Anchorage	48.4
6	Lansing, Mich.	47.6
7	Appleton-Oshkosh, Wis.	47.1
8	Evansville, Ind.	44.7
9	Altoona, Pa.	44.6
9	Davenport, Ill.	44.6
11	South Bend, Ind.	44.4
12	Modesto, Ca.	44.2
13	Binghamton, N.Y.	43.4
14	Corpus Christi, Tex.	43.0
15	Billings, Mont.	42.5

Lowest

Rank	Market area	Market-share
1	West Palm Beach	14.6
2	Columbus, Ga.	15.5
3	New York	16.6
4	Houston	16.8
5	Beaumont, Tex.	18.1
6	Sarasota	19.0
7	Montgomery, Ala	19.3
8	Birmingham	20.5
9	Milwaukee	20.7
10	Miami	20.9
10	Kansas City, Mo.	20.9

	Lowest	
10	Chicago	20.9
13	Baltimore	21.2
13	St. Louis	21.2
15	Jackson, Miss.	21.6

274. Audiences for Country Music

Country-music stations increased their share of the radio audience from 9.3% in 1977 to 12.6% in 1982. The country-music audience covers a broad age range, with 4.2% under 18, 31.8% ages 18 – 34, 32.6% ages 35 – 49, and 31.4% age 50 or over. The markets where country music claims a large market-share are spread across the interior of the country from Alabama to the Dakotas. Very few country-music listeners are found in the markets of New England, in the eastern portion of the Middle Atlantic states, in Honolulu or in Miami (where Spanish language radio stations tap 22% of the audience, far above the national average 2% share for such stations).

Table: Country-Music Markets
Date: 1982
Source: *American Radio*
Description: The 15 best and 13 worst markets for country-music programs by share of total area market.
U. S. Average: 12.6%

COUNTRY-MUSIC MARKETS
Highest

Rank	Market area	Market-share
1	Asheville, N.C.	46.3
2	Springfield, Mo.	41.8
3	Waco, Tex.	41.0
4	Fargo, N.Dak.	40.5
5	Johnson City-Kingsport, Va.	38.3
6	Lubbock, Tex.	38.1
7	Knoxville	37.4
8	Tulsa	35.9
9	Amarillo, Tex.	35.4
10	Beaumont, Tex.	35.3
11	Austin, Tex.	34.8
12	Huntington, W.Va.	34.6
13	Sioux Falls, S.Dak.	33.3
14	Oklahoma City	32.7
15	Huntsville, Ala.	32.3

	Lowest	
1	Boston	1.2
2	Bridgeport	2.1
3	Hartford	2.2
4	Worcester, Mass.	2.3

	Lowest	
5	Manchester, N.H.	2.6
6	Springfield, Mass.	3.5
6	Honolulu	3.5
8	Providence	3.6
9	New Haven	4.0
10	Miami	4.3
11	New York	4.6
12	Atlantic City	5.3
13	Philadelphia	5.9

275. Audiences for Classical Music

The classical music audience is small, relatively mature (33.3% in the 35 – 49 age range, 40.3% in the range 50 and up) and did not change very much as a percentage of the total audience from 1977 to 1982. Higher shares are found in the stylish or upscale western cities and selected markets in the Midwest and the East.

Table: Classical Music Markets
Date: 1982
Source: *American Radio*
Description: The 15 best markets for classical music programs by share of total area market.
U. S. Average: 1.2%

CLASSICAL MUSIC MARKETS

Rank	Market area	Market share
1	San Diego	4.8
2	San Francisco	3.9
3	Denver	3.7
4	Albuquerque	3.6
5	Seattle	3.3
6	Washington, D.C.	3.1
7	Milwaukee	2.6
7	Salinas, Calif.	2.6
9	Cleveland	2.5
9	New York	2.5
9	San Antonio	2.5
12	Philadelphia	2.2
12	Phoenix	2.2
14	Wilmington, D.C.	2.1
15	Norfolk	2.0

276. Audiences for Religious Programming

Stations featuring religious themes primarily appeal to older persons (75.0% of listeners are 35 or over, 54.9% are 50 or over) and to women (two-thirds of all listeners). The audience-share for religious stations increased somewhat from 1977 to 1982, but it is still small. Most of the areas with high audience-shares for this format are in the South and the Pacific Northwest. The top station, KJIC in Shreveport, relies on good gospel music to hold its market-share.

Table: Religious Format Markets
Date: 1982
Source: *American Radio*
Description: The 15 best markets for religious programs by share of the total area market.
U. S. Average: 1.4%

RELIGIOUS FORMAT MARKETS

Rank	Market area	Market-share
1	Shreveport, La.	13.1
2	Jacksonville	9.5
3	Huntington, W.Va.	6.9
4	Lancaster, Pa.	6.6
5	Birmingham	6.4
6	Memphis	5.7
7	Eugene, Oreg.	5.6
8	Greensboro-Winston-Salem	5.5
9	Billings, N.Dak.	5.2
10	Fresno, Calif.	4.9
11	Yakima, Wash.	4.8
12	Seattle	4.6
12	Pueblo, Colo.	4.6
14	Johnson City-Kingsport, Tenn.	4.5
14	Tulsa	4.5

277. TELEVISION

Television watching is far and away the most important form of mass amusement in America. The amount of viewing has increased steadily, though more slowly of late, since the fist sets were introduced in 1939. Viewing habits have not changed much in recent years, but new technologies are bringing about vast shifts in the structure of the TV broadcasting industry. The network share of the audience dropped from 90% in 1977 to 78% early in 1983. Independent stations, the Public Broadcasting System (now with over 5% of the audience) and especially cable TV have registered steady gains. There are now over 30 million households with cable TV. With increases of about 350,000 viewers per month, cable viewing was up by 42% from 1981 to 1982. Cable subscribers are able to choose from a wider variety of specialized programming. They also have access, usually at a price, to services syndicated by satellites such as Home Box Office, Showtime, the ESPN sports channel, Music TV (featur-

ing video performances of hit tunes), and news and business news services. The new video recording technologies, home video games and plug-in computer consoles are also using up more hours of time on TV sets—which have been transformed from simple receivers to "home entertainment centers" or, in some cases, "work stations." Two-way uses of TV—for banking, shopping and requesting information in the form of printouts—are still on the horizon. The first studies of these forms seem to show that Americans, already bewildered by new TV set capabilities, may not yet be ready to shift quickly in this direction.

The most recent audience surveys by A.C. Nielsen & Co. show that there is a set in almost every American home, that 89% of all households have a color set and that 55% have two or more sets. In an average American household, on an average day in 1982, there was a TV set tuned to a broadcast channel for 6 hours and 48 minutes (up four minutes from 1981). This comes to over 47.5 hours of viewing per week. The highest levels of personal viewing are found among adults, especially older women (over 35 hours per week), while busy teenagers are the least constant viewers (but still over 20 hours per week). A 1983 National Association of Broadcasters survey shows, however, that interest in broadcast TV has weakend in recent years and that over 40% of all Americans are dissatisfied with the quality of TV programs in general.

Educators concerned with declining performances in school and on standardized tests note that by age 16 most children have spent over 10,000 hours with the TV set, more time than they spend in school. A National Institute of Mental Health report in 1982 concluded that "violence on television does lead to aggressive behavior by children and teenagers," and law enforcement officials continue to worry about "copy-cat" incidents. (This includes copying fictional behavior. At least 29 persons are said to have shot themselves while imitating a Russian-roulette sequence from "The Deer Hunter" shortly after it was televised.) Behavioral scientists have shown that TV viewing seems to produce shorter attention spans and that the act of watching seems to stimulate emotional responses and suppress more rational approaches to experience. Studies at Purdue University have indicated that turning on the TV and turning off certain mental functions are related activities, since over 90% of tested individuals were unable to remember accurately the key facts in commercial messages only moments after viewing them. Those who emphasize the bright side of the TV habit usually stick to generalizations about beneficial effects for the family (keeps family members together, at home), for the nation (a source of information and motivation separate from government) or for the social order (gives all of us something in common). The debate on the personal and social effects of TV, more heated than ever, continues to occupy us; meanwhile TV sets work a little bit harder every day.

The tables in this section show the areas of the country in which certain forms of programming or certain representative shows are most popular. (Information on televised sports programs can be found in the section on Sports.) The data come from Arbitron surveys. ADI ratings indicate the percentage of TV sets in a given Area of Dominant Influence (of signals originating from that area) that are tuned to a particular program or type of programming during a typical quarter hour. Areas are listed below according to the principal city in a given transmitting area, usually the point of origin of signals covering a wide area. In addition to the ADI ratings, the Arbitron ADI index is presented. This index is set at 100 for areas with ADI ratings (percentage of TV sets) at the national average level, 200 for areas with ADI ratings twice the national average, and so forth. The index values, which are used for rankings in the tables, do not precisely match the ADI scores because of special adjustments that take overlapping broadcast areas and other details into account. A table on cable penetration of leading TV markets will be found at the end of the section.

277. Cable TV Households in 20 Large Market
Areas

Cable TV may never penetrate all American households in the way that broadcast TV does, since it involves significant installation charges and monthly service and maintenance fees; but it is a fair bet that the great majority of households will be "wired" for cable within the next 10 years. Cable promoters are active in all the major markets, and the indicated percentages of households with cable service in November 1982 have probably already been surpassed in each of these 20 areas. The pace at which cable hookups proceed in a given area is at present strongly dependent on the process of negotiation between promoters and the local governments that control the rights to install cable systems. In New York City, for example, cable is now available only in Manhattan. In Brooklyn and the other boroughs final approval is still pending. When franchises are granted, there will be a mad rush to sign up customers and a sudden jump in the figure reported here for New York as a whole. In general, it appears that this process is moving relatively slowly in the big Midwestern cities.

Table: Cable Penetration in the T.V. Top 20 Markets
Date: 1982
Source: A.C. Nielsen & Co.
Description: Cable penetration in the 20 top television markets.

CABLE PENETRATION IN THE TOP 20 TELEVISION MARKETS

Rank	Market area	Percentage of penetration
1	Pittsburgh	51.1
2	San Francisco-Oakland	44.1
3	Seattle-Tacoma	42.0
4	Philadelphia	36.3
5	Houston	33.3
6	Atlanta	32.8
7	Cleveland-Akron	30.4
8	Miami-Fort Lauderdale	30.0
9	Tampa-St. Petersburg-Sarasota	29.9
10	New York	29.7
11	Boston-Worcester-Manchester, N.H.	27.1
12	Dallas-Fort Worth	26.8
13	Los Angeles-Palm Springs	23.8
14	Denver	19.5
15	Baltimore	18.3
16	Washington, D.C. Hagerstown, Md.	16.7
17	St. Louis	15.3
18	Detroit	13.4
19	Chicago	11.9
20	Minneapolis-St. Paul	11.6

278. Audiences for Network Prime Time

About 12% of all households are tuned to prime-time shows on ABC, CBS or NBC during an average quarter hour on any given evening. The biggest audience is on Sunday night, followed by Monday night (in the football season). Friday night has the lowest audience levels. Rates of viewing do not vary that much around the country. In Lafayette and Lake Charles, the top viewing areas, audience levels are only about 40% above the national norm. The top 10 areas are all located in the South, four in Louisiana alone. This is a pattern that will reappear many times in the tables below.

Table: Best Markets for Network Prime Time
Date: 1982
Source: Arbitron
Description: The 10 market areas with the highest ADI rating for network prime time.

BEST MARKETS FOR NETWORK PRIME TIME

Rank	Market area	ADI rating	ADI index
1	Lafayette, La.	16	140
1	Lake Charles, La.	16	140
3	Columbia, S.C.	16	134
4	Dothan, Ala.	16	133
5	Alexandria, La.	16	132
5	Greenwood-Greenville, Miss.	16	132
7	Baton Rouge	15	131
7	Beaumont-Port Arthur, Tex.	15	131
9	Columbus, Ga.	15	130
9	Mobile-Pensacola	15	130

279. Audiences for Daytime Serials

"Daytime serial" is the industry's name for a soap opera, the form of never-ending melodrama that dominates network programming on weekday afternoons. A great deal of interest in the soaps ("General Hospital" in particular) was generated in the early 1980s. This interest, together with the great success of "Dallas," spawned a number of serial melodramas on prime-time television. In the afternoons, characters continue to churn through predictable crises of life, romance and family situations though less predictable crises involving more risqué situations have recently come to be displayed more explicitly. Things may not be going well for us and for the people around us, but is a sure bet that things will always be worse for our daytime video friends. About 7% of all TV sets are tuned to the soaps on any given afternoon. The largest audiences are found in the South. Five of the areas on this list are also among the top 10 prime-time viewing areas. The size of the audience is more variable than the size of the prime-time audience in different parts of the country, with index levels more than twice the national norm in the Greenwood, Mississippi area.

Table: Best Markets for Daytime Serials
Date: 1982
Source: Arbitron
Description: The 10 market areas with the highest ADI rating for daytime serials.
United States total ADI rating: 7

BEST MARKETS FOR DAYTIME SERIALS

Rank	Market area	ADI rating	ADI index
1	Greenwood-Greenville, Miss.	15	223

Rank	Market area	ADI rating	ADI index
2	Lafayette, La.	13	198
3	Jackson, Tenn.	12	187
3	Charleston	12	186
3	Lake Charles, La.	12	182
3	Jackson, Miss.	12	181
3	Monroe-Eldorado, Ark., La., Miss.	12	181
8	Columbus, Ga.	11	172
8	Shreveport-Texarkana, La., Tex., Ark.	11	172
8	Baton Rouge	11	169

280. Audiences for Late Night Television

The audiences for the talk shows, old movies and reruns of such programs as "Saturday Night Live" is relatively small, averaging just 3% of all households. Midwesterners are the night owls of the nation. The degree of late night viewing (or falling asleep in front of the set?) is remarkably high in Chicago, nearly triple the national average.

Table: Best Markets for Late Night Television
Date: 1982
Source: Arbitron
Description: The 10 market areas with the highest ADI rating for late night television.
U.S. total ADI rating: 3

BEST MARKETS FOR LATE NIGHT TELEVISION

Rank	Market area	ADI rating	ADI index
1	Chicago	8	277
2	Duluth-Superior	5	175
2	Springfield, Mo.	5	173
2	Davenport-Rock Island-Moline, Ill.	5	170
2	Southbend-Elkart, Ind.	5	168
2	Minot-Bismark-Dickinson, N.Dak., S.Dak.	5	158
7	North Platte, Nebr.	4	152
7	San Angelo, Tex.	4	148
7	Sioux Falls-Mitchell, Iowa, Minn., S.Dak.	4	147
7	Terre Haute, Ind.	4	147

281. Audiences for "Dallas"

"Dallas" is popular all across the country, but especially popular in the South, where several local index values indicate levels of attention double the national average. The famous "Who Shot J.R.?" episode a few years back held the single program viewing record before the final episode of M*A*S*H established a new standard.

Table: Best Markets for "Dallas"
Date: 1982
Source: Arbitron
Description: The 10 market areas with the highest ADI rating for "Dallas."
U.S. total ADI rating: 15

BEST MARKETS FOR "DALLAS"

Rank	Market area	ADI rating	ADI index
1	Charleston	35	234
2	Beaumont-Port Arthur, Tex.	33	224
3	Monroe-El Dorado, Ark., La., Miss.	32	216
3	Selma, Ala.	32	213
5	Savannah	29	199
5	Alexandria, La.	29	196
7	Lafayette, La.	28	190
7	Tallahassee, Fla., Thomasville, Ga.	28	189
9	Dothan, Ala.	27	182
9	Florence, S.C.	27	181

282. Audiences for "Diff'rent Strokes"

This show is a popular situation comedy with a black cast. It has a strong following among both black and white viewers, but in relative terms it is more appealing to blacks. This can be traced in the figures below, which indicate high regional interest in areas of the South with relatively large numbers of black residents.

Table: Best Markets for "Diff'rent Strokes"
Date: 1982
Source: Arbitron
Description: The 10 market areas with the highest ADI rating for "Diff'rent Strokes."
U.S. total ADI rating: 16

BEST MARKETS FOR "DIFF'RENT STROKES"

Rank	Market area	ADI rating	ADI index
1	Albany, Ga.	39	239
2	Lake Charles, La.	34	211
3	Charleston-Huntington, W.Va.	30	187
3	Montgomery, Ala.	30	186
3	Alexandria, La.	30	183
6	Bristol-Kingsport-Johnson City, Tenn.	29	178

Rank	Market area	ADI rating	ADI index
7	Greenwood-Greenville, Miss.	28	174
7	Laurel-Hattiesburg, Miss.	28	173
7	Beckley-Bluefield, Oak Hill, W.Va.	28	172
7	Wilmington, N.C.	28	171

283. Audiences for "General Hospital"

The most loyal followers of "General Hospital," the raciest of the soap operas, are found in many of the same areas of the South that appear above as centers of interest in all sorts of melodrama.

Table: Best Markets for "General Hospital"
Date: 1982
Source: Arbitron
Description: The 10 market areas with the highest ADI rating for "General Hospital."
U.S. total ADI rating: 11

BEST MARKETS FOR "GENERAL HOSPITAL"

Rank	Market area	ADI rating	ADI index
1	Greenwood-Greenville, Miss.	28	258
2	Jackson, Tenn.	26	240
3	Birmingham	25	236
4	Columbus, Ga.	23	214
5	Augusta, Ga.	21	197
5	Jonesboro, Ark.	21	197
5	Anniston, Ala.	21	194
5	Harrisonburg, Va.	21	194
9	Twin Falls, Idaho	20	181
10	Chattanooga	19	172

284. Audiences for "Good Morning, America"

Early risers in the South and other more rural sections of the country are the leading fans of this early morning program, which in recent years has successfully challenged the domination of the "Today" program. Index values suggest that regional and local variation in fondness for the program are substantial.

Table: Best Markets for "Good Morning, America"
Date: 1982
Source: Arbitron

Description: The 10 market areas with the highest ADI rating for "Good Morning, America."
U.S. total ADI rating: 5

BEST MARKETS FOR "GOOD MORNING, AMERICA"

Rank	Market area	ADI rating	ADI index
1	Jonesboro, Ark.	16	322
2	Meridian, Miss.	15	307
3	Presque Isle, Maine	14	288
3	Amarillo, Tex.	14	285
3	Bowling Green, Ky.	14	274
6	Harrisonburg, W.Va.	13	271
6	Ottumwa-Kirksville, Iowa, Mo.	13	258
8	Jackson, Tenn.	12	251
8	Greenwood-Greenville, Miss.	12	249
8	Biloxi-Gulfport, Miss.	12	238

285. Audiences for "Hill Street Blues"

"Hill Stree Blues"—a kind of police variety show featuring strong dramatic scripts, sharply defined characters and semicontinuous plot development from show to show—has gradually developed a loyal following throughout the country. Many of the high audience areas in the South appear on this list of top markets, but with the exception of concentrations in Lake Charles and Albany the highest index levels are only 45% to 60% above the national average, levels comparable to those for M*A*S*H.

Table: Best Markets for "Hill Street Blues"
Date: 1982
Source: Arbitron
Description: The 10 market areas with the highest ADI rating for "Hill Street Blues."
U.S. total ADI rating: 17

BEST MARKETS FOR "HILL STREET BLUES"

Rank	Market area	ADI rating	ADI index
1	Lake Charles, La.	32	190
2	Albany, Ga.	31	187
3	Ardmore-Adla, Okla.	27	160
4	Alexandria, La.	26	160
4	Columbia, S.C.	26	157
6	Wheeling-Steubenville, W.Va., Ohio	25	151
6	La Crosse-Eau Claire, Wis.	25	148

Rank	Market area	ADI rating	ADI index
8	Beaumont-Port Arthur, Wis. 8montgomery,Ala.	24 24	146 146
8	Watertown-Carthage, N.Y.	24	146

286. Audiences for "Little House on the Prairie"

"Little House" was the best example of wholesome, family drama on TV during the late 1970s and early 1980s. Areas of strong viewer interest are located throughout the country in more or less "rurally oriented" market areas. Interest in these areas was highly intense, with the top 10 areas all showing index levels more than twice the national average.

Table: Best Markets for "Little House on the Prairie"
Date: 1982
Source: Arbitron
Description: The 10 market areas with the highest ADI rating for "Little House on the Prairie."
U.S. total ADI rating: 11

BEST MARKETS FOR "LITTLE HOUSE ON THE PRAIRIE"

Rank	Market area	ADI rating	ADI index
1	Presque Island, Maine	39	346
2	Laurel-Hattiesburg, Miss.	29	257
2	Alexandria, La.	29	254
4	Lake Charles, La.	28	244
5	Columbia, S.C.	26	231
5	Montgomery, Ala.	26	226
5	Rapid City, S.Dak.	26	224
8	North Platte, Nebr.	25	220
8	Albany, Ga.	25	219
8	Columbus-Tupelo, Miss.	25	216

287. Audiences for "Magnum, P.I."

"Magnum," with good-looking Tom Selleck in the title role as a kind of one-man counterpart to all three of Charlie's Angels, has been near the top of the ratings for the past few seasons. Six of the top 10 "Dallas" markets are also top markets for this show, though the presence of a pair of top markets outside the South indicates a somewhat more differentiated appeal.

Table: Best Markets for "Magnum, P.I."
Date: 1982

Source: Arbitron
Description: The 10 market areas with the highest ADI rating for "Magnum, P.I."
U.S. total ADI rating: 18

BEST MARKETS FOR "MAGNUM, P.I."

Rank	Market area	ADI rating	ADI index
1	Fayetteville, La.	39	213
1	Fort Myers-Naples, Fla.	39	211
3	Florence, S.C.	38	206
4	Monroe-El Dorado, La., Ark.	37	200
4	Dothan, Ala.	37	200
6	Ardmore-Adla, Okla.	35	193
7	Savannah	34	183
8	Selma, Ala.	32	178
8	Charleston	32	176
10	Twin Falls, Idaho	30	166

288. Audiences for "M*A*S*H"

The 251st and final M*A*S*H episode, aired in early 1983, set records for viewers of a single program. It was a successful conclusion to a successful 11-year run in prime time (debut: September 17, 1972). The syndicated reruns will be on the air for many years to come. The format of the show is too familiar to require explanation, and the characters have become part of contemporary folklore. The broad appeal of the show, which climbed year by year from 46th to 3rd place in the program ratings, is reflected in the absence of a clear regional pattern among the top viewing areas. M*A*S*H was just plain popular all over. The index values for the top areas are lower than those for "Dallas," for example, indicating that there were no regional or local pockets of exceptionally enthusiastic followers.

Table: Best Markets for "M*A*S*H"
Date: 1982
Source: Arbitron
Description: The 10 market areas with the highest ADI rating for "M*A*S*H".
U.S. total ADI rating: 19

BEST MARKETS FOR "M*A*S*H"

Rank	Market area	ADI rating	ADI index
1	Presque Isle, Maine	36	187
2	Watertown-Carthage, N.Y.	34	177
3	Beaumont-Port Arthur, Tex.	29	150
4	Binghamton, N.Y.	28	146

Rank	Market area	ADI rating	ADI index
4	Twin Falls, Idaho	28	146
4	Mobile-Pensacola	28	145
4	Cheyenne-Scottsbluff-Sterling, Wyo., Nebr., Colo.	28	144
4	Alpena, Mich.	28	144
4	Charleston	28	143
4	Dayton	28	142

289. Audiences for the 1982 Miss Universe Pageant

Pretty girls in bathing suits are always popular on TV, but for the folks near Monroe, Beaumont and Terre Haute that truism seems to go double (or nearly double, according to index values). With few exceptions, areas on the list for this one-time spectacular are familiar from the tables above as places in which people simply watch lots of TV.

Table: Best Markets for the 1982 Miss Universe Pageant
Date: 1982
Source: Arbitron
Description: The 10 market areas with the highest ADI rating for the 1982 Miss Universe Pageant
U.S. total ADI rating: 25

BEST MARKETS FOR THE 1982 MISS UNIVERSE PAGEANT

Rank	Market area	ADI rating	ADI index
1	Monroe-El Dorado La., Ark.	51	200
2	Beaumont-Port Arthur, Tex.	48	187
3	Terre Haute, Ind.	47	184
4	Baton Rouge	44	171
5	New Orleans	42	166
6	Evansville, Ind.	41	162
7	Wausau-Rhinelander, Wis.	39	152
8	Columbus, Ga.	38	149
8	Little Rock	38	151
8	Charleston	38	149

290. Audiences for "60 Minutes"

"60 Minutes" is a popular and potent mixture of genial humor (including Andy Rooney), general reporting, and exposes in which petty and mean spirited characters are oftebn embarassed right on camera. It has been the leading after dinner entertainment on Sunday nights for several years, always at or near the top of the ratings among all shows. During 1982, nearly one household in five was tuned in to an average performance. This show is popular among mature Americans (high ratings in Florida) and in a number of cities scattered across the middle of the country where it may be suspected that an interest in current events is coupled with the tough sense of justice, fairness and responsibility that characterizes the editorial policy of the program.

Table: Best Markets for "60 Minutes"
Date: 1982
Source: Arbitron
Description: The 10 market areas with the highest ADI rating for "60 Minutes".
U.S. total ADI rating: 19

BEST MARKETS FOR "60 MINUTES"

Rank	Market area	ADI rating	ADI index
1	Fort Myers-Naples, Fla.	37	193
2	Marquette, Mich.	33	168
3	West Palm Beach	30	154
3	Ardmore-Ada, Okla.	30	154
5	Topeka	29	149
6	Alexandria, Minn.	28	145
6	Helena, Mont.	28	143
8	Tucson	27	141
8	Austin, Tex.	27	140
8	Traverse City-Cadillac, Mich.	27	139

291. Audiences for "Smurfs"

"Smurfs" the biggest news in television marketing for children since the advent of "Sesame Street" and "The Muppet Show," are spin-offs of a show especially popular among southern kids in more rural settings.

Table: Best Markets for "Smurfs"
Date: 1982
Source: Arbitron
Description: The 10 market areas with the highest ADI rating for "Smurfs".
U.S. total ADI rating: 7

BEST MARKETS AUDIENCES FOR "SMURFS"

Rank	Market area	ADI rating	ADI index
1	Bluefield-Beckley-Oak Hill, Va., W.Va.	17	258
1	Albany, Ga.	17	250
3	Zanesville, Ohio	15	219
4	Charleston	14	211
4	Charleston-Huntington, W.Va.	14	210
4	Columbia, S.C.	14	207
4	Bristol-Kingsport-Johnson City, Ky., Tenn., Va.	14	201
8	Greenville-Spartanburg-Asheville, Ga., N.C., S.C.	13	197
8	Laurel-Hattiesburg, Miss.	13	194
8	Lake Charles, La.	13	186

DRINK

Drinking habits vary to a surprising extent in different parts of the country. Religious and ethnic diversity, together with other aspects of regional and local culture, are reflected in these differences. The tables in this section review the consumption of alcohol and soft drinks around the nation and provide a glimpse of bygone days with summaries on the remnants of prohibition and seizures of moonshine whiskey.

Affluence and its anxieties have contributed to rising alcohol consumption in the past 20 years. To a certain extent alcohol has even become a substitute for food—the percentage of average calorie consumption accounted for by alcohol rose from 5.2% to 6.9% between 1955 and 1972. The consumption of wine has increased dramatically in recent years, up 100% between 1969 and 1981. Consumption of beer increased by 30% in the same period, and consumption of distilled spirits by 11%. The recent pattern of increasing beer consumption dates from 1963, while use of distilled spirits has been climbing more or less steadily since 1959. The taste for wine first made a definite upswing in 1967, and it has accelerated in the last few years. It appears that wine is gaining ground on distilled spirits as the drink to serve at parties and to dinner guests.

Although alcohol consumption has increased, America still lags behind Europeean countries such as Austria, West Germany, France and Italy in overall consumption. The tables on alcoholic beverages should be used cautiously, since the information is based on wholesale shipments. Shipments do not necessarily lead to retail sales and sales do not necessarily lead to the drinking of every drop. Some alcohol is also produced at home or otherwise acquired outside of regular commercial channels. These factors probably do not distort the picture too much, but it is important to note that wholesale shipments to a given state may lead to actual consumption by residents of other states (visitors on vacation, or clever buyers who cross state lines to take advantage of lower taxes or prices).

292. Alchohol Consumption

This table shows how much alcohol there was in all the alcoholic beverages apparently consumed in 1978. The word "apparently" simply means that figures are based on shipments to wholesalers in a given state. The per capita calculation is based on the number of persons of legal drinking age in the state.

Nevada and New Hampshire stand head and shoulders above the other states in alcohol consumption per capita. To be fair to the residents of these states, it should be noted that a good bit of this drinking is probably done by out-of-state residents. Gamblers on holiday inflate the figure for Nevada, while the relatively low New Hampshire alcohol tax brings in many buyers from Massachusetts. A good deal of Bay State drinking may be hidden in the data for New Hampshire.

These two states aside, consumption varies from about 3½ gallons in Alaska to about 1¾ gallons in Utah (that is, per adult, per year). The most intemperate state thus outdrinks the most temperate by about 2 to 1. Low consumption is apparently associated with religious prohibitions. Mormon strictures on drink clearly play a part in suppressing consumption in Utah and Idaho to levels far below those in neighboring states (compare Colorado, Wyoming, Montana, Oregon, Nevada and Arizona). The 10 states just above Utah, in positions 40 through 49, form a geographical block that corresponds to the definition of the 'Bible Belt' — the states where fundamentalist churches have a relatively broad influence. Untaxed homemade liquor (moonshine) that escapes measurement may also partly explain these figures.

States near the top of the list may be there for a variety of reasons, including the prevalence of recreation and vacation areas (Nevada, California, Arizona, Florida, Hawaii) or cold winter nights (Alaska, New Hampshire, Vermont, Wyoming, Wisconsin).

Does it seem alarming that the average American adult drinks about 2¾ gallons of alcohol per year? Some consolation may be drawn from historical statistics suggesting a corresponding figure for the period from 1810 to 1830 of about seven gallons.

Table: Alcohol Consumption
Date: 1978
Source: Fourth Special Report to the U.S. Congress on Alcohol and Health from the Secretary of Health and Human Services (1981).
Description: Apparent consumption of pure ethyl alcohol (gallons per year) per member of the legal drinking age population.
U.S. Average: 2.73 gallons

ALCOHOL CONSUMPTION

Rank	State	Gallons consumed per capita
1	Nevada	6.78
2	New Hampshire	5.45
3	Alaska	3.59
4	Vermont	3.57
5	California	3.42
6	Colorado	3.41
6	Wyoming	3.41
8	Wisconsin	3.34
9	Arizona	3.31
10	Florida	3.29
11	Hawaii	3.17
11	Rhode Island	3.17
13	Montana	3.12
14	Maryland	3.05
15	Massachusetts	3.04
16	Washington	3.01
17	New Mexico	2.95
18	Delaware	2.93
19	Illinois	2.87
20	Oregon	2.80
21	Texas	2.76
22	Michigan	2.75
22	New York	2.75
24	North Dakota	2.72
25	Minnesota	2.70
26	New Jersey	2.69
27	Louisiana	2.67
27	Maine	2.67
29	Connecticut	2.66
30	Idaho	2.62
31	South Carolina	2.60
32	Nebraska	2.58
33	Georgia	2.45
34	South Dakota	2.42
35	Iowa	2.37
36	Virginia	2.34
37	Missouri	2.32
38	Pennsylvania	2.31
39	Ohio	2.23
40	Tennessee	2.19
41	Mississippi	2.18

Rank	State	Gallons consumed per capita
42	North Carolina	2.16
43	Indiana	2.13
44	Oklahoma	2.05
45	Alabama	1.97
46	Kansas	1.91
47	Kentucky	1.85
48	West Virginia	1.84
49	Arkansas	1.80
50	Utah	1.73

293 Beer Consumption

Americans spend much more money on beer than on wine or distilled spirits. Beer sales accounted for close to one-third of the total U.S. market for all beverages in 1978, compared to less than 5% for wine and distilled spirits.

As noted above, the figures for Nevada and New Hampshire should be treated cautiously. The position of Wisconsin is not surprising if we remember what "made Milwaukee famous." The positions of states like Wyoming, Montana and Texas—much higher here than for total alcohol consumption—suggest a link between the culture of the cattle lands and a preference for beer over the other alcoholic alternatives. The end of the list is much like the end of the list for overall alcohol consumption, except that Ohio and Indiana have moved out of the lower group while Connecticut, where beer is not well liked, has dropped close to the bottom.

The overall pattern is close to the pattern in the preceeding table: people in the top states drink about twice as much beer as the people in Utah. Nationwide, per capita beer consumption increased by about six gallons per year—more that 20%—between 1974 and 1981. All states participated in the increase.

Table: Beer Consumption
Date: 1981
Source: *Beverage World*, May 1982
Description: Apparent consumption of beer (gallons per year) per member of the legal drinking age population, by state (adjusted to exclude dry countries), for the 50 states.
United States average: 33.9 Gallons.

BEER CONSUMPTION

Rank	State	Gallons consumed per capita
1	Nevada	53.5
2	Wisconsin	47.1

Rank	State	Gallons consumed per capita
3	New Hampshire	46.4
4	Wyoming	45.7
5	Montana	45.1
5	Texas	45.1
7	Arizona	43.9
8	Hawaii	41.9
9	Colorado	40.0
9	New Mexico	40.0
11	Alaska	39.7
12	Florida	38.4
13	Nebraska	37.9
14	North Dakota	37.1
15	Delaware	36.9
16	Massachusetts	36.7
17	Vermont	36.0
18	California	35.9
19	Idaho	35.3
20	Louisiana	35.0
20	Pennsylvania	35.0
22	Illinois	34.4
23	Maryland	34.2
24	Missouri	34.0
25	Rhode Island	33.9
25	Washington	33.9
27	Iowa	33.8
28	Minnesota	33.5
29	Ohio	32.2
29	Oregon	32.2
31	Maine	31.7
32	Michigan	31.5
33	New York	30.7
33	South Dakota	30.7
35	New Jersey	30.5
36	Indiana	30.4
36	Virginia	30.4
38	Kansas	30.1
39	South Carolina	29.9
40	Oklahoma	29.0
41	Georgia	28.0
42	Tennessee	27.5
42	Mississippi	27.5
44	Kentucky	26.8
45	North Carolina	26.7
46	Connecticut	26.1
47	Arkansas	25.2
47	West Virginia	25.2
49	Alabama	24.0
50	Utah	22.1

294. Consumption of Distilled Spirits

Whiskies (including bourbon, blends, scotch, etc.) are the most popular distilled spirits in the nation. Whiskies account for about 49% of this market, and for more than 60% of the market in the states of Mississippi, West Virginia, Kanas, Kentucky, Louisiana, Missouri and South Dakota. Vodka is in second place with about 20% of the national market (but close to 30% in the Carolinas). Gin controls about 10% of the market, and smaller shares belong to rum, brandy, cordials, tequila and ready-made cocktails.

At the time the table was produced, there were 24 states where the legal age for purchasing distilled spirits was 21, six states where this age was 20 and 13 states where the age was 19. The legal age was 18 in the remaining seven states: Connecticut, Hawaii, Louisiana, New York, Vermont, West Virginia and Wisconsin. Eighteen states had a state monopoly on sales of distilled spirits for off-premises consumption (two at the wholesale level and 16 at the retail level).

The spread between the bottom of this list and the top (excluding Nevada and New Hampshire) is slightly greater than 2 to 1. Vermont, Maryland, Connecticut and New York stand much highter on this list than on the list for beer, while Texas, Idaho, Iowa, Missouri and Ohio show the reverse pattern. Easterners in general (except Pennsylvanians) seem to prefer their alcohol in concentrated form. In Texas over 21 gallons of beer, in Connecticut only about eight, are consumed for each gallon of distilled spirits. The national average is about 12½.

Table: Distilled Spirits Consumption
Date: 1981
Source: *Beverage World*, May 1982
Description: Apparent consumption of distilled spirits (gallons per year), adjusted to exclude dry countries, per member of the legal drinking age population.

DISTILLED SPIRITS CONSUMPTION

Rank	State	Gallons consumed per capita
1	Nevada	8.0
2	New Hampshire	7.3
3	Alaska	4.4
4	Vermont	4.1
5	Maryland	3.7
6	Delaware	3.5
6	Florida	3.5
8	California	3.4
8	Massachusetts	3.4
10	Connecticut	3.2
10	New York	3.2
10	Wisconsin	3.2
13	Colorado	3.0
13	Illinois	3.0
13	Montana	3.0
13	New Jersey	3.0
13	North Dakota	3.0
13	Wyoming	3.0

Rank	State	Gallons consumed per capita
19	Hawaii	2.9
19	Louisiana	2.9
19	Rhode Island	2.9
19	South Carolina	2.9
19	Washington	2.9
24	Georgia	2.8
24	Maine	2.8
26	South Dakota	2.6
27	Michigan	2.5
27	Oregon	2.5
29	Minnesota	2.4
29	Virginia	2.4
31	Arizona	2.3
31	Nebraska	2.3
33	Mississippi	2.2
33	New Mexico	2.2
35	North Carolina	2.1
35	Oklahoma	2.1
35	Pennsylvania	2.1
35	Texas	2.1
39	Alabama	2.0
39	Idaho	2.0
39	Iowa	2.0
39	Missouri	2.0
39	Ohio	2.0
39	West Virginia	2.0
45	Indiana	1.9
45	Kansas	1.9
47	Arkansas	1.8
47	Kentucky	1.8
49	Tennessee	1.7
50	Utah	1.4

295.   Wine Consumption

Setting aside Nevada and New Hampshire, for reasons noted in the introduction to Table 292, it is clear that California, the nation's leading wine producer, is also the heaviest consumer of wine by a wide margin. The ready availability of California wines probably also accounts for the fact that Washington and Oregon make a stronger showing on this "wine list" than on the lists for other alcoholic beverages, and it may also explain why temperate Utah has been nudged from the bottom of this list.

An examination of the lower half of the list shows that wine is extremely unpopular in the South and lower Midwest. Tennessee is not a heavy beer drinking state (see Table 293), but its people still manage to drink 28 times more beer than wine. Beer is more popular in Rhode Island than in Tennessee, but beer drinking there outpaces wine drinking only by about 7 to 1. Nationwide, beer consumption exceeds wine consumption in volume by about 11 to 1.

The taste for wine differs among the states more widely than the taste for beer or distilled spirits: the ratio between states at the top of the list (starting from Alaska) and states at the bottom is on the order of 4 or 5 to 1.

Table 295: Wine Consumption
Date: 1981
Source: *Beverage World*, May 1982
Description: Apparent consumption of wine (gallons per year) per member of the legal drinking age population, by state (adjusted to exclude dry countries), for the 50 states.
United States average: 3.0 gallons.

WINE CONSUMPTION

Rank	State	Gallons consumed per capita
1	Nevada	7.2
2	California	6.3
3	New Hampshire	5.1
4	Alaska	4.6
4	Rhode Island	4.6
4	Washington	4.6
7	New Jersey	4.4
8	Massachussetts	4.3
9	Oregon	4.2
9	Vermont	4.2
11	New York	4.0
12	Connecticut	3.8
13	Colorado	3.7
13	Hawaii	3.7
15	Arizona	3.6
16	Florida	3.5
17	Illinois	3.0
17	Maryland	3.0
19	Delaware	2.7
19	Idaho	2.7
19	Montana	2.7
19	Wisconsin	2.7
23	Maine	2.6
23	New Mexico	2.6
25	Michigan	2.4
26	Louisiana	2.3
26	Minnesota	2.3
26	Virginia	2.3
29	Texas	2.1
30	Wyoming	2.0
31	Pennsylvania	1.9
32	Mississippi	1.8
32	North Carolina	1.8
32	Ohio	1.8
35	Georgia	1.7
35	Nebraska	1.7
37	Alabama	1.6
37	South Carolina	1.6
37	South Dakota	1.6
40	Indiana	1.5
40	North Dakota	1.5

Rank	State	Gallons consumed per capita
42	Oklahoma	1.3
43	Iowa	1.2
44	Kansas	1.1
44	Utah	1.1
44	West Virginia	1.1
47	Arkansas	1.0
48	Tennessee	.96
49	Mississippi	.85
50	Kentucky	.83

296.   Soft Drink Consumption

The southern states, where alcohol is relatively unpopular, are grouped together at the top of the soft drink consumption list. This list, in fact, looks much like the beer consumption list turned upside down, with one additional feature: all the states of the Northwest (including Utah) are clustered at the bottom. The Carolinas maintain a comfortable lead over the other states. If we compare Tennessee, the third place state, with Wyoming at the bottom, we find the familiar 2 to 1 ratio between the heaviest and lightest levels of consumption.

Nationwide, soft drinks are more popular than beer, with consumption of soft drinks at 37.3 gallons per year for every person in the population as opposed to 33.9 gallons of beer per year in the (smaller) legal drinking age population.

Table: Soft Drink Consumption
Date: 1981
Source: *Beverage World*, April 1982
Description: Soft drink consumption (gallons per year) per member of the general population.
United States average: 37.3 gallons

SOFT DRINK CONSUMPTION

Rank	State	Gallons consumed per capita
1	North Carolina	55.4
2	South Carolina	51.4
3	Tennessee	46.9
4	Georgia	46.2
5	Mississippi	44.3
6	Alabama	42.4
7	West Virginia	40.4
8	Virginia	40.1
9	Kentucky	39.9
10	Maryland	39.7
11	Texas	39.2

Rank	State	Gallons consumed per capita
12	Louisiana	38.7
13	Missouri	38.6
14	Delaware	38.5
15	Minnesota	37.4
16	Illinois	36.9
16	Kansas	36.9
18	Michigan	36.8
19	Florida	36.7
20	New York	36.4
21	Massachusetts	36.3
22	Ohio	36.1
22	Nebraska	36.1
22	Nevada	36.1
25	Oklahoma	36.0
26	Pennsylvania	35.1
27	Arkansas	35.0
28	Hawaii	34.9
29	California	34.8
29	New Jersey	34.8
29	Wisconsin	34.8
32	Iowa	34.6
33	Rhode Island	34.3
34	Connecticut	33.9
34	Indiana	33.9
36	Colorado	33.6
37	Alaska	32.6
38	Maine	32.0
39	South Dakota	32.0
40	Utah	31.9
41	Arizona	31.8
42	New Mexico	31.3
43	New Hampshire	29.8
44	North Dakota	29.3
45	Vermont	29.1
45	Washington	29.1
47	Oregon	28.5
48	Idaho	26.3
49	Montana	25.6
50	Wyoming	23.9

297.   Prohibition

The unpopularity of alcohol in the South as revealed by consumption patterns is also reflected in the fact that there are 12 southern states (plus South Dakota, Kansas and Nebraska) where some counties currently excercise the option provided in their state constitutions to prohibit sales of distilled spirits. The effect of these prohibitions is shown as the percentage of state population that resides in legally dry areas. Prohibition is significant in only a few states, and its influence is on the wane; since 1976 the proportion of population in dry counties has dropped from 31.2% to 6.9% in Tennessee and from 10.5% to 0.7% in Texas as counties have reversed earlier stands on their options. Only 2.3% of the American population lived in a dry county in 1981.

Table: Prohibition
Date: 1981
Source: Distilled Spirits Council of the United States
Description: Percentage of the population living in dry areas in states having provision for local option as of December 1981.

PROHIBITION

Rank	State	Percent of population living in dry areas
1	Kentucky	42.3
2	Mississippi	27.6
3	Alabama	24.9
4	Georgia	17.9
5	Arkansas	8.2
6	South Dakota	6.9
7	Virginia	2.5
8	North Carolina	2.2
9	South Carolina	1.9
10	Louisiana	1.5
11	Florida	1.4
12	Tennessee	0.7
13	Washington	0.4
14	Kansas	0.3
15	Nebraska	0.1

298. Moonshine Seized

The Treasury Department seized 4,610 gallons of "nontaxpaid whiskey" in 1980, down from 15,604 gallons in 1975. Since the average American adult drinks about 2.7 gallons of distilled spirits per year, the equivalent of a year's supply for just about 1,707 persons was hauled in. Successful raids occurred in only four states.

Table: Moonshine Seized
Date: 1980
Source: Treasury Department
Description: Total number of gallons of nontaxpaid whiskey seized by agents of the Bureau of Alcohol, Tobacco and Firearms by state for fiscal 1980.

MOONSHINE SEIZED

Rank	State	Gallons
1	Georgia	2,477
2	Virginia	1,563
3	North Carolina	565
4	Nebraska	5

TRANSPORTATION

This section is devoted largely to the automobile, the chief means of personal transportation in the United States and a characteristic feature of the American scene. Ever since Henry Ford's Model T and other standard makes brought prices within the range of the average family during 1920s, the use of the automobile has been a dynamic force in the transformation of American life. Suburban areas originally quite distant from centers of employment and the suburban areas of employment that eventually developed around them are the product of the automobile. Highway development opened up formerly remote areas of the nation to drivers on tour. During the dust bowl days of the 1930s it became clear that the ability to travel long distances cheaply and in relative comfort encourages migration between regions, chiefly towards the West. Roadside facilities ranging from snack bars to motels (derived from "motor hotel," as some may remember), and from drive-in movies to drive-in churches, have become typical features of the landscape. The auto industry was the leading branch of American production for many years before falling victim to the energy crisis of the 1970s and increased international competition.

It is clear that the nation is now fully automobile-dependent. The tables in this section show that most workers in the country would simply never arrive on the job if deprived of motor transport. Mass transit facilities, especially railroads, have fallen on hard times as one battle after another has been lost to the more accessible, more private automobile. As a consequence of all this, motor-vehicle emissions on a fantastic scale have become the leading cause of air pollution.

The first four tables in this section document the extent of auto ownership, the speeds at which autos are typically driven, and the frequency of that most American way of death, the highway fatality. Four subsequent tables on the ways that residents of various states travel to and from work offer evidence of automotive predominance in comparison to the time honored methods of walking or use of public transportation. The final table looks at another characteristic mode of transportation in modern America, the airplane. The 20 busiest airports in the country are listed and compared.

299: Registered Automobiles

For every two people in the United States there is one registered automobile. The 1980 national ratio of 544 autos per 1,000 persons represents an increase of 24% from the 1970 ratio of 438 per thousand. The actual number of registered autos increased 38% during the decade to an all time high of 123,467,000. State by state ratios per 1,000 population range from 746 in Montana (up an astounding 66% from 449 in just 10 years) to 387 in Alaska. Regional patterns are not particularly strong. A few states from every major region are found in all parts of the table. Alaska and New York are the exceptional cases. Data in the following tables help to explain the situation in New York.

Table: Automobiles Registered
Date: 1980
Source: Federal Highway Administration
Description: Automobiles registered per 1,000 population.
United States average: 544
State median: 542

AUTOMOBILES REGISTERED

Rank	State	Automobiles per 1,000 population
1	Montana	746
2	Connecticut	662
3	Illinois	659
4	Florida	651
5	Wyoming	609
6	Colorado	608
7	Oklahoma	607
8	Iowa	603

Rank	State	Automobiles per 1,000 population
9	Minnesota	602
10	North Carolina	593
11	Kansas	588
11	New Hampshire	588
13	New Jersey	586
14	Massachusetts	579
14	Ohio	579
16	Oregon	574
17	Virginia	571
18	Michigan	566
19	Maryland	562
20	North Dakota	560
21	Washington	557
22	Nebraska	556
23	Georgia	554
24	Delaware	547
25	Alabama	543
26	Rhode Island	542
26	South Dakota	542
28	California	541
29	Indiana	536
30	Wisconsin	535
31	Hawaii	533
32	Nevada	523
33	New Mexico	521
34	Tennessee	516
34	Texas	516
36	Vermont	508
37	Idaho	506
38	Kentucky	501
39	Missouri	498
40	West Virginia	497
41	South Carolina	493
42	Pennsylvania	489
43	Arizona	485
44	Maine	471
45	Louisiana	468
46	Utah	466
47	Mississippi	462
48	Arkansas	442
49	New York	408
50	Alaska	387

300: Households With No Access to Motor Vehicles

In most cases "access" to a motor vehicle simply means owning one or more cars, but long-term leasing deals, shared access among households (usually within a family), truck ownership, and other arrangements also count as access for the present table. On this basis, 87.2% of all households had access to a vehicle in 1980 and over half had access to multiple vehicles. Access to two vehicles was reported by 33.8% of households, to three or more vehicles by 17.7%. Only 12.8% of households were without access. New York is the special case in this table, in a state containing the urban region where over half of all daily use of public transportation in the nation goes on, many households are perfectly resigned to do without a car. The problems of maintaining a car, not to mention parking a car, in New York City are so formidable that taking taxis and renting cars for special occasions are wise alternatives. Other states with high proportions of non-access households either feature large metropolitan areas with conditions similar to New York—including good access to public transportation—or they are relatively poor states where ownership is still beyond the means of many families and individuals. The households of the Midwest and the Plains almost always have access to a car.

Table: Households without Motor Vehicles
Date: 1980
Source: Census Bureau
Description: Percentage of households without motor vehicles.
United States average: 12.8%
State median: 10.2%

HOUSEHOLDS WITHOUT MOTOR VEHICLES

Rank	State	Percent
1	New York	32.8
2	Pennsylvania	16.5
3	Massachusetts	16.0
4	Illinois	15.1
5	New Jersey	15.0
6	Louisiana	13.6
7	Maryland	13.4
8	Alaska	13.3
9	West Virginia	13.1
9	Rhode Island	13.1
11	Mississippi	13.0
12	Kentucky	12.7
13	South Carolina	12.1
14	Georgia	11.6
14	Alabama	11.6
16	Missouri	11.5
17	Maine	11.3
17	Tennessee	11.3
19	Connecticut	11.1
20	Arkansas	10.8
20	Florida	10.8
20	Hawaii	10.8
20	North Carolina	10.8
24	Virginia	10.6
25	Ohio	10.2
25	Wisconsin	10.2
27	Michigan	10.1
27	Vermont	10.1
29	California	9.9
29	Delaware	9.9
31	Minnesota	9.7

Rank	State	Percent
32	New Hampshire	9.5
33	Indiana	9.3
34	Washington	9.1
35	Oregon	8.9
36	Iowa	8.2
36	Nebraska	8.2
38	Texas	7.7
39	New Mexico	7.6
39	North Dakota	7.6
39	Oklahoma	7.6
42	Montana	7.5
43	South Dakota	7.1
44	Kansas	7.0
45	Colorado	6.8
46	Nevada	6.6
47	Utah	6.2
48	Arizona	5.9
49	Idaho	5.4
50	Wyoming	4.1

301: Speeding Motorists

There were over 145 million licensed drivers in the United States in 1980, about 20 million more licensed drivers than registered autos. This comes to about 640 drivers per 1,000 persons in the population. Driving is the great American pastime. Since most people must drive if they are to work and to eat, it is fortunate that driving is so popular. Most people enjoy driving fast when they get the chance. Transportation Department observations show that about half of all vehicles on American roads are doing better than 55 mph at any given time. The national speed limit imposed in 1974 is generally ignored in many states. Since these observations cover a sample of all types of roads in a given state, it is clear that most vehicles on the limited-access highways are doing better than 55 most of the time. Data for the states show that the proportions of speeders (drivers going faster that 55) vary between 67% and 27% of all cars on the road. Some of the drivers doing under 55 are also speeders, of course, in zones with lower posted limits. States near the top of the list tend to be in the West, but since a higher fraction of all roads in the West are of the high-speed, limited-access variety, the data may simply indicate greater opportunities to do what drivers in the East wish they could do more often. More or less severe policing systems probably play a part in these figures as well.

Table: Speeding Motorists
Date: 1980
Source: Transportation Department

Description: Percentage of vehicles clocked at over 55 miles per hour.
United States average: 49.3%
State median: 48.8%

SPEEDING MOTORISTS

Rank	State	Percent of speeding vehicles
1	New Mexico	67.4
2	Texas	64.7
3	Arizona	63.2
4	Utah	61.9
5	California	61.7
6	North Dakota	58.3
7	Kansas	58.1
8	Delaware	57.9
9	Montana	57.8
10	Florida	57.6
11	Wyoming	57.5
12	Indiana	56.6
13	Nevada	56.0
14	Minnesota	55.2
14	Ohio	55.2
16	Vermont	54.9
17	Alabama	53.7
18	Nebraska	53.1
19	Mississippi	52.6
20	Rhode Island	52.4
21	Wisconsin	50.2
22	Missouri	50.1
23	South Dakota	50.0
24	Tennessee	49.7
25	Washington	48.9
26	Connecticut	48.8
27	Iowa	48.6
28	West Virginia	48.4
29	Massachusetts	48.3
30	Michigan	47.9
30	Oklahoma	47.9
32	Maine	46.0
32	Pennsylvania	46.0
34	Arkansas	45.9
34	New Jersey	45.9
36	South Carolina	45.5
37	New York	45.4
38	Illinois	45.0
39	North Carolina	44.7
40	Kentucky	43.1
41	Louisiana	41.3
42	Virginia	39.9
43	Idaho	39.0
44	Hawaii	38.7
45	Oregon	38.1
46	Georgia	37.6
47	Colorado	35.9
48	New Hampshire	35.1
49	Alaska	30.3
50	Maryland	27.0

302: Vehicle Traffic Fatalities

It seems plain that the chances of dying in an auto accident should be directly related to the average vehicle speed when something goes wrong. This assumption would mean that the rankings in this table and the previous table should be closely related. But the comparison is not as close as might be expected. In Louisiana and Idaho, where measured speeding is relatively uncommon, death rates on a per mile basis are alarmingly high. West Virginia presents a similar case, though its notoriously winding mountain roads may be the real culprit here. Delaware, Ohio and Minnesota present countercases. There is plenty of speeding in each of these states, but the fatality levels are relatively low. Are drivers in some states simply more careful than drivers in other states at any given speed? In general, higher rates in this table appear in the West and South, lower rates in the North and East.

Table 302: Motor Vehicle Traffic Deaths
Date: 1981
Source: National Safety Council
Description: Death rate per 100 million vehicle miles and number of traffic deaths.
United States average: 3.3 per 100 million vehicle miles
State median: 3.2 per 100 million vehicle miles

MOTOR VEHICLE TRAFFIC DEATHS

Rank	State	Death rate per 100 million vehicle miles	Number of traffic deaths
1	Wyoming	5.2	264
2	Louisiana	5.0	1,233
3	Montana	5.0	338
4	Arizona	4.8	916
4	Nevada	4.8	295
6	New Mexico	4.7	544
7	Mississippi	4.4	745
8	Idaho	4.2	293
8	Texas	4.2	4,701
10	West Virginia	4.0	439
11	Florida	3.9	3,121
12	South Carolina	3.7	846
13	Alaska	3.6	97
13	North Carolina	3.6	1,497
13	Oklahoma	3.6	1,000
16	California	3.3	5,170
16	Colorado	3.3	754
16	Kansas	3.3	578
16	Nebraska	3.3	378
16	Oregon	3.3	645
16	Tennessee	3.3	1,119
16	Utah	3.3	364
23	Alabama	3.2	944
23	Arkansas	3.2	537
23	Georgia	3.2	1,418
23	Iowa	3.2	610
23	Kentucky	3.2	830
23	New York	3.2	2,508
29	Idaho	3.1	1,173
29	Missouri	3.1	1,055
29	North Dakota	3.1	166
29	Vermont	3.1	116
33	Washington	3.0	872
34	Wisconsin	2.9	927
35	Illinois	2.8	1,852
35	Maine	2.8	211
35	Pennsylvania	2.8	2,049
35	South Dakota	2.8	117
39	Connecticut	2.7	527
39	Maryland	2.7	792
41	Delaware	2.6	112
41	Hawaii	2.6	150
41	Minnesota	2.6	763
41	Virginia	2.6	1,012
45	Michigan	2.5	1,589
46	Ohio	2.4	1,780
47	New Hampshire	2.3	148
47	New Jersey	2.3	1,162
49	Massachusetts	2.1	752
50	Rhode Island	2.0	111

303: Commuters Who Drive Alone

Nearly two of every three working Americans drives to and from the job alone. Solo commuting is most common in Ohio and Michigan (where, as shown in the next table, driving to work in groups is fairly unpopular). The lowest figures are found in states with large rural segments where many people work at home, and in states with large metropolitan transport systems. More than half of all workers drive to the job alone in every state except New York.

Table: Commuters Driving Private Cars Alone
Date: 1980
Source: Census Bureau
Description: Percentage of commuters driving private cars to work alone.
United States average: 64.5%
State median: 65.0%

COMMUTERS DRIVING PRIVATE CARS ALONE

Rank	State	Percent
1	Ohio	72.4
2	Michigan	72.3
3	Oklahoma	70.9

Rank	State	Percent
4	Florida	69.8
5	Indiana	69.5
6	Alabama	69.3
7	Texas	69.2
7	Tennessee	69.2
9	Nevada	68.9
10	Arizona	68.4
11	Arkansas	68.0
12	California	67.8
12	Georgia	67.8
14	Connecticut	67.4
14	New Mexico	67.4
16	Kansas	67.1
16	Louisiana	67.1
18	Delaware	66.5
19	North Carolina	66.4
20	Kentucky	66.3
21	Iowa	66.2
22	Mississippi	66.1
23	Missouri	65.6
24	South Carolina	65.2
24	Washington	65.2
26	Rhode Island	64.8
27	Oregon	64.4
28	West Virginia	64.3
29	Colorado	63.7
29	Utah	63.7
31	New Jersey	63.6
32	Wisconsin	63.5
33	Idaho	63.1
34	Nebraska	62.8
35	Virginia	62.3
36	New Hampshire	62.1
37	Illinois	61.5
38	Pennsylvania	61.4
39	Minnesota	61.0
40	Maryland	60.7
41	Massachusetts	60.6
42	Wyoming	60.2
43	Montana	59.2
44	South Dakota	58.6
45	North Dakota	55.9
46	Vermont	55.8
47	Hawaii	55.3
48	Maine	53.9
49	Alaska	51.1
50	New York	46.7

304: Commuters Who Drive With Others

Nearly 20% of all commuters get to work by driving in groups of two or more, a statistic that includes family members who travel together as well as members of formal or informal car pools. Combining this group with the larger group of commuters who drive alone we find that 84.3% of all American workers depend on automobiles to get between home and the job. Group commuting appears to be most popular in the South and in New England. Hawaii, Utah and Alaska are regional outsiders that also belong in this group.

Table: Commuters Who Share Private Cars
Date: 1980
Source: Census Bureau
Description: Percentage of commuters who drive or ride in private cars to work with others.
United States Average: 19.8%
State Median: 20.2%

COMMUTERS WHO SHARE PRIVATE CARS

Rank	State	Percent
1	Virginia	25.5
2	South Carolina	25.4
3	Mississippi	25.3
4	Vermont	25.2
5	North Carolina	24.9
6	West Virginia	24.6
7	New Hampshire	24.1
8	Alabama	23.8
9	Hawaii	23.5
10	Maryland	23.3
10	Wyoming	23.3
12	Arkansas	23.1
12	Kentucky	23.1
12	Maine	23.1
12	Utah	23.1
16	Tennessee	22.3
17	Alaska	22.2
17	Georgia	22.2
19	Delaware	21.6
20	Louisiana	21.5
21	Texas	21.4
22	Missouri	21.2
23	Rhode Island	21.0
24	Florida	20.4
25	New Mexico	20.3
26	Indiana	20.2
27	Kansas	20.0
28	Pennsylvania	19.9
29	Colorado	19.7
29	Massachusetts	19.7
31	Arizona	19.6
31	Connecticut	19.6
31	Oklahoma	19.6
34	Nevada	19.2
35	Wisconsin	19.0
36	Washington	18.9
37	Minnesota	18.7
38	New Jersey	18.3
39	Iowa	18.3
40	Oregon	18.2
41	Illinois	17.9
42	Michigan	17.7
43	Idaho	17.6
43	Nebraska	17.6

Rank	State	Percent
45	Montana	17.2
46	California	17.1
46	North Dakota	17.1
48	Ohio	16.7
49	New York	16.1
50	South Dakota	14.3

305: Commuters Who Use Public Transportation

New York City has the largest percentage of all mass transit ridership in the country. The cities of Chicago, Boston, Washington, D.C. and Philadelphia are centers for the only other public transportation systems that carry a really significant fraction of daily commuter traffic. Below Oregon, in 13th position, there are 37 states in which public transportation is the way to work for fewer than five commuters in 100. Mass transit is essential for the daily operation of the great metropolitan centers of America, but outside of these centers it is almost unknown.

Table: Percentage of Commuters Using Public Transportation
Date: 1980
Source: Census Bureau
Description: Percentage of commuters using public transportation.
United States average: 6.3%
State median: 2.6%

PERCENTAGE OF COMMUTERS USING PUBLIC TRANSPORTATION

Rank	State	Percent
1	New York	25.4
2	Illinois	11.8
3	New Jersey	9.6
4	Massachusetts	9.2
5	Maryland	9.0
6	Hawaii	8.4
7	Pennsylvania	8.3
8	California	5.6
9	Connecticut	5.5
10	Minnesota	5.4
10	Washington	5.4
12	Virginia	5.2
13	Oregon	5.1
14	Colorado	4.7
14	Rhode Island	4.7
16	Ohio	4.3
17	Louisiana	4.1

Rank	State	Percent
17	Missouri	4.1
19	Delaware	4.0
19	Georgia	4.0
21	Wisconsin	3.7
22	Utah	3.4
23	Alaska	3.3
24	Florida	2.6
24	Tennessee	2.6
26	Nebraska	2.5
27	Idaho	2.3
27	Michigan	2.3
27	Texas	2.3
30	Kentucky	2.2
31	Arizona	1.9
31	Iowa	1.9
31	Nevada	1.9
31	New Mexico	1.9
31	Wyoming	1.9
36	Indiana	1.8
36	West Virginia	1.8
38	Maine	1.6
39	North Carolina	1.5
39	Vermont	1.5
41	Alabama	1.4
41	New Hampshire	1.4
43	South Carolina	1.3
44	Mississippi	1.2
44	Montana	1.2
46	Arkansas	1.0
46	Kansas	1.0
46	Oklahoma	1.0
49	North Dakota	.7
50	South Dakota	.5

306: Commuters Who Walk

The idea of walking to work represents a kind of unattainable ideal for many Americans, a dim reflection of bygone days when working life and home life were more closely coordinated. The overwhelming majority of people who actually do walk to work are found in rural occupations or in very small towns, expecially in New England and on the Plains. About one worker in 20 walks to and from the job, a slightly smaller group than the group of mass transit riders (though a comparison of state median values shows that in most *states* the number of pedestrians is larger than the number of mass transit riders). Pedestrian commuting is especially infrequent in the South.

Table: Workers Walking to Work
Date: 1980
Source: Census Bureau
Description: Percentage of workers walking to work.

United States average: 5.5%
State median: 5.6%

WORKERS WALKING TO WORK

Rank	State	Percent
1	Alaska	16.6
2	North Dakota	14.8
3	Montana	14.1
4	South Dakota	12.7
5	Vermont	11.3
6	Iowa	9.4
6	Maine	9.4
8	Wyoming	8.8
9	New York	8.6
10	Nebraska	8.4
11	New Hampshire	8.2
12	Minnesota	8.1
12	Wisconsin	8.1
14	Idaho	7.8
14	Hawaii	7.8
16	Massachusetts	7.6
17	Pennsylvania	7.5
18	Rhode Island	7.4
19	Kansas	6.3
19	West Virginia	6.3
21	Colorado	6.1
21	Oregon	6.1
23	New Jersey	6.0
24	Nevada	5.8
25	Illinois	5.7
26	Utah	5.5
27	New Mexico	5.3
28	Washington	5.2
29	Indiana	5.0
30	Connecticut	4.8
30	South Carolina	4.8
32	California	4.7
33	Delaware	4.6
33	Kentucky	4.6
33	Michigan	4.6
36	Mississippi	4.5
36	Oklahoma	4.5
38	North Carolina	4.4
39	Arkansas	4.3
39	Missouri	4.3
41	Arizona	4.2
41	Maryland	4.2
43	Ohio	3.9
44	Louisiana	3.8
44	Texas	3.8
46	Virginia	3.5
47	Tennessee	3.4

Rank	State	Percent
47	Florida	3.4
47	Georgia	3.4
50	Alabama	3.0

307: The 20 Busiest Airports

The airports of Chicago and Atlanta, which handle large volumes of commercial passengers making stopovers or connecting flights on longer distance journeys, were the busiest airports in 1980. Air traffic in these areas was exceeded only by the combined traffic of three New York City airports (J.F.K., LaGuardia and Newark), which amounted to 53.5 million passengers. With one exception, this list of busy airports is in effect a list of the major metropolitan areas of the United States. Can you spot the odd case? You bet you can.

Table: 20 Busiest Airports for Commercial Aviation
Date: 1980
Source: International Civil Aviation Organization
Description: Passenger traffic in the 20 busiest airports.

BUSIEST AIRPORTS FOR COMMERCIAL AVIATION

Rank	State	Passengers (in millions)
1	Chicago (O'Hare)	43.1
2	Atlanta	41.7
3	Los Angeles	33.1
4	New York (J.F.K.)	26.8
5	Dallas-Fort Worth	21.5
5	San Francisco	21.5
7	Denver	20.8
8	Miami	20.5
9	New York (LaGuardia)	17.5
10	Boston (Logan)	14.7
11	Washington, D.C. (National)	14.5
12	Honolulu	14.0
13	Pittsburgh	11.5
14	Houston	10.7
15	Detroit	9.9
15	Las Vegas	9.9
17	Philadelphia	9.6
18	Newark	9.2
18	Seattle	9.2
20	Minneapolis	9.0

GOVERNMENT

This section covers selected aspects of the structure, size and cost of government activity in the United States. The first table shows how seats in the U.S. House of Representatives are apportioned among the states and how the 1980 census results changed this distribution. The following table also deals with the structure of the legislative branch of government, but here the composition of the legislatures in each of the 50 states is at issue. The size of government is the subject of tables on employment in state and local governments. There were 16.2 million Americans employed in all levels of government in 1980, up from 6.4 million in 1950. Of the 9.8 million new government jobs added during this period, about 92% were in state and local governments. Federal government employment was up 37% over a period of 30 years, but state and local government employment jumped by 211% in the same period. State and local governments accounted for 13.3 million workers, or 82.1% of all government employment, in 1980. The tables trace state by state variations in these principal forms of public employment. Information on the general costs of government can be found in tables throughout this book, especially in the section on taxation and in tables on government expenses in various sections. Here we treat only three special themes: the salaries of governors, the salaries of state legislators, and the amount of federal defense spending in each state.

308. Congressional Apportionment and Changes from 1970 to 1980

One of the central tasks of the census is to determine the distribution of population by state for the purpose of assigning a proportional number of seats in the U.S. House of Representatives. The population shifts recorded at each census are used to change seat assignments, thus touching of political wars over the new boundaries of congressional districts in the states that are affected. The

1980 census results were first used for the 1982 elections. There were 11 states that gained a total of 17 seats on the basis of population shifts between 1970 and 1980. Florida (4 seats), Texas (3) and California (2) gained multiple seats in the House and eight other states gained one seat each: Tennessee, Washington, Colorado, Oregon, Arizona, Utah, New Mexico and Nevada. The states with strengthened representation are all in the West and the South. Ten states lost these same 17 seats. New York lost five, Pennsylvania, Illinois and Ohio each lost two, and single seat losses occurred in Michigan, New Jersey, Massachusetts, Indiana, Missouri and South Dakota.

Table: Congressional Apportionment
Date: 1980
Source: Census Bureau
Description: Congressional apportionment in the U.S. House of Representatives based on the 1980 census with increase or decrease from the 1970 census.
United States total: 435 representatives

CONGRESSIONAL APPORTIONMENT

Rank	State	Number of representatives	Increase or decrease 1970–1980
1	California	45	2
2	New York	34	−5
3	Texas	27	3
4	Pennsylvania	23	−2
5	Illinois	22	−2
6	Ohio	21	−2
7	Florida	19	4
8	Michigan	18	−1
9	New Jersey	14	−1
10	Massachusetts	11	−1
10	North Carolina	11	0
12	Georgia	10	0
12	Indiana	10	−1
12	Virginia	10	0
15	Missouri	9	−1
15	Tennessee	9	1

Rank	State	Number of representatives	Increase or decrease 1970–1980
15	Wisconsin	9	0
18	Louisiana	8	0
18	Maryland	8	0
18	Minnesota	8	0
18	Washington	8	1
22	Alabama	7	0
22	Kentucky	7	0
24	Colorado	6	1
24	Connecticut	6	0
24	Iowa	6	0
24	Oklahoma	6	0
24	South Carolina	6	0
29	Arizona	5	1
29	Kansas	5	0
29	Mississippi	5	0
29	Oregon	5	1
33	Arkansas	4	0
33	West Virginia	4	0
35	Nebraska	3	0
35	New Mexico	3	1
35	Utah	3	1
38	Hawaii	2	0
38	Idaho	2	0
38	Maine	2	0
38	Montana	2	0
38	Nevada	2	1
38	New Hampshire	2	0
38	Rhode Island	2	0
45	Alaska	1	0
45	Delaware	1	0
45	North Dakota	1	0
45	South Dakota	1	−1
45	Vermont	1	0
45	Wyoming	1	0

309. Number of State Senate Seats and State House Seats

The size of legislative bodies in the states reflects diverging historical traditions and conceptions of government. The lower house (House of Representatives) in New Hampshire is about twice as large as Pennsylvania's, the second largest lower house. The 424 state representatives in New Hampshire, 400 in the lower house plus 24 in the upper house (Senate), form an unusually large group. About one in every 2,500 citizens of the state holds a position in the legislature, by far the highest quotient in the nation. New Hampshire government is rooted in the town meeting, a thriving institution that dates from the colonial period. The legislature seems to be conceived as a kind of large-scale town meeting. Many of the participants in this most participatory of democracies retain a more or less "amateur" political status (compare

salaries for legislators given below). The town meeting style of government practiced in New Hampshire is found to some degree throughout New England. States in this area crowd close to the top of the list for the lower houses.

The single-chamber, or unicameral, system in Nebraska is the only one of its kind. Listed among the upper houses, the Nebraska chamber ranks 13th in size, but these 49 representatives make up the smallest overall legislative body in any state. The frugal citizens of the state shifted from a bicameral to a unicameral system in 1934, hoping to save "time, talk and money" during the Depression years. (The same referendum vote legalized drinking beer and betting on horse races.)

On the average, lower houses tend to be about 2.5 times larger than upper houses. The ratio is especially high for New Hampshire. The lowest ratios, 2 to 1, are found in states that prefer the neatness of round numbers like 100 and 50, 80 and 40, or 40 and 20. Wisconsin, Tennessee and Ohio use the 3 to 1 ratio of 99 and 33 seats.

Table: State Legislatures
Date: 1981
Source: Council of State Governments
Description: Size of state legislatures and number of house and senate seats.
United States total: 7,658 seats
State median—total: 148
State median—upper house: 100
State median—lower house: 38

STATE LEGISLATURES

Rank	State	Total seats	House seats	Senate seats
1	New Hampshire	424	400	24
2	Pennsylvania	253	203	50
3	Georgia	236	180	56
3	Illinois	236	177	59
5	New York	210	150	60
6	Minnesota	201	134	67
7	Massachusetts	200	160	40
8	Missouri	197	163	34
9	Maryland	188	141	47
10	Connecticut	187	151	36
11	Maine	184	151	33
12	Texas	181	150	31
13	Vermont	180	150	30
14	Mississippi	174	122	52
15	North Carolina	170	120	50
15	South Carolina	170	124	46
17	Kansas	165	125	40
18	Florida	160	120	40
19	Indiana	150	100	50
19	Iowa	150	100	50
19	Montana	150	100	50
19	North Dakota	150	100	50

Rank	State	Total seats	House seats	Senate seats
19	Rhode Island	150	100	50
24	Oklahoma	149	101	48
25	Michigan	148	110	38
26	Washington	147	98	49
27	Louisiana	144	105	39
28	Alabama	140	105	35
28	Virginia	140	100	40
30	Kentucky	138	100	38
31	Arkansas	135	100	35
32	West Virginia	134	100	34
33	Ohio	132	99	33
33	Tennessee	132	99	33
33	Wisconsin	132	99	33
36	California	120	80	40
36	New Jersey	120	80	40
38	New Mexico	112	70	42
39	Idaho	105	70	35
39	South Dakota	105	70	35
41	Utah	104	75	29
42	Colorado	100	65	35
43	Wyoming	92	62	30
44	Arizona	90	60	30
44	Oregon	90	60	30
46	Hawaii	76	51	25
47	Delaware	62	41	21
48	Alaska	60	40	20
48	Nevada	60	40	20
50	Nebraska	39		

unicameral

310. State Government Employees per 10,000 Residents

Alaska and Hawaii lead the rest of the nation by a wide margin in the area of state government employment per resident. A comparison with rates in the table following shows that these are also the only states in which state workers outnumber local government workers. In general, there are two types of states that appear near the top of the present table. One type—represented by Alaska, New Mexico, Montana and Wyoming—combines a great deal of territory with relatively sparse and scattered settlement. In this situation there tend to be many small-scale local governments with meager resources, so the state must make a relatively strong effort to supply services over a wide area. A second type—represented by Hawaii, Delaware and Rhode Island—is simply a state with very little territory. In this situation the state government tends to directly supply services that are the business of local governments in larger states (note which three states are at the bottom of the next table). So, the formula for relatively intensive state government seems to be *either* small territory *or* sparse population in a large

territory. Hawaii and Alaska are the extreme examples of these types. Near the bottom of this list we find that states tend to be large and heavily populated.

Table: State Government Employment
Source: Census Bureau
Description: Full-time equivalent employment in state government per 10,000 population.
United States average: 169.7 employees per 10,000 population
State median: 158 employees per 10,000 population

STATE GOVERNMENT EMPLOYMENT

Rank	State	State government employees per 10,000 population
1	Alaska	416
2	Hawaii	378
3	Delaware	262
4	New Mexico	259
5	Vermont	215
6	Rhode Island	211
7	West Virginia	204
8	Montana	199
9	South Carolina	196
10	Maryland	194
11	Louisiana	193
11	North Dakota	193
11	Wyoming	193
14	Oklahoma	186
15	Nebraska	180
15	South Dakota	180
17	Utah	177
18	Virginia	176
19	Washington	173
20	Arkansas	164
20	Oregon	164
22	Alabama	161
22	Maine	161
24	Kansas	160
25	Mississippi	159
26	Idaho	158
26	Kentucky	158
28	New Hampshire	156
29	Iowa	155
30	Georgia	152
30	Nevada	152
32	Connecticut	149
33	Colorado	147
33	North Carolina	147
35	Arizona	137
35	Tennessee	137
37	Massachusetts	136
37	Michigan	136
39	Minnesota	135
40	Missouri	133
41	Wisconsin	127

Rank	State	State government employees per 10,000 population
42	New York	123
43	Indiana	121
44	New Jersey	119
44	Texas	119
46	Illinois	108
47	Florida	107
47	Ohio	107
47	Pennsylvania	107
50	California	105

311. Local Government Employees per 10,000 Residents

Nationwide, local governments (counties, towns and cities) employ more than twice as many people as state governments. The ratio between these two types of employer is a fair indicator of the way that responsibilities are shared out in a given state. Hawaii, deeply entrenched in 50th position here, is largely managed by state government. Alaska, on the other hand, has many local government officials to complement the large state government work force. Its combined state and local government work force comes to 903 employees per 10,000 residents of Alaska, by far the highest ratio in the nation. Local governments, especially the governments in metropolitan areas, are relatively important in states like California, New York and Florida. Outside of industrial Massachusetts, the local governments of New England tend to have relatively few full-time employees.

Table: Local Government Employment
Date: 1980
Source: Census Bureau
Description: Full-time equivalent employment in local governments per 10,000 population.
United States average: 335.4 employees
State median: 338 employees

LOCAL GOVERNMENT EMPLOYMENT

Rank	State	Local government employees per 10,000 population
1	Wyoming	450
2	New York	416
3	Georgia	410
3	Nebraska	410
5	Alaska	387
6	New Jersey	384
7	Kansas	376
8	Texas	370
9	Arizona	368
9	Colorado	368
11	Florida	364
11	Massachusetts	364
11	Minnesota	364
14	California	363
15	North Carolina	360
16	Montana	357
17	Mississippi	355
18	Wisconsin	354
19	Iowa	353
19	Maryland	353
19	Tennessee	353
22	Oregon	350
23	Nevada	349
24	Alabama	344
25	Louisiana	339
26	Illinois	338
26	Oklahoma	338
28	Michigan	334
29	Missouri	332
30	Ohio	331
31	Indiana	330
31	New Mexico	330
33	Virginia	327
34	Idaho	323
35	Washington	322
36	South Dakota	320
37	South Carolina	319
38	North Dakota	309
39	West Virginia	307
40	Arkansas	301
41	Maine	297
42	Connecticut	296
43	New Hampshire	293
43	Pennsylvania	293
45	Utah	287
46	Vermont	267
47	Delaware	265
47	Kentucky	265
49	Rhode Island	260
50	Hawaii	125

312. Salaries of the Governors

Salaries for state governors range from $35,000 to $85,000 a year, with a median value near $50,000. The salaries of governors and legislators are not very closely related, as shown by a comparison with the rankings in the next table. In Virginia, the governor makes almost 10

Rank	State	Annual salary
42	New Hampshire	$44,520
43	Montana	43,360
44	Connecticut	42,000
45	Idaho	40,000
45	Massachusetts	40,000
45	Nebraska	40,000
48	Arkansas	35,000
48	Delaware	35,000
48	Maine	35,000

times as much as a legislator. In California, the ratio is less than two to one. Ratios between the salaries of governors and legislators (which can be readily worked out from the given tables) may provide some clues as to the relative scope or power of the legislative and executive branches in the states.

Table: Governors' Salaries
Date: 1982
Source: *World Almanac*
Description: Annual salaries of governors.
State average: $55,107
State median: $51,500

GOVERNORS' SALARIES

Rank	State	Annual salary
1	New Jersey	$85,000
1	New York	85,000
3	Virginia	75,000
4	Alaska	74,196
5	Louisiana	73,440
6	Texas	71,400
7	Michigan	70,000
8	Tennessee	68,226
9	Minnesota	66,500
10	Pennsylvania	66,000
11	Georgia	65,934
12	Wisconsin	65,801
13	Washington	63,000
14	Florida	60,498
15	Iowa	60,000
15	Maryland	60,000
15	New Mexico	60,000
15	South Carolina	60,000
15	West Virginia	60,000
20	Illinois	58,000
21	North Carolina	57,864
22	Oregon	55,423
23	Missouri	55,000
23	Wyoming	55,000
25	Mississippi	53,000
26	Alabama	50,000
26	Arizona	50,000
26	Colorado	50,000
26	Hawaii	50,000
26	Kentucky	50,000
26	Nevada	50,000
26	Ohio	50,000
33	Rhode Island	49,500
34	California	49,100
35	Indiana	48,000
35	Oklahoma	48,000
35	Utah	48,000
38	North Dakota	47,000
39	South Dakota	46,750
40	Kansas	45,000
41	Vermont	44,850

313. Salaries of State Legislators

Basic legislative salaries vary across a wide range, from a token $100 per year in New Hampshire to over $30,000 per year in Michigan and New York. These figures generally indicate the degree of professionalism that states expect of their legislators, that is, the degree to which representation is treated as a full-time job, with representatives expected to devote their full energy to the job. States with large populations and complex administrative problems tend to be near the top of the list. Legislatures in these states are in session for much of the year every year. (In some states the legislature meets only every other year: Arkansas, Kentucky, Maine, Montana, Nevada, New Hampshire, North Carolina, Oregon, Texas, Washington and Wyoming.) California, with the fewest legislators per capita in the country, may well provide the highest overall level of compensation. The state supports legislative offices in the home districts as well as in the capital, Sacramento.

The 10 states listed at the bottom pay no fixed salaries. Earnings depend on the number of days that the legislature is in session, up to a certain maximum. Total earnings in all these states are relatively low, with a top figure of only about $6,000 per annum (in Nevada). Arkansas and South Carolina combine regular salaries with per diem payments (which can add as much as $10,000 per annum to earnings in South Carolina).

Over and above the amounts listed here, legislators in all states are compensated for some travel and living expenses, although these payments vary considerably from state to state. There are 18 states that distribute special bonus payments for attending special legislative sessions.

Table: Salaries of State Legislators
Date: 1982
Source: Council of State Governments
Description: Annual salaries of state legislators.

SALARIES OF STATE LEGISLATORS

Rank	State	Annual salaries
1	Michigan	$31,000
2	New York	30,804
3	California	28,110
4	Illinois	28,000
5	Pennsylvania	25,000
6	Wisconsin	22,638
7	Ohio	22,500
8	Massachusetts	19,125
9	Alaska	18,768
10	Maryland	18,500
10	Minnesota	18,500
12	New Jersey	18,000
12	Oklahoma	18,000
14	Louisiana	16,800
15	Arizona	15,000
15	Missouri	15,000
17	Colorado	14,000
18	Iowa	13,700
19	Hawaii	13,650
20	Florida	12,000
21	Delaware	11,400
22	Washington	11,200
23	North Carolina	10,000
24	Indiana	9,600
25	Oregon	8,400
26	Tennessee	8,308
27	Mississippi	8,100
28	Virginia	8,000
29	Connecticut	7,500
29	Arkansas	7,500
31	Georgia	7,200
31	Texas	7,200
33	South Carolina	6,936
34	West Virginia	5,136
35	Nebraska	4,800
36	Idaho	4,200
37	North Dakota	2,800
38	Maine	2,500
39	Vermont	2,000
40	New Hampshire	100

	Nevada	104 per day
	Kentucky	50 per day
	Montana	44 per day
	Kansas	42 per day
	New Mexico	40 per day
	Wyoming	30 per day
	Utah	25 per day
	Alabama	10 per day
	North Dakota	5 per day
	Rhode Island	5 per day

Copyright © Council of State Governments

314. Defense Spending

The data in this table represent dollars spent for military operations in the 50 states plus dollars awarded to domestic contractors for weapons and supplies. Defense Department funds spent outside the country are not included here. Total domestic defense spending in 1982 amounted to $768.00 for every living soul in the country. Per capita spending levels in the states varied across a wide range, with a 20 to 1 ratio between rates at the high and low extremes—the neighboring states of Virginia and West Virginia. Since the Pentagon building is located in Arlington, Virginia, with many associated central defense management facilities clustered nearby, it is not surprising to find Virginia at the top of the list. The other three states with high per capita spending—Alaska, Connecticut and Hawaii—have major air defense or naval facilities, combined with relatively small populations. California is the leading state on a dollar expenditure basis. The Golden State absorbed 18% of domestic defense spending in 1982.

Table: Defense Spending
Source: Census Bureau
Description: Domestic defense spending in billions of dollars and per capita expenditure.
United States total spending: $179 billion
United States average: $768 per capita
State median: $604 per capita

DEFENSE SPENDING

Rank	State	Per capita expenditure	Defense spending (in billions of dollars)
1	Virginia	$2,234	12.1
2	Alaska	2,091	.9
3	Connecticut	2,013	6.3
4	Hawaii	1,969	1.9
5	California	1,336	32.3
6	Missouri	1,283	6.3
7	Maryland	1,197	5.1
8	Washington	1,179	5.0
9	Massachusetts	1,036	6.0
10	New Hampshire	980	.9
11	Maine	936	1.1
12	Kansas	910	2.2
13	New Mexico	887	1.2
14	Arizona	876	2.4
15	Mississippi	851	2.2
16	Utah	819	1.2
17	Colorado	816	2.4
18	Texas	792	11.7
19	Florida	759	7.7
20	Georgia	737	4.1
21	Louisiana	728	3.1
22	Delaware	723	.4
23	South Carolina	716	2.3
24	Oklahoma	639	2.0
25	Alabama	617	2.4
26	Rhode Island	590	.6
27	New Jersey	554	4.1
28	Nevada	551	.5

Rank	State	Per capita expenditure	Defense spending (in billions of dollars)	Rank	State	Per capita expenditure	Defense spending (in billions of dollars)
29	North Carolina	$519	3.1	40	Wyoming	$354	.2
30	New York	505	8.9	41	South Dakota	314	.2
31	Vermont	481	.2	42	Tennessee	292	1.3
32	North Dakota	476	.3	43	Idaho	246	.2
33	Indiana	473	2.6	44	Illinois	242	2.8
34	Arkansas	429	1.0	45	Michigan	241	2.2
35	Pennsylvania	420	5.0	46	Montana	230	.2
36	Ohio	419	4.5	47	Wisconsin	229	1.1
37	Minnesota	412	1.7	48	Oregon	191	.5
38	Nebraska	368	.6	49	Iowa	164	.5
39	Kentucky	366	1.3	50	West Virginia	117	.2

POLITICS

The tables in this section focus on political participation, documenting recent levels of general interest in politics (voter registration and turnout), the distribution of party loyalties and the positions of several important groups (women, blacks and Hispanics) in the political system.

Low levels of political interest (i.e., high levels of political apathy) have been viewed with concern by political observers for many years. Our political institutions are thought to be legitimate because they express the will of the people. When people are reluctant to express their will, we are led to wonder whether this reflects general satisfaction and indifference or, more ominously, a general withdrawal from public concerns or dissatisfaction with available alternatives. During the past 50 years the proportion of the voting age population that actually voted in presidential elections has never been *higher* than 62.8% (in 1960). The proportion voting for members of the House of Representatives has never been higher than 58.5% (also 1960). Since 1960 the decline in participation has been continuous, with one exception: The off-year congressional elections of 1982, widely viewed as a referendum on the Reagan presidency, attracted a turnout equal to 43.2% of the total voting age population—up from 35.5% in the off-year elections of 1978. Although this represents a turnaround in an otherwise disturbing trend, the very low level at which the reversal occurred is itself disturbing. What would happen if an election were announced and nobody showed up? The American political system has been successful (if often slow) in accommodating the challenges of new groups and new demands, but we do not know if it can survive this deep indifference on the part of so many of those it claims to represent.

The two-party system in the United States, which emerged during the 19th century and which has remained dominant despite several realignments of major regions and voting groups over the years, has come under renewed pressure in recent years. The candidacy of John Anderson in 1980 demonstrated the importance of a growing block of voters who feel that they have no real home in the major parties. Split-ticket voting has greatly increased of late. The fundamental divergence between the major parties remains much the same as it has been throughout this century—the Democrats have a considerable lead in the number of registered voters, while the Republicans are well ahead in access to campaign contributions from wealthy individuals and groups—but there have been some shifts in the content of their activities. With the overwhelming importance of television advertising in campaigns, the introduction of computerized fund raising systems, and the greater influence of Political Action Committees (PACs) in lobbying for the interests of special groups, members of Congress have been pursuing "free-lance" strategies rather than conforming to party discipline. The parties have become rather loose associations of political stars who are now less likely to follow a party line on a given issue and more likely to act according to their own best opportunities. The negative side of this apparent gain in political independence appears in the difficulty of establishing consistent national policies and in the greater openness of representatives of the people to the enticements of wealthy interest groups.

At the same time that our political system seems threatened by public disaffection and loss of internal coherence, new groups have begun to make their presence felt in the political process. Black citizens have recently emerged as a significant collective force in national politics, having fought a long struggle against systematic exclusionary practices. By 1980 the Republican Party had entered the competition for black votes, which previously it had been content to concede to the Democrats. Americans of Hispanic origin are only now beginning to play a major part in the political life of Florida and the Southwest. The position of women in the political process now occupies the attention of all political strategists. The "gender gap" that appeared during the 1980 elections—a significantly lower level of support for President Reagan among women voters—became a prominent issue in planning for the 1984 campaigns. To some extent, the widening scope of political inclusion has now appeared in the rising numbers of blacks and women who hold public offices. Progress in this area has so far shown up mainly at the local level, particularly in the office of mayor in a number of large cities.

315. Voter Registration by Party Affiliation

This table covers 26 states for which data on registration by party are available. Most of the other 24 states do not register voters by party, in a few cases data are simply unavailable. The states here are ranked according to the percentage of voters registered with either of the two major parties. Major-party affiliation is still the rule in most states. States near the bottom of this list generally have high percentages of voters registered as independents, though registrations by members of minor parties account for the loss of a few percentage points here and there. Alaskans are the great pioneers of independent politics. Since Democratic registrations are generally more numerous than Republican registrations, the states at the top of the list also tend to have the largest contingents of registered Democrats. Louisiana is the extreme case. Registered Republicans outnumber registered Democrats in just five of the 26 states: Nebraska, Wyoming, South Dakota, New Hampshire and Kansas. In Iowa the parties run neck and neck on registrations, but both trail the independents by four percentage points.

Table: Voter Registration by Party Affiliation
Date: 1980
Source: *Almanac of American Politics*
Description: Percentage of registered voters who are registered as Democrats or Republicans.
26-State median: Democrats or Republicans 87%
26-State median: Democrats 44% and Republicans 31%

VOTER REGISTRATION BY PARTY AFFILIATION

Rank	State	Percent registered as Democrats or Republicans	Percent Democrat	Percent Republican
1	Oklahoma	98	72	26
1	West Virginia	98	67	31
3	Kentucky	97	68	29
4	North Carolina	95	71	24
5	Florida	94	64	30
5	Louisiana	94	87	7
5	Nebraska	94	44	50
5	Pennsylvania	94	53	41
9	New Mexico	93	63	30

Rank	State	Percent registered as Democrats or Republicans	Percent Democrat	Percent Republican
10	Maryland	92	69	23
10	Nevada	92	53	39
12	South Dakota	91	45	46
13	California	88	53	35
14	Oregon	86	50	36
14	Wyoming	86	37	49
16	Delaware	77	44	33
17	New Hampshire	73	33	40
18	New York	71	37	34
19	Connecticut	65	39	26
20	Iowa	64	32	32
21	Colorado	63	32	31
22	Maine	61	32	29
23	Kansas	56	24	32
24	New Jersey	54	33	21
25	Ohio	44	26	18
26	Alaska	43	26	17

316. Percentage of Voting Age Population Registered to Vote

Just over 71% of voting age Americans were potentially able to vote in the presidential election of 1980, down a fraction of a percentage point from 1976. States with high registration figures are mainly scattered across the northern frontier of the country, with concentrations in the upper Midwest and northern Plains and in New England. Mississippi and Alabama, where registration has been a focal point of the ongoing campaign for civil rights, are the main exceptions to this pattern of northern-rim concentration. In the warm-weather states of the South and the Southwest, together with Hawaii and the states of the Middle Atlantic region, the attitude toward registration (and voting, see tables following) is apparently more casual. Important upward shifts in registration between 1976 and 1980 occurred in Alaska, Iowa and Ohio. Sharp downward shifts were recorded in Utah, Washington, West Virginia, Colorado and Texas. Statewide registration was not required in North Dakota in either 1976 or 1980, in Mississippi in 1976, and in Wisconsin in 1980—as indicated by asterisks.

Table: Percentage of Voting Age Population Registered to Vote
Date: 1980
Source: National Republican Congressional Committee
Description: Percentage of the voting age population registered to vote in 1980 and 1976.

United States average: 1980 (48 states) 71.7%; 1976 (49 states) 71.4%
State median: 1980 (48 states) 74.0%; 1976 (49 states) 72.7%

PERCENTAGE OF VOTING AGE POPULATION REGISTERED TO VOTE

Rank	State	Percent in 1980	Percent in 1976
1	Minnesota	95.6	94.0
2	Alaska	95.1	80.9
3	Maine	94.2	93.7
4	South Dakota	92.1	90.4
5	Idaho	90.9	93.0
6	Montana	89.0	88.2
7	Michigan	87.6	83.6
8	Mississippi	86.8	*
9	Vermont	85.2	86.1
10	Utah	84.8	90.4
11	Iowa	83.4	70.1
12	New Hampshire	83.0	82.7
13	Oregon	81.9	85.6
14	Missouri	79.7	75.4
15	Alabama	78.2	74.4
16	Rhode Island	77.7	81.5
17	Indiana	76.2	82.4
18	Ohio	76.1	63.2
19	Nebraska	76.0	77.6
20	Illinois	75.6	80.2
21	Kansas	75.1	67.9
22	Washington	74.5	81.1
23	Connecticut	74.3	75.4
24	West Virginia	74.2	83.8
25	Massachusetts	73.8	70.5
26	New Mexico	73.5	68.7
27	Arkansas	73.3	69.4
28	Tennessee	71.4	64.3
29	Delaware	70.1	74.5
30	Louisiana	69.9	72.7
31	Kentucky	69.7	72.1
32	New Jersey	69.6	72.7
33	Colorado	68.8	75.3
34	Oklahoma	67.5	71.4
35	Maryland	67.3	67.6
35	Wyoming	67.3	72.5
37	Texas	66.7	73.5
38	North Carolina	65.6	67.1
38	Pennsylvania	65.6	68.0
40	California	65.5	65.1
41	Florida	64.9	66.9
42	Georgia	64.4	67.9
43	New York	60.9	63.7
44	Virginia	59.4	59.7
45	Hawaii	58.2	60.0
46	Arizona	58.0	64.2
47	South Carolina	56.6	57.9
48	Nevada	50.0	59.1
49	North Dakota	*	*
49	Wisconsin	*	80.4

* Registration not required

317. 1980 Voter Turnout as a Percentage of Voting Age Population

Only 53.2% of the potential electorate cast votes in the election that carried Ronald Reagan to the White House in 1980. The percentages varied between 70.6% in politically conscious Minnesota and 41% in apathetic South Carolina. In general, actual turnout reflected the rankings on registration given above. Alaska, Mississippi and Alabama are the major exceptions to this. Since only about 60% of the *registered* voters turned out in these states, they have much lower rankings in this table. High turnouts of over 80% of the registered voters in Colorado, Connecticut, Nevada, Virginia, Wyoming and Massachusetts pushed these states to relatively higher rankings here. In the 12 states at the bottom of the table fewer than half of all eligible adults participated in the 1980 election.

Table: Voter Turnout as a Percentage of Voting Age Population
Date: 1980
Source: Election Research Center and Census Bureau
Description: Voter turnout in the 1980 presidential election as a percentage of voting age population.
United States average: 53.2%
State median: 55.5%

VOTER TURNOUT AS A PERCENTAGE OF VOTING AGE POPULATION

Rank	State	Percent
1	Minnesota	70.6
2	Idaho	68.6
3	Wisconsin	67.9
4	South Dakota	67.6
5	Montana	65.6
5	Utah	65.6
7	North Dakota	65.4
8	Maine	65.1
9	Iowa	63.1
10	Oregon	61.9
11	Connecticut	61.5
12	Michigan	60.1
13	Massachusetts	59.4
14	Missouri	59.1
14	Rhode Island	59.1
16	Alaska	58.5
17	Vermont	58.2
17	Washington	58.2
19	Illinois	58.1
20	Indiana	57.9
20	New Hampshire	57.9
22	Kansas	57.2
23	Nebraska	57.1
24	Colorado	56.9
25	Ohio	55.6
26	New Jersey	55.4
27	Delaware	55.1

Rank	State	Percent
28	Wyoming	54.5
29	Louisiana	53.9
30	West Virginia	53.1
31	Oklahoma	53.0
32	Mississippi	52.3
33	Pennsylvania	52.2
34	Arkansas	51.9
35	New Mexico	51.7
36	Maryland	50.5
37	Kentucky	50.2
38	Florida	50.0
39	California	49.7
40	Alabama	49.2
41	Tennessee	49.1
42	New York	48.2
42	Virginia	48.2
44	Texas	45.8
45	Arizona	45.4
46	Hawaii	44.0
46	North Carolina	44.0
48	Nevada	42.5
49	Georgia	41.8
50	South Carolina	41.0

318. 1982 Voter Turnout as a Percentage of Voting Age Population

Congressional elections do not attract as much voter interest as presidential contests. This fact is clearly reflected here. Except for Alaska, where participation actually increased by about six percentage points from 1980, all states registered declines, generally in the range of 5 to 15 percentage points. The decline in Arkansas was below average (–3.7 points), while very large drops occurred in Idaho (–18.3 points) and Wisconsin (–22.3 points).

Table: Voter Turnout as a Percentage of Voting Age Population
Date: 1982
Source: Committee for the Study of the American Electorate, Center on Political Education, AFL-CIO
Description: Voter turnout in 1982 congressional elections as a percentage of voting age population.
United States average: 43.2%
State median: 43%

VOTER TURNOUT AS A PERCENTAGE OF VOTING AGE POPULATION

Rank	State	Percent of turnout of potential voters	Potential voters (in thousands)
1	Alaska	64.8	287
2	Minnesota	61.2	2,988
3	South Dakota	57.9	482
4	Maine	55.2	831
5	Utah	54.5	986
6	Montana	54.0	569
7	North Dakota	52.5	473
8	Oregon	50.7	1,954
9	Idaho	50.3	661
10	Iowa	49.1	2,094
11	Arkansas	48.2	1,650
12	Massachusetts	47.9	4,394
13	Wyoming	47.6	354
14	Nebraska	47.3	1,144
15	Indiana	46.0	3,904
16	Michigan	45.8	6,554
17	Wisconsin	45.6	3,464
18	Hawaii	45.5	716
18	Rhode Island	45.5	726
20	New Mexico	44.7	936
21	Connecticut	44.6	2,378
22	Washington	44.5	3,154
23	Vermont	44.0	379
24	Kansas	43.4	1,759
25	Delaware	43.1	443
26	Ohio	43.0	7,793
27	Missouri	42.4	3,640
28	Colorado	41.7	2,225
28	Illinois	41.7	8,346
30	California	41.0	18,277
31	Pennsylvania	40.8	8,883
32	New Hampshire	40.6	697
33	Alabama	40.1	2,812
34	West Virginia	39.3	1,408
35	Oklahoma	39.2	2,299
36	New Jersey	39.1	5,544
37	New York	39.0	13,153
38	Tennessee	37.3	3,375
39	Nevada	36.7	661
40	Arizona	36.0	2,061
40	Mississippi	36.0	1,745
42	Maryland	35.7	3,190
43	Virginia	34.7	4,078
44	Florida	32.4	8,169
45	North Carolina	29.9	4,417
46	South Carolina	29.3	2,291
47	Texas	29.1	10,793
48	Georgia	28.9	4,040
49	Kentucky	26.7	2,620
50	Louisiana	*	3,055

* candidates ran unopposed.

319. Percentage of the Voting Age Population That Is Black

The civil rights movement that began to gather momentum some 25 years ago has helped to guarantee equal protection under the law and equal access to public resources and services for all citizens. The principal activities of this movement necessarily occurred outside regular political channels, since the exclusion of black citizens from the political process was one of the major forms of inequality against which the movement was directed. With the overthrow of discriminatory voting laws and with the success of voter registration drives, the inclusion of black citizens in American political institutions has emerged as an important legacy of the movement. The increasing importance of black voters in the electoral process is now beginning to show up in the increasing numbers of black elected officials in local offices (see Table 321).

The figures in this table indicate the potential black vote in the 50 states. These data refer to the racial distribution in the entire adult population. Since registration and voting levels among blacks are still generally lower than those for whites, despite the improvements brought about by registration drives, the actual proportional voting strength of black citizens is somewhat lower in most cases than these figures would suggest. Still, it is clear that the voice of black voters is now of tremendous importance throughout the South. In states where the proportion of black voting potential exceeds about 5%—the top 26 states on the list—politicians who ignore the will of their black constituents now do so at great risk to their careers.

Table: Percent of Voting Age Population That Is Black
Date: 1980
Source: Census Bureau
United States average: 10.5%
State median: 5.6%

PERCENT OF VOTING AGE POPULATION THAT IS BLACK

Rank	State	Percent
1	Mississippi	31.0
2	South Carolina	27.3
3	Louisiana	26.6
4	Georgia	24.3
5	Alabama	22.9
6	Maryland	20.8
7	North Carolina	20.3
8	Virginia	17.5
9	Delaware	14.2
9	Tennessee	14.2
11	Arkansas	14.1
12	Illinois	12.9
13	New York	12.4
14	Michigan	11.7
15	Florida	11.3
16	Texas	11.1
17	New Jersey	11.0

Rank	State	Percent
18	Missouri	9.3
19	Ohio	9.2
20	Pennsylvania	8.1
21	California	7.1
22	Indiana	6.8
23	Kentucky	6.7
24	Connecticut	6.0
24	Oklahoma	6.0
26	Nevada	5.3
27	Kansas	4.8
28	Alaska	3.4
28	Massachusetts	3.4
30	Colorado	3.2
30	West Virginia	3.2
30	Wisconsin	3.2
33	Nebraska	2.6
34	Arizona	2.5
34	Rhode Island	2.5
36	Washington	2.4
37	Hawaii	1.9
38	New Mexico	1.7
39	Iowa	1.2
39	Oregon	1.2
41	Minnesota	1.1
42	Utah	.7
42	Wyoming	.7
44	New Hampshire	.4
44	North Dakota	.4
46	Idaho	.3
46	Maine	.3
46	South Dakota	.3
49	Montana	.2
49	Vermont	.2

320. Percentage of the Voting Age Population that is of Hispanic Origin

The political significance of Spanish-speaking Americans has increased rapidly during the past decade. A steady stream of migrants from Mexico and the Caribbean has supplemented the political strength of Spanish-speaking groups that have been established for many years in certain parts of the country. These figures on the potential Hispanic vote show that areas of strength are presently limited to about 12 states (using 4% of potential voters as the cutoff point for significant strength). Adults of Hispanic origin in Hawaii form a group distinct from the others found in this table, since their more immediate origins are not in Mexico and the Caribbean but rather in the Philippines and other Pacific islands. Among the other 11 states at the top, the majority are located in the Southwest. Florida and the states associated with the New York City and Chicago metropolitan areas are the other members of this group. Just as the figures in the previous table suggest that blacks will exercise great political influence in the Southeast in the decades to come, it is clear from these data that Americans of Hispanic origin will be a major factor in the future political development of the Southwest.

Table: Percent of Voting Age Population of Hispanic Origin
Date: 1980
Source: Census Bureau
United States average: 5.5%
State median: 1.4%

PERCENT OF VOTING AGE POPULATION OF HISPANIC ORIGIN

Rank	State	Percent
1	New Mexico	33.1
2	Texas	17.7
3	California	16.1
4	Arizona	13.3
5	Colorado	9.8
6	Florida	8.5
7	New York	8.3
8	Hawaii	6.0
9	Nevada	5.8
10	New Jersey	5.7
11	Illinois	4.6
12	Wyoming	4.4
13	Utah	3.6
14	Idaho	3.2
15	Connecticut	3.1
16	Louisiana	2.3
16	Washington	2.3
18	Kansas	2.2
19	Alaska	2.1
20	Oregon	2.0
21	Massachusetts	1.9
22	Rhode Island	1.8
23	Oklahoma	1.5
24	Maryland	1.4
24	Michigan	1.4
24	Nebraska	1.4
24	Virginia	1.4
28	Delaware	1.3
28	Indiana	1.3
30	Georgia	1.1
30	Wisconsin	1.1
32	Montana	1.0
32	Pennsylvania	1.0
32	South Carolina	1.0
35	Mississippi	.9
35	Missouri	.9
35	North Carolina	.9
35	Ohio	.9
39	Alabama	.8
40	Arkansas	.7
40	Iowa	.7
40	Kentucky	.7

Rank	State	Percent
40	Tennessee	.7
44	Minnesota	.6
44	Vermont	.6
44	West Virginia	.6
47	New Hampshire	.5
47	North Dakota	.5
47	South Dakota	.5
50	Maine	.4

321. Black Elected Officials

The data in this table reflect the situation as of July 1981. The 5,014 officials covered here included 343 members of the U.S. Congress and state legislatures, 2,863 city and county officials, 549 law enforcement officials (judges, sheriffs, etc.), and 1,259 members of the boards of public schools and colleges. Although this definition of elected officials is relatively broad, the numbers of blacks included remains very small. During the past decade, however, the situation has been changing rapidly. The figures comparable to 5,014 for 1981 were 1,472 in February 1970 and 3,503 in April 1975. There are now black elected officials in 42 of the 50 states. The area of highest representation is in the South.

Table: Black Elected Officials
Date: 1981
Source: Joint Center for Political Studies
Description: Black elected officials.
United States total: 5,014
State average: 100
State median: 27

BLACK ELECTED OFFICIALS

Rank	State	Number of blacks in office
1	Mississippi	436
2	Louisiana	367
3	Illinois	313
4	Michigan	291
5	Georgia	266
6	North Carolina	255
7	Alabama	247
8	California	233
9	South Carolina	227
10	Arkansas	218
11	Ohio	199
12	New York	197
13	Texas	195
14	New Jersey	158
15	Missouri	134

Rank	State	Number of blacks in office
16	Pennsylvania	125
17	Tennessee	123
18	Florida	110
19	Virginia	91
20	Kentucky	88
21	Oklahoma	85
22	Maryland	78
23	Indiana	67
24	Connecticut	53
25	Massachusetts	28
26	Kansas	26
27	Wisconsin	18
28	West Virginia	16
29	Arizona	15
29	Colorado	15
29	Delaware	15
32	Washington	14
33	Minnesota	10
34	Nevada	8
34	Rhode Island	8
36	Iowa	6
36	Nebraska	6
36	Oregon	6
39	New Mexico	5
40	Alaska	3
40	Maine	3
42	Hawaii	2
43	Utah	1
44	Idaho	0
44	Montana	0
44	New Hampshire	0
44	North Dakota	0
44	South Dakota	0
44	Vermont	0
44	Wyoming	0

322. Women Holding State and Local Public Office

The number of women holding office in states and localities increased from 7,089 in 1975 to 16,585 in 1981. Women now hold a total of 12% of all offices included in this category. The offices, with 1981 figures for the percentage of women among all such officials in parentheses, are the following: state legislators (12%), county commission members (7%), mayors (9%) and members of township and other local councils (14%). This last group of officials—the town and local council members—accounts for 12,792, or 77%, of all the offices held by women that are considered in this table.

Michigan is the leading state, though 90% of the women who hold office there fall into the relatively less significant category of local council members. There are now women in the legislatures of all 50 states, including 124 of 424 legislators in New Hampshire. Women are mayors of cities in every state except Rhode Island, where there are, actually, not many places with mayors' positions to be filled.

Table: Women Holding State and Local Public Office
Date: 1981
Source: Center for the American Woman in Politics
Description: Women holding state and local public office.
United States total: 16,585
State average: 332
State median: 225

WOMEN HOLDING STATE AND LOCAL PUBLIC OFFICE

Rank	State	Number of women in office
1	Michigan	2,584
2	Ohio	783
3	Texas	740
4	Illinois	669
5	Iowa	624
6	Kansas	550
7	Minnesota	546
8	Pennsylvania	533
9	California	468
10	Kentucky	457
11	New Jersey	435
12	Missouri	424
13	Arkansas	375
14	Florida	362
15	Indiana	353
16	Oregon	347
17	Colorado	339
18	North Carolina	336
19	Washington	333
20	Alabama	327
21	Oklahoma	298
22	Connecticut	297
23	Maine	270
24	Nebraska	229
25	West Virginia	228
26	Georgia	222
27	Tennessee	218
28	Virginia	217
29	Massachusetts	212
30	New Hampshire	207
31	Alaska	199
32	Mississippi	191
33	North Dakota	189
34	South Carolina	185
35	New York	171
35	South Dakota	171
37	Louisiana	161
38	Maryland	160

Rank	State	Number of women in office
39	Idaho	153
40	Utah	137
41	Montana	133
42	Arizona	118
42	Wisconsin	118
44	Vermont	116

Rank	State	Number of women in office
45	New Mexico	115
46	·Wyoming	106
47	Delaware	71
48	Rhode Island	57
49	Hawaii	20
50	Nevada	19

BUSINESS

The United States emerged as a nation at a time in history when the worldwide expansion of commerce was changing the traditional structures of all societies. Traditional elite groups, tracing their strength to feudal times, continued to hold sway in the nations of Europe and in Japan until the present century, but such groups never really established a foothold in the New World (or at least this part of it). Consequently, the United States is the oldest pure business civilization on earth. Many of our folk heroes and villains and many of our national leaders have been closely associated with commercial life in one way or another—as heads of businesses, lawyers or lobbyists, as robber barons or philanthropists, as inheritors of business fortunes or, more recently, as advertisers or spokespeople for commercial interests.

Business conditions are perhaps the most constant theme in national politics. The business conditions of a given state are a key to the quality of life that it offers to residents. There are numberless ways in which the state of business affects our daily lives and there are many ways in which these influences can be presented statistically. The tables in this section highlight only a few important indicators of commercial conditions. A table presenting the number of business concerns per state serves as a starting point. This is followed by two tables tracing the scale of the economic enterprises in which people work. Two further tables on manufacturing pinpoint the leading industrial states and show the extent to which state economies depend on foreign trade. A table on bank assets identifies the great financial centers, and the final table covers the extent of our most popular "decentralized" financial institution—individual participation in American corporations through ownership of stock.

323. Industrial and Commercial Firms

In 1980 there were about 2.8 million industrial and commercial firms doing business in the United States. Almost all of these firms were organized as corporations,

but real estate and financial companies not organized as corporations are included in these totals. Over 14 million other businesses, not considered in this table, were organized as proprietorships or partnerships. The gross receipts of the 2.8 million firms included here came to more than five trillion dollars in 1980, about 10 times the amount received by all of the proprietorships and partnerships.

The rankings and the spread of values among the states show that the number of business firms is closely related to the size of the population in a given state. A comparison with state population data presented in chapter 3 indicates some slight variation in this relationship from state to state, but by and large the propensity to form business firms is about the same in all parts of the country.

Table: Business Concerns
Date: 1980
Source: Commerce Department
Description: Total number (in thousands) of industrial and commercial firms including real estate and insurance companies doing business in 1980.
United States total: 2.8 million firms
State median: 40,000 firms

BUSINESS CONCERNS

Rank	State	Firms (in thousands)
1	California	307
2	New York	228
3	Texas	189
4	Illinois	138
5	Pennsylvania	130
6	Florida	129
7	Ohio	120
8	Michigan	97
9	New Jersey	93
10	Massachusetts	74
11	North Carolina	68
12	Georgia	64
13	Missouri	62

Rank	State	Firms (in thousands)
14	Indiana	59
15	Wisconsin	57
16	Minnesota	54
17	Virginia	53
18	Tennessee	51
19	Louisiana	50
20	Washington	47
21	Connecticut	46
22	Colorado	44
23	Oklahoma	43
24	Iowa	42
25	Alabama	40
25	Kentucky	40
25	Maryland	40
28	Oregon	36
29	Kansas	34
30	South Carolina	33
31	Arizona	30
32	Arkansas	29
33	Mississippi	27
34	Nebraska	24
35	Utah	19
36	West Virginia	18
37	Maine	16
37	New Mexico	16
39	Rhode Island	15
40	New Hampshire	14
41	Idaho	13
41	Montana	13
43	Hawaii	11
43	Nevada	11
43	South Dakota	11
46	North Dakota	10
47	Wyoming	9
48	Vermont	8
49	Delaware	6
50	Alaska	5

324. Employment in Large Establishments

A business establishment, as opposed to a business firm, is a specific physical location (plant, office, etc.) at which business is conducted. A given firm may have any number of component establishments. The data in this table therefore serve to indicate the percentage of employees in a given state who do their jobs in a large-scale workplace—a workplace with 500 or more people at work. Many people who spend their time working in smaller establishments are actually employed, of course, by larger firms with well over 500 people on the payroll.

For the nation as a whole, there is a relatively even breakdown of private-sector employees across four levels of workplace scale: establishments with 1–19 workers (24.0% of all employees), 20–99 workers (26.7%), 100–499 workers (24.5%), and 500 or more workers

(24.7%). There is wide variation among the states in the percentage of employees in large establishments. Michigan and Ohio, where 149 of the 280 American motor-vehicle production establishments are (or were) located, head the list. The 16 states with percentages above the national average include the major industrial and mining states in the East and the Midwest (but not New Jersey or Rhode Island) plus Texas, California and Nevada. The 12 states at the bottom of the list include Alaska (where there are no large establishments) and New Mexico along with states in upper New England and all across the northern Plains from the Dakotas across the Rockies to Oregon.

Table: Establishments with 500 or More Employees
Date: 1979
Source: Bureau of Labor Statistics
Description: Percentage of business establishments with 500 or more employees.
United States average: 25%
State median: 19%

ESTABLISHMENTS WITH 500 OR MORE EMPLOYEES

Rank	State	Percent
1	Michigan	37
2	Ohio	32
3	Illinois	31
3	Nevada	31
5	Texas	30
6	Connecticut	29
6	Pennsylvania	29
6	Virginia	29
9	California	28
9	Massachusetts	28
9	New York	28
9	West Virginia	28
13	Tennessee	27
14	Indiana	26
15	South Carolina	25
15	Wisconsin	25
17	Alabama	24
17	Missouri	24
19	Iowa	23
19	North Carolina	23
21	Maryland	22
22	Delaware	21
22	Hawaii	21
24	New Jersey	20
25	Kansas	19
25	Minnesota	19
27	Georgia	18
27	Kentucky	18
27	Washington	18
30	Louisiana	17
30	Mississippi	17
32	Arizona	16
32	Florida	16
34	Oklahoma	15

Rank	State	Percent
35	Rhode Island	13
36	Arkansas	12
37	Colorado	11
37	Nebraska	11
39	Maine	10
39	New Hampshire	10
41	Oregon	9
42	Utah	6
43	Idaho	4
43	New Mexico	4
43	North Dakota	4
43	South Dakota	4
47	Montana	3
47	Vermont	3
47	Wyoming	3
50	Alaska	0

Rank	State	Percent
5	North Dakota	44
5	Vermont	44
7	Idaho	42
8	New Mexico	40
9	Nebraska	35
10	Utah	34
11	Arkansas	32
11	Maine	32
11	Oregon	32
14	Colorado	31
15	Delaware	30
15	Hawaii	30
15	Iowa	30
15	Kansas	30
15	New Hampshire	30
15	Oklahoma	30
15	Rhode Island	30
15	Washington	30
23	Florida	29
23	Mississippi	29
25	Arizona	27
25	Kentucky	27
25	Nevada	27
28	Minnesota	26
28	West Virginia	26
30	Alabama	25
30	Georgia	25
30	Louisiana	25
30	Maryland	25
34	Missouri	24
34	New Jersey	24
34	New York	24
34	South Carolina	24
34	Virginia	24
39	California	23
39	Connecticut	23
39	Wisconsin	23
42	Indiana	22
42	North Carolina	22
42	Tennessee	22
42	Texas	22
46	Massachusetts	21
46	Pennsylvania	21
48	Michigan	19
48	Ohio	19
50	Illinois	17

325. Employment in Small Establishments

Small establishment are defined here as those with fewer than 20 employees. About 24% of all private-sector employees work in such small-scale surroundings. Generally speaking, this table is like the previous table turned upside down. Ten of the 12 states at the top of this list were among the bottom 12 in the previous list, and eight of the 12 states at the bottom here were among the top 12 on that list. Nevada and West Virginia are the only states with very high rankings for employees in large establishments that also have fairly high rankings here (25th and 28th). There are relatively few middle-sized establishments (20–499 employees) in these states. The tendency is for people to work either in the big enterprises—casinos/hotels and mines, respectively—or in small-scale establishments.

Table: Establishments with Fewer than 20 Employees
Date: 1979
Source: Bureau of Labor Statistics
Description: Percentage of business establishments with fewer than 20 employees.
United States average: 24%
State median: 27%

ESTABLISHMENTS WITH FEWER THAN 20 EMPLOYEES

Rank	State	Percent
1	Montana	48
2	Alaska	45
2	South Dakota	45
2	Wyoming	45

326. Manufacturing Output

This table provides a portrait of the "industrial states" of America, using the gross value of manufacturers' shipments as a measure. Many readers will be surprised to find that California and Texas are far ahead of the other states in their level of manufacturing output. The states that are most often immediately identified as industrial fall in positions three through eight. California and Texas, the two new production centers in the West, together create about as much manufacturing value as the three older centers of Illinois, Ohio and New York.

Oil is the major product manufactured (i.e., refined) in Texas, and the high value of oil products and chemical products accounts for the strong showing of Louisiana on this list. Although Louisiana ranks only 19th in total number of business firms, it occupies rank 11 here. Conversely, the state of Missouri is found at rank 32 here despite the fact that it ranks 13th in number of business firms. Many of the states near the bottom here have a predominantly rural, nonmanufacturing orientation. All of them have relatively small populations.

Table: Value of Manufacturers' Shipments
Date: 1980
Source: Department of Commerce
Description: Value of manufacturers' shipments (in billions of dollars).
United States total: $1.8 trillion
State median: $23 billion

VALUE OF MANUFACTURERS' SHIPMENTS

Rank	State	Value (in billions)
1	California	$177
2	Texas	160
3	Illinois	120
4	Ohio	114
5	New York	112
6	Pennsylvania	108
7	Michigan	93
8	New Jersey	69
9	Indiana	63
10	North Carolina	56
11	Louisiana	51
12	Wisconsin	50
13	Massachusetts	44
14	Georgia	43
15	Tennessee	36
15	Washington	36
17	Florida	33
17	Minnesota	33
17	Virginia	33
20	Iowa	31
21	Alabama	29
21	Kentucky	29
23	Connecticut	28
24	South Carolina	25
25	Kansas	24
26	Oklahoma	22
27	Maryland	20
28	Oregon	19
29	Arkansas	16
29	Colorado	16
29	Mississippi	16
32	Missouri	14
32	Nebraska	14

Rank	State	Value (in billions)
34	Arizona	$11
34	West Virginia	11
36	Utah	9
37	Delaware	8
37	Maine	8
37	Rhode Island	8
40	New Hampshire	7
41	Idaho	5
41	Montana	5
43	Hawaii	3
43	New Mexico	3
43	South Dakota	3
43	Vermont	3
43	Wyoming	3
48	Alaska	2
48	North Dakota	2
50	Nevada	1

327. Manufacturing Exports

Exported goods account for about 14% of all manufacturing activity in the United States, whether this is measured by the value of goods that are exported or by the number of jobs supported by foreign trade. About 4.8 million jobs can be directly traced to international trade in manufactured goods. These figures tend to underestimate the true contribution of foreign trade, since they do not include the value of or the employment attached to goods initially purchased by domestic firms that are ultimately included in goods that are exported.

The rankings below are in terms of value. Percentages of employment are roughly parallel to percentages of value. Near the top of the table value percentages generally exceed employment percentages, indicating that the export industries are relatively capital intensive. The reverse is true to some extent in the lower part of the table. States found here do not export very much and the goods that they do manage to export are relatively labor-intensive products.

Alaska and Washington are the clear leaders in this table, with about one-third of their manufacturing output bound for points beyond the borders, especially Canada. Arizona maintains a lively trade with Mexico (but neighboring New Mexico, rank 45, does not). Exports of West Virginia coal are a vital aspect of its economy. Leaving aside these two most export-oriented states and the states of Hawaii and Wyoming, where there is little manufacturing of any kind and almost all of the output is consumed domestically, the manufacturing export sector comes to between 9% and 22% of manufacturing activity in the main sequence of 46 states.

Table: Shipments Related to Manufactured Exports
Date: 1980
Source: Department of Commerce
Description: Percentage of the value of manufacturing shipments and percentage of manufacturing employment related to manufactured exports.
United States average: 14.1% shipments; 13.7% employment
State median: 13.4% shipments; 12.8% employment

SHIPMENTS RELATED TO MANUFACTURED EXPORTS

Rank	State	Percent of value of manufacturing shipments	Percent of manufacturing employment
1	Alaska	36.9	34.7
2	Washington	29.6	24.0
3	Arizona	21.8	21.3
4	West Virginia	19.2	15.5
5	Connecticut	17.3	15.9
6	Idaho	17.2	13.2
7	South Carolina	17.0	13.8
8	Massachusetts	16.7	15.0
9	Oregon	16.1	15.4
9	Rhode Island	16.1	16.3
11	Ohio	15.9	15.9
12	Vermont	15.4	14.6
13	Michigan	15.3	13.5
14	Florida	15.1	14.7
15	Virginia	14.9	12.0
16	New Hampshire	14.5	14.5
16	Tennessee	14.5	11.4
18	Indiana	14.3	13.9
19	California	14.2	15.1
20	Illinois	14.1	13.8
21	Nevada	13.8	11.1
21	North Carolina	13.8	11.7
21	Pennsylvania	13.8	13.7
24	Alabama	13.7	11.4
25	New York	13.5	12.2
26	Arkansas	13.4	10.0
27	Kentucky	13.3	11.4
28	Utah	13.1	10.0
29	Iowa	13.0	13.1
30	Louisiana	12.9	11.7
31	Wisconsin	12.6	14.0
32	Texas	12.3	13.6
33	New Jersey	12.2	12.7
34	Minnesota	12.0	13.1
35	Maryland	11.8	11.4
35	Montana	11.8	6.6
37	Mississippi	11.6	8.9
37	Missouri	11.6	11.3
39	Georgia	11.5	12.3
40	Oklahoma	11.1	12.7
41	Colorado	10.9	12.9
42	Kansas	10.1	12.5
42	North Dakota	10.1	10.8
44	Maine	10.0	8.8
45	New Mexico	9.7	6.0
46	Nebraska	9.5	9.1
47	Delaware	9.3	13.6
48	South Dakota	9.1	8.5
49	Hawaii	5.0	4.9
50	Wyoming	4.4	5.8

328. Business Failures

For the year 1980, Dun & Bradstreet recorded 11,742 business failures among some 2.8 million enterprises listed in their *Reference Book*. This was the highest total of failures since 1967, but far below the record of 31,822 in 1932. The failure rate of 42 per 10,000 listed companies was the highest since 1975, but still far below the record of 154 per 10,000 companies, again in 1932. Increasing business failure rates indicate an economic recession, when declining activity brings pressure to bear on weak firms. The total liabilities of failing companies—the amount owed to creditors—came to over $4.6 billion in 1980, an all-time record.

The business failure rate in Washington was exceptionally high. The rate in neighboring Oregon was twice the national average. Very low failure rates were recorded among the businesses of Wyoming, Arizona, Vermont and New Hampshire. Failure rates provide some sense of the severity of the recession in various areas, but there are enough compounding factors that a cautious interpretation along these lines is called for. The tendency of businesses in certain areas to take more risks or to operate with narrower margins of financial leeway is one such factor. Perhaps the business style in the Pacific Northwest is simply more wide open than the style in upper New England.

Table: Business Failures
Date: 1980
Source: *Dun & Bradstreet Business Failure Record*
Description: Business failures per 10,000 listed concerns.
United States average: 42 per 10,000 listed concerns
State median: 39 per 10,000 listed concerns

BUSINESS FAILURES

Rank	State	Rate per 10,000 listed concerns
1	Washington	177.8
2	Tennessee	101.1

Rank	State	Rate per 10,000 listed concerns
3	Oregon	85.9
4	Montana	79.3
5	Michigan	76.3
6	South Dakota	74.5
7	California	70.0
7	North Dakota	70.0
9	Oklahoma	69.0
10	Minnesota	59.7
11	Illinois	58.0
12	Nebraska	57.5
12	Texas	57.5
14	New Jersey	53.6
15	Virginia	52.3
16	Kansas	51.8
17	Pennsylvania	50.2
18	Idaho	49.5
19	Kentucky	46.3
20	Georgia	45.7
21	Maine	45.6
22	Alabama	45.2
23	Ohio	44.4
24	Indiana	43.5
25	Nevada	40.5
26	Wisconsin	39.1
27	Arkansas	38.8
27	Mississippi	38.8
29	Maryland	37.2
29	New Mexico	37.2
31	Massachusetts	37.0
32	Delaware	36.4
33	North Carolina	34.2
34	Colorado	33.0
35	Louisiana	31.9
36	Connecticut	29.5
36	Iowa	29.5
38	New York	28.8
39	West Virginia	24.8
40	Florida	24.7
41	Missouri	22.1
42	Utah	15.7
43	Connecticut	13.7
44	New Hampshire	11.9
45	Vermont	7.1
46	Arizona	6.3
47	Wyoming	2.6
	South Carolina	Not available
	Hawaii	Not available
	Alaska	Not available

329. Bank Assets

Only 353 of the 15.039 banks in the United States are located in the state of New York, but they control about one-quarter of all banking assets in the country. California, home of the richest individual bank, the Bank of America, is the West Coast banking center. Illinois and Texas control the finances in the center of the country, and Pennsylvania is a secondary center in the East. Bank assets in these five top states are greater than those in all of the other 45 states combined.

Table: Bank Assets
Date: 1982
Source: *Polk's World Bank Directory*
Description: Total assets (in billions of dollars) of banks.
United States total: $2.26 trillion
State median: $20 billion

BANK ASSETS

Rank	State	Assets (in billions)
1	New York	$588
2	California	269
3	Illinois	159
4	Texas	151
5	Pennsylvania	115
6	Massachusetts	66
7	Ohio	60
8	Michigan	59
9	Florida	54
10	New Jersey	41
11	Missouri	38
12	Minnesota	37
13	Indiana	36
14	Connecticut	32
15	Louisiana	31
15	Washington	31
17	North Carolina	29
17	Wisconsin	29
19	Oklahoma	28
19	Virginia	28
21	Georgia	27
21	Tennessee	27
23	Iowa	24
24	Kentucky	22
25	Maryland	20
26	Alabama	19
27	Colorado	18
27	Kansas	18
29	Arizona	16
30	Oregon	14
31	Arkansas	13
31	Mississippi	13
31	Nebraska	13
34	West Virginia	12
35	Rhode Island	10
36	South Carolina	9
37	South Dakota	8
38	New Hampshire	7
38	New Mexico	7
38	Utah	7
41	Delaware	6
41	Hawaii	6

Rank	State	Assets (in billions)
41	Iowa	6
41	Maine	6
41	Montana	6
41	North Dakota	6
47	Nevada	4
47	Vermont	4
47	Wyoming	4
50	Alaska	3

330. Stock Ownership

In mid-1981 there were 32.2 million individuals with funds invested in shares of American corporations listed on the major exchanges—including the over-the-counter market—or invested in shares of stock mutual funds. The number of shareholders increased by two million from 1980 to 1981, when the group of shareholders made up over 14% of the general population. The distribution of shares among individuals is, of course, highly uneven. A very small fraction of all shareowners hold the bulk of all common stock. The median household income of shareholders was $29,200, well above the national median income of $17,700. About 58% of shareholders also hold down white-collar jobs, while 11% hold blue-collar jobs and 31% are not employed (including homemakers, retired persons, etc. along with independently wealthy coupon-clippers). Although about 25% of the population lives in nonmetropolitan areas, only 16.5% of shareholders are found outside the SMSAs.

The highest levels of stock ownership are found in states along the East Coast, from Maryland to Massachusetts; on the West Coast, in California and Washington; in the interior, in Illinois, Colorado and Michigan; and in the outlying states of Alaska and Hawaii. Virginia and Florida are the only states in the South with relatively high shareholder levels. Wyoming occupies a similar distinctive position among its neighbors.

Table: Stock Ownership
Date: 1981
Source: New York Stock Exchange
Description: Percentage of the total state population owning stock.
United States average: 14.4%

State median: 13.3%

STOCK OWNERSHIP

Rank	State	Percent
1	Connecticut	20.0
2	New York	19.5
3	Alaska	19.1
4	Hawaii	18.1
5	Massachusetts	17.6
6	Illinois	17.1
7	California	17.0
8	New Jersey	16.9
9	Maryland	15.5
10	Colorado	15.4
11	Michigan	15.2
12	Delaware	15.1
13	Washington	15.0
14	Rhode Island	14.8
14	Wyoming	14.8
16	Nevada	14.6
17	Ohio	14.2
18	Florida	13.9
18	Virginia	13.9
20	Arizona	13.8
20	Pennsylvania	13.8
22	Wyoming	13.7
23	Minnesota	13.5
23	New Hampshire	13.5
25	Nebraska	13.3
25	Texas	13.3
27	Kansas	13.1
28	Missouri	12.7
29	Indiana	12.6
29	Iowa	12.6
29	Oregon	12.6
29	Utah	12.6
33	Vermont	12.2
34	New Mexico	11.8
35	Oklahoma	11.5
36	Maine	11.4
37	North Carolina	11.3
38	Georgia	11.1
39	North Dakota	11.0
40	Montana	10.9
41	West Virginia	10.8
42	Idaho	10.7
43	Louisiana	10.5
44	South Dakota	10.3
45	Tennessee	10.1
46	South Carolina	9.5
47	Kentucky	8.9
48	Alabama	8.8
48	Arkansas	8.8
50	Mississippi	7.2

STATE SUMMARIES

Alabama

Located smack-dab in the heart of Dixie, Alabama is a medium-sized state by national standards, with a total population and a population density also close to national median levels. The topography of the state is diverse, ranging from the Appalachian highlands along the northern border with Tennessee to the lowlands along Mobile Bay where a narrow corridor of Alabama territory touches the Gulf of Mexico. The large central region of the state is a fertile coastal plain that once was the most productive cotton-growing area in the nation. The economy of Alabama today is centered on manufacturing, as shown by its second place ranking in proportion of blue-collar jobs among all jobs. The Birmingham metropolitan area, where 22% of the state population resides, is the largest iron- and steel-producing center in the South. This industrial focus helps to explain why Alabama had one of the highest unemployment rates during the most recent recession.

Income levels are generally low. Nearly 15% of all families are poor by federal standards. State tax revenue is low and so is state spending on social services, especially in the area of education. High spending on health programs is mainly a reflection of state action in passing on federal health dollars to the poor. The rate of recent population increase has been close to the national average, but a low ranking with respect to residents born out of state shows that Alabama has been fairly isolated in recent decades. Alabamians are active in religious affairs but inactive as voters. They do not appear to consume much alcohol and they perpetrate few violent crimes.

Alcohol consumption: 45
Area: 29
Church adherents: 14
College graduates: 45
Crime, property: 37
Crime, violent: 25
Education, public
school expenditures: 50
Elderly, % in
total pop: 23
Health expenditures,
state and local: 5
Income, personal: 47
Labor, blue-collar: 2
Manufacturing output: 21
Mobility, interstate: 45
Population: 22

Population change: 29
Population density: 26
Poverty, % of people
living in: 5
Tax burden, state: 42

Unemployment: 3
Voter turnout as % of
voting age pop.: 40
Welfare, state and
local expenditures: 30

Alaska

The state of Alaska is exceptional in almost every way. It is extremely large, better than twice the size of Texas, but it has the smallest state population in the nation. Some 44% of all Alaskans live in the Anchorage metropolitan area on the southern coast of the main body of the state. Other residents are mostly found in the southeastern corridor where Juneau, the state capital, is located. The main body of Alaska is a virtually uninhabited, permanently frozen wasteland. Most of the territory of our "last frontier" is owned by the federal government. Alaskan energy resources as well as the inspirational and strategic value of its location are of national importance.

Except for Nevada, Alaska has the largest percentage of residents born out of state. Alaskans are on the average exceptionally young and very well educated. Their dollar incomes are by far the highest in the nation, but much of this advantage is immediately lost to the extremely high prices they must pay for essential commodities. They may not attend church regularly and their rate of alcohol consumption may be well above the national norm, but these indicators largely reflect the youth of our vigorous Alaskans. If the age distribution of the state population moves closer to the national standard in years to come, the extreme values in these cultural dimensions will also be smoothed out. The revenues of the state government are astronomical thanks to special income from the development of natural resources, especially oil. Chronic budget surpluses allow high rates of spending for health, education and welfare, as well as the direct payment of special bonuses to each citizen—a feature for which the state has become noted.

Alcohol consumption: 3
Area: 1
Church adherents: 49
College graduates: 2
Crime, property: 14
Crime, violent: 20
Education, public
  school expenditures: 1
Elderly, % in
  total pop.: 50
Health expenditures,
  state and local: 16
Income, personal: 1
Labor, blue-collar: 40

Manufacturing output: 48
Mobility, interstate: 2
Population: 50
Population change: 6
Population density: 50
Poverty, % of people
  living in: 35
Tax burden, state: 1
Unemployment: 22
Voter turnout as % of
  voting age pop.: 16
Welfare, state and
  local expenditures: 5

Population: 29
Population change: 2
Population density: 40
Poverty, % of people
  living in: 24
Tax burden, state: 23

Unemployment: 20
Voter turnout as % of
  voting age pop.: 45
Welfare, state and
  local expenditures: 50

Arizona

Arizona, one of the largest states in the country, is a land of deserts, bluffs, mesas and rugged mountains. The Grand Canyon is located in the northwestern part of the state, while the Petrified Forest National Park is found in the northeast, close to the Painted Desert and the large Navajo and Hopi reservations. The climate is warm and dry, making the state a popular winter resort and an attractive retirement home for many Americans. Although overall population density is rather low, the rate of increase was extremely high during the 1970s due to massive migration from other parts of the country. Only about two of every five Arizonans were born in the state. There are two major urban centers in southern Arizona—the metropolitan Phoenix area, with 55% of state population, and the Tucson area, with 20%.

The economy of the state centers on services and commerce. Manufacturing output is still low, although many new manufacturing operations have settled in the state in recent years. White-collar jobs are predominant. The state raises an average amount of tax revenue, but spending for all social services is low. The individualistic ethos of Arizona is clearly reflected in its ranking as the nation's least generous provider of welfare services. Voter turnout rates are among the lowest in the nation. A further indicator of the tendency of Arizonans to take things into their own hands is the high rate of property and violent crime.

Alcohol consumption: 9
Area: 6
Church adherents: 42
College graduates: 19
Crime, property: 2
Crime, violent: 8
Education, public
  school expenditures: 39

Elderly, % in
  total pop: 23
Health expenditures
  state and local: 34
Income, personal: 31
Labor, blue-collar: 38
Manufacturing output: 34
Mobility, interstate: 3

Arkansas

The medium-sized state of Arkansas lies just west of the Mississippi River, bordered by Missouri to the north and louisiana to the south. Much of the state consists of wooded hill country, crisscrossed by many rivers and streams. Waterborne traffic from the gulf of Mexico travels up to Little Rock via the Mississippi and the Arkansas rivers.

The population of the state is not particularly large or densely concentrated, but is scattered broadly across the small towns and rural areas of the state. The largest metropolitan area is the one that surrounds Little Rock, the capital; but only 17% of the population lives here. Population increase has recently been above the national norm and the percentage of residents born out of state is close to the national median. The average age of the Arkansas population is exceeded only in Florida, a special case. No other state has a smaller percentage of college graduates. Only one of every 10 residents over age 25 has completed college.

Although Arkansas calls itself The Land of Opportunity, average income is quite low and the percentage of poor families is very high. Manufacturing, including mining and timber production, is the mainstay of the economy. Blue-collar jobs are predominant. The state raises relatively little revenue and does not spend much on services for its citizens, particularly in the area of education. Church affiliation is fairly extensive and rate of crime, especially property crime, is rather low. Arkansans consume less alcohol per capita than the residents of any other state except Utah.

Alcohol consumption: 49
Area: 27
Church adherents: 16
College graduates: 50
Crime, property: 44
Crime, violent: 34
Education, public
  school expenditures: 45
Elderly, % in
  total pop.: 2
Health expenditures,
  state and local: 33
Income, personal: 48
Labor, blue-collar: 10

Manufacturing output: 29
Mobility, interstate: 23
Population: 33
Population change: 17
Population density: 35
Poverty, % of people
  living in: 4
Tax burden, state: 44
Unemployment: 19
Voter turnout as % of
  voting age pop.: 34
Welfare, state and
  local expenditures: 31

California

The third largest state in the nation, after Alaska and Texas, California encompasses several different climates and environments. The much renowned scenic coastline is over 1,200 miles long. The vast Sierra Nevada range forms the border with Nevada and provides the setting for such attractions as the Yosemite and Sequoia national parks. The central San Joaquin Valley—not to be confused with the San Fernando Valley near Los Angeles, habitat of the "Valley Girls"—is the most productive agricultural area in the world. The Mojave Desert is the dominant topographical feature in the south. The cool, moist, seasonal climate of San Francisco and the north is quite different from the dry and year-round warmth of Los Angeles, San Diego and the sunny, smoggy south.

The population of California is about the same size as the entire population of Canada. One American in 10 lives in the Golden State. Although the rapid growth rate of the state in the 1950s and 1960s has slowed in recent years, thousands of Americans and Mexicans still move to California every year. The proportion of college graduates is well above average and white-collar jobs are predominant in the labor force. The state ranks number one in manufacturing output and number four in average personal income. California government, former governor Ronald Reagan's best efforts notwithstanding, is big government. The state generates surging streams of tax revenue and has high spending levels despite repeated efforts to control its budget by executive action and popular referendum. Voter turnout, meanwhile, is subnormal. Although new religious groups often originate in freewheeling California, ties with established churches are not especially important. As our leading wine-producing state, California is also among the leaders in alcohol consumption. High crime rates are an unfortunate complement of the good life on the West Coast.

Alcohol consumption: 5	Manufacturing output: 1
Area: 3	Mobility, interstate: 15
Church adherents: 46	Population: 1
College graduates: 7	Population change: 18
Crime, property: 5	Population density: 14
Crime, violent: 4	Poverty, % of people
Education, public	living in: 25
school expenditures: 15	Tax burden, state: 8
Elderly, % in	Unemployment: 16
total pop.: 34	Voter turnout as % of
Health expenditures,	voting age pop.: 38
state and local: 14	Welfare, state and
Income, personal: 4	local expenditures: 6
Labor, blue-collar: 40	

Colorado

The Rocky Mountains rise out of the Great Plains in central Colorado. The Continental Divide—a line marking the place from which all rivers flow either east or west—slices through the center of the state. Colorado is large, ranking eighth in area, while overall population density is still rather low. The population picture has been changing in recent decades. The 31% growth rate during the 1970s was among the highest in the nation. The state is one of only seven in which residents born out of state are in the majority. Denver is the capital and the Denver-Boulder metropolitan area is the home of 56% of all Coloradoans. The population is young and very well educated. The percentage of college graduates among adults (23%) is the highest in the nation.

Mineral resources and agricultural land in the eastern part of the state were the original basis of the economy. Tourism, services and high-technology industries have now become more important. The percentage of blue-collar workers is already low and it is declining. Income levels, however, are relatively high. State government revenue flows in at a low to moderate level and government services in areas other than education are not heavily funded. Voter participation is only about average, and church participation is well below average, as is the case in many western states. Alcohol consumption and property crime both run at high levels, with above normal rates of violent crime as well.

Alcohol consumption: 6	Manufacturing output: 29
Area: 8	Mobility, interstate: 6
Church adherents: 44	Population: 28
College graduates: 1	Population change: 8
Crime, property: 6	Population density: 38
Crime, violent: 16	Poverty, % of people
Education, public	living in: 40
school expenditures: 12	Tax burden, state: 39
Elderly, % in	Unemployment: 28
total pop.: 45	Voter turnout as % of
Health expenditures,	voting age pop.: 24
state and local: 26	Welfare, state and
Income, personal: 11	local expenditures: 33
Labor, blue-collar: 42	

Connecticut

The state of Connecticut is small and heavily settled. Much of the state consists of wooded areas that have grown back over the cleared farmland of pre-Civil War days. There are many small towns that preserve classic New England style, but there are also several old and gritty industrial centers. The southern part of the state includes many of the more exclusive suburbs of New York City. This is the main reason why the average income level is the highest in the nation except for Alaska; although state tax rates are fairly low, this wealth still generates an above average level of government revenue. Spending for education and welfare is relatively high, but Connecticut is one of only 10 states where per capita health spending is under $100. Voter participation is high and so is church participation, boosted by a large Catholic segment in the general population. Alcohol consumption and crime rates are moderate.

Alcohol consumption: 29	Manufacturing output: 23
Area: 48	Mobility, interstate: 20
Church adherents: 9	Population: 25
College graduates: 3	Population change: 45
Crime, property: 19	Population density: 4
Crime, violent: 27	Poverty, % of people
Education, public	living in: 46
school expenditures: 11	Tax burden, state: 17
Elderly, % in	Unemployment: 42
total pop.: 18	Voter turnout as % of
Health expenditures,	voting age pop.: 11
state and local: 41	Welfare, state and
Income, personal: 2	local expenditures: 13
Labor, blue-collar: 33	

Delaware

Delaware, the first state to ratify the Constitution in 1787, lies on the eastern side of the peninsula separating Delaware Bay and Chesapeake Bay. Except for a few hills in the northwestern corner, the state lies on a coastal plain with elevations not much above sea level. Dover is the capital and Wilmington is the largest city. The state has never had a major port city on Delaware Bay, because Philadelphia, located further north on the Delaware River, has been the principal seaport on this body of water since colonial times. The total area of just over 2,000 square miles makes Delaware the second tiniest state after Rhode Island. The state population of about 600,000 is also relatively small; more people than this live in the city of Milwaukee and three times as many people live in the city of Philadelphia. Overall density of settlement is nevertheless high for a state.

The average income in Delaware is comfortably above the national norm. This, in part, is related to the fact that the state serves as residential base for wealthy families with connections to the major East Coast cities. Delaware is also the legal headquarters of over 70,000 corporations that enjoy the convenience of its laws of incorporation. State government enjoys, in turn, a healthy stream of revenue. But education is the only area in which state

social spending reflects this level of public wealth. Aside from its paper transactions, Delaware economy is noted as a center of chemical production. Among the other indicators tabulated here, the high level of property crime and a sub-par ranking for religious participation are the most notable.

Alcohol consumption: 18	Manufacturing output: 37
Area: 49	Mobility, interstate: 12
Church adherents: 39	Population: 47
College graduates: 21	Population change: 31
Crime, property: 8	Population density: 7
Crime, violent: 21	Poverty, % of people
Education, public	living in: 22
school expenditures: 8	Tax burden, state: 4
Elderly, % in	Unemployment: 40
total pop.: 35	Voter turnout as % of
Health expenditures,	voting age pop.: 27
state and local: 46	Welfare, state and
Income, personal: 13	local expenditures: 24
Labor, blue-collar: 33	

Florida

The Sunshine State is a broad, flat peninsula protruding from the southeastern corner of the United States. Florida boasts over 1,300 miles of Atlantic and Gulf coastline and a subtropical climate that many people find most attractive. The Everglades wilderness and the Florida Keys—a chain of islands curling back into the gulf—are the most notable topographical features. The beaches and the warm weather are the basis of Florida's prosperity. The capital city is Tallahassee, located in the thin northern strip of land that binds the state to Georgia. Jacksonville is the largest city, but the big metropolitan areas are located at Miami in the southeast and Tampa-St. Petersburg on the western coast.

The population of Florida is just under 10 million, the seventh largest state population. Average density of settlement is high and most settlements are close to the Atlantic coast. With a 43% growth rate during the 1970s, third highest in the country, Florida was the only state east of the Mississippi among the leaders in this area. The proportion of residents born out of state is also quite high. A single ranking accounts for much of what is distinctive about the state population statistics—its number one ranking in percentage of residents aged 65 and over. The flow of retired persons to Florida, particularly from the Northeast, has been high for decades. The past 15 years have also witnessed increasing migration to Florida from the Caribbean and Central America. The language of the European nation that first discovered and conquered

Florida, the language of Spain, has returned with the new migrants.

High rates of violent and property crime reflect an unfortunate mix of wealth and poverty in the state, which disappears in the statistics by averaging out to mid-range values in the income and poverty variables. State government revenue is fairly low and state welfare spending is very low, considering that the proportion of poor families is above the national norm. Voter participation and religious participation are also below par.

Alcohol consumption: 10
Area: 22
Church adherents: 43
College graduates: 34
Crime, property: 3
Crime, violent: 2
Education, public
  school expenditures: 22
Elderly, % in
  total pop.: 1
Health expenditures,
  state and local: 13
Income, personal: 26
Labor, blue-collar: 32

Manufacturing output: 17
Mobility, interstate: 5
Population: 7
Population change: 3
Population density: 11
Poverty, % of people
  living in: 19
Tax burden, state: 41
Unemployment: 24
Voter turnout as % of
  voting age pop.: 38
Welfare, state and
  local expenditures: 49

Georgia

Georgia ranks 21st in total area, but it is the largest state east of the Mississippi River. Atlanta is the capital city and the largest metropolitan area, with 37% of state population. Population growth was relatively high during the 1970s, the decade in which former Georgia governor Jimmy Carter went on to become President. This was also the decade in which Atlanta consolidated its position as the transportation hub and the business center of the South. Industrial activity also increased markedly. Manufacturing output now ranks at about the level that would be expected on the basis of population. The balance between blue-collar and white-collar work is now close to the national norm. Unemployment was not severe during the last recession, since the new industries that have come to Georgia were not hit as hard as the steel industry and automobile manufacturing. In any event, the average income level in this largely nonunion state is rather low and the percentage of poor families is high. State tax receipts are on the low side and so are levels of spending for education and welfare. Health spending, on the other hand, aided by federal contributions, is the highest in the nation. Georgia voters had the second lowest turnout rate in the country for the 1980 election in which Ronald Reagan trounced Carter. Crime rates are somewhat above average and church activity is at a lower level than in most southern states.

Alcohol consumption: 33
Area: 21
Church adherents: 31
College graduates: 27
Crime, property: 21
Crime, violent: 13
Education, public
  school expenditures: 44
Elderly, % in
  total pop.: 40
Health expenditures,
  state and local: 1
Income, personal: 37
Labor, blue-collar: 15

Manufacturing output: 14
Mobility, interstate: 27
Population: 13
Population change: 16
Population density: 22
Poverty, % of people
  living in: 8
Tax burden, state: 37
Unemployment: 38
Voter turnout as % of
  voting age pop.: 49
Welfare, state and
  local expenditures: 39

Hawaii

The state of Hawaii comprises a chain of islands based on ancient undersea volcanos, some still mildly active, that poke above the surface near the center of the northern Pacific Ocean. The closely grouped main islands are about 2,400 miles from San Francisco. The entire chain stretches some 1,500 miles further west. The climate of Hawaii is just about perfect. This is the basis of the tourist industry that has brought prosperity to the islands. Hawaii also functions as the command center of American military operations in the Pacific, just as it did in 1941 when the Japanese raid on Pearl Harbor touched off the new phase of World War II that ended at Hiroshima and Nagasaki. Hawaii entered the Union in 1959 as the 50th state. The capital of Hawaii is Honolulu, located on the island of Oahu where 70% of the state population resides.

Total land area is small, about the size of Connecticut and Rhode Island combined. Population density is fairly high and the rate of growth during the 1970s was rapid. Some growth has come in the form of migration from the U.S. mainland and from elsewhere in the Pacific, but the birth rate among Hawaiians is also very high. This also shows up in the low representation of the elderly in the population. Hawaiians are more likely to have completed college than other Americans and the average income level is high. There are few blue-collar jobs, as might be expected in an economy centered on spending for national defense and tourist services. The unemployment rate was the lowest in the nation during the recent recession. The state extracts a high level of tax revenue from citizens and enterprises, but spending in areas other than welfare is only about average. There is not much religious participation in Hawaii and there is a curious disproportion in the rankings for the two types of crime considered here. Violent crime is infrequent, but the appropriation of property belonging to others runs at a very high rate.

Alcohol consumption: 11	Manufacturing output: 43
Area: 47	Mobility, interstate: 30
Church adherents: 47	Population: 39
College graduates: 4	Population change: 12
Crime, property: 4	Population density: 15
Crime, violent: 38	Poverty, % of people
Education, public	living in: 32
school expenditures: 27	Tax burden, state: 3
Elderly, % in	Unemployment: 50
total pop.: 47	Voter turnout as % of
Health expenditures,	voting age pop.: 46
state and local: 21	Welfare, state and
Income, personal: 14	local expenditures: 9
Labor, blue-collar: 49	

Idaho

Idaho is a northwestern state of rugged mountain beauty. The economy is centered on agricultural production—especially the potato crop—and mining activity. Fewer than one million people occupy an area of over 83,000 square miles. Boise is the state capital and the largest urban area, with a population of just 102,000. State population increase was rapid during the 1970s, with both migration and high birth rates contributing to growth. Almost half of all residents were born out of state. Manufacturing output is relatively low, as is the average income level. Voters are among the most active in the country; only Minnesota had a higher turnout in 1980. State revenue per capita and social spending levels are all subpar. Crime rates are fairly low.

Alcohol consumption: 30	Manufacturing output: 41
Area: 13	Mobility, interstate: 8
Church adherents: 27	Population: 41
College graduates: 22	Population change: 6
Crime, property: 38	Population density: 43
Crime, violent: 35	Poverty, % of people
Education, public	living in: 16
school expenditures: 42	Tax burden, state: 34
Elderly, % in	Unemployment: 21
total pop.: 36	Voter turnout as % of
Health expenditures,	voting age pop.: 2
state and local: 30	Welfare, state and
Income, personal: 36	local expenditures: 42
Labor, blue-collar: 22	

Illinois

The greater part of Illinois consists of rolling farm country. In the northeastern corner by the shore of Lake Michigan sits Chicago, the great midwestern metropolis which has historically been the gateway to the world for the products of the vast agricultural empire in the heart of America. Over 60% of the population of Illinois lives in the vicinity of Chicago, which is a great manufacturing center and generator of paperwork as well as a great commercial center. Illinois ranks fifth in population among the states, though there was very little growth during the 1970s. The income level is high on the average, but the state was also subject to extensive unemployment during the recession. The general decline of basic industries that carried the state to the number three rank in manufacturing output is a major source of employment problems. Rankings for state government revenue and spending, religious participation, voting and crime rates all fall fairly close to national norms. If the state could be separated into Chicago and the downstate regions, some of these average rankings would be more extreme for both regions. The strong representation of Catholics in Chicago, for example, balances the high rates of church participation in the metropolis against lower rates characteristic of Protestant downstate areas.

Alcohol consumption: 19	Manufacturing output: 3
Area: 24	Mobility, interstate: 37
Church adherents: 17	Population: 5
College graduates: 35	Population change: 43
Crime, property: 29	Population density: 10
Crime, violent: 18	Poverty, % of people
Education, public	living in: 25
school expenditures: 21	Tax burden, state: 28
Elderly, % in	Unemployment: 7
total pop.: 28	Voter turnout as % of
Health expenditures,	voting age pop.: 19
state and local: 40	Welfare, state and
Income, personal: 6	local expenditures: 12
Labor, blue-collar: 20	

Indiana

Indiana, the Hoosier State, lies immediately to the east of Illinois. Along the short stretch of Lake Michigan in the northwest corner of the state are a number of industrial towns belonging to the Chicago metropolitan area. Further south, to the east of the Wabash River, there is a broad band of rich farmland dotted with towns, giving way to hill country in the area close to the Ohio River, the southern border with Kentucky. The largest metropolitan area is at Indianapolis, the state capital, where 21% of all Hoosiers make their homes. Indiana has one of the larger state populations, but growth has been slow in recent years. The proportion of elderly residents is slightly below average, while the percentage of college graduates is well below average.

The economy involves a mixture of industry and

agriculture. Manufacturing output is strong, average income is fairly high and white-collar and farm jobs are emphasized. The high ranking for unemployment illustrates once again the crisis conditions prevailing in certain sectors, such as observed in Illinois. State government in Indiana operates at a low level of revenue and spending. Voter participation is at about the same level as Illinois and the rates of violent crime, alcohol consumption and religious participation are about at the level that would be observed in Illinois if Chicago were excluded.

Alcohol consumption: 43	Manufacturing output: 9
Area: 38	Mobility, interstate: 28
Church adherents: 32	Population: 12
College graduates: 46	Population change: 35
Crime, property: 34	Population density: 13
Crime, violent: 31	Poverty, % of people
Education, public	living in: 41
school expenditures: 41	Tax burden, state: 43
Elderly, % in	Unemployment: 6
total pop.: 30	Voter turnout as % of
Health expenditures,	voting age pop.: 20
state and local: 25	Welfare, state and
Income, personal: 32	local expenditures: 44
Labor, blue-collar: 8	

Iowa

The geographical character of Iowa is almost uniform throughout the state—a rolling plain covered with farms as far as the eye can see. Located in the middle of the nation, Iowa is also in the middle as regards area and population. Iowa farms are highly productive, specializing in hogs and corn. About eight of every 10 jobs in Iowa depend on agriculture, if jobs in the production of farm equipment and farm services are added in. The population is evenly distributed across the land. Des Moines is the capital and the largest metropolitan area, but only 12% of the population lives there. The rate of population growth was low during the 1970s and a high proportion of Iowans are Iowa natives. The elderly are well represented in the population, which partly accounts for the fact that the present percentage of college graduates is not high.

The income level is just above the national average and there is little poverty. State government raises only an average amount of revenue per capita. Levels of social-services spending rank at somewhat higher positions. Given the low poverty rate, the level of welfare spending seems remarkably high. Iowa voters participate actively in the political process, a fact noted every four years when the early primary elections here and in New Hampshire kick off the presidential political season. The road to power for Jimmy Carter began with a strong showing in

the 1976 Democratic primary in Iowa. Religious participation is strong, hard liquor is not very popular, and the benefits of relatively low crime rates are enjoyed by the citizens.

Alcohol consumption: 35	Manufacturing output: 20
Area: 25	Mobility, interstate: 41
Church adherents: 10	Population: 27
College graduates: 38	Population change: 42
Crime, property: 35	Population density: 32
Crime, violent: 43	Poverty, % of people
Education, public	living in: 45
school expenditures: 16	Tax burden, state: 22
Elderly, % in	Unemployment: 30
total pop.: 4	Voter turnout as % of
Health expenditures,	voting age pop.: 9
state and local: 9	Welfare, state and
Income, personal: 19	local expenditures: 16
Labor, blue-collar: 30	

Kansas

Kansas, set in the center of the country, is a relatively large state consisting of prairie land planted in crops in the eastern half of the state and more elevated plains given over to grazing in the west. Wheat and cattle are the characteristic agricultural products. Topeka is the capital and Wichita is the largest city. Kansas City, is another large city, though its sister, Kansas City, Missouri is three times larger.

total population, population density, and rate of growth during the 1970s were all somewhat below national average levels. A moderately high percentage of elderly residents is one notable feature of the state's population structure. The diversity of the economy built up around agricultural occupations is indicated by the below average ranking for percent of blue-collar jobs, low state government sensitivity to industrial unemployment, and the degree of prosperity that shows up in the income and poverty rankings. Levels of religious and political participation are just about average. State revenues are fairly low and spending is emphasized only in the area of education. Crime rates are moderate and drinking is unpopular.

Alcohol consumption: 46	Health expenditures,
Area: 14	state and local: 27
Church adherents: 25	Income, personal: 15
College graduates: 25	Labor, blue-collar: 36
Crime, property: 22	Manufacturing output: 25
Crime, violent: 30	Mobility, interstate: 17
Education, public	Population: 32
school expenditures: 10	Population change: 38
Elderly, % in	Population density: 37
total pop.: 8	

Poverty, % of people living in: 38	Voter turnout as % of voting age pop.: 22
Tax burden, state: 35	Welfare, state and
Unemployment: 42	local expenditures: 25

Kentucky

Kentucky is a border state between the South and the Midwest, generally consisting of a bumpy plain sloping down toward the Mississippi River in the west. The capital is Frankfort and the principal metropolitan area is found on the Ohio River at Louisville, where about 20% of the population resides. The Kentucky Derby is run each year at Louisville and the nation's gold reserves are stored about 30 miles further south at Fort Knox.

The population is of moderate size, including many native sons and daughters among its members. The percentage of college graduates is quite low. Coal, tobacco, whiskey and racehorses are products of the Bluegrass State. Blue is also the color of a large fraction of work shirt collars in Kentucky. Sensitivity to unemployment is high and rankings for income and poverty disclose a general weakness in the economy. State government raises an average amount of revenue, but spending levels on social welfare are low, particularly in view of the poverty rate. There is not too much crime, not too much interest in politics on the part of voters, and only an average degree of religious activity. Kentucky may produce a good deal of high-quality alcohol, but it consumes very little of it if the statistics are to be trusted.

Alcohol consumption: 47	Manufacturing output: 21
Area: 37	Mobility, interstate: 46
Church adherents: 21	Population: 23
College graduates: 48	Population change: 25
Crime, property: 46	Population density: 23
Crime, violent: 39	Poverty, % of people living in: 3
Education, public school expenditures: 46	Tax burden, state: 24
Elderly, % in total pop.: 26	Unemployment: 14
Health expenditures, state and local: 44	Voter turnout as % of voting age pop.: 37
Income, personal: 44	Welfare, state and local expenditures: 22
Labor, blue-collar: 12	

Louisiana

Louisiana guards the mouth of the Mississippi River at the Gulf of Mexico. It is a kind of border state where the South meets Texas and the West. Rolling hills in the north give way to marshy bayous along the Gulf Coast. Except for Canadian border areas in New England, southern Louisiana is the only place in the country where there is a large French-speaking minority. The great port of New Orleans, now part of a metropolitan area where 28% of state population resides, was originally a key French outpost in the New World. This city, situated below sea level, still preserves a spirit and a style unique in the United States—one part continental heritage, one part heritage of the old South as this is preserved in the musical styles of the great black musicians who created dixieland jazz.

The largely native-born Louisiana population grew at about the national rate during the 1970s. There are relatively few elderly individuals and the proportion of college graduates is below average. The economy, based on oil and chemical production plus river trade, is strong in manufacturing output but weak as a provider of personal income. Poverty is extensive. Revenue flows into state coffers at an adequate rate, but spending on social services outside of federally backed health programs is not impressive. The crime rates indicate a violent streak in the Louisiana temperament; property crime rank lags far behind violent crime.

Alcohol consumption: 27	Manufacturing output: 11
Area: 31	Mobility, interstate: 46
Church adherents: 15	Population: 19
College graduates: 41	Population change: 22
Crime, property: 28	Population density: 21
Crime, violent: 6	Poverty, % of people living in: 2
Education, public school expenditures: 37	Tax burden, state: 19
Elderly, % in total pop.: 38	Unemployment: 18
Health expenditures, state and local: 6	Voter turnout as % of voting age pop.: 29
Income, personal: 34	Welfare, state and local expenditures: 27
Labor, blue-collar: 16	

Maine

Maine is the largest and the most remote of the New England states, noted for its rugged, rocky coast and its deep forests. The weather is cool all year round, very cold in winter. Most of the population lives in towns no more than 25 miles distant from the coast. The interior is given over to specialized settlements that support skiing, wilderness recreation, and the timber and paper industries. Lobster, potatos, poultry and dairy products are important to the economy of the state.

Fairly high proportions of the population are elderly and native born. Population growth was only about 13% during the 1970s, but New Hampshire and Vermont were the only states in the Northeast with higher rates. Maine's economy is not yet sufficiently diverse to support many white-collar jobs. Although unemployment was not so bad during the recession, income levels remain rather low. State government spending for welfare is strong, but health spending is the lowest in the nation. Voters are active but churches are not especially strong in Maine. Crime rates are quite low.

Alcohol consumption: 27	Manufacturing output: 37
Area: 39	Mobility, interstate: 39
Church adherents: 38	Population: 38
College graduates: 39	Population change: 28
Crime, property: 41	Population density: 36
Crime, violent: 44	Poverty, % of people
Education, public	living in: 17
school expenditures: 31	Tax burden, state: 28
Elderly, % in	Unemployment: 35
total pop.: 11	Voter turnout as % of
Health expenditures,	voting age pop.: 8
state and local: 50	Welfare, state and
Income, personal: 41	local expenditures: 11
Labor, blue-collar: 3	

Maryland

Maryland is a small eastern state that surrounds the Chesapeake Bay. The capital is Annapolis, site of the U. S. Naval Academy. The Baltimore metropolitan area is home for over half of the state's people. Many of the others live in the Maryland suburbs of Washington, D.C. The eastern shore area, sharing a peninsula with Delaware, is not heavily populated; overall density of settlement is nevertheless high. Relatively few residents were born in Maryland, college educated adults are not hard to find, and the elderly do not make up a large share of the population. These qualities are consistent with and in part attributable to the attractions provided by the nation's capital for talented younger adults from all across the country. Income levels are high and white-collar work is prevalent for Maryland residents. This is not surprising in a state where government activities dominate the economic scene, but the subpar rate of voter turnout is puzzling in this light. Church activities are not too important and crime is a significant problem.

Alcohol consumption: 14	Elderly, % in
Area: 42	total pop: 41
Church adherents: 39	Health expenditures
College graduates: 7	state and local: 19
Crime, property: 13	Income, personal: 8
Crime, violent: 5	Labor, blue-collar: 46
Education, public	Manufacturing output: 27
school expenditures: 18	Mobility, interstate: 13

Population: 18	Unemployment: 37
Population change: 32	Voter turnout as % of
Population density: 5	voting age pop.: 36
Poverty, % of people	Welfare, state and
living in: 42	local expenditures: 21
Tax burden, state: 15	

Massachusetts

Massachusetts is the leading state in New England and the capital, Boston, is in effect the capital of New England. One of the smaller states in area, Massachusetts has the 11th largest population in the nation, and the third highest population density. About 48% of all residents live in the Boston area, but there are several other centers of population and economic activity in the state. The western section features scenic mountains overlooking the Connecticut River Valley. Cape Cod and the islands of Martha's Vineyard and Nantucket are interesting offshore features. They are the areas to which Bay Staters resort in the summertime.

In colonial days the fisheries and the Atlantic trade were at the heart of the state's economy. These were succeeded by farming and manufacturing during the 19th century. Since the second world war the economy has shifted strongly toward services finance, and the development of new kinds of industry growing out of the research conducted at the great educational centers such as the Massachusetts Institute of Technology, in the Boston area. The Route 128 beltway around Boston was an early version of California's "Silicon Valley"—a locale where firms like Polaroid developed innovative technologies.

Even though a large proportion of the Massachusetts population is over 65 years of age, the percentage of college graduates is high. It is interesting to note that this level of education has not come about due to the sudden arrival of young people born and educated out of state as, for example, in Alaska. A strong system of public institutions of higher education complements a broad group of outstanding private colleges and universities. Massachusetts actually has one of the lowest proportions of nonnative residents. Manufacturing output is high, but there is a balance between blue- and white-collar jobs. Income levels remained high and unemployment was not too serious during the recent recession because of economic diversity. State tax revenue is high and social services spending is generous. The level of church participation is high in this predominantly Catholic state.

Alcohol consumption: 15	College graduates: 6
Area: 45	Crime, property: 18
Church adherents: 6	Crime, violent: 12

Education, public
   school expenditures: 3
Elderly, % in
   total pop.: 10
Health expenditures,
   state and local: 17
Income, personal: 12
Labor, blue-collar: 27
Manufacturing output: 13
Mobility, interstate: 48

Population 11: 47
Population change: 3
Population density
   Poverty % of people: 34
   living in: 34
Tax burden, state: 12
   voting age pop.: 13
Welfare, state and
   local expenditures: 3

Michigan

Michigan is a medium-sized state in the upper Midwest, split into two widely separated parts the Lower Peninsula and the smaller Upper Peninsula, by Lake Michigan. Lansing is the capital and Detroit, the Motor City, is the leading urban area. The state population is the eighth largest in the nation, with 47% of all residents living in the Detroit area. Population growth has been slowed almost to a standstill in recent years, however, as economic opportunities have evaporated. Michigan is a key industrial state, seventh in manufacturing output. Blue-collar jobs are predominant. The steep decline of the American auto industry has led to devastating unemployment in Michigan.

state tax revenue and spending on education are only about average, but levels of spending on health and welfare are fairly high. While religious participation is not very strong, Michigan voters are fairly active, spurred on, no doubt, by the political activism of the labor unions. Crime rates are high. As in the case of Chicago and Illinois, widely divergent rankings on many indicators would be observed if the Detroit area were to be separated from the smaller cities, towns and rural areas of the rest of the state.

Alcohol consumption: 22
Area: 23
Church adherents: 36
College graduates: 29
Crime, property: 10
Crime, violent: 9
Education, public
   school expenditures: 20
Elderly, % in
   total pop.: 36
Health expenditures,
   state and local: 8
Income, personal: 16
Labor, blue-collar: 13

Manufacturing output: 7
Mobility, interstate: 35
Population: 8
Population change: 40
Population density: 12
Poverty, % of people
   living in: 27
Tax burden, state: 24
Unemployment: 2
Voter turnout as % of
   voting age pop.: 12
Welfare, state and
   local expenditures: 4

Minnesota

Minnesota is a large state in the north central part of the country. Rolling hills and over 15,000 natural lakes grace the landscape. About half of the population lives in the metropolitan area around the twin cities, Minneapolis and St. Paul. The most famous city in the state, however, may be little Lake Wobegon, the fictional "town that time forgot," which has become a kind of second home to millions who listen to Garrison Keillor's *Prairie Home Companion* program, broadcast from St. Paul every Saturday on National Public Radio. This is a typical American heartland town where "the women are strong, the men are good-looking, and the children are above average—every last one of them."

The real state of Minnesota has a population of moderate size that has recently been growing at a moderate rate. The numbers of elderly people and college-educated adults are just a shade above average. The economy is mixed, with extensive dairy farming, grain production, mining, manufacturing and management functions. Manufacturing output is strong although the blue-collar segment of the labor force is small. Income is above average and there is little poverty. Minnesotans are politically active, they had the highest voter turnout in the nation in 1980. State government raises much money and spends it actively for social programs. The political sentiments of the state are well-expressed by Walter Mondale, 1984 Democratic presidential hopeful, former Vice President under Jimmy Carter, former three-term senator from Minnesota.

Alcohol consumption: 25
Area: 12
Church adherents: 5
College graduates: 20
Crime, property: 33
Crime, violent: 40
Education, public
   school expenditures: 19
Elderly, % in
   total pop.: 17
Health expenditures,
   state and local: 12
Income, personal: 17
Labor, blue-collar: 45

Manufacturing output: 17
Mobility, interstate: 38
Population: 21
Population change: 33
Population density: 33
Poverty, % of people
   living in: 44
Tax burden, state: 6
Unemployment: 26
Voter turnout as % of
   voting age pop.: 1
Welfare, state and
   local expenditures: 8

Mississippi

Mississippi is located deep in the Southeast on the eastern side of the river from which its name is taken. Near the river the land is flat and fertile. Other parts of the state are generally wrapped in hills. The 44-mile stretch of Gulf

Coast in the far south includes a national seashore and several small port cities situated between Mobile on the east and New Orleans on the west. The area and population of the state rank somewhat below national averages. Recent population growth has been moderate and most Mississippians are native born. The proportion of college-educated adults is low. About 46% of the population lives in the area near Jackson, the state capital.

Per capita income in Mississippi is the lowest in the nation by a wide margin. One family in five is poor—the highest rate in the country and more than twice the national average. The economy mixes agricultural and industrial production. Oil and natural gas, chemicals and textiles are important products. Low wages and the absence of unions have made the state attractive to footloose firms from other parts of the country. Blue-collar jobs are prevalent and periodic unemployment is thus a serious problem. The state is unable to raise much tax revenue. The level of welfare spending is very low considering the extent of poverty. The federal government helps out to some extent in the area of health, but spending on education is abysmally low. Religion is of no more than moderate importance to the average resident. Both crime rates, are low, but the difference in rankings is worth noting. Similar disparities, where violent crimes turn out to be more frequent, are also observed in other southern states.

Alcohol consumption: 41	Manufacturing output: 29
Area: 32	Mobility, interstate: 42
Church adherents: 18	Population: 31
College graduates: 44	Population change: 25
Crime, property: 48	Population density: 31
Crime, violent: 33	Poverty, % of people
Education, public	living in: 1
school expenditures: 48	Tax burden, state: 40
Elderly, % in	Unemployment: 13
total pop.: 20	Voter turnout as % of
Health expenditures,	voting age pop.: 32
state and local: 10	Welfare, state and
Income, personal: 50	local expenditures: 26
Labor, blue-collar: 6	

Missouri

Missouri, nicknamed the Show Me State in honor of the reputed scepticism and stubborness of its residents, lies in the middle of the country on the west bank of the Mississippi. The city of St. Louis, located at the confluence of the Missouri and the Mississippi rivers, was the key jumping-off point for the migrations that pushed back the western frontier during the 19th century. Jefferson city, the capital, is located in the center of the

state. The other major city is Kansas City on the western border. State population is sizable, but the rate of growth was low during the 1970s. One the other hand, migration from the South to St. Louis and Kansas City has been high enough over the past several decades to place the state near the middle in ranking according to percentage of nonnative residents. The elderly segment of the population is large and the percentage of college graduates is subpar.

The farm, the factory, the warehouse and the office building are all significant sites of economic activity in Missouri. This diversity shows up in the medium ranking for percentage of blue-collar jobs and in the medium unemployment level, sustained despite industrial decline in St. Louis. However, the overall performance of the economy in generating personal income is not very strong. State government collects very little money per capita and spends for social purposes only at an average rate. Missouri voters are somewhat more active than voters in most parts of the country. Church ties and crime rates are not too different from national averages. Drinking is not very popular.

Alcohol consumption: 37	Manufacturing output: 32
Area: 19	Mobility, interstate: 24
Church adherents: 24	Population: 15
College graduates: 39	Population change: 38
Crime, property: 25	Population density: 27
Crime, violent: 14	Poverty, % of people
Education, public	living in: 20
school expenditures: 29	Tax burden, state: 48
Elderly, % in	Unemployment: 23
total pop.: 5	Voter turnout as % of
Health expenditures,	voting age pop.: 14
state and local: 24	Welfare, state and
Income, personal: 33	local expenditures: 35
Labor, blue-collar: 28	

Montana

Montana is called Big Sky country for reasons obvious to anyone who has seen the sky there. This very large state in the interior Northwest consists of beautifully open high plains in the eastern half and the northern Rockies in the west. The population of Montana is almost exactly equivalent to the population of the city of Baltimore, the tenth largest city in the nation. But Baltimore has an area of just 80 square miles, a drop in the bucket compared to the 147,046 square miles of Montana. The only states with lower population density are Wyoming and Alaska. The Billings metropolitan area is the largest in the state, but its population of 108,000 makes up only 14% of the state population. The growth of population exceeded the national norm during the 1970s, and 40% of all residents have arrived from elsewhere at some time in the recent past. Percentages of the elderly and of college-educated adults are roughly normal.

Mines, forests and ranches are the basic units of Montana's economic life. Agricultural employment, cowpunching included, is more important than regular blue-collar jobs. The income level is somewhat low. State government raises an average amount of revenue and spends at a high level on social services only in the field of education. Montana residents flocked to the voting booths in 1980. Property crime is moderate and violent crime is relatively infrequent. Churches are not especially strong.

Alcohol consumption: 13	Manufacturing output: 41
Area: 4	Mobility, interstate: 14
Church adherents: 35	Population: 44
College graduates: 15	Population change: 27
Crime, property: 27	Population density: 48
Crime, violent: 42	Poverty, % of people
Education, public	living in: 21
school expenditures: 5	Tax burden, state: 26
Elderly, % in	Unemployment: 27
total pop.: 30	Voter turnout as % of
Health expenditures,	voting age pop.: 5
state and local: 42	Welfare, state and
Income, personal: 35	local expenditures: 34
Labor, blue-collar: 43	

Nebraska

Nebraska is a rather large state in the northwestern corner of the highly productive granary that occupies the middle of the continent. The landscape consists largely of rolling grasslands in the eastern sector, with hills and high plains in the west. The economy is rooted in agriculture and the processing and shipment of food products. Cattle, hogs, dairy products, corn and wheat are the leading commodities. The nation's largest meat-packing center is Omaha, a metropolitan area on the Missouri River border with Iowa, where 31% of Nebraskans live. Farm jobs are more important than blue-collar jobs, so Nebraska is not very sensitive to layoffs and unemployment during downswings of the economic cycle. The state holds revenue collection at a low level and spends for social programs at no better than an average rate. The religious life of Nebraska towns is very active and crime rates are low. Elderly Nebraskans make up a relatively large share of the population.

Alcohol consumption: 32	College graduates: 22
Area: 15	Crime, property: 42
Church adherents: 8	Crime, violent: 41

Education, public	Population change: 35
school expenditures: 28	Population density: 41
Elderly, % in	Poverty % of people
total pop.: 7	living in: 34
Health expenditures,	Tax burden, state: 45
state and local: 20	Unemployment: 46
Income, personal: 21	Voter turnout as % of
Labor, blue-collar: 37	voting age pop: 23
Manufacturing output: 32	Welfare, state and
Mobility, interstate: 26	local expenditures: 43
Population: 35	

Nevada

Nevada is a large western state located in a desolate basin between the Rockies and the Sierras. The climate is dry and most of the land is uninhabited. The population is concentrated in a small number of settlement areas, especially the mountainous Lake Tahoe district near the California border, and the Las Vegas desert area in the southern corner of the state near the Hoover Dam and Lake Mead. There is a small amount of farming based on irrigation and there is some mining, but Nevada's economy is largely based on tourism, which in turn is based on the legality of gambling, certain forms of prostitution and fast-and-loose marriage and divorce procedures. The income level is high, there is little measurable poverty, most jobs are white-collar jobs and unemployment does not appear to be a major problem. This is very impressive for a state that ranks dead last in manufacturing output.

The rate of population growth in Nevada was by far the highest in the country during the 1970s. Of all the states, Nevada has the fewest native-born residents. There are few elderly people in the population, nevertheless the percentage of adults with college educations is low. The state realizes high levels of revenue, skimming from the gambling tables and avoiding any tax burden on residents. Rankings for the three forms of social spending (health, education and welfare) vary sharply, with health funded at a high level and welfare funded poorly (in part because there is little poverty). In other areas Nevada also displays extremes in the rankings that might be expected of an eccentric and wide-open state. Crime rates are extremely high. Vast quantities of alcohol are consumed—most, to be sure, by visitors to the state. Finally, Nevada is apparently the least religious state in the nation.

Alcohol consumption: 1	College graduates: 31
Area: 7	Crime, property: 1
Church adherents: 50	Crime, violent: 3

Education, public
school expenditures: 25
Elderly, % in
total pop.: 46
Health expenditures,
state and local: 7
Income, personal: 6
Labor, blue-collar: 50
Manufacturing output: 50
Mobility, interstate: 1
Population: 43

Population change: 1
Population density: 47
Poverty, % of people
living in: 49
Tax burden, state: 6
Unemployment: 10
Voter turnout as % of
voting age pop: 48
Welfare, state and
local expenditures: 47

New Hampshire

New Hampshire is a mountainous, heavily forested state projecting northward from Massachusetts to the Canadian border, dividing Vermont from Maine. A small corner of the state fronts on the Atlantic Ocean. The capital is Concord and the largest cities are Manchester and Nashua, down near the Massachusetts border. They are the leading centers in an area where most of the state population lives, within the larger orbit of Boston. This is not a large population, but the rate of growth during the 1970s was the highest in the Northeast. The nonnative segment of the population is large. Some recent migration to New Hampshire derives from the expansion of the Boston metropolis, some from the increasing popularity of winter sports and rural lifestyles in New England.

The income distribution in New Hampshire is relatively flat. Though average income is just under the national average, the poverty rate is very low. Government is strongly rooted at the local level of the town meeting, with its dignified version of the free-for-all of participatory democracy. State government is lean. Per capita state tax revenue is the lowest in the nation. Welfare is the only area in which the state spends much money. The high rate of alcohol consumption is deceptive because low tax rates on liquor encourage many buying trips from purchasers living outside the state.

Alcohol consumption: 2
Area: 44
Church adherents: 33
College graduates: 14
Crime, property: 36
Crime, violent: 47
Education, public
school expenditures: 32
Elderly, % in
total pop.: 26
Health expenditures,
state and local: 49
Income, personal: 30
Labor, blue-collar: 21

Manufacturing output: 40
Mobility, interstate: 9
Population: 42
Population change: 13
Population density: 20
Poverty, % of people
living in: 48
Tax burden, state: 50
Unemployment: 42
Voter turnout as % of
voting age pop.: 20
Welfare, state and
local expenditures: 18

New Jersey

A small, heavily populated state on the Atlantic coast, New Jersey is wedged in between New York and Pennsylvania. Known as The Garden State, its topography includes choppy hills in the northwest, flat farmland in the center and a sandy wilderness, the Pine Barrens, toward the southeast. The 130-mile shoreline is studded with summer resort towns, including the year-round playground of Atlantic City, where Miss America is crowned each year and gambling casinos are now crowding out cabanas. The main New Jersey population centers adjoin New York City and Philadelphia. Some are affluent suburbs, others are disabled cities like Camden and Newark. There was little population increase during the 1970s, but then there is little need for population increase. The garden is full of people; New Jersey is the most densely settled state in the Union.

The state is an economic powerhouse, ranking eighth in manufacturing output and third in personal income. The economy is diverse and fairly well protected against unemployment by virtue of a high proportion of more recession-proof white-collar jobs. State government raises revenue at a rate just above the national norm, spending heavily on education but not much on health. Crime rates are high, especially in the older urban areas. The capital of New Jersey is Trenton, situated on the Delaware not far from where Washington made his historic crossing.

Alcohol consumption: 26
Area: 46
Church adherents: 21
College graduates: 13
Crime, property: 12
Crime, violent: 11
Education, public
school expenditures: 7
Elderly, % in
total pop.: 18
Health expenditures,
state and local: 37
Income, personal: 3
Labor, blue-collar: 35

Manufacturing output: 8
Mobility, interstate: 21
Population: 9
Population change: 44
Population density: 1
Poverty, % of people
living in: 32
Tax burden, state: 15
Unemployment: 32
Voter turnout as % of
voting age pop.: 26
Welfare, state and
local expenditures: 14

New Mexico

New Mexico, one of the largest states, is situated on the Mexican border between Arizona and Texas. It is known for its remarkable physical features and inspiring landscape. In the desert south the Carlsbad Caverns burrow into the earth not far to the east of Alamogordo, the site where the first atomic bomb was detonated in 1945. On the plateaus and the mountaintops of the north the nights are cool and clear. Monuments to earlier American civilizations, like the Chaco Canyon cliff dwellings, adorn the landscape.

The population of New Mexico remains small despite several decades of rapid increase. The main area of settlement is in the north central part of the state close by the Rio Grande. Santa Fe is the capital and Albuquerque is the metropolis, home of 35% of all residents of the state. There are few elderly New Mexicans, indicating that the state has yet to develop its full potential as a retirement area.

Ranches and mines are the key economic units. The development of electronics and energy-related manufacturing is still in its early stages. The Los Alamos Scientific Laboratory, where that first atomic device was developed, continue with their mission to advance atomic energy research. The general income level in the state is low and poverty is widespread, particularly among the members of the large American Indian minorities. The state collects ample taxes, but comparatively little money goes toward spending on health, education, or, especially, welfare. Religious participation is strong while political participation is rather weak. Crime, the violent sort in particular, runs at a fairly high level.

Alcohol consumption: 17	Manufacturing output: 43
Area: 5	Mobility, interstate: 11
Church adherents: 12	Population: 37
College graduates: 15	Population change: 9
Crime, property: 20	Population density: 44
Crime, violent: 10	Poverty, % of people
Education, public	living in: 6
school expenditures: 24	Tax burden, state: 5
Elderly, % in	Unemployment: 25
total pop.: 44	Voter turnout as % of
Health expenditures,	voting age pop.: 35
state and local: 23	Welfare, state and
Income, personal: 42	local expenditures: 41
Labor, blue-collar: 38	

New York

Small by national standards, New York has the largest area of any northeastern state. Hills and two groups of mountains—the Catskills and the Adirondacks—dominate the landscape in the east. The state gradually flattens toward the west as it approaches Buffalo on the shores of Lake Erie. The Finger Lakes region in the center of the state, below Rochester and Syracuse, offers recreational opportunities in a lovely setting. Niagra Falls is in the far western end of the state above Buffalo. Albany, the state capital, is located on the Hudson River 150 miles above New York harbor. Across from the towers of the Island of Manhattan, the boroughs of Brooklyn and

Queens are situated on the southern tip of Long Island, a kind of giant aircraft carrier of an island bearing most of the New York City suburbs that are actually part of New York State.

New York is the second most populous state in the country, with one of the highest population densities. Although thousands of people flow into the state, and especially the city, each year to seek their fortunes, the population is so large that they leave few statistical traces. New York is the state with the highest percentage of native-born residents. The population actually declined during the 1970s as changing economic conditions forced the flight of manufacturing operations from cities all across the state, but especially from New York City and Buffalo. The loss of jobs eventually led to loss of residents. New York may be declining as a manufacturing state, but it still ranks fifth nationally in output. The proportion of blue-collar jobs is already low, however, and it will probably decline further. The prominence of managerial, professional and service occupations now provides a certain buffer against high unemployment. Personal income is high on the average, but as there are significant disparities in income among different groups the poverty rate is rather high also.

State government in New York is extremely active, getting and spending funds for social programs at high rates. The rate of property crime is high and New York leads the nation in the rate of violent crime. The influence of conditions in New York City on all these statewide rates is decisive. The metropolis is the residence of 45% of state population. When the suburban areas within the state, especially on lower Long Island, are added in, over 60% of the entire state population is accounted for.

Alcohol consumption: 22	Manufacturing output: 5
Area: 30	Mobility, interstate: 50
Church adherents: 28	Population: 2
College graduates: 12	Population change: 50
Crime, property: 11	Population density: 6
Crime, violent: 1	Poverty, % of people
Education, public	living in: 14
school expenditures: 2	Tax burden, state: 10
Elderly, % in	Unemployment: 33
total pop.: 13	Voter turnout as % of
Health expenditures,	voting age pop.: 42
state and local: 3	Welfare, state and
Income, personal: 9	local expenditures: 1
Labor, blue-collar: 43	

North Carolina

The state of North Carolina extends from the Atlantic coast to the Blue Ridge Mountains. The Piedmont Plateau in the center of the state is the location of several medium-sized cities, including Raleigh, the capital. The state is heavily wooded, not least in forests of pine, the state tree. The North Carolina population is the largest in the Southeast outside of Florida. The growth rate during the 1970s was about average, there is a large native element in the population and there are relatively few college graduates among adults.

Textile manufacturing is the key economic activity and blue-collar jobs are strongly represented in the labor force. Chickens, dairy products and tobacco are the main products of the land. There has been some shift toward new industries and white-collar jobs in recent years, focused around the universities in the Durham-Chapel Hill area, but the movement toward greater diversity has not yet taken hold in the economy as a whole. The level of personal income is fairly low and poverty is extensive. The state government operates at income and spending levels below national averages. Voter turnout and alcohol consumption are low and so is crime—at least property crime.

Alcohol consumption: 42	Manufacturing output: 10
Area: 28	Mobility, interstate: 38
Church adherents: 23	Population: 46
College graduates: 41	Population change: 21
Crime, property: 40	Population density: 17
Crime, violent: 24	Poverty, % of people
Education, public	living in: 12
school expenditures: 36	Tax burden, state: 31
Elderly, % in	Unemployment: 28
total pop.: 33	Voter turnout as % of
Health expenditures,	voting age pop.: 46
state and local: 31	Welfare, state and
Income, personal: 40	local expenditures: 36
Labor, blue-collar: 4	

North Dakota

North Dakota is situated on the Canadian border, across the Red River to the west of Minnesota. The surface of the state consists generally of wide, open plains, with the rugged Badlands in the west. Wheat is a leading product of a largely agricultural economy supplemented by some coal mining. Manufacturing output is very low and there are few blue-collar industrial jobs. The farms of North Dakota generate a moderate level of personal income and provide a cushion against severe unemployment. The populations of North Dakota and Memphis, Tennessee, our 14th largest city, are about the same size. Population density is low and settlements are scattered evenly all across the state. The two largest urban areas, at Fargo and the state capital of Bismarck, together

account for only 26% of all inhabitants. State tax revenue is a bit above average. The various types of social spending are all more or less below the national norm. The Lutherans and Catholics of North Dakota are sufficiently active to give the state one of the highest rates of church affiliation in the country. Political participation is also high. Violent crime is rare in North Dakota and only in West Virginia is the rate of property crime lower.

Alcohol consumption: 24	Manufacturing output: 48
Area: 17	Mobility, interstate: 32
Church adherents: 3	Population: 46
College graduates: 30	Population change: 37
Crime, property: 49	Population density: 45
Crime, violent: 50	Poverty, % of people
Education, public	living in: 18
school expenditures: 30	Tax burden, state: 14
Elderly, % in	Unemployment: 37
total pop.: 13	Voter turnout as % of
Health expenditures,	voting age pop.: 7
state and local: 47	Welfare, state and
Income, personal: 25	local expenditures: 32
Labor, blue-collar: 47	

Ohio

Ohio is a heavily populated state bounded by Lake Erie on the north and the Ohio River, an important tributary of the Mississippi, on the south. Much of the state consists of contoured hills and valleys, flattening out as the land approaches the Great Lakes, and in many other spots throughout the state. Columbus, the capital and the main campus of the state university, is centrally located. There are many rural towns scattered across the farmlands of the state, but industrial cities like Cleveland, Cincinnati, Dayton, Toledo, Akron and Youngstown are the hallmark of Ohio. The present crisis of these blue-collar cities is evident in several rankings—the weakened position on measures of industrial output, the slow pace of recent population growth and the very high level of unemployment. Per capita personal income has slipped in relation to other states and poverty is now more widespread. The crisis in the steel and auto industries, with side effects on associated industries such as rubber and glass, has plagued the state for years. Ohio government does not raise much tax revenue, but levels of social spending are held close to the national averages. Church participation and crime rates are moderate.

Alcohol consumption: 39	Crime, property: 24
Area: 35	Crime, violent: 17
Church adherents: 29	Education, public
College graduates: 33	school expenditures: 26

Elderly, % in total pop.: 29	Population density: 46
Health expenditures, state and local: 15	Poverty, % of people living in: 29
Income, personal: 23	Tax burden, state: 46
Labor, blue-collar: 13	Unemployment: 4
Manufacturing output: 4	Voter turnout as % of voting age pop.: 25
Mobility, interstate: 32	Welfare, state and local expenditures: 23
Population: 6	
Population change: 46	

Oklahoma

Oklahoma is a fairly large state in the southwestern interior. Cattle ranching and the production of oil and natural gas are the characteristic economic sectors. The state ranks near the middle on most economic indicators, though the level of unemployment was distinctly low near the bottom of the recent recession. The population is of medium size, growing at a rate just above the national average. Urbanized areas centered on Tulsa and the state capital, Oklahoma City, account for a combined total of 50% of all state residents. Oklahoma raises revenue at a high rate thanks to taxes on the depletion of oil and gas. Spending on social services is only at moderate levels. Oklahomans are not avid voters, but they do support their churches and avoid strong drink. Crime rates are at medium levels.

Alcohol consumption: 44	Manufacturing output: 26
Area: 13	Mobility, interstate: 18
Church adherents: 13	Population: 26
College graduates: 25	Population change: 19
Crime, property: 31	Population density: 34
Crime, violent: 26	Poverty, % of people living in: 15
Education, public school expenditures: 34	Tax burden, state: 9
Elderly, % in total pop.: 12	Unemployment: 47
Health expenditures, state and local: 32	Voter turnout as % of voting age pop.: 31
Income, personal: 24	Welfare, state and local expenditures: 19
Labor, blue-collar: 24	

Oregon

Oregon is a relatively large state in the Pacific Northwest. The climate is cool and moist along the coast, drier, with more diurnal and seasonal temperature variation, in the eastern part of the state beyond the Cascade Range. Crater Lake National Park is only one of many beautiful features in the mountain landscape. The forests of Oregon are vast, supporting the role of the state

as the leading producer of lumber and paper products. The population grew rapidly during the 1970s. There is a large percentage of residents born elsewhere in the country. The capital city of Salem is located in the northwestern part of the state near Portland, the metropolis on the Columbia River where 40% of the population resides.

The economy is mixed, somewhat sensitive to unemployment and productive of a modest level of prosperity. State government revenue is low, but spending for public education is emphasized. Oregonians are active voters and reluctant churchgoers. Crime rates, especially for property crime, are relatively high.

Alcohol consumption: 20	Manufacturing output: 28
Area: 10	Mobility, interstate: 7
Church adherents: 45	Population: 30
College graduates: 17	Population change: 11
Crime, property: 9	Population density: 39
Crime, violent: 19	Poverty, % of people living in: 30
Education, public school expenditures: 4	Tax burden, state: 38
Elderly, % in total pop.: 20	Unemployment: 10
Health expenditures, state and local: 36	Voter turnout as % of voting age pop.: 10
Income, personal: 29	Welfare, state and local expenditures: 20
Labor, blue-collar: 28	

Pennsylvania

The Keystone State is large for an eastern state. Its population of nearly 12 million is the fourth largest in the nation. There was very little increase during the 1970s. Since there has not been much migration to Pennsylvania in recent decades, the native-born segment of the population is large, second only to the native-born segment in New York. The elderly population is sizable and the proportion of college-educated adults is rather low. Harrisburg, a small city on the Susquehanna River near the Pennsylvania Dutch country, is the capital. The Philadelphia metropolitan area in the southeast is the home of 31% of state residents, while another 19% live in the coal- and steel-producing region around Pittsburgh in the southwest.

Pennsylvania is a leading industrial state with significant representation of blue-collar workers in the labor force. The decline of the steel industry in the western part of the state has contributed to high unemployment rates. General strength and diversity in the economy has been sufficient, however, to support a moderate income level and to hold down the poverty rate. State government revenue is just about average, but social spending is strong, particularly for education and welfare. The degree of church affiliation is high and the crime rates are lower than might be expected, given its industrial character.

Alcohol consumption: 38
Area: 33
Church adherents: 11
College graduates: 43
Crime, property: 45
Crime, violent: 32
Education, public
    school expenditures: 66
Elderly, % in
    total pop.: 9
Health expenditures,
    state and local: 43
Income, personal: 20
Labor, blue-collar: 11

Manufacturing output: 6
Mobility, interstate: 49
Population: 4
Population change: 48
Population density: 8
Poverty, % of people
    living in: 37
Tax burden, state: 21
Unemployment: 8
Voter turnout as % of
    voting age pop.: 33
Welfare, state and
    local expenditures: 10

Rhode Island

A tiny state of just 1,212 square miles, Rhode Island is squeezed between Connecticut and Massachusetts on the Atlantic coast in lower New England. Providence is the capital and the main city. The city of Newport may be better known around the country, however. It was once the most exclusive resort town on this side of the Atlantic and today is the rallying point of the Americas' Cup yacht races.

State population is not large, but density of settlement is of course very high. Rhode Island was one of only two states to experience population decline during the 1970s. The fraction of elderly residents is high. Manufacturing is the cornerstone of the economy. Blue-collar jobs predominate and the income level is moderate. The state raises a normal amount of revenue and concentrates on welfare spending. Political participation is on the active side and religious participation in this overwhelmingly Catholic state is the highest in the nation.

Alcohol consumption: 11
Area: 50
Church adherents: 1
College graduates: 27
Crime, property: 17
Crime, violent: 28
Education, public
    school expenditures: 17
Elderly, % in
    total pop.: 3
Health expenditures,
    state and local: 18
Income, personal: 27
Labor, blue-collar: 9

Manufacturing output: 37
Mobility, interstate: 36
Population: 40
Population change: 49
Population density: 2
Poverty, % of people
    living in: 31
Tax burden, state: 20
Unemployment: 17
Voter turnout as % of
    voting age pop.: 14
Welfare, state and
    local expenditures: 2

South Carolina

The state of South Carolina is of modest size. About two-thirds of the state lies on a low coastal plain featuring many lakes and marshes. From these the land rises into hills and finally into the Blue Ridge Mountains in the northwestern corner. Much of the land is covered with forest and scrub. Population density and the recent rate of population increase are both just above the national average. The distribution of settlements and people is fairly uniform. The capital city, Columbia, and the exquisite old port city of Charleston are the focal points of the two leading urbanized areas. But these areas encompass between them only 27% of the population.

Subsistence farming is still a common way of life in South Carolina. The level of personal income is very low and the poverty rate is high. Over the past few decades a low-wage textile industry has displaced dairy and tobacco farming as the core economic activity. Blue-collar jobs are prevalent. The state raises little revenue and spends very little for education and welfare. Federal Medicaid funds for the poor account for the high level of health spending. South Carolinians are the most apathetic voters in the nation. Property crime is moderate but violent crimes are not infrequent.

Alcohol consumption: 31
Area: 40
Church adherents: 26
College graduates: 36
Crime, property: 30
Crime, violent: 7
Education, public
    school expenditures: 47
Elderly, % in
    total pop.: 43
Health expenditures,
    state and local: 4
Income, personal: 49
Labor, blue-collar: 7

Manufacturing output: 24
Mobility, interstate: 31
Population: 24
Population change: 15
Population density: 19
Poverty, % of people
    living in: 9
Tax burden, state: 33
Unemployment: 15
Voter turnout as % of
    voting age pop.: 50
Welfare, state and
    local expenditures: 45

South Dakota

The wide Missouri River slices South Dakota in half, dividing the farm country in the east from the Great Plains, the Badlands and the Black Hills in the west. The Mount Rushmore National Monument is located near Rapid City in the southwestern corner of the state. The capital is Pierre. The largest urban area is Sioux Falls in the farmlands to the east, where the bulk of the population is in fact settled. It is a small population in which the elderly are well represented. Farming and ranching are the state's characteristic economic activities. Manufacturing output is low and there are relatively few blue-collar industrial jobs. The employment situation does not depend directly on general swings in economic conditions, but the level of income is rather low. State government does not raise or spend much money. Spending for health and hospitals is quite low. Crime rates are close to rock bottom. North Dakotans flock to both voting booths and church pews in great numbers, by and large avoiding barstools.

Alcohol consumption: 34	Manufacturing output: 43
Area: 16	Mobility, interstate: 25
Church adherents: 4	Population: 45
College graduates: 36	Population change: 41
Crime, property: 47	Population density: 46
Crime, violent: 49	Poverty, % of people
Education, public	living in: 10
school expenditures: 35	Tax burden, state: 47
Elderly, % in	Unemployment: 49
total pop.: 5	Voter turnout as % of
Health expenditures,	voting age pop.: 4
state and local: 48	Welfare, state and
Income, personal: 38	local expenditures: 28
Labor, blue-collar: 48	

Tennessee

Tennessee is a southern state with a proud heritage as a part of the early American frontier in the 18th and early 19th centuries. Andrew Jackson served as a senator from Tennessee prior to gaining the presidency in 1829. The state can be viewed as consisting of three distinct regions. The western third of the state, between the Mississippi and the Tennessee rivers, is farmland. Memphis is the chief city. From the Tennessee River to the Cumberland Mountains further east there is a central basin in which Nashville is the dominant city and industrial production is the mainstay of the economy. Nashville is not just the state capital, it is the capital of country music, the site of the Grand Ole Opry and the Graceland museum in honor of Tennessee's favorite son, Elvis Presley. The eastern third of the state, beyond the Cumberlands, is mountain and mining country, with Knoxville as the principal urban center.

Overall population density in Tennessee is a bit higher than the national average. Just under 40% of the population can be found in the Memphis and Nashville metropolitan areas. Manufacturing is generally the leading economic sector. The Tennessee Valley Authority generates the electrical energy that keeps the engines turning. Blue-collar employment is relatively important to the state and unemployment hit hard during the recent recession. Average income is rather low and there are

many poor families. The state collects few taxes, spends very little on education and not much on welfare. Voter turnout in 1980 was below average. Violent crime appears to be somewhat more of a problem than property crime.

Alcohol consumption: 40	Manufacturing output: 15
Area: 34	Mobility, interstate: 28
Church adherents: 20	Population: 17
College graduates: 47	Population change: 20
Crime, property: 43	Population density: 18
Crime, violent: 23	Poverty, % of people
Education, public	living in: 7
school expenditures: 49	Tax burden, state: 49
Elderly, % in	Unemployment: 5
total pop.: 23	Voter turnout as % of
Health expenditures,	voting age pop.: 41
state and local: 11	Welfare, state and
Income, personal: 43	local expenditures: 38
Labor, blue-collar: 5	

Texas

Texas is the largest state in the Union after Alaska. Bounded on the south by the Rio Grande and the Gulf of Mexico, Texas generally presents a flat landscape rising from the coast toward the rangeland of the panhandle. Known as The Lone Star State, Texas looks back with pride upon its brief history as an independent republic. The population is the third largest in the nation. If patterns of growth continue as in the 1970s, Texas will move ahead of New York in population by the turn of the century. The major metropolitan areas are Houston and Dallas-Fort Worth, each with close to three million residents. Together they make up 41% of state population. The capital city is Austin.

The economy is massive, complex and dynamic. Texas leads the nation in number of farms and amount of farm acreage. Many of these farms are cattle ranches. Manufacturing output, second in the nation to California, is rooted first and foremost in the oil business. Blue-collar, white-collar and farm employment are balanced in the labor market. The state maintained a high employment level through the recent recession despite strong growth of the labor force. State government is lean in Texas and perhaps a bit mean too, to judge by the level of spending on welfare. Although crime rates are high in certain areas of the state, Houston for example, the overall state crime rates are not at all extreme.

Alcohol consumption: 21	Crime, property: 15
Area: 2	Crime, violent: 15
Church adherents: 19	Education, public
College graduates: 24	school expenditures: 38

Elderly, % in
   total pop.: 38
Health expenditures,
   state and local: 29
Income, personal: 18
Labor, blue-collar: 19
Manufacturing output: 2
Mobility, interstate: 34
Population: 3
Population change: 10

Population density: 30
Poverty, % of people
   living in: 11
Tax burden, state: 32
Unemployment: 40
Voter turnout as % of
   voting age pop.: 44
Welfare, state and
   local expenditures: 46

Utah

Utah is one of the larger states, famous as the location of Great Salt Lake and the huge Great Salt Lake desert where land speed records are tested on the Bonneville Salt Flats. The state also offers beautiful mountain scenery and spectacular canyons in the southern section. The dominance of the Mormon Church in religious affairs is what makes Utah special; most state residents are members. Utah is virtually tied with Rhode Island as the state with the highest rate of religious participation. The Mormon Tabernacle is located in Salt Lake City, the state capital. The rate of alcohol consumption in Utah is the lowest in the country.

The population is not very large, but recent growth has been rapid. Because of the high birthrate and the migration of young people to Utah the percentage of elderly residents is very low. Many adults have been to college. The economy does not produce a high average income level, but unemployment is not a leading problem and there are very few poor families. Agriculture, industry, services and commerce all play a part in the economy. State government revenue is moderate. Spending levels on social services are below national norms across the board. Utah voters are among the most active in the nation. There is not much violent crime, though property crime appears to be a problem.

Alcohol consumption: 50
Area: 11
Church adherents: 2
College graduates: 5
Crime, property: 16
Crime, violent: 37
Education, public
   school expenditures: 43
Elderly, % in
   total pop.: 49
Health expenditures,
   state and local: 39
Income, personal: 46
Labor, blue-collar: 23

Manufacturing output: 36
Mobility, interstate: 22
Population: 36
Population change: 5
Population density: 42
Poverty, % of people
   living in: 37
Tax burden, state: 27
Unemployment: 30
Voter turnout as % of
   voting age pop.: 5
Welfare, state and
   local expenditures: 39

Vermont

Vermont is located deep in New England, up along the Canadian border. The Connecticut River divides Vermont from New Hampshire to the east. Part of the western border with New York is formed by Lake Champlain. The state includes the Green Mountains, plenty of rolling hills and very rocky soil. It is almost entirely forested. The capital is Montpellier and the largest urban area is at Burlington, on the shore of Lake Champlain, where 22% of all Vermonters make their homes. Only two other states have fewer residents than Vermont. Other population statistics fall in the middle range, though the proportion of college graduates is high. Maple sugar is the characteristic agricultural product. Granite is the characteristic mineral product. There are many dairy farms, small factories and lumber processing businesses. Winter sports enthusiasts bring a great deal of money into the state each year. There is little unemployment, but the general income level is low. State tax revenue is moderate, while rankings on social spending vary considerably from a low in health spending to a high in welfare spending. Although Vermonters drink freely there is very little violent crime.

Alcohol consumption: 4
Area: 43
Church adherents: 30
College graduates: 9
Crime, property: 26
Crime, violent: 48
Education, public
   school expenditures: 33
Elderly, % in
   total pop.: 22
Health expenditures,
   state and local: 45
Income, personal: 39
Labor, blue-collar: 25

Manufacturing output: 43
Mobility, interstate: 19
Population: 48
Population change: 23
Population density: 29
Poverty, % of people
   living in: 28
Tax burden, state: 28
Unemployment: 47
Voter turnout as % of
   voting age pop.: 17
Welfare, state and
   local expenditures: 17

Virginia

The state of Virginia is roughly triangular in shape. It meets Washington, D.C. near the northern corner. The main body of the state joins Chesapeake Bay below the mouth of the Potomac River. A detached section projecting south from Maryland divides the bay from the Atlantic Ocean. The Blue Ridge Mountains fill northwestern Virginia. The largest urban complex occupies both sides of the Hampton roads inlet at the southeastern extremity of the state. The main cities here are Norfolk and Newport News. This is the site of a large U.S. Navy installation. The capital of Virginia is Richmond, located at the eastern edge of the beautiful plateau that forms the central part of the state. Arlington and a number of other towns are part of an extensive suburban complex below Washington.

The population is relatively large, including a generous share of people born out of state. College graduates are well represented in the population. The economy is extremely varied, leading to balanced rankings on most indicators. State revenue is on the low side and social spending is about average. Political participation is lower than might be expected in this part of the country, so near the nation's capital. Religious participation and crime rates are also a bit below average.

Alcohol consumption: 36	Manufacturing output: 17
Area: 36	Mobility, interstate: 16
Church adherents: 37	Population: 14
College graduates: 10	Population change: 24
Crime, property: 39	Population density: 16
Crime, violent: 36	Poverty, % of people
Education, public	living in: 22
school expenditures: 23	Tax burden, state: 36
Elderly, % in	Unemployment: 34
total pop.: 41	Voter turnout as % of
Health expenditures,	voting age pop.: 42
state and local: 28	Welfare, state and
Income, personal: 22	local expenditures: 29
Labor, blue-collar: 26	

Washington

Washington occupies the extreme northwestern corner of the 48 contiguous states. The Cascade Range divides the state into two different climate zones in much the same way that Oregon is divided. (Washington has about 30% less area than Oregon, but its population is about 60% larger.) West of the Range the Pacific Ocean dominates the weather, bringing sudden wind shifts and frequent showers. Continental weather prevails east of the mountains, more reliable but also more severe. Eastern Washington is an agricultural area, a patchwork of rangeland, wheat fields and orchards. Western Washington is a more heavily settled area with a more complex economic structure. The bulk of the state population resides by the shores of puget Sound. The Seattle metropolitan area alone accounts for 39% of the population.

Washington is a state of great natural beauty. The Olympic Peninsula to the west of the Puget Sound is a kind of northern rain forest. Mount Ranier is perhaps the most majestic peak in the Cascades, an awesome sight clearly visible from the streets of Seattle when the cloud cover lifts. Another peak in the Cascades has attracted

world attention—the active Mount St. Helens volcano which first exploded in March 1980.

The economy of western Washington sets the tone for the state as a whole. Manufacturing output is high,—especially in the defense industry, centered in Seattle, and in the aircraft and electronics industries. The recent slump brought heavy unemployment. The overall income level is high, however, and the presence of a well-educated adult population is one of the state's economic strong points. The state government raises considerable revenues and concentrates on education and welfare spending. Church ties are not strongly developed in Washington. The rate of property crime is high.

Alcohol consumption: 16	Manufacturing output: 15
Area: 20	Mobility, interstate: 9
Church adherents: 48	Population: 20
College graduates: 11	Population change: 14
Crime, property: 7	Population density: 28
Crime, violent: 22	Poverty, % of people
Education, public	living in: 42
school expenditures: 13	Tax burden, state: 11
Elderly, % in	Unemployment: 8
total pop.: 32	Voter turnout as % of
Health expenditures,	voting age pop.: 17
state and local: 35	Welfare, state and
Income, personal: 10	local expenditures: 15
Labor, blue-collar: 31	

West Virginia

West Virginia is a small, mountainous state tucked away behind the Appalachians where the South meets the Middle Atlantic region and the Midwest. Some of the most remote rural areas in the nation are found here. There are also dozens of towns centered around the production of the state's leading commodity—coal. The largest metropolitan area in the state is at Charleston, the state capital; but this area accounts for only 14% of the population.

The heavy concentration on mining explains why the state ranks first in proportion of blue-collar jobs and, unfortunately, first in unemployment. The general income level is low and many families live in poverty. There is a large native segment in the population, a fairly large group of elderly people, and few college graduates. The state collects a normal amount of revenue, yet social spending is low. Very little alcohol is consumed, it would appear. Crime rates are extremely low.

Alcohol consumption: 48	College graduates: 49
Area: 41	Crime, property: 50
Church adherents: 41	Crime, violent: 45

Education, public
    school expenditures: 40
Elderly, % in
    total pop.: 15
Health expenditures,
    state and local: 38
Income, personal: 45
Labor, blue-collar: 1
Manufacturing output: 34
Mobility, interstate: 43
Population: 34

Population change: 34
Population density: 25
Poverty, % of people
    living in: 12
Tax burden, state: 17
Unemployment: 1
Voter turnout as % of
    voting age pop: 30
Welfare, state and
    local expenditures: 37

Wisconsin

The state of Wisconsin is located on the western shore of Lake Michigan, north of Illinois. Endless rolling hills, crystal lakes and clear, crisp air are the characteristic environmental amenities. Most of the population is settled in the south, including the 30% of state residents who live in the Milwaukee metropolitan area. Madison, the capital, is about 75 miles due west from Milwaukee. The population is moderately large and growing slowly but steadily. Dairy farms and machine shops are the typical economic enterprises. Unemployment can be severe during recessions. The income level is just average, but the distribution must be fairly even since there are few poor families. The state is politically active. Voters pay attention to elections and the state raises and distributes funds at a high level. Residents are active churchgoers and heavy drinkers (these need not be the same individuals, of course). Violent crime is infrequent and property crime is low.

Alcohol consumption: 8
Area: 26
Church adherents: 7
College graduates: 32
Crime, property: 32
Crime, violent: 46
Education, public
    school expenditures: 9
Elderly, % in
    total pop.: 16
Health expenditures,
    state and local: 22
Income, personal: 28
Labor, blue-collar: 18

Manufacturing output: 12
Mobility, interstate: 44
Population: 16
Population change: 34
Population density: 24
Poverty, % of people
    living in: 47
Tax burden, state: 13
Unemployment: 10
Voter turnout as % of
    voting age pop: 3
Welfare, state and
    local expenditures: 7

Wyoming

Wyoming is a large state with a very small population. Population has been growing rapidly of late due to migration from other states, but the overall density of settlement is still the lowest in the country outside of Alaska. Located in the north-central part of the country where the Great Plains meet the Rockies, Wyoming includes such geographical spectaculars as the Devil's Tower National Monument and the Yellowstone and Grant Teton national parks. The capital city is Cheyenne. Farms, ranches, mines and oil wells are the key sites of economic life. Recent growth in the state is attributable to increased energy-resource development following world oil price shifts. This boom has been translated into very high incomes for many residents. Energy-resource depletion taxes have filled state coffers, but spending has been rather selective. Crime rates in Wyoming are moderate and alcohol consumption is high.

Alcohol consumption: 6
Area: 9
Church adherents: 34
College graduates: 17
Crime, property: 23
Crime, violent: 29
Education, public
    school expenditures: 14
Elderly, % in
    total pop.: 47
Health expenditures,
    state and local: 2
Income, personal: 5
Labor, blue-collar: 16

Manufacturing output: 43
Mobility, interstate: 4
Population: 49
Population change: 4
Population density: 49
Poverty, % of people
    living in: 49
Tax burden, state: 2
Unemployment: 35
Voter turnout as % of
    voting age pop.: 28
Welfare, state and
    local expenditures: 48

BIBLIOGRAPHY

American Association of Retired Persons. *A Profile of Older Americans.* Washington, D.C.: American Association of Retired Persons, 1980.

American Bar Association. *Membership Report.* November 1982.

American Bowling Congress. *Annual Report, 1981–1982.*

American Council of Life Insurance. *1982 Life Insurance Fact Book.* Washington, D.C.: American Council of Life Insurance, 1982.

Arbitron Ratings Company. *Arbitron Ratings: Television Audience Estimates. Network Program Analysis.* New York: July 1982.

Audit Bureau of Circulation. "Selected Magazine Circulation Data." Unpublished computer survey, 1982.

Bacheller, Martin A., ed. *The Hammond Almanac 1983.* Maplewood, N.J.: Hammond Almanac Inc., 1982.

"Backing Down on Benefits." *Time.* October 21, 1981, pp. 32–44.

Barone, Michael, and Ujifusa, Grant. *Almanac of American Politics 1982.* Washington, D.C.: Barone and Company, 1981.

"The Battle Over Abortion." *Time.* April 6, 1981, pp. 20–28.

Bowman, Thomas F., Giuliani, George A., and Mingé, Ronald M. *Finding Your Best Place to Live in America.* New York: Red Lion Books, 1981.

Boyer, Richard, and Savageau, David. *Places Rated Almanac.* New York: Rand McNally & Company, 1981.

"Cheating by the Millions." *Time.* March 28, 1983, pp. 26–33.

The College Board. *College Board Scores Rise for the First Time since 1963.* New York: The College Board, September 1982.

Council of State Governments. *The Book of States 1982–1983.* Vol. 24. Lexington, Ky.: Council of State Governments, 1982.

Council on Environmental Quality. *Environmental Quality 1981: The 12th Annual Report of the Council on Environmental Quality.* Washington, D.C.: 1981.

"Defense Money—Where It Goes." *U.S. News & World Report.* February 21, 1983, p. 15.

Distilled Spirits Council of the United States. *Annual Statistical Review, 1981.* 1982.

Dun & Bradstreet Inc. *Business Failure Record: 1980.* New York: 1982.

Duncan, James, Jr. *American Radio Spring 1982 Report.* Kalamazoo, Mich.: Duncan Media Enterprises, 1982.

Eckforth, Marcy. "Libraries Check Out National Celebration." *USA Today.* April 23, 1983, p. 4A.

"F.B.I. Says Crime is Down in U.S., but Houston Reports Rise of 17%." *New York Times.* October 20, 1982, p. A20.

Gest, Ted. "The Noose Gets Tighter on Death Row." *U.S. News & World Report.* July 18, 1983, p. 21.

Hacker, Andrew, ed. *U.S. A Statistical Portrait of the American People.* New York: Viking Press, 1983.

Information Please Publishers. *Information Please Almanac: Atlas & Yearbook 1983.* 37th ed. New York: A & W Publishers, Inc., 1982.

Lesko, Matthew. *Information U.S.A.* New York: Viking Press, 1983.

"Low Teacher Pay and Status Faulted." *New York Times.* August 24, 1983, p. A12.

"Most Dangerous U.S. Waste Dumps Identified." *Chemical and Engineering News.* January 3, 1983, p.8.

National Collegiate Athletic Association. "National College Basketball Attendance, 1982." *NCAA Statistics Service—Bulletin.* 1982.

National Collegiate Athletic Association. "1981 College Football Attendance." *NCAA Statistics Service—Bulletin.* 1981.

National Council of the Churches of Christ in the U.S.A. *Churches and Church Membership in the United States, 1980.* Atlanta, Ga.: Glenmary Research Center, 1982.

National Football League. *National Football League 1982*

Media Information Book. New York: National Football League, 1982.

National Marine Manufacturers Association. *Boat Registration Statistics 1981.* New York: National Marine Manufacturers Association, 1982.

N.Y. Stock Exchange. *Shareownership, 1981.* New York: April 1982.

"1980 Survey of Manufactures Provides State Export Data." *Business America.* February 22, 1982, pp. 12–13.

"The 1982 Beverage Market Index/Part I." *Beverage World.* April 1982, p. 30.

"1982's Beverage Market Index & Sales Planning Guide/Part II." *Beverage World.* May 1982, p. 30.

North American Soccer League. "Attendance Figures 1975–1981." Unpublished material, 1982.

"No Way Out." *U.S. News & World Report.* August 16, 1982, pp. 31–35.

"Picking Up the Pieces." *Time.* April 25, 1983, p. 10 ff.

Polk, R.L., & Co. *Polk's World Bank Directory.* North American ed., 176th issue. Nashville, Tenn.: R.L. Polk & Co., 1982.

Raasch, Chuck. "Over-65's Will Outnumber Teens in July." *USA Today.* April 20, 1983, p. 1.

"The Social-Security Crisis." *Newsweek.* January 24, 1983, p. 18.

"States' Income at $300 Billion for First Time, U.S. Reports." *New York Times.* October 25, 1982, p. A12.

Tax Foundation. *Facts and Figures on Government Finance.* 21st biennial ed. New York: 1981.

"10 Million People without Jobs—Who They Are." *U.S. News & World Report.* March 15, 1982, pp. 71–74.

"The Trauma and Tedium of a Lawsuit." *U.S. News & World Report.* November 1, 1982, pp. 51–54.

"Unemployment on the Rise." *Time.* February 8, 1982. p. 22.

U.S. Amateur Confederation of Roller Skating. *1982 Press Information and Media Guide.* Lincoln, Neb.: 1982.

U.S. Department of Agriculture. Economic Research Service. *Farm Data Summary, U.S.* Washington D.C.: 1982.

U.S. Department of Agriculture. Statistical Reporting Service. Crop Reporting Service. *Poultry: Production, Disposition & Income 1980–1981.* Washington, D.C.: 1982.

U.S. Department of Commerce. *1980 Annual Survey of Manufactures.* Washington, D.C.: 1982.

U.S. Department of Commerce. Bureau of the Census. *Census of Population and Housing.* PHC 80-51-1. Washington, D.C.: March 1982.

U.S. Department of Commerce. Bureau of the Census. *Environmental Quality Control: Governmental Finances: Fiscal Year 1980.* State and Local Government Special Studies No. 103. Washington, D.C.: October 1982.

U.S. Department of Commerce. Bureau of the Census. *Farm Population of the United States.* P-27, No. 54. Washington, D.C.: September 1981.

U.S. Department of Commerce. Bureau of the Census. *Governmental Finances in 1980–81.* G.F. 81, No. 5 Washington, D.C.: 1982.

U.S. Department of Commerce. Bureau of the Census. *Housing Starts.* No. C 20-82-6. Washington, D.C.: August 1982.

U.S. Department of Commerce. Bureau of the Census. *Housing Statistics.* No. 6. Washington, D.C.: December 1981; Reprinted November 1982.

U.S. Department of Commerce. Bureau of the Census. *1980 Census of Population. Rate of the Population by States: 1980.* PC 80-51-3. Washington, D.C.: 1981.

U.S. Department of Commerce. Bureau of the Census. *State and Metropolitan Area Data Book 1982: A Statistical Abstract Supplement.* Washington, D.C.: August 1982.

U.S. Department of Commerce. Bureau of the Census. *State Government Finances in 1981.* G.F. 81, No. 3. Washington, D.C.: 1982.

U.S. Department of Commerce. Bureau of the Census. *State Government Tax Collections in 1982.* G.F. 82, No. 1. Washington, D.C.: 1983.

U.S. Department of Commerce. Bureau of the Census. *State Tax Collections in 1981.* Washington, D.C.: 1982.

U.S. Department of Commerce. Bureau of the Census. *Statistical Abstract of the United States, 1982–83.* 103rd ed. Washington, D.C.: 1982.

U.S. Department of Commerce. Bureau of the Census, and U.S. Department of Housing and Urban Development. *New Residential Construction in Standard Metropolitan Statistical Areas, First Quarter, 1982.* Washington, D.C.: 1982.

U.S. Department of Commerce. Bureau of the Census. Construction Reports. *Housing Units Authorized by Building Permits and Public Contracts: January 1983.* No. C40-83-1. Washington, D.C.: 1983.

U.S. Department of Commerce. Bureau of the Census. Current Population Reports. *Ancestry and Language in the United States.* P-23, No. 116. Washington, D.C.: March 1982.

U.S. Department of Commerce. Bureau of the Census. Current Population Reports. *Characteristics of Households and Persons Receiving Non-Cash Benefits.* P-23, No. 110. Washington, D.C.: March 1981.

U.S. Department of Commerce. Bureau of the Census. Current Population Reports. *Consumer Income: Characteristics of Households and Persons Receiving Selected Noncash Benefits: 1980.* Series P-60, No. 131. Washington, D.C.: 1982.

U.S. Department of Commerce. Bureau of the Census. Current Population Reports. *Consumer Income: Characteristics of the Population below the Poverty Level: 1980.* Series P-60, No. 133. Washington, D.C.: 1982.

U.S. Department of Commerce. Bureau of the Census. Current Population Reports. *Consumer Income: Illustrative Projections of Money Income Size Distributions, for Households: 1980 to 1995.* Series P-60, No. 122. Washington, D.C.: 1980.

U.S. Department of Commerce. Bureau of the Census. Current Population Reports. *Educational Attainment in the United States.* P-20, No. 356. Washington, D.C.: August 1980.

U.S. Department of Commerce. Bureau of the Census. Current Population Reports. *Fertility of American Women.* P-20, No. 364. Washington, D.C.: August 1981.

U.S. Department of Commerce. Bureau of the Census. Current Population Reports. *Household and Family Characteristics.* P-20, No. 366. Washington, D.C.: September 1981.

U.S. Department of Commerce. Bureau of the Census. Current Population Reports. *Population Characteristics. Geographical Mobility: March 1980 to March 1981.* Series P-20, No. 377. Washington, D.C.: 1983.

U.S. Department of Commerce. Bureau of the Census. Current Population Reports. *Population Profile of the United States.* P-20, No. 363. Washington, D.C.: June 1981.

U.S. Department of Commerce. Bureau of the Census. Current Population Reports. *Voting and Registration in the Election of 1980.* P-20, No. 370. Washington, D.C.: April 1982.

U.S. Department of Commerce. Bureau of Economic Analysis. *1980 Personal Income Data for Counties.* B.E.A., No. 82–27. Washington, D.C.: May 23, 1982.

U.S. Department of Commerce. Bureau of Economic Analysis. *Survey of Current Business.* Washington, D.C.: July 1982.

U.S. Department of Commerce. Bureau of Economic Analysis. *Survey of Current Business.* Washington, D.C.: August 1982.

U.S. Department of Commerce. Bureau of Industrial Economics. *1982 U.S. Industrial Outlook for 200 Industries with Projections for 1986.* Washington, D.C.: 1982.

U.S. Department of Commerce. Bureau of Industrial Economics. *1983 U.S. Industrial Outlook.* Washington, D.C.: 1983.

U.S. Department of Commerce. Economic Development Administration. *1981 Annual Report: Economic Development Administration.* Washington, D.C.: 1982.

U.S. Department of Commerce. National Oceanic and Atmospheric Administration. *Comparative Climatic Data for the U.S. through 1980.* Washington, D.C.: 1981.

U.S. Department of Education. National Center for Education Statistics. Digest of Education Statistics, Washington: D.C.: 1981.

U.S. Department of Education. National Center for Education Statistics. *Statistics of Public Elementary and Secondary School Systems.* Washington, D.C.: Fall 1979.

U.S. Department of Education. National Center for Education Statistics. *Statistics of Public School Systems, Fall 1980.* Washington, D.C.: 1981.

U.S. Department of Health and Human Services. Alcohol, Drug Abuse, and Mental Health Administration. *First Statistical Compendium on Alcohol and Health.* No. (ADM) 81-1115. Washington, D.C.: 1981.

U.S. Department of Health and Human Services. National Center for Health Statistics. *Vital Statistics Report: Final Mortality Statistics, 1978.* DHHS *Publication* No. (PHS) 80-1120, Vol. 29, No. 6. Washington, D.C.: September 1980.

U.S. Department of Health and Human Services. Office of Research and Demonstrations. *The Medicare and Medicaid Data Book, 1981.* Washington, D.C.: 1982.

U.S. Department of Health and Human Services. Public Health Service. *Monthly Vital Statistics Report,* Vol. 3, No. 6 (Supplement). Washington, D,C.: September 28, 1981.

U.S. Department of Health and Human Services. Public Health Service. Centers for Disease Control. "Abortion Surveillance." *Annual Summary, 1978.* November 1980.

U.S. Department of Health and Human Services. Public Health Service. Centers for Disease Control. "Morbidity and Mortality Weekly Report." *Annual Summary, 1980.* Vol. 29, No. 54, September 1981.

U.S. Department of Health and Human Services. Social Security Administration. *Social Security Bulletin Annual Statistical Supplement, 1980.*

U.S. Department of Justice. "Probation and Parole 1981." *Bureau of Justice Statistics Bulletin.* August 1982.

U.S. Department of Justice. Bureau of Justice Statistics. *Prisoners in State and Federal Institutions.* Washington, D.C.: May 1980.

U.S. Department of Justice. Drug Enforcement Administration. *Drug Enforcement Statistical Report: Enforcement Activity, Drug Abuse Indicators, Organization and Training Data.* Washington, D.C.: 1980.

U.S. Department of Justice. Federal Bureau of Investigation. *Uniform Crime Reports. Crime in the United States: 1980.* Washington, D.C.: 1981.

U.S. Department of Justice. Immigration and Naturalization Service. *Annual Report of Immigration and Naturalization Service.* Washington, D.C.: 1979.

U.S. Department of Labor. Bureau of Labor Statistics. *Analysis of Labor Statistics.* Bulletin 2120. Washington, D.C.: March 1982.

U.S. Department of Labor. Bureau of Labor Statistics. *Analysis of Work Stoppages, 1980.* Bulletin 2120. Washington, D.C.: March 1982.

U.S. Department of Labor. Bureau of Labor Statistics. *Current Wage Developments.* Washington, D.C.: January 1981.

U.S. Department of Labor. Bureau of Labor Statistics. *Directory of National Unions and Employee Associations, 1979.* Bulletin 2079. Washington, D.C.: September 1980.

U.S. Department of Labor. Bureau of Labor Statistics. *Geographic Profile of Employment and Unemployment, 1980.* Bulletin 2111. Washington, D.C.: March 1982.

U.S. Department of Labor. Bureau of Labor Statistics. *National Survey of Professional, Administrative, Technical, and Clerical Pay.* Bulletin 2145. Washington, D.C.: March 1982.

U.S. Department of Labor. Bureau of Labor Statistics. *News Release.* U.S.D.L. No. 82-99 March 18, 1982; U.S.D.L. No. 82-241 July 12, 1982; U.S.D.L. No. 82-334 September 23, 1982; U.S.D.L. No. 83-5 January 7, 1983; U.S.D.L. No. 83-75 February 15, 1983. Washington, D.C.: 1982–1983.

U.S. Department of Labor, Bureau of Labor Statistics. "Urban Family Budgets and Comparative Indexes for Selected Urban Areas." Press release, April 1982.

U.S. Department of Transportation. Federal Aviation Administration. *FAA Statistical Handbook of Aviation. Calendar Year 1980.* Washington, D.C.: 1980.

U.S. Department of Transportation. Office of the Secretary of Transportation. *Grant Awards Fiscal Year 1980.* Washington, D.C.: 1981.

United States Figure Skating Association. "Membership in the U.S. Figure Skating Association." Unpublished material, 1982.

U.S. House of Representatives. 97th Congress, First Session. Hearing before the Subcommittee on Housing and Consumer Interests of the Select Committee on Aging. *Housing the Elderly: Present Problems and Future Conditions.* No. 97-318. Washington, D.C.: July 29, 1981.

U.S. House of Representatives. 97th Congress, Second Session. Committee on Aging and the Subcommittee on Health and Long-Term Care of the Select Committee on Aging. *Impact on the Elderly of Proposed Medicare and Medicaid Cuts.* No. 97-346. Washington, D.C.: March 19, 1982.

U.S. House of Representatives. 97th Congress, Second Session. Select Committee on Aging. *Every Ninth American.* 1982 ed. No. 97-332. Washington, D.C.: July 1982.

U.S. Small Business Administration. *The State of Small Business: A Report to the President.* Washington, D.C.: 1982.

"When States Run Out of Funds for Jobless." *U.S. News & World Report.* August 30, 1982, p. 65.

Women's International Bowling Congress. *Annual Report, 1981–1982.*

The World Almanac and Book of Facts 1983. New York: Newspaper Enterprise Association, Inc., November 1982.

INDEX